International Management

FIFTH EDITION

International Management

Managing Across Borders and Cultures

Helen Deresky

State University of New York–Plattsburgh

PEARSON

Prentice
Hall

Upper Saddle River, New Jersey 07458

Library of Congress Cataloging-in-Publication Data

Deresky, Helen.
  International management : managing across borders and cultures / Helen
  Deresky.-- 5th ed.
      p. cm.
  Includes bibliographical references and index.
  ISBN 0-13-109597-8
  1. International business enterprises--Management. 2. International business
  enterprises--Management--Case studies. 3. Industrial management. I. Title.

HD62.4.D47 2006
658'.049--dc22   2004026620

Editorial Director: Jeff Shelstad
Senior Acquisition Editor: David Parker
Project Manager: Ashley Santora
Editorial Assistant: Denise Vaughn
Marketing Manager: Anke Braun
Marketing Assistant: Patrick Danzusa
Managing Editor: John Roberts
Production Editor: Renata Butera
Permissions Supervisor: Charles Morris
Manufacturing Buyer: Michelle Klein
Cover Design: Bruce Kenselaar
Cover Photos/Photo: Getty Images
Composition/Full-Service Project Management: Carlisle Communications
Printer/Binder: Courier–Westford
Typeface: 10/12 Times Ten Roman

Credits and acknowledgments borrowed from other sources and reproduced, with permission, in this textbook appear on appropriate page within the text.

Microsoft® and Windows® are registered trademarks of the Microsoft Corporation in the U.S.A. and other countries. Screen shots and icons reprinted with permission from the Microsoft Corporation. This book is not sponsored or endorsed by or affiliated with the Microsoft Corporation.

Pearson Education LTD.   Pearson Education Australia PTY, Limited
Pearson Education Singapore, Pte. Ltd   Pearson Education North Asia Ltd
Pearson Education, Canada, Ltd   Pearson Educación de Mexico, S.A. de C.V.
Pearson Education–Japan   Pearson Education Malaysia, Pte. Ltd

10 9 8 7 6 5 4
ISBN 0-13-109597-8

To my husband, John,
and my children, John, Mark, and Lara,
for their love and support

Brief Contents

Contents

COMPREHENSIVE CASES   309

Preface

The hypercompetitive global arena of the twenty-first century mandates that managers develop the skills necessary to design and implement global strategies, to conduct effective cross-national interactions and to manage daily operations in foreign subsidiaries. Global companies are faced with varied and dynamic environments in which they must accurately assess the political, legal, technological, competitive, and cultural factors that shape their strategies and operations. In addition, companies operating abroad often report that their global strategies are undermined by the ineffective management of intercultural relations. The fate of overseas operations depends at least in part on the international manager's cultural skills and sensitivity, as well as the ability to carry out the company's strategy within the context of the host country's business practices and environment.

Clearly, the skills needed for effective management of people and processes in a global context are crucial for the twenty-first century. There is thus a pronounced need for a comprehensive textbook that addresses the actual management functions and behaviors necessary to develop global vision and management skills at both a *strategic* (macro) level and an *interpersonal* (micro) level.

International Management: Managing Across Borders and Cultures, 5th edition, fills this need. This text places the student in the role of a manager of any nationality, encouraging the student to take a truly global perspective in dealing with dynamic management issues in both foreign and diverse host environments. Cross-cultural management and competitive strategy are evaluated in the context of global changes—the expanding European Union (EU), the North American Free Trade Agreement (NAFTA), and the rapidly growing economies in Asia—that require new management applications. Throughout, the text emphasizes how the variable of culture interacts with other national and international factors to affect managerial processes and behaviors. In addition, the growing competitive influence of technology is emphasized throughout the text, with E-Biz Boxes showcasing the use of e-business for globally competitive strategic positioning.

This textbook is designed for undergraduate and graduate students majoring in international business or general management. Graduate students might be asked to focus more heavily on the comprehensive cases that conclude each part of the book and to complete the term project in greater detail. It is assumed, though not essential, that most students using *International Management: Managing Across Borders and Cultures,* 5th edition, will have taken a basic principles of management course. Although this text is primarily intended for business students, it is also useful for practicing managers and for students majoring in other areas, such as political science or international relations, who would benefit from a background in international management.

NEW TO THIS EDITION

The entire text has been revised to reflect current research, current events and global developments, and company examples from the field of international management. Particular attention is paid to contemporary issues such as the globalization of human capital, outsourcing, knowledge management, virtual teams, and the growing economies of China and India. Other revisions to the text material include the following:

- **Comprehensive cases:** Nine of the sixteen comprehensive cases are new and current; seven are favorites rolled over from the 4th edition. The selection of cases has been drawn from a broad array of geographical settings: Russia, Brazil, Germany, India, Malaysia, China, West Indies, Indonesia, and Japan, as well as "global" cases. The new integrative case presents the student-manager with a variety of strategic, cultural, and political issues involved in Wal-Mart's expansion into Germany.

- **E-Business:**   The increasing emphasis on technology in global business transactions is highlighted in every chapter with text coverage, such as that in Chapter 6: "Using E-Business for Global Expansion," and with the E-Biz Boxes in every chapter.
- **Eleven** *New* **Chapter Opening Profiles**
- **Seven** *New* **Management Focus Boxes**
- **Seven** *New* **Chapter-Ending Cases**
- *New* **or Updated Comparative Management in Focus sections**

DISTINCTIVE TEXT FEATURES

- **Streamlined text** in eleven chapters, with particular focus on global strategic positioning, entry strategies and alliances, effective cross-cultural understanding and management, and developing and retaining an effective global management cadre.
- **Comprehensive cases** placing the student in the decision-making role of the manager regarding issues of strategy, culture, HRM, social responsibility, technology, and politics in the global arena. Examples are Reebok's "ethical" issues in Asia, Dell's negotiating experiences in Brazil, the alliance between G.M. and AvtoVAZ of Russia, Global E-Commerce at UPS, Management of Human Assets at Infosys in India, Starbucks in China, TelSys International (dealing with a cross-cultural negotiation situation set in Malaysia make it useful as a negotiation simulation as well or instead of the case).
- **Chapter-Opening Profiles** giving practical and current illustrations of the chapter topics, such as "Adjusting Business to Saudi Arabian Culture," "Cemex Mexico," "France's Thomson and China's TCL to Join TV Units."
- **Comparative Management in Focus sections** providing in-depth comparative application of chapter topics in specific countries, such as the growing Indian economy, and updated sections such as "Strategy for the EU market", "IJVs in the Russian Federation," and "Communicating with Arabs."
- **Management Focus Boxes** giving management and company examples around the world to highlight the chapter topics, such as "CEO Speaks Out: Ethics Abroad," "The Body Shop's Anita Roddick," "Indian Companies Are Adding Western Flavor," and "Japan's Neglected Resource: Female Workers."
- **E-Biz Boxes** demonstrating the application of IT, specifically B2B, around the world, such as "eBay," "Companies Must Localize E-Commerce to Avoid Culture–Internet Clash," and "Bikeworld Goes Global."
- **Chapter-Ending Cases** including short cases, such as " NTT DoComo, Japan," "ABB, Sweden," "Vodafone UK.," and "Avon China."
- **Experiential Exercises** at the end of each chapter, challenging students on topics such as ethics in decision making, cross-cultural negotiations, and strategic planning.
- **Internet Study Guide,** chapter quizzes are available on the text's Web site. These quizzes ask a variety of multiple choice, true/false, and essay questions which provide student's with immediate feedback. Go to www.prenhall.com/deresky.
- **Integrative Term Project** outlined at the end of the text and providing a vehicle for research and application of the course content.
- **Integrative Case** "Wal-Mart's German Misadventure."

SUPPLEMENTS PACKAGE

Instructor's Manual: The Instructor's Manual has been completely revised. For each chapter, the Instructor's Manual provides a comprehensive lecture outline with references to slides in the PowerPoint package, chapter discussion questions and answers, as well as additional Teaching Resources, a list of related Web sites, and additional Experiential Exercises for selected chapters.

Test Item File: The Test Item File consists of multiple choice questions, discussion questions, and comprehensive essay questions. Each question is followed by a page reference, a difficulty rating of easy, moderate, or difficult, and a classification of either application or recall to help you build a well-balanced test.

Instructor's Resource Center on CD-ROM: The Instructor's Resource Center, available on CD, includes presentation and classroom resources. Instructors can collect the materials, edit them to create powerful class lectures, and upload them to an online course management system.

Using the Instructor's Resource Center, instructors can easily create custom presentations. Select a chapter from the table of contents to see a list of available resources or simply search by keyword. After you've found the files you'd like to use, click on each to select, and place in your export list for exporting to your computer's hard drive or other disk. The Instructor's Resource Center on CD will organize your newly created files into folders according to file type.

With the Instructor's Resource Center, you will find the following faculty supplements:

PowerPoints: A fully revised, comprehensive package of approximately 350 slides, which outline each chapter and include exhibits from the text. The PowerPoint package is designed to aid the educator and supplement in-class lectures.

TestGen software: Containing all of the questions in the printed Test Item File, TestGen is a comprehensive suite of tools for testing and assessment.

Converted TestGen software for **WebCT, Blackboard,** and **CourseCompass**
Instructor's Manual
Test Item File

Custom Videos on DVD: This DVD, drawn from Prentice Hall's custom video series, features experts discussing a wide range of issues in the global marketplace. Topics include:

The Debate on Globalization
Global Business & Ethics
Impact of Culture-Latin America
Entering Chinese Market
Entering Global Markets: Lands' End and Yahoo!
Global Human Resource Management

Companion Web site: The companion Web site for this text, located at http://www.prenhall.com/deresky, contains valuable resources for both students and professors, including an interactive student study guide.

ACKNOWLEDGMENTS

The author would like to acknowledge, with thanks, the individuals who made this text possible. For the fifth edition, these people include the following:

Barbara Hastings, University of South Carolina
Ram Subramanian, Valley State University
Marion White, James Madison University
Manisha Singal, Radford University
Davina Vora, University of Texas at Dallas
Annette Crow, University of Central Oklahoma
Constance Bates, Florida International University
Bonita Barger, Tennessee Tech University
Lauryn Migenes, University of Central Florida

—Helen Deresky

Part I: The Global Manager's Environment

CHAPTER

1

Assessing the Environment

Political, Economic, Legal, Technological

Outline

Opening Profile: Business Goes on in Jakarta Despite Threat of Terrorism

"If you want to be a player in Southeast Asia, you need to be here," said Stuart Dean, president of G.E. International's Southeast Asian operations.

While security concerns prompted President Bush's schedulers to limit his Indonesian visit in October 2003 to three hours, U.S. companies continue to operate in Indonesia despite the constant danger of terrorist attack. A year after the bombing in Bali and two months after the attack at the J. W. Marriott Hotel in Jakarta, security experts consider Indonesia as dangerous as ever.

The Ford Motor Company, for one, is undeterred. Last month, Ford introduced a seven-seat sport utility vehicle with full-page advertisements in Indonesia's largest daily newspaper, part of an effort to break into a fast-growing auto market dominated by Japanese manufacturers. "There's no thought of taking people out," said Will Angove, an Australian who is Ford Motor Indonesia's president. "Indonesia is strategically an important market."

U.S. business people in Indonesia say the country offers so much opportunity, dangerous or not, that they cannot allow themselves to be scared off. Since the bombing at the Marriott, businesses have battened down, and the hotels serving foreigners resemble military compounds. However, few of the roughly 10,000 U.S. citizens in Indonesia are leaving. "They've been here a long time and understand the risks," said Brian C. Watters, a principal at Assessments Group Indonesia, a security consulting firm in Jakarta.

Security problems and corruption have been significant drags on foreign investment in Indonesia for a long time. In 2004, foreign interest actually seemed to be rising. Government approvals of foreign projects increased 3.7 percent in the first nine months of the year, compared with the same period in 2002, and foreign investors poured more than a half billion dollars into the Jakarta stock market. Still, the economy had not been growing fast enough to create sufficient jobs to help defuse terrorism at its roots.

Some of the largest investors, Western oil companies, have learned to cope with almost daily threats. Exxon Mobil operates gas fields in Aceh Province at the northwest tip of Sumatra, where the Indonesian army has been trying to suppress a long-simmering separatist rebellion; after a spate of attacks against its employees two years ago, the company suspended operations for four months but did not pull out. Some expatriates say they see no more chance of being bombed in Indonesia than, say, being hit by a bus at home. Still, the terrorist threat is real.

In response, many companies are trying to run their Indonesia operations with more unmarried expatriates and to transfer those with families to other countries. Functions for expatriates are usually kept secret until the day before the event.

SOURCE: W. Arnold, "Business Goes on in Jakarta Despite Threat of Terrorism," www.nytimes.com, *October 22, 2003.* Copyright © 2003 *The New York Times Company,* Used with permission.

The Jack Welch of the future cannot be me. I spent my entire career in the United States. The next head of General Electric will be somebody who spent time in Bombay, in Hong Kong, in Buenos Aires. We have to send our best and brightest overseas and make sure they have the training that will allow them to be the global leaders who will make GE flourish in the future.
—*Jack Welch (former GE CEO),*
in a speech to GE employees, 2001

Managers in the twenty-first century are being challenged to operate in an increasingly complex, interdependent, and dynamic global environment. Those involved in global business have to adjust their strategies and management styles to those regions of the world in which they want to operate, whether directly or through some form of alliance. One aspect of this global arena requiring increasing attention is that of the potential for terrorism where businesses operate, as illustrated in the opening profile.[1] Other typical challenges that managers must face involve politics, culture, and the use, transfer, and protection of technology. In addition, the opportunities and risks of the global marketplace increasingly bring with them the societal obligations of operating in a global community. An example is the dilemma faced by Western drug manufacturers of how to fulfill their responsibilities to stockholders, acquire capital for research, and protect their patents while also being good global citizens by responding to the cry for free or low-cost drugs for AIDS in poor countries.[2] Managers in those companies are struggling to find ways to balance their social responsibilities, their images, and their competitive strategies.

To compete aggressively, firms must make considerable investments overseas—not only capital investment but also investment in well-trained managers with the skills essential to working effectively in a multicultural environment. In any foreign environment, managers need to handle a set of dynamic and fast-changing variables, including the all-pervasive variable of culture that affects every facet of daily management. Added to that "behavioral software" are the challenges of the burgeoning use of technological software and the borderless Internet, which are rapidly changing the dynamics of competition and operations.

Global management, then, is the process of developing strategies, designing and operating systems, and working with people around the world to ensure sustained competitive advantage. Those management functions are shaped by the prevailing conditions and ongoing developments in the world, as outlined in the following sections.

THE GLOBAL BUSINESS ENVIRONMENT

Following is a summary of global situations and trends which managers need to monitor and incorporate in their strategic and operational planning.

Globalism

Business competitiveness has now evolved to a level of sophistication that many term **globalism**—global competition characterized by networks of international linkages that bind countries, institutions, and people in an interdependent global economy. The invisible hand of global competition is being propelled by the phenomenon of an increasingly borderless world. As described by Kenichi Ohmae, "The nation-state itself—that artifact of the eighteenth and nineteenth centuries—has begun to crumble, battered by a pent-up storm of political resentment, ethnic prejudice, tribal hatred, and religious animosity."[3]

As a result of global economic integration, extrapolation of current trends will lead to world exports of goods and services of $11 trillion in 2005, or 28 percent of world gross domestic product (GDP).[4]

As reported by the World Trade Organization, differences in regional output growth rates have narrowed as economic activity picked up in Western Europe and the transition economies. It is clear that world trade is phenomenal and growing and, importantly, is increasingly including the developing nations.

Almost all firms around the world are affected to some extent by globalism. Firms from any country now compete with your firm both at home and abroad, and your domestic competitors are competing on price by outsourcing resources anywhere in the world. It is essential, therefore, for managers to go beyond operating only in their domestic market. If they do not, they will be even farther behind the majority of managers who have already recognized that they must have a global vision for their firms, beginning with preparing themselves with the skills and tools of managing in a global environment. Companies that desire to remain globally competitive and to expand their operations to other countries will have to develop a cadre of top management with experience operating abroad and an understanding of what it takes to do business in other countries and to work with people of other cultures.

Another indicator of globalism is that foreign direct investment has grown more than three times faster than the world output of goods. The European Union (EU) has caught up with the United States to share the position of the world's largest investor. The United Kingdom has been the most active source of merger and acquisition investment. The United States is the largest home for foreign investment, with China the second-largest recipient. Many global companies produce and sell more of their global brands abroad than domestically. Avon, for example, realized 62 percent of its $7 billion revenue for 2003 in international markets.[5] Nestlé has 50 percent of its sales outside of its home market, Coca-Cola has 80 percent, and Procter & Gamble 65 percent. Investment by global companies around the world means that this aspect of globalism benefits developing economies—through the transfer of financial, technological, and managerial resources, as well as through the development of local allies that later become self-sufficient and have other operations. Global companies are becoming less tied to specific locations, and their operations and allies are spread around the world, as they source and coordinate resources and activities in the most suitable areas and as technology allows faster and more flexible interactions and greater efficiencies. This phenomenon is not limited to large companies.

> *Almost everyone can take advantage of trade-lead Web sites or can go to global conferences or trade shows. The small businesses of today are the multinationals of tomorrow.*[6]

> DONNA SHARP,
> *World Trade Institute of Pace University*
> *in New York, January 1, 2004*

Small companies are also affected by and, in turn, affect globalism. They play a vital role in contributing to their national economies—through employment, new job creation, development of new products and services, and international operations, typically exporting. The vast majority (about 98 percent) of businesses in developed economies are small and medium-sized enterprises (SMEs), which are typically referred to as those companies having fewer than 500 employees. Small businesses are rapidly discovering foreign markets. In the United States alone, companies with fewer than 100 employees that export goods increased to 213,000 in 2001, up from 96,000 in 1992, generating a combined $130 billion in exported merchandise, according to the Department of Commerce.[7] Although many small businesses are affected by globalism only to the extent that they face competing products from abroad, an increasing number of entrepreneurs are being approached by potential offshore customers, thanks to the burgeoning number of trade shows, federal and state export initiatives, and the growing use of Web sites, with the ease of making contact and placing orders online. One example of a very small global business (two people) is that of Ms. Warwick, based in London, as described in the accompanying Management Focus.

Management Focus

Small Company, Global Approach

Gayle Warwick Fine Linen is a multinational player. Its high-end, handmade bed and table linens are woven in Europe, embroidered in Vietnam, and sold in Britain and the United States. Sales are soaring, and its full-time staff recently doubled—to two: Gayle Warwick and the assistant she hired in March.

Just because you are a U.S. citizen does not mean your business has to be based in the United States. Ms. Warwick discovered that with barriers to trade and investment falling everywhere, she was free to roam the world to make the contacts she needed to put her business together, then to return to her home base in London to run the show. At first, Ms. Warwick, who is fifty, operated from an office and a dining-room-turned-showroom in her London home in the Pimlico district. Then in September, the upscale British retailer Thomas Goode did away with its linen department in the Mayfair district and turned the space over to her company.

Gayle Warwick's company, which is based in London, has its handmade bed and table linens woven in Europe, embroidered in Vietnam, and sold in Britain and the United States.

SOURCE: Courtesy of Jonathan Player.

The catalyst was a social encounter in the early 1990s with the Vietnamese wife of one of her husband's business colleagues, a woman who showed her a hand-embroidered tablecloth from her native country and invited Ms. Warwick to visit her in Vietnam. The two women made the trip in 1995, had samples made, and ordered other linens, which they shipped home and sold at charity Christmas fairs.

It was a start—but just a start. "I thought there might be something in this, but I wasn't sure what," Ms. Warwick said. "There was no connect-the-dots from my past to that moment and idea."

When the Vietnamese woman moved away the next year, Ms. Warwick decided to go to Vietnam on her own to explore the possibility of setting up a linen business. That trip convinced her that she needed to do more research. With the help of $16,000 in savings, she spent the next three years traveling to Italy, Ireland, and Switzerland to talk with linen and organic-cotton spinners, weavers, and finishers; to France and Germany to attend textile trade fairs; and to Vietnam to find embroiderers. "You have to be really tenacious," she said of her learning experience.

Her increasing expertise and the contacts she made paid off. For example, executives of a French quality-control company in Ho Chi Minh City, once known as Saigon, put her in touch with exporters in Hanoi, who in turn helped her find skilled craftspeople in northern Vietnamese villages to work on her designs. She hired a French freight forwarder, SDV International Logistics, to handle her far-flung business by shipping unfinished and finished fabrics within Europe and to Vietnam, then delivering the embroidered linens to London and the United States. Although they do not do so for Ms. Warwick, freight forwarders can also manage payments, a potential godsend for small exporters dealing with partners scattered around the globe.

SOURCE: "A Small Company, a Global Approach" by Jane L. Levere, www.nytimes.com, Small Business section, January 1, 2004. Copyright © 2004 by *The New York Times Co.* Reprinted with permission.

Regional Trading Blocs—The TRIAD

The dominance of the United States is already over. What is emerging is a world economy of blocs represented by the North American Free Trade Agreement (NAFTA), the EU, and the Association of Southeast Asian Nations (ASEAN). There's no one center in this world economy.[8]

PETER DRUCKER,
Fortune, January 12, 2004

Much of today's world trade takes place within three regional free-trade blocs (Western Europe, Asia, and North America), called the TRIAD market, grouped around the three dominant currencies (the euro, the yen, and the dollar). In 2004, these trade blocs were expanding their borders to include neighboring countries, either directly or with separate agreements. One researcher summarizes the impact this new order has had on our perception of national boundaries in the following way:

Today, if you look closely at the world TRIAD companies inhabit, national borders have effectively disappeared and, along with them, the economic logic that made them useful lines of demarcation in the first place.[9]

The European Union
The EU's long-awaited eastward enlargement becomes a reality, bringing into the union 10 new countries, 75 million people, and an ocean of individual hopes and frustrations.[10]

FINANCIAL TIMES,
April 27, 2004

> *The EU is a club that new member states clearly want to join. Romania, Bulgaria, and Turkey are in the queue to come next.[11]*
>
> FINANCIAL TIMES,
> *September 17, 2003*

The European Union now comprises a twenty-five-nation unified market of over 400 million people. This "borderless" market now includes ten Central and Eastern Europe (CEE) countries—the Czech Republic, Estonia, Hungary, Latvia, Lithuania, Poland, the Slovak Republic, and Slovenia- as well as Malta and Cyprus. They joined the EU in May 2004, having met the EU accession requirements, including privatizing state-run businesses, improving the infrastructure, and revamping their finance and banking systems.[12] With the euro now a legally tradable currency, Europe's business environment is being transformed. The vast majority of legislative measures have been adopted to create an internal market with free movement of goods and people among the EU countries. The elimination of internal tariffs and customs, as well as financial and commercial barriers, have not eliminated national pride. Although most people in Europe are being thought of simply as Europeans, they still think of themselves first as British, French, Danish, Italian, and such and are wary of giving up too much power to centralized institutions or of giving up their national culture. The continuing enlargement of the EU to include many less prosperous countries has also promoted divisions among the "older" members.[13]

Global managers face two major tasks. One is strategic (dealt with more fully in Chapter 6): how firms outside of Europe can deal with the implications of the EU and of what some have called a "Fortress Europe"—that is, a market giving preference to insiders. The other task is cultural: how to deal effectively with multiple sets of national cultures, traditions, and customs within Europe, such as differing attitudes about how much time should be spent on work versus leisure activities.

Asia

> *A new east Asian economy is emerging, focused on greatly increased trade within the region and based on China rather than Japan.[14]*
>
> FINANCIAL TIMES,
> *January 6, 2004*

Japan and the Four Tigers—Singapore, Hong Kong, Taiwan, and South Korea, each of which has abundant natural resources and labor—have provided most of the capital and expertise for Asia's developing countries. Now the focus is on China's role in driving closer integration in the region through its rapidly growing exports. Japan continues to negotiate trade agreements with its neighbors; China is negotiating with the entire thirteen-member ASEAN, while ASEAN is negotiating for earlier development of its own free trade area, Asean Free Trade Area(AFTA).[15]

China

> *The Chinese market offers big opportunities for foreign investment, but you must learn to tolerate ambiguity and find a godfather to look after your political connections.[16]*
>
> FINANCIAL TIMES,
> *August 26, 2003*

China has enjoyed recent success as an export powerhouse, a status built on its strengths of low costs and a constant flow of capital. Its GDP growth rate (9.01 percent in 2003) has been the fastest growth rate in the world for several consecutive years. While considerable differences are found among the country's regions, making for quite varied markets, it is clear that China is slowly opening its doors. China seems to be stuck halfway between a command economy and a market economy, with capital allocation still largely state-controlled.[17] Central, regional, and local political influences create unpredictability for businesses, as do the arbitrary legal systems, suspect data, and underdeveloped infrastructure. In addition to foreign investment, China continues to enjoy significant inflows of money from the ethnic Chinese outside of China, often called the "Bamboo Network" or the "Overseas Chinese" network (further discussed in Chapter 8).

In September 2001, China completed its fifteen-year quest to become a member of the **World Trade Organization (WTO)**. The deal, which opens China's state-dominated economy to imports and also increases their exports, became effective in 2002; lower tariffs make foreign products more affordable for the Chinese, opening up huge, untapped markets.[18] In addition, an increasing number of non-Chinese firms are setting up manufacturing and service facilities in China, as well as joint ventures.

South Asia   In 2004, an agreement was signed to form the South Asia Association of Regional Cooperation (SAARC), a free trade pact among seven South Asian nations: Bangladesh, Bhutan, India, the Maldives, Nepal, Pakistan, and Sri Lanka, effective January 1, 2006. The agreement will lower tariffs to 25 percent within three to five years and eliminate them within seven years. The member nations comprise 1.5 billion people, with an estimated one-third of them living in poverty. Trade in South Asia is estimated at $14 billion when the agreement takes effect, though the majority of that trade will be between India and Pakistan, the two largest countries in the region.[19] Officials in those countries hope to follow the success of the other Asian regional bloc, the ASEAN.

North America
Consider the following observations:

> *NAFTA gave us a big push. Mexico's $594 billion economy is now the ninth largest in the world, up from No. 15 a dozen years ago. It gave us jobs. It gave us knowledge, experience, technological transfer.[20]*

> MEXICAN PRESIDENT VICENTE FOX,
> *December 22, 2003*

> *On balance, NAFTA's been rough for rural Mexicans. . . . It takes more than just trade liberalization to improve the quality of life for poor people around the world.[21]*

> THE CARNEGIE ENDOWMENT REPORT,
> *November, 2003*

> *NAFTA has brought significant economic and social benefits to the Mexican economy.[22]*

> THE WORLD BANK REPORT,
> *November, 2003*

The goal of the NAFTA between the United States, Canada, and Mexico was to bring faster growth, more jobs, better working conditions, and a cleaner environment for all as a result of increased exports and trade. This trading bloc—"one America"—has 421 million consumers. Now, after ten years, the debate continues about the extent to which those goals have been accomplished. That perspective varies, of course, among the three NAFTA countries and also varies according to how it has affected individual business firms and employees in various parts of those countries. (This subject is discussed in further detail in the Comparative Management in Focus section in Chapter 2.)

However, some changes for Mexico from 1993 to 2003 are not debatable, whether or not they all are attributable to the NAFTA. These include an increase in GDP from $403 billion to $594 billion; a doubling of exports as a percentage of GDP from 15 percent to 30 percent; and also, interestingly, an increase in remittances by migrants in the United States from $2.4 billion to $14 billion.[23] One has to wonder this then: If more jobs are available in Mexico and if people are being paid fairly, why are so many crossing the border to find jobs? Certainly, recent competition from China for outsourced jobs from foreign firms has put downward pressure on opportunities for Mexico, as manufacturing facilities and some service facilities migrate from Mexico to China in a race for the lowest cost operations.[24]

Central America   In December 2003, the United States completed negotiations for a new regional trade pact with four Central American countries: El Salvador, Guatemala, Honduras, and Nicaragua. In 2004, Costa Rica, the most wealthy nation in Central America, agreed to join. As when NAFTA was being considered, debate remains considerable as to what benefits and trade-offs the Central American Free Trade Agreement (CAFTA) would bring.[25]

Other Regions in the World

Sweeping political, economic, and social changes around the world present new challenges to global managers. The worldwide move away from communism, together with the trend toward **privatization**, has had an enormous influence on the world economy. Economic freedom is a critical factor in the relative wealth of nations.

One of the most striking changes today is that almost all nations have suddenly begun to develop decentralized, free market systems in order to manage a global economy of intense competition, the complexity of high-tech industrialization, and an awakening hunger for freedom.[26]

The Russian Federation

Today's Russia is an exciting place for investors. Five years after a financial crisis, Moscow is humming with construction sites and there is a fresh optimism in the air. Reforms in the financial system have opened up Russia to foreign investment. But there remain many pitfalls for the unwary.[27]

FINANCIAL TIMES SPECIAL REPORT,
October 9, 2003

The tossing of Russian oil oligarch Mikhail Khodorkovsky into the slammer on tax evasion charges and freezing 44 percent of the stock of Yukos—the giant energy concern—was a fresh reminder that when investing in emerging markets ... politics matter. (Khodorkovsky was considered a political rival to President Putin.)[28]

AMERICAN BANKER-BOND BUYER,
January 2, 2004

Clearly, Russia is faring well as it continues its transition to a capitalist economic system. According to the Russian economic ministry, the economy grew by 6.8 percent in 2003.[29] There has been more confidence by foreign investors since President Vladimir Putin imposed fiscal management policies that upgraded Russia's debt ratings. Until recently Russia has been regarded as more politically stable; New land, legal, and labor codes, as well as a more stable rouble, have encouraged foreign firms to take advantage of opportunities in that immense area, in particular the vast natural resources and the well-educated population of 145 million.[30] Moscow, in particular, is teeming with new construction sites, high-end cars, and new restaurants. The real GDP growth for Russia, at percent about 4.0 percent for 2004, is considered to be controlled by the so-called business "oligarchs"—a small group of businesspeople with political influence who capitalized on the privatization of Russia's economy and who limit competitive opportunities for small businesses.[31] In late 2004, however, foreign investors became very wary after President Putin reasserted controls over the oil sector after the Yukos affair, and reigned in some regional elections after the school siege in Beslan.

Less Developed Countries

Less developed countries (LDCs) are characterized by change that has come about more slowly as they struggle with low gross national product (GNP) and low per capita income, as well as the burdens of large, relatively unskilled populations and high international debt. Their economic situation and the often unacceptable level of government intervention discourage the foreign investment they need. Many countries in Central and South America, the Middle East, India, and Africa desperately hope to attract foreign investment to stimulate economic growth. Africa, for example, has been virtually ignored by most of the world's investors, although it does receive increasing investment from companies in South Africa, which has the region's biggest economy. South African companies no doubt realize that they have a competitive edge on the African continent that they do not have in more developed parts of the world.[32] Vodacom of South Africa, for example, promotes cell phone service in Kindu, Congo.

For firms willing to take the economic and political risks, the LDCs offer considerable potential for **international business**. Assessing the risk–return trade-offs and keeping up with political developments in these developing countries are two of the many demands on international managers. India is one country whose economy is booming as a result of

An ad on a shop in Kindu, Congo, promotes cellphone service from Vodacom of South Africa.

SOURCE: Copyright Adam Roberts. Reprinted by permission.

opening up to global business and providing highly skilled and educated workers to foreign companies. (For further discussion of the effects of globalization on India's landscape and culture see Comparative Management in Focus: Opening Economy Revitalizes India.)

Comparative Management in Focus
Opening Economy Revitalizes India

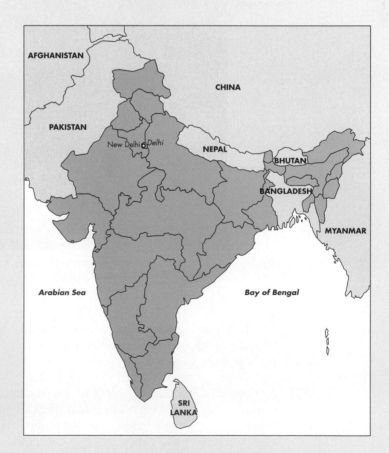

Map 1-1

Gurgaon, India—Tarun Narula, a 25-year-old computer instructor, celebrated Mohandas K. Gandhi's birthday on Oct. 2 by going to the Metropolitan Mall. So did so many thousands of others that the parking lot was full, as were those of the other two malls across and down the street. Indian-made sport utility vehicles, cars, and motorcycles fought for space, choking the roads of this satellite city south of Delhi.

Inside the malls, young people sipped coffee at Barista Coffee, the Starbucks of India. They wandered through Indian department stores, Marks and Spencer, Lacostee and Reebok. Families took children to McDonald's or the Subway sandwich shop. Moviegoers chose between "Boom," a Bollywood film with a decidedly Western touch of vulgarity, and "2 Fast 2 Furious."

He's everywhere. McDonalds is in Gurgaon, India—indicative of the global economy.

SOURCE: Amy Waldman, NYTimes

This is no longer the India of Gandhi, among history's most famous ascetics.

The change in values, habits and options in India—not just from his day, but from a mere decade ago—is undeniable, and so is the sense of optimism about India's economic prospects.

Much of India is still mired in poverty, but just over a decade after the Indian economy began shaking off its statist shackles and opening to the outside world, it is booming. The surge is based on strong industry and agriculture, rising Indian and foreign investment and American-style consumer spending by a growing middle class, including the people under age 25 who now make up half the country's population.

After growing just 4.3 percent last year, India's economy, the second fastest growing in the world, after China, is widely expected to grow close to 7 percent this year.

The growth of the past decade has put more money in the pockets of an expanding middle class, 250 million to 300 million strong, and more choices in front of them. Their appetites are helping to fuel demand-led growth for the first time in decades.

India is now the world's fastest growing telecom market, with more than one million new mobile phone subscriptions sold each month. Indians are buying about 10,000 motorcycles a day. Banks are now making $15 billion a year in home loans, with the lowest interest rates in decades helping to spur the spending, building and borrowing. Credit and debit cards are slowly gaining.

The potential for even more market growth is enormous, a fact recognized by multinationals and Indian companies alike. In 2001, according to census figures, only 31.6 percent of India's 192 million households had a television, and only 2.5 percent a car, jeep, or van.

Foreign institutional investors have poured nearly $5 billion into the Indian market this year, already more than six times last year's total. The Bombay Stock Exchange's benchmark Sensitive Index has risen by more than 50 percent since April, hitting a three-year high. Foreign exchange reserves are at a record $90 billion.

After huffing and puffing in place for eight or nine years, "the train has left the station," C. K. Prahalad, a professor at the University of Michigan Business School, said of the Indian economy.

More than a decade after India began opening its economy by reducing protectionism and red tape, slowly lifting restrictions on foreign investment and reforming its financial sector, the changes are starting to show substantial results.

Companies that stumbled in the face of recession and new competitive pressures in the 1990's have increased productivity and are showing record profits. India is slowly making a name not just for software exports and service outsourcing, but also as an exporter of autos, auto parts, and motorcycles.

Nature has played a part as well. The seasonal monsoon that ended recently was the best this agriculture-dependent economy has seen in at least five years, with normal or excess rainfall in 33 of 36 of the country's sub-regions. That, in turn, is putting income and credit in rural pockets, spurring a run on consumer goods that will only strengthen when the harvest comes in later this year.

In some places, the economic transformation is startling. Look at islands of prosperity like Gurgaon, or Bangalore, and you see an India that many Americans—not to speak of Indians—would not recognize.

It is a place where a young fashion designer like Swati Bhargava, 27, who works for a company that exports clothes to American and French chains, can buy stylish Indian clothes, eat at Pizza Hut, drink at Barista, and contemplate the country mutating around her.

SOURCE: "Sizzling Economy Revitalizes India" by Amy Waldman, The *New York Times*, October 20, 2003. Copyright © 2003 by *The New York Times Co.* Reprinted with permission.

Information Technology

From his London office, Richard J. Callahan, the U.S. West International chief, begins a turbocharged conference call with seven division presidents in five countries. They hash over cellular-phone sales in the Czech Republic, forecast long-distance hookups in Russia, and give a thumbs-up to opening an office in Japan.[33]

Of all the developments propelling global business today, the one that is transforming the international manager's agenda more than any other, is the rapid advance in **information technology (IT)**. The speed and accuracy of information transmission are changing the nature of the global manager's job by making geographic barriers less relevant. Indeed, the necessity of being able to access IT is being recognized by managers and families around the world, who are giving priority to being "plugged in" over other lifestyle accoutrements.

Information can no longer be centrally or secretly controlled by governments; political, economic, market, and competitive information is available almost instantaneously to anyone around the world, permitting informed and accurate decision making. Even cultural barriers are being lowered gradually by the role of information in educating societies about one another. Indeed, as consumers around the world become more aware, through various media, of how people in other countries live, their tastes and preferences begin to converge:

> *Global brands of colas, blue jeans, athletic shoes, and designer ties and handbags are as much on the mind of the taxi driver in Shanghai as they are in the home of the schoolteacher in Stockholm.*[34]

The explosive growth of information technology is both a cause and an effect of globalism. The information revolution is boosting productivity around the world. In addition, use of the Internet is propelling electronic commerce around the world (as discussed later in this chapter). Companies around the world are linked electronically to their employees, customers, distributors, suppliers, and alliance partners in many countries. Technology, in all its forms, gets dispersed around the world by **multinational corporations (MNCs)** and their alliance partners in many countries. However, some of the information intended for electronic transmission is currently subject to export controls by an EU directive intended to protect private information about its citizens. So, perhaps IT is not yet "borderless" but rather is subject to the same norms, preferences, and regulations as "human" cross-border interactions.

The Globalization of Human Capital

> *Of the 500 [U.S.] firms we surveyed, 45 percent indicate that they are currently using a global sourcing model. . . . The percentage of jobs being offshored (now averaging 13 percent for those 500 firms) will roughly double in the next three years.*[35]
>
> HEWITT ASSOCIATES STUDY PRESS RELEASE QUOTED ON CNBC,
> *March 5, 2004*

> *Globalization means we share jobs as well as goods.*[36]
>
> FINANCIAL TIMES,
> *August 27, 2003*

While firms around the world have been outsourcing manufacturing jobs to low-cost countries for decades, many are now also outsourcing—or "offshoreing"—white-collar jobs to India, China, Mexico, and the Phillippines:

> *Customer support, medical analysis, technical work, computer programming, form-filling and claims-processing—all these jobs can now move around the globe in the same way that farming and factory jobs could a century ago.*[37]
>
> FINANCIAL TIMES,
> *August 27, 2003*

Forrester Research predicted that 3.3 million (U.S.) jobs would be lost in service-sector offshore outsourcing by 2015, and added that "the information technology industry will lead the initial overseas exodus."[38] A programmer in India, for example—well educated and skilled and English-speaking—earns about $20,000 a year, compared to $80,000 in the United States. In Bangalore, India, MNCs such as Intel, Dell, IBM, Yahoo, and AOL employ 109,000 workers in chip design, software, call-centers, and tax processing.[39]

In China—long the world's low-cost manufacturing hub—jobs are on the upswing for back-office support for financial services and for telecom and retail companies in Asia. Such employees communicate to people in Hong Kong and Taiwan in local languages.[40] While backlash from some firms' clients has resulted in firms such as Dell repatriating their high-end jobs, white-collar job migration is still on the rise for firms around the world, bringing with it a new phase in economic globalization and competition.

The Global Manager's Role

Whatever your level of involvement, it is important to understand the global business environment and its influence on the manager's role. This complex role demands a contingency approach to dynamic environments, each of which has its own unique requirements. Within the larger context of global trends and competition, the rules of the game for the global

EXHIBIT 1-1   An Open Systems Model: The Contingency Role
of the Global Manager

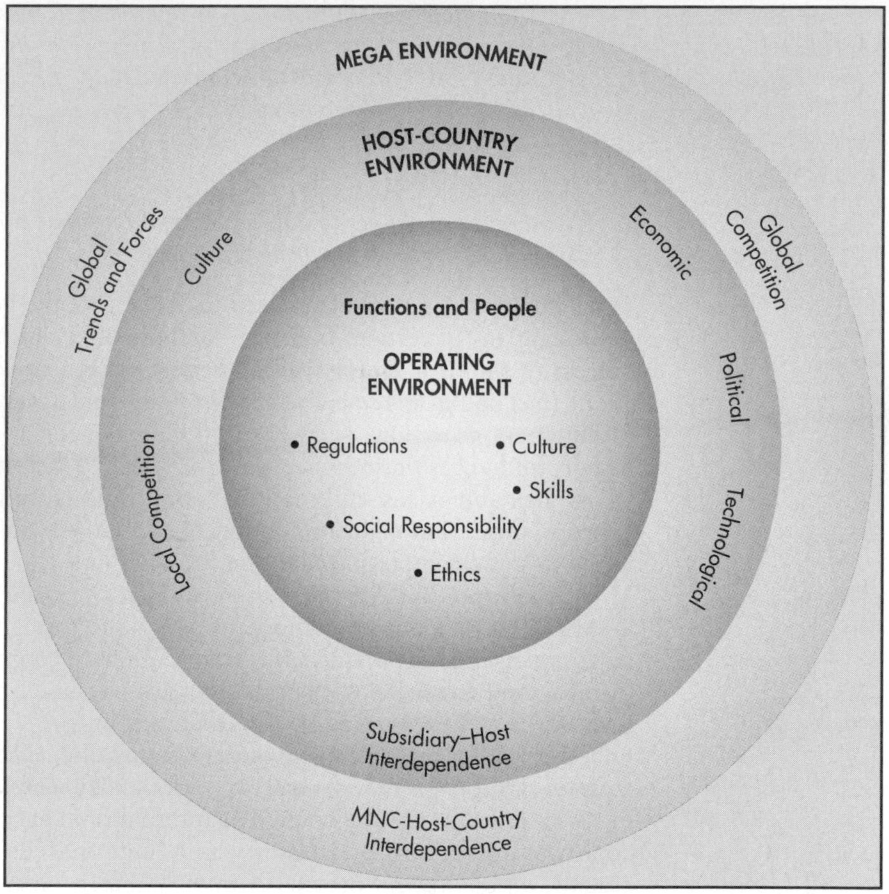

MEGA ENVIRONMENT

HOST-COUNTRY
ENVIRONMENT

Global Trends and Forces

Culture

Economic

Global Competition

Local Competition

Political

Technological

Functions and People

**OPERATING
ENVIRONMENT**

- Regulations
- Culture
- Skills
- Social Responsibility
- Ethics

Subsidiary–Host
Interdependence

MNC-Host-Country
Interdependence

manager are set by each country (see Exhibit 1-1): its political and economic agenda, its technological status and level of development, its **regulatory environment**, its comparative and competitive advantages, and its cultural norms. The astute manager will analyze the new environment, anticipate how it may affect the future of the home company, and then develop appropriate strategies and operating styles.

THE POLITICAL AND ECONOMIC ENVIRONMENT

Proactive globally oriented firms maintain an up-to-date profile of the political and economic environment of the countries in which they maintain operations (or have plans for future investment).

An important aspect of the political environment is the phenomenon of ethnicity—a driving force behind political instability around the world. In fact, many uprisings and conflicts that are thought to be political in nature are actually expressions of differences among ethnic groupings. Often, religious disputes lie at the heart of those differences. Uprisings based on religion operate either in conjunction with ethnic differences (as probably was the case in the former Yugoslavia) or as separate from them (as in Northern Ireland). Many terrorist activities are also based on religious differences, as in the Middle East. Managers must understand the ethnic and religious composition of the host country in order to anticipate problems of general instability, as well as those of an operational nature, such as effects on the workforce, on production and access to raw materials, and on the market.[41] For example, consider the following:[42]

In Pakistan one must understand the differences between Punjabi and Sindi. In Malaysia it is essential to recognize the special economic relationship between Chinese and Malay. In the Philippines it is important to understand the significant and lead financial role played by the Filipino-Chinese.

Political Risk

President Nestor Kirchner stripped the French-owned company, Thales Spectrum, defence contractor, of its operating license, marking the most aggressive action against a foreign investor in Argentina since his election. . . . The cabinet secretary said, "This service can't be conceded to the private sector. The results of the privatization have not been positive."[43]

www.FT.com,
January 27, 2004

Increasingly, investors are understanding that projects can be derailed by little "p" political risk . . . the death from 1,000 cuts.[44]

The managers of a global firm need to investigate the political risks to which they expose their company in certain countries—and the implications of those risks for the economic success of the firm. **Political risks** are any governmental action or politically motivated event that could adversely affect the long-run profitability or value of a firm.[45] The Middle East, as we have seen, has traditionally been an unstable area where political risk heavily influences business decisions.

In unstable areas, multinational corporations weigh the risks of nationalization or expropriation. **Nationalization** refers to the forced sale of an MNC's assets to local buyers, with some compensation to the firm, perhaps leaving a minority ownership with the MNC. **Expropriation**, very rare in the last decade, occurs when a local government seizes and provides inadequate compensation for the foreign-owned assets of an MNC; when no compensation is provided, it is confiscation. In countries that have a proven history of stability and consistency, the political risk to a multinational corporation is relatively low. The risk of expropriation is highest in countries that experience continuous political upheaval, violence, and change. An event that affects all foreign firms doing business in a country or region is called a **macropolitical risk event**. In the Middle East, Iraq's invasion of Kuwait in 1990 abruptly halted all international business with and within both of those countries and caught businesses wholly unprepared. In China, the Tiananmen Square crackdown on student protestors in 1989 interrupted much foreign business in the Far East. After years of increasing international investment in China (at the time of the crackdown, the United States had reached the $3 billion mark in direct foreign investment), many companies closed and withdrew their personnel. Concerned about the government's response to student unrest, these businesses were wary about the future.[46]

In many regions, terrorism poses a severe and random political risk to company personnel and assets and can, obviously, interrupt the conduct of business. According to Micklous, **terrorism** is "the use, or threat of use, of anxiety-inducing . . . violence for ideological or political purposes."[47] The increasing incidence of terrorism, especially in Latin America, concerns MNCs. In particular, the kidnapping of business executives has become quite common. An event that affects one industry or company or only a few companies is called a **micropolitical risk event**.[48] Such events have become more common than macropolitical risk events. Such micro action is often called "**creeping expropriation**," indicating a government's gradual and subtle action against foreign firms.[49] This is when a "death from a 1,000 cuts" comes in—"when you haven't been expropriated, but it takes ten times longer to do anything."[50] Typically, such continuing problems with an investment present more difficulty for foreign firms than do major events that are insurable by political-risk insurers. The following list describes seven typical political risk events common today (and possible in the future):

1. Expropriation of corporate assets without prompt and adequate compensation
2. Forced sale of equity to host-country nationals, usually at or below depreciated book value
3. Discriminatory treatment against foreign firms in the application of regulations or laws
4. Barriers to **repatriation** of funds (profits or equity)
5. Loss of technology or other intellectual property (such as patents, trademarks, or trade names)
6. Interference in managerial decision making
7. Dishonesty by government officials, including canceling or altering contractual agreements, extortion demands, and so forth[51]

Political Risk Assessment

International companies must conduct some form of **political risk assessment** to manage their exposure to risk and to minimize financial losses. Typically, local managers in each country assess potentially destabilizing issues and evaluate their future impact on their company, making suggestions for dealing with possible problems. Corporate advisers then establish guidelines for each local manager to follow in handling these problems. Dow Chemical has a program in which it uses line managers trained in political and economic analysis, as well as executives in foreign subsidiaries, to provide risk analyses of each country.[52]

Risk assessment by multinational corporations usually takes two forms. One uses experts or consultants familiar with the country or region under consideration. Such consultants, advisers, and committees usually monitor important trends that may portend political change, such as the development of opposition or destabilizing political parties. They then assess the likelihood of political change and develop several plausible scenarios to describe possible future political conditions.

A second and increasingly common means of political risk assessment used by MNCs is the development of internal staff and in-house capabilities. This type of assessment may be accomplished by having staff assigned to foreign subsidiaries, by having affiliates monitor local political activities, or by hiring people with expertise in the political and economic conditions in regions critical to the firm's operations. Frequently, all means are used. The focus must be on monitoring political issues before they become headlines; the ability to minimize the negative effects on the firm—or to be the first to take advantage of opportunities—is greatly reduced once a major media source, such as CNN, has put out the news.

No matter how sophisticated the methods of political risk assessment become; however, nothing can replace timely information from people on the front line. In other words, sophisticated techniques and consultations are useful as an addition to, but not as a substitute for, the line managers in foreign subsidiaries, many of whom are host-country nationals. These managers represent the most important resource for current information on the political environment, and how it might affect their firm, because they are uniquely situated at the meeting point of the firm and the host country. Prudent MNCs, however, weigh the subjectivity of these managers' assessments and also realize that similar events will have different effects from one country to another.

An additional technique, the assessment of political risk through the use of computer modeling, is now becoming fairly common. One firm, American Can, uses a program called PRISM (Primary Risk Investment Screening Matrix), which digests information from overseas managers and consultants on 200 variables and reduces them to an index of economic desirability and an index of political and economic stability. Those countries with the most favorable PRISM indices are then considered by American Can for investment.[53] Such a program, of course, is only as good as its input data—which is often of doubtful quality because of inadequate information systems in many countries and because the information is processed subjectively.

To analyze their data regarding potential risks, some companies attempt to quantify variables into a ranking system for countries. They use their staff or outside consultants to allocate a minimum and a maximum score for criteria they deem important to them on (1) the political and economic environment, (2) domestic economic conditions, and (3) external economic relations. The sum of the individual scores for each variable represents a total risk evaluation range for each country.[54] One drawback of these quantitative systems is that they rely on information based primarily on past events. They are therefore limited in their ability to predict political events in a volatile environment.

Still another method, more rapidly responsive to and predictive of political changes, is called the **early-warning system**. This system uses lead indicators to predict possible political dangers, such as signs of violence or riots, developing pressure on the MNC to hire more local workers, or pending import–export restrictions.[55] The early-warning analysis is typically separated into macrorisk and microrisk elements.

In addition to assessing the political risk facing a firm, alert managers also examine the specific types of impact that such risks may have on the company. For an autonomous international **subsidiary**, most of the impact from political risks (nationalization, terrorism) will be at the level of the ownership and control of the firm because its acquisition by the host country would provide the state with a fully operational business.[56] For global firms, the primary risks are likely to be from restrictions (on imports, exports, currency, and so forth), with the impact at the level of the firm's transfers (or exchanges) of money, products, or component parts.[57]

Managing Political Risk

After assessing the potential political risk of investing or maintaining current operations in a country, managers face perplexing decisions on how to manage that risk. On one level, they can decide to suspend their firm's dealings with a certain country at a given point—either by the **avoidance** of investment or by the withdrawal of current investment (by selling or abandoning plants and assets). On another level, if they decide that the risk is relatively low in a particular country or that a high-risk environment is worth the potential returns, they may choose to start (or maintain) operations there and to accommodate that risk through **adaptation** to the political regulatory environment. That adaptation can take many forms, each designed to respond to the concerns of a particular local area. The following are some means of adaptation suggested by Taoka and Beeman:

1. **Equity sharing** includes the initiation of joint ventures with nationals (individuals or those in firms, labor unions, or government) to reduce political risks.
2. **Participative management** requires that the firm actively involve nationals, including those in labor organizations or government, in the management of the subsidiary.
3. **Localization of the operation** includes the modification of the subsidiary's name, management style, and so forth, to suit local tastes. Localization seeks to transform the subsidiary from a foreign firm to a national firm.
4. **Development assistance** includes the firm's active involvement in infrastructure development (foreign-exchange generation, local sourcing of materials or parts, management training, technology transfer, securing external debt, and so forth).[58]

In addition to avoidance and adaptation, two other means of risk reduction available to managers are **dependency** and **hedging**. Some means that managers might use to maintain dependency—keeping the subsidiary and the host nation dependent on the parent corporation—follow:

1. **Input control** means that the firm maintains control over key inputs, such as raw materials, components, technology, and know-how.
2. **Market control** requires that the firm keep control of the means of distribution (for instance, by only manufacturing components for the parent firm or legally blocking sales outside the host country).
3. **Position control** involves keeping certain key subsidiary management positions in the hands of expatriate or home-office managers.
4. **Staged contribution strategies** mean that the firm plans to increase, in each successive year, the subsidiary's contributions to the host nation (in the form of tax revenues, jobs, infrastructure development, hard-currency generation, and so forth). For this strategy to be most effective, the firm must inform the host nation of these projected contributions as an incentive.[59]

Finally, even if the company cannot diminish or change political risks, it can minimize the losses associated with these events by hedging. Following are some means of hedging:

1. **Political risk insurance** is offered by most industrialized countries. In the United States, the Overseas Private Investment Corporation (OPIC) provides coverage for new investments in projects in friendly, less developed countries. Insurance minimizes losses arising from specific risks—such as the inability to repatriate profits, expropriation, nationalization, or confiscation—and from damage as a result of war, terrorism, and so forth.[60] The Foreign Credit Insurance Association (FCIA) also covers political risks caused by war, revolution, currency inconvertibility, and the cancellation of import or export licenses. However, political risk insurance covers only the loss of a firm's assets, not the loss of revenue resulting from expropriation.[61]
2. **Local debt financing** (money borrowed in the host country), where available, helps a firm hedge against being forced out of operation without adequate compensation. In such instances, the firm withholds debt repayment in lieu of sufficient compensation for its business losses.

Multinational corporations also manage political risk through their global strategic choices. Many large companies diversify their operations both by investing in many countries and by operating through joint ventures with a local firm or government or through local licensees. By involving local people, companies, and agencies, firms minimize the risk of negative outcomes due to political events. (See Chapters 6 and 7 for further discussion of these and other global strategies.)

Managing Terrorism Risk

No longer is the risk of terrorism for global businesses focused only on certain areas such as South America or the Middle East. That risk now has to be considered in countries such as the United States, which had previously been regarded as safe. Eighty countries lost citizens in the World Trade Center attack on September 11, 2001. Many companies from Asia and Europe had office branches in the towers of the World Trade Center; most of those offices, along with the employees from those countries, were destroyed in the attack. Thousands of lives and billions of dollars were lost, not only by those immediately affected by the attack but also by countless small and large businesses impacted by the ripple effect; global airlines and financial markets were devastated.

As incidents of terrorism accelerate around the world, many companies are also increasingly aware of the need to manage the risk of terrorism. In high-risk countries, both IBM and Exxon try to develop a benevolent image through charitable contributions to the local community. They also try to maintain low profiles and minimize publicity in the host countries by using, for example, discreet corporate signs at company sites.[62]

Some companies have put together teams to monitor the patterns of terrorism around the world. Kidnappings are common in Latin America (as a means of raising money for political activities). Abductions in Colombia hit a record 3,029 in 2000.[63] In the Middle East, airplane hijackings, kidnapping of foreigners, and blackmail (for the release of political prisoners) are common. In Western Europe, terrorists typically aim bombs at U.S.-owned banks and computer companies. Almost all MNCs have stepped up their security measures abroad, hiring consultants in counterterrorism (to train employees to cope with the threat of terrorism) and advising their employees to avoid U.S. airlines when flying overseas.[64] For many firms, however, the opportunities outweigh the threats, even in high-risk areas such as Jakarta (see beginning of this chapter).

Economic Risk

The Chilean power companies, forestry firms, soda bottlers, and supermarkets that plowed billions of dollars into Argentina are now retrenching or revising their strategies. The moves follow Argentina's currency devaluation, which brought the economy to a virtual standstill and sapped the population of much of its remaining buying power.[65]

WALL STREET JOURNAL,
February 20, 2002

Closely connected to a country's political stability is its economic environment—and the relative risk that it may pose to foreign companies. A country's level of economic development generally determines its economic stability and, therefore, its relative risk to a foreign firm. Most industrialized nations pose little risk of economic instability; less developed nations pose more risk. This risk was illustrated when Argentina's economic woes, expected to result in the country's economy shrinking up to 15 percent in 2002, negatively affected foreign firms doing business there.

A country's ability or intention to meet its financial obligations determines its **economic risk**. The economic risk incurred by a foreign corporation usually falls into one of two main categories. Its subsidiary (or other investment) in a specific country may become unprofitable if (1) the government abruptly changes its domestic monetary or fiscal policies or (2) the government decides to modify its foreign-investment policies. The latter situation would threaten the company's ability to repatriate its earnings and would create a financial or interest-rate risk. Furthermore, the risk of exchange-rate volatility results in currency translation exposure to the firm when the balance sheet of the entire corporation is consolidated and may cause a negative cash flow from the foreign subsidiary. Currency translation exposure occurs when the value of one country's currency changes relative to that of another. For a U.S. company operating in Mexico, the peso devaluation in the late 1990s meant that the company's assets in that country were worth less when translated into dollars on the financial statements, but the firm's liabilities in Mexico were also less. When exchange-rate changes are radical, repercussions are felt around the world. For example, when the Russian ruble was devalued in 1998, it was unfortunate for the Russian people because their money could buy so much less and for Russian firms because they did not have enough buying power to purchase products from overseas, which meant that the sales of foreign companies declined. On the other hand, foreign companies suddenly had more purchasing power in Russia to outsource raw materials, labor, and so on.

Because every MNC operating overseas exposes itself to some level of economic risk, often affecting its everyday operational profitability, managers constantly reassess the level of risk their companies may face in any specific country or region of the world. Four methods of analyzing economic risk, or a country's creditworthiness, are recommended by John Mathis, a professor of international economics who has also served as senior financial policy analyst for the World Bank. These methods are (1) the quantitative approach, (2) the qualitative approach, (3) a combination of both of these approaches, and (4) the checklist approach.

The **quantitative method**, says Mathis, "attempts to measure statistically a country's ability to honor its debt obligation."[66] This measure is arrived at by assigning different weights to economic variables in order to produce a composite index used to monitor the country's creditworthiness over time and to make comparisons with other countries. A drawback of this approach is that it does not take into account different stages of development among the countries it compares.

The **qualitative approach** evaluates a country's economic risk by assessing the competence of its leaders and analyzing the types of policies they are likely to implement. This approach entails a subjective assessment by the researcher in the process of interviewing those leaders and projecting the future direction of the economy.

The **checklist approach**, explains Mathis, "relies on a few easily measurable and timely criteria believed to reflect or indicate changes in the creditworthiness of the country."[67] Researchers develop various vulnerability indicators that categorize countries in terms of their ability to withstand economic volatility. Most corporations recognize that neither this, nor any single approach, can provide a comprehensive economic risk profile of a country. Therefore, they try to use a combination of approaches.

THE LEGAL ENVIRONMENT

The prudent global manager consults with legal services, both locally and at headquarters, to comply with host-country regulations and to maintain cooperative long-term relationships in the local area. If the manager waits until a problem arises, little legal recourse may be available outside of local interpretation and enforcement. Indeed, this has been the experience of many foreign managers in China, where financial and legal systems remain rudimentary in spite of attempts to show the world a capitalist face. Managers there often simply ignore their debts to foreign companies as they did under the old socialist system.[68] The painful lesson to many foreign companies in China is that they are losing millions because Beijing often does not stand behind the commitments of its state-owned enterprises. Although no guarantee is possible, the risk of massive losses may be minimized, among other ways, by making sure you get approval from related government offices (national, provincial, and local), seeing that you are not going to run amok of long-term government goals, and getting loan guarantees from the headquarters of one of Beijing's main banks.[69] In addition, one cannot assume that there will be legal recourse in China. Mr. Cheng, a U.S. businessman who grew up in Hunan, China, was thrown in jail in China because a Chinese businessman changed his mind about investing in Mr. Cheng's safety-helmet factory in Zhuhai. Only after two months and his son's visit to the U.S.

embassy in Beijing was Mr. Cheng freed. Mr. Cheng asks, "[without even a trial], how could the court render a decision just one hour after Mr. Liu and my general manager had signed a new contract?"[70] Some of the contributing factors, he has realized since then, were the personal connections—*guanxi*—involved and the fact that some courts offer their services to the business community for profit. In addition, many judges get their jobs through nepotism rather than by virtue of a law degree.

Although the regulatory environment for the international manager consists of the many local laws and the court systems in those countries in which he or she operates, certain other legal issues are covered by international law, which governs relationships between sovereign countries, the basic units in the world political system.[71] One such agreement, which regulates international business by spelling out the rights and obligations of the seller and the buyer, is the United Nations Convention on Contracts for the International Sale of Goods (CISG). This convention became law on January 1, 1988, and applies to contracts for the sale of goods between countries that have adopted the convention.

Generally speaking, the manager of the foreign subsidiary or foreign operating division will comply with the host country's legal system. Such systems, derived from common law, civil law, or Muslim law, are a reflection of the country's culture, religion, and traditions. Under **common law**, used in the United States and twenty-six other countries of English origin or influence, past court decisions act as precedents to the interpretation of the law and to common custom. **Civil law** is based on a comprehensive set of laws organized into a code. Interpretation of these laws is based on reference to codes and statutes. About seventy countries, predominantly in Europe (e.g., France and Germany), are ruled by civil law, as is Japan. In Islamic countries, such as Saudi Arabia, the dominant legal system is **Islamic law**; based on religious beliefs, it dominates all aspects of life. Islamic law is followed in approximately twenty-seven countries and combines, in varying degrees, civil, common, and indigenous law.[72]

Contract Law

In China, the old joke goes, a contract is a pause in the negotiation.[73]

VANESSA CHANG,
KPMG Peat Marwick

A **contract** is an agreement by the parties concerned to establish a set of rules to govern a business transaction. Contract law plays a major role in international business transactions because of the complexities arising from the differences in the legal systems of participating countries and because the host government in many developing and communist countries is often a third party in the contract. Both common law and civil law countries enforce contracts, although their means of resolving disputes differ. Under civil law, it is assumed that a contract reflects promises that will be enforced without specifying the details in the contract; under common law, the details of promises must be written into the contract to be enforced.[74] Astute international managers recognize that they will have to draft contracts in legal contexts different from their own, and so they prepare themselves accordingly by consulting with experts in international law before going overseas. In China, for example, "The risk is, you could have a contract torn up or changed. We're just going to have to adjust to that in the West," says Robert Broadfoot, who heads the Political & Economic Risk Consultancy in Hong Kong. He says that Western companies think they can avoid political risk by spelling out every detail in a contract, but "in Asia, there is no shortcut for managing the relationship."[75] In other words, the contract is in the relationship, not on the paper, and the way to ensure the reliability of the agreement is to nurture the relationship.

Even a deal that has been implemented for some time may start to get watered down at a time when you cannot do anything about it. A Japanese-led consortium experienced this problem after it built an expressway in Bangkok. The Thai government later lowered the toll that it had agreed could be charged for use of the road. This is a subtle form of expropriation, since a company cannot simply pack up a road and leave.[76] Neglect regarding contract law may leave a firm burdened with an agent who does not perform the expected functions, or a firm may be faced with laws that prevent management from laying off employees (often the case in Belgium, the Netherlands, Germany, Sweden, and elsewhere).[77]

Other Regulatory Issues

Differences in laws and regulations from country to country are numerous and complex. These and other issues in the regulatory environment that concern multinational firms are briefly discussed here.

Countries often impose protectionist policies, such as tariffs, quotas, and other trade restrictions, to give preference to their own products and industries. The Japanese have come under much criticism for protectionism, which they use to limit imports of foreign goods while they continue exporting consumer goods (e.g., cars and electronics) on a large scale. The U.S. auto industry continues to ask the U.S. government for protection from Japanese car imports. Calls to "Buy American," however, are thwarted by the difficulty of identifying cars that are truly U.S.-made; the intricate web of car-manufacturing alliances between Japanese and American companies often makes it difficult to distinguish the maker.

A country's tax system influences the attractiveness of investing in that country and affects the relative level of profitability for an MNC. Foreign tax credits, holidays, exemptions, depreciation allowances, and taxation of corporate profits are additional considerations the foreign investor must examine before acting. Many countries have signed tax treaties (or conventions) that define such terms as "income," "source," and "residency" and spell out what constitutes taxable activities.

The level of government involvement in the economic and regulatory environment varies a great deal among countries and has a varying impact on management practices. In Canada, the government has a significant involvement in the economy. It has a powerful role in many industries, including transportation, petrochemicals, fishing, steel, textiles, and building materials—forming partly owned or wholly owned enterprises. Wholly owned businesses are called Crown Corporations (Petro Canada, Ontario Hydro Corporation, Marystown Shipyard, Saskatchewan Telephones, and so forth), many of which are as large as major private companies. The government's role in the Canadian economy, then, is one of both control and competition.[78] Government policies, subsidies, and regulations directly affect the manager's planning process, as do other major factors in the Canadian legal environment, such as the high proportion of unionized workers (30 percent). In Quebec, the law requiring official bilingualism imposes considerable operating constraints and expenses. For a foreign subsidiary, this regulation forces managers to speak both French and English and to incur the costs of language training for employees, translators, the administration of bilingual paperwork, and so on.[79]

THE TECHNOLOGICAL ENVIRONMENT

The effects of technology around the world are pervasive—both in business and in private lives. In many parts of the world, whole generations of technological development are being skipped over. For example, many people will go straight to a digital phone without ever having had their houses wired under the analog system. Even in a remote village such as Bario, Malaysia—still lacking many traditional roads—an information highway is underway.[80] Advances in information technology are bringing about increased productivity—for employees, for companies, and for countries.

> *The Internet, the submarine fiber-optic cable, and the communications satellite are now cast in the role once played by the iron-hulled ocean-going steamship.*[81]

Now that we are in a global information society, it is clear that corporations must incorporate into their strategic planning and their everyday operations the accelerating macro-environmental phenomenon of **technoglobalism**—in which the rapid developments in information and communication technologies (**ICTs**) are propelling globalization and vice versa.[82] Investment-led globalization is leading to global production networks, which results in global diffusion of technology to link parts of the value-added chain in different countries. That chain may comprise parts of the same firm, or it may comprise suppliers and customers, or technology-partnering alliances among two or more firms. Either way, technological developments are facilitating, indeed necessitating, the network firm structure that allows flexibility and rapid response to local needs. Clearly, the effects of technology on global trade and business transactions cannot be ignored; in addition, the Internet is propelling electronic commerce around the world. The ease of use and pervasiveness of the Internet raise difficult questions about ownership of intellectual property, consumer protection, residence location, taxation, and other issues.[83]

New technology specific to a firm's products represents a key competitive advantage to firms and challenges international businesses to manage the transfer and diffusion of proprietary technology, with its attendant risks. Whether it is a product, a process, or a management technology, an MNC's major concern is the **appropriability of technology**—that is, the ability of the innovating firm to profit from its own technology by protecting it from competitors.

An MNC can enjoy many technological benefits from its global operations. Advances resulting from cooperative research and development (R&D) can be transferred among affiliates around the world, and specialized management knowledge can be integrated and shared. However, the risks of technology transfer and pirating are considerable and costly. Although firms face few restrictions on the creation and dissemination of technology in developed countries, less developed countries often impose restrictions on licensing agreements, royalties, and so forth, as well as on patent protection.

In Germany, for example, royalties on patents are limited to 10 percent of sales, but the patent and trademark durations are twenty years and ten years, respectively, with 45 percent being the highest tax bracket allowed on royalties. Less developed countries tend to be comparatively more restrictive on the patent and trademark durations and on the range of unpatentable items. Egypt has no limits on royalties but will only patent production processes, and then only for fifteen years.

In most countries, governments use their laws to some extent to control the flow of technology. These controls may be in place for reasons of national security. Other countries, LDCs in particular, use their investment laws to acquire needed technology (usually labor-intensive technology to create jobs), increase exports, use local technology, and train local people.

The most common methods of protecting proprietary technology are the use of patents, trademarks, trade names, copyrights, and trade secrets. Various international conventions do afford some protection in participating countries; more than eighty countries adhere to the International Convention for the Protection of Industrial Property, often referred to as the Paris Union, for the protection of patents. However, restrictions and differences in the rules in some countries not signatory to the Paris Union, as well as industrial espionage, pose continuing problems for firms trying to protect their technology.

One risk to a firm's intellectual property is the inappropriate use of the technology by joint-venture partners, franchisees, licensees, and employees (especially those who move to other companies). Some countries rigorously enforce employee secrecy agreements.

Another major consideration for global managers is the need to evaluate the appropriateness of technology for the local environment—especially in less developed countries. Studying the possible cultural consequences of the transfer of technology, managers must assess whether the local people are ready and willing to change their values, expectations, and behaviors on the job to use new technological methods, whether applied to production, research, marketing, finance, or some other aspect of business. Often, a decision regarding the level of technology transfer is dominated by the host government's regulations or requirements. In some instances, the host country may require that foreign investors import only their most modern machinery and methods so that the local area may benefit from new technology. In other cases, the host country may insist that foreign companies use only labor-intensive processes, which can help to reduce high unemployment in an area. When the choice is left to international managers, experts in economic development recommend that managers make informed choices about appropriate technology. The choice of technology may be capital-intensive, labor-intensive, or intermediate, but the key is that it should suit the level of development in the area and the needs and expectations of the people who will use it.[84]

Patel, a small manufacturer of detergent in India, provides an example of the successful use of appropriate technology. Patel has taken over three-quarters of the detergent market from Lever, a multinational company whose Surf detergent had formerly dominated the market in India. Managers at Patel realized that Surf was a high-quality, high-priced product but that it was not suitable for a poor country. They set up a chain of stores in which people mixed their own detergent ingredients by hand. This primitive method enabled Patel to tailor its technology to the conditions and expectations in India and to outsell Lever on the basis of price; its annual sales are now over $250 million.[85]

Global E-Business

B2B clearly helps companies find suppliers and customers in other countries.[86]

Andy Kyte,
Gartner Inc., England, May 17, 2001

The biggest U.S. internet companies {such as eBay, Yahoo!, and AOL} enjoy huge economies of scale, and, in some cases, overseas revenues are expected soon to overtake domestic sales.[87]

Financial Times,
June 10, 2004

In spite of global trade's slower-than-expected pace of advancement over the Internet, without doubt the Internet has had a considerable impact on how companies buy and sell goods around the world—mostly raw materials and services going to manufacturers. Internet-based electronic trading and data exchange are changing the way companies do business, while breaking down global barriers of time, space, logistics, and culture. It has introduced a new level of global competition by providing efficiencies through reducing numbers of suppliers and slashing administration costs throughout the value chain. **E-business** is "the integration of systems, processes, organizations, value chains, and entire markets using Internet-based and related technologies and concepts."[88] **E-commerce** refers directly to the marketing and sales process via the Internet. Firms use e-business to help build new relationships between businesses and customers.[89] The Internet and e-business provide a number of uses and advantages in global business, including the following:

1. Convenience in conducting business worldwide; facilitating communication across borders contributes to the shift toward globalization and a global market.
2. An electronic meeting and trading place, which adds efficiency in conducting business sales.
3. A corporate Intranet service, merging internal and external information for enterprises worldwide.
4. Power to consumers as they gain access to limitless options and price differentials.
5. A link and efficiency in distribution.[90]

Although most early attention was on e-commerce, experts now believe the real opportunities are in business-to-business (**B2B**) transactions. In addition, while the scope, complexity, and sheer speed of the B2B phenomenon, including e-marketplaces, have global executives scrambling to assess the impact and their own competitive roles, estimates for growth in the e-business marketplace may have been overzealous. The global economic slowdown and its resultant dampening of corporate IT spending have caused various research groups, such as AMR Research and the Gartner Group, to revise their projections downward for B2B Internet transactions. Still, the growth projections are considerable, with an estimated $6 trillion in B2B transactions for 2004.

While we hear mostly about large companies embracing B2B, it is noteworthy that a large proportion of current and projected B2B use is by small and medium-sized firms, for three common purposes: supply chain, procurement, and distribution channel.

A successful Internet strategy—especially on a global scale—is, of course, not easy to create. Potential problems abound, as experienced by the European and U.S. companies surveyed by Forrester Research. Such problems include internal obstacles and politics, difficulties in regional coordination and in balancing global versus local e-commerce, and cultural differences. Such a large-scale change in organizing business clearly calls for absolute commitment from the top, empowered employees with a willingness to experiment, and good internal communications.[91]

Barriers to the adoption and progression of e-business around the world include lack of readiness of partners in the value chain, such as suppliers. If companies want to have an effective marketplace, they usually must invest in increasing their trading partners' readiness and their customers' capabilities. Other barriers are cultural. In Europe, for example, "Europe's e-commerce excursion has been hindered by a laundry list of cultural and regulatory obstacles, like widely varying tax systems, language hurdles, and currency issues."[92]

In spite of such problems, as well as the global technology bust, companies in Europe purchased more than $200 billion in goods and services in 2003. However, it is noteworthy that only 20 percent of B2B e-commerce flowed through e-marketplaces, with most passing through industry consortium exchanges, such as Covisint for the automobile industry and Exostar for the aerospace industry. The other 80 percent comprised online sales through company Web sites.[93]

In other areas of the world, barriers to creating global e-businesses include differences in physical, information, and payment infrastructure systems. In such countries, innovation is required to use local systems for implementing a Web strategy. In Japan, for example, very few transactions are conducted using credit cards. Typically, bank transfers and COD are used to pay for purchases. Also, many Japanese use convenience stores, such as 7-Eleven Japan, to pay for their online purchases by choosing that option online.[94]

For these reasons, B2B e-business is likely to expand globally faster than B2C (business-to-consumer transactions). In addition, consumer e-commerce depends on each country's level of access to computers and the Internet, as well as the relative efficiency of home delivery. Clearly, companies who want to go global through e-commerce must localize to globalize, which means much more than just presenting online content in local languages.

> *Localizing . . . also means recognizing and conforming to the nuances, subtleties and tastes of multiple local cultures, as well as supporting transactions based on each country's currency, local connection speeds, payment preferences, laws, taxes and tariffs.[95]*

In spite of various problems, use of the Internet to facilitate and improve global competitiveness continues to be explored and discovered. In the public sector in Europe, for example, the European Commission advertises tender invitations online in order to transform the way public sector contracts are awarded, using the Internet to build a truly single market:

> *Other global professional service organizations are successfully using all aspects of e-business and are helping their clients to do so. One example is PricewaterhouseCoopers. The company's employees, operating in over 150 countries, provide clients with expertise in solving complex business problems, including the sectors of Global Human Resources, Business Process Outsourcing, Financial Advisory, Audit and Advisory, Management Consulting, and Global Tax Services.[96]*

As the PricewaterhouseCoopers executives claim, e-business is not only a new Web site on the Internet but also "a source of significant strategic advantage; one that will distinguish one company from another and transform business relationships as they are known today."[97] Hoping to capture this strategic advantage, the European Airbus venture—a public and private sector combination—has joined a global aerospace B2B exchange for aircraft parts (see E-Biz Box: Europe's Airbus Joins Global Aerospace B2B

Exchange). The exchange illustrates two major trends in global competition: (1) those of cooperative global alliances, even among competitors, to achieve synergies and (2) the use of technology to enable those connections and synergies.

E-BIZ BOX

Europe's Airbus Joins Global Aerospace B2B Exchange

France's Airbus Industrie is joining the Global Aerospace and Defense Exchange for aircraft parts under development by Boeing, Lockheed Martin, Raytheon, and BAE Systems. The open aerospace and defense exchange is based on the Commerce One MarketSite Portal Solution, which provides an electronic marketplace where buyers and sellers around the world can conduct business. The founding industry partners have an agreement to share equal ownership stakes in the new entity, with adjustments over time to be based on each partner's flow of its e-commerce through the exchange. Commerce One has a 5 percent equity; and 20 percent equity has been set aside for other industry participants and employees of the new venture.

The partner companies, their manufacturers, and their suppliers expect to realize enormous cost savings in the $400 billion industry by buying and selling parts over the Internet in the online exchange. The companies involved currently do business with over 37,000 suppliers, hundreds of airlines, and national governments globally, all of which will be invited to join the Web-based marketplace. Most commercial airplanes contain up to six million parts and are supported by millions of pages of technical data. The partners expect to be able to deliver greater value and to realize significantly lower transaction costs. The exchange will also be an e-marketplace for the indirect products and services that the partner companies, the airlines, and their suppliers need for daily operations.

Plans for the Web site now include the world's five largest aerospace companies and the biggest manufacturers of commercial airliners, Boeing and Airbus. Airbus Industrie is a European consortium comprising France's Aerospatiale Matra, Germany's DaimlerChrysler Aerospace, Spain's Construcciones Aeronauticas, and UK's BAE Systems.

While the combined exchange is being developed, the partners involved continue their own e-commerce sites, such as Raytheon's www.Everythingaircraft.com and Airbus Online Services. Meanwhile, other alliances among various partners continue, such as that between Aerospatiale, DaimlerChrysler Aerospace, and Construcciones, which formed the European Aeronautic Defence and Space Company. The company also plans to pull Italy's Finmeccanica into the fold. The Brits, retaining their usual independence, have decided to keep their aerospace company BAE Systems, 20 percent owner of Airbus, independent. But no one said it would be easy. Commerce One, developer of the five-member Global aerospace site, faces considerable technical hurdles because of the tremendous red tape and regulatory clearances involved with aerospace transactions.

SOURCES: Adapted from www.commerceone.com, www.Airbus.com, www.herring.com, www.FT.com, www.Boeing.com, www.baesystems.com, www.raytheon.com, and www.lockheedmartin.com (all 2000).

CONCLUSION

A skillful global manager cannot develop a suitable strategic plan or consider an investment abroad without first assessing the environment—political, economic, legal, and technological—in which the company will operate. This assessment should result not so much in a comparison of countries as in a comparison of (1) the relative risk and (2) the projected return on investments among these countries. Similarly, for ongoing operations, both the subsidiary manager and headquarters management must continually

EXHIBIT 1-2   The Environment of the Global Manager

Political Environment	Economic Environment
Form of government	Economic system
Political stability	State of development
Foreign policy	Economic stability
State companies	GNP
Role of military	International financial standing
Level of terrorism	Monetary/fiscal policies
Restrictions on imports/exports	Foreign investment

Regulatory Environment	Technological Environment
Legal system	Level of technology
Prevailing international laws	Availability of local technical skills
Protectionist laws	Technical requirements of country
Tax laws	Appropriability
Role of contracts	Transfer of technology
Protection for proprietary property	Infrastructure
	Environmental protection

Cultural Environment (see Part II)

monitor the environment for potentially unsettling events or undesirable changes that may require the redirection of certain subsidiaries or the entire company. Some of the critical factors affecting the global manager's environment (and therefore requiring monitoring) are listed in Exhibit 1-2.

Environmental risk has become the new frontier in global business. The skills of companies and the measures taken to manage their exposure to environmental risk on a world scale will soon largely replace their ability to develop, produce, and market global brands as the key element in global competitive advantage.

The pervasive role of culture in **international management** will be discussed fully in Part II, with a focus on how the managerial functions and the daily operations of a firm are also affected by a subtle, but powerful, environmental factor in the host country—that of culture.

Chapter 2 presents some more subtle, but critical, factors in the global environment—those of social responsibility and ethical behavior. We will consider a variety of questions: What is the role of the firm in the future of other societies and their people? What stakeholders must managers consider in their strategic and operational decisions in other countries? How do the expectations of firm behavior vary around the world, and should those expectations influence the international manager's decisions? What role does long-term global economic interdependence play in the firm's actions in other countries?

Summary of Key Points

1. Competing in the twenty-first century requires firms to invest in the increasingly refined managerial skills needed to perform effectively in a multicultural environment. Managers need a global orientation to meet the challenges of world markets and rapid, fundamental changes in a world of increasing economic interdependence.

2. Global management is the process of developing strategies, designing and operating systems, and working with people around the world to ensure sustained competitive advantage.

3. One major direction in world trade is the development of regional free-trade blocs. The TRIAD market refers to the three trade blocs of Western Europe, Asia, and North America.

4. Drastic worldwide changes present dynamic challenges to global managers, including the political and economic trend toward the privatization of businesses, rapid advances in information technology, and the management of offshore **human capital**.

5. Global managers must be aware of political risks around the world. Political risks are any governmental actions or politically motivated events that adversely affect the long-run profitability or value of a firm.

6. The risk of terrorist activity represents an increasing risk around the world. Managers have to decide how to incorporate that risk factor in their strategic and operational plans.

7. Political risk assessment by MNCs usually takes two forms: consultation with experts familiar with the area and the development of internal staff capabilities. Political risk can be managed through (1) avoiding or withdrawing investment; (2) adapting to the political regulatory environment; (3) maintaining the host country's dependency on the parent corporation; and (4) hedging potential losses through political risk insurance and local debt financing.

8. Economic risk refers to a country's ability to meet its financial obligations. The risk is that the government may change its economic policies, thereby making a foreign company unprofitable or unable to repatriate its foreign earnings.

9. The regulatory environment comprises the many different laws and courts of those nations in which a company operates. Most legal systems derive from the common law, civil law, or Muslim law.

10. Use of the Internet in e-commerce—in particular, in business-to-business (B2B) transactions—and for intracompany efficiencies, is rapidly becoming an important factor in global competitiveness.

11. The appropriability of technology is the ability of the innovating firm to protect its technology from competitors and to obtain economic benefits from that technology. Risks to the appropriability of technology include technology transfer and pirating and legal restrictions on the protection of proprietary technology. Intellectual property can be protected through patents, trademarks, trade names, copyrights, and trade secrets.

Discussion Questions

1. Discuss examples of recent macropolitical risk events and the effect they have or might have on a foreign subsidiary. What are micropolitical risk events? Give some examples and explain how they affect international business.

2. What means can managers use to assess political risk? What do you think is the relative effectiveness of these different methods? At the time you are reading this, what countries or areas do you feel have political risk sufficient to discourage you from doing business there?

3. Can political risk be "managed"? If so, what methods can be used to manage such risk, and how effective are they? Discuss the lengths to which you would go to manage political risk relative to the kinds of returns you would expect to gain.

4. Explain what is meant by the economic risk of a nation. Use a specific country as an example. Can economic risk in this country be anticipated? How?

5. Discuss the importance of contracts in international management. What steps must a manager take to ensure a valid and enforceable contract?

6. Discuss the effects of various forms of technology on international business. What role does the Internet play? Where is all this leading? Explain the meaning of the "appropriability of technology." What role does this play in international competitiveness? How can managers protect the proprietary technology of their firms?

7. Discuss the risk of terrorism. What means can managers use to reduce the risk or the effects of terrorism? Where in the world, and from what likely sources, would you anticipate terrorism?

Application Exercises

1. Do some further research on the technological environment. What are the recent developments affecting businesses and propelling globalization? What problems have arisen regarding use of the Internet for global business transactions, and how are they being resolved?

2. Consider recent events and the prevailing political and economic conditions in the Russian Federation. As a manager who has been considering investment there, how do you assess the political and economic risks at this time? What should be your company's response to this environment?

Experiential Exercise

In groups of three, represent a consulting firm. You have been hired by a diversified multinational corporation to advise on the political and economic environment in different countries. The company wants to open one or two manufacturing facilities in Europe to take advantage of the EU agreement. Choose a specific type of company and two specific countries in Europe and present them to the class, including the types of risks that would be involved and what steps the firm could take to manage those risks.

Internet Resources

Visit the Deresky companion Web site at www.prenhall.com/deresky for this chapter's Internet resources.

The EC Shatters Microsoft's Windows

The EU Commission concluded that Microsoft had "failed to provide the information needed by its rivals in the market for computer servers and by making the supply of Windows . . . conditional on the inclusion of its Media Player program."[1]

Political and legal differences around the world can hit home and restrict strategic options and growth opportunities. Enter the era of the global reach of regulatory bodies. In March 2004, the European Commission (EC), the executive arm of the European Union (EU), ordered Microsoft to open up more of its technology to competitors and to provide Europe with a version of its Windows operating system without a media player. The EC had brought two main charges against Microsoft: (1) that the company had failed to share critical technical information with Sun Microsystems and (2) that it illegally bundled Windows Media Player into its dominant Windows operating system. As a punishment, the EC imposed a fine on Microsoft of 497 million euros (around $605 million) for attempting to shut out competitors in other markets. The EC justified its steep fine on the basis of Microsoft's ability to pay—with an estimated cash hoard totaling $52.8 billion—and therefore the necessity to make the fine high enough to have a deterrent effect.[2]

Whereas U.S. antitrust regulation tends to focus on whether consumers would be harmed by a company's actions, European antitrust regulators focus on the potential harm to business competition. Commissioner Mario Monti's decision was based on the position that competitors would be put at an unfair disadvantage by Microsoft's withholding codes that allow Windows-based computers to work better with servers. The EC ruled that Microsoft had 120 days in which to share that information with its competitors with rival server products and to promise to keep that information current. Under the ruling, Microsoft also had to offer a version of Windows without Media Player within 90 days.

For its part, Microsoft argued that consumers and software developers benefit from product integration, which results in product innovation. The company commented thus:

The Commission is seeking to make new law that will have an adverse impact on intellectual property rights and the ability of dominant firms to innovate.

This adverse impact will not be confined to the software industry or to Europe . . . and . . . would spell bad news for the European and global economies.[3]

Microsoft argued that such rulings jeopardize the economic incentives for a range of companies and industries. However, the EC countered that high technology must be subject to the same antitrust rules that govern other industries. For its part, Microsoft offered a compromise—to include its rivals' programs on personal computers—but the offer was rejected, with Monti saying that the deal would have failed to constrain Microsoft in other cases.

Microsoft appealed the decision, charging that the EC ruling was made without showing evidence of consumer harm:

The decision goes well beyond established legal precedents by asserting a broad and ill-defined duty on dominant firms to share the fruits of their research and development.[4]

Microsoft asked the Court of First Instance, the EU's second-highest court, to suspend the EC's demands. On June 27, 2004, the EC said it would not enforce the June 28th deadline for ordering Microsoft to start selling a modified version of its Windows operating system; instead the Commission said the order would wait until the European appeals court in Luxembourg decides whether to suspend the order.[5] The appeal, as a whole, is likely to drag on for years. At the heart of the legal battle over the landmark decision is the question of how other firms will be affected as they do business in Europe.

Meanwhile, with ten additional countries in the EU as of May 1, 2004, the EU has decided to abandon a system of centralized antitrust enforcement in Brussels. Now everything but mergers is subject to enforcement by regulators in each country. The fear is of a nationalistic approach and the inconsistent application of regulatory practices.

EU competition chief Mario Monti won't be the only bane of Microsoft; the software giant now will have 25 mini-Marios to tangle with. . . . That may be good for consumers and antitrust lawyers, but it will make life tough for companies doing business in the EU.[6]

CASE QUESTIONS

1. What were the consequences of the EC's decision to punish Microsoft? Who did the EC want to protect?
2. Do some research to update the Microsoft case at the time of your reading. What is there in the different historic, political, legal, and business practices background that gave rise to this situation? Are there differences in the approach to globalization?
3. Have there been similar rulings by the EC about other MNCs since the time of this report?

4. What are the implications and potential fallout of the EC's decision for strategic planning of other companies around the world?
5. Does this mean that companies can now be governed in every way by any of the countries or regions in which they do business, or is there hope of future "globalization" of regulations such as these?

REFERENCES

1. Daniel Dombey, "Brussels Rejected Microsoft Deal Amid Concerns Over Next Version of Windows," *Financial Times,* March 24, 2004.
2. "The High Cost of Microsoft's Wealth," www.businessweek.com, April 22, 2004.
3. Ina Fried, "Microsoft Commentary Slams EU Ruling," CNETNews.com, April 21, 2004.

4. "Software Giant to Outline Case for Consumer," *Financial Times,* April 22, 2004.
5. Paul Meller, "Europeans delay enforcement of order against Microsoft," www.nytimes.com, June 28, 2004.
6. "Europe Braces for the Mini-Marios," *Fortune,* May 3, 2004.

CHAPTER

Managing Interdependence

Social Responsibility and Ethics

Outline

Opening Profile: The Collapse of Parmalat — Italy's "Enron"

*Europe's businesses have much to learn from the unfolding
drama at Italy's Parmalat.*

—The Economist,
January 17, 2004

Global business mandates that companies manage their worldwide operations efficiently and effectively on the basis of openness, corporate integrity, and ethical standards. Although global markets have become a reality in many countries, national rules and the regulatory environment continue to be local, often providing loopholes for the companies because of weaker supervision by the enforcement agencies. In the past fifteen years, many companies have been found abusing their corporate powers and breaking rules that led to massive corporate losses and bankruptcies (for example, Allied Irish Bank, Arthur Andersen, Banco Ambrosiano and the Vatican Bank, Bank of Credit and Commerce International, Barings Bank, Bre-X, Credit Lyonnais, Daiwa Bank, Enron, World.com, and other dot.com companies). A close history of corporate scandals reveals that companies either become victims of their own lax corporate environments or intentionally break laws to profit from unscrupulous activities. An Italian multinational food company, Parmalat, is a classic example that fits in this category. To everybody's surprise, the company went bankrupt in December 2003 because of a $10 billion corporate fraud and massive deception. Parmalat's bankruptcy was the largest corporate failure ever in Europe, with debts exceeding $18 billion. It is interesting to note that since the 1990s, Parmalat often used derivatives and a web of complex financial transactions to expand in the international markets and manage its day-to-day operations. The *Wall Street Journal* wrote, "Behind Parmalat Chief's rise: Ties to Italian power structure; after the old system began to fade, it became harder to keep funds flowing." *Financial Times* commented, "Milk money earned through a tangled web of lies and deceit." At the time of filing Chapter 11, Parmalat was Italy's eighth-largest company, maintained 139 production facilities worldwide, and employed 36,000 workers in thirty countries. The company was well respected in Italy and even owned a soccer team. The Parmalat scandal broke when the company was unable to fulfill its financial liabilities and massive debt.

A brief history of Parmalat reveals that in 1961, at the age of twenty-two, Calisto Tanzi founded the company out of his small family food business. Over the years, the company grew from a small Italian business to one of the major food brands in the world. Parmalat was listed on the Milan Stock Exchange in 1990. In 2003, the Tanzi family controlled 51 percent of Parmalat. The whole corporate drama started in February 2003 when Parmalat tried to float 500 million euros of bonds because of financial difficulties. In December 2003, Bank of America found out that a document of 3.9 billion euros provided by Parmalat was bogus. After this unusual discovery by the bank, Parmalat fell like a house of cards. Tanzi and other top company officials were arrested by the police. Because of the severity of corporate fraud and deceit, the Italian government, and others, got involved in the case since Parmalat had operations in thirty countries. In January 2004, auditors announced that the company's debt exceeded 14.3 billion euros. Another report revealed that the company had been losing about 450 million euros per year since the mid-1990s, although Parmalat's auditors in Italy and other countries continuously failed to detect and report any wrongdoings. Regarding the Italian corporate system, Melis (2004) points out that the country's corporate governance is often hampered by a "complex accountability and monitoring system" that is based on concentrated control by the families.

As of May 2004, the Parmalat case (also called "Italy's Enron") was scheduled to go to court in September 2004. The Italian prosecutors indicted twenty-nine company officials, the Italian units of Bank of America, and the company's two ex-auditors, Deloitte & Touche and Grant Thornton's Italian unit. In the meantime, Enrico Bondi, a government-appointed administrator of Parmalat, was given the charge to restructure the company. Parmalat may swap its debt of 14.8 billion euros ($17.7 billion) into equity and may re-list the company shares on the stock market. According to analysts, Bondi may also unload other company assets and retain only milk and fruit juice operations. In April 2004, Switzerland's highest court rejected a request by Italy for access to Parmalat's bank accounts that had been frozen during the enquiry. Officials on both sides of the border had been cooperating closely in an attempt to track Parmalat's fraudulent activities. During investigations of possible money laundering by former Parmalat executives, Switzerland also froze deposits in two of Parmalat's Swiss subsidiaries.

Regardless of the outcome of the Parmalat case, the corporate world has learned that international business ethics is a major priority and that companies must pay attention to their relationships with society and other entities. The Parmalat case is one of the visible cases in business ethics that will be having repercussions for years to come in world markets, and for other companies around the world that were linked with their operations. *The Economist* correctly commented, "Europe's businesses have much to learn from the unfolding disaster at Italy's Parmalat." Beyond national origins and corporate size, only those companies adhering to ethical standards and responsibility at the global level will succeed in their markets and future plans. Social responsibility and ethical standards are not options but rather integral parts of a company's global operations.

Written exclusively for this book by Syed Tariq Anwar, West Texas A&M University. Copyright © 2004 by Syed Tariq Anwar. Used with permission.

SOURCES: M. Bianco and P. Casavola, "Italian Corporate Governance: Effects on Financial Structure and Firm Performance," *European Economic Review,* vol. 43, 1999, 1,057–1,069; "Parmalat Debt Grows to 14 Billion Euros," news.bbc.co.uk, January 26, 2004, 1–2; "Parmalat: Timeline to Turmoil," news.bbc.co.uk, January 26, 2004, 1–3; "How Parmalat Went Sour," *Business Week,* January 12, 2004, 46–47; "Parma Splat," *The Economist,* January 17, 2004, 59–61; "Milk Money Earned through a Tangled Web of Lies and Deceit," *Financial Times,* January 2, 2004, 13; "Of Milk and Money: Arrests Multiply as Investigators Cast Their Net Wider in Parmalat's Unfolding $10 Billion Fraud," *Financial Times,* January 9, 2004, 13; "How Parmalat Differs from U.S. Scandals," knowledge.Wharton.upenn.edu, January 15, 2004, 1–4; A. Melis, "On the Role of the Board of Statutory Auditors in Italian Listed Companies," *Corporate Governance,* January, 2004, 74–84; "New Audit Details Fall of Parmalat," www.nytimes.com, April 17, 2004, 1–4; "Court Rejects Italy's Bid for Parmalat Documents," www.nytimes.com, April 26, 2004; "Parmalat Prosecutors Claim Important Break," *Wall Street Journal,* December 30, 2003, A3.

UN ethics guidelines may alarm multinationals.[1]
—*Financial Times,*
August 11, 2003

No hiding place for the irresponsible business. Technology factories face "sweatshops probe." Social concerns edge into the mainstream.[2]
—*Financial Times,*
September 29, 2003

Global interdependence is a compelling factor in the global business environment, creating demands on international managers to take a positive stance on issues of social responsibility and ethical behavior, economic development in host countries, and ecological protection around the world.

Managers today are usually quite sensitive to issues of social responsibility and ethical behavior because of pressures from the public, from interest groups, from legal and governmental concerns, and from media coverage. In August 2003, for example, the United Nations published draft guidelines for the responsibilities of transnational corporations and called for companies to be subject to monitoring, verification, and censure. Though many companies agree with the guidelines, they resist the notion that corporate responsibility should be regulated and question where to draw the line between socially responsible behavior and the concerns of the corporation's other stakeholders.[3] In the domestic arena, managers are faced with numerous ethical complexities. In the international arena, such concerns are compounded by the larger numbers of stakeholders involved, including customers, communities, allies, and owners in various countries.

This chapter's discussion focuses separately on issues of social responsibility and ethical behavior, though considerable overlap can be observed. The difference between the two is a matter of scope and degree. Whereas ethics deals with decisions and interactions on an individual level, decisions about social responsibility are broader in scope, tend to be made at a higher level, affect more people, and reflect a general stance taken by a company or a number of decision makers.

THE SOCIAL RESPONSIBILITY OF MNCs

Multinational corporations (MNCs) have been and—to a lesser extent—continue to be at the center of debate regarding social responsibility, particularly the benefits versus harm wrought by their operations around the world, especially in less developed countries. The criticisms of MNCs have been lessened in recent years by the decreasing economic differences among countries, by the emergence of less developed countries' (LDCs) multinationals, and by the greater emphasis on social responsibility by MNCs. However, concerns remain about the exploitation of LDCs, fueled by such incidents as the Union Carbide gas leak in Bhopal, India, in December 1984, which killed 2,500 people and injured more than 200,000. Such incidents raise questions about the use of hazardous technology in developing economies.

Issues of social responsibility continue to center on the poverty and lack of equal opportunity around the world, the environment, consumer concerns, and employee safety and welfare. Many argue that, since MNCs operate in a global context, they should use their capital, skills, and power to play proactive roles in handling worldwide social and economic problems and that, at the least, they should be concerned with host-country welfare. Others argue that MNCs already have a positive impact on LDCs by providing managerial training, investment capital, and new technology, as well as by creating jobs and improving infrastructure. Certainly, multinational corporations (now often called **transnational corporations** [TNCs]) constitute a powerful presence in the world economy and often have a greater capacity than local governments to induce change. The sales, debts, and resources of the largest multinationals exceed the gross national product, the public and private debt, and the resources, respectively, of some nations.[4]

The concept of **international social responsibility** includes the expectation that MNCs concern themselves with the social and economic effects of their decisions. The issue is how far that concern should go and what level of planning and control that concern should take. Such dilemmas are common for MNC managers. Del Monte managers, for example, realize that growing pineapples in the rich coastal lands of Kenya brings mixed results there. Although badly needed foreign-exchange earnings are generated for Kenya, poor Kenyans living in the region experience adverse effects because less land is available for subsistence agriculture to support them.[5]

Opinions on the level of social responsibility that a domestic firm should demonstrate range from one extreme—the only responsibility of a business is to make a profit, within the confines of the law, in order to produce goods and services and serve its shareholders' interests[6]—to another extreme—companies should anticipate and try to solve problems in society. Between these extremes are varying positions described as socially reactive, in which companies respond, to some degree of currently prevailing social expectations, to the environmental and social costs of their actions.[7]

The stance toward social responsibility that a firm should take in its international operations, however, is much more complex—ranging perhaps from assuming some responsibility for economic development in a subsidiary's host country to taking an active role in identifying and solving world problems. The increased complexity regarding the social responsibility and ethical behavior of firms across borders is brought about by the additional stakeholders in the firm's activities through operating overseas. As illustrated in Exhibit 2-1, managers are faced with not only considering stakeholders in the host country but also with weighing their rights against the rights of their domestic stakeholders. Most managerial decisions will have a trade-off of the rights of these stakeholders—at least in the short term. For example, a decision to discontinue using children in Pakistan to sew soccer balls means the company will pay more for adult employees and will, therefore, reduce the profitability to its owners. That same decision—while taking a stand for human rights according to the social and ethical expectations in the home country and bowing to consumers' demands—may mean that those children and their families go hungry or are forced into worse working situations. Another decision to keep jobs at home to satisfy local employees and unions will mean higher prices for consumers and less profit for stakeholders. In addition, if competitors take their jobs to cheaper overseas factories, a company may go out of business, which will mean no jobs at all for the domestic employees and a loss for the owners.

With the growing awareness of the world's socioeconomic interdependence, global organizations are beginning to recognize the need to reach a consensus on what should constitute moral and ethical behavior. Some think that such a consensus is emerging because of the development of a **global corporate culture**—an integration of the business environments in which firms currently operate.[8] This integration results from the gradual

EXHIBIT 2-1   MNC Stakeholders

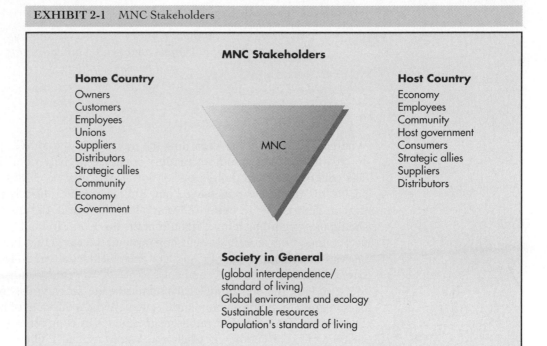

dissolution of traditional boundaries and from the many intricate interconnections among MNCs, internationally linked securities markets, and communication networks.[9]

Although it is very difficult to implement a generalized code of morality and ethics in individual countries, such guidelines do provide a basis of judgment regarding specific situations. Bowie uses the term **moral universalism** to address the need for a moral standard that is accepted by all cultures.[10] Although, in practice, it seems unlikely that a universal code of ethics will ever be a reality, Bowie says that this approach to doing business across cultures is far preferable to other approaches, such as ethnocentrism or ethical relativism. With an **ethnocentric approach**, a company applies the morality used in its home country—regardless of the host country's system of ethics.

A company subscribing to **ethical relativism**, on the other hand, simply adopts the local moral code of whatever country in which it is operating. With this approach, companies run into value conflicts, such as continuing to do business in China despite home-country objections to China's continued violation of human rights. In addition, public pressure in the home country often forces the MNC to act in accordance with ethnocentric value systems anyway. In one instance, public outcry in the United States and most of the world resulted in major companies (IBM, General Motors, Coca-Cola, and Eastman Kodak) either selling or discontinuing their operations in South Africa during the 1980s to protest that country's apartheid policies. More recently, the Food and Drug Administration (FDA) has been pressuring U.S. manufacturers of silicone-filled breast implants (prohibited in the United States for cosmetic surgery because of health hazards) to adopt a voluntary moratorium on exports. While Dow Corning has ceased its foreign sales—citing its responsibility to apply the same standards internationally as it does domestically—other major manufacturers continue to export the implants, often from their factories in other countries.

The difficulty, even in adopting a stance of moral universalism, is in deciding where to draw the line: Which kinds of conflicts of values, asks Wicks, are "conversation stoppers" or "cooperation enders"? Individual managers must at some point decide, based on their own morality, when they feel a situation is simply not right and to withdraw their involvement.

There are practical limitations on our ability to act in the modern world, but a systematic infringement of basic personal rights is generally grounds for ending cooperation. Less blatant violations, or practices that are not abhorrent to our basic values, are treated as items which are negotiable.[11]

MNC Responsibility Toward Human Rights

So far, 42 U.S. companies and 24 in the U.K. have endorsed the U.N.'s Voluntary Global Compact governing human rights, labour rights, and the environment.[12]

FINANCIAL TIMES,
August 11, 2003

Whereas many situations regarding the morality of the MNC's presence or activities in a country are quite clear, other situations are not, especially when dealing with human rights. The role of MNCs in pulling out of South Africa in the 1980s as part of the movement against apartheid has now played out, and many are cautiously returning to the now multiracial democracy. In many other areas of the world, the question of what role MNCs should play regarding human rights is at the forefront. So loud has been the cry about products coming from so-called sweatshops around the world that President Clinton established an Anti-Sweatshop Code of Conduct, which includes a ban on forced labor, abuse, and discrimination, and it requires companies to provide a healthy and safe work environment and to pay at least the prevailing local minimum wage, among other requirements. A group has been named to monitor compliance; enforcement is difficult, of course, but publicity helps. The Department of Labor publishes the names of companies that comply with the code, including Nike, Reebok, Liz Claiborne, Wal-Mart, and Phillips-Van Heusen.[13] Those companies can be identified on the department's home page Web site (www.dol.gov/ilab). Even so, in a study commissioned by Nike in 2000 to review personnel activities at its contractors in Indonesia, it was found that 56 percent of the 4,004 workers told researchers that they had witnessed supervisors verbally, sexually, or physically abusing other employees.[14]

The study, by nonprofit Global Alliance, concludes that workers at the Indonesian factories contracted by Nike had limited access to medical care, were exposed to sexual molestation by managers, and were often forced to work overtime. What constitutes "human rights" is clouded by the perceptions and priorities of people in different countries. While the United States often takes the lead in the charge against what it considers human rights violations around the world, other countries point to the homelessness and high crime statistics in the United States. Often the discussion of human rights centers around Asia because many of the products in the West are imported from Asia by Western companies using manufacturing facilities located there.[15] It is commonly held in the West that the best chance to gain some ground on human rights issues is for large MNCs and governments around the world to take a unified stance; many global players now question the morality of trading for goods that have been produced by forced labor or child labor. Although laws in the United States ban prison imports, shady deals between the manufacturers and companies acting as intermediaries make it difficult to determine the origin of many products—and make it easy for companies wanting access to cheap products or materials to ignore the law. However, under pressure from their labor unions (and perhaps their consciences), a number of large image-conscious companies have established corporate codes of conduct for their buyers, suppliers, and contractors and have instituted strict procedures for auditing their imports.[16] Reebok has audited all its suppliers in Asia.[17] Levi Strauss has gone a step further. After sending teams of investigators around the world, Levi Strauss announced a new company policy: "We should not initiate or renew contractual relationships in countries where there are pervasive violations of basic human rights."[18]

Codes of Conduct

A considerable number of organizations have developed their own codes of conduct; some have gone further to group together with others around the world to establish standards to improve the quality of life for workers around the world. Companies such as Avon, Sainsbury Plc., Toys "R" Us, and Otto Versand have joined with the Council on Economic Priorities (CEP) to establish SA8000 (Social Accountability 8000, on the lines of the manufacturing quality standard ISO9000). Their proposed global labor standards would be monitored by outside organizations to certify whether plants are meeting those standards, among which are the following:

- Do not use child or forced labor.
- Provide a safe working environment.
- Respect workers' rights to unionize.
- Do not regularly require more than 48-hour work weeks.
- Pay wages sufficient to meet workers' basic needs.[19]

In addition, four **international codes of conduct** provide some consistent guidelines for multinational enterprises (MNEs). These codes were developed by the International Chamber of Commerce, the Organization for Economic Cooperation and Development, the International Labor Organization, and the United Nations Commission on Transnational Corporations. Getz has integrated these four codes and organized their common underlying principles, thereby establishing MNE behavior toward governments, publics, and people, as shown in Exhibit 2-2 (the originating institutions are in parentheses). She concludes, "As international organizations and institutions (including MNEs themselves) continue to refine the codes, the underlying moral issues will be better identified, and appropriate MNE behavior will be more readily apparent."[20]

EXHIBIT 2-2   International Codes of Conduct for MNEs

MNE and Host Governments

Economic and developmental policies
- MNEs should consult with governmental authorities and national employers' and workers' organizations to assure that their investments conform to the economic and social development policies of the host country. (ICC; OECD; ILO; UN/CTC)
- MNEs should not adversely disturb the balance-of-payments or currency exchange rates of the countries in which they operate. They should try, in consultation with the government, to resolve balance-of-payments and exchange rate difficulties when possible. (ICC; OECD; UN/CTC)
- MNEs should cooperate with governmental policies regarding local equity participation. (ICC; UN/CTC)
- MNEs should not dominate the capital markets of the countries in which they operate. (ICC; UN/CTC)
- MNEs should provide the information necessary for correctly assessing taxes to be paid to host government authorities. (ICC; OECD)
- MNEs should not engage in transfer pricing policies that modify the tax base on which their entities are assessed. (OECD; UN/CTC)
- MNEs should give preference to local sources for components and raw materials if prices and quality are competitive. (ICC; ILO)
- MNEs should reinvest some profits in the countries in which they operate. (ICC)

Laws and regulations
- MNEs are subject to the laws, regulations, and jurisdiction of the countries in which they operate. (ICC; OECD; UN/CTC)
- MNEs should respect the right of every country to exercise control over its natural resources, and to regulate the activities of entities operating within its territory. (ICC; OECD; UN/CTC)

- MNEs should use appropriate international dispute settlement mechanisms, including arbitration, to resolve conflicts with the governments of the countries in which they operate. (ICC; OECD)
- MNEs should not request the intervention of their home governments in disputes with host governments. (UN/CTC)
- MNEs should resolve disputes arising from expropriation by host governments under the domestic law of the host country. (UN/CTC)

Political involvement
- MNEs should refrain from improper or illegal involvement in local political activities. (OECD; UN/CTC)
- MNEs should not pay bribes or render improper benefits to any public servant. (OECD; UN/CTC)
- MNEs should not interfere in intergovernmental relations. (UN/CTC)

MNEs and the Public

Technology transfer
- MNEs should cooperate with governmental authorities in assessing the impact of transfers of technology to developing countries and should enhance the technological capacities of developing countries. (OECD; UN/CTC)
- MNEs should develop and adapt technologies to the needs and characteristics of the countries in which they operate. (ICC; OECD; ILO)
- MNEs should conduct research and development activities in developing countries, using local resources and personnel to the greatest extent possible. (ICC; UN/CTC)
- When granting licenses for the use of industrial property rights, MNEs should do so on reasonable terms and conditions. (ICC; OECD)

EXHIBIT 2-2 (cont.)

- MNEs should not require payment for the use of technologies of no real value to the enterprise. (ICC)

Environmental protection
- MNEs should respect the laws and regulations concerning environmental protection of the countries in which they operate. (OECD; UN/CTC)
- MNEs should cooperate with host governments and with international organizations in the development of national and international environmental protection standards. (ICC; UN/CTC)
- MNEs should supply to appropriate host governmental authorities, information concerning the environmental impact of the products and processes of their entities. (ICC; UN/CTC)

MNEs and Persons

Consumer protection
- MNEs should respect the laws and regulations of the countries in which they operate with regard to consumer protection. (OECD; UN/CTC)
- MNEs should preserve the safety and health of consumers by disclosure of appropriate information, proper labeling, and accurate advertising. (UN/CTC)

Employment practices
- MNEs should cooperate with host governments' efforts to create employment opportunities in particular localities. (ICC)
- MNEs should support representative employers' organizations. (ICC; ILO)
- MNEs should try to increase employment opportunities and standards in the countries in which they operate. (ILO)
- MNEs should provide stable employment for their employees. (ILO)
- MNEs should establish nondiscriminatory employment policies and promote equal employment opportunities. (OECD; ILO)
- MNEs should give priority to the employment and promotion of nationals of the countries in which they operate. (ILO)

- MNEs should assure that adequate training is provided to all employees. (ILO)
- MNEs should contribute to the managerial and technical training of nationals of the countries in which they operate, and should employ qualified nationals in managerial and professional capacities. (ICC; OECD; UN/CTC)
- MNEs should respect the right of employees to organize for the purpose of collective bargaining. (OECD; ILO)
- MNEs should provide workers' representatives with information necessary to assist in the development of collective agreements. (OECD; ILO)
- MNEs should consult with workers' representatives in all matters directly affecting the interests of labor. (ICC)
- MNEs, in the context of negotiations with workers' representatives, should not threaten to transfer the operating unit to another country. (OECD; ILO)
- MNEs should give advance notice of plant closures and mitigate the resultant adverse effects. (ICC; OECD; ILO)
- MNEs should cooperate with governments in providing income protection for workers whose employment has been terminated. (ILO)
- MNEs should provide standards of employment equal to or better than those of comparable employers in the countries in which they operate. (ICC; OECD; ILO)
- MNEs should pay, at minimum, basic living wages. (ILO)
- MNEs should maintain the highest standards of safety and health, and should provide adequate information about work-related health hazards. (ILO)

Human rights
- MNEs should respect human rights and fundamental freedoms in the countries in which they operate. (UN/CTC)
- MNEs should not discriminate on the basis of race, color, sex, religion, language, social, national and ethnic origin, or political or other opinion. (UN/CTC)
- MNEs should respect the social and cultural objectives, values, and traditions of the countries in which they operate. (UN/CTC)

International agency sources:
OECD: The Organization for Economic Cooperation and Development Guidelines for Multinational Enterprises.
ILO: The International Labor Office Tripartite Declarations of Principles Concerning Multinational Enterprises and Social Policy.
ICC: The International Chamber of Commerce Guidelines for International Investment.
UN/CTC: The United Nations Universal Declaration of Human Rights.
The UN Code of Conduct on Transnational Corps.

ETHICS IN GLOBAL MANAGEMENT

WorldCom, which changed its name recently to MCI, committed the greatest fraud in U.S. financial history, reporting what now appears to be $11bn in profits it never made.[21]

FINANCIAL TIMES,
July 29, 2003

These banks [JP Morgan, Chase, and Citigroup, who were aware of the Enron fraud] serve as yet another reminder that you can't turn a blind eye to the consequences of your actions—if you know or have reason to know that you are helping a company mislead its investors, you are committing securities fraud.[22]

FINANCIAL TIMES,
July 20, 2003

Italy's Parmalat, a $9.6 billion dairy giant, implodes in Europe's biggest corporate-accounting scandal.[23]

TIME,
January 12, 2004

Globalization has multiplied the ethical problems facing organizations. Yet business ethics have not yet been globalized. Attitudes toward ethics are rooted in culture and business practices. Swee Hoon Ang found, for example, that, while East Asians tended to be less ethical than their expatriate counterparts from the United States and Britain, it was because they considered deception as amoral and acceptable if it has a positive effect on larger issues such as the company, the extended family, or the state.[24] For an MNC, it is very difficult to reconcile consistent and acceptable behavior around the world with home-country standards. One question, in fact, is whether they should be reconciled. It seems that, while the United States has been the driving force to legislate moral business conduct overseas, perhaps more scrutiny should have been applied to those global MNCs headquartered in the United States, such as Enron and WorldCom, that so greatly defrauded their investors, employees, and all who had business with them.

The term **international business ethics** refers to the business conduct or morals of MNCs in their relationships with individuals and entities. Such behavior is based largely on the cultural value system and the generally accepted ways of doing business in each country or society, as we have discussed throughout this book. Those norms, in turn, are based on broadly accepted guidelines from religion, philosophy, professional organizations, and the legal system. The complexity of the combination of various national and cultural factors in a particular host environment that combine to determine ethical or unethical societal norms is illustrated in Exhibit 2-3. The authors, Robertson and Crittenden, note,

"Varying legal and cultural constraints across borders have made integrating an ethical component into international strategic decisions quite challenging."[25]

Should managers of MNC subsidiaries, then, base their ethical standards on those of the host country or those of the home country—or can the two be reconciled? What is the moral responsibility of expatriates regarding ethical behavior, and how do these issues affect business objectives? How do expatriates simultaneously balance their responsibility to various stakeholders—to owners, creditors, consumers, employees, suppliers, governments, and societies? The often conflicting objectives of host and home governments and societies also must be balanced.

The approach to these dilemmas varies among MNCs from different countries. While the American approach is to treat everyone the same by making moral judgments based on general rules, managers in Japan and Europe tend to make such decisions based on shared values, social ties, and their perceptions of their obligations. According to many U.S. executives, there is little difference in ethical practices among the United States, Canada, and Northern Europe. According to Bruce Smart, former U.S. Undersecretary of Commerce for International Trade, the highest ethical standards seem to be practiced by the Canadians, British, Australians, and Germans. As he says, "a kind of noblesse oblige still exists among the business classes in those countries"—compared with the prevailing attitude among many U.S. managers that condones making it whatever way one can.[26] Another who experienced few problems with ethical practices in Europe is Donald Petersen, former CEO of Ford Motor Company. However, he warns us about

EXHIBIT 2-3   A Moral Philosophy of Cross-cultural Societal Ethics

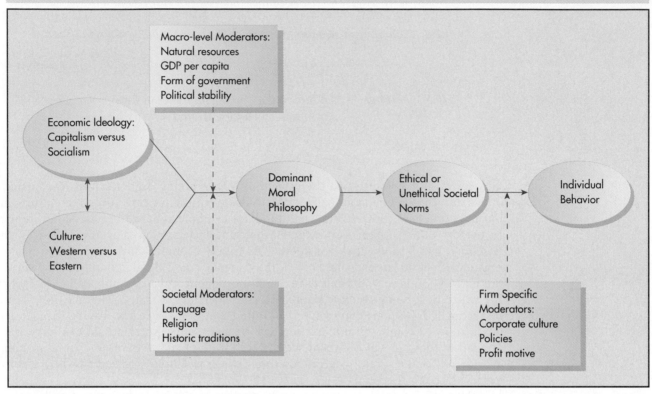

SOURCE: C. J. Robertson and W. F. Crittenden, "Mapping Moral Philisophies: Strategic Implications for Multinational Firms," *Strategic Management Journal*, 24: 385–392 (2003) © John Wiley & Sons, Inc. Reproduced with permission.

underdeveloped countries, in particular those under a dictatorship, where bribery is generally accepted practice.[27] Petersen's experience has been borne out by research, which draws on fourteen surveys from seven independent institutions, by Transparency International, a German nongovernmental organization (NGO) that fights corruption. The organization's year 2003 Corruption Perceptions Index (see Exhibit 2-4) shows results of research on the level of corruption among public officials and politicians in various countries, as perceived by businesspeople, academics, and risk analysts. Finland was rated number one, or least corrupt, followed by Denmark, New Zealand, and Iceland. The United States was number sixteen. Transparency International's British arm noted that corruption was "worryingly high" in Greece, number forty-four, and Italy, number thirty-one. Transparency International's chairman concludes that "Rich countries must provide practical support to developing country governments that demonstrate the political will to curb corruption."[28]

EXHIBIT 2-4   The 2003 Corruption Perceptions Index

Country Rank	Country	CPI 2002 score	Surveys used	Standard deviation	High-low range
1	Finland	9.7	8	0.4	8.9–10.0
2	Denmark	9.5	8	0.3	8.9–9.9
	New Zealand	9.5	8	0.2	8.9–9.6
4	Iceland	9.4	6	0.4	8.8–10.0
5	Singapore	9.3	13	0.2	8.9–9.6
	Sweden	9.3	10	0.2	8.9–9.6
7	Canada	9.0	10	0.2	8.7–9.3
	Luxembourg	9.0	5	0.5	8.5–9.9
	Netherlands	9.0	9	0.3	8.5–9.3

EXHIBIT 2-4   (cont.)

Country Rank	Country	CPI 2002 score	Surveys used	Standard deviation	High-low range
10	United Kingdom	8.7	11	0.5	7.8–9.4
11	Australia	8.6	11	1.0	6.1–9.3
12	Norway	8.5	8	0.9	6.9–9.3
	Switzerland	8.5	9	0.9	6.8–9.4
14	Hong Kong	8.2	11	0.8	6.6–9.4
15	Austria	7.8	8	0.5	7.2–8.7
16	USA	7.7	12	0.8	5.5–8.7
17	Chile	7.5	10	0.9	5.6–8.8
18	Germany	7.3	10	1.0	5.0–8.1
	Israel	7.3	9	0.9	5.2–8.0
20	Belgium	7.1	8	0.9	5.5–8.7
	Japan	7.1	12	0.9	5.5–7.9
	Spain	7.1	10	1.0	5.2–8.9
23	Ireland	6.9	8	0.9	5.5–8.1
24	Botswana	6.4	5	1.5	5.3–8.9
25	France	6.3	10	0.9	4.8–7.8
	Portugal	6.3	9	1.0	5.5–8.0
27	Slovenia	6.0	9	1.4	4.7–8.9
28	Namibia	5.7	5	2.2	3.6–8.9
29	Estonia	5.6	8	0.6	5.2–6.6
	Taiwan	5.6	12	0.8	3.9–6.6
31	Italy	5.2	11	1.1	3.4–7.2
32	Uruguay	5.1	5	0.7	4.2–6.1
33	Hungary	4.9	11	0.5	4.0–5.6
	Malaysia	4.9	11	0.6	3.6–5.7
	Trinidad & Tobago	4.9	4	1.5	3.6–6.9
36	Belarus	4.8	3	1.3	3.3–5.8
	Lithuania	4.8	7	1.9	3.4–7.6
	South Africa	4.8	11	0.5	3.9–5.5
	Tunisia	4.8	5	0.8	3.6–5.6
40	Costa Rica	4.5	6	0.9	3.6–5.9
	Jordan	4.5	5	0.7	3.6–5.2
	Mauritius	4.5	6	0.8	3.5–5.5
	South Korea	4.5	12	1.3	2.1–7.1
44	Greece	4.2	8	0.7	3.7–5.5
45	Brazil	4.0	10	0.4	3.4–4.8
	Bulgaria	4.0	7	0.9	3.3–5.7
	Jamaica	4.0	3	0.4	3.6–4.3
	Peru	4.0	7	0.6	3.2–5.0
	Poland	4.0	11	1.1	2.6–5.5
50	Ghana	3.9	4	1.4	2.7–5.9
51	Croatia	3.8	4	0.2	3.6–4.0
52	Czech Republic	3.7	10	0.8	2.6–5.5
	Latvia	3.7	4	0.2	3.5–3.9
	Morocco	3.7	4	1.8	1.7–5.5
	Slovak Republic	3.7	8	0.6	3.0–4.6
	Sri Lanka	3.7	4	0.4	3.3–4.3
57	Colombia	3.6	10	0.7	2.6–4.6
	Mexico	3.6	10	0.6	2.5–4.9
59	China	3.5	11	1.0	2.0–5.6

EXHIBIT 2-4 (cont.)

Country Rank	Country	CPI 2002 score	Surveys used	Standard deviation	High-low range
	Dominican Rep.	3.5	4	0.4	3.0–3.9
	Ethiopia	3.5	3	0.5	3.0–4.0
62	Egypt	3.4	7	1.3	1.7–5.3
	El Salvador	3.4	6	0.8	2.0–4.2
64	Thailand	3.2	11	0.7	1.5–4.1
	Turkey	3.2	10	0.9	1.9–4.6
66	Senegal	3.1	4	1.7	1.7–5.5
67	Panama	3.0	5	0.8	1.7–3.6
68	Malawi	2.9	4	0.9	2.0–4.0
	Uzbekistan	2.9	4	1.0	2.0–4.1
70	Argentina	2.8	10	0.6	1.7–3.8
71	Cote d'Ivoire	2.7	4	0.8	2.0–3.4
	Honduras	2.7	5	0.6	2.0–3.4
	India	2.7	12	0.4	2.4–3.6
	Russia	2.7	12	1.0	1.5–5.0
	Tanzania	2.7	4	0.7	2.0–3.4
	Zimbabwe	2.7	6	0.5	2.0–3.3
77	Pakistan	2.6	3	1.2	1.7–4.0
	Philippines	2.6	11	0.6	1.7–3.6
	Romania	2.6	7	0.8	1.7–3.6
	Zambia	2.6	4	0.5	2.0–3.2
81	Albania	2.5	3	0.8	1.7–3.3
	Guatemala	2.5	6	0.6	1.7–3.5
	Nicaragua	2.5	5	0.7	1.7–3.4
	Venezuela	2.5	10	0.5	1.5–3.2
85	Georgia	2.4	3	0.7	1.7–2.9
	Ukraine	2.4	6	0.7	1.7–3.8
	Vietnam	2.4	7	0.8	1.5–3.6
88	Kazakhstan	2.3	4	1.1	1.7–3.9
89	Bolivia	2.2	6	0.4	1.7–2.9
	Cameroon	2.2	4	0.7	1.7–3.2
	Ecuador	2.2	7	0.3	1.7–2.6
	Haiti	2.2	3	1.7	0.8–4.0
93	Moldova	2.1	4	0.6	1.7–3.0
	Uganda	2.1	4	0.3	1.9–2.6
95	Azerbaijan	2.0	4	0.3	1.7–2.4
96	Indonesia	1.9	12	0.6	0.8–3.0
	Kenya	1.9	5	0.3	1.7–2.5
98	Angola	1.7	3	0.2	1.6–2.0
	Madagascar	1.7	3	0.7	1.3–2.5
	Paraguay	1.7	3	0.2	1.5–2.0
101	Nigeria	1.6	6	0.6	0.9–2.5
102	Bangladesh	1.2	5	0.7	0.3–2.0

Explanatory notes
CPI 2003 Score relates to perceptions of the degree of corruption as seen by business people, academics and risk analysts, and ranges between 10 (highly clean) and 0 (highly corrupt).

A more detailed description of the CPI 2003 methodology is available at
http://www.transparency.org/cpi/index.html#cpi or at www.gwdg.de/~uwvw/2002.html

SOURCE: Transparency International, 2003

The biggest single problem for MNCs in their attempt to define a corporatewide ethical posture is the great variation of ethical standards around the world. Many practices that are considered unethical or even illegal in some countries are accepted ways of doing business in others. More recently, this dilemma has taken on new forms because of the varied understandings of the ethical use of technology around the world, as illustrated in the accompanying E-Biz Box: EU Imposes Cross-Border.

E-BIZ BOX

EU Imposes Cross-Border

ELECTRONIC DATA PRIVACY

Most people in the United Sates have wished for more privacy of personal data; they receive mailings, solicitations, and other information about themselves that make them wonder where that source acquired the personal information. Not so in Europe. In fact, the Europeans are determined that they won't get on any unwanted mailing list from the United States or elsewhere. As of October 25, 1998, when the European Union Directive on Data Protection went into effect, commissioners in Brussels have resolved to prosecute companies and block Web sites that fail to live up to Europe's standards on data privacy. The directive guarantees European citizens absolute control over data concerning them. A U.S. company wanting personal information must get permission from that person and explain what the information will be used for; the company must also guarantee that the information won't be used for anything else without the person's consent. European Union (EU) citizens have the right, under this directive, to file suits against a company if they feel it is abusing their private data and force them to change it.

Such protections seem admirable, but free marketers across the Atlantic Ocean are worried about the prospect of Europe being able to regulate the computer databases and the Internet, which are vital to the information economy. They feel that regulations should be agreed upon for a global system. It is a stalemate situation of protection of privacy versus freedom of information, which is protected by the First Amendment in the United States. At the heart of the standoff is a basic cultural difference: Europeans trust their governments over companies, whereas in the United States, it is the opposite. Already, European inspectors travel to Sioux City, South Dakota, to Citigroup's giant data processing center, where computers store financial information about millions of German credit card holders, to make sure that Citigroup is complying with the privacy data protection law. Citigroup accepted the supervision as a condition to market a credit card in Germany.

U.S. companies are concerned that the EU directive will force them to establish separate data networks for Europe, making it impossible to conduct business as usual with EU member countries. The privacy rules are already having an effect—prohibiting U.S. airlines and hotels, for example, from storing information about their clients that they would normally use to provide better service for them. Third parties to business transactions, such as FedEx delivering a package across the Atlantic Ocean, could also be held responsible. There is considerable concern that the EU directive will imperil the future of electronic commerce.

The question of protection of private data export is but one of the complexities brought about by the use of technology in international business. For now, on your next trip to Europe, bringing back the contact information that you entered on your laptop computer is illegal!

SOURCE: "Rules of Global Economy Are Set in Brussels," *Wall Street Journal*, April 23, 2002; "Europe's Privacy Cops," *Business Week*, November 2, 1998; "Eurocrats Try to Stop Data at the Border," *Wall Street Journal*, October 30, 1998.

*The computer is on the dock, it's raining, and you have to pay $100 [bribe]
to get it picked up.*

WILLIAM C. NORRIS,
Control Data Corporation

U.S. companies are often caught between being placed at a disadvantage by refusing to go along with a country's accepted practices, such as bribery, or being subject to criticism at home for using "unethical" tactics to get the job done. Large companies that have refused to participate have led the way in taking a moral stand because of their visibility, their potential impact on the local economy, and, after all, their ability to afford such a stance.

Whereas the upper limits of ethical standards for international activities are set by the individual standards of certain leading companies—or, more realistically, by the moral values of their top managers—it is more difficult to set the lower limits of those standards. Laczniak and Naor explain:

> *The laws of economically developed countries generally define the lowest common denominator of acceptable behavior for operations in those domestic markets. In an underdeveloped country or a developing country, it would be the actual degree of enforcement of the law that would, in practice, determine the lower limit of permissible behavior.* [29]

The bribery of officials is prohibited by law in many countries, but it still goes on as an accepted practice; often, it is the only way to get anything done. In such cases, the MNC managers have to decide which standard of behavior they will follow. What about the $100 bribe to get the computer off the rainy dock? William Norris says he told his managers to pay the $100 because to refuse would be taking things too far. Generally, Control Data did not yield to such pressure, though it said sales were lost as a result.[30]

Questionable Payments

A specific ethical issue for managers in the international arena is that of **questionable payments**. These are business payments that raise significant questions of appropriate moral behavior either in the host nation or in other nations. Such questions arise out of differences in laws, customs, and ethics in various countries, whether the payments in question are political payments, extortion, bribes, sales commissions, or "grease money"— payments to expedite routine transactions.[31] Other common types of payments are made to speed the clearance of goods at ports of entry and to obtain required certifications. They are called different names in different countries: tokens of appreciation, *la mordida* (the bite, in Mexico), *bastarella* ("little envelope" in Italy), *pot-de-vin* (jug of wine in France). For the sake of simplicity, all these different types of questionable payments are categorized in this text as some form of bribery. In Mexico, for example, companies make monthly payments to the mail carriers or their mail gets "lost."

In South Korea, for another example, the bribery scandal that put former president Roh Tae Woo behind bars in 1996 spread to the top 30 *chaebol* (the large industrial conglomerates of financially linked, and often family-linked, companies that do business among themselves whenever possible), which account for 14 percent of South Korea's gross domestic product. Any ensuing changes to the close relationship between politics and business in South Korea are likely to reshape, and perhaps slow down, the Korean economy. However, executives in those *chaebol* say they still expect to pay the *huk kab,* or "rice-cake expenses," which run thousands of dollars, as "holiday gifts" to cabinet ministers as a hedge against disadvantageous treatment.

Exhibit 2-5 shows research results from Transparency International, called the 2003 Bribe Payers Index. This ranks the leading exporting countries in terms of the degree to which their companies are perceived to be paying bribes abroad.

The dilemma for Americans operating abroad is how much to adhere to their own ethical standards in the face of foreign customs or how much to follow local ways to be competitive. Certainly, in some societies, gift giving is common to bind social and familial

EXHIBIT 2-5   2003 Bribe Payers Index

Rank	Country	Score	Rank	Country	Score
1	Australia	8.5	12	France	5.5
2	Sweden	8.4	13	United States	5.3
	Switzerland	8.4		Japan	5.3
4	Austria	8.2	15	Malaysia	4.3
5	Canada	8.1		Hong Kong	4.3
6	Netherlands	7.8	17	Italy	4.1
	Belgium	7.8	18	South Korea	3.9
8	United Kingdom	6.9	19	Taiwan	3.8
9	Singapore	6.3	20	People's Republic of China	3.5
	Germany	6.3			
11	Spain	5.8	21	Russia	3.2

SOURCE: Transparency International, 2003.

ties, and such gifts incur obligation. Nevertheless, a bribe is different from a gift or other reciprocation, and those involved know that by whether it has a covert nature. According to Noonan:

> *Bribery is universally shameful. Not a country in the world does not treat bribery as criminal on its books.... In no country do bribetakers speak publicly of their bribes, nor do bribegivers announce the bribes they pay. No newspaper lists them. No one advertises that he can arrange a bribe. No one is honored precisely because he is a big briber or bribee. No one writes an autobiography in which he recalls the bribes he has taken or paid.... Not merely the criminal law—for the transaction could have happened long ago and prosecution be barred by time—but an innate fear of being considered disgusting restrains briber and bribee from parading their exchange. Significantly, it is often the Westerner with ethnocentric prejudice who supposes that a modern Asian or African society does not regard the act of bribery as shameful in the way Westerners regard it.[32]*

However, Americans must be able to distinguish between harmless practices and actual bribery, between genuine relationships and those used as a cover-up. To help them distinguish, the **Foreign Corrupt Practices Act** (FCPA) of 1977 was established, which prohibits U.S. companies from making illegal payments, or other gifts, or political contributions to foreign government officials for the purposes of influencing them in business transactions. The goal was to stop MNCs from contributing to corruption in foreign government and to upgrade the image of the United States and its companies operating overseas. The penalties include severe fines and sometimes imprisonment. Many managers feel the law has given them a more even playing field, and so they have been more willing to do business in certain countries where it seemed impossible to do business without bribery and kickbacks.

Unfortunately, bribery continues, mostly on a small scale, where it often goes undetected. Still, the U.S. government does vigorously pursue and prosecute bribery cases. Even the mighty IBM's Argentine subsidiary has been accused of paying a bribe of $249 million to get the contract to install computers at all the branches of Argentina's largest commercial bank, Banco de la Nación. Companies from the United States claim that they are placed at a competitive disadvantage in Latin America and elsewhere because their competitors overseas do not face the same home-country restrictions on bribery.

If we agree with Carson that "accepting a bribe involves the violation of an implicit or explicit promise or understanding associated with one's office or role, and that, therefore, accepting (or giving) a bribe is always prima facie wrong,"[33] then our decisions as managers, salespersons, and so on are always clear, no matter where we are.

If, however, we acknowledge that in some cases—in "morally corrupt contexts," as Philips calls them—"there may be no prima facie duty to adhere to the agreements implicit in one's role or position," then the issue becomes situational and a matter of judgment, with few consistent guidelines. If our perspective, continues Philips, is that "the action purchased from the relevant official does not count as a violation of his [or her] duty," then the U.S. managers or other foreign managers involved are actually victims of extortion rather than guilty of bribery.[34] That is the position taken by Gene Laczniak of Marquette Company, who says that it is just part of the cost of doing business in many countries to pay small bribes to get people simply to do their jobs. However, he is against paying bribes to persuade people to make decisions that they otherwise would not have made.[35]

Whatever their professed beliefs, many businesspeople are willing to engage in bribery as an everyday part of meeting their business objectives. Many corporate officials, in fact, avoid any moral issue by simply "turning a blind eye" to what goes on in subsidiaries. Some companies avoid these issues by hiring a local agent who takes care of the paperwork and pays all the so-called fees in return for a salary or consultant's fee.[36] However, while the FCPA does allow "grease" payments to facilitate business in a foreign country, if those payments are lawful there, other payments prohibited by the FCPA remain subject to prosecution even if the company says it did not know that its agents or subsidiaries were making such payments—the so-called "reason to know" provision.[37]

Critics of the FCPA contend that the law represents an ethnocentric attempt to impose U.S. standards on the rest of the world and puts U.S. firms at a competitive disadvantage.[38] Indeed, the United States is the only country prohibiting firms from making payments to secure contracts overseas.[39] In any event, many feel that business activities that cannot stand scrutiny are clearly unethical, corrupt, and, in the long run, corrupting.[40] Bribery fails three important tests of ethical corporate actions: (1) Is it legal? (2) Does it work (in the long run)? (3) Can it be talked about?[41]

Many MNCs have decided to confront concerns about ethical behavior and social responsibility by developing worldwide practices that represent the company's posture. Among those policies are the following:

- Develop worldwide codes of ethics.
- Consider ethical issues in strategy development.
- Develop periodic "ethical impact" statements.
- Given major, unsolvable, ethical problems, consider withdrawal from the problem market.[42]

Most of the leadership in developing ethical postures in international activities comes from the United States. Although this move toward ethics and social responsibility is spreading, both in the United States and around the world, problems still abound in many countries.

Heightened global competition encourages companies to seek advantages through questionable tactics. A U.S. Commerce Department study revealed many incidents of improper inducements by companies and governments around the world (such as Germany's Siemens and the European airframe consortium Airbus Industrie) that undercut U.S. companies. Yet U.S. companies are not all clean. In October 1995, Lockheed Martin Corporation's former vice president was sentenced to eighteen months in prison and given a $125,000 fine for bribing a member of the Egyptian Parliament to win an order for three C-130 cargo planes.[43] So much for Lockheed's consent decree to refrain from corrupt practices, which it signed twenty years ago following its bribery scandal in Japan.

Japan also continues to have its share of internal problems regarding the ethical behavior of its officials and businesspeople. In the scandal involving Nippon Telephone and Telegraph Company (NTT), the chairman of the board of NTT was involved in obtaining cut-rate stock in a real estate subsidiary of the Recruit Company in exchange for helping the company obtain two U.S. supercomputers. When the stock went public, the chairman and other NTT executives made a lot of money, and they were later arrested and charged with accepting bribes.[44] As the scandal unfolded, it appeared that government members were involved, including the prime minister, Noboru Takeshita, who had received $1.4 million in questionable, albeit legal, donations from the Recruit Company. Takeshita subsequently resigned, as did other government officials, and the incident became known as "Recruitgate," in reference to the Watergate scandal that forced President Nixon to resign.[45]

Making the Right Decision

How is a manager operating abroad to know what is the "right" decision when faced with questionable or unfamiliar circumstances of doing business? The first line of defense is to consult the laws of both the home and the host countries—such as the FCPA. If any of those laws would be violated, then you, the manager, must look to some other way to complete the business transaction, or withdraw altogether.

Second, you could consult the International Codes of Conduct for MNEs (see Exhibit 2-2). These are broad and cover various areas of social responsibility and ethical behavior; even so, many issues are subject to interpretation.

If legal consultation does not provide you with a clear answer about what to do, you should consult the company's code of ethics (if there is one). You, as the manager, should realize that you are not alone in making these kinds of decisions. It is also the responsibility of the company to provide guidelines for the actions and decisions made by its employees. In addition, you are not the first, and certainly not the last, to be faced with this kind of situation—which also sets up a collective experience in the company about what kinds of decisions your colleagues typically make in various circumstances. Those norms or expectations (assuming they are honorable) can supplement the code of ethics or substitute for the lack of a formal code. If your intended action runs contrary to the norms or the formal code, discontinue that plan.

If you are still unsure of what to do, you have the right and the obligation to consult your superiors. Unfortunately, often the situation is not that clear-cut, or your boss will tell you to "use your own judgment." Sometimes your superiors in the home office just want you to complete the transaction to the benefit of the company and don't want to be involved in what you have to do to consummate the deal.

If your dilemma continues, you must fall back upon your own moral code of ethics. One way to consider the dilemma is to ask yourself what the rights of the various stakeholders involved are (see Exhibit 2-1), and how you should weigh those rights. First, does the proposed action (rigged contract bid, bribe, etc.) harm anyone? What are the likely consequences of your decision in both the short run and long run? Who would benefit from your contemplated action? What are the benefits to some versus potential harm to others? In the case of a rigged contract bid through bribery, for example, people are put at a disadvantage, especially over the long term, with a pattern of this behavior. This is because, if competition is unfair, not only are your competitors harmed by losing the bid, but also the consumers of the products or services are harmed because they will pay more to attain them than they would under an efficient market system.

In the end, you have to follow your own conscience and decide where to draw the line in the sand in order to operate with integrity—otherwise the line moves further and further away with each transgression. In addition, what can start with a small bribe or cover-up here—a matter of personal ethics—can, over time, and in the aggregate of many people covering up, result in a situation of a truly negligent, and perhaps criminal, stance toward social responsibility to society, like that revealed by investigations of the tobacco industry in the United States. Indeed, executives are increasingly being held personally and criminally accountable for their decisions; this is true even for people operating on the board of directors of a company. Criminal charges were brought against fifteen executives of WorldCom in 2003, for example, and the noose was widening surrounding the Enron debacle as international banks such as Citigroup and JP Morgan Chase were charged with "taking part in sham deals to disguise Enron's financial problems."[46]

Richard Rhodes, CEO of Rhodes Architectural Stone, Inc., is one executive who has drawn a line in the sand for himself and his company, and who holds himself and his employees accountable to a high moral standard when it comes to issues of bribery and human rights. He explains how they deal with difficult situations abroad in the accompanying Management Focus, "CEO Speaks Out: Ethics Abroad—Business Fundamentals, Value Judgments."

Management Focus

CEO Speaks Out: Ethics Abroad—Business Fundamentals, Value Judgments

You've just finished negotiating the deal, and it's time for a celebration, drinks and dinner all around, and you go to bed only to wake up the next morning to learn that the other side wants to start all over again.

Or, you try to buy something–say a collection of antique vessels for resale for decorative uses–and you're told that the artifacts are yours but only for a price. You wonder, should I agree to pay a bribe just this once?

So it goes sometimes when it comes to the business of doing business abroad, which has been the case for my company, Rhodes Architectural Stone, Inc., ever since its launch (under another name) in 1998. Ours is the business of buying artifacts slated for demolition in areas of the world, such as Africa, China, India, and Indonesia, and, in turn, selling to discriminating clients in the United States.

If there is one thing we've learned, it is that the ethical landscape is different in the third world. In the United States–notwithstanding the recent spate of corporate scandals that have set a woefully new low for ethical business behavior–the fact remains that standards do exist against which improprieties can be measured.

Not so in some other countries. The tenets that underlie our U.S. business language–that your word is your bond, that transparency is expected in joint ventures and contractual engagements, that each party walks away from the table getting as well as giving something–are not always understood in all parts of the world.

This inherent conflict between first- and third-world business standards has meant that our journey as a design-driven firm has been at times extremely difficult. A core value of the company, which we call "value in the round," meaning that value must be created for all parties in the deal, has involved familiarizing ourselves with an alien environment in order to establish business fundamentals. Needing to respect cultural differences must be carefully investigated and evaluated while all the time taking care not to cross the line to engage in practices we abhor.

BUSINESS BLACK AND WHITE

In short, in the world of grays that characterizes business dealings in countries in which ethics are at best rudimentary by U.S. standards, and at worst nonexistent, we've taken the position that we must establish a black and white.

Let me explain. Take the word "transparency," for example, which in the United States involves a baseline understanding of capitalism, allowing that each party is able to get something in a negotiation without necessarily having cheated another. With that common understanding, negotiators don't need to resort to taking money out of the game–bribing, to be precise–because all of the money is in the game.

Nor is there a need to have to renegotiate a deal that has already been agreed upon because of a belief that the deal that was struck couldn't be good–or why would the parties have agreed to it?

In countries whose business laws are nascent, if they exist at all, and whose thinking has been shaped by philosophies vastly different from our own, our first challenge is to take what I call the "entry-level" business players, who disproportionately populate the developing countries in which we do business, and bring them up to speed in the business fundamentals of the U.S.

In the all-too-common instance of being asked that a deal be renegotiated, we see it as our duty to teach the fundamentals that underlie the business practices of the West, such as your word is your bond, and that, while it's all right to take as much time as you need to negotiate a deal, once you've agreed, you stand by it.

In the wake of a request to go back to the table after the celebratory dinner, for example, I begin by outlining what it's going to take for them to do business with us. We put it down in writing, even though I've learned that such documents are unenforceable. And, if they ask again to renegotiate, we walk.

In short, in a world in which business fundamentals are shades of gray, we've determined a black-and-white process that is our blueprint for doing business.

MORAL BLACK AND WHITE

Back to the bribes: Simply put, we don't do them. In the case of our wanting to buy the collection of antique vessels, for example, we walked when told we would have to make such a payment. The good news in that case was that we were actually invited back a year later to make the purchase on our terms.

The matter of bribes, however, is more than just shall we or shall we not. It goes to the heart of the other issue underlying doing business in the third world, and that is the need for a way to respect cultural differences without crossing the line to engage in practices that are inappropriate or immoral by Western standards.

Looked at this way, Rhodes Architectural Stone not only draws the line at paying bribes, but also at child labor and the mistreatment of women. The matter of child labor will serve to illustrate the dilemma. Imagine an American entrepreneur, traveling in the bitter cold in the remote countryside dressed in a Gortex parka, thinsulite socks, and the most comfortable and technologically advanced clothing money can buy. We arrive and state that we will not buy anything fabricated or procured with child labor. Now contrast that with the local reality of the labor of the entire family required to put bread on the table and a roof over one's head.

If my children were starving, I suppose I would do the same. In fact, our own forbearers in the United States did employ children in factories well into the twentieth century, and because of that, we don't have to do it any more.

Into this moral gray area, we've established another black and white: namely, that we cannot and will not do business with entities that engage in the practice of child labor, but we will not go the next step and preach. In other words, we will not tell them they are wrong.

Surely, we bring a powerful lever when it comes to backing up this moral stance. Unlike foreign companies that go into native countries to sell products to people who can't afford to buy them, we are there to buy what they have to sell. We bring the twin carrots of hard currency and jobs.

That advantage notwithstanding, the decision to establish a moral black and white wasn't easy. It's one thing to come to that imperative in the matter of formulating business standards where none exist, for that involves the neutral task of teaching. It's quite another to tread into territory in which the actions are criminal or immoral by Western standards and, yet, understandable within the context of the foreign culture.

The decision to do so, therefore, is actually a process, one of thought and reflection and, in the final analysis, leadership.

PUTTING IT ALL TOGETHER

In coming to the imperatives that Rhodes Architectural Stone has determined for its business dealings overseas, I was fortunate to have the counsel of a member of our board, a former Whirlpool executive, who had extensive business experience throughout the world.

This individual taught me that when dealing with the grays that characterize the business landscape in the third world, it is necessary to establish a black and white, both for the way you will conduct business and account for your moral imperatives. And, if the reality differs considerably when you are actually at the table, it is necessary to be strong enough to walk away.

In sum, you must ask yourself questions such as: Who am I? How do I feel about this or that action? Can I sleep at night if I so engage in this or that behavior?

In the milieu of grays that characterizes the world beyond our oceans, be strong enough to formulate your black and whites, which, in turn, will become your guiding principles.

MANAGING INTERDEPENDENCE

Because multinational firms (or other organizations, such as the Red Cross) represent global interdependency, their managers at all levels must recognize that what they do, in the aggregate, has long-term implications for the socioeconomic interdependence of nations. Simply to describe ethical issues as part of the general environment does not address the fact that managers must control their activities at all levels—from simple, daily business transactions involving local workers, intermediaries, or consumers to global concerns of ecological responsibility—for the future benefit of all concerned. Whatever the situation, the powerful long-term effects of MNC and MNE action (or inaction) should be planned for and controlled—not haphazardly considered part of the side effects of business. The profitability of individual companies depends on a cooperative and constructive attitude toward global interdependence.

Foreign Subsidiaries in the United States

Much of the preceding discussion has related to U.S. subsidiaries around the world. However, to globally highlight the growing interdependence and changing balance of business power foreign subsidiaries in the United States should also be considered. Since much criticism about a lack of responsibility has been directed toward MNCs with headquarters in the United States, we must think of these criticisms from an outsider's perspective. The number of foreign subsidiaries in the United States has grown and continues to grow dramatically; **foreign direct investment (FDI)** in the United States by other countries is, in many cases, far more than U.S. investment outward. Americans are thus becoming more sensitive to what they perceive as a lack of control over their own country's business.

Things look very different from the perspective of Americans employed at a subsidiary of an overseas MNC. Interdependence takes on a new meaning when people "over there" are calling the shots regarding strategy, expectations, products, and personnel. Often, Americans' resentment about different ways of doing business by "foreign" companies in the United States inhibits cooperation, which gave rise to the companies' presence in the first place.

Today, managers from all countries must learn new ways, and most MNCs are trying to adapt. Sadahei Kusumoto, president and CEO of the Minolta Corporation, says that Japanese managers in the United States must recognize that they are "not in Honshu [Japan's largest island] anymore" and that one very different aspect of management in the United States is the idea of corporate social responsibility.[47]

In Japan, corporate social responsibility has traditionally meant that companies take care of their employees, whereas in the United States the public and private sectors are expected to share the responsibility for the community. Part of the explanation for this difference is that U.S. corporations get tax deductions for corporate philanthropy, whereas Japanese firms do not; nor are Japanese managers familiar with community needs. For these and other reasons, Japanese subsidiaries in the United States have not been active in U.S. philanthropy. However, Kusumoto pinpoints why they should become more involved in the future:

> *In the long run, failure to play an active role in the community will brand these companies as irresponsible outsiders and dim their prospects for the future.*[48]

Whether Kusomoto's motives for change are humanitarian or just good business sense does not really matter. The point is that he recognizes interdependence in globalization and acts accordingly.

Managing Subsidiary–Host-Country Interdependence

When **managing interdependence**, international managers must go beyond general issues of social responsibility and deal with the specific concerns of the MNC subsidiary–host-country relationship. Outdated MNC attitudes that focus only on profitability and autonomy are shortsighted and usually result in only short-term realization of those goals. MNCs must learn to accommodate the needs of other organizations and countries:

> *Interdependence rather than independence, and cooperation rather than confrontation are at the heart of that accommodation . . . the journey from independence to interdependence managed badly leads to dependence, and that is an unacceptable destination.*[49]

Most of the past criticism levied at MNCs has focused on their activities in LDCs. Their real or perceived lack of responsibility centers on the transfer-in of inappropriate technology, causing unemployment, and the transfer-out of scarce financial and other resources, reducing the capital available for internal development. In their defense, MNCs help LDCs by contributing new technology and managerial skills, improving the infrastructure, creating jobs, and bringing in investment capital from other countries by exporting products. The infusion of outside capital provides foreign-exchange earnings that can be used for further development. The host government's attitude is often referred to as a love–hate relationship: It wants the economic growth that MNCs can provide, but it does not want the incursions on national sovereignty or the technological dependence that may result. Most criticisms of MNC subsidiary activities, whether in less developed or more developed countries, are along the following lines:

1. MNCs locally raise their needed capital, contributing to a rise in interest rates in host countries.
2. The majority (sometimes even 100 percent) of the stock of most subsidiaries is owned by the parent company. Consequently, host-country people do not have much control over the operations of corporations within their borders.

3. MNCs usually reserve the key managerial and technical positions for expatriates. As a result, they do not contribute to the development of host-country personnel.

4. MNCs do not adapt their technology to the conditions that exist in host countries.

5. MNCs concentrate their research and development activities at home, restricting the transfer of modern technology and know-how to host countries.

6. MNCs give rise to the demand for luxury goods in host countries at the expense of essential consumer goods.

7. MNCs start their foreign operations by purchasing existing firms rather than by developing new productive facilities in host countries.

8. MNCs dominate major industrial sectors, thus contributing to inflation, by stimulating demand for scarce resources and earning excessively high profits and fees.

9. MNCs are not accountable to their host nations but only respond to home-country governments; they are not concerned with host-country plans for development.[50]

Specific MNCs have been charged with tax evasion, union busting, and interference in host-country politics. Of course, MNCs have both positive and negative effects on different economies. For every complaint about MNC activities (whether about capital markets, technology transfer, or employment practices), we can identify potential benefits (see Exhibit 2-6.)

Numerous conflicts arise between MNC companies or subsidiaries and host countries, including conflicting goals (both economic and noneconomic) and conflicting concerns, such as the security of proprietary technology, patents, or information. Overall, the resulting trade-offs create an interdependent relationship between the subsidiary and the host government, based on relative bargaining power. The power of MNCs is based on their large-scale, worldwide economies, their strategic flexibility, and their control over technology and production location. The bargaining chips of the host governments include their control of raw materials and market access and their ability to set the rules

---

EXHIBIT 2-6   MNC Benefits and Costs to Host Countries

Benefits	Costs
Capital Market Effects	
■ Broader access to outside capital	■ Increased competition for local scarce capital
■ Foreign-exchange earnings	■ Increased interest rates as supply of local capital decreases
■ Import substitution effects allow governments to save foreign exchange for priority projects	■ Capital service effects of balance of payments
■ Risk sharing	
Technology and Production Effects	
■ Access to new technology and R&D developments	■ Technology is not always appropriate
■ Infrastructure development and support	■ Plants are often for assembly only and can be dismantled
■ Export diversification	■ Government infrastructure investment is higher than expected benefits
Employment Effects	
■ Direct creation of new jobs	■ Limited skill development and creation
■ Opportunities for indigenous management development	■ Competition for scarce skills
■ Income multiplier effects on local community business	■ Low percentage of managerial jobs for local people
	■ Employment instability because of ability to move production operations freely to other countries

SOURCE: R. H. Mason and R. S. Spich, *Management: An International Perspective, 202* (Homewood, Ill. Irwin, 1987).

regarding the role of private enterprise, the operation of state-owned firms, and the specific regulations regarding taxes, permissions, and so forth.[51]

MNCs run the risk of their assets becoming hostage to host control, which may take the form of nationalism, protectionism, or governmentalism. Under **nationalism**, for example, public opinion is rallied in favor of national goals and against foreign influences. Under **protectionism**, the host institutes a partial or complete closing of borders to withstand competitive foreign products, using tariff and nontariff barriers, such as those used by Japan. Under **governmentalism**, the government uses its policy-setting role to favor national interests, rather than relying on market forces. An example is Britain's decision to privatize its telephone system.[52]

Ford Motor Company came up against many of these controls when it decided to produce automobiles in Spain. The Spanish government set specific restrictions on sales and export volume: the sales volume was limited to 10 percent of the previous year's total automobile market, and the export volume had to be at least two-thirds of the entire production in Spain. Ford also had to agree that it would not broaden its model lines without the authorization of the government.[53]

The intricacies of the relationship and the relative power of an MNC subsidiary and a host-country government are situation specific. Clearly, such a relationship should be managed for mutual benefit; a long-term, constructive relationship based on the MNC's socially responsive stance should result in progressive strategic success for the MNC and economic progress for the host country. The effective management of subsidiary–host-country interdependence must have a long-term perspective. Although temporary strategies to reduce interdependence via controls on the transnational flows by firms (for example, transfer-pricing tactics) or by governments (such as new residency requirements for skilled workers) are often successful in the short run, they result in inefficiencies that must be absorbed by one or both parties, with negative long-term results.[54] In setting up and maintaining subsidiaries, managers are wise to consider the long-term trade-offs between strategic plans and operational management. By finding out for themselves the pressing local concerns and understanding the sources of past conflicts, they can learn from mistakes and recognize the consequences of the failure to manage problems. Furthermore, managers should implement policies that reflect corporate social responsibility regarding local economic issues, employee welfare, or natural resources.[55] At the least, the failure to effectively manage interdependence results in constraints on strategy. In the worst case, it results in disastrous consequences for the local area, for the subsidiary, and for the global reputation of the company.

The interdependent nature of developing economies and the MNCs operating there is of particular concern when discussing social responsibility because of the tentative and fragile nature of the economic progression in those countries. MNCs must set a high moral standard and lay the groundwork for future economic development. At the minimum, they should ensure that their actions will do no harm. Some recommendations by De George for MNCs operating in and doing business with developing countries are as follows:

1. Do no intentional harm. This includes respect for the integrity of the ecosystem and consumer safety.
2. Produce more good than harm for the host country.
3. Contribute by their activity to the host country's development.
4. Respect the human rights of their employees.
5. To the extent that local culture does not violate ethical norms, respect the local culture and work with and not against it.
6. Pay their fair share of taxes.
7. Cooperate with the local government in developing and enforcing just background (infrastructure) institutions (i.e., laws, governmental regulations, unions, and consumer groups, which serve as a means of social control).[56]

One issue that illustrates conflicting concerns about social responsibility is the interdependence between Mexico and the United States, which has resulted from the North American Free Trade Agreement (NAFTA) (see Comparative Management in Focus, "Interdependence:— NAFTA at 10—Growing Pains in Mexico, Canada, and the United States").

Comparative Management in Focus

Interdependence: NAFTA at 10—Growing Pains in Mexico, Canada, and the United States

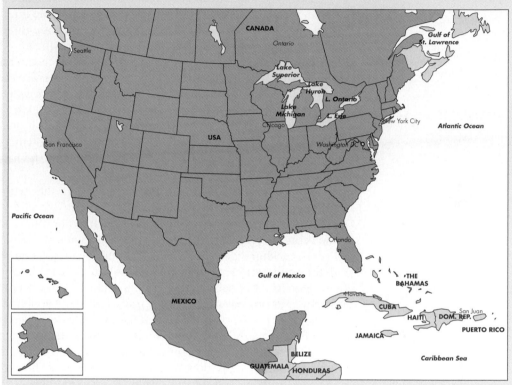

Map 2-1

The North American Free Trade Agreement (NAFTA)took hold 10 years ago, after a bruising, arm-twisting debate. Today, it is more than ever a politically charged symbol of the promises and perils of free trade.

The accord, known as NAFTA, brought under one canopy three hugely different economies: the wealthy United States, middle-class Canada, and striving Mexico. The disparities made NAFTA the boldest gamble ever on the proposition that free trade could benefit all.

Leaders promised the accord would create millions of good jobs, curb illegal immigration, and raise living standards "from the Yukon to the Yucatan." A decade later, the verdict, even among NAFTA's strongest supporters, is that for those goals free trade by itself is not enough.

NAFTA's effects cannot be isolated from the broader changes in a globalizing economy; however, many economists and political analysts say that while the accord stimulated trade and overall growth, it also brought jarring dislocations. For better or worse—or both—NAFTA transformed the continent's economic landscape with startling speed.

Gary Hufbauer, a senior analyst at the Institute for International Economics, a Washington research group that supports free trade, said the gains for the United States—lower priced consumer goods and increased corporate earnings—are large compared to the losses.

"However, the gains are so thinly spread across the country that people don't thank NAFTA when they buy a mango or inexpensive auto parts," he said.

The pain, he said, is concentrated in places like the Midwest, where manufacturing jobs have been lost to Mexico and Canada, and now to China. "NAFTA-related job loss and lower income may be small, but the echo is very large because of all the other jobs lost to globalization," he said. "NAFTA is the symbol for all of that pain."

The debate over NAFTA continues to shape the future of free trade, even as more nations line up for its presumed benefits, like the four Central American countries that reached their own accord with the United States in December 2003.

But even that agreement is likely to face agonizing debate in Congress during an election year as NAFTA's wrenching changes provide a rallying point for opponents who say it was too much too fast and paid too little attention to the impact on workers.

With the national consensus on free trade fraying and the loss of jobs looming as a campaign issue, it is doubtful whether any Democratic candidate or President Bush will stand unapologetically behind deeper trade liberalization in the coming year.

But for NAFTA's supporters, the accord, which lowered or eliminated tariffs on everything from agricultural goods to auto parts, still left all three nations better off than they would have been without it.

"It has definitely created export-related job growth," said Bill Richardson, the governor of New Mexico. As the Democratic whip, he helped pushed through passage of NAFTA in the House.

"On the whole NAFTA's been a plus, but still, with a lot of alarmingly bad follow-up on commitments made on the border," he said. Promises to protect workers' rights and the environment have "failed alarmingly." So have pledges to close the economic gap between the United States and Mexico.

"The whole idea that NAFTA would create jobs on the Mexican side and thus deter immigration has just been dead wrong," he said. "That was oversold."

Robert B. Zoellick, the United States Trade Representative, says NAFTA achieved its objective of increasing trade, especially doubling American agricultural exports to Mexico. Though the United States' trade deficit with Canada and Mexico grew nine-fold to nearly $90 billion, total trade among the three nations grew by 109 percent.

"NAFTA has been pulling American goods and grains into Mexico, benefiting consumers and supporting quality U.S. jobs here at home," he said, referring to rising pay for manufacturing jobs. That 14.4 percent boost still lagged behind the overall increase in household incomes.

For retail giants like Wal-Mart, government-subsidized American agricultural businesses and America's biggest makers of automobiles and automobile parts, borderless trade meant bigger profits for themselves and their stockholders.

But the benefits of stable prices and rising 401(k)'s are largely invisible compared with the blight of a shuttered factory. The consumers of the United States or Mexico or Canada are also each nation's workers, farmers, and small town residents, and NAFTA left many with lower consumer costs at the expense of their old way of life.

In Canada, where NAFTA helped shape a more competitive economy, those growing pains were cushioned by a strong social safety net. Not so in Mexico and the United States.

"We're the losers," said Bonnie Long, one of at least half a million American manufacturing workers who lost their jobs due to NAFTA, despite the surge in trade. "We lost our health care, our living wages. The winners are the corporate executives who don't even live here and can locate their factories wherever they find the cheapest labor."

GOSHEN, INDIANA, U.S.

Social Tensions and Vanishing Jobs

Indiana, like the rest of the United States, has enjoyed a growth in exports under NAFTA But, Goshen is also like thousands of towns across the nation that have seen jobs and health benefits disappear with the accord.

What is also disappearing is a way of life in Goshen, home to 30,000 people and the seat of Elkhart County in northern Indiana. The town once lived by making things. It was the "widget capital" of the United States, says its mayor, Allan Kauffman.

Gerald A. Trolz has refused to relocate Goshen Stamping, his small hardware manufacturing firm in Indiana, despite pressure from low-wage competition abroad. "The experts don't see what's happening here, on the shop floor," he said.

SOURCE: Copyright Joe Raymond. Reprinted by permission.

"NAFTA has not had a positive impact," he explained. "Goshen makes widgets. It has always made widgets. And, any company that makes widgets that are easy to transport—those are gone or are going to go."

Half of Elkhart County depends on manufacturing. Once dozens of locally owned factories across the state churned out parts for all sorts of products, electronics, pharmaceuticals, furniture, pianos, and especially for the automotive industry.

Few manufacturers have been able to resist the seemingly tidal pull of globalization that includes NAFTA. One is Gerald A. Trolz, a local hero because he would not sell or relocate Goshen Stamping, his small hardware manufacturing firm, even after his main customer moved to Mexico and half his sales went with it.

He said the only reason he has been able to keep his firm in Goshen is that he owns it: he does not answer to stockholders. "The experts don't see what's happening here, on the shop floor, so it's easy for them to say that NAFTA was good or bad," Mr. Trolz said. "Until this levels out, it is just plain havoc."

The increasing competition from cheap labor abroad has deepened a decades-old trend toward depressed wages, as has another unexpected impact of NAFTA—the arrival of hundreds of Mexican migrants looking for work in the United States.

CIUDAD ACUÑA, MEXICO

A Fleeting Boom and Disillusionment
One of the promises of NAFTA was that it would close the great gaps in wages and living standards between the United States and Mexico and keep Mexicans working on their side of the border.

Nowadays in Mexico, "When you argue that free trade benefits poor people," said Luis de la Calle, a chief NAFTA negotiator for Mexico, "no one believes you." A strong supporter of the accord, Mr. de la Calle, an economist, nonetheless believes NAFTA's benefits for Mexico are dwindling as manufacturing moves to countries where wages are even lower, particularly China.

Some Mexican companies successfully exploited the new American market, especially those allied with American corporations, like big tomato growers that sell to companies like Del Monte, or food processors that turn American pigs into bacon.

But by every measurable standard, the gap between rich and poor in Mexico widened. Unemployment is up and real wages, eroded by a collapse of the peso in 1995, are flat or down for many millions of workers.

Etelvina Vázquez, an assembly-line worker, and her son, Pedro, have a subsidized house in Acuña but no spare money.
SOURCE: Courtesy of Taylor Jones.

NAFTA created jobs, but not fast enough to keep pace with rising competition from China, or with a labor force that swelled with Mexican farmers displaced by subsidized American imports.

Millions of Mexican workers crossed into the United States. A million more moved north to the border looking for work, in a movement comparable to the migration of Americans from the rural South to Northern cities like Chicago and Detroit in the first half of the 20th century. For Mexico, the change happened in a decade.

Many ended up in the trade-driven assembly lines known as *maquiladoras*, most of which stand in hard-bitten border towns like Ciudad Juárez and Ciudad Acuña. The *maquiladoras* produced $78 billion in exports during 2002, nearly two-thirds of that sum from American parts assembled in Mexico and re-exported to the United States.

"The promises made about how life would be were not real," said Etelvina Vázquez, 43, an assembly-line worker in an Alcoa auto-supplies plant. She is one of 27,000 people who moved to Ciudad Acuña from the southern state of Veracruz alone, according to the city's *maquiladoras* owners' association.

After five years, Ms. Vázquez takes home $45 for a 48-hour week, after deductions for the costs of her government-built house. Though her income is higher than it was back home, what she has left after paying the bills is about the same. "Life is different," she said, "but just as hard."

Many of these *maquiladoras* jobs are now disappearing, as the one relative advantage Mexico once had—cheap labor—erodes in an expanding global marketplace. Of the 700,000 new *maquiladora* jobs generated in NAFTA's first seven years, 300,000 have been eliminated since 2000.

Inside and outside the *maquiladoras*, "all the jobs gained in manufacturing, thanks to, have vanished," said Edgar Amador, an economist in Mexico City. "Ten years after, there is no conclusive evidence that real wages have increased because of NAFTA."

To Angelica Morales, a *maquiladora* worker transplanted to Ciudad Acuña from Monclova, four hours south, the reason is clear enough. "There are no independent unions," she said. "Workers have no say over what happens to them."

Such arguments do not persuade Cuauhtemoc Hernández, 31, who represents the city's Maquiladora Association—34 assembly-line plants, all but two owned by American companies, employing 32,000 Mexican workers. The benefits for American business—cheap labor, high productivity, generous tax breaks—flow throughout the city, he says.

"The growth of Acuña was fast, fast, fast," he said—so fast that the city has a severe lack of housing, hospitals, and schools.

"Everybody says the local situation—unpaved streets, no workers' health institutions, no housing that workers deserve—is the *maquiladoras*' fault," Mr. Hernández said. "Even some government authorities say, 'No more *maquiladoras*.' What is our answer? Our answer is: 'You cannot stop progress.'"

DURHAM, ONTARIO, CANADA

Industries Forced to Adapt or Die

Canada was far better situated than Mexico to benefit from free trade. It has a well-educated middle class. Ninety percent of Canadians live within 100 miles of the border. They enjoy liberal unemployment benefits and universal health insurance.

"Of course, you've got some pain that has to be endured," said Jean Chrétien, who stepped down this month as Canada's prime minister.

Progress proved wrenching for Canada, as well. It had a separate 1988 free-trade accord with the United States, five years before NAFTA. Those years were a cold shower for Canada: from 1989 to 1991, 450,000 manufacturing jobs, roughly one in five, were lost.

Some survivors came out stronger. NAFTA's proponents point to a future where the promises of free trade may yet be fulfilled.

In the small Ontario manufacturing town of Durham, the managers of the Durham Furniture factory got a phone call from Toronto on February. 10, 1992. Their parent company, Strathearn House Group, had gone bankrupt. All 150 employees were summoned to the cafeteria to hear the news: their 93-year-old plant would soon close.

"The entire town was like a wake," recalled Lloyd Love, now vice president for manufacturing.

Then, the managers found financing to reopen the plant as a stand-alone company called Durham Furniture. Under the direction of an American marketing specialist named John Scarsella, now president and chief executive, Durham remade itself, investing more than $15 million in new technology and aiming for American customers.

Durham's sales rose eight-fold since 1994 to over $75 million this year. Eighty percent of that goes to the United States. From 100 employees in 1993, the company now has 800 workers, a sales office in Canfield, Ohio, and a showroom in High Point, North Carolina.

"The border is seamless for us," Mr. Scarsella said. "We went from a Canadian company with a 30 million population market to a 300 million market. We do not treat the border as a border."

David Hanna, executive vice president of the Ontario Furniture Manufacturing Association, said perhaps half a dozen company members were driven out of business by NAFTA, which let American giants like Ethan Allen flood the Canadian market. Ontario's premier furniture manufacturers have lost about half of the roughly 7,200 workers they had a decade ago, he said.

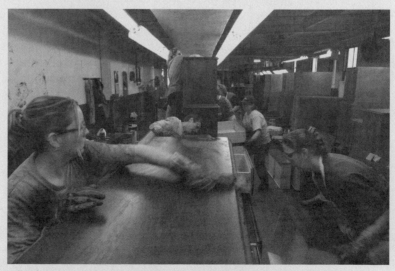

After its parent company went backrupt, Durham Furniture thrived under NAFTA by shifting focus to the American market.

SOURCE: Copyright Lana Slezic. Reprinted by permission.

"Once barriers went down, Canadian industry was very exposed," said Perrin Beatty, president of the Manufacturers and Exporters Association and a cabinet minister in the government who negotiated the agreement. "It meant a psychological shift of gears. You either adapted or you died."

Today Canada's businesses are far more export-oriented than a generation ago. They created 500,000 jobs last year, even as they, too, feel growing Chinese competition. Exports to the United States more than doubled and now represent more than a third of Canada's economy. Several sectors—communications equipment, chemicals, oil and gas services, aircraft manufacturing, and electronics—are growing fast.

Managing Environmental Interdependence

International managers—and all people for that matter—can no longer afford to ignore the impact of their activities on the environment. As Ward and Dubois put it:

> Now that mankind is in the process of completing the colonization of the planet, learning to manage it intelligently is an urgent imperative. [People] must accept responsibility for the stewardship of the earth. The word stewardship implies, of course, management for the sake of someone else. . . . As we enter the global phase of human evolution, it becomes obvious that each [person] has two countries, his [or her] own and the planet earth.[57]

Effectively **managing environmental interdependence** includes considering ecological interdependence as well as the economic and social implications of MNC activities. There is an ever-increasing awareness of, and a mounting concern, worldwide, about the effects of global industrialization on the natural environment. This concern was evidenced by the gathering of world leaders in 2000 at the Earth Summit in Rio de Janeiro to discuss and decide on action for ecological preservation. Government regulations and powerful interest groups are demanding ecological responsibility regarding the use of scarce natural resources and production processes that threaten permanent damage to the planet. MNCs have to deal with each country's different policies and techniques for environmental and health protection. Such variations in approach reflect different levels of industrialization, living standards, government–business relations, philosophies of collective intervention, patterns of industrial competition, and degrees of sophistication in public policy.[58] For an MNC to take advantage of less stringent regulations (or expectations) is not only irresponsible but also invites disaster, as illustrated by the Union Carbide accident in Bhopal in December 1984.

In recent years, the export of hazardous wastes from developed countries to less developed ones has increased considerably. One instance was the dumping of over 8,000 drums of waste, including drums filled with polychlorinated biphenyl (PCB), a highly toxic compound, in Koko, Nigeria.[59] While not all dumping is illegal, the large international trade in hazardous wastes (as a result of the increasing barriers to domestic disposal) raises disturbing questions regarding social responsibility. Although the importer of waste must take some blame, it is the exporter who shoulders the ultimate responsibility for both generation and disposal. Often, companies choose to dispose of hazardous waste in less developed countries to take advantage of weaker regulations and lower costs. Until we have strict international regulation of trade in hazardous wastes, companies should take it upon themselves to monitor their activities, as Singh and Lakhan demand:

> To export these wastes to countries which do not benefit from waste-generating industrial processes or whose citizens do not have lifestyles that generate such wastes is unethical. It is especially unjust to send hazardous wastes to lesser developed countries which lack the technology to minimize the deleterious effects of these substances.[60]

The exporting of pesticides poses a similar problem, with the United States and Germany being the main culprits. The United States exports about 200 million pounds of pesticides each year that are prohibited, restricted, or not registered for use in the United States.[61] One MNC, Monsanto Chemical Corporation, for example, sells DDT to many foreign importers, even though its use in the United States has been essentially banned. Apart from the lack of social responsibility toward the people and the environment in the countries that import DDT, this action is also irresponsible to U.S. citizens because many of their fruits and meat products are imported from those countries.[62]

These are only two of the environmental problems facing countries and large corporations today. According to Graedel and Allenby, the path to truly sustainable development is for corporations to broaden their concept of industrial ecology:

> *The concept [of industrial ecology] requires that an industrial system be viewed not in isolation from its surrounding systems, but in concert with them. It is a systems view in which one seeks to optimize the total materials cycle from virgin material, to finished material, to component, to product, to obsolete product, and to ultimate disposal.*[63]

Essentially, this perspective supports the idea that environmental citizenship is necessary for a firm's survival as well as responsible social performance.[64]

It is clear, then, that MNCs must take the lead in dealing with ecological interdependence by integrating environmental factors into strategic planning. Along with an investment appraisal, a project feasibility study, and operational plans, such planning should include an environmental impact assessment.[65] At the least, MNC managers must deal with the increasing scarcity of natural resources in the next few decades by (1) looking for alternative raw materials, (2) developing new methods of recycling or disposing of used materials, and (3) expanding the use of byproducts.[66]

Multinational corporations already have had a tremendous impact on foreign countries, and this impact will continue to grow and bring about long-lasting changes. Even now, U.S. MNCs alone account for about 10 percent of the world's gross national product (GNP). Because of interdependence at both the local and global level, it is not only moral but also in the best interest of MNCs to establish a single clear posture toward social and ethical responsibilities worldwide and to ensure that it is implemented. In a real sense, foreign firms enter as guests in host countries and must respect the local laws, policies, traditions, and culture as well as those countries' economic and developmental needs.

CONCLUSION

When research findings and anecdotal evidence indicate differential attitudes toward ethical behavior and social responsibility across cultures, MNCs must take certain steps. For example, they must be careful when placing a foreign manager in a country whose values are incongruent with his or her own because this could lead to conflicts with local managers, governmental bodies, customers, and suppliers. As discussed earlier, expatriates should be oriented to the legal and ethical ramifications of questionable foreign payments, the differences in environmental regulations, and the local expectations of personal integrity. They should also be supported as they attempt to integrate host-country behaviors with the expectations of the company's headquarters.[67]

Social responsibility, ethical behavior, and interdependence are important concerns to be built into management control—not as afterthoughts but as part of the ongoing process of planning and controlling international operations for the long-term benefit of all.

Part II focuses on the pervasive and powerful influence of culture in the host-country environment in which the international manager operates. Chapter 3 examines the nature of culture—what are its various dimensions and roots? How does culture affect the behavior and expectations of employees, and what are the implications for how managers operating in other countries should behave?

Summary of Key Points

1. The concept of international social responsibility includes the expectation that MNCs should be concerned about the social and economic effects of their decisions on activities in other countries.
2. Moral universalism refers to the need for a moral standard that is accepted by all cultures.
3. Concerns about MNC social responsibility revolve around issues of human rights in other countries, such as South Africa and China. Many organizations develop codes of conduct for their approach to business around the world.
4. International business ethics refers to the conduct of MNCs in their relationships to all individuals and entities with whom they come into contact. Ethical behavior is judged and based largely on the cultural value system and the generally accepted ways of doing business in each country or society. MNC managers must decide whether to base their ethical standards on those of the host country or those of the home country and whether these different standards can be reconciled.
5. MNCs must balance their responsibility to various stakeholders, such as owners, creditors, consumers, employees, suppliers, governments, and societies.
6. Questionable payments are those payments that raise significant questions about appropriate moral behavior in either the host nation or other nations. The Foreign Corrupt Practices Act prohibits most questionable payments by U.S. companies doing business in other countries.
7. Managers must control their activities relative to interdependent relationships at all levels—from simple, daily business transactions involving local workers, intermediaries, or consumers to global concerns of ecological responsibility.
8. The MNC–host-country relationship is generally a love–hate relationship from the host country's viewpoint in that it wants the economic growth that the MNC can provide but does not want the dependency and other problems that result.
9. The failure to effectively manage interdependence will result in constraints on strategy, in the least, or in disastrous consequences for the local area, the subsidiary, and the global reputation of the company.
10. Managing environmental interdependence includes the need to consider ecological interdependence as well as the economic and social implications of MNC activities.

Discussion Questions

1. Discuss the concept of international social responsibility. What role does it play in the relationship between a company and its host country?
2. Discuss the criticisms that have been leveled against MNCs in the past regarding their activities in less-developed countries. What counterarguments are there to those criticisms?
3. What does moral universalism mean? Discuss your perspective on this concept. Do you think the goal of moral universalism is possible? Is it advisable?
4. What do you think should be the role of MNCs toward human rights issues in other countries—for example, China or South Africa? What are the major human rights concerns at this time? What ideas do you have for dealing with these problems? What is the role of corporate codes of conduct in dealing with these concerns?
5. What is meant by international business ethics? How does the local culture affect ethical practices? What are the implications of such local norms for ethical decisions by MNC managers?
6. As a manager in a foreign subsidiary, how can you reconcile local expectations of questionable payments with the Foreign Corrupt Practices Act? What is your stance on the problem of "payoffs?" How does the degree of law enforcement in a particular country affect ethical behavior in business?
7. Explain what is meant by managing interdependence in the global business arena. Discuss the love–hate relationship between MNCs and host countries.
8. What do you think are the responsibilities of MNCs toward the global environment? Give some examples of MNC activities that run counter to the concepts of ecological interdependence and environmental responsibility.
9. Discuss the ethical issues that have developed regarding the use of IT in cross-border transactions. What new conflicts have developed since the printing of this book? What solutions can you suggest?

Application Exercises

Do some research to determine the codes of conduct of two MNCs. Compare the issues that they cover and share your findings with the class. After several students have presented their findings, prepare a chart showing the commonalities and differences of content in the codes presented. How do you account for the differences?

Experiential Exercise

Consider the ethical dilemmas in the following situation and decide what you would do. Then meet in small groups of students and come to a group consensus. Discuss your decisions with the class.

> I am CEO of an international trading company in Turkey. One state-owned manufacturing company (Company A) in one of the Middle East countries opened a tender for 15,000 tons PVC granule K value 70. Company A makes all its purchases through tenders. For seven years in that market, my company has never been able to do any business with Company A (though we have sold many bulk materials to other state-owned companies in that market). One of our new managers had a connection with the purchasing manager of Company A, who promised to supply us with all of our competitors' bids if we pay him a 2 percent commission on all of our sales to his company. Our area manager accepted this arrangement. He got the competing bids, made our offer, and we got the tender. I learned of this situation when reviewing our income and expenses chart, which showed the 2 percent commission.

> What shall I do, given the following: (1) If I refuse to accept the business without any legitimate reasons (presently there are none) my company will be blacklisted in that country—where we get about 20 percent of our gross yearly profit. (2) If I accept the business and do not pay the 2 percent commission, the purchasing manager will make much trouble for us when he receives our shipment. I am sure that he will not release our 5 percent bank guarantee letter about the quality and quantity of the material. (3) If I accept the business and pay the 2 percent commission, it will go against everything I have achieved in the thirty years of my career.

You have three ethical problems here: First, your company has won a rigged bid. Second, you must pay the person who rigged it or he will make life miserable for you. Third, you have to decide what to do with the area manager who accepted this arrangement.

SOURCE: J. Delaney and D. Sockell, "Ethics in the Trenches," *Across the Board* (October 1990): 17.

Internet Resources

Visit the Deresky companion Web site at www.prenhall.com/deresky for this chapter's Internet resources.

GM Returns to South Africa 10 Years After End of Apartheid

JOHANNESBURG, Jan. 29, 2004—Ten years after the end of apartheid, one of the largest companies to divest itself of its South African holdings is coming back. The *General Motors Corporation*, which sold its operations here to local management in 1987, will buy back the remaining 51 percent of the Delta Motor Corporation under a deal approved earlier this week by South African regulators.

Delta, which has been 49 percent owned by GM since 1997, will become General Motors South Africa and join GM's money-losing Latin America, Africa, and Middle East division.

Seventeen years after General Motors pulled out of South Africa because of the country's policies of racial segregation and pressure from shareholders, analysts say it is still hard to count the costs of the company's decision to divest.

GM is one of the last major companies that left during apartheid to return, and while its cars—made and sold under license by Delta—are known, the name of the parent company is less familiar.

Terms of the deal, like the terms of the original sale, were not disclosed, although Tony Twine, an economist, estimated Delta's value at $6 billion rand or about $849 million. The company, based in Port Elizabeth, has about 3,400 employees and assembles Opal cars and Isuzu pickups. It also imports Suzukis and, since November, Chevrolets.

When Delta was formed in 1987, many analysts expected it to fail. But it survived and, by maintaining the popularity of affordable brands like Opels, slightly increased its share of the South African market, to about 10.7 percent last year, from 9.3 percent in 1985, the last full year GM had operations here.

But Mr. Twine, of the South African consultant firm Econometrix, and other analysts say Delta has yet to do what most rivals have done: transform itself into an export-oriented business. That failure, he says, is a result of the continued private ownership of a majority of Delta shares. The company is the last of South Africa's major automobile makers to remain privately held.

"The simple equation is that the multinational parent will produce vehicles wherever it can take the lion's share of the profits," Mr. Twine said, "and obviously if the majority of equity is held by someone else, you're not going to give them the right to make exports for the global market because you're not going to get all of the profits."

South Africa's automobile exports are booming, making cars one of the country's fastest-growing industries, largely because of new trade agreements and domestic regulations that give companies credits for cars and parts they export. Most of South Africa's major manufacturers—BMW, *Volkswagen*, and *Toyota*—used to make small numbers of a wide variety of cars for domestic sale but now manufacture one or two models for domestic sale and export. Other models are imported.

But Delta's factory still produces primarily for local sale. According to the National Association of Automobile Manufacturers of South Africa, Delta exported 1,370 vehicles last year, 1 percent of the country's total, mostly to neighboring countries. The company also exports auto parts.

Without a strong export program, GM is at a disadvantage when it imports cars made elsewhere in its 32-country network and especially as it tries to introduce brands previously not available in South Africa, like Chevrolet. Though a small market in global terms, South Africa is the second largest after Brazil in GM's Latin America, Africa, and Middle East division. That division lost $331 million in 2003, largely because of weak economic conditions.

"One of the expected outcomes of General Motors taking control and reinvesting would be that South Africa would be more fully integrated into the global General Motors strategy and sourcing plans," said Nico Vermeulen, director of the automakers' association. "It will open up export opportunities."

In an interview earlier this week, GM executives declined to comment on specific plans for Delta, except to say a planned 1.5 billion rand ($213 million) capital program would go ahead. But they did say that they planned to use South Africa as a hub for growth in Africa and were considering exports to elsewhere in the world. Analysts said Australia and Europe would be the most likely overseas destinations for South African-produced GM cars.

Maureen Kempston Darkes, a GM group vice president who met with South African President Thabo Mbeki Wednesday, said the buy out was a vote of confidence in the new South Africa and its role in a changing Africa.

"Certainly we're here because South Africa has changed and we see political and economic stability in the country," she said. "We hope our involvement will lead to growth."

CASE QUESTIONS

1. Why did GM leave South Africa ten years ago? What was the dilemma facing foreign firms at that time?

2. Why did some firms decide to continue operating in South Africa at the time of racial segregation? Do you think they were being more or less socially responsible to the people of South Africa? Research some MNCs that did not leave during the period of apartheid. Do you think they are better off now than those which left?

3. How can foreign firms balance their strategic interests and their social responsibility when faced with similar situations?

4. Is GM in a better position in South Africa now? Is the South African economy in a better position now that GM has returned?

5. What other similar situations prevail in the world now, and how do you think MNCs should respond?

Case 1 Reebok: Managing Human Rights Issues "Ethically"?

I do not know that anybody has bought a pair of Reebok shoes because of its human rights program.
But we are a global corporation and we have an obligation to give back to the communities
in which we live and work.

—Doug Cahn, Director of Human Rights Programmes,
Reebok International Limited[1]

In January 2002, China Labor Watch[2] published a report on working conditions in six factories in China. These factories manufactured footwear products for the U.S. based Reebok International Limited (Reebok), one of the leading footwear and apparel companies in the world. The report highlighted the poor working conditions in these factories. A similar report had been published in 1997 by two Hong Kong-based non-profit organizations, which had accused Reebok's sub-contractors[3] of violating some of the provisions of Chinese labor laws in footwear factories in China.

With over a 100 years of operations in the footwear industry, a large workforce (estimated to be over 75,000 in 2002), and operations in over 170 countries across the world, Reebok's dominance in the global footwear industry was unquestionable. However, with the focus of the international community drifting to human rights issues in Chinese footwear and apparel factories, Reebok joined the ranks of those companies that were accused of not paying sufficient attention to human rights issues.

Reebok had taken several measures to prevent human rights violations in its Asian footwear manufacturing operations (see Exhibit C1-1). It had established an exclusive human rights department (HRD) in 1998 to address human rights issues in its operations across the globe, and it had also instituted a Code of Conduct, also known as Reebok's Human Rights Production Standards (see Exhibit C1-2), to regulate working conditions in the factories of its subcontractors. However, in spite of the measures taken by the company, it had to face several allegations regarding the violation of labor laws in its Chinese operations. Analysts felt that the efforts made by the company were not adequate and that the company needed to be more committed to the protection of human rights to enhance its image as a socially responsible company.

COMPANY HISTORY

In 1885, Joseph William Foster (Foster), a famous athlete in the English Running Club (Bolton, UK) made spiked running shoes in his garden shed. In the early 1890s, he set up a company called "JW Foster & Sons, Inc.," to make handmade spike shoes. Foster believed that due to their superior quality, such shoes could help athletes improve their performance in long distance track events. By 1900, the company developed a clientele of internationally reputed athletes. In 1933, Foster expired and the company was renamed "The Olympic Works." In the 1950s, Foster's grandsons—Jeff and Joe—started a new company called Reebok Sports Limited."[4]

In the 1960s and 1970s, as Reebok's business expanded, the company established its distribution outlets in several countries all over the world. In the 1970s, the company was renamed Reebok International Limited. By 1981, the company's sales touched $1.5 million. In 1982, Reebok launched 'Freestyle,' an athletic shoe for women, pioneering the concept of sports gear for aerobics. In the same year, the company also launched its first tennis and fitness shoe for men. In 1984, Reebok got its shares listed on the New York Stock Exchange.

This case was written by K. Prashanth, under the direction of Vivek Gupta, ICFAI Center for Management Research (ICMR).

© 2003, ICFAI Center for Management Research. All rights reserved. No part of this publication may be reproduced, stored in a retrieval system, used in a spreadsheet, or transmitted in any form or by any means—electronic or mechanical, without permission.

To order copies, call 0091-40-2343-046213164 or write to ICFAI Center for Management Research, Plot # 49, Nagarjuna Hills, Hyderabad 500 082, India or e-mail icmr@icfai.org. Web site: www. icmrindia.org

[1]As quoted in the article, "Reebok in China: Worker Elections in Two Supplier Factories," written by Alison Maitland in the *Financial Times*, dated December 12, 2002.

[2]A New York-based independent non-profit organization for Chinese labor and human rights, which works towards improving Chinese workers' living and working conditions, defending their rights, upholding international labor and human rights standards, and preparing independent labor union organizations that are true representatives of the workers.

[3]In most Asian countries, Reebok manufactured its footwear and sports goods through subcontractors. Subcontractors were essentially middlemen who contracted workers on a daily wage basis. Reebok paid a negotiated amount to the subcontractors according to the size of contract. In most cases, the factories were owned by the subcontractors.

[4]The company was named after the African gazelle, which was known for its incredible speed.

EXHIBIT C1-1   Reebok's Asian Operations

China
Brave Win Rubber Factory, Dongguan, China
Elegant Top Shoes Co. Ltd., Dongguan, China
Freetrend Industrial Ltd., Dean Shoes, Shenzhen, China
Fu Tai Plastic Material Factory, Dongguan, China
Fujian Ching Luh Shoes Group Co. Ltd., Chemical Section, Fuzhou, China
Hung Ye Shoes Mfg. Co. Ltd., Dongguan, China
Kenmate Industrial Co. Ltd., Ping Hu Shoe City, Shenzhen City, China
Kong Tai Shoes Mfg. Co. Ltd., Shenzhen, China
Nority Limited Co. Ltd., Dongguan, China
Pou-Yuen Industrial (Holdings) Ltd., Zhongshan, China
Shang Sheng Rubber Factroy Co. Ltd., Dongguan, China
Shiang Yi Shoes, Emphatic Enterprise Co. Ltd., Putian, China
Asian Sourcing, Shanghai, China
Xinqi Garment Company Ltd., Yantai Shandong, China

Indonesia
P.T. Dong Joe Indonesia, Tangerang, Indonesia
P.T. Golden Adishoes, Karawang, Indonesia
P.T. Seni Sulam Adiwarna, Bekasi, Indonesia
P.T. Tampukyudha Inti, Bekasi, Indonesia
P.T. Tirai Tapak Tiara, Bekasi, Indonesia
P.T. Tong Yang Indonesia, Bekasi, Indonesia

India
Sant Rubber Corporation, Jalandhar City, India
Sarup Tanneries Ltd., Jalandhar City, India
Moja Shoes Pvt. Ltd., Sonepat (HR), India
Lakhani India Ltd., Faridabad, India

Taiwan
Pou Yue Enterprises Ltd., Changhua Hsien, Taiwan
Taiwan Ching Luh Shoes Co. Ltd., TaiNan Hsien, Taiwan
King First/Young-Der Garment Fact., Wu–Je Village I-Lan Hsien, Taiwan
On Asia/Yen San Manufacture Co., Don San Area, Taiwan
Ping Yang Mei-Chou, I-Lan Hsien, Taiwan
Tung Heleh Hats Mfg. Co., Hsien Li Ching Shui Chan Taichung, Hsien, Taiwan
Willow Company Limited, Taipei, Taiwan

Thailand
Rangsit Footwear Co. Ltd., Ayuthaya, Thailand
Modern Technology Component Co. Ltd., Prachinburi, Thailand
Siam Unisole Co. Ltd./Wongpaitoon Group, Public Co. Ltd., Samutsakorn, Thailand
Wongpaitoon Group Public Co. Ltd., Bangkok, Thailand
Srisuree Co. Ltd., Ayuthaya, Thailand
Future Garment Co. Ltd., Yamawa, Bangkok, Thailand

Vietnam
HSV–Hwaseung Vina Co. Ltd., Dong Nai, Vietnam
Pou-Yuen Vietnam Enterprise, Ho Chi Minh City, Vietnam
Thai Binh Shoes Co., Ltd., Binh Duong, Vietnam
Yueh Lead Industrial Co. Ltd., Binh Duong Province, Vietnam

SOURCE: www.reebok.com.

Reebok's name was first heard in connection with human rights issues when, in 1986, it withdrew its operations from the Republic of South Africa (RSA) to protest against *apartheid*.[5] In 1988, Reebok's HRD was established to address human rights issues in the company's operations across the world. The company also instituted an annual Reebok Human Rights Award to recognize and reward the contributions of young people (below the age of 30) across the world who made efforts to prevent

---

[5]An official policy of racial segregation involving political, legal, and economic discrimination against non-whites.

EXHIBIT C1-2   Reebok Human Rights Production Standards

1. Non-retaliation Policy
Every factory producing Reebok products will publicize and enforce a non-retaliation policy that permits factory workers to speak with Reebok staff without fear of retaliation by factory management.

2. Non-discrimination
Reebok will seek business partners who do not discriminate in hiring and employment pratices and who make decisions about hiring, salary, benefits, advancement, discipline, termination, and retirement solely on the basis of a person's ability to do the job.

3. Working Hours/Overtime
Workers shall not work more than 60 hours per week, including overtime, except in extraordinary business circumstances. In countries where the maximum work week is less, that standard shall apply. Workers shall be entitled to at least one day off in every seven day period.

4. Forced or Compulsory Labor
Reebok will not work with business partners that use forced or other compulsory labor, including labor that is used as a means of political coercion or as punishment for holding or for peacefully expressing political views, in the manufacture of its products. Reebok will not purchase materials that were produced by forced prison or other compulsory labor and will terminate business relationships with any sources found to utilize such labor.

5. Fair Wages
Reebok will seek business partners who share our commitment to the betterment of wage and benefit levels that address the basic needs of workers and their families as far as possible and appropriate in the light of national practices and conditions. Reebok will not select business partners that pay less than the minimum wage required by local law or that pay less than prevailing local industry practices (whichever is higher).

6. Child Labor
Reebok will not work with business partners that use child labor. The term "child" generally refers to a person who is younger than 15 (or 14 where the law of the country of manufacture allows) or younger than the age for completing compulsory education in the country of manufacture where such age is higher than 15.

7. Freedom of Association
Reebok will seek business partners that share its commitment to the right of employees to establish and join organizations of their own choosing. Reebok recognizes and respects the right of all employees to organize and bargain collectively.

8. Safe and Healthy Work Environment
Reebok will seek business partners that strive to assure employees a safe and healthy workplace and that do not expose workers to hazardous conditions.

SOURCE: www.reebok-usa.com.

human rights violations in their countries. In the same year, Reebok also asked its subcontractors in China to certify that they did not employ child labor in their factories. The company also organized a concert called "Human Rights Now," along with Amnesty International,[6] to mark the 40th anniversary of the United Nations' adoption of the Universal Declaration of Human Rights.

In 1992, Reebok established its Code of Conduct— "Reebok Human Rights Production Standards." According to the company, these standards were strictly implemented by all factories which produced Reebok's products. The implementation of these standards was monitored by the concerned employees of Reebok's HRD. Reebok felt that these standards would serve as a benchmark for assessing working conditions in its footwear and sports goods manufacturing operations all over the world. The company also felt that the owners of the factories could judge the working conditions on their own by benchmarking against these standards.

In the same year, the company tied up with the Lawyers Committee for Human Rights[7] to start "Witness," a project that equipped its HRD staff with video cameras, fax machines, and computers to help it closely monitor issues relating to human rights abuse in its affiliated facilities across the world. That year, Reebok also became a founding member of Business for Social Responsibility.[8]

In 1994, Reebok hired the consultancy firm, Ernst & Young, to conduct the industry's first independent audit of working conditions in Reebok's Indonesian footwear

---

[6]An internationally recognized non-governmental organization that works for the protection of human rights. Financed by subscriptions and donations from its worldwide membership, it has more than a million members and supporters in over 140 countries and territories.

[7]Established in 1978 in the U.S., its mission is to create a secure and humane world by advancing justice, human dignity, and respect for the rule of law.

[8]A U.S. based global nonprofit organization that helps member companies achieve commercial success in ways that respect ethical values, people, communities, and the environment.

operations. During the year, Reebok also resumed its operations in RSA.

In 1995, Reebok started manufacturing soccer balls in its facilities in Asia. In 1996, some media reports stated that child labor was being used in the company's operations in Sialkot, Pakistan, to manufacture soccer balls. Reebok responded quickly to these reports. Its HRD staff monitored these facilities to ensure that people aged below fifteen years were not employed. The company even stuck a label on the balls (manufactured by the concerned factory) which declared "Guarantee: Manufactured without Child Labor" (see Exhibit C1-3). In 1997, Reebok shifted its manufacturing activities to a newly built factory in Sialkot.

In order to provide elementary education and vocational training to the children who lost their jobs because of its anti-child labor drive, Reebok launched a $1 million project called Reebok Educational Assistance to Pakistan (REAP) in mid-1997. As part of the project, the company tied up with the Society for Advancement of Education[9] to establish a school called Chaanan Institute for Child Labor Rehabilitation. The school employees encouraged the families involved in manufacturing soccer balls in the Sialkot region to send their children to school instead of work. All these initiatives helped improve the social image of the company.

In 1997, Reebok introduced a "Workers Communication System" in its operations in Indonesia to enable workers to express their grievances so that necessary action could be taken. The workers were assured of not being victimized by the management of the factory for expressing their grievances. Complaint boxes were installed in places like toilets (in the factories) to ensure that workers could drop their complaints without fear. Printed prepaid mailers were also made available to the workers. Subsequently, the system was installed in other Asian countries such as China, Thailand, and Vietnam.

EXHIBIT C1-3   Label on Reebok's Soccer Balls Manufactured in Sialkot, Pakistan

By labeling soccer balls in the above manner, Reebok communicated to consumers and stakeholders its policy of not employing child labor.

---

[9]An NGO based in Islamabad, which undertakes several human rights related activities.

In 1998, Reebok started conducting seminars in Indonesian factories to teach workers how to organize unions and engage in collective bargaining.[10] In May 2000, elections were held in a factory in Indonesia, which marked the beginning of the democratization of the workforce in the country. In the same year, Reebok helped the American Center for International Labor Solidarity (ACILS) conduct training programs in five factories in Indonesia to encourage the company's workers to set up unions to address work related problems.

REEBOK'S PROBLEMS IN CHINA

Multinational shoe companies (MNSCs) entered the People's Republic of China (PRC) in the mid-1980s, following the liberalization of the Chinese economy in 1984. Due to large scale unemployment in China, the workers were ready to work for low wages, thus resulting in low wage-related expenditures for MNSCs. Moreover, labor laws were not strictly implemented by local governments within the PRC, which competed with each other to attract foreign investment, especially in labor-intensive industries such as shoe manufacturing.

Like most of its competitors, Reebok entered the Chinese market through the contract manufacturing route, i.e., through subcontractors. By doing so, the company could absolve itself of responsibilities relating to footwear production, while at the same time take advantage of low production costs to earn higher margins. The company could also bargain with subcontractors to fix production deadlines and manufacturing price. By the end of 1996, China accounted for nearly 35 percent of Reebok's worldwide footwear production. The figure reached 44 percent by 1999 (see Exhibit C1-4).

However, Reebok soon found that, by using the contract manufacturing route, it could not absolve itself of its responsibilities relating to footwear production. The company had to deal with allegations by independent research agencies about human rights violation in its footwear manufacturing operations in China. In 1996, a report published by two Hong Kong based research groups—the Asia Monitor Resource Centre[11] and the Hong Kong Christian Industrial Committee[12]—highlighted the poor working conditions and inhuman treatment of workers in footwear factories in China that manufactured products for Reebok.

---

[10]Collective bargaining consists of negotiations between an employer and a group of employees so as to determine the conditions of employment. The result of collective bargaining procedures is a collective agreement. Employees are often represented in bargaining by a union or other labor organization.
[11]An independent non-government organization (NGO), which focuses on Asian labor problems. The center's main goal is to support democratic and independent labor movements in Asia.
[12]Established in 1967, it is an independent non-government organization (NGO), which supports workers' movements in China and Hong Kong.

EXHIBIT C1-4 Reebok's Athletic Footwear Production in Asia (1999)

Country	% Production
People's Republic of China	44%
Indonesia	29%
Thailand	16%
Vietnam	2%
The Philippines	2%
Taiwan	2%

SOURCE: www.cbae.nmsu.edu.

In September 1997, another report was published by the same research agencies alleging violation of the provisions of the Chinese Labor Law and Reebok's Human Rights Production Standards in four Chinese footwear factories. The report also highlighted the ineffectiveness of Reebok's monitoring mechanism in preventing human rights abuse in its subcontracted manufacturing units in China.

According to the report, Reebok's subcontractors were not paying wages as per Chinese labor laws. For example, in one factory in the Dongguan Province of China, the legal minimum wage was US$1.93 per day, while the actual wages paid ranged from $1.20 to $1.45 per day. In another factory, the legal minimum monthly wage was $42.17, while the workers actual pay ranged from $30 to $42 per month. Similarly, provisions relating to the payment of overtime wages were also violated.

The workers in the factories, mostly women, were not treated properly. They were forced to do early-morning calisthenics[13] every day, and those who missed out on these sessions were fined. Talking during working hours was not allowed. The fines for violating these rules ranged between $7.23 and $21.69 (more than half the monthly wage of the workers). This practice was in contravention of Chinese Labor Law, which stated that deducting disciplinary fines was illegal.

The workers were also deprived of their basic right of freedom of association. The management of the factories did not permit the setting up of unions by the workers. The only recognized union in the country was The All China Federation of Trade Unions (ACFTU), which was controlled by the Chinese government. Analysts had accused the union of favoring the management. Workers' agitations were often suppressed by the management. In one such instance, in March 1997, when the entire assembly production department in one factory went on strike over non-payment of wages, all of them were fired.

According to the 1997 report, while Reebok's Human Rights Production Standards clearly stipulated that children below the age of fifteen years should not be

employed by its subcontractors, it was found that the factories employed children aged between thirteen and fifteen. The report also mentioned that there were serious violations of the provisions of Chinese labor law regarding working hours and the use of overtime. The normal permissible working hours per week were 44 hours (as per Chinese Law) and 60 hours (as per Reebok's Human Rights Production Standards). However, in practice, the normal working hours per week were 72 hours (twelve hours daily). In addition, workers were forced to do overtime from two to five hours every day. It was also found that the management of footwear factories pressured the employees to work overtime. Those who refused to do overtime were fined between $7.23 and $21.67; and those who refused to work overtime for three consecutive days were fired. Many workers were expected to fulfill high production targets, failing which they had to work beyond the working hours, without being paid overtime. All these practices were strictly non-permissible as per the Chinese Labor Law.

Workers had to work in extremely hazardous conditions. They were exposed to dust and noise pollution, excessive heat, and dangerous fumes that could cause suffocation. As a result, most of the workers suffered from headaches, dyspnea (difficult and painful breathing), dizziness, and skin irritations. The safety mechanisms in these factories were also found to be inadequate.

Workers were abused, both verbally as well as physically. The management of the subcontracted factories fired workers for reasons such as becoming pregnant and becoming overaged. The food and accommodations provided by the management were also not up to the mark. The workers were required to stay in overcrowded dormitories in extremely unhygienic conditions. The management did not provide any benefits such as childcare, social security, medical insurance, maternity leave, and bereavement leave, although Chinese Labor Law required these benefits to be provided to workers. The report also revealed that the workers in these factories were not aware of the existence of the company's human rights production standards though the managements of the concerned factories were required to translate it into the local language and educate the employees regarding its provisions.

Responding to the charges mentioned in the report, Doug Cahn, director, Reebok's Human Rights program said, "Any violations are unacceptable to us, and we demand that factories take corrective action if the charges are found to be true."[14]

REEBOK'S RESPONSE

In response to the increasing allegations of human rights violations in China, Reebok took few steps to assess and

[13]Warm up exercises conducted by workers before commencing work.

[14]"Study: Chinese workers abused making Nikes, Reeboks" posted on the Web site www.news-star.com dated September 20, 1997.

EXHIBIT C1-5 Business Principles Framed by the U.S. Business Corporations Operating in China (May 1999)

As companies doing business in China, we seek to hear and respond to the concerns of workers making our products. We want to ensure that our business practices in China respect basic labor standards defined by the International Labor Organization, and basic human rights defined by the United Nations Universal Declaration of Human Rights and encoded in the International Covenants on Economic, Social and Cultural Rights, and Civil and Political Rights, signed by the Chinese government, as well as in China's national laws. To this end, we agree to implement and promote the following principles in the People's Republic of China:

No goods or products produced within our company-owned facilities or those of our suppliers shall be manufactured by bonded labor, forced labor within prison camps or as part of reform-through-labor or reeducation-through-labor programs.

Our facilities and suppliers shall provide wages that meet workers' basic needs, and fair and decent working hours, at a minimum adhering to the wage and hour guidelines provided by China's national labor laws and policies.

Our facilities and suppliers shall prohibit the use of corporal punishment, as well as any physical, sexual or verbal abuse or harassment of workers.

Our facilities and suppliers shall use production methods that do not negatively affect the occupational safety and health of workers.

Our facilities and suppliers shall not seek police or military intervention to prevent workers from exercising their rights.

We shall undertake to promote the following freedoms among our employees and the employees of our suppliers: freedom of association and assembly, including the right to form unions and to bargain collectively; freedom of expression; and freedom from arbitrary arrest or detention.

Employees working in our facilities and those of our suppliers shall not face discrimination in hiring, remuneration, or promotion based on age, gender, marital status, pregnancy, ethnicity, or region of origin.

Employees working in our facilities and those of our suppliers shall not face discrimination in hiring, remuneration or promotion based on labor, political or religious activity, or on involvement in demonstrations, past records of arrests or internal exile for peaceful protest, or membership in organizations committed to non-violent social or political change.

Our facilities and suppliers shall use environmentally responsible methods of production that have minimum adverse impact on land, air, and water quality.

Our facilities and suppliers shall prohibit child labor, at a minimum complying with guidelines on minimum age for employment within China's national labor laws.

We will work cooperatively with human rights organizations to ensure that our enterprises and suppliers are respecting these principles and, more broadly, to promote respect for these principles in China. We will issue an annual statement to the Human Rights for Workers in China Working Group detailing our efforts to uphold these principles.

SOURCE: "Mattel, Levi Strauss, Reebok Endorse New Code," www.cleanclothes.com, June 05, 1999.

improve the working conditions in its manufacturing facilities. In May 1999, Reebok, along with Mattel[15] and Levi Strauss[16] (which had large operational interests in China), teamed up with twenty-one human rights, fair trade, and social investment groups to endorse a set of principles (see Exhibit C1-5) for corporations doing business in China. Through these measures, Reebok attempted to address issues such as the use of forced labor, child labor, inadequate wages, long working hours, and physical or other kinds of abuse of employees. This was one of the first major initiatives taken by leading U.S. business corporations in China to address human rights issues.

In March 2001, Reebok along with Nike and Adidas Salomon AG[17] (global footwear companies), teamed up with three Taiwan-based subcontractors and four Hong Kong-based NGOs to institute a project called China Capacity Building Project in China. As part of the project, ninety people, including workers, supervisors, and managers belonging to the three footwear companies, participated in a four-day training workshop. Training was imparted in various areas including occupational safety and health principles. Over the next three months, health and safety committees were set up and workers were also asked to express their views to help management evaluate and improve health, safety, and environmental conditions in manufacturing facilities in China. An attempt was made to encourage workers to report the problems they faced to the management, external observers and NGOs. One of the NGOs, which participated in the program—China Working Women's Network—set up a mobile resource center to educate women workers in the factories about issues such as health, gender consciousness, and labor rights. The program covered 21,000 female workers working in Reebok's, Nike's, and Adidas Salomon's manufacturing facilities in South China.

In an effort to ensure lasting improvement in working conditions in the factories, workers were encouraged to set up forums to interact with the management. The

[15]Mattel is one of the world's leading toy manufacturing companies. Its products include Barbie dolls, Fisher-Price toys, Hot Wheels and Matchbox cars, American Girl dolls and books, and various Sesame Street, Barney, and other licensed items.

[16]A famous U.S. based apparel company established in 1853. It became reputed for its blue jeans.

[17]A U.S.-based sports goods company, which produces and markets sports equipment, footwear, and apparel under the brand names of Adidas, Salomon, Taylor Made, and Mavic.

management was also asked to conduct elections in their factories. In July 2001, elections were held in the Kong Tai plant in the Guangdong province in China. This was the first election conducted at a Reebok footwear factory in China. External observers were also invited to the factory to observe the election. The elections were conducted without much hype and the publicity was minimal. Reebok also imparted training to the workers' representatives in handling union matters such as conducting meetings, recording complaints, and handling grievances.

Through the previously mentioned measures, Reebok made an attempt to demonstrate its commitment towards human rights. Over the years, Reebok's HRD increased the scope of its activities. Reebok's annual human rights awards remained the only corporate-sponsored human rights awards that recognized the efforts of young non-violent human rights activists.[18] Reebok was also among the first few companies in the U.S. to have joined the Fair Labor Association.[19]

THE INEFFECTIVE MEASURES

Though Reebok improved working conditions in its Chinese and other Asian factories, analysts felt that a lot still remained to be done. Reports continued to be published regularly about poor working conditions in Reebok's footwear operations in China.

In January 2002, the China Labor Watch published a report after investigating working conditions (between June 2001 and January 2002) in six Reebok shoe factories in China. The report concluded that the steps taken by Reebok to improve working conditions and prevent human rights abuse were not sufficient. According to the report, some of the measures taken by Reebok were not delivering the desired results.

It was found that Reebok's non-discrimination policy (see Exhibit C1-2), under which management must not discriminate between men and women while recruiting and during employment, was not being implemented. In the Chinese factories, female workers outnumbered male workers by 10 to 1, indicating a bias toward the recruitment of female workers. Analysts felt that the management of these factories preferred female workers primarily because they were submissive and could be easily exploited. They were sexually harassed by supervisors and risked losing their job if they voiced their grievances.

Moreover, the management did not provide accommodation to married couples, forcing them to live separately. All these factors had a negative impact on the workers' psyche. Some workers complained of mental distress while some took to drinking. Some workers even committed suicide.

The report also revealed that Reebok's experiment with elections in Kong Tai factory left much to be desired and that the labor union was still under the management's control. The chairman of the union was nominated by the official union, ACFTU (All China Federation of Trade Unions), in contravention of the Chinese Trade Union Law, which stated that the head of the union must be freely elected. In addition, the factory management did not pay the activity fee (2 percent of the total wages of the workforce) to the union as stipulated by the law.

Violations were also reported with regard to working hours and overtime. The workers were asked to work overtime, on an average, eighty-six hours per month. Though Reebok's HRD staff conducted inspections at these factories, the factory management warned workers against expressing their plight to the staff. Deviations were also found in the legal minimum wages and the actual wages paid. While the legal minimum wage ranged between 32 cents to 42 cents per hour in most of the cities where the factories were located, the wages paid were less than 28 cents. Workers who decided to hand in their resignations did not receive severance pay as required by Chinese law.

Employees were exposed to toxic fumes and had to spend long hours in high temperatures, which led to nausea and respiratory problems. According to the report, management did not provide a safe and healthy working environment to workers. The management even fired workers who used the complaint box set up by the company to get feedback regarding workers' grievances.

THE EFFORTS CONTINUE

Even though doubts were raised about the efficacy of Reebok's measures for preventing the violation of human rights, the company continued with its efforts to improve working conditions at the Chinese factories. In August 2002, Reebok took measures to reduce overtime working hours in these factories to thirty-six hours per month.

In November 2002, elections were conducted in Reebok's Taiwanese owned Fuh Luh footwear factory in the Fujian province of China. Reebok had to negotiate with the factory management and the ACFTU for several months to develop a framework for the conduct of the elections. Explaining the difficulty faced during the negotiation process, Cahn said: "Freedom of association is going to be one of the most difficult issues in the future as global brands attempt to find appropriate ways to respect the rights of workers while not getting others involved in the process of negotiations between workers and the managers/owners of the factories."[20]

[18]As quoted in the article, "Advantage Reebok," written by Margery Gordon, posted on www.callbaptist.edu, dated May 9, 2001.
[19]An initiative under which corporates work with labor and human rights advocates to establish voluntary workplace standards and monitoring requirements for footwear and apparel industries.
[20]"Reebok—Freedom of association in Indonesia," posted on the Web site, www.iblf.org.

Reportedly, the elections, which were supervised by external observers, were conducted in a fair manner.

Unlike elections at the Kong Tai factory, these elections allowed proportional representation of workers belonging to each of the seven departments of the factory. In addition, elections were conducted for all posts, including the Union Chairman's post, which was not contestable before. Explaining the significance of empowering the workers in the Chinese factories by conducting elections, sources at Reebok said, "We have inspections of factories, both announced and unannounced. But you just don't have the assurance that things will be the same the next day. Factories in China are incredibly sophisticated at finding ways to fool us. The best monitors are the workers themselves."[21]

QUESTIONS FOR DISCUSSION

1. Reebok is one of the very few companies in the U.S. footwear and apparel industry that has consistently made efforts to improve its labor management practices and working conditions in its operations in Third World countries. Explain the measures taken by the company over the years to improve working conditions and prevent human rights violations in its footwear manufacturing operations.

2. In spite of the continuous efforts made by Reebok to prevent workers' abuse, on two different occasions human rights violations in Reebok's Chinese operations were reported. Discuss the problems faced by workers in China. In light of the problems faced by Chinese workers, critically analyze the efficacy of the measures taken by Reebok to improve working conditions and prevent human rights violation.

3. According to analysts, Reebok's measures for improving working conditions in its Chinese factories were not sufficient. What other measures should Reebok take to tackle the problem of human rights violations in its Chinese operations? Explain in detail.

ADDITIONAL REFERENCES

"Executive Summary of Report on Nike and Reebok in China," www.globalexchange.org, September 1997.

"Study: Chinese Workers Abused Making Nikes, Reeboks," www.news-star.com, September 21, 1997.

"Football Child Labor Lives On," news.bbc.co.uk, April 16, 1998.

"Nike, Reebok Compete to Set Labor Rights Pace," www.cleanclothes.org, March 25, 1999.

"Mattel, Levi Strauss, Reebok Endorse New Code," www.cleanclothes.org, June 5, 1999.

Tom Kirchofer, "Reebok Admits Problems at Indonesian Factories," www.cleanclothes.org, October 18, 1999.

"Best Foot Forward at Reebok," *Economist,* October 23, 1999.

Aaron Bernstein, "Sweatshops: No More Excuses," *BusinessWeek,* November 8, 1999.

Jon Fallon, "Reebok's Façade of Respectability," groups. www.northwestern.edu, Spring 2000.

Aaron Bernstein, Michael Shari, Elisabeth Malkin, "A World of Sweatshops," *BusinessWeek,* November 6, 2000.

Margery Gorden, "Advantage Reebok," www.calbaptist. edu, May 9, 2001.

"Getting Organized, with Western Help," *Economist,* December 12, 2001.

"Reebok's Human Rights Standard and Chinese Workers' Working Conditions," www.chinalaborwatch. org, January 2002.

"First Free Trade Union Elections Held in Chinese Reebok's Factory," www.labourbehindthelabel.org, March 2002.

"China Capacity Building Project—Occupational Health and Safety," mhssn.igc.org, May 29, 2002.

"Ethically Unemployed," *Economist,* November 30, 2002.

Alison Maitland, "Reebok in China: Worker Elections in Two Supplier Factories," www.cleanclothes.org, December 12, 2002.

Reebok Human Rights Programs, geocities.com.

E. Nancy Landrum, M. David Boje, "Kairos: Strategies Just in Time in the Asian Athletic Footwear Industry," cbae.nmsu.edu.

"Reebok—Setting an Example for Freedom of Association?" www.iblf.org.

www.reebok.co.uk

www.reebokus.com

cbae.nmsu.edu

RELATED CASE STUDIES

Nike's Labor Practices, Reference No. 702-021-1.

---

[21]"First Free Trade Union Elections Held in Chinese Reebok factory," in the Web site www.labourbehindthelabel.org, March 2002.

Case 2 Treating AIDS: A Global Ethical Dilemma

In spite of a worldwide offensive against AIDS, in March 2004 shortages of money and battles over patents have kept antiretroviral drugs from reaching more than 90 percent of the poor people who need them.[1]

Ninety percent of the world's 33 million HIV/AIDS cases are in Africa, Latin America and Asia. The vast majority of infected people in those areas can't afford the cocktails of miracle drugs that can make AIDS a chronic disease rather than a death sentence.[2]

The dilemma for drug companies, governments, and world health organizations is how to make those cocktails—which cost about $750 a month in the United States—affordable in countries like South Africa, where annual income is around $6,000 per capita, and where 8 percent of the 38 million people there are infected with the AIDS virus.[3] Western drug companies are faced with issues of social responsibility in both the short- and the long-term. In the short term, they are faced with concerns of compassion for people who can be treated with their drugs, pressure from health organizations around the world, global competition, and the need to maintain a benevolent image. For the long term, the pharmaceutical industry is faced with maintaining sufficient revenue to support the goal of developing a cure for AIDS and other diseases—a process that takes years of research and development.

In a related concern, the pharmaceutical industry is fighting to protect intellectual-property rights—the patents on their drugs which protect the companies from generic copies. This goes to the heart of what drug companies are in business to do—to invest large sums of money over a long period to develop drugs, which are then patented in order for those companies to recoup their investment cost. The executives of those companies feel that if they cannot maintain global patent protection, then their businesses would not survive. This in itself is a dilemma for world health, because then who would develop and produce the drugs the world needs? Those managers also have the responsibility to maximize shareholder wealth.

This complex, global situation continues to unfold with various parties trying to find a solution to the overall problem, which comes down to one of who should pay for AIDS drugs around the world?

For its part, the South African government passed a law in 1997 to empower the government to secure cheaper drugs for its people by allowing small local companies to copy patented drugs. The provision was also made to allow AIDS drugs to be imported from countries such as India which do not enforce patent rights.[4] Needless to say, this led to an ongoing legal battle with the multinational drug companies with branches in South Africa. In an attempt to combat such actions, in May 2000, five major multinational pharmaceutical companies offered to sell the AIDS combination therapies at reduced prices to developing nations.[5] However, the annual cost of $1,000 was still regarded as too high for most patients. In addition, those companies pointed out that the administration of therapies is far more complicated and expensive than simply handing out pills. Various groups, such as Oxfam and Doctors Without Borders (a humanitarian group of doctors who volunteer their time) continue to pressure drug companies to reduce their prices further for poor countries; they also have been working to enable generic versions to be imported to those countries without trade penalties.[6]

On another front in this war, an Indian company, Cipla, announced, in February 2001, that it would provide its generic version of the triple-combination therapy to Doctors Without Borders at a cost of $350 per patient per year. Indian law allows that local firms there can manufacture drugs without regard to whether they are patented in other countries, "if they employ processes different from the original patented process."[7] Through its action, Cipla has triggered a price war, causing GlaxoSmithKline and Merck to match prices for poor countries. Yusuf Hamied, Cipla's chairman, is glad to see that trend because he is concerned about the alarming rate of increase of cases of HIV in India—currently four million, and says that his company could not produce enough by itself.[8] He believes that patents should be only between countries which are technological equals.

---

[1]D. G. McNeil, Jr., "Plan to fight AIDS overseas is foundering," www.nytimes.com, March 28, 2004.

[2]D. Rosenberg and John Barry, "No money, no meds: South Africa needs access to cheap AIDS medicine, but drug companies want a say in what they get and how they get it," *Newsweek*, July 12, 1999, v134, i2, p 32.

[3]Ibid.

[4]Ibid.

[5]"AIDS and the drug companies," *America*, March 26, 2001, 3.

[6]Ibid.

[7]Ibid.

[8]K. S. Jayaraman, "Opinion interview: Yusuf Hamied, chairman of Indian drug company, Cipla," *New Scientist*, March 31, 2001, v169, i2284, p 42.

Patent laws are national laws; they are not international laws. There is no one patent that applies to the whole world; patent laws are designed with national interests in mind. . . .Every country must be allowed to decide its own destiny.[9]

This was the reasoning that led India to change its patent law in 1972 to prohibit product patents in food and health. However, if India is to be allowed to join the WTO it will have to change its patent laws by 2005, making many of its drugs illegal, although its process patents can run for seven years after that.

South Africa and India are claiming a state of "national emergency," which allows governments to ignore foreign patents under WTO's rules. In Brazil, also, local pharmaceutical firms, under pressure from the Brazilian government, have been making their own anti-retroviral drugs and distributing them free to patients. As a result, AIDS deaths have dropped by 50 percent since 1994.[10]

Western pharmaceutical companies regard the actions by the Brazilian and Indian governments as infringing on their intellectual property rights. The counter-argument is that since most of those large companies sell anti-AIDS drugs mostly to wealthy countries, it is not necessary for them to keep up their prices.[11]

In April 2001, the world pharmaceutical industry dropped its lawsuit against the South African government because the primary companies (Merck, GlaxoSmithKline PLC, Bristol-Myers Squibb., Boehringer Ingelheim GmbH, and Abbott Laboratories) concluded that, by fighting it, their image was being severely tarnished by the general opinion in the world about their insensitivity to the plight of poor people.[12] The suit had been filed by the industry, in 1998, challenging the South African law allowing generic drugs to be imported without the permission of the patent holders.[13] The agreement to drop the suit was based on a promise by the South African government to comply with the WTO rules in implementing the disputed medicines law.[14] Confounding efforts by many parties, however, has been the attitude by President Thabo Mbeki towards the AIDS problem in his country. He has stated on several occasions that he believes that AIDS is "simply a disease of poverty, not of infection with the HIV virus."[15] Foot dragging over approval of the use of free drugs offered by Boehringer for 90,000 expectant mothers is creating the impression that the South African government lacks the political will to use the AIDS drugs.[16]

The South African government came under further pressure in January 2002 when Doctors Without Borders (the Nobel-prize winning humanitarian group, *Medicins sans Frontieres*—MSF) took action which ignored the South African patent law. Supported by local AIDS activists in Johannesburg, the group demanded the government make the drugs more widely available and imported cheap generic drugs from Brazil to use in their clinic near Capetown.[17] While Western manufacturers "have steadily dropped their prices, to the point where executives say they are making no profit or are selling their drugs at a loss," those prices are still being undercut by generic manufacturers in India, Thailand, and Brazil.[18] The MSF group is no doubt counting on the belief that the two companies holding patents on the drugs they imported from Brazil to South Africa—GlaxoSmithKline PLC and Boehringer Ingelheim GmbH—will not sue such a well-respected charitable organization. Even so, Glaxo executives expressed surprise because their company has an agreement with a South African generics producer to manufacture some of Glaxo's drugs.[19] The problem, however, is that South African regulatory approval has not yet been granted for such drugs. Such obstructionist tactics are coming under fire from the MSF group. While the South African Department of Health claims that about 25 percent of the country's adults are infected with HIV, President Mbeki continues to question whether HIV causes AIDS and even whether AIDS is actually the leading cause of death in South Africa, a stance which is bringing criticism and pressure from various groups in the country.[20] The South African government refused to pay for the drugs imported by the Treatment Action Campaign (TAC) for use by the MSF doctors, at a cost of $3.20 to $1.55 per daily treatment.[21]

Meanwhile, as this situation of global interdependence brings challenges of social responsibility conflicting with capitalism, the UN established a board to oversee the Global Fund for HIV, tuberculosis, and malaria. While there is pressure to use that money to buy generic drugs, the World Health Organization is working with the major pharmaceutical companies to intensify their efforts to find cures for diseases in developing countries.[22]

Advocates of cheap drugs say the Bush administration yielded to pressure from the pharmaceutical lobby to find ways to reject the generics.[23] However, in the

[9]Ibid.

[10]"AIDS and the Drug Companies," *America.*

[11]Ibid.

[12]R. Block and G. Harris, "Drug Makers Agree to Drop South Africa Suit," *Wall Street Journal,* April 19, 2001.

[13]Ibid.

[14]Ibid.

[15]Ibid.

[16]Ibid.

[17]M. Schoofs, "Doctor Group Defies South Africa AIDS Policy," *Wall Street Journal,* January 30, 2002.

[18]Ibid.

[19]Ibid.

[20]Ibid.

[21]S. Boseley, "AIDS Drugs Bring Hope to South Africa—AIDS Activists Bring Gift of Life to South Africa," *The Guardian—United Kingdom,* January 30, 2002.

[22]Ibid.

[23]D. G. McNeil, Jr., "Plan to Fight AIDS Overseas Is Foundering," www.nytimes.com, March 28, 2004.

face of dwindling funding from the U.S., a group including the United Nations, the World Bank, the Global Fund to Fight AIDS, Tuberculosis and Malaria, and former President Bill Clinton announced in April 2004 a joint plan to buy and distribute cheap, generic AIDS drugs in poor countries. The generic drugs will be purchased primarily from companies based in India at around $140 per person per year. Additional hope was offered by the World Trade Organization in August 2003, when it agreed to give poor nations greater access to inexpensive life-saving medicine by altering international trade rules. The agreement will permit poor countries to import generic versions of expensive patented medicines, buying them from countries such as India and Brazil, without running afoul of trade laws protecting patent rights.[24]

QUESTIONS FOR DISCUSSION

1. Do a stakeholder analysis of this global situation—that is, name the various parties involved and explain the goals of each, the rationale for their positions, and the short- and long-term implications of the situation each party faces.
2. What ethical philosophy should apply to this situation: moral ethnocentrism, ethical relativism, or moral universalism? Explain the rationale for your answer and relate it to the parties you identified in question 1.
3. Is a universal code of ethics possible for the global pharmaceutical industry? Explain how that could work.
4. What should, or can, the managers of the Western pharmaceutical companies do to resolve this problem? Is it entirely their responsibility? What other parties could, or should, help pay for the drugs? Draw up a plan of action from the perspective of a company executive.
5. Do a follow-up on this case situation. What has happened since this writing in April 2004? Has the position of the world's companies changed? If so, how? What changes have there been for the other major stakeholders?
6. What lessons are there for MNCs from the way this situation has evolved and the responses of various stakeholders.

[24]E. Becker, "Poor Nations Can Purchase Cheap Drugs Under Accord," www.nytimes.com, August 30, 2003.

Case 3   Footwear International

John Carlson frowned as he studied the translation of the front-page story from the afternoon's edition of the *Meillat,* a fundamental newspaper with close ties to an opposition political party. The story, titled "Footwear's Unpardonable Audacity," suggested that the company had knowingly insulted Islam by including the name of Allah in a design used on the insoles of sandals it was manufacturing. To compound the problem, the paper had run a photograph of one of the offending sandals on the front page. As a result, student groups were calling for public demonstrations against Footwear the next day. As managing director of Footwear Bangladesh, Carlson knew he would have to act quickly to defuse a potentially explosive situation.

ABOUT THE COMPANY

Footwear International is a multinational manufacturer and marketer of footwear. Operations span the globe and include more than eighty-three companies in seventy countries. These include shoe factories, tanneries, engineering plants producing shoe machinery and moulds, product development studios, hosiery factories, quality control laboratories, and approximately 6,300 retail stores and 50,000 independent retailers.

Footwear employs more than 67,000 people and produces and sells in excess of 270 million pairs of shoes every year. The head office acts as a service center and is staffed with specialists drawn from all over the world. These specialists, in areas such as marketing, retailing, product development, communications, store design, electronic data processing, and business administration, travel for much of the year to share their expertise with the various companies. Training and technical education, offered through company-run colleges and the training facility at headquarters, provide the latest skills to employees from around the world.

Although Footwear requires standardization in technology and the design of facilities, it also encourages a high degree of decentralization and autonomy in its operations. The companies are virtually self-governing, which means their allegiance belongs to the countries in which they operate. Each is answerable to a board of directors that includes representatives from the local business community. The concept of "partnership" at the local level has made the company welcome internationally and has allowed it to operate successfully in countries where other multinationals have been unable to survive.

BANGLADESH

With a population approaching 110 million in an area of 143,998 square kilometers (see Exhibit C3-1), Bangladesh is the most densely populated country in the world. It is also among the most impoverished, with a 1987 per capita gross national product of $160 and a high reliance on foreign aid. More than 40 percent of the gross domestic product is generated by agriculture, and more than 60 percent of its economically active population works in the agriculture sector. Although the land in Bangladesh is fertile, the country has a tropical monsoon climate and suffers from the ravages of periodic cyclones. In 1988, the country experienced the worst floods in recorded history.

The population of Bangladesh is 85 percent Muslim, and Islam was made the official state religion in 1988. Approximately 95 percent of the population speaks Bengali, with most of the remainder speaking tribal dialects.

Bangladesh has had a turbulent history in the twentieth century. Most of the country was part of the British-ruled East Bengal until 1947. In that year, it joined with Assam to become East Pakistan, a province of the newly created country of Pakistan. East Pakistan was separated from the four provinces of West Pakistan by 1,600 kilometers of Indian territory, and although the East was more populous, the national capital was established in West Pakistan. Over the following years, widespread discontent built in the East whose people felt that they received a disproportionately small amount of development funding and were under-represented in government.

Following a period of unrest starting in 1969, the Awami League, the leading political party in East Pakistan, won an overwhelming victory in local elections held in 1970. The victory promised to give the league, which was pro-independence, control in the National Assembly. To prevent that happening, the national government suspended the convening of the Assembly indefinitely. On March 26, 1971, the Awami League proclaimed the independence of the People's Republic of Bangladesh, and civil war quickly followed. In the ensuing conflict, hundreds of thousands of refugees fled to safety across the border in India. In December, India, which supported the independence of Bangladesh, declared war, and twelve days later Pakistan surrendered. Bangladesh had won its independence, and the capital of the new country was established at Dhaka. In the years immediately following independence, industrial output declined in major industries as the result of the departure of many of the largely non-Bengali financier and managerial class.

Throughout the subsequent years, political stability proved elusive for Bangladesh. Although elections were held, stability was threatened by the terrorist tactics resorted to by opposition groups from both political extremes. Coups and countercoups, assassinations, and suspension of civil liberties became regular occurrences.

Since 1983, Bangladesh had been ruled by the self-proclaimed President General H. M. Ershad. Despite demonstrations in 1987 that led to a state of emergency being declared, Ershad managed to retain power in elections held the following year. The country remains politically volatile, however. Dozens of political parties continually maneuver for position, and alliances and coalitions are the order of the day. The principal opposition party is the Awami League, an alliance of eight political parties. Many of the parties are closely linked with so-called opposition newspapers, which promote their political positions. Strikes and demonstrations are frequent and often result from cooperation among opposition political parties, student groups, and unions.

FOOTWEAR BANGLADESH

Footwear became active in what was then East Bengal in the 1930s. In 1962, the first major investment took place with the construction of a footwear manufacturing facility at Tongi, an industrial town located thirty kilometers north of Dhaka. During the following years, the company expanded its presence in both conventional and unconventional ways. In 1971, the then managing director became a freedom fighter, while continuing to oversee operations. He subsequently became the only foreigner to be decorated by the government with the "*Bir Protik*" in recognition of both his and the company's contribution to the independence of Bangladesh.

In 1985, Footwear Bangladesh went public and two years later spearheaded the largest private-sector foreign

EXHIBIT C3-1

investment in the country, a tannery and footwear factory at Dhamrai. The new tannery produced leather for local Footwear needs and the export market, and the factory produced a variety of footwear for the local market.

By 1988, Footwear Bangladesh employed 1,800 employees and sold through eighty-one stores and fifty-four agencies. The company introduced approximately 300 new products a year to the market using their in-house design and development capability. Footwear managers were particularly proud of the capability of the personnel in these departments, all of whom were Bangladeshi.

Annual sales in excess of ten million pairs of footwear gave the company 15 percent of the national market in 1988. Revenues exceeded $30 million and after-tax profit was approximately $1 million. Financially, the company was considered a medium contributor within the Footwear organization. With a population approaching 110 million, and per capita consumption of one pair of shoes every two years, Bangladesh was perceived as offering Footwear enormous potential for growth both through consumer education and competitive pressure.

The managing director of Footwear Bangladesh was John Carlson, one of only four foreigners working for the company. The others were the managers of production, marketing, and sales. All had extensive and varied experience within the Footwear organization.

THE INCIDENT

On Thursday, June 22, 1989, John Carlson was shown a copy of that day's *Meillat*, a well-known opposition newspaper with pro-Libyan leanings. Under the headline "Footwear's Unpardonable Audacity," the writer suggested that the design on the insole of one model of sandal produced by the company included the Arabic spelling of the word *Allah* (see Exhibit C3-2). The story suggested that Footwear was under Jewish ownership and to link the alleged offense with the gunning down of

many people in Palestine by Jews. The story highlighted the fact that the design was on the insole of the sandal and therefore, next to the bottom of the foot, a sign of great disrespect to Muslims.

Carlson immediately contacted the supervisor of the design department and asked for any information he could provide on the design on the sandals. He already knew that they were from a medium-priced line of women's footwear that had the design on the insole changed often as a marketing feature. Following his investigation, the supervisor reported that the design had been based on a set of Chinese temple bells that the designer had purchased in the local market. Pleased by the appearance of the bells, she had used them as the basis for a stylized design, which she submitted to her supervisor for consideration and approval (see Exhibit C3-3).

All the employees in the development and marketing department were Muslims. The supervisor reported that the woman who had produced the offending design was a devout Bengali Muslim who spoke and read no Arabic. The same was true of almost all the employees in the department. The supervisor confirmed to Carlson that numerous people in the department had seen the new design prior to its approval, and no one had seen any problem or raised any objection to it. Following the conversation, Carlson compared the design to the word *Allah,* which he had arranged to have written in Arabic (see Exhibit C3-4).

Carlson was perplexed by the article and its timing. The sandals in question were not new to the market and had not been subject to prior complaints. As he reread the translation of the *Meillat* article, he wondered why the Jewish reference had been made when the family that owned Footwear International was Christian. He also wondered if the fact that students from the university had taken the sandals to the paper was significant.

As the day progressed, the situation got worse. Carlson was shown a translation of a proclamation that had been circulated by two youth groups calling for

---

EXHIBIT C3-2   Translation of the *Meillat* Story*

Unpardonable Audacity of Footwear

In Bangladesh a Sandal with Allah as Footwear trade mark in Arabic designed in calligraphy has been marketed although last year Islam was made the State Religion in Bangladesh. The Sandal in black and white contains Allah in black. Prima facie it appears it has been designed and the Alif "the first letter in Arabic" has been jointly written. Excluding Alif it reads LILLAH. In Bangladesh after the Satan Rushdie's† Satanic Verses which has brought unprecedented demonstration and innumerable strikes (Hartels). This International shoe manufacturing organization under Jewish ownership with the design of Allah has made religious offense. Where for sanctity of Islam one million people of Afghanistan have sacrificed their lives and wherein occupied Palestine many people have been gunned down by Jews for sanctity of Islam in this country the word Allah under this guise has been put under feet.

Last night a group of students from Dhaka university came to Meillat office with a couple of pairs of Sandal. The management staff of Footwear was not available over telephone. This sandal has got two straps made of foam.

*The translation is identical to that which Carlson was given at work.
†Salman Rushdie was the author of the controversial book *The Satanic Verses.* The author had been sentenced to death, *in absentia*, by Ayatollah Khomeini, the late leader of Iran, for crimes against Islam.

EXHIBIT C3-3   The Temple Bells and the Design Used on the Sandal

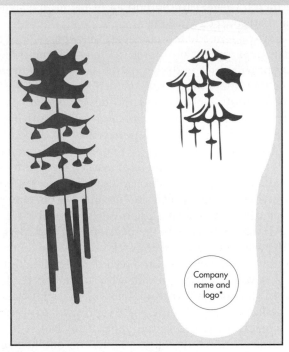

The company's name and logo appeared prominently on the insole of the sandal. Both of the images in the exhibit were redrawn from copies of facsimiles sent to headquarters by John Carlson.

demonstrations against Footwear to be held the next day (see Exhibit C3-5). The proclamation linked Footwear, Salman Rushdie, and the Jewish community and ominously stated that "even at the cost of our lives we have to protest against this conspiracy."

EXHIBIT C3-4   The Arabic Spelling of Allah

This exhibit was redrawn from a facsimile sent to headquarters by John Carlson.

More bad news followed. Calls had been made for charges to be laid against Carlson and four others under a section of the criminal code that forbade "deliberate and malicious acts intended to outrage feelings of any class by insulting its religion or religious believers" (see Exhibit C3-6). A short time later, Carlson received a copy of a statement that had been filed by a local lawyer although no warrants were immediately forthcoming (see Exhibit C3-7).

While he was reviewing the situation, Carlson was interrupted by his secretary. In an excited voice, she informed him that the prime minister was being quoted as calling the sandal incident an "unforgivable crime." The seriousness of the incident seemed to be escalating rapidly, and Carlson wondered what he should do to try to minimize the damage.

EXHIBIT C3-5   Translation of the Student Group's Proclamation*

The audacity through the use of the name "Allah" in a sandal.

Let Rushdie's Jewish Footwear Company be prohibited in Bangladesh.

Dear people who believe in one God it is announced in the holy Quran Allahs name is above everything but shoe manufacturing Jewish Footwear Shoe Company has used the name Allah and shown disrespect of unprecedented nature and also unpardonable audacity. After the failure of Rushdie's efforts to destroy the beliefs of Muslims in the Quran, Islam and the prophet (SM) who is the writer of Satanic verses the Jewish People have started offending the Muslims. This time it is a fight against Allah. In fact Daud Haider, Salman Rushdie Viking Penguin and Footwear Shoe Company all are supported and financed by Jewish community. Therefore no compromise with them. Even at the cost of our lives we have to protest against this conspiracy.

For this procession and demonstration will be held on 23rd, June Friday after Jumma prayer from Baitul Mukarram Mosque south gate. Please join this procession and announce we will not pardon Footwear Shoe Company's audacity. Footwear Shoe Company has to be prohibited, don't buy Jewish products and Footwear shoes. Be aware Rushdie's partner.

Issued by Bangladesh Islamic Jubashibir (Youth Student Forum) and Bangladesh Islamic Satrashbir (Student Forum)

This translation is identical to that which Carlson was given at work.

EXHIBIT C3-6   Section 295 of the Criminal Code

295-A. *Deliberate and malicious acts intended to outrage religious feelings of any class by insulting its religion or religious believers.* Whoever, with deliberate and malicious intention of outraging the religious feelings of any class of [the citizens of Bangladesh], by words, either spoken or written, or by visible representations, insults, or attempts to insult the religion or religious beliefs of that class, shall be punished with imprisonment . . .

. . . In order to bring a matter under S. 295-A it is not the mere matter of discourse or the written expression but also the manner of it which has to be looked to. In other words the expressions should be such as are bound to be regarded by any reasonable man as grossly offensive and provocative and maliciously and deliberately intended to outrage the feelings of any class of citizens. . . . If the injurious act was done voluntarily without a lawful excuse, malice may be presumed.

EXHIBIT C3-7   The Statement of the Plaintiff

The plaintiff most respectfully states that:

1) The plaintiff is a lawyer, and a Bangladeshi Citizen and his religion is Islam. He is basically a devout Muslim. According to Islamic tradition he regularly performs his daily work.

2) The first accused of this . . . is the Managing Director of Footwear Shoe Company, the second accused is the Production Manager of the said company, the third accused is the Marketing Manager, the fourth accused is the Calligrapher of the said company and last accused is the Sales Manager of the said company. The said company is an international organization having shoe business in different countries.

3) The accused persons deliberately wanted to outrage the religion of Muslims by engraving the calligraphy of "Allah" in Arabic on a sandal thereby to offend the religion of majority this Muslim Country. By marketing this sandal with the calligraphy of "Allah" they have offended the religious feelings of millions of Muslims. It is the solemn religious duty and responsibility of every devout Muslim to protect the sanctity of "Allah." The plaintiff first saw the sandal with this calligraphy on 22nd June 1989 at Elephant road shop.

The accused persons collectively and deliberately wanted this calligraphy under the feet thereby to offend the religion of mine and many other Muslims and have committed a crime under provisions of section 295A of the Penal Code. At the time of the hearing the evidence will be provided.

Therefore under the provisions of section 295A of the Penal Code the accused persons to be issued with warrant of arrest and be brought to court for justice.

The names of the Witnesses
1)
2)
3)

QUESTIONS FOR DISCUSSION

1. You are in John Carlson's position. Analyze the situation facing Footwear, and prepare a detailed plan of action to deal with your immediate responsibilities as well as the entire situation and a long-term plan. The following suggestions may help you develop your plan:

    - Use a stakeholder analysis to assess the role and objectives of various interest groups and evaluate what is going on and why, and to look beyond the immediate situation.
    - Consider what role or roles local politics play in the Footwear case, and who are the principal actors in this real-life business drama.

    - What issues are of greatest concern to Footwear Bangladesh? To Footwear International?

2. These events actually happened. Ask your professor for the information on the follow-up events. Do you think this situation could happen again?

CHAPTER

Understanding the Role of Culture

Opening Profile: Adjusting Business to Saudi Arabian Culture

For most outsiders, Saudi Arabia is a land of contrasts and paradoxes. (Map 3-1 shows its location.) It has supermodern cities, but its strict Islamic religious convictions and ancient social customs, on which its laws and customs depend, often clash with modern economic and technical realities. Saudi Arabians sometimes employ latitude in legal formation and enforcement to ease these clashes and sometimes accommodate different behaviors from foreigners. Nevertheless, many foreigners misunderstand Saudi laws and customs or find them contrary to their own value systems. Foreign companies have had mixed success in Saudi Arabia, due in large part to how well they understood and adapted imaginatively to Saudi customs.

Companies from countries with strict separation between state and religion or where few people actively engage in religion find Saudi Arabia's pervasiveness of religion daunting. Religious decrees have sometimes made companies rescind activities. For example, an importer halted sales of the children's game Pokémon because the game might encourage the un-Islamic practice of gambling, and a franchisor was forced to remove the face under the crown in Starbucks' logo because Saudi authorities felt the public display of a woman's face was religiously immoral. However, most companies know the requirements in advance. For instance, Coty Beauty omits models' faces on point-of-purchase displays that it depicts in other countries. Companies know that they must remove the heads and hands from mannequins and must not display them scantily clad. Companies, such as McDonald's, dim their lights, close their doors, and stop attending to customers

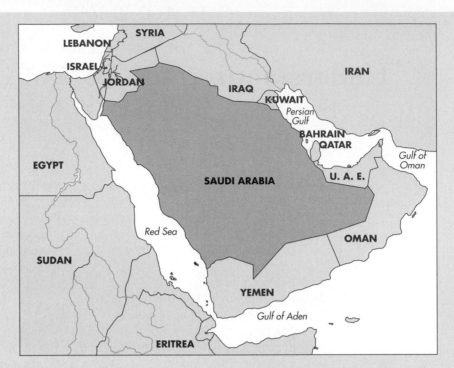

Map 3-1   Saudi Arabia comprises most of the Arabian peninsula. All of the countries bordering Saudi Arabia are Arab countries (meaning that the first language is Arabic), and all are predominately Islamic.

during the five times per day that men are called to pray. Companies also adjust voluntarily to gain the good will of customers—for example, by converting revenue-generating space to prayer areas. (Saudi Arabian Airlines does this in the rear of its planes, and the U.K.'s Harvey Nichols does this in its department store.) During the holy period of Ramadan, people are less active during the day because they fast, so many stores shift some operating hours to the evenings when people prefer to shop.

In 2000, Saudi Arabia ratified an international agreement designed to eliminate the discrimination of women; however, its prescribed behaviors for women appear paradoxical to outsiders. On the one hand, women now outnumber men in Saudi Arabian universities and own about 20 percent of all Saudi businesses. (There are separate male and female universities, and female-owned businesses can sell only to women.) Women also comprise a large portion of Saudi teachers and doctors. On the other hand, women account for only about 7 percent of the workforce. They cannot have private law or architectural firms, nor can they be engineers. They are not permitted to drive, because this may lead to evil behavior. They must wear abayas (robes) and cover their hair completely when in public. They cannot work alongside men except in the medical profession, and they cannot sell directly to male customers. If they are employed where men work, they must have separate work entrances and be separated from males by partitions. They must be accompanied by an adult male relative when dealing with male clerks.

The female prescriptions have implications for business operations. For example, the Saudi American Bank established branches for and staffed only by women. Pizza Hut installed two dining rooms—one for single men and one for families. (Women do not eat there without their families.) Both Harvey Nichols and Saks Fifth Avenue have created women-only floors in their department stores. On lower levels, there is mixed shopping, all male salespeople (even for products like cosmetics and bras), and no changing rooms or places to try cosmetics. On upper floors, women can check their *abayas* and shop in jeans, spandex, or whatever. The stores have also created drivers' lounges for their chauffeurs. A downside is that male store managers can visit upper floors only when the stores are closed, which limits their observations of situations that might improve service and performance. Similarly, market research companies cannot rely on discussions with family-focused groups to determine marketing needs. Because men do much more of the household purchasing, companies target them more in their marketing than in other countries.

Why do high-end department stores and famous designers operate in Saudi Arabia where women cover themselves in *abayas* and men typically wear *thobes* (long robes)? Simply, the many very rich people in Saudi Arabia are said to keep Paris couture alive. Even though Saudi Arabia prohibits fashion magazines and movies, this clientele knows what is in fashion. (The government also prohibits satellite dishes, but some estimates say that two-thirds of Saudi homes have them.) Women buy items from designers' collections, which they wear abroad or in Saudi Arabia only in front of their husbands and other women. Underneath their *abayas*, they often wear very expensive jewelry, makeup, and clothing. Wealthy men also want the latest high-end fashions when traveling abroad.

Another paradox is that about 60 percent of the Saudi private workforce is foreign, even though the unemployment rate is about 30 percent. Changing economic conditions are at least partially responsible for this situation. In the early 1980s, Saudi oil revenues caused per capita income to jump to about $28,000, but this plummeted below $7,000 by the early 2000s. When incomes were high, Saudis brought in foreigners to do most of the work. At the same time, the government liberally supported university training, including study abroad. Saudis developed a mentality of expecting foreigners to do all the work, or at least some of the work, for them. The New Zealand head of National Biscuits & Confectionery said that Saudis now want only to be supervisors and complain if they have to work at the same level as people from Nepal, Bangladesh, and India. Although the government has taken steps to replace foreign workers with Saudis, prevailing work attitudes impede this transition. For example, the acceptance by a Saudi of a bellboy job at the Hyatt Regency hotel in Jidda was so unusual that Saudi newspapers put his picture on their front pages.

Saudi Arabian legal sanctions seem harsh to many outsiders. Religious patrols may hit women if they show any hair in public. The government carries out beheadings and hand-severances in public and expects passers-by to observe the punishments, some of which are for crimes that would not be offenses in other countries. For example, the government publicly beheaded three men in early 2002 for being homosexuals. However, there are inconsistencies. For example, religious patrols are more relaxed about women's dress codes in some Red Sea resorts, and they are more lenient toward the visiting female executives of MNEs than toward Saudi women. Whereas they don't allow Saudi women to be flight attendants on Saudi Arabian Airlines because they would have to work alongside men, they permit women from other Arab countries to do so. Further, in foreign investment compounds where almost everyone is a foreigner, these religious patrols make exceptions to most of the strict religious prescriptions.

Interesting situations concern the charging of interest and the purchase of accident insurance, both of which are disallowed under strict Islamic interpretations of the Koran. In the case of interest, the Saudi government gives interest-free loans for mortgages. This worked well when Saudi Arabia was awash with oil money, but borrowers must now wait about 10 years for a loan. In the case of accident insurance (by strict Islamic doctrine, there are no accidents, only preordained acts of God), the government eliminated prohibitions because businesses needed the insurance.

Personal interactions between cultures are tricky, and those between Saudis and non-Saudis are no exception. For example, Parris-Rogers International (PRI), a British publishing house, sent two salesmen to Saudi Arabia and paid them on a commission basis. They expected that by moving aggressively, the two men could make the same number of calls as they could in the United Kingdom. They were used to working eight-hour days, to having the undivided attention of potential clients, and to restricting conversation to the business transaction. To them, time was money. However, they found that appointments seldom began at the scheduled time and most often took place at cafés where the Saudis would engage in what the salesmen considered idle chitchat. Whether in a café or in the office, drinking coffee or tea and talking to acquaintances seemed to take precedence over business matters. The salesmen began showing so much irritation at "irrelevant" conversations, delays, and interruptions from friends that they caused irrevocable damage to the company's objectives. The Saudi counterparts considered them rude and impatient.

Whereas businesspersons from many countries invite counterparts to social gatherings at their homes to honor them and use personal relationships to cement business arrangements, Saudis view the home as private and even consider questions about their families as rude and an invasion of privacy. In contrast, Saudi businessmen seldom regard business discussions as private; they thus welcome friends to sit in. The opposite is true in many countries.

In spite of contrasts and paradoxes, foreign companies find ways to be highly successful in Saudi Arabia. In some cases, legal barriers to some products, such as to alcoholic beverages and pork products, have created boons for other products, such as soft drinks and turkey ham. In addition, some companies have developed specific practices in response to Saudi conditions and have later benefited from them in their home countries. For example, companies, such as Fuji and Kodak, created technology for while-you-wait photo development for Saudi Arabia because customers wanted to retrieve photos without anyone else seeing them. They transferred this technology to the United States several years later.

SOURCE: John D. Daniels, Lee H. Radebaugh, Sullivan Daniel P., *International Business: Environments and Operations*, 10th ed. © 2004. Reprinted by permission of Pearson Education, Inc., Upper Saddle River, NJ.

This chapter's opening profile describes how an understanding of the local culture and business environment can give managers an advantage in competitive industries. Foreign companies—no matter how big—can ignore those aspects to their peril. Such differences in culture and the way of life in other countries necessitate that managers develop international expertise to manage on a contingency basis according to the host-country environment. Powerful, interdependent factors in that environment—political, economic, legal, technological, and cultural—influence management strategy, functions, and processes.

A critical skill for managing people and processes in other countries is **cultural savvy**—that is, a working knowledge of the cultural variables affecting management decisions. Managers have often seriously underestimated the significance of cultural factors. According to numerous accounts, many blunders made in international operations can be attributed to a lack of cultural sensitivity.[1] Examples abound. Scott Russell, senior vice president for human resources at Cendant Mobility in Danbury, Connecticut, recounts the following:

> An American company in Japan charged its Japanese HR manager with reducing the workforce. The Japanese manager studied the issue but couldn't find a solution within cultural Japanese parameters; so when he came back to the Americans, he reduced the workforce by resigning—which was not what they wanted.[2]

Cultural sensitivity, or **cultural empathy**, is an awareness and an honest caring about another individual's culture. Such sensitivity requires the ability to understand the perspective of those living in other (and very different) societies and the willingness to put oneself in another's shoes.

International managers can benefit greatly from understanding the nature, dimensions, and variables of a specific culture and how these affect work and organizational processes. This cultural awareness enables them to develop appropriate policies and determine how to plan, organize, lead, and control in a specific international setting. Such a process of adaptation to the environment is necessary to successfully implement strategy. It also leads to effective interaction in a workforce of increasing cultural diversity, in both the United States and other countries.

Company reports and management studies make it clear that a lack of cultural sensitivity costs businesses money and opportunities. One study of U.S. multinational corporations found that poor intercultural communication skills still constitute a major management problem. Managers' knowledge of other cultures lags far behind their understanding of other organizational processes.[3] In a synthesis of the research on cross-cultural training, Black and Mendenhall found that up to 40 percent of expatriate managers leave their assignments early because of poor performance or poor adjustment to the local environment. About half of those who do remain are considered only marginally effective. Furthermore, they found that cross-cultural differences are the cause of failed negotiations and interactions, resulting in losses to U.S. firms of over $2 billion a year for failed expatriate assignments alone.[4]

Other evidence indicates, however, that cross-cultural training is effective in developing skills and enhancing adjustment and performance. In spite of such evidence, U.S. firms do little to take advantage of such important research and to incorporate it into their ongoing training programs, whose purpose is ostensibly to prepare managers before sending them overseas. Too often, the importance of such training in developing cultural sensitivity is realized much too late, as seen in the following account of the unhappy marriage between America's AT&T and Italy's Olivetti, the office-equipment maker:

> One top AT&T executive believes that most of the problems in the venture stemmed from cultural differences. "I don't think we or Olivetti spent enough time understanding behavior patterns," says Robert Kayner, AT&T group executive. "We knew the culture was different, but we never really penetrated. We would get angry, and they would get upset." Mr. Kayner says AT&T's attempts to fix the problems, such as delays in deliveries, were transmitted in curt memos that offended Olivetti officials. "They would get an attitude, 'Who are you to tell us what to do,'" he says. Or, the Olivetti side would explain its own problems, and AT&T managers would simply respond, "Don't tell me about your problems. Solve them." AT&T executives are the first to admit, now, that one of the greatest challenges of putting a venture together is that partners frequently see the world in very different—and potentially divisive—ways.[5]

This chapter provides a conceptual framework with which companies and managers can assess relevant cultural variables and develop cultural profiles of various countries. This framework is then used to consider the probable effects of cultural differences on an organization and their implications for management. To do this, the powerful environmental factor of cultural context is examined. The nature of culture and its variables and dimensions are first explored, and then specific differences in cultural values and their implications for the on-the-job behavior of individuals and groups are considered. Cultural variables, in general, are also discussed in this chapter. The impact of culture on specific management functions and processes is discussed in later chapters as appropriate.

CULTURE AND ITS EFFECTS ON ORGANIZATIONS

As generally understood, the **culture** of a society comprises the shared values, understandings, assumptions, and goals that are learned from earlier generations, imposed by present members of a society and passed on to succeeding generations. This shared outlook results, in large part, in common attitudes, codes of conduct, and expectations that subconsciously guide and control certain norms of behavior.[6] One is born into, not with, a given culture, and gradually internalizes its subtle effects through the socialization process. Culture results in a basis for living grounded in shared communication, standards, codes of conduct, and expectations.[7] Over time, cultures evolve as societies adapt to transitions in their external and internal environments and relationships. A manager assigned to a foreign subsidiary, for example, must expect to find large and small differences in the behavior of individuals and groups within that organization. As depicted in Exhibit 3-1, these differences result from the societal, or sociocultural, variables of the culture, such as religion and language, in addition to prevailing national variables, such as economic, legal, and political factors. National and sociocultural variables, thus, provide the context for the development and perpetuation of cultural variables. These cultural variables, in turn, determine basic attitudes toward work, time, materialism, individualism, and change. Such attitudes affect an individual's motivation and expectations regarding work and group relations, and they ultimately affect the outcomes that can be expected from that individual.

A policy change made by KLM Royal Dutch Airlines, with which the organizational culture responded to national cultural values and accepted practices, illustrated the way these sets of variables can interact. The culture of social responsiveness in the Netherlands was incorporated into business policy when the airline revised its travel-benefits policy for families of employees. For some time, many KLM stewards had protested the rule that only immediate family members were eligible for low fares on KLM flights. They found it discriminatory that even just-married heterosexual spouses received the benefit, while long-term homosexual partners were not eligible. Upon reconsideration, KLM responded that any couple who formally registered as living together, which is a normal legal practice in the Netherlands, would be eligible for the low fares. However, a year had to elapse between partners before a new partner could be registered. By changing its policy, KLM put the emphasis on committed relationships rather than on marital status or sexual preference.[8]

McDonald's provides another example, with its 58 restaurants in Russia. The company's experience with setting up businesses there for the eleven years since the first restaurant opened in Moscow demonstrates the combined effects of national and cultural variables on work. In Russia, local employees require lengthy training to serve up "Bolshoi Maks" in the "McDonald's way." Unfortunately, Russians are still, for the most part, not familiar with working under the capitalist system; they have been victims of the inertia brought about by the old system of central planning for so long that productivity remains low. As a result, Russians have few goods to buy, and the new

EXHIBIT 3-1   Environmental Variables Affecting Management Functions

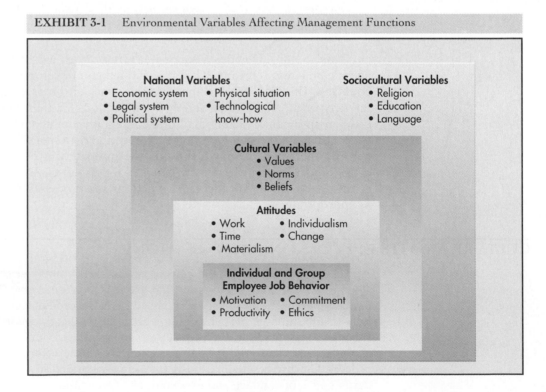

free-market prices are so high that there is little motivation for them to work for rubles that won't buy anything.[9]

It is clear that cultural variables—shared beliefs, values, and attitudes—can greatly affect organizational processes. One example of how culture affects organizational processes is frequently evident as the use of technological applications in those processes spreads around the world. The result can be culture–technology clashes. In particular, companies that conduct global business via the Internet are finding many areas of culture–Internet clash that they must resolve if they are to achieve success in foreign markets (see E-Biz Box: Companies Must Localize E-Commerce to Avoid Culture–Internet Clash).

E-BIZ BOX

Companies Must Localize E-Commerce to Avoid Culture–Internet Clash

With 75 percent of the world's Internet market living outside the United States, multinational e-businesses are learning the hard way that their Web sites must reflect local markets, customs, languages, and currencies to be successful in foreign markets. Different legal systems, financial structures, tastes, and experiences necessitate attention to every detail to achieve global appeal. In other words, e-businesses must localize to globalize, which means much more than translating online content to local languages. Lycos Europe, for example, based its privacy policies upon German law since it is the most stringent.

One problem area often beyond the control of e-business is the costs of connecting to the Internet for people in other countries. In Asia, for example, such costs are considerably higher than in the United States. Other practical problems in Asia, as well as in Germany, the Netherlands, and Sweden, include the method of payment, which in most of these places still involves cash or letters of credit and written receipts. Dell tackled this problem by offering debit payments from consumers' checking accounts. Some companies have learned the hard way that they need to do their homework before launching sites aimed at overseas consumers. Dell, for example, committed a faux pas when it launched an e-commerce site in Japan with black borders on the site; black is considered negative in the Japanese culture, so many consumers took one look and didn't want anything else to do with it. Dell executives learned that the complexity of language translation into Japanese was only one area in which they needed to localize.

The complexities of localizing don't stop there. Legal and political issues and local support centers require forethought, as do simple content design factors such as the icons used. Mailboxes, for example, are not used in Europe, and shopping carts are rare in many areas where people shop only in small stores.

In spite of all the challenges, e-business presents significant opportunities for companies of all sizes to go global and to do well if they do their homework where they hope to do business and come to understand how to mesh their technology with local cultures and lifestyles. Some companies outsource their Web design and processes for foreign markets to make up for a lack of internal skills; others use various "global software" packages and services designed to help firms expand into foreign markets.

SOURCES: D. Gareiss, "Business on the World Wide Web: It's Not Enough to Have Web Pages That Sell Wares in English," *Information Week,* December 11, 2000, p. 69; "The Net Is Transforming the West, But Companies in the East Lag Behind," www.businessweek.com, October 23, 2000; A. Chen and M. Hicks, "Going Global? Avoid Culture Clashes: Sites Must Reflect Local Customs and Ways of Doing Business to Achieve Success in Foreign Markets," *PC Week,* April 3, 2000, p. 65; "World Organization of Webmaster and Web of Culture Announce Partnership for Web Globalization Education and Certification," *Internet Wire,* February 12, 2003, p. 3; "Outsourcing—Following the Leaders May Well Lead to Failure (Systems)," *Information Systems Auditor,* December 2002, p. 8.

Which organizational processes—technical and otherwise—are most affected by cultural differences, and how, is the subject of ongoing cross-cultural management research and debate.[10] Some argue that the effects of culture are more evident at the individual level of personal behavior than at the organizational level, as a result of convergence.[11] **Convergence** describes the phenomenon of the shifting of individual management styles to become more similar to one another. The convergence argument is based on the belief that the demands of industrialization, worldwide coordination, and competition tend to factor out differences in organizational-level processes, such as choice of technology and structure. In a 2000 study of Japanese and Korean firms, Lee, Roehl, and Choe found that globalization and firm size were sources of convergence of management styles.[12] These factors are discussed in more detail later in this chapter.

The effects of culture on specific management functions are particularly noticeable when we attempt to impose our own values and systems on another society. Exhibit 3-2 gives some examples of the values typical of U.S. culture, compares some common perspectives held by people in other countries, and shows which management functions might be affected, clearly implying the need for the differential management of organizational processes. For example, American managers plan activities, schedule them, and judge their timely completion based on the belief that people influence and control the future, rather than assuming that events will occur only at the will of Allah, as managers in an Islamic nation might believe.

EXHIBIT 3-2   U.S. Values and Possible Alternatives

Aspects of U.S. Culture*	Alternative Aspect	Examples of Management Function Affected
The individual can influence the future (where there is a will there is a way).	Life follows a preordained course, and human action is determined by the will of God.	Planning and scheduling
The individual can change and improve the environment.	People are intended to adjust to the physical environment rather than to alter it.	Organizational environment, morale, and productivity
An individual should be realistic in his or her aspirations.	Ideals are to be pursued regardless of what is "reasonable."	Goal setting and career development
We must work hard to accomplish our objectives (Puritan ethic).	Hard work is not the only prerequisite for success; wisdom, luck, and time are also required.	Motivation and reward system
Commitments should be honored (people will do what they say they will do).	A commitment may be superseded by a conflicting request, or an agreement may only signify intention and have little or no relationship to the capacity for performance.	Negotiating and bargaining
One should effectively use one's time (time is money that can be saved or wasted).	Schedules are important, but only in relation to other priorities.	Long- and short-range planning
A primary obligation of an employee is to the organization.	The individual employee has a primary obligation to his or her family and friends.	Loyalty, commitment, and motivation
The employer or employee can terminate the relationship.	Employment is for a lifetime.	Motivation and commitment to the company
The best-qualified people should be given the positions available.	Family, friendship, and other considerations should determine employment practices.	Employment, promotions, recruiting selection, and reward

*Aspect here refers to a belief, value, attitude, or assumption that is a part of a culture in that it is shared by a large number of people in that culture.

SOURCE: Excerpted from *Managing Cultural Differences* by Philip R. Harris and Robert T. Moran, 5th ed. Copyright © 2000 by Gulf Publishing Company, Houston, TX. Used with permission. All rights reserved.

Many people in the world understand and relate to others only in terms of their own culture. This unconscious reference point of one's own cultural values is called a **self-reference criterion**.[13] The result of such an attitude is illustrated in the following story:

> *Once upon a time there was a great flood, and involved in this flood were two creatures, a monkey and a fish. The monkey, being agile and experienced, was lucky enough to scramble up a tree and escape the raging waters. As he looked down from his safe perch, he saw the poor fish struggling against the swift current. With the very best of intentions, he reached down and lifted the fish from the water. The result was inevitable.[14]*

The monkey assumed that its frame of reference applied to the fish and acted accordingly. Thus, international managers from all countries must understand and adjust to unfamiliar social and commercial practices—especially the practices of that mysterious and unique nation, the United States. Japanese workers at a U.S. manufacturing plant learned to put courtesy aside and interrupt conversations with Americans when there were problems. Europeans, however, are often confused by Americans' apparent informality, which then backfires when the Europeans do not get work done as the Americans expect.[15]

As a first step toward cultural sensitivity, international managers should understand their own cultures. This awareness helps to guard against adopting either a parochial or an ethnocentric attitude. **Parochialism** occurs, for example, when a Frenchman expects those from or in another country to automatically fall into patterns of behavior common in France. **Ethnocentrism** describes the attitude of those who operate from the assumption that their ways of doing things are best—no matter where or under what conditions they are applied. Companies both large and small have demonstrated this lack of cultural sensitivity in countless subtle (and not so subtle) ways, with varying disastrous effects.

Procter & Gamble (P&G) was one such company. In an early Japanese television commercial for Camay soap, a Japanese woman is bathing when her husband walks into the bathroom. She starts telling him about her new beauty soap. Her husband, stroking her shoulder, hints that he has more on his mind than suds. The commercial, which had been popular in Europe, was a disaster in Japan. For the man to intrude on his wife "was considered bad manners," says Edwin L. Artzt, P&G's vice chairman and international chief. "And the Japanese didn't think it was very funny." P&G has learned from its mistakes and now generates about half of its revenue from foreign sales.[16]

After studying his or her own culture, the manager's next step toward establishing effective cross-cultural relations is to develop cultural sensitivity. Managers not only must be aware of cultural variables and their effects on behavior in the workplace but also must appreciate cultural diversity and understand how to build constructive working relationships anywhere in the world. The following sections explore cultural variables and dimensions. Later chapters suggest specific ways in which managers can address these variables and dimensions to help build constructive relationships.

CULTURAL VARIABLES

Given the great variety of cultures and subcultures around the world, how can a student of cross-cultural management, or a manager wishing to be culturally savvy, develop an understanding of the specific nature of a certain people? With such an understanding, how can a manager anticipate the probable effects of an unfamiliar culture within an organizational setting and thereby manage human resources productively and control outcomes?

One approach is to develop a cultural profile for each country or region with which the company does or is considering doing business. Developing a cultural profile requires some familiarity with the cultural variables universal to most cultures. From these universal variables, managers can identify the specific differences found in each country or people—and hence anticipate their implications for the workplace.

Managers should never assume that they can successfully transplant American, or Japanese, or any other country's styles, practices, expectations, and processes. Instead, they should practice a basic tenet of good management—contingency management.

Contingency management requires managers to adapt to the local environment and people and to manage accordingly. That adaptation can be complex because the manager may confront differences not only in culture, but also in business practices. (See Management Focus: The Body Shop's Anita Roddick.)

Management Focus

The Body Shop's Anita Roddick: Advocacy for Awareness

Dame Anita Roddick

The time has come to change the way we think about business. Success shouldn't be measured only in financial statements, profits, and losses. It should be about people, life, and developing the human spirit—including that of your suppliers, customers, and employees. But, I didn't start my business to change the world—I started out in 1976 with a vision merely to survive. It took me about a year to raise the equivalent of $7,000 to open my first personal-care products shop in Brighton, England.

That first The Body Shop was wedged between two funeral parlors. They immediately slapped an attorney's letter on me, telling me to cease and desist. They said it was disrespectful of the coffins passing by. But I couldn't change the name—I'd spent a quarter of my money on the sign. So, I called a local newspaper, which immediately thought I had opened a sex shop.

Between the press and the undertakers, I learned that you don't need to spend money on advertising when people will spread your name for free. Soon people were coming to me, wanting to open their own The Body Shop. Today it's an international business, publicly traded, with franchisees in 49 countries.

DIFFERENT COUNTRIES, DIFFERENT NEEDS

As we spread into other countries, I found that while people are basically alike, you still have to respect the culture you're in. For example, people in the West think white is for weddings, but in some Asian countries, it's the color of death. In Saudi Arabia, you can't have

women working in the stores. You can't show any part of the human body except the eyes, feet, and hands. That's caused us quite a bit of stress.

Particular words and language may not work in some cultures. We've always tried to be creative with our marketing, but sometimes it gets us into trouble. When we introduced industrial hemp products, we were banned in France because the government claimed the point-of-sale material glamorized marijuana! And, in the Far East, because of the intense humidity, people won't buy heavy-duty oil and oil-and-water emulsions. So, we give each market the right to choose 25 percent of the types of products they want to sell, with our authority and formulations.

In the United States, it was a different issue. Americans seem to care more about availability than the spiritual meaning behind the products. They want to know they can always get their particular favorite, and that it will always be of very high quality. They also like variety more than anyone else—they'll want fifteen different fragrances for the same product and would be more than happy if we introduced thousands of new products every year.

SUPPORTING THE DEVELOPING WORLD

As a source for ingredients for our products, the company tries to establish relationships with small cooperatives or farming communities—in developing countries and even in the United States—because we believe that the best way to improve people's lives is to give them a chance at self-reliance. It's one of the only ways the gap between the Western nations and the Third World can ever be closed. We try to sustain small economic-reliance groups by increasing our community trade purchasing programs, and we work alongside strategic alliances like fair-trade associations, Oxfam or Max Havelaar in Holland.

Values make a difference, too. Our people in New Zealand said they wanted to open only four shops because they wanted to have time for their children—and that's okay with us. We haven't forced our franchisees to grow if they don't want to.

We set up a project called the *Kayapo* with the indigenous people in the most remote part of Brazil, on the Xingu Reserve, who are terribly difficult to work with because every three years they split the village and move on. And then, we get notices saying, "Sorry, gone fishing for three months." There's a real forgiveness level to reach when products are slower off the mark, or you raise the product profile and suddenly it's not there any more. But, you make a story out of it. We have patient customers who seem intrigued when we explain that we don't have their favorite product because the Brazilian tribespeople would rather catch fish right now.

DEALING WITH GROWING PAINS

The dark side of growing as large as we have is institutionalizing our success. Indeed, all true entrepreneurs hate hierarchy. With hierarchy come rules and regulations that kill creativity. An entrepreneur really should never be in any organization that gets so big that it loses intimacy.

Also, as you grow bigger, there seems to be this strange belief in the comfort of strangers. We've spent shedloads of money on management consultants, who tend to make things worse because they come in with a template and try to superimpose it onto your company.

There's a dark side when new people come on board and don't understand the company's heritage. We've been struggling with that problem recently. A hundred new people in product development designed products our customers didn't want. Then, they said our old market was dull and boring, and that we should target a new market—it didn't matter how much we antagonized our core customers and shareholders. Of course, it didn't work. The organization has had to be humble and bring the old products back.

MEASURING UP TO A MISSION

We've held focus groups for all of our stakeholders—employees, franchisees, customers, suppliers, people who have received money from our foundations, and our investors—and asked them to question us about how we measure up to our mission statement.

The Body Shop has always been about more than selling products, and we wanted to protect that side of things. So, we legitimized our values. We put them into our Articles of Association Memoranda, the legal document you draw up when you incorporate a company in England. The company is dedicated to social and environmental change and human rights advocacy. No matter what else happens, 70 percent of our shareholders would have to get together to vote those values out in the future.

In the old days, we were never an economic threat because we were so small. Now, we've become the threat of good example. An international business can factor human rights, social justice, education, and even the cost of cleaning up the mess it makes into its bottom line. Indeed, some of the most intriguing entrepreneurial initiatives have started out as a cry for freedom. We don't want to act like a big corporation. We want to thank the community for giving us our wealth and put time and effort into giving something back.

SOURCE: "Advocacy for Awareness" by Anita Roddick, The Body Shop, as appeared on Web site www.entreworld.org. Reprinted by permission.

Subcultures

Managers should recognize, of course, that generalizations in cultural profiles will produce only an approximation, or stereotype, of national character. Many countries comprise diverse subcultures whose constituents conform only in varying degrees to the national character. In Canada, distinct subcultures include anglophones and francophones (English-speaking and French-speaking people) and indigenous Canadians. The United States, too, has varying subcultures. Americans abroad are almost always dealt with in the context of the stereotypical American, but, at home, Americans recognize differences among themselves due to ethnic, geographic, or other subcultural backgrounds. Americans should apply the same insight toward people in other countries and be extremely careful not to overgeneralize or oversimplify. For example, although Americans tend to think of Chinese as homogeneous in their culture, considerable differences among Chinese people occur owing to regional diversity—including distinct ethnic groups with their own local customs and a multitude of dialects. A study by Ralston, YU Kai-Ceng, Xun Wang, Terpstra, and He Wei, concluded that, although adherence to traditional Confucian values was common to all regions, regions differed considerably on variables such as individualism and openness to change (with Guangzhou and Shanghai ranking the highest on those dimensions, followed by Beijing and Dalian and then Chengdu and Lanzhou).[17] This implies that Chinese in Guangzhou and Shanghai may be somewhat more "westernized" and more open to doing business with westerners.

Above all, good managers treat people as individuals, and they consciously avoid any form of **stereotyping**. However, a cultural profile is a good starting point to help managers develop some tentative expectations—some cultural context—as a backdrop to managing in a specific international setting. It is useful, then, to look at what cultural variables have been studied and what implications can be drawn from the results.

Influences on National Culture

To develop cultural profiles, we first need to be familiar with the kinds of universal cultural variables found in most societies that make up unique clusters and provide a snapshot of the overall character of a specific group. Although there are countless individual variables, one approach to categorizing interdependent variables is given by Harris and Moran, who have identified eight categories that form the subsystems in any society.[18] This systems approach to understanding cultural and national variables—and their effects on work behavior—is consistent with the model shown in Exhibit 3-1. The following sections describe these eight categories and explain their implications.

Kinship   A kinship system is the system adopted by a given society to guide family relationships. Whereas in the United States this system consists primarily of the nuclear family (which is increasingly represented by single-parent families), in many other parts of the world the kinship system consists of an extended family with many members, spanning several generations. This extended, closely knit family, typical in many Eastern nations, may influence corporate activities in cases where family loyalty is given primary consideration—such as when contracts are awarded or when employees are hired (and a family member is always selected over a more suitable candidate from outside the family). In these family-oriented societies, such practices are pervasive and are taken for granted. Foreign managers often find themselves locked out of important decisions when dealing with family businesses. If, however, they take the time to learn the local cultural expectations regarding families, they will notice predictable patterns of behavior and be better prepared to deal with them. Such traditional practices are exemplified in the experience of an Asian MBA, educated in the United States, when he presented a more up-to-date business plan to his uncle, the managing director of a medium-sized firm in India:

> *The family astrologer attended the meeting and vetoed the plan. Later, the nephew persisted and asked the astrologer to reconsider the plan. The astrologer recommended various ceremonies after which the astral signs would probably bend toward the plan.*[19]

Education   The formal or informal education of workers in a foreign firm, received from whatever source, greatly affects the expectations placed on those workers in the workplace. It also influences managers' choices about recruitment and staffing practices, training programs, and leadership styles. Training and development programs, for example, need to be consistent with the general level of educational preparation in that country.

Economy   Whatever the economic system, the means of production and distribution in a society (and the resulting effects on individuals and groups) has a powerful influence on such organizational processes as sourcing, distribution, incentives, and repatriation of capital. At this time of radically changing political systems, it appears that the drastic differences between capitalist and socialist systems will have less effect on multinational corporations (MNCs) than in the past.

Politics   The system of government in a society, whether democratic, communist, or dictatorial, imposes varying constraints on an organization and its freedom to do business. It is the manager's job to understand the political system and how it affects organizational processes to negotiate positions within that system and to manage effectively the mutual concerns of the host country and guest company. As demonstrated by the difficulties that McDonald's had in training Russian workers for its Moscow restaurant (discussed previously in this chapter), the political and economic subsystems of a country often dominate other cultural systems.

Religion   The spiritual beliefs of a society are often so powerful that they transcend other cultural aspects. Religion commonly underlies both moral and economic norms. In the United States, the effects of religion in the workplace are limited (other than a generalized belief in hard work, which stems from the Protestant work ethic), whereas in other countries religious beliefs and practices often influence everyday business transactions and on-the-job behaviors. For example, in India, McDonald's does not serve beef or pork out of respect for Hindu and Muslim customers. Also, in a long-standing tradition based on the Qur'an and the sayings of Muhammad, Arabs consult with senior members of the ruling families or the community regarding business decisions. Hindus, Buddhists, and some Muslims believe in the concept of destiny, or fate. In Islamic countries, the idea of *insha Allah,* that is, "God willing," prevails. In some Western countries, religious organizations, such as the Roman Catholic Church, play a major cultural role through moral and political influence.

One of the ways that the Islamic faith affects the operations of international firms involves the charging of interest:

> *The kingdom of Saudi Arabia observes Sharia, which is Islamic law based on both the Qur'an and the Hadith—the traditions of the Prophet Muhammad. Under these codes, interest is banned, and both the giver and the taker of interest are equally damned. This means that the modern Western banking system is technically illegal. A debate has begun on the interpretation of the concept of interest. The kingdom's religious scholars, the ulema, view all interest, or rib'a, as banned. Some have challenged that interpretation as too restrictive, however, and have called for a more liberal interpretation. Their view is that Muhammad referred only to excessive interest when he condemned usury. Should something come of this debate, it would help establish a legal framework for dealing with Saudi Arabia's banking problems, such as steep drops in profits, and end the legal limbo of Western-style banking in the kingdom.*[20]

Associations   Many and various types of associations arise out of the formal and informal groups that make up a society. Whether these associations are based on religious, social, professional, or trade affiliations, managers should be familiar with them and the role they may play in business interactions.

Health   The system of health care in a country affects employee productivity, expectations, and attitudes toward physical fitness and its role in the workplace. These expectations will influence managerial decisions regarding health care benefits, insurance, physical facilities, sick days, and so forth.

Recreation   Closely associated with other cultural factors, recreation includes the way in which people use their leisure time, as well as their attitudes toward leisure and their choice of with whom to socialize. Workers' attitudes toward recreation can affect their work behavior and their perception of the role of work in their lives.

CULTURAL VALUE DIMENSIONS

Cultural variables result from unique sets of shared values among different groups of people. Most of the variations between cultures stem from underlying value systems, which cause people to behave differently under similar circumstances. **Values** are a society's ideas about what is good or bad, right or wrong—such as the widespread belief that stealing is immoral and unfair. Values determine how individuals will probably respond in any given circumstance. As a powerful component of a society's culture, values are communicated through the eight subsystems just described and are passed from generation to generation. Interaction and pressure among these subsystems (or more recently from foreign cultures) may provide the impetus for slow change. The dissolution of the Soviet Union and the formation of the Commonwealth of Independent States is an example of extreme political change resulting from internal economic pressures and external encouragement to change.

Project GLOBE Cultural Dimensions

Recent research results on cultural dimensions have been made available by the GLOBE (Global Leadership and Organizational Behavior Effectiveness) Project team. The team comprises 170 researchers who have collected data over seven years on cultural values and practices and leadership attributes from 18,000 managers in sixty-two countries. Those managers were from a wide variety of industries and sizes of organizations from every corner of the globe. The team identified nine cultural dimensions that distinguish one society from another and have important managerial implications: assertiveness, future orientation, performance orientation, humane orientation, gender differentiation, uncertainty avoidance, power distance, institutional collectivism versus individualism, and in-group collectivism. Only the first four are discussed here; this avoids confusion for readers since the other five dimensions are similar to those researched by Hofstede, which are presented in the next section. (Other research results from the GLOBE Project are presented in subsequent chapters where applicable, such as in the Leadership section in Chapter 11.) The descriptions are as follows and selected results are shown in Exhibit 3-3.[21]

EXHIBIT 3-3   Selected Cultural Dimensions Rankings from the Globe Research Project

Country Rankings on Assertiveness

Least Assertive Countries in GLOBE		Medium Assertive Countries in GLOBE		Most Assertive Countries in GLOBE	
Sweden	3.38	Egypt	3.91	Spain	4.42
New Zealand	3.42	Ireland	3.92	United States	4.55
Switzerland	3.47	Philippines	4.01	Greece	4.58
Japan	3.59	Ecuador	4.09	Austria	4.62
Kuwait	3.63	France	4.13	Germany (Former East)	4.73

Country Rankings on Performance Orientation

Least Performance-Oriented Countries in GLOBE		Medium Performance-Oriented Countries in GLOBE		Most Performance-Oriented Countries in GLOBE	
Russia	2.88	Sweden	3.72	United States	4.49
Argentina	3.08	Israel	3.85	Taiwan	4.56
Greece	3.20	Spain	4.01	New Zealand	4.72
Venezuela	3.32	England	4.08	Hong Kong	4.80
Italy	3.58	Japan	4.22	Singapore	4.90

Country Rankings on Future Orientation

Least Future-Oriented Countries in GLOBE		Medium Future-Oriented Countries in GLOBE		Most Future-Oriented Countries in GLOBE	
Russia	2.88	Slovenia	3.59	Denmark	4.44
Argentina	3.08	Egypt	3.86	Canada (English-speaking)	4.44
Poland	3.11	Ireland	3.98	Netherlands	4.61
Italy	3.25	Australia	4.09	Switzerland	4.73
Kuwait	3.26	India	4.10	Singapore	5.07

Country Rankings on Humane Orientation

Least Humane-Oriented Countries in GLOBE		Medium Humane-Oriented Countries in GLOBE		Most Humane-Oriented Countries in GLOBE	
Germany (Former West)	3.18	Hong Kong	3.90	Indonesia	4.69
Spain	3.32	Sweden	4.10	Egypt	4.73
France	3.40	Taiwan	4.11	Malaysia	4.87
Singapore	3.49	United States	4.17	Ireland	4.96
Brazil	3.66	New Zealand	4.32	Philippines	5.12

SOURCE: Adapted from Mansour Javidan and Robert J. House, "Cultural Acumen for the Global Manager: Lessons from Project GLOBE," *Organizational Dynamics* (Spring 2001): 289–305.

Assertiveness   This dimension refers to how much people in a society are expected to be tough, confrontational, and competitive versus modest and tender. Austria and Germany, for example, are highly assertive societies that value competition and have a "can-do" attitude. This compares with Sweden and Japan, less assertive societies, which tend to prefer warm and cooperative relations and harmony. The GLOBE team concluded that those countries have sympathy for the weak and emphasize loyalty and solidarity.

Future Orientation   This dimension refers to the level of importance a society attaches to future-oriented behaviors such as planning and investing in the future. Switzerland and Singapore, high on this dimension, are inclined to save for the future and have a longer time horizon for decisions. This perspective compares with societies such as Russia and Argentina, which tend to plan more in the shorter term and place more emphasis on instant gratification.

Performance Orientation   This dimension measures the importance of performance improvement and excellence in society and refers to whether or not people are encouraged to strive for continued improvement. Singapore, Hong Kong, and the United States score high on this dimension; typically, this means that people tend to take initiative and have a sense of urgency and the confidence to get things done. Countries like Russia and Italy have low scores on this dimension; they hold other priorities ahead of performance, such as tradition, loyalty, family, and background, and they associate competition with defeat.

Humane Orientation   This dimension measures the extent to which a society encourages and rewards people for being fair, altruistic, generous, caring, and kind. Highest on this dimension are the Philippines, Ireland, Malaysia, and Egypt, indicating a focus on sympathy and support for the weak. In those societies paternalism and patronage are important, and people are usually friendly and tolerant and value harmony. This compares with Spain, France, and the former West Germany, which scored low on this dimension; people in these countries give more importance to power and material possessions, as well as self-enhancement.

Clearly, research results such as these are helpful to managers seeking to be successful in cross-cultural interactions. Anticipating cultural similarities and differences allows managers to develop the behaviors and skills necessary to act and decide in a manner appropriate to the local societal norms and expectations.

Cultural Clusters

Gupta et al (2002). from the GLOBE research team also analyzed their data on the nine cultural dimensions to determine where similarities cluster geographically. Their results support the existence of ten cultural clusters: South Asia, Anglo, Arab, Germanic Europe, Latin Europe, Eastern Europe, Confucian Asia, Latin America, Sub-Sahara Africa, and Nordic Europe. They point out the usefulness to managers of these clusters:

> *Multinational corporations may find it less risky and more profitable to expand into more similar cultures rather than those which are drastically different.[22]*

These clusters are shown in Exhibit 3-4. To compare two of their cluster findings, for example, Gupta et al (2002). describe the Germanic cluster as masculine, assertive, individualistic and result-oriented. This compares with the Latin American cluster, which they characterize as practicing high power distance, low performance orientation, uncertainty avoidance, and collective:

> *"Latin American societies tend to enact life as it comes, taking its unpredictability as a fact of life, and not overly worrying about results"[23]*

Hofstede's Value Dimensions

Earlier research resulted in a pathbreaking framework for understanding how basic values underlie organizational behavior; this framework was developed by Hofstede, based

EXHIBIT 3-4   Geographic Culture Clusters

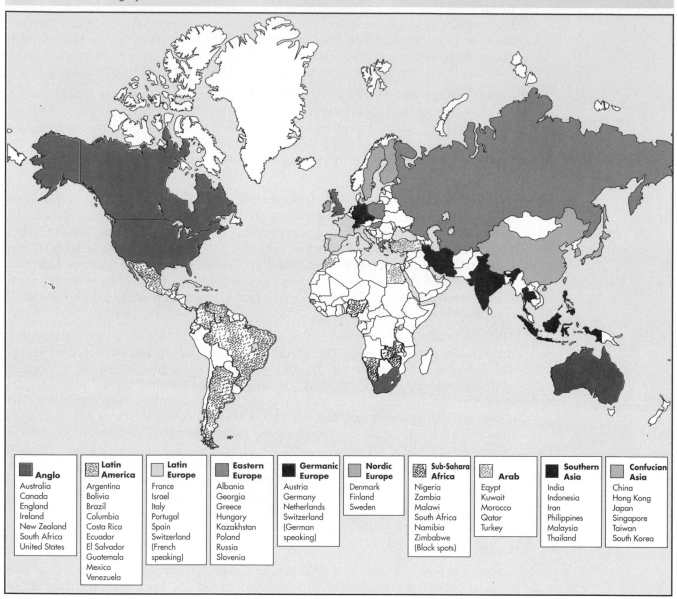

Anglo	**Latin America**	**Latin Europe**	**Eastern Europe**	**Germanic Europe**	**Nordic Europe**	**Sub-Sahara Africa**	**Arab**	**Southern Asia**	**Confucian Asia**
Australia	Argentina	France	Albania	Austria	Denmark	Nigeria	Egypt	India	China
Canada	Bolivia	Israel	Georgia	Germany	Finland	Zambia	Kuwait	Indonesia	Hong Kong
England	Brazil	Italy	Greece	Netherlands	Sweden	Malawi	Morocco	Iran	Japan
Ireland	Columbia	Portugal	Hungary	Switzerland		South Africa	Qatar	Philippines	Singapore
New Zealand	Costa Rica	Spain	Kazakhstan	(German		Namibia	Turkey	Malaysia	Taiwan
South Africa	Ecuador	Switzerland	Poland	speaking)		Zimbabwe		Thailand	South Korea
United States	El Salvador	(French	Russia			(Black spots)			
	Guatemala	speaking)	Slovenia						
	Mexico								
	Venezuela								

SOURCE: Data from V. Gupta, P. J. Hanes, and P. Dorfman, *Journal of World Business,* 37, 1 (Spring 2002): 13.

on his research on over 116,000 people in 50 countries. He proposed four value dimensions: power distance, uncertainty avoidance, individualism, and masculinity.[24] We should be cautious when interpreting these results, however, because his research findings are based on a sample drawn from one multinational firm, IBM, and because he does not account for within-country differences in multicultural countries. Although we introduce these value dimensions here to aid in the understanding of different cultures, their relevance and application to management functions will be discussed in later chapters.

The first of these value dimensions, **power distance**, is the level of acceptance by a society of the unequal distribution of power in institutions. In the workplace, inequalities in power are normal, as evidenced in hierarchical boss–subordinate relationships. However, the extent to which subordinates accept unequal power is societally determined. In countries in which people display high power distance (such as Malaysia, the Philippines, and Mexico), employees acknowledge the boss's authority simply by respecting that individual's formal position in the hierarchy, and they seldom bypass the chain of command. This respectful response results, predictably, in a centralized structure and autocratic leadership. In countries where people display low power distance (such as

Austria, Denmark, and Israel), superiors and subordinates are apt to regard one another as equal in power, resulting in more harmony and cooperation. Clearly, an autocratic management style is not likely to be well received in low power-distance countries.

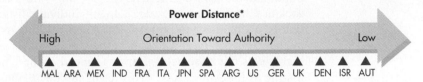

Power Distance*

High   Orientation Toward Authority   Low

MAL ARA MEX IND FRA ITA JPN SPA ARG US GER UK DEN ISR AUT

*Not to scale—indicates relative magnitude.
Note: ARA = Arab Countries
        AUT = Austria

SOURCE: Based on G. Hofstede, "National Cultures in Four Dimensions," *International Studies of Management and Organization*, Spring–Summer 1983.

The second value dimension, **uncertainty avoidance**, refers to the extent to which people in a society feel threatened by ambiguous situations. Countries with a high level of uncertainty avoidance (such as Japan, Portugal, and Greece) tend to have strict laws and procedures to which their people adhere closely, and a strong sense of nationalism prevails. In a business context, this value results in formal rules and procedures designed to provide more security and greater career stability. Managers have a propensity for low-risk decisions, employees exhibit little aggressiveness, and lifetime employment is common. In countries with lower levels of uncertainty avoidance (such as Denmark, Great Britain, and, to a lesser extent, the United States), nationalism is less pronounced, and protests and other such activities are tolerated. As a consequence, company activities are less structured and less formal, some managers take more risks, and high job mobility is common.

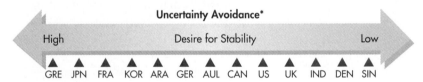

Uncertainty Avoidance*

High   Desire for Stability   Low

GRE JPN FRA KOR ARA GER AUL CAN US UK IND DEN SIN

*Not to scale—indicates relative magnitude.
Note: AUL = Australia

SOURCE: Based on G. Hofstede, 1983.

The third of Hofstede's value dimensions, **individualism**, refers to the tendency of people to look after themselves and their immediate families only and to neglect the needs of society. In countries that prize individualism (such as the United States, Great Britain, and Australia), democracy, individual initiative, and achievement are highly valued; the relationship of the individual to organizations is one of independence on an emotional level, if not on an economic level.

In countries such as Pakistan and Panama, where low individualism prevails—that is, where **collectivism** predominates—one finds tight social frameworks, emotional dependence on belonging to "the organization," and a strong belief in group decisions. People from a collectivist country, like Japan, believe in the will of the group rather than that of the individual, and their pervasive collectivism exerts control over individual members through social pressure and the fear of humiliation. The society valorizes harmony and saving face, whereas individualistic cultures generally emphasize self-respect, autonomy, and independence. Hiring and promotion practices in collectivist societies are based on paternalism rather than achievement or personal capabilities, which are valued in individualistic societies. Other management practices (such as the use of quality circles in Japanese factories) reflect the emphasis on group decision-making processes in collectivist societies.

Hofstede's findings indicate that most countries scoring high on individualism have both a higher gross national product and a freer political system than those countries scoring low on individualism—that is, there is a strong relationship among individualism, wealth, and a political system with balanced power. Other studies have found that the output of individuals working in a group setting differs between individualistic and collectivist societies. In the United States, a highly individualistic culture, social loafing is common—that is, people tend to perform less when working as part of a group than when working alone.[25] In a comparative study of the United States and the People's Republic of China (a highly collectivist society), Earley found that the Chinese did not exhibit as much social loafing as the Americans.[26] This result can be attributed to Chinese cultural values, which subordinate personal interests to the greater goal of helping the group succeed.

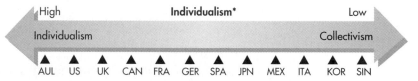

*Not to scale—indicates relative magnitude.

SOURCE: Based on G. Hofstede, 1983.

The fourth value dimension, **masculinity**, refers to the degree of traditionally "masculine" values—assertiveness, materialism, and a lack of concern for others—that prevail in a society. In comparison, femininity emphasizes "feminine" values—a concern for others, for relationships, and for the quality of life. In highly masculine societies (Japan and Austria, for example), women are generally expected to stay home and raise a family. In organizations, one finds considerable job stress, and organizational interests generally encroach on employees' private lives. In countries with low masculinity (such as Switzerland and New Zealand), one finds less conflict and job stress, more women in high-level jobs, and a reduced need for assertiveness. The United States lies somewhat in the middle, according to Hofstede's research. American women typically are encouraged to work, and families are often are able to get some support for child care (through day-care centers and maternity leaves).

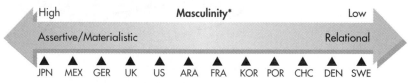

*Not to scale—indicates relative magnitude.

SOURCE: Based on G. Hofstede, 1983.

The four cultural value dimensions proposed by Hofstede do not operate in isolation; rather, they are interdependent and interactive—and thus complex—in their effects on work attitudes and behaviors. For example, in a 2000 study of small to medium-sized firms in Australia, Finland, Greece, Indonesia, Mexico, Norway, and Sweden, based on Hofstede's dimensions, Steensma, Marino, and Weaver found that "entrepreneurs from societies that are masculine and individualistic have a lower appreciation for cooperative strategies as compared to entrepreneurs from societies that are feminine and collectivist. Masculine cultures view cooperation in general as a sign of weakness and individualistic societies place a high value on independence and control."[27] In addition, they found that high levels of uncertainty avoidance prompted more cooperation, such as developing alliances to share risk.

Trompenaars's Value Dimensions

Fons Trompenaars also researched value dimensions; his work was spread over a ten-year period, with 15,000 managers from 28 countries, representing 47 national cultures. Some of those dimensions, which we are not discussing elsewhere and which affect daily business activities, are shown in Exhibit 3-5, along with the descriptions and the placement of nine of the countries in approximate relative order.[28] If we view the placement of these countries along a range from personal to societal, based on each dimension, some interesting patterns emerge.[29] One can see from the exhibit that the same countries tend to be at similar positions on all dimensions, with the exception of the emotional orientation.

EXHIBIT 3-5   Trompenaars's Value Dimensions

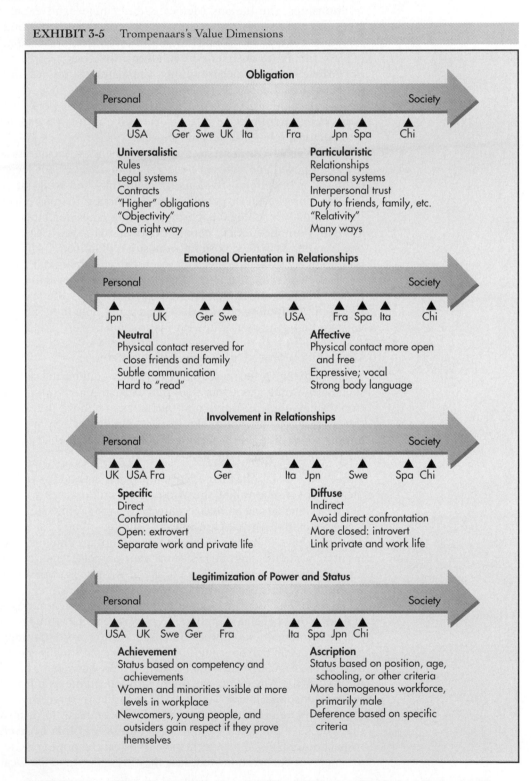

SOURCE: Adapted from Lisa Hoecklin, *Managing Cultural Differences* (Wokingham, England: Addison-Wesley and The Economist Intelligence Unit, 1995. Based on F. Trompenaars, *Riding the Waves of Culture* (London: Nicholas Brealey, 1993).

Looking at Trompenaars's dimension of **universalism versus particularism,** we find that the universalistic approach applies rules and systems objectively, without consideration for individual circumstances, whereas the particularistic approach—more common in Asia and in Spain, for example—puts the first obligation on relationships and is more subjective. Trompenaars found, for example, that people in particularistic societies are more likely to pass on insider information to a friend than those in universalistic societies.

In the **neutral versus affective** dimension, the focus is on the emotional orientation of relationships. The Italians, Mexicans, and Chinese, for example, would openly express emotions even in a business situation, whereas the British and Japanese would consider such displays unprofessional; they, in turn would be regarded as "hard to 'read'."

As far as involvement in relationships goes, people tend to be either **specific or diffuse** (or somewhere along that dimension). Managers in specific-oriented cultures—the United States, United Kingdom, France—separate work and personal issues and relationships; they compartmentalize their work and private lives, and they are more open and direct. In diffuse-oriented cultures—Sweden, China—work spills over into personal relationships and vice versa.

In the **achievement versus ascription** dimension, the question that arises is "What is the source of power and status in society?" In an achievement society, the source of status and influence is based on individual achievement—how well one performs the job and what level of education and experience one has to offer. Therefore, women, minorities, and young people usually have equal opportunity to attain position based on their achievements. In an ascription-oriented society, people ascribe status on the basis of class, age, gender, and so on; one is more likely to be born into a position of influence. Hiring in Indonesia, for example, is more likely to be based on who you are than is the case in Germany or Australia.

It is clear, then, that a lot of what goes on at work can be explained by differences in people's innate value systems, as described by Hofstede and Trompenaars, based on their research. Awareness of such differences and how they influence work behavior can be very useful to you as a future international manager.

Critical Operational Value Differences

After studying various research results about cultural variables, it helps to identify some specific culturally based variables that cause frequent problems for Americans in international management. Important variables are those involving conflicting orientations toward time, change, material factors, and individualism. We try to understand these operational value differences because they strongly influence a person's attitudes and probable response to work situations.

Time   Americans often experience much conflict and frustration because of differences in the concept of time around the world—that is, differences in temporal values. To Americans, time is a valuable and limited resource; it is to be saved, scheduled, and spent with precision, lest we waste it. The clock is always running—time is money. Therefore, deadlines and schedules have to be met. When others are not on time for meetings, Americans may feel insulted; when meetings digress from their purpose, Americans tend to become impatient. Similar attitudes toward time are found in Western Europe and elsewhere.

In many parts of the world, however, people view time from different and longer perspectives, often based on religious beliefs (such as reincarnation, in which time does not end at death), on a belief in destiny, or on pervasive social attitudes. In Latin America, for example, a common attitude toward time is *mañana,* a word that literally means "tomorrow." A Latin American person using this word, however, usually means an indefinite time in the near future. Similarly, the word *bukra* in Arabic can mean "tomorrow" or "some time in the future." While Americans usually regard a deadline as a firm commitment, Arabs often regard a deadline imposed on them as an insult. They feel that important things take a long time and therefore cannot be rushed. To ask an Arab to rush something, then, is to imply that you have not given him an important task or that he would not treat that task with respect. International managers have to be careful not to offend people—or lose contracts or employee cooperation—because they misunderstand the local language of time.

Change   Based largely on long-standing religious beliefs, values regarding the acceptance of change and the pace of change can vary immensely among cultures. Western people generally believe that an individual can exert some control over the future and can manipulate events, particularly in a business context—that is, individuals feel they have some internal control. In many non-Western societies, however, control is considered external; people generally believe in destiny, or the will of their God, and therefore adopt a passive attitude or even feel hostility toward those introducing the "evil" of change. In societies that place great importance on tradition (such as China), one small area of change may threaten an entire way of life. Webber describes just how difficult it is for an Asian male, concerned about tradition, to change his work habits:

> *To the Chinese, the introduction of power machinery meant that he had to throw over not only habits of work but a whole ideology; it implied dissatisfaction with the ways of his father's way of life in all its aspects. If the old loom must be discarded, then 100 other things must be discarded with it, for there are somehow no adequate substitutes.[30]*

International firms are agents of change throughout the world. Some changes are more popular than others; for example, McDonald's hamburgers are apparently one change the Chinese are willing to accept.

The New Idea

SOURCE: Courtesy McDonald's Corporation.

Material Factors   In large part, Americans consume resources at a far greater rate than most of the rest of the world. Their attitude toward nature—that it is there to be used for their benefit—differs from the attitudes of Indians and Koreans, for example, whose worship of nature is part of their religious beliefs. Whereas Americans often value physical goods and status symbols, many non-Westerners find these things unimportant; they value the aesthetic and the spiritual realm. Such differences in attitude have implications for management functions, such as motivation and reward systems, because the proverbial carrot must be appropriate to the employee's value system.

Individualism   In general, Americans tend to work and conduct their private lives independently, valuing individual achievement, accomplishments, promotions, and wealth

EXHIBIT 3-6   Fundamental Differences Between Japanese and Mexican Culture That Affect Business Organizations

Dimension	Japanese Culture	Mexican Culture
Hierarchical nature	Rigid in rank and most communication; blurred in authority and responsibility	Rigid in all aspects
Individualism vs. collectivism	Highly collective culture; loyalty to work group dominates; group harmony very important	Collective relative to family group; don't transfer loyalty to work group; individualistic outside family
Attitudes toward work	Work is sacred duty; acquiring skills, working hard, thriftiness, patience and perseverance are virtues	Work is means to support self and family; leisure more important than work
Time orientation	Balanced perspective; future oriented; monochronic in dealings with outside world	Present oriented; time is imprecise; time commitments become desirable objectives
Approach to problem solving	Holistic, reliance on intuition, pragmatic, consensus important	Reliance on intuition and emotion, individual approach
Fatalism	Fatalism leads to preparation	Fatalism makes planning, disciplined routine unnatural
View of human nature	Intrinsically good	Mixture of good and evil

SOURCE: J. J. Lawrence and Ryh-song Yeh, "The Influence of Mexican Culture on the Use of Japanese Manufacturing Techniques in Mexico," *Management International Review* 34, no. 1 (1994): 49–66.

above any group goals. In many other countries, individualism is not valued (as discussed previously in the context of Hofstede's work). In China, for example, much more of a "we" consciousness prevails, and the group is the basic building block of social life and work. For the Chinese, conformity and cooperation take precedence over individual achievement, and the emphasis is on the strength of the family or community—the predominant attitude being, "We all rise or fall together."

International managers often face conflicts in the workplace as a result of differences in these four basic values of time, change, materialism, and individualism. If these operational value differences and their likely consequences are anticipated, managers can adjust expectations, communications, work organization, schedules, incentive systems, and so forth to provide for more constructive outcomes for the company and its employees. Some of these operational differences are shown in Exhibit 3-6, using Japan and Mexico as examples. Note, in particular, the factors of time, individualism change (fatalism), and materialism (attitudes toward work) expressed in the exhibit.

THE INTERNET AND CULTURE

Koreans are an impatient people, and we like technology. So everyone wants the fastest Internet connection.

HWANG KYU-JUNE[31]

We would be remiss if we did not acknowledge the contemporary phenomenon of the increasingly pervasive use of the Internet in society, for it seems to be encroaching on many of the social variables discussed earlier—in particular associations, education, and the economy. In South Korea, for example, where information technology makes up about 30 percent of the gross domestic product (GDP), there is an obsession for anything digital. Over 70 percent of homes are connected to a high-speed Internet service. That compares with 50 percent in Canada—the next highest user—and 23 percent in the United States.[32] This phenomenon seems to be changing the lives of many Koreans. Teenagers, used to hanging out at the mall, now do so at the country's 20,000 personal computer (PC) parlors to watch movies, check e-mail, and surf the Net for as little as $1US. Korean housewives are on a waiting list for ADSL lines when the $35 billion high-speed government telecommunications project is completed in 2005. By then 95 percent of Korean households will have Internet access.[33]

At the same time that the Internet is affecting culture, culture is also affecting how the Internet is used. One of the pervasive ways that culture is determining how the Internet may be used in various countries is through the local attitude to **information privacy**—the right to control information about oneself—as observed in the following quote:

You Americans just don't seem to care about privacy, do you?

SWEDISH EXECUTIVE [34]

While Americans collect data about consumers' backgrounds and what they buy, often trading that information with other internal or external contacts, the Swedes, for example, are astounded that this is done, especially without governmental oversight.[35] The Swedes are required to register all databases of personal information with the Data Inspection Board (DIB), their federal regulatory agency for privacy, and to get permission from that board before that data can be used. Indeed, the Swedish system is typical of most countries in Europe in their societal approaches to privacy.[36] One example of a blocked data transfer occurred when Sweden would not allow U.S. airlines to transmit passenger information, such as wheelchair need and meal preferences, to the United States.[37]

Generally, in Europe, each person must be informed, and given the chance to object, if the information about that person is going to be used for direct marketing purposes or released to another party. That data cannot be used for secondary purposes if the consumer objects.

> *In Italy, data cannot be sent outside—even to other EU countries—without the explicit consent of the data subject.*
>
> *In Spain, all direct mail has to include the name and address of the data owner so that the data subject is able to exercise his rights of access, correction, and removal.*[38]

The manner in which Europe views information privacy has its roots in culture and history, leading to a different value set regarding privacy. The preservation of privacy is considered a human right, perhaps partially as a result of an internalized fear about how personal records were used in war times in Europe. In addition, research by Smith on the relationship between level of concern about privacy and Hofstede's cultural dimensions revealed that high levels of uncertainty avoidance were associated with the European approach to privacy, whereas higher levels of individualism, masculinity, and power distance were associated with the U.S. approach.[39]

It seems, then, that societal culture and the resultant effects on business models can render the assumptions about the "global" nature of information technology incorrect. U.S. businesspeople, brought up on a strong diet of the market economy, need to realize that they will often need to "localize" their use of IT to different value sets about its use.

DEVELOPING CULTURAL PROFILES

Managers can gather considerable information on cultural variables from current research, personal observation, and discussions with people. From these sources, managers can develop cultural profiles of various countries—composite pictures of working environments, people's attitudes, and norms of behavior. As we have previously discussed, these profiles are often highly generalized; many subcultures, of course, may exist within a country. However, managers can use these profiles to anticipate drastic differences in the level of motivation, communication, ethics, loyalty, and individual and group productivity that may be encountered in a given country. More such homework may have helped the GM–Daewoo joint venture in Korea, which ended after years of acrimonious relations. Executives from both sides acknowledge that they "seriously underestimated the obstacles posed to their three-continent car-making experiment by divergent cultures and business aspirations, not to mention the different languages."[40]

It is relatively simple for Americans to pull together a descriptive profile of U.S. culture, even though regional and individual differences exist, because Americans know themselves and because researchers have thoroughly studied U.S. culture. The results of one such study by Harris and Moran are shown in Exhibit 3-7, which provides a basis of comparison with other cultures and, thus, suggests the likely differences in workplace behaviors.

EXHIBIT 3-7   Americans at a Glance

1. *Goal and achievement oriented*—Americans think they can accomplish just about anything, given enough time, money, and technology.
2. *Highly organized and institutionally minded*—Americans prefer a society that is institutionally strong, secure, and tidy or well kept.
3. *Freedom-loving and self-reliant*—Americans fought a revolution and subsequent wars to preserve their concept of democracy, so they resent too much control or interference, especially by government or external forces. They believe in an ideal that all persons are created equal; though they sometimes fail to fully live that ideal, they strive through law to promote equal opportunity and to confront their own racism or prejudice.

    They also idealize the self-made person who rises form poverty and adversity, and think they can influence and create their own futures. Control of one's destiny is popularly expressed as "doing your own thing." Americans think, for the most part, that with determination and initiative, one can achieve whatever one sets out to do and thus, fulfill one's individual human potential.
4. *Work oriented and efficient*—Americans possess a strong work ethic, though they are learning in the present generation to constructively enjoy leisure time. They are conscious of time and efficient in doing things. They tinker with gadgets and technological systems, always searching for easier, better, more efficient ways to accomplish tasks.
5. *Friendly and informal*—Americans reject the traditional privileges of royalty and class but defer to those with affluence and power. Although informal in greeting and dress, they are a noncontact culture (e.g., usually avoid embracing in public) and maintain a certain physical/psychological distance with others (e.g., about 2 feet).
6. *Competitive and aggressive*—Americans in play or business generally are so oriented because of their drives to achieve and succeed. This is partially traced to their heritage of having to overcome a wilderness and hostile elements in their environment.
7. *Values in transition*—Traditional American values of family loyalty, respect and care of the aged, marriage and the nuclear family, patriotism, material acquisition, forthrightness, and the like are undergoing profound reevaluation as people search for new meanings.
8. *Generosity*—Although Americans seemingly emphasize material values, they are a sharing people, as has been demonstrated in the Marshall Plan, foreign aid programs, refugee assistance, and their willingness at home and abroad to espouse a good cause and to help neighbors in need. They tend to be altruistic and some would say naive as a people.

SOURCE: From *Managing Cultural Differences* by Philip R. Harris and Robert T. Moran, 5th ed. Copyright © 2000 by Gulf Publishing Company, Houston, TX. Used with permission. All rights reserved.

It is not so easy, however, to pull together descriptive cultural profiles of peoples in other countries unless one has lived there and been intricately involved with those people. Still, managers can make a start by using what comparative research and literature are available. The following Comparative Management in Focus section provides brief, generalized country profiles based on a synthesis of research, primarily from Hofstede[41] and England,[42] as well as numerous other sources.[43] These profiles illustrate how to synthesize information and gain a sense of the character of a society—from which implications may be drawn about how to manage more effectively in that society. More extensive implications and applications related to managerial functions are drawn in later chapters.

In 2004, however, anecdotal evidence pointed to some convergence with Western business culture is taking place—resulting from Japan's economic contraction and subsequent bankruptcies. Focus on the group, lifetime employment, and a pension has given way to a more competitive business environment with job security no longer guaranteed and an emphasis on performance-based pay. This has led Japan's "salarymen" to recognize the need for personal responsibility on the job and in their lives. Although only a few years ago emphasis was on the group, Japan's long economic slump seems to be causing some cultural restructuring of the individual. Corporate Japan is changing from a culture of consensus and groupthink to one touting the need for an "era of personal responsibility" as a solution to revitalize its competitive position in the global marketplace.[44]

To tell you the truth, it's hard to think for yourself, says Mr. Kuzuoka . . . [but, if you don't] . . . in this age of cutthroat competition, you'll just end up drowning.[45]

Comparative Management in Focus

Profiles in Culture

Japan, Germany, and South Korea

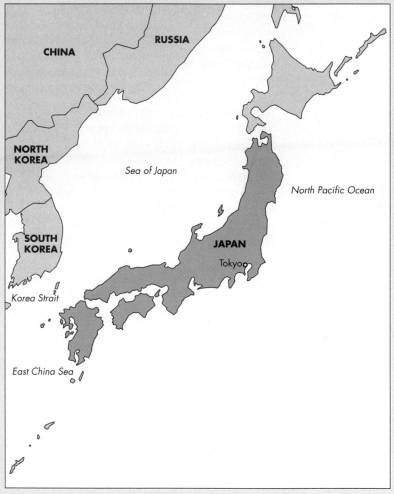

Map 3-2

JAPAN

Now I have to stand firmly on my own and think for myself. I wish I had realized this earlier in life.... Building my life around the company was a big mistake.

—Forty-year employee at a Japanese company[46]

As a result of economic decline and global competition (discussed at the end of this section), in 2004 we see evidence in cities of changes in Japan's business culture. However, the underlying cultural values still predominate—for now anyway.

Much of Japanese culture—and the basis of working relationships—can be explained by the principle of *wa*, "peace and harmony." This principle, embedded in the value the Japanese attribute to *amae* ("indulgent love"), probably originated in the Shinto religion, which focuses on spiritual and physical harmony. *Amae* results in *shinyo*, which refers to the mutual confidence, faith, and honor necessary for successful business relationships. Japan ranks high on pragmatism, masculinity, and uncertainty avoidance, and fairly high on power distance. At the same time, much importance is attached to loyalty, empathy, and the guidance of subordinates. The result is a mix of authoritarianism and humanism in the workplace, similar to a family system. These cultural roots are evident in a very homogeneous managerial value system, with strong middle management, strong working relationships, strong seniority systems that stress rank, and an emphasis on looking after employees. The principle of *wa* carries forth into the work group—the building block of Japanese business. The Japanese strongly identify and thus seek to cooperate with their work groups. The emphasis is on participative management, consensus problem solving, and decision making with a patient, long-term perspective. Open expression and conflict are discouraged, and it is of paramount importance to avoid the shame of not fulfilling one's duty. These elements of work culture result in a devotion to work, collective responsibility, and a high degree of employee productivity.

If we extend this cultural profile to its implications for specific behaviors in the workplace, we can draw a comparison with common American behaviors. Most of those behaviors seem to be opposite to those of their counterparts; it is no wonder that many misunderstandings and conflicts in the workplace arise between Americans and Japanese (see Exhibit 3-8). For example, a majority of the attitudes and behaviors of many Japanese stems from a high level of collectivism, compared with a high level of individualism common to Americans. This contrast is highlighted in the center of Exhibit 3-8—"Maintain the group"—compared with "Protect the individual." In addition, the strict social order of the Japanese permeates the workplace in adherence to organizational hierarchy and seniority and in loyalty to the

EXHIBIT 3-8   The American–Japanese Cultural Divide

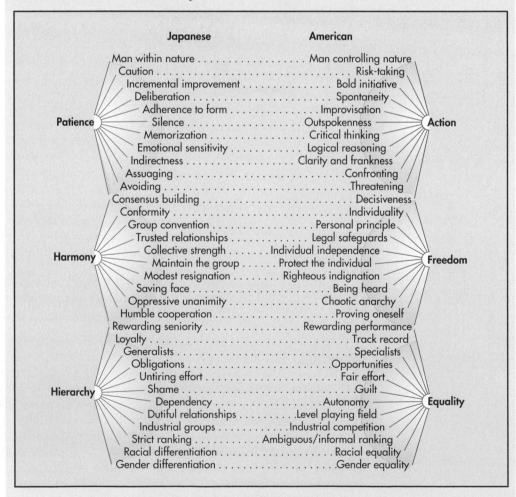

SOURCE: R. G. Linowes, "The Japanese Manager's Traumatic Entry into the United States: Understanding the American-Japanese Cultural Divide," *The Academy of Management Executive VII,* no. 4 (November 1993): 24.

firm. This contrasts markedly with the typical American responses to organizational relationships and duties based on equality. In addition, the often blunt, outspoken American businessperson offends the indirectness and sensitivity of the Japanese for whom the virtue of patience is paramount, causing the silence and avoidance that so frustrates Americans.[47] As a result, Japanese businesspeople tend to think of American organizations as having no spiritual quality and little employee loyalty, and of Americans as assertive, frank, and egotistic. Their American counterparts, in turn, respond with the impression that Japanese businesspeople have little experience and are secretive, arrogant, and cautious.[48]

GERMANY

The reunited Germany is somewhat culturally diverse inasmuch as the country borders several nations. Generally, Germans rank quite high on Hofstede's dimension of individualism, although their behaviors seem less individualistic than those of Americans. They score fairly high on uncertainty avoidance and masculinity and have a relatively small need for power distance. These cultural norms show up in the Germans' preference for being around familiar people and situations; they are also reflected in their propensity to do a detailed evaluation of business deals before committing themselves.

Christianity underlies much of German culture—more than 96 percent of Germans are Catholics or Protestants. This may be why Germans tend to like rule and order in their lives, and why there is a clear public expectation of acceptable and the unacceptable ways to act. Public signs everywhere in Germany dictate what is allowed or *verboten* (forbidden). Germans are very strict with their use of time, whether for business or pleasure, frowning on inefficiency or on tardiness. In business, Germans tend to be assertive, but they downplay aggression. Decisions are not as centralized as one would expect, with hierarchical processes often giving way to consensus decision making. However, strict departmentalization is present in organizations, with centralized and final authority at the departmental manager level. Hall and Hall describe the German preference for closed doors and private space as evidence of the affinity for compartmentalization in organizations and in their own lives. They also prefer more physical space around them in conversation than do most other Europeans, and they seek privacy so as not to be overheard. German law prohibits loud noises in public areas on weekend afternoons. Germans are conservative, valuing privacy, politeness, and formality; they usually use last names and titles for all except those close to them.

In negotiations, Germans want detailed information before and during discussions, which can become lengthy. They give factors such as voice and speech control much weight. However, since Germany is a low-context society, communication is explicit, and Americans find negotiations easy to understand.[49]

SOUTH KOREA

Koreans rank high on collectivism and pragmatism, fairly low on masculinity, moderate on power distance, and quite high on uncertainty avoidance. Although greatly influenced by U.S. culture, Koreans are still very much bound to the traditional Confucian teachings of spiritualism and collectivism. Korea and its people have undergone great changes, but the respect for family, authority, formality, class, and rank remain strong. Koreans are demonstrative, friendly, quite aggressive and hard-working, and very hospitable. For the most part, they do not subscribe to participative management. Family and personal relationships are important, and connections are vital for business introductions and transactions. Business is based on honor and trust; most contracts are oral. Although achievement and competence are important to Koreans, the priority of guarding both parties' social and professional reputations is a driving force in relationships. Thus, praise predominates, and honest criticism is rare.

Further insight into the differences between U.S. and Korean culture can be derived from the following excerpted letter from Professor Jin K. Kim in Plattsburgh, New York, to his high school friend, MK, in South Korea, who just returned from a visit to the United States. MK, whom Dr. Kim had not seen for twenty years, planned to emigrate to the United States, and Dr. Kim wanted to help ward off his friend's culture shock by telling him about U.S. culture from a Korean perspective.

Dear MK,

I sincerely hope the last leg of your trip home from the five-week fact-finding visit to the United States was pleasant and informative. Although I may not have expressed my sense of exhilaration about your visit through the meager lodging accommodations and "barbaric" foods we provided, it was sheer joy to spend four weeks with you and Kyung-Ok. (Please refrain from hitting the ceiling. My use of your charming wife's name, rather than the usual Korean expression "your wife" or "your house person," is not an indication of my amorous intentions toward her as any red-blooded Korean man would suspect. Since you are planning to immigrate to this country soon, I thought you might as well begin to get used to the idea of your wife exerting her individuality. Better yet, I thought you should be warned that the moment the plane touches U.S. soil, you will lose your status as the center of your familial universe.) At any rate, please be assured that during your stay here my heart was filled with memories of our three years together in high school when we were young in Pusan.

During your visit, you called me, on several occasions, an American. What prompted you to invoke such a reference is beyond my comprehension. Was it my rusty Korean expressions? Was it my calculating mind? Was it my pitifully subservient (at least when viewed through your cultural lens) role that I was playing in my family life? Or, was it my familiarity with some facets of the cultural landscape? This may sound bewildering to you, but it is absolutely true that through all the years I have lived in this country, I never truly felt like an American. Sure, on the surface, our family followed closely many ritualistic routines of the American culture: shopping malls, dining out, PTA, Little League, picnics, camping trips, credit card shopping sprees, hot dogs, and so on. But mentally I remained stubbornly in the periphery. Naturally, then, my subjective cultural attitudes stayed staunchly Korean. Never did the inner layers of my Korean psyche yield to the invading American cultural vagaries, I thought. So, when you labeled me an American for the first time, I felt a twinge of guilt.

Several years ago, an old Korean friend of mine, who settled in the United States about the same time I did, paid a visit to Korea for the first time in some fifteen years. When he went to see his best high school friend, who was now married and had two sons, his friend's wife made a bed for him and her husband in the master bedroom, declaring that she would spend the night with the children. It was not necessarily the sexual connotation of the episode that made my friend blush; he was greatly embarrassed by the circumstance in which he imposed himself to the extent that the couple's privacy had to be violated. For his high school friend and his wife, it was clearly their age-old friendship to which the couple's privacy had to yield. MK, you might empathize rather easily with this Korean couple's state of mind, but it would be a gross mistake even to imagine there may be occasions in your adopted culture when a gesture of friendship breaks the barrier of privacy. Zealously guarding their privacy above all, Americans are marvelously adept at drawing the line where friendship—that elusive "we" feeling—stops and privacy begins…

Indeed, one of the hardest tasks you will face as an "alien" is how to find that delicate balance between your individuality (for example, privacy) and your collective identity (for example, friendship or membership in social groups).

Privacy is not the only issue that stems from this individuality–collectivity continuum. Honesty in interpersonal relationships is another point that may keep you puzzled. Americans are almost brutally honest and frank about issues that belong to public domains; they are not afraid of discussing an embarrassing topic in most graphic details as long as the topic is a matter of public concern. Equally frank and honest gestures are adopted when they discuss their own personal lives once the presumed benefits from such gestures are determined to outweigh the risks involved. Accordingly, it is not uncommon to encounter friends who volunteer personally embarrassing and even shameful information lest you find it out from other sources. Are Americans equally straightforward and forthcoming in laying out heartfelt personal criticisms directed at their friends? Not likely. Their otherwise acute sense of honesty becomes significantly muted when they face the unpleasant task of being negative toward their personal friends. The fear of an emotion-draining confrontation and the virtue of being polite force them to put on a facade or mask.

The perfectly accepted social behavior of telling "white lies" is a good example. The social and personal virtues of accepting such lies are grounded in the belief that the potential damage that can be inflicted by directly telling a friend the hurtful truth far outweighs the potential benefit that the friend could gain from it. Instead of telling a hurtful truth directly, Americans use various indirect communication channels to which their friend is likely to be tuned. In other words, they publicize the information in the form of gossip or behind-the-back recriminations until it is transformed into a sort of collective criticism against the target individual. Thus objectified and collectivized, the "truth" ultimately reaches the target individual with a minimal cost of social discomfort on the part of the teller. There is nothing vile or insidious about this communication tactic, since it is deeply rooted in the concern for sustaining social pleasantry for both parties.

This innocuous practice, however, is bound to be perceived as an act of outrageous dishonesty by a person deeply immersed in the Korean culture. In the Korean cultural context, a trusted personal relationship precludes such publicizing prior to direct, "honest" criticism to the individual concerned, no matter what the cost in social and personal unpleasantry. Indeed, as you are well aware, MK, such direct reproach and even recrimination in Korea is in most cases appreciated as a sign of one's utmost love and concern for the target individual. Stressful and emotionally draining as it is, such a frank expression of criticism is done out of "we" feeling. Straight-talking friends did not want me to repeat undesirable acts in front of others, as it would either damage "our reputation" or go against the common interest of "our collective identity." In Korea, the focus is on the self-discipline that forms a basis for the integrity of "our group." In America, on the other hand, the focus is on the feelings of two individuals. From the potential teller's viewpoint, the primary concern is how to maintain social politeness, whereas from the target person's viewpoint, the primary concern is how to maintain self-esteem. Indeed, these two diametrically opposed frames of reference—self-discipline and self-esteem—make one culture collective and the other individualistic.

It is rather amazing that for all the mistakes I must have made in the past twenty years, only one non-Korean American friend gave me such an "honest" criticism. In a sense, this concern for interpersonal politeness conceals disapproval of my undesirable behavior for a time and ultimately delays the adjustment or realignment of my behavior, since it is likely to take quite a while for the collective judgment to reach me through the "publicized" channels of communication. So many Korean immigrants express their indignation about their U.S. colleagues who smile at them but who criticize them behind their backs. If you ever become a victim of such a perception, MK, please take heart that you are not the only one who feels that pain.

MK, the last facet of the individualism–collectivism continuum likely to cause a great amount of cognitive dissonance in the process of your assimilation to American life is the extent to which you have to assert your individuality to other people. You probably have no difficulty remembering our high school principal, K. W. Park, for whom we had a respect–contempt complex. He used to lecture, almost daily at morning assemblies, on the virtue of being modest. As he preached it, it was a form of the Confucian virtue of self-denial. Our existence or presence among other people, he told us, should not be overly felt through communicated messages (regardless of whether they are done with a tongue or pen). . . . One's existence, we were told, should be noticed by others in the form of our acts and conduct. One is obligated to provide opportunities for others to experience one's existence through what he or she does. Self-initiated effort for public recognition or self-aggrandizement was the most shameful conduct for a person of virtue.

This idea is interesting and noble as a philosophical posture, but when it is practiced in America, it will not get you anywhere in most circumstances. The lack of self-assertion is translated directly into timidity and lack of self-confidence. This is a culture where you must exert your individuality to the extent that it would make our high school principal turn in his grave out of shame and disgust. Blame the size of the territory or the population of this country. You may even blame the fast-paced cadence of life or the social mobility that moves people around at a dizzying speed. Whatever the specific reason might be, Americans are not waiting to experience you or your behaviors as they exist. They want a "documented" version of you that is eloquently summarized, decorated, and certified. What they are looking for is not your raw, unprocessed being with rich texture; rather, it is a slickly processed self, neatly packaged, and, most important, conveniently delivered to them. Self-advertising is encouraged almost to the point of pretentiousness. Years ago in Syracuse, I had an occasion to introduce a visiting Korean monk–scholar to a gathering of people who wanted to hear something about Oriental philosophies. After taking an elegantly practiced bow to the crowd, this humble monk declared, "My name is. . . . Please teach me, as I do not know anything." It took quite a bit of probing and questioning for us to extract something to chew on from that monk with the mysterious smile. Contrast this with an American colleague of mine applying for a promotion several years ago, who literally hauled in two cabinets full of documented evidence of his scholarly achievements.

The curious journey toward the American end of the individualism–collectivism continuum will be inevitable, I assure you. The real question is whether it will be in your generation, your children's, or their children's. Whenever it happens, it will be a bittersweet revenge for me, since only then will you realize how it feels to be called an American by your best high school chum.

SOURCE: Excerpted from a letter by Dr. Jin K. Kim, State University of New York—Plattsburgh. Copyright © 2001 by Dr. Jin K. Kim. Used with permission of Dr. Kim.

CULTURE AND MANAGEMENT STYLES AROUND THE WORLD

As an international manager, once you have researched the culture of a country in which you may be going to work or with which to do business, and after you have developed a cultural profile, it is useful then to apply that information to develop an understanding of the expected management styles and ways of doing business that predominate in that region, or with that type of business setting. Two examples follow: Saudi Arabia and Chinese Small Family Businesses.

Saudi Arabia

Understanding how business is conducted in the modern Middle East requires an understanding of the Arab culture, since the Arab peoples are the majority there and most of them are Muslim. The Arab culture is intertwined with the pervasive influence of Islam. Even though not all Middle Easterners are Arab, Arab culture and management style predominate in the Arabian Gulf region. Shared culture, religion, and language underlie behavioral similarities throughout the Arab world. Islam "permeates Saudi life—Allah is always present, controls everything, and is frequently referred to in conversation."[50] Employees may spend more than two hours a day in prayer as part of the life pattern that intertwines work with religion, politics, and social life.

Arab history and culture are based on tribalism, with its norms of reciprocity of favors, support, obligation, and identity passed on to the family unit, which is the primary structural model. Family life is based on closer personal ties than in the West. Arabs value personal relationships, honor, and saving face for all concerned; these values take precedence over the work at hand or verbal accuracy. "Outsiders" must realize that establishing a trusting relationship and respect for Arab social norms has to precede any attempts at business discussions. Honor, pride, and dignity are at the core of "shame" societies, such as the Arabs. As such, shame and honor provide the basis for social control and motivation. Circumstances dictate what is right or wrong and what is acceptable behavior.[51]

Arabs avoid open admission of error at all costs because weakness *(muruwwa)* is a failure to be manly. It is sometimes difficult for westerners to get at the truth because of the Arab need to avoid showing weakness; instead, Arabs present a desired or idealized situation. Shame is also brought on someone who declines to fulfill a request or a favor; therefore, a business arrangement is left open if something has yet to be completed.

The communication style of Middle Eastern societies is high context (that is, implicit and indirect), and their use of time is polychronic: Many activities can be taking place at the same time, with constant interruptions commonplace. The imposition of deadlines is considered rude, and business schedules take a backseat to the perspective that events will occur "sometime" when Allah wills *(bukra insha Allah).* Arabs give primary importance to hospitality; they are cordial to business associates and lavish in their entertainment, constantly offering strong black coffee (which you should not refuse) and banquets before considering business transactions. Westerners must realize the importance of personal contacts and networking, socializing and building close relationships and trust, practicing patience regarding schedules, and doing business in person. Exhibit 3-9 gives some selected actions and nonverbal behaviors that may offend Arabs. The relationship between cultural values and norms in Saudi Arabia and managerial behaviors is illustrated in Exhibit 3-10.

Chinese Small Family Businesses

The predominance of small businesses in China and the region highlights the need for managers from around the world to gain an understanding of how such businesses operate. Many small businesses—most of which are family or extended-family businesses—become part of the value chain (suppliers, buyers, retailers, etc.) within industries in which "foreign" firms may compete.

EXHIBIT 3-9   Behavior That Will Likely Cause Offense in Saudi Arabia

- Bringing up business subjects until you get to know your host, or you will be considered rude.
- Commenting on a man's wife or female children over 12 years of age.
- Raising colloquial questions that may be common in your country but possibly misunderstood in Saudi Arabia as an invasion of privacy.
- Using disparaging or swear words and off-color or obscene attempts at humor.
- Engaging in conversations about religion, politics, or Israel.
- Bringing gifts of alcohol or using alcohol, which is prohibited in Saudi Arabia.
- Requesting favors from those in authority or esteem, for it is considered impolite for Arabs to say no.
- Shaking hands too firmly or pumping—gentle or limp handshakes are preferred.
- Pointing your finger at someone or showing the soles of your feet when seated.

SOURCE: P. R. Harris and R. T. Moran, *Managing Cultural Differences*, 5th ed. (Houston: Gulf Publishing, 2000).

EXHIBIT 3-10   The Relationship Between Culture and Managerial Behaviors in Saudi Arabia

Cultural Values	Managerial Behaviors
Tribal and family loyalty	Work group loyalty Paternal sociability Stable employment and a sense of belonging A pleasant workplace Careful selection of employees Nepotism
Arabic language	Business as an intellectual activity Access to employees and peers Management by walking around Conversation as recreation
Close and warm friendships	A person rather than task and money orientation Theory Y management Avoidance of judgment
Islam	Sensitivity to Islamic virtues Observance of the Qur'an and Sharia Work as personal or spiritual growth Consultative management A full and fair hearing Adherence to norms
Honor and shame	Clear guidelines and conflict avoidance Positive reinforcement Training and defined job duties Private correction of mistakes Avoidance of competition
An idealized self	Centralized decision making Assumption of responsibility appropriate to position Empathy and respect for the self-image of others
Polychronic use of time	Right- and left-brain facility A bias for action Patience and flexibility
Independence	Sensitivity to control Interest in the individual
Male domination	Separation of sexes Open work life; closed family life

SOURCE: R. R. Harris and R. T. Moran, *Managing Cultural Differences* 4th ed. (Houston: Gulf Publishing, 1996).

Exhibit 3-11 presents a general framework for comparing Western and Chinese cultures; the resulting differences in Chinese attitudes and behavior are shown, along with implications for managers. (Further discussion of the Chinese culture continues in Chapter 5 in the context of negotiation.) Some specifics of Chinese management style and practices in particular are presented here as they apply to small businesses. It is important to note that no matter the size of a company, but especially in small businesses, it is the all-pervasive presence and use of *guanxi* that provides the little red engine of business transactions in China. *Guanxi* means "connections"—the network of relationships the Chinese cultivate through friendship and affection; it entails the exchange of favors and gifts to provide an obligation to reciprocate favors. Those who share a *guanxi* network share an unwritten code.[52] The philosophy and structure of Chinese businesses comprise paternalism, mutual obligation, responsibility, hierarchy, familialism, personalism, and connections.[53] Autocratic leadership is the norm, with the owner using his or her power—but with a caring about other people that may predominate over efficiency.[54]

According to Lee, the major differences between Chinese management styles and those of their Western counterparts are human-centeredness, family-centeredness,

EXHIBIT 3-11   A Summary of Western and Chinese Cultural Differences and the Implications for Management

Comparing pertinent features of the West with those of China, we can make the following distinctions:

The West	China
Individual rights	Individual duty and collective obligations
Rule by law	Rule by personality and imperial authority
The collective right to grant, question, and reject political authority	Unquestioning submission to hereditary authority backed by force
Political and ethnic pluralism	Monolithic power and homogeneity
Cultural interaction	Cultural isolation
Sufficient resources to support early urbanization, specialization of labor, and large-scale trade	An agrarian, subsistence economy and endless hardship, both natural and imposed
An external orientation	An internal orientation
Physical and social mobility	Permanence *in situ*
Reliance on reason and the scientific method	Reliance on precedent, intuition, and wisdom
An aggressive, active approach to nature, technology, and progress	Passive, fatalistic submission

Resulting differences in Chinese values, attitudes, and behavior with managerial implications:

1. Larger power distance—a greater willingness to accept the authority of others
2. Collectivism
   a. Deriving satisfaction less from task competence and achievement and more from a sense of contribution to a group effort
   b. More value placed on the comfort and availability of mutual support and affiliation with a group than on independence, self-reliance, privacy, and personal space
   c. More cooperativeness and less competitiveness as individuals
   d. Harmony and humility rather than aggressiveness
   e. High-content communication rather than directness and forthrightness
   f. Recognition of group—rather than individual—performance
   g. More relativistic, particularistic ethical standards
3. An external locus of control
4. More reliance on accumulated wisdom than on reason and objectivity
5. Holistic thinking and synthesis rather than linear thinking and analysis

SOURCE: J. Scarborough, "Comparing Chinese and Western Cultural Roots: Why East Is East and . . . ," *Business Horizons* (November–December 1998): 15–24.

centralization of power, and small size.[55] Their human-centered management style puts people ahead of a business relationship and focuses on friendship, loyalty, and trustworthiness.[56] The family is extremely important in Chinese culture, and any small business tends to be run like a family.

The centralized power structure in Chinese organizations, unlike those in the West, splits into two distinct levels: At the top is the boss and a few family members, and at the bottom are the employees, with no ranking among the workers.[57]

As Chinese firms in many modern regions in the Pacific Rim seek to modernize and compete locally and globally, a tug of war has begun between the old and the new: the traditional Chinese management practices and the increasingly "imported" Western management styles. As discussed by Lee, this struggle is encapsulated in the different management perspectives of the old and young generations. A two-generational study of Chinese managers by Ralston et al. also found generational shifts in work values in China. They concluded that the new generation manager is more individualistic, more independent, and takes more risks in the pursuit of profits. However, they also found the new generation holding on to their Confucian values, concluding that the new generation may be viewed as "crossverging their Eastern and Western influences, while on the road of modernization."[58]

CONCLUSION

This chapter has explored various cultural values and how managers can understand them with the help of cultural profiles. The following chapters focus on application of this cultural knowledge to management in an international environment (or, alternatively in a domestic multicultural environment)—especially as relevant to cross-cultural communication (Chapter 4), negotiation and decision making (Chapter 5), and motivating and leading (Chapter 11). Culture and communication are essentially synonymous; what happens when people from different cultures communicate, and how can international managers understand the underlying process and adapt their styles and expectations accordingly? For the answers, read the next chapter.

Summary of Key Points

1. The culture of a society comprises the shared values, understandings, assumptions, and goals that are passed down through generations and imposed by members of the society.
2. Cultural and national differences strongly influence the attitudes and expectations and therefore the on-the-job behavior of individuals and groups.
3. Managers must develop cultural sensitivity to anticipate and accommodate behavioral differences in different societies.
4. Managers must avoid parochialism—an attitude that assumes one's own management techniques are best in any situation or location and that other people should follow one's patterns of behavior.
5. Harris and Moran take a systems approach to understanding cultural and national variables and their effects on work behavior. They identify eight subsystems of variables: kinship, education, economy, politics, religion, associations, health, and recreation.
6. From his research in fifty countries, Hofstede proposes four underlying value dimensions that help to identify and describe the cultural profile of a country and affect organizational processes: power distance, uncertainty avoidance, individualism, and masculinity. Through the research of Hofstede and others, we can cluster countries based on intercultural similarities.
7. On-the-job conflicts in international management frequently arise out of conflicting values and orientations regarding time, change, material factors, and individualism.
8. Managers can use research results and personal observations to develop a character sketch, or cultural profile, of a country. This profile can help managers anticipate how to motivate people and coordinate work processes in a particular international context.

Discussion Questions

1. What is meant by the culture of a society, and why is it important that international managers understand it? Do you notice cultural differences among your classmates? How do those differences affect the class environment? Your group projects?
2. Describe the four dimensions of culture proposed by Hofstede. What are the managerial implications of these dimensions?
3. Discuss the types of operational conflicts that could occur in an international context because of different attitudes toward time, change, material factors, and individualism. Give examples relative to specific countries.
4. Give some examples of countries in which the family and its extensions play an important role in the workplace. How are managerial functions affected, and what can a manager do about this influence?
5. Discuss collectivism as it applies to the Japanese workplace. What managerial functions does it affect?
6. Discuss the role of Islam in cross-cultural relations and business operations.

Application Exercises

1. Develop a cultural profile for one of the countries in the following list. Form small groups of students and compare your findings in class with those of another group preparing a profile for another country. Be sure to compare specific findings regarding religion, kinship, recreation, and other subsystems. What are the prevailing attitudes toward time, change, material factors, and individualism?

   Any African country
   People's Republic of China
   Saudi Arabia
   Mexico
   France
   India

2. In small groups of students, research Hofstede's findings regarding the four dimensions of power distance, uncertainty avoidance, masculinity, and individualism for one of countries below in comparision to the United States. (Your instructor can assign the countries to avoid duplication.) Present your findings to the class. Assume you are a U.S. manager of a subsidiary in the foreign country and explain how differences on these dimensions are likely to affect your management tasks. What suggestions do you have for dealing with these differences in the workplace?

Brazil
Italy
People's Republic of China
Russia

Experiential Exercises

1. A large Baltimore manufacturer of cabinet hardware had been working for months to locate a suitable distributor for its products in Europe. Finally invited to present a demonstration to a reputable distributing company in Frankfurt, it sent one of its most promising young executives, Fred Wagner, to make the presentation. Fred not only spoke fluent German but also felt a special interest in this assignment because his paternal grandparents had immigrated to the United States from the Frankfurt area during the 1920s. When Fred arrived at the conference room where he would be making his presentation, he shook hands firmly, greeted everyone with a friendly *guten tag,* and even remembered to bow the head slightly as is the German custom. Fred, a very effective speaker and past president of the Baltimore Toastmasters Club, prefaced his presentation with a few humorous anecdotes to set a relaxed and receptive atmosphere. However, he felt that his presentation was not very well received by the company executives. In fact, his instincts were correct, for the German company chose not to distribute Fred's hardware products.
   What went wrong?

2. Bill Nugent, an international real estate developer from Dallas, had made a 2:30 P.M. appointment with Mr. Abdullah, a high-ranking government official in Riyadh, Saudi Arabia. From the beginning things did not go well for Bill. First, he was kept waiting until nearly 3:45 P.M. before he was ushered into Mr. Abdullah's office. When he finally did get in, several other men were also in the room. Even though Bill felt that he wanted to get down to business with Mr. Abdullah, he was reluctant to get too specific because he considered much of what they needed to discuss sensitive and private. To add to Bill's sense of frustration, Mr. Abdullah seemed more interested in engaging in meaningless small talk than in dealing with the substantive issues concerning their business.
   How might you help Bill deal with his frustration?

3. Tom Forrest, an up-and-coming executive for a U.S. electronics company, was sent to Japan to work out the details of a joint venture with a Japanese electronics firm. During the first several weeks, Tom felt that the negotiations were proceeding better than he had expected. He found that he had very cordial working relationships with the team of Japanese executives, and in fact, they had agreed on the major policies and strategies governing the new joint venture. During the third week of negotiations, Tom was present at a meeting held to review their progress. The meeting was chaired by the president of the Japanese firm, Mr. Hayakawa, a man in his mid-forties, who had recently taken over the presidency from his eighty-two-year-old grandfather. The new president, who had been involved in most of the negotiations during the preceding weeks, seemed to Tom to be one of the strongest advocates of the plan that had been developed to date. Hayakawa's grandfather, the recently retired president, also was present at the meeting. After the plans had been discussed in some detail, the octogenarian past president proceeded to give a long soliloquy about how some of the features of this plan violated the traditional practices on which the company had been founded. Much to Tom's amazement, Mr. Hayakawa did nothing to explain or defend the policies and strategies that they had taken weeks to develop. Feeling extremely frustrated, Tom then gave a fairly strong argued defense of the plan. To Tom's further amazement, no one else in the meeting spoke up in defense of the plan. The tension in the air was quite heavy, and the meeting adjourned shortly thereafter. Within days the Japanese firm completely terminated the negotiations on the joint venture.
   How could you help Tom better understand this bewildering situation?

SOURCE: Gary P. Ferraro, *The Cultural Dimensions of International Business,* 2nd ed. (Upper Saddle River, NJ, Prentice Hall, 1994).

Internet Resources

Visit the Deresky Web site at www.prenhall.com/deresky for this chapter's Internet resources.

Trouble at Computex Corporation

Mr. Peter Jones
Vice President—Europe
Computex Corporation
San Francisco/USA
Göteborg

Dear Mr. Jones:

The writers of this letter are the head count of the Sales Department of Computex Sweden, A.S., except for the Sales Manager.

We have decided to bring to your attention a problem which unsolved probably will lead to a situation where the majority among us will leave the company within a rather short period of time. None of us want to be in this situation, and we are approaching you purely as an attempt to save the team to the benefit of ourselves as well as Computex Corporation.

We consider ourselves an experienced, professional, and sales-oriented group of people. Computex Corporation is a company for which we are proud to work. The majority among us have been employed for several years. Consequently, a great number of key customers in different areas of Sweden see us as representatives of Computex Corporation. It is correct to say that the many excellent contacts we have made have been established over years; many of them are friends of ours.

These traits give a very short background because we have never met you. What kind of problem forces us to such a serious step as to contact you?

Problems arise as a result of character traits and behavior of our General Manager, Mr. Miller.

Firstly, we are more and more convinced that we are tools that he is utilizing in order to "climb the ladder." In meetings with us individually, or as a group, he gives visions about the future, how he values us, how he wants to delegate and involve us in business, the importance of cooperation and communication, and so on. When it comes to the point, these phrases turn out to be only words.

Mr. Miller loses his temper almost daily, and his outbursts and reactions are not equivalent to the possible error. His mood and views can change almost from hour to hour. This fact causes a situation where we feel uncertain when facing him and consequently are reluctant to do so. Regarding human relationships, his behavior is not acceptable, especially for a manager.

The extent of the experience of this varies within the group due to our location. Some of us are seldom in the office.

Secondly, we have clearly experienced that he has various means of suppressing and discouraging people within the organization.

The new "victim", now, is our Sales Manager, Mr. Johansson. Because he is our boss, it is obvious that we regret such a situation, which to a considerable extent influences our working conditions.

There are also other victims among us. It is indeed very difficult to carry through what is stated in our job descriptions.

We feel terribly sorry and wonder how it can be possible for one person to almost ruin a whole organization.

If this group consisted of people less mature, many of us would have left Computex Corporation already. So far only one has left the company due to the previously mentioned reasons.

From September 1, two new Sales Representatives are joining the company. We regret very much that new employees get their first contact with the company under the present circumstances. An immediate action is therefore required.

It is not our objective to get rid of Mr. Miller as General Manager. Without going into details, we are thankful for what he has done to the company from a business point of view. If he could control his mood, show some respect for his colleagues, keep words, and stick to plans, we believe that we can succeed under his leadership.

We are fully aware of the seriousness of contacting you, and we have been in doubt whether or not to contact you directly before talking to Mr. Miller.

After serious discussions and considerations, we have reached the conclusion that a problem of this nature unfortunately cannot be solved without some sort of action from the superior. If possible, direct confrontation must be avoided. It can only make things worse.

We are hoping for a positive solution.

Six of Your Sales Representatives in Sweden

Peter Jones let out a long sigh as he gazed over the letter from Sweden. "What do I do now?" he thought and began to reflect on the problem. He wondered who was right and who was wrong in this squabble, and he questioned whether he would ever get all the information necessary to make a wise decision. He didn't know much about the Swedes and was unsure whether this was strictly a work problem or a "cross-cultural" problem. "How can I tease those two issues apart?" he asked himself, as he locked his office and made his way down the hallway to the elevator.

As Peter pulled out of the parking garage and onto the street, he began to devise a plan to deal with the problem. "This will be a test of my conflict management skills," he thought. "No doubt about it!" As he merged into the freeway traffic from the on-ramp and began his commute home, he began to wish that he had never sent Miller to Sweden in the first place. "But would Gonzalez or Harris have done any better? Would I have done any better?" Few answers seemed to come to him as he plodded along in the bumper-to-bumper traffic on Interstate 440.

CASE QUESTION

1. You are Peter. How would you deal with this problem now? What should have been done differently in the first place?

SOURCE: Martin Hilb, University of St. Gallen, Switzerland.

CHAPTER 4

Communicating across Cultures

Opening Profile: On Keeping Your Foot Safely Out of Your Mouth

Joe Romano found out on a business trip to Taiwan how close a one-syllable slip of the tongue can come to torpedoing a deal.

Mr. Romano, a partner of High Ground, an emerging technology-marketing company in Boston, has been traveling to Asia for ten years and speaks fluent Mandarin and Taiwanese. Or so he thought, until he nearly blew an important deal when he met the chief executive of a major Taiwanese manufacturer.

"You're supposed to say 'Au-ban,' which means basically, 'Hello, No. 1 Boss,' " Mr. Romano explained. "But being nervous, I slipped and said 'Lau-ban ya,' which means, 'Hello, wife of the boss.' "

"So I basically called him a woman in front of twenty senior Taiwanese executives, who all laughed," he said. "He looked at me like he was going to kill me because in Asia, guys are hung up on being seen as very manly. I had to keep asking them to forgive 'the stupid American' before the C.E.O. would accept my apologies."

This is why translators are worth the investment for delicate business negotiations overseas, suggests Heike Estey, who leads cultural-sensitivity training as director of sales for Express Visa Service in Washington.

Even in the same language, communication miscues can occur. Lee Bowden, the managing director of the Sagamore, was staying at a 350-room resort on Lake George in Bolton Landing, New York. where he overheard a British guest ask the

116

desk clerk for "a rubber." While the clerk hemmed and hawed, Mr. Bowden, having worked in Britain, knew that the guest was requesting an eraser, not a condom. The confusion was quickly erased, and the requested device was delivered to the guest.

Stephen Schechter, professor of political science at the Sage Colleges in Troy, New York, and co-director of Civitas, an international civic education group, recalls a bilingual blooper so stark that it could have caused a permanent rift. At the end of a visit to Syracuse in the early 1990's, Yakov Sokolov, a Russian partner in the organization, raised a glass to his local hosts. "My dear friends, thank you so much for your hostility," he said, flubbing the word "hospitality."

"It could have been a terrible diplomatic error," Dr. Schechter said, "but thanks to good humor it has become a thing of beauty, a metaphor for our ability to overcome cultural misunderstandings."

It is not just spoken language that can create havoc for those trying to make their way in an unfamiliar culture. Body language can also send out the wrong signals.

Neil Alumkal, an associate vice president of 5W Public Relations, a Manhattan firm, recounted the time he and some associates were in Bangkok taking a motorcycle taxi known as a *tuk tuk* to the Royal Dragon, a restaurant so large that waiters use roller skates to move around. Giving directions, they tried to demonstrate which establishment they meant by raising their feet toward the non-English-speaking driver and pointing to them, as though they were wearing skates.

He immediately pulled over in a rage and ordered them out of his vehicle. Unbeknownst to them, showing the soles of your feet to someone is a serious insult in Thailand and most other Asian countries as well as in much of the Middle East.

Even ingrained mannerisms that no one would pay attention to at home can make an unfavorable impression abroad. For Stacie Krajchir, who has worked on TV commercial shoots around the world and is a co-author of *The Itty Bitty Guide to Business Travel*, it was the posture she took when she was engaged in conversations that got her in hot water.

"I have a habit of putting my hands on my hips when I talk," said Ms. Krajchir, who lives in Venice Beach, California. "But in Bali, it was politely but pointedly noted that when you stand that way it's seen as a sign of rudeness or defiance."

She committed an even worse blunder in Thailand. While working on a commercial with children, she affectionately patted one of them on the head. Alas, in that country, she said, the gesture was seen as "a grave offense because the head is considered sacred." Once again, the cultural gaffe was brought to her attention, and she apologized.

The question of physical contact is one of the great imponderables of international travel. The rules on whom to touch, where, when, why, for how long, and with what degree of enthusiasm vary starkly from country to country.

"With touching, it's very complicated because it's so deeply embedded not just as a cultural thing but as an emotional thing," said Sheida Hodge, the worldwide managing director of the cross-cultural division of Berlitz International in Princeton, New Jersey. "Generally, American culture is not a touching culture, so when we are abroad we just have to watch closely and try to adapt."

For example, in France, a relationship-oriented culture, good friends greet members of the opposite sex with a peck on each cheek. To the French, a handshake is much more than a simple ritual for saying hello or goodbye but rather a means of making a personal connection, Ms. Hodge said. The Japanese bow to one another at varying angles, depending on their relative social standing, she said, but "because they are familiar with American habits, a handshake is O.K." Latin Americans like to throw their arms around colleagues' backs or grab them by the arm to show their friendliness, physical acts that can startle or discomfit Yankee visitors.

In general, she said, people in southern Europe and the Middle East are much more physical than Americans, though in most Muslim countries, social touching never takes place between the sexes.

With so many cultural land mines out there, is there any hope for the untutored American business traveler? Ms. Hodge, who is the author of *Global Smarts: The Art of Communicating and Deal Making Anywhere in the World* has a reassuring answer. "None of these faux pas are deal breakers," she said. "People think, 'Oh, I crossed my legs. There goes the contract.' It's not true."

Ms. Estey suggested that "it behooves anyone doing business in a country that is foreign to them to do some cultural homework." One source she recommended is a Web site called CultureGrams.com, a primer on the customs and geography of 180 countries ($199 a year for up to five users).

When Americans do make the effort to learn their international colleagues' communication styles, it can pay off. Donald C. Dowling, Jr.—a senior counsel at Proskauer Rose, a Manhattan law firm speaks fluent Spanish, but he admits his French "is awful." So it was all the more surprising when the head of the Paris office, where he was doing a stint, toasted him at a Christmas party, throwing his arm around Mr. Dowling and announcing, "I love this guy because he speaks French."

"It took me a minute to figure out he wasn't making fun of me," Mr. Dowling said. "I think he just appreciated that I tried, unlike one American stationed in that office for two years, who managed to pick up a total of three words."

SOURCE: Perry Garfinkel, "On Keeping Your Foot Safely Out of Your Mouth," www.nytimes.com, July 13, 2004. Reprinted by permission of The New York Times.

Cultural communications are deeper and more complex than spoken or written messages. The essence of effective cross-cultural communication has more to do with releasing the right responses than with sending the "right" messages.
—Hall and Hall[1]

Multi-local online strategy. . . is about meeting global business objectives by tuning in to the cultural dynamics of their local markets.
—"Think Globally, Interact Locally,"
New Media Age[2]

As the opening profile suggests, communication is a critical factor in the cross-cultural management issues discussed in this book, particularly those of an interpersonal nature, involving motivation, leadership, group interactions, and negotiation. Culture is conveyed and perpetuated through communication in one form or another. Culture and communication are so intricately intertwined that they are, essentially, synonymous.[3] By understanding this relationship, managers can move toward constructive intercultural management.

Communication, whether in the form of writing, talking, listening, or via the Internet, is an inherent part of a manager's role and takes up the majority of a manager's time on the job. Studies by Mintzberg demonstrate the importance of oral communication; he found that most managers spend between 50 and 90 percent of their time talking to people.[4] The ability of a manager to effectively communicate across cultural boundaries will largely determine the success of international business transactions or the output of a culturally diverse workforce. It is useful, then, to break down the elements involved in the communication process, both to understand the cross-cultural issues at stake and to maximize the process.

THE COMMUNICATION PROCESS

The term **communication** describes the process of sharing meaning by transmitting messages through media such as words, behavior, or material artifacts. Managers communicate to coordinate activities, to disseminate information, to motivate people, and to negotiate future plans. It is of vital importance, then, for a receiver to interpret the meaning of a particular communication in the way the sender intended. Unfortunately, the communication process (see Exhibit 4-1) involves stages during which meaning can be distorted. Anything that serves to undermine the communication of the intended meaning is typically referred to as **noise**.

The primary cause of noise stems from the fact that the sender and the receiver each exist in a unique, private world thought of as her or his life space. The context of that private world, largely based on culture, experience, relations, values, and so forth, determines the interpretation of meaning in communication. People filter, or selectively understand, messages consistent with their own expectations and perceptions of reality and their values and norms of behavior. The more dissimilar the cultures of those involved, the more the likelihood of misinterpretation. In this way, as Samovar, Porter, and Jain state, cultural factors pervade the communication process:

> Culture not only dictates who talks with whom, about what, and how the communication proceeds, it also helps to determine how people encode messages, the meanings they have for messages, and the conditions and circumstances under which various messages may or may not be sent, noticed, or interpreted. In fact, our entire repertory of communicative behaviors is dependent largely on the culture in which we have been raised. Culture, consequently, is the foundation of communication. And, when cultures vary, communication practices also vary.[5]

Communication, therefore, is a complex process of linking up or sharing the perceptual fields of sender and receiver; the perceptive sender builds a bridge to the life space of the receiver.[6] After the receiver interprets the message and draws a conclusion about what the sender meant, he or she will, in most cases, encode and send back a response, making communication a circular process.

The communication process is rapidly changing, however, as a result of technological developments, therefore propelling global business forward at a phenomenal growth rate. These changes are discussed later in this chapter.

EXHIBIT 4-1 The Communication Process

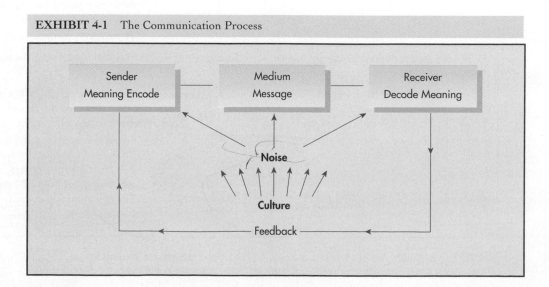

Cultural Noise in the Communication Process

*In Japanese there are several words for "I" and several words for "you" but
their use depends on the relationship between the speaker and the other person.
In short, there is no "I" by itself; the "I" depends on the relationship.*

H. C. TRIANDIS,
The Blackwell Handbook of Cross-cultural Management[7]

Because the focus in this text is on effective cross-cultural communication, it is important to understand what cultural variables cause noise in the communication process. This knowledge of **cultural noise**—the cultural variables that undermine the communications of intended meaning—will enable us to take steps to minimize that noise and so to improve communication.

When a member of one culture sends a message to a member of another culture, **intercultural communication** takes place. The message contains the meaning intended by the encoder. When it reaches the receiver, however, it undergoes a transformation in which the influence of the decoder's culture becomes part of the meaning.[8] Exhibit 4-2 provides an example of intercultural communication in which the meaning got all mixed up. Note how the attribution of behavior differs for each participant. **Attribution** is the process in which people look for an explanation of another person's behavior. When they realize that they do not understand another, they tend, say Hall and Hall, to blame their confusion on the other's "stupidity, deceit, or craziness."[9]

In the situation depicted in Exhibit 4-2, the Greek employee gets frustrated and resigns after experiencing communication problems with his American boss. How could this outcome have been avoided? We do not have much information about the people or the context of the situation, but we can look at some of the variables that might have been involved and use them as a basis for analysis.

EXHIBIT 4-2   Cultural Noise in International Communication

Behavior	Attribution
American: "How long will it take you to finish this report?"	*American:* I asked him to participate. *Greek:* His behavior makes no sense. He is the boss. Why doesn't he tell me?
Greek: "I don't know. How long should it take?"	*American:* He refuses to take responsibility. *Greek:* I asked him for an order.
American: "You are in the best position to analyze time requirements."	*American:* I press him to take responsibility for his actions. *Greek:* What nonsense: I'd better give him an answer.
Greek: "10 days."	*American:* He lacks the ability to estimate time; this time estimate is totally inadequate.
American: "Take 15. Is it agreed? You will do it in 15 days?"	*American:* I offer a contract. *Greek:* These are my orders: 15 days.

In fact, the report needed 30 days of regular work. So the Greek worked day and night, but at the end of the 15th day, he still needed to do one more day's work.

American: "Where is the report?"	*American:* I am making sure he fulfills his contract. *Greek:* He is asking for the report. (Both attribute that it is not ready.)
Greek: "It will be ready tomorrow."	
American: "But we agreed it would be ready today."	*American:* I must teach him to fulfill a contract. *Greek:* The stupid, incompetent boss! Not only did he give me the wrong orders, but he doesn't even appreciate that I did a 30-day job in 16 days.
The Greek hands in his resignation.	The American is surprised. *Greek:* I can't work for such a man.

SOURCE: Adapted from H. C. Triandis, *Interpersonal Behavior* (Monterey, California Brooks/Cole, 1997), 248; reported in Simcha Ronen, *Comparative and Multinational Management* (New York: John Wiley and Sons, 1986), 101–102.

THE CULTURE–COMMUNICATION LINK

The following sections examine underlying elements of culture that affect communication. The degree to which one is able to effectively communicate largely depends on how similar the other person's cultural expectations are to our own. However, cultural gaps can be overcome by prior learning and understanding of those variables and how to adjust to them.

Trust in Communication

The key ingredient in a successful alliance is trust.

JAMES R. HOUGHTON,
Former Chairman, Corning, Inc.[10]

Effective communication, and therefore collaboration in alliances across national boundaries, depends on the informal understandings among the parties that are based on the trust that has developed between them. However, the meaning of trust and how it is developed and communicated vary across societies. In China and Japan, for example, business transactions are based on networks of long-standing relationships based on trust, rather than on the formal contracts and arm's-length relationships typical of the United States. When there is trust between parties, implicit understanding arises within communications. This understanding has numerous benefits in business, including encouraging communicators to overlook cultural differences and minimize problems. It allows communicators to adjust to unforeseen circumstances with less conflict than would be the case with formal contracts, and it facilitates open communication in exchanging ideas and information.[11] From his research on trust in global collaboration, John Child suggests the following guidelines for cultivating trust:

- Create a clear and calculated basis for mutual benefit. There must be realistic commitments and good intentions to honor them.
- Improve predictability: strive to resolve conflicts and keep communication open.
- Develop mutual bonding through regular socializing and friendly contact.[12]

What can managers anticipate with regard to the level of trust in communications with people in other countries? If trust is based on how trustworthy we consider a person to be, then it must vary according to that society's expectations about whether that culture supports the norms and values that predispose people to behave credibly and benevolently. Are there differences across societies in those expectations of trust? Research by the World Values Study Group of 90,000 people in forty-five societies provides some insight on cultural values regarding predisposition to trust.[13] Exhibit 4-3 shows the percentage of respondents in each society who responded that "most people can be trusted." As you can see, the Nordic countries and China had the highest predisposition to trust, while Brazil, Turkey, Romania, Slovenia, and Latvia had the lowest.

The GLOBE Project

Results from the GLOBE research on culture, discussed in Chapter 3, provide some insight into culturally appropriate communication styles and expectations for the manager to use abroad. GLOBE researchers Javidan and House make the following observations:[14] For people in societies that ranked high on performance orientation—for example, the United States—presenting objective information in a direct and explicit way is an important and expected manner of communication; this compares with people in Russia or Greece—which ranked low on performance orientation—for whom hard facts and figures are not readily available or taken seriously. In those cases, a more indirect approach is preferred. People from countries ranking low on assertiveness, such as Sweden, also recoil from explicitness; their preference is for much two-way discourse and friendly relationships.

People ranking high on the "humane" dimension, such as those from Ireland and the Philippines, make avoiding conflict a priority and tend to communicate with the goal of being supportive of people rather than of achieving objective end results. This compares to people from France and Spain whose agenda is achievement of goals.

EXHIBIT 4-3   Level of General Trust in People

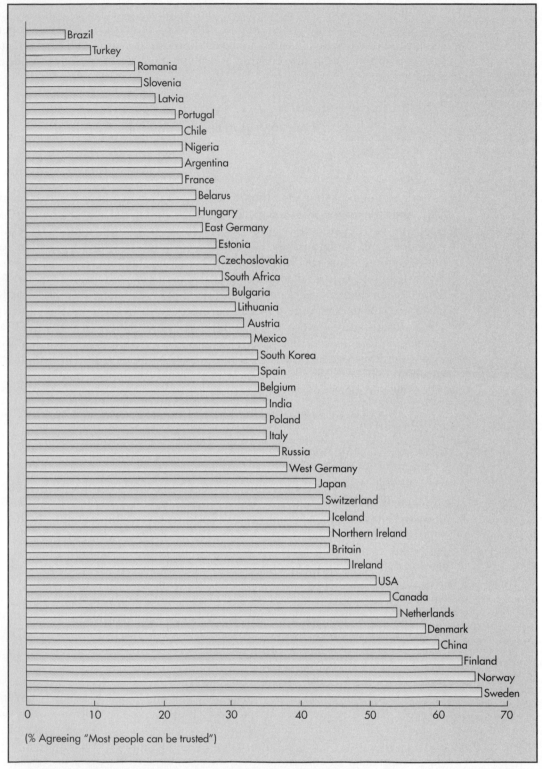

(% Agreeing "Most people can be trusted")

SOURCE: J. L. Johnson and J. B. Cullen, "Trust in Cross-Cultural Relationships," in M. J. Gannon and K. L. Newman, *The Blackwell Handbook of Cross-Cultural Management* (Oxford, England: Blackwell Publishers, 2002), P. 349.

The foregoing provides examples of how to draw implications for appropriate communication styles from the research findings on cultural differences across societies. Astute global managers have learned that culture and communication are inextricably linked and that they should prepare themselves accordingly. Most will also suggest that you carefully watch and listen to how your hosts are communicating and to follow their lead.

Cultural Variables in the Communication Process

On a different level, it is also useful to be aware of cultural variables that can affect the communication process by influencing a person's perceptions; some of these variables have been identified by Samovar and Porter and discussed by Harris and Moran, and others.[15] These variables are as follows: attitudes, social organization, thought patterns, roles, language (spoken or written), nonverbal communication (including kinesic behavior, proxemics, paralanguage, and object language), and time. Although these variables are discussed separately in this text, their effects are interdependent and inseparable—or, as Hecht, Andersen, and Ribeau put it, "Encoders and decoders process nonverbal cues as a conceptual, multichanneled gestalt."[16]

Attitudes   We all know that our attitudes underlie the way we behave and communicate and the way we interpret messages from others. Ethnocentric attitudes are a particular source of noise in cross-cultural communication. In the incident described in Exhibit 4-2, both the American and the Greek are clearly attempting to interpret and convey meaning based on their own experiences of that kind of transaction. The American is probably guilty of stereotyping the Greek employee by quickly jumping to the conclusion that he is unwilling to take responsibility for the task and the scheduling.

This problem, **stereotyping**, occurs when a person assumes that every member of a society or subculture has the same characteristics or traits. Stereotyping is a common cause of misunderstanding in intercultural communication. It is an arbitrary, lazy, and often destructive way to find out about people. Astute managers are aware of the dangers of cultural stereotyping and deal with each person as an individual with whom they may form a unique relationship.

Social Organization   Our perceptions can be influenced by differences in values, approach, or priorities relative to the kind of social organizations to which we belong. These organizations may be based on one's nation, tribe, or religious sect, or they may consist of the members of a certain profession. Examples of such organizations include the Academy of Management or the United Auto Workers (UAW).[17]

Thought Patterns   The logical progression of reasoning varies widely around the world and greatly affects the communication process. Managers cannot assume that others use the same reasoning processes, as illustrated by the experience of a Canadian expatriate in Thailand:

> *While in Thailand a Canadian expatriate's car was hit by a Thai motorist who had crossed over the double line while passing another vehicle. After failing to establish that the fault lay with the Thai driver, the Canadian flagged down a policeman. After several minutes of seemingly futile discussion, the Canadian pointed out the double line in the middle of the road and asked the policeman directly, "What do these lines signify?" The policeman replied, "They indicate the center of the road and are there so I can establish just how far the accident is from that point." The Canadian was silent. It had never occurred to him that the double line might not mean "no passing allowed."[18]*

In the Exhibit 4-2 scenario, perhaps the American did not realize that the Greek employee had a different rationale for his time estimate for the job. Because the Greek was not used to having to estimate schedules, he just took a guess, which he felt he had been forced to do.

Roles   Societies differ considerably in their perceptions of a manager's role. Much of the difference is attributable to their perceptions of who should make the decisions and who has responsibility for what. In the Exhibit 4-2 example, the American assumes that his role as manager is to delegate responsibility, to foster autonomy, and to practice participative management. He prescribes the role of the employee without any consideration of whether the employee will understand that role. The Greek's frame of reference leads him to think that the manager is the boss and should give the order about when to have the job completed. He interprets the American's behavior as breaking that frame of reference, and therefore he feels that the boss is "stupid and incompetent" for giving him the wrong order and for not recognizing and appreciating his accomplishment. The manager should have considered what behaviors Greek workers would expect of him and then either should have played that role or discussed the situation carefully, in a training mode.

Language   Spoken or written language, of course, is a frequent cause of miscommunication, stemming from a person's inability to speak the local language, a poor or too-literal translation, a speaker's failure to explain idioms, or a person missing the meaning conveyed through body language or certain symbols. Even among countries that share the same language, problems can arise from the subtleties and nuances inherent in the use of the language, as noted by George Bernard Shaw: "Britain and America are two nations separated by a common language." This problem can exist even within the same country among subcultures or subgroups.[19]

Many international executives tell stories about lost business deals or lost sales because of communication blunders:

> When Pepsi Cola's slogan "Come Alive with Pepsi" was introduced in Germany, the company learned that the literal German translation of "come alive" is "come out of the grave."
>
> A U.S. airline found a lack of demand for its "rendezvous lounges" on its Boeing 747s. They later learned that "rendezvous" in Portuguese refers to a room that is rented for prostitution.[20]

More than just conveying objective information, language also conveys cultural and social understandings from one generation to the next.[21] Examples of how language reflects what is important in a society include the 6,000 different Arabic words used to describe camels and their parts and the fifty or more classifications of snow used by the Inuit, the Eskimo people of Canada.

In as much as language conveys culture, technology, and priorities, it also serves to separate and perpetuate subcultures. In India, 14 official and many unofficial languages are used, and over 800 languages are spoken on the African continent.

Because of increasing workforce diversity around the world, the international business manager will have to deal with a medley of languages. For example, assembly-line workers at the Ford plant in Cologne, Germany, speak Turkish and Spanish as well as German. In Malaysia, Indonesia, and Thailand, many of the buyers and traders are Chinese. Not all Arabs speak Arabic; in Tunisia and Lebanon, for example, French is the language of commerce.[22]

International managers need either a good command of the local language or competent interpreters. The task of accurate translation to bridge cultural gaps is fraught with difficulties, as Schermerhorn discovered in his study of 153 Hong Kong Chinese bilinguals. He found a considerable difference in interpretation and response according to whether the medium used was Chinese or English, even after many experts were involved in the translation process.[23]

Even the direct translation of specific words does not guarantee the congruence of their meaning, as with the word "yes" used by Asians, which usually means only that they have heard you, and, often, that they are too polite to disagree. The Chinese, for example, through years of political control, have built into their communication culture a cautionary stance to avoid persecution by professing agreement with whatever opinion was held by the person questioning them.[24]

Politeness and a desire to say only what the listener wants to hear create noise in the communication process in much of the world. Often, even a clear translation does not help a person to understand what is meant because the encoding process has obscured the true message. With the poetic Arab language—replete with exaggeration, elaboration, and repetition—meaning is attributed more to how something is said rather than what is said.

For the American supervisor and Greek employee cited in Exhibit 4-2, it is highly likely that the American could have picked up some cues from the employee's body language, which probably implied problems with the interpretation of meaning. How might body language have created noise in this case?

Nonverbal Communication   Behavior that communicates without words (although it often is accompanied by words) is called **nonverbal communication**. People will usually believe what they see over what they hear—hence the expression, "A picture is worth a thousand words." Studies show that these subtle messages account for between 65 and 93 percent of interpreted communication.[25] Even minor variations in body language, speech rhythms, and punctuality, for example, often cause mistrust and misperception of the situation among cross-national parties.[26] The media for such nonverbal communication can be categorized into four types: (1) kinesic behavior, (2) proxemics, (3) paralanguage, and (4) object language.

The term **kinesic behavior** refers to communication through body movements—posture, gestures, facial expressions, and eye contact. Although such actions may be universal, often their meaning is not. Because kinesic systems of meaning are culturally specific and learned, they cannot be generalized across cultures. Most people in the West would not correctly interpret many Chinese facial expressions; sticking out the tongue expresses surprise, a widening of the eyes shows anger, and scratching the ears and cheeks indicates happiness.[27] Research has shown for some time, however, that most people worldwide can recognize displays of the basic emotions of anger, disgust, fear, happiness, sadness, surprise, and contempt.[28]

Many business people and visitors react negatively to what they feel are inappropriate facial expressions, without understanding the cultural meaning behind them. In his studies of cross-cultural negotiations, Graham observed that the Japanese feel uncomfortable when faced with the Americans' eye-to-eye posture. They are taught since childhood to bow their heads out of humility, whereas the automatic response of Americans is "look at me when I'm talking to you!"[29]

Subtle differences in eye behavior (called *oculesics*) can throw off a communication badly if they are not understood. Eye behavior includes differences not only in eye contact but also in the use of eyes to convey other messages, whether or not that involves mutual gaze. Edward T. Hall, author of the classic *The Silent Language,* explains the differences in eye contact between the British and the Americans. During speech, Americans will look straight at you, but the British keep your attention by looking away. The British will look at you when they have finished speaking, which signals that it is your turn to talk. The implicit rationale for this is that you can't interrupt people when they are not looking at you.[30]

It is helpful for U.S. managers to be aware of the many cultural expectations regarding posture and how they may be interpreted. In Europe or Asia, a relaxed posture in business meetings may be taken as bad manners or the result of poor upbringing. In Korea you are expected to sit upright, with feet squarely on the floor, and to speak slowly, showing a blending of body and spirit.

Managers can also familiarize themselves with the many different interpretations of hand and finger signals around the world, some of which may even represent obscene gestures. Of course, we cannot expect to change all of our ingrained, natural kinesic behavior, but we can be aware of what it means to others. We also can learn to understand the kinesic behavior of others and the role it plays in their society, as well as how it can affect business transactions. Misunderstanding the meanings of body movements—or an ethnocentric attitude toward the "proper" behavior—can have negative repercussions, as illustrated in the opening profile of this chapter.

Proxemics deals with the influence of proximity and space on communication—both personal space and office space or layout. Americans expect office layout to provide private space for each person, and usually a larger and more private space as one goes up the hierarchy. In much of Asia, the custom is open office space, with people at all levels working and talking in close proximity to one another. Space communicates power in both Germany and the United States, evidenced by the desire for a corner office or one on the top floor. The importance of French officials, however, is made clear by a position in the middle of subordinates, communicating that they have a central position in an information network, where they can stay informed and in control.[31]

Do you ever feel vaguely uncomfortable and start moving backward slowly when someone is speaking to you? This is because that person is invading your "bubble"—your personal space. Personal space is culturally patterned, and foreign spatial cues are a common source of misinterpretation. When someone seems aloof or pushy, it often means that she or he is operating under subtly different spatial rules.

Hall and Hall suggest that cultural differences affect the programming of the senses and that space, perceived by all the senses, is regarded as a form of territory to be protected.[32] South Americans, Southern and Eastern Europeans, Indonesians, and Arabs are **high-contact cultures**, preferring to stand close, touch a great deal, and experience a "close" sensory involvement. On the other hand, North Americans, Asians, and Northern Europeans are **low-contact cultures** and prefer much less sensory involvement, standing farther apart and touching far less. They have a "distant" style of body language.[33]

Interestingly, high-contact cultures are mostly located in warmer climates, and low-contact cultures in cooler climates. Americans are relatively nontouching, automatically standing at a distance so that an outstretched arm will touch the other person's ear.[34] Standing any closer than that is regarded as invading intimate space. However, Americans and Canadians certainly expect a warm handshake and maybe a pat on the back from closer friends, though not the very warm double handshake of the Spaniards (clasping the forearm with the left hand). The Japanese, considerably less **haptic**, do not shake hands; an initial greeting between a Japanese and a Spanish businessperson would be uncomfortable for both parties if they were untrained in cultural haptics.

When considering high- and low-contact cultures, we can trace a correlation between Hofstede's cultural variables of individualism and collectivism and the types of kinesic and proxemic behaviors people display. Generally, people from individualistic cultures are more remote and distant, whereas those from collectivist cultures are interdependent: They tend to work, play, live, and sleep in close proximity.[35]

The term **paralanguage** refers to how something is said rather than the content—the rate of speech, the tone and inflection of voice, other noises, laughing, or yawning. The culturally aware manager learns how to interpret subtle differences in paralanguage, including silence. Silence is a powerful communicator. It may be a way of saying no, of being offended, or of waiting for more information to make a decision. There is considerable variation in the use of silence in meetings. While Americans get uncomfortable after ten or fifteen seconds of silence, Chinese prefer to think the situation over for thirty seconds before speaking. The typical scenario between Americans and Chinese, then, is that the American gets impatient, says something to break the silence, and offends the Chinese by interrupting his chain of thought and comfort level with the subject.[36] Graham, a researcher on international negotiations, taped a bargaining session held at Toyota's U.S. headquarters in California. The U.S. executive had made a proposal to open a new production facility in Brazil and was waiting for a response from the three Japanese executives, who sat with lowered eyes and hands folded on the table. After about thirty seconds—an eternity to Americans, accustomed to a conversational response time of a few tenths of a second—the American blurted out that they were getting nowhere—and the meeting ended in a stalemate. More sensitivity to cultural differences in communication might have led him to wait longer or perhaps to prompt some further response through another polite question.[37]

The term **object language**, or **material culture**, refers to how we communicate through material artifacts, whether architecture, office design and furniture, clothing, cars, or cosmetics. Material culture communicates what people hold as important. In Mexico, a visiting international executive or salesperson is advised to take time out, before negotiating business, to show appreciation for the surrounding architecture, which is prized by Mexicans.

Time   Another variable that communicates culture is the way people regard and use time (see also Chapter 3). To Brazilians, relative punctuality communicates the level of importance of those involved. To Middle Easterners, time is something controlled by the will of Allah.

To initiate effective cross-cultural business interactions, managers should know the difference between *monochronic time systems* and *polychronic time systems* and how they affect communications. Hall and Hall explain that in **monochronic cultures** (Switzerland, Germany, and the United States), time is experienced in a linear way, with a past, a present, and a future, and time is treated as something to be spent, saved, made up, or wasted. Classified and compartmentalized, time serves to order life. This attitude is a learned part of Western culture, probably starting with the Industrial Revolution. Monochronic people, found in individualistic cultures, generally concentrate on one thing at a time, adhere to time commitments, and are accustomed to short-term relationships.

In contrast, **polychronic cultures** tolerate many things occurring simultaneously and emphasize involvement with people. Two Latin friends, for example, will put an important conversation ahead of being on time for a business meeting, thus communicating the priority of relationships over material systems. Polychronic people—Latin Americans, Arabs, and those from other collectivist cultures—may focus on several things at once, be highly distractible, and change plans often.[38]

The relationship between time and space also affects communication. Polychronic people, for example, are likely to hold open meetings, moving around and conducting transactions with one party and then another, rather than compartmentalizing meeting topics, as do monochronic people.

The nuances and distinctions regarding cultural differences in nonverbal communication are endless. The various forms are listed in Exhibit 4-4; wise intercultural managers will take careful account of the role that such differences might play.

What aspects of nonverbal communication might have created noise in the interactions between the American supervisor and the Greek employee in Exhibit 4-2? Undoubtedly, some cues could have been picked up in the kinesics behavior of each person. It was the responsibility of the manager, in particular, to notice any indications from the Greek that could have prompted him to change his communication pattern or assumptions. Face-to-face communication permits the sender of the message to get immediate feedback, verbal and nonverbal, and thus to have some idea as to how that message is being received and whether additional information is needed. What aspects of the Greek employee's kinesic behavior or paralanguage might have been evident to a more culturally sensitive manager? Did both parties' sense of time affect the communication process?

Context

A major differentiating factor that is a primary cause of noise in the communication process is that of context—which actually incorporates many of the variables just discussed. The **context** in which the communication takes place affects the meaning and interpretation of the interaction. Cultures are known to be high- or low-context cultures, with a relative range in between.[39] In **high-context cultures** (Asia, the Middle East, Africa, and the Mediterranean), feelings and thoughts are not explicitly expressed; instead, one has to read between the lines and interpret meaning from one's general understanding. Two such high-context cultures are those of South Korea and Arab cultures. In such cultures, key information is embedded in the context rather than made explicit. People make assumptions about what the message means through their knowledge of the person or the

EXHIBIT 4-4   Forms of Nonverbal Communication

- Facial expressions
- Body posture
- Gestures with hands, arms, head, etc.
- Interpersonal distance (proxemics)
- Touching, body contact
- Eye contact
- Clothing, cosmetics, hairstyles, jewelry
- Paralanguage (voice pitch and inflections, rate of speech, and silence)
- Color symbolism
- Attitude toward time and the use of time in business and social interactions
- Food symbolism and social use of meals

surroundings. In these cultures, most communication takes place within a context of extensive information networks resulting from close personal relationships. See the following Management Focus for further explanation of the Asian communication style.

In **low-context cultures** (Germany, Switzerland, Scandinavia, and North America), where personal and business relationships are more compartmentalized, communication

---

Management Focus

Oriental Poker Face: Eastern Deception or Western Inscrutability?

Among many English expressions that are likely to offend those of us whose ancestry may be traced to the Far East, two stand out quite menacingly for me: "Oriental poker face" and "idiotic Asian smile." The former refers to the supposedly inscrutable nature of a facial expression that apparently reflects no particular state of mind, while the latter pokes fun at a face fixed with a perpetually friendly smile. Westerners' perplexity, when faced with either, arises from the impression that these two diametrically opposed masquerading strategies prevent them from extracting useful information—at least the type of information that at least they could process with a reasonable measure of confidence—about the feelings of the person before them. An Asian face that projects no signs of emotion, then, seems to most Westerners nothing but a facade. It does not matter whether that face wears an unsightly scowl or a shining ray; a facial expression they cannot interpret poses a genuine threat.

Compassionate and sympathetic to their perplexity as I may be, I am also insulted by the Western insensitivity to the significant roles that subtle signs play in Asian cultures. Every culture has its unique modus operandi for communication. Western culture, for example, apparently emphasizes the importance of direct communication. Not only are the communicators taught to look directly at each other when they convey a message, but they also are also encouraged to come right to the point of the message. Making bold statements or asking frank questions in a less than diplomatic manner (i.e., "That was really a very stupid thing to do!" or "Are you interested in me?") is rarely construed as rude or indiscreet. Even embarrassingly blunt questions such as "Senator Hart, have you ever had sexual intercourse with anyone other than your wife?" are tolerated most of the time. Asians, on the other hand, find this direct communicative communication style quite unnerving. In many social interactions, they avoid direct eye contact. They "see" each other without necessarily looking directly at each other, and they gather information about inner states of mind without asking even the most discreet or understated questions. Many times they talk around the main topic, and, yet, they

succeed remarkably well in understanding one another's position. (At least they believe they have developed a reasonably clear understanding.)

To a great extent, Asian communication is listening-centered; the ability to listen (and a special talent for detecting various communicative cues) is treated as equally important as, if not more important than, the ability to speak. This contrasts clearly with the American style of communication that puts the utmost emphasis on verbal expression; the speaker carries most of the burden for ensuring that everyone understands his or her message. An Asian listener, however, is prone to blame himself or herself for failing to reach a comprehensive understanding from the few words and gestures performed by the speaker. With this heavier burden placed on the listener, an Asian speaker does not feel obliged to send clearly discernible message cues (at least not nearly so much as he or she is obliged to do in American cultural contexts). Not obliged to express themselves without interruption, Asians use silence as a tool in communication. Silence, by most Western conventions, represents discontinuity of communication and creates a feeling of discomfort and anxiety. In the Orient, however, silence is not only comfortably tolerated but is considered a desirable form of expression. Far from being a sign of displeasure or animosity, it serves as an integral part of the communication process, used for reflecting on messages previously exchanged and for carefully crafting thoughts before uttering them.

It is not outlandish at all, then, for Asians to view Americans as unnecessarily talkative and lacking in the ability to listen. For the Asian, it is the American who projects a mask of confidence by being overly expressive both verbally and nonverbally. Since the American style of communication places less emphasis on the act of listening than on speaking, Asians suspect that their American counterparts fail to pick up subtle and astute communicative signs in conversation. To one with a cultural outlook untrained in reading those signs, an inscrutable face represents no more than a menacing or amusing mask.

SOURCE: Dr. Jin Kim, State University of New York–Plattsburgh. Copyright © 1995 by Dr. Jin Kim. Used with permission of Dr. Kim.

EXHIBIT 4-5   Cultural Context and Its Effects on Communication

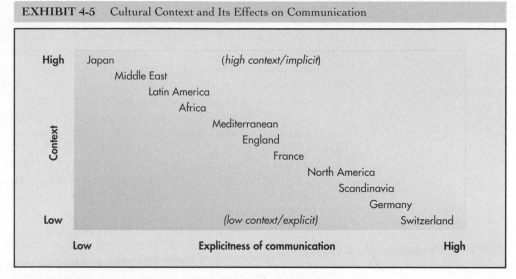

SOURCE: Based on information drawn from Edward T. Hall and M. R. Hall, *Understanding Cultural Differences* (Yarmouth, ME: Intercultural Press, 1990); and Martin Rosch, "Communications: Focal Point of Culture," *Management International Review* 27, no. 4 (1987): 60.

media have to be more explicit. Feelings and thoughts are expressed in words, and information is more readily available.

In cross-cultural communication between high- and low-context people, a lack of understanding may preclude reaching a solution, and conflict may arise. Germans, for example, will expect considerable detailed information before making a business decision, whereas Arabs will base their decisions more on knowledge of the people involved—the information is present, but it is implicit.

People in high-context cultures expect others to understand unarticulated moods, subtle gestures, and environmental clues that people from low-context cultures simply do not process. Misinterpretation and misunderstanding often result.[40] People from high-context cultures perceive those from low-context cultures as too talkative, too obvious, and redundant. Those from low-context cultures perceive high-context people as nondisclosing, sneaky, and mysterious.[41] Research indicates, for example, that Americans find talkative people more attractive, whereas Koreans, high-context people, perceive less verbal people as more attractive. Finding the right balance between low- and high-context communication can be tricky, as Hall and Hall point out: "Too much information leads people to feel they are being talked down to; too little information can mystify them or make them feel left out."[42] Exhibit 4-5 shows the relative level of context in various countries.

The importance of understanding the role of context and nonverbal language to avoid misinterpretation is illustrated in Comparative Management in Focus: Communicating with Arabs.

Comparative Management in Focus

Communicating with Arabs

In the Middle East, the meaning of a communication is implicit and interwoven, and consequently much harder for Americans, accustomed to explicit and specific meanings, to understand.

Arabs are warm, emotional, and quick to explode: "Sounding off" is regarded as a safety valve.[43] In fact, the Arabic language aptly communicates the Arabic culture, one of emotional extremes. The language contains the means for overexpression, many adjectives, words that allow for exaggeration, and metaphors to emphasize a position. What is said is often not as important as how it is said.[44] Eloquence and flowery speech are admired for their own sake, regardless of the content. Loud speech is used for dramatic effect.

At the core of Middle Eastern culture are friendship, honor, religion, and traditional hospitality. Family, friends, and connections are very important on all levels in the Middle East and will take precedence over business transactions. Arabs do business with people, not companies, and they make commitments to people, not contracts. A phone call to the right person can help to get around seemingly insurmountable obstacles. An Arab expects loyalty from friends, and it is understood that giving and receiving favors is an inherent part of the relationship; no one says no to a request for a favor. A lack of follow-through is assumed to be beyond the friend's control.[45]

Because hospitality is a way of life and highly symbolic, a visitor must be careful not to reject it by declining refreshment or rushing into business discussions. Part of that hospitality is the elaborate system of greetings and the long period of getting acquainted, perhaps taking up the entire first meeting. While the handshake may seem limp, the rest of the greeting is not. Kissing on the cheeks is common among men, as is hand-holding between male friends. However, any public display of intimacy between men and women is strictly forbidden by the Arab social code.

Women play little or no role in business or entertainment; the Middle East is a male-dominated society, and it is impolite to inquire about women. Other nonverbal taboos include showing the soles of one's feet and using the left (unclean) hand to eat or pass something. In discussions, slouching in a seat or leaning against a wall communicates a lack of respect.

The Arab society also values honor. Harris and Moran explain: "Honor, social prestige, and a secure place in society are brought about when conformity is achieved. When one fails to conform, this is considered to be damning and leads to a degree of shame."[46] Shame results not just from doing something wrong but from having others find out about that wrongdoing. Establishing a climate of honesty and trust is part of the sense of honor. Therefore, considerable tact is needed to avoid conveying any concern or doubt. Arabs tend to be quite introverted until a mutual trust is built, which takes a long time.[47]

In their nonverbal communication, most Arab countries are high-contact cultures. Arabs stand and sit closer and touch people of the same sex more than Westerners. They do not have the same concept of "public" and "private" space, or as Hall puts it, "Not only is the sheer noise level much higher, but the piercing look of the eyes, the touch of the hands, and the mutual bathing in the warm moist breath during conversation represent stepped-up sensory inputs to a level which many Europeans find unbearably intense.[48] On the other hand, the distance preferred by North Americans may leave an Arab suspicious of intentions because of the lack of olfactory contact.[49]

The Muslim expression *Bukra insha Allah*—"Tomorrow if Allah wills"—explains much about the Arab culture and its approach to business transactions. A cultural clash typically occurs when an American tries to give an Arab a deadline. "I am going to Damascus tomorrow morning and will have to have my car tonight," is a sure way to get the mechanic to stop work," explains Hall, "because to give another person a deadline in this part of the world is to be rude, pushy, and demanding."[50] In such instances, the attitude toward time communicates as loudly as words.

In verbal interactions, managers must be aware of different patterns of Arab thought and communication. Compared to the direct, linear fashion of American communication, Arabs tend to meander: They start with social talk, discuss business for a while, loop round to social and general issues, then back to business, and so on.[51] American impatience and insistence on sticking to the subject will "cut off their loops," triggering confusion and dysfunction.

EXHIBIT 4-6   *Miscommunication Between Americans and Arabs Caused by Cross-cultural Noise*

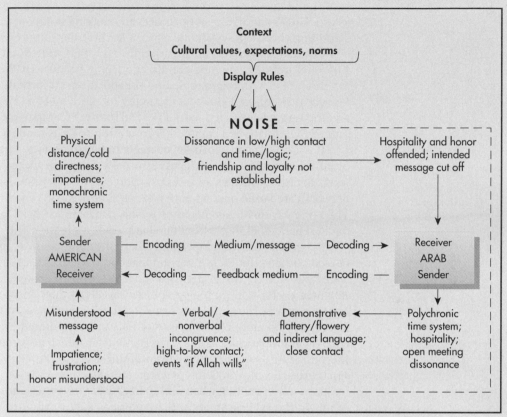

Exhibit 4-6 illustrates some of the sources of noise that are likely to interfere in the communication process between Americans and Arabs.

For people doing business in the Middle East, the following are some useful guidelines for effective communication:

- Be patient. Recognize the Arab attitude toward time and hospitality—take time to develop friendship and trust, for these are prerequisites for any social or business transactions.
- Recognize that people and relationships matter more to Arabs than the job, company, or contract—conduct business personally, not by correspondence or telephone.
- Avoid expressing doubts or criticism when others are present—recognize the importance of honor and dignity to Arabs.
- Adapt to the norms of body language, flowery speech, and circuitous verbal patterns in the Middle East, and don't be impatient to "get to the point."
- Expect many interruptions in meetings, delays in schedules, and changes in plans.[52]

Communication Channels

In addition to the variables related to the sender and receiver of a message, the variables linked to the channel itself and the context of the message must be taken into consideration. These variables include fast or slow messages and information flows, as well as different types of media.

Information Systems   Communication in organizations varies according to where and how it originates, the channels, and the speed at which it flows, whether it is formal or informal, and so forth. The type of organizational structure, the staffing policies, and the leadership style will affect the nature of an organization's information system.

As an international manager, it is useful to know where and how information originates and the speed at which it flows, both internally and externally. In centralized organizational structures, as in South America, most information originates from top managers. Workers take less responsibility to keep managers informed than in a typical company in the United States, where delegation results in information flowing from the staff to the managers. In a decision-making system where many people are involved, such as the **Ringi system** of consensus decision making in Japan, the expatriate needs to understand that there is a systematic pattern for information flow.[53]

Context also affects information flow. In high-context cultures (such as in the Middle East), information spreads rapidly and freely because of the constant close contact and the implicit ties among people and organizations. Information flow is often informal. In low-context cultures (such as Germany or the United States), information is controlled and focused, and thus it does not flow so freely.[54] Compartmentalized roles and office layouts stifle information channels; information sources tend to be more formal.

It is crucial for an expatriate manager to find out how to tap into a firm's informal sources of information. In Japan, employees usually have a drink together on the way home from work, and this becomes an essential source of information. However, such communication networks are based on long-term relationships in Japan (and in other high-context cultures). The same information may not be readily available to "outsiders." A considerable barrier in Japan separates strangers from familiar friends, a situation that discourages communication.

Americans are more open and talk freely about almost anything, whereas Japanese will disclose little about their inner thoughts or private issues. Americans are willing to have a wide "public self," disclosing their inner reactions verbally and physically. In contrast, the Japanese prefer to keep their responses largely to their "private self." The Japanese expose only a small portion of their thoughts; they reduce, according to Barnlund, "the unpredictability and emotional intensity of personal encounters."[55] Barnlund depicts this difference diagrammatically, as shown in Exhibit 4-7, which illustrates the cultural clash between the public and private selves in intercultural communication between Americans and Japanese. The plus and minus signs indicate the areas of agreement or disagreement (respectively) resulting when each party forces its cultural norms of communication on the other. In the American style, the American's cultural norms of explicit communication impose on the Japanese by invading the person's private self. The Japanese style of implicit communication causes a negative reaction from the American because of what is perceived as too much formality and ambiguity, which wastes time.[56]

Cultural variables in information systems and context underlie the many differences in communication style between Japanese and Americans. Exhibit 4-8 shows some specific differences. The Japanese *ningensei* ("human beingness") style of communication refers to the preference for humanity, reciprocity, a receiver orientation, and an underlying distrust of words and analytic logic.[57] The Japanese believe that true intentions are not readily revealed in words or contracts but are, in fact, masked by them. In contrast to the typical American's verbal agility and explicitness, Japanese behaviors and communications are directed to defend and give face for everyone concerned; to do so, they avoid public disagreements at all costs. In cross-cultural negotiations, this last point is essential.

The speed with which we try to use information systems is another key variable that needs attention to avoid misinterpretation and conflict. Americans expect to give and receive information very quickly and clearly, moving through details and stages in a linear fashion to the conclusion. They usually use various media for fast messages—letters giving all the facts and plans up front, faxes, and familiar relationships. In contrast, the French use the slower message channels of deep relationships, culture, and sometimes mediators to exchange information. A French written communication will be tentative, with subsequent letters slowly building up to a new proposal. The French preference for written communication, even for informal interactions, echoes the formality of their relationships—and results in a slowing down of message transmission that often seems unnecessary to Americans. Jean-Louis Reynal, a plant manager at Citröen, explains that "it wouldn't be too much of an exaggeration to say that, until they are written, until they are entrusted to the blackboard, the notepad, or the flip chart, ideas have no reality for the French manager. You could even say that writing is an indispensable aid to 'being' for us."[58]

In short, it behooves Americans to realize that, because most of the world exchanges information through slower message media, it is wise to schedule more time for transactions, develop patience, and learn to get at needed information in more subtle ways—after building rapport and taking time to observe the local system for exchanging information.

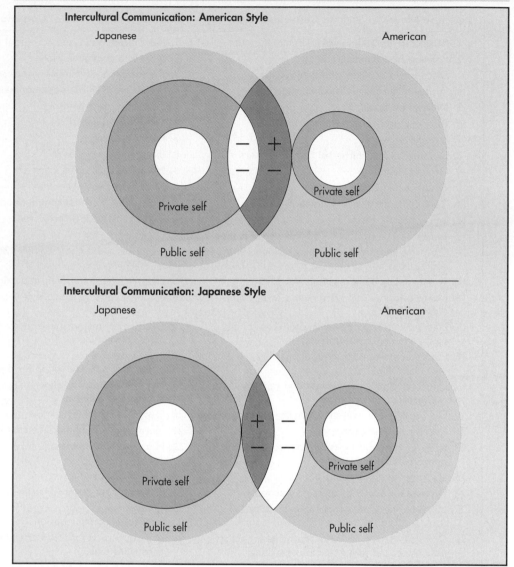

EXHIBIT 4-7   Intercultural Communication Conflicts Between Americans and Japanese

SOURCE: Dean C. Barnlund, "Public and Private Self in Communicating with Japan," *Business Horizons* (March–April 1989): 37. Reprinted with permission from Business Horizons, © 1989 by the Trustees at Indiana University, Kelley School of Business.

We have seen that cross-cultural misinterpretation can result from noise in the actual transmission of the message—the choice or speed of media. Interpreting the meaning of a message can thus be as much a function of the transmission channel (or medium) as it is of examining the message itself.

INFORMATION TECHNOLOGY: GOING GLOBAL AND ACTING LOCAL

All information is local; IT systems can connect every corner of the globe, but IT managers are learning they have to pay attention to regional differences.

COMPUTERWORLD,
April 10, 2000[59]

Deploying B2B e-commerce technology [globally] ... becomes exponentially more difficult because systems must address concerns not germane to domestic networks, such as language translation, currency conversion and even cultural differences.

INTERNET WEEK,
October 9, 2000[60]

EXHIBIT 4-8 Difference Between Japanese and American Communication Styles

Japanese *Ningensei* Style of Communication	U.S. Adversarial Style of Communication
1. Indirect verbal and nonverbal communication	1. More direct verbal and nonverbal communication
2. Relationship communication	2. More task communication
3. Discourages confrontational strategies	3. Confrontational strategies more acceptable
4. Strategically ambiguous communication	4. Prefers more to-the-point communication
5. Delayed feedback	5. More immediate feedback
6. Patient, longer-term negotiators	6. Shorter-term negotiators
7. Uses fewer words	7. Favors verbosity
8. Distrustful of skillful verbal communicators	8. Exalts verbal eloquence
9. Group orientation	9. More individualistic orientation
10. Cautious, tentative	10. More assertive, self-assured
11. Complementary communicators	11. More publicly critical communication
12. Softer, heartlike logic	12. Harder, analytic logic preferred
13. Sympathetic, empathetic, complex use of pathos	13. Favors logos, reason
14. Expresses and decodes complex relational strategies and nuances	14. Expresses and decodes complex logos, cognitive nuances
15. Avoids decision making in public	15. Frequent decision making in public
16. Makes decisions in private venues, away from public eye	16. Frequent decision in public at negotiating tables
17. Decisions via *ringi* and *nemawashi* (complete consensus process)	17. Decisions by majority rule and public compromise is more commonplace
18. Uses go-betweens for decision making	18. More extensive use of direct person-to-person, player-to-player interaction for decisions
19. Understatement and hesitation in verbal and nonverbal communication	19. May publicly speak in superlatives, exaggerations, nonverbal projection
20. Uses qualifiers, tentativeness, humility as communicator	20. Favors fewer qualifiers, more ego-centered
21. Receiver/listening-centered	21. More speaker- and message-centered
22. Inferred meanings, looks beyond words to nuances, nonverbal communication	22. More face-value meaning, more denotative
23. Shy, reserved communicators	23. More publicly self-assertive
24. Distaste for purely business transactions	24. Prefers to "get down to business" or "nitty gritty"
25. Mixes business and social communication	25. Tends to keep business negotiating more separated from social communication
26. Utilizes *matomari* or "hints" for achieving group adjustment and saving face in negotiating	26. More directly verbalizes management's preference at negotiating tables
27. Practices *haragei* or "belly logic" and communication	27. Practices more linear, discursive, analytical logic; greater reverence for cognitive than for affective

SOURCE: Reprinted from A. Goldman, "The Centrality of 'Ningensei' to Japanese Negotiating and Interpersonal Relationships: Implications for U.S. Japanese Communication," *International Journal of Intercultural Relations* 18, no. 1 (Winter 1994), with permission from Elsevier.

Using the Internet as a global medium for communication has enabled companies of all sizes to quickly develop a presence in many markets around the world—and, in fact, has enabled them to "go global." However, their global reach cannot alone translate into global business. Those companies are learning that they have to adapt their e-commerce and their enterprise resource planning (ERP) applications to regional idiosyncrasies beyond translation or content management issues; even asking for a name or an e-mail address can incur resistance in many countries where people do not like to give out personal information.[61] While communication over the Internet is clearly not as personal as face-to-face cross-cultural communication, those transactions must still be regionalized and personalized to adjust to differences in language, culture, local laws, and business models, as well as differences in the level of development in the local telecommunications infrastructure. Yet, if the Internet is a global medium for communication, why do so many U.S. companies treat the Web as a U.S.-centric phenomenon?

Giving preference to some geographic regions, languages, and cultures is "a short-sighted business decision that will result in diminished brand equity, market share, profits and global leadership."[62] With an annual predicted growth rate of 70 percent in non–English-language sites and usage, this soon puts English-language sites in the minority.[63]

It seems essential, then, that a global online strategy must also be multilocal. The impersonal nature of the Web must somehow be adapted to local cultures to establish relationships and create customer loyalty. Effective technological communication requires even more cultural sensitivity than face-to-face communication because of the inability to assess reactions and get feedback, or even to retain contact in many cases. It is still people, after all, who respond to and interact with other people through the medium of the Internet, and those people interpret and respond according to their own languages and cultures, as well as their local business practices and expectations. In Europe, for example, significant differences in business cultures and e-business technology have slowed e-business progress there. However, some companies are making progress in pan-European integration services, such as *leEurope*, which aims to cross language, currency, and cultural barriers. Specifically, *leEurope* is building a set of services "to help companies tie their back-end e-business systems together across European boundaries through a series of mergers involving regional e-business integrators in more than a dozen countries."[64]

Manheim Auctions, featured in the accompanying E-Biz Box: Manheim Auctions Adds Localized B2B System to Its Global Operations, is one global company that has successfully added a multilocal online strategy to its long-established bricks-and-mortar facilities.

E-BIZ BOX

Manheim Auctions Adds Localized B2B System to Its Global Operations

With headquarters in Atlanta, Georgia, Manheim Auctions is the largest and highest volume wholesale automobile auction company in the world. The company operates more than 115 auction facilities worldwide and employs more than 30,000 people. Manheim remarkets vehicles for wholesale consignors. These sellers include car dealers, manufacturers, rental car operators, fleet/lease companies, and financial institutions. The buyers of the vehicles are licensed franchise and independent auto dealers. Thousands of dealers conduct business using Manheim's global network, which shares a massive database of vehicle information, including prices, histories, and digital photos—through www.Manheimauctions.com and www.Autotrader.com, as well as localized addresses.*

Mainheim has had its share of challenges as it attempts to localize its "cyberlots" while expanding globally. New partners in the United Kingdom and Australia, for example, unknown to Manheim, had lines of business that Manheim's online site did not support. The company also had to make adjustments for different measurement standards, such as kilometers, and different terminology for car parts, such as a "boot" in the United Kingdom instead of "trunk."** In addition, with feedback from its Australian acquisition partner, Manheim made changes to its corporate logo, shown below. Those partners down under naturally felt left out when they saw that the globe logo showed only North and South America.***

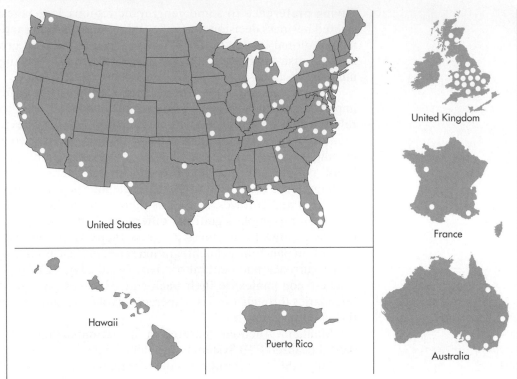

*With more than **115** locations worldwide, Manheim's global network shares a massive database of vehicle information including prices, histories, and digital photos.*

Map 4-1

*www.manheimauctions.com, April 2001.
**D. Shand, "All Information Is Local: IT Systems Can Connect Every Corner of the Globe, But IT Managers Are Learning They Have to Pay Attention to Regional Differences," *Computerworld*, April 10, 2000, 88 (1).
***Ibid.

SOURCE: www.manheimauctions.com/HTML/history.html.

MANAGING CROSS-CULTURAL COMMUNICATION

Steps toward effective intercultural communication include the development of cultural sensitivity, careful encoding, selective transmission, careful decoding, and appropriate followup actions. These steps are discussed as follows and are illustrated in the accompanying

---

Management Focus

Indian Companies Are Adding Western Flavor

By SARITHA RAI
   August 19, 2003

HYDERABAD, India - Arun Kumar had never shaken hands with a foreigner nor needed to wear a necktie. He vaguely thought that raising a toast had something to do with eating bread. If it was dark outside, he greeted people with a "good night."

But Mr. Kumar, 27, and six other engineers graduating from the local university with master's degrees in computer applications, were recently recruited by the Hyderabad offices of Sierra Atlantic, a software company based in Fremont, California And, before they came face to face with one of Sierra's 200 or so American customers, the new employees went through a grueling four-week training session aimed at providing them with global-employee skills like learning how to speak on a conference call, how to address colleagues (as Mr. or Ms.), and how to sip wine properly.

"Teetotalers practice by sipping Coke out of their wine glasses," Mr. Kumar said at the session in early July.

As more and more service- and knowledge-intensive jobs migrate to India, such training programs, covering some substance as well as style, are increasingly common at companies with large numbers of Indian employees.

It is particularly imperative for employees of software companies to appear culturally seamless with Americans. American clients account for more than two-thirds of India's software and services export revenues. Growing at 30 percent a year despite a global downturn, the sectors account for 18 percent of the country's total exports.

Sierra Atlantic, a midsize software services company whose clients include the Oracle Corporation of Redwood City, California, says that one-fourth of its 400 employees, all but a handful of them Indian and most of them working out of the Hyderabad offices, are constantly interacting with foreigners.

For Sierra and others, including the Bangalore-based Wipro and Infosys Technologies, two of India's largest software and services exporters, the training in Western ways is intended not only to help employees perform daily business interactions with American or European colleagues and customers but to help the companies transcend their image as cheap labor.

As India's software companies expand, they are competing to hire the most skilled engineers. And, Mr. Kumar is typical of the thousands of eager young engineering graduates from small-town India who are thronging India's technology hubs—cities like Hyderabad, Bangalore, and Chennai—in search of these jobs.

Though he and his peers are technologically adept and fluent in English, most lack the sophistication needed to flourish in a global business setting.

"It is not always understood that speaking a common language, English, is rarely a guarantee of communicating the same way," said Partha Iyengar, vice president for research at Gartner India Research and Advisory Services.

That point has been increasingly driven home as top Indian software companies like Infosys, Wipro, and the Bombay-based Tata Consultancy Services have moved to the next level of competition by offering product development, call centers, support services, and bidding on multimillion-dollar deals.

Such companies already provide services for some multinationals, primarily those based in the United States, including General Electric, American Express and Nike. They are expected to gross an estimated $12 billion in export revenues this year, up from $9.5 billion last year, according to the National Association of Software and Service Companies, the industry trade group known as Nasscom. And that means more contact with customers and clients abroad—and more often as full professional partners. "Your interaction with people of alien cultures will only increase," Colonel Gowri Shankar, a 30-year veteran of the Indian Army and Sierra's trainer, told Mr. Kumar and half a dozen other young engineers that morning in July, "and you should be equally at ease whether in Hyderabad or Houston."

Colonel Shankar and some other trainers are on the staff of their companies, though some companies, like Wipro, bring in Americans.

The Sierra programmers listened raptly as Colonel Shankar listed common complaints: speaking one of India's many languages in front of foreigners, questioning colleagues about their compensation and cracking ethnic jokes. Some things he covers are not acceptable in any corporate setting and some are particular sore points with foreigners.

He is fiendish about punctuality and a stickler for protocol.

"Americans are friendly, but do not slap an American on his back or call him by his first name in the first meeting," said Colonel Shankar, whose training materials are fine-tuned by information from programmers returning from trips abroad.

Across the world, Global Savvy, a consulting company in Palo Alto, California, trains high-tech employees to work together in projects around the world. "The training in American culture is not to make Indian software professionals less Indian," said Lu Ellen Schafer, the executive director. "It is to make them more globally competent."

Among Ms. Schafer's clients are Cisco Systems and the LexisNexis unit of Reed Elsevier as well as Wipro and other Indian companies. Ms. Schafer says she urges her American clients to refer to Indians as "consultants and partners," not "contractors and vendors." She prefers to train Americans and Indians together, to stress that globalizing is a two-way street.

For the Indian software companies that have expanded their lines of business, there are new cultural challenges.

"The Indian programmer mind-set is to provide only what is asked, but the consultant is trained to offer alternative viewpoints," said Ranjan Acharya, corporate vice president for human resources development at Wipro, which has trained 650 of its employees in what it calls "power consulting." Still, he said, "we train our people to appear right," without appearing to be the final authority.

The pressure in consulting, a business many of the top software companies are trying to ramp up, has become intense as global giants like Accenture expand in India. "While Indian companies do very well at the low end," said Andrew Holland, executive vice president for DSP Merrill Lynch, "global corporations still prefer to look at large consultancies like Accenture higher up the chain."

And, the competition on the low end will soon include software companies from countries like China and Russia.

Companies that distinguish themselves as strategic partners will separate from the low-cost pack, said Marc Hebert, Sierra Atlantic's executive vice president for marketing.

Whether the cultural training will make a difference is unclear.

"As an aggregate, Indian software professionals have not changed in the way they present themselves," said Peter Nag, vice president and global program management officer for Lehman Brothers in New York, which is a client of Wipro. "We find that Indians hesitate to say no even though we ask them all the time to speak their minds. Then, there are small things like getting up from the seat when a senior colleague enters the room. This feels strange."

"But there are many good individuals technically qualified and culturally sophisticated," he added. "They are the types we would hire here on Wall Street."

Still, some companies training their employees say they are already seeing the benefits. Sierra said that in February its Indian unit won a bid against a technically able Indian competitor because the Sierra employees were seen as a better fit. "It all adds up to better rates and bigger projects," said the project leader, Kalyani Manda.

Ms. Manda said she noticed a difference when she herself conformed, even in a seemingly minor way. On her first trip to the United States three years ago, she wore a *salwar kameez*, a loose-fitting Indian garment, and felt totally out of place. "On the next trip," she said, "I wore pants, fit in better, and delivered more."

As the training of Sierra's fresh recruits progressed, Mr. Kumar, who has never written a letter before except to his family, exulted, "I wrote a business letter to my project head which I began with 'Dear Mr. Hari.'"

A colleague, Aastha Vij, 23, was equally jubilant.

"I'm actually looking forward to meeting my first American client," Ms. Vij said. "I'm no longer nervous."

Management Focus: Indian Companies Are Adding Western Flavor, which describes how Indian software professionals working for high-tech Western companies in India are taking training in cross-cultural sensitivity and communication to make them more globally competent.

Developing Cultural Sensitivity

When acting as a sender, a manager must make it a point to know the receiver and to encode the message in a form that will most likely be understood as intended. On the manager's part, this requires an awareness of his or her own cultural baggage and how it affects the communication process. In other words, what kinds of behaviors does the message imply, and how will they be perceived by the receiver? The way to anticipate the most likely meaning that the receiver will attach to the message is to internalize honest cultural empathy with that person. What is the cultural background—the societal, economic, and organizational context—in which this communication is taking place? What are this person's expectations regarding the situation, what are the two parties' relative positions, and what might develop from this communication? What kinds of transactions and behaviors is this person used to? Cultural sensitivity (discussed in Chapter 3) is really just a matter of understanding the other person, the context, and how the person will respond to the context.

Careful Encoding

In translating his or her intended meaning into symbols for cross-cultural communication, the sender must use words, pictures, or gestures that are appropriate to the receiver's frame of reference. Of course, language training is invaluable, but senders should also avoid idioms and regional sayings (such as "Go fly a kite" or "Foot the bill") in a translation, or even in English when speaking to a non-American who knows little English.

Literal translation, then, is a limited answer to language differences. Even for people in English-speaking countries, words may have different meanings—as experienced by a U.S. banker in Australia after a business dinner. To show appreciation, he said he was "full" (interpreted by his hosts as drunk); as the silence spread at the table, he tried to correct himself by saying he was "stuffed" (a word used locally only in a sexual context).[65] Ways to avoid such problems are to speak slowly and clearly, avoid long sentences and colloquial expressions, and explain things in several different ways and through several media, if possible.[66] However, even though English is in common use around the world for business transactions, the manager's efforts to speak the local language will greatly improve the climate. Sometimes people from other cultures resent the assumption by English-speaking executives that everyone else will speak English.

Language translation is only part of the encoding process; the message also is expressed in nonverbal language. In the encoding process, the sender must ensure congruence between the nonverbal and the verbal message. In encoding a message, therefore, it is useful to be as objective as possible and not to rely on personal interpretations. To further clarify their messages, managers can hand out written summaries of verbal presentations and use visual aids, such as graphs or pictures. A good general guide is to move slowly, wait, and take cues from the receivers.

Selective Transmission

The type of medium chosen for the message depends on the nature of the message, its level of importance, the context and expectations of the receiver, the timing involved, and the need for personal interaction, among other factors. Typical media include e-mail, letters or memos, reports, meetings, telephone calls, teleconferences, videoconferences, or face-to-face conversations. The secret is to find out how communication is transmitted in the local organization—how much is downward versus upward or vertical versus horizontal, how the grapevine works, and so on. In addition, the cultural variables discussed earlier need to be considered: whether the receiver is from a high- or low-context culture, whether he or she is used to explicit or implicit communication, and what speed and routing of messages will be most effective.

For the most part, it is best to use face-to-face interaction for relationship building or for other important transactions, particularly in intercultural communications, because of the lack of familiarity between parties. Personal interactions give the manager the opportunity to get immediate verbal and visual feedback and to make rapid adjustments in the communication process.

International dealings are often long-distance, of course, limiting the opportunity for face-to-face communication. However, personal rapport can be established or enhanced through telephone calls or videoconferencing and through trusted contacts. Modern electronic media can be used to break down communication barriers by reducing waiting periods for information, clarifying issues, and allowing instant consultation. Global telecommunications and computer networks are changing the face of cross-cultural communication through the faster dissemination of information within the receiving organization. Ford of Europe uses videoconferencing for engineers in Britain and Germany to consult about quality problems. Through the video monitors, they examine one another's engineering diagrams and usually find a solution that gets the factory moving again in a short time.[67]

Careful Decoding of Feedback

Timely and effective feedback channels can also be set up to assess a firm's general communication about the progression of its business and its general management principles. The best means for getting accurate feedback is through face-to-face interaction because this allows the manager to hear, see, and immediately sense how a message is being interpreted. When visual feedback on important issues is not possible or appropriate, it is a good idea to use several means of attaining feedback, in particular, employing third parties.

Decoding is the process of translating the received symbols into the interpreted message. The main causes of incongruence are (1) the receiver misinterprets the message, (2) the receiver encodes his or her return message incorrectly, or (3) the sender misinterprets the feedback. Two-way communication is thus essential for important issues so that successive efforts can be made until an understanding has been achieved. Asking other colleagues to help interpret what is going on is often a good way to break a cycle of miscommunication.

Perhaps the most important means for avoiding miscommunication is to practice careful decoding by improving one's listening and observation skills. A good listener practices projective listening, or empathetic listening—listening without interruption or evaluation to the full message of the speaker, attempting to recognize the feelings behind the words and nonverbal cues, and understanding the speaker's perspective.

At the multinational corporation (MNC) level, avenues of communication and feedback among parent companies and subsidiaries can be kept open through telephone calls, regular meetings and visits, reports, and plans—all of which facilitate cooperation, performance control, and the smooth running of the company. Communication among far-flung operations can be best managed by setting up feedback systems and liaison people. The headquarters people should maintain considerable flexibility in cooperating with local managers and allowing them to deal with the local context as they see fit.

Follow-up Actions

Managers communicate through both action and inaction. Therefore, to keep open the lines of communication, feedback, and trust, managers must follow through with action on what has been discussed and then agreed upon—typically a contract, which is probably the most important formal business communication. Unfortunately, the issue of contract follow-through is a particularly sensitive one across cultures because of the different interpretations regarding what constitutes a contract (perhaps a handshake, perhaps a full legal document) and what actions should result. Trust, future communications, and future business are based on such interpretations, and it is up to managers to understand them and to follow through on them.

The management of cross-cultural communication depends largely on a manager's personal abilities and behavior. Those behaviors that researchers indicate to be most important to intercultural communication effectiveness (ICE) are listed here, as reviewed by Ruben:

1. Respect (conveyed through eye contact, body posture, voice tone, and pitch)
2. Interaction posture (the ability to respond to others in a descriptive, nonevaluative, and nonjudgmental way)
3. Orientation to knowledge (recognizing that one's knowledge, perception, and beliefs are valid only for oneself and not for everyone else)
4. Empathy
5. Interaction management
6. Tolerance for ambiguity
7. Other-oriented role behavior (one's capacity to be flexible and to adopt different roles for the sake of greater group cohesion and group communication)[68]

Whether at home or abroad, certain personal capabilities facilitate effective intercultural communication; these abilities can help the expatriate to adapt to the host country and enable productive working relations to develop in the long term. Researchers have established a relationship between personality traits and behaviors and the ability to adapt to the host-country's cultural environment.[69] What is seldom pointed out, however, is that communication is the mediating factor between those behaviors and the relative level of adaptation the expatriate achieves. The communication process facilitates cross-cultural adaptation through this process, expatriates learn the dominant communication patterns of the host society. Therefore, we can link those personality factors shown by research to ease adaptation with those necessary for effective intercultural communication.

Kim has consolidated the research findings of these characteristics into two categories: (1) **openness**—traits such as open-mindedness, tolerance for ambiguity, and extrovertedness; and (2) **resilience**—traits such as having an internal locus of control, persistence, a tolerance of ambiguity, and resourcefulness.[70] These personality factors, along with the expatriate's cultural and racial identity and the level of preparedness for change, comprise that person's potential for adaptation. The level of preparedness can be improved by the manager before his or her assignment by gathering information about the host country's verbal and nonverbal communication patterns and norms of behavior. Kim incorporates these factors in a communication model of cross-cultural adaptation. Exhibit 4-9 shows the major variables that affect the level of communication competence achieved between the host and the expatriate. These are the adaptive predisposition of the expatriate and the conditions of receptivity and conformity to pressure in the host environment. These factors affect the process of personal and social communication, and, ultimately, the adaptation outcome. Explains Kim, "Three aspects of strangers' adaptive change—increased functional fitness, psychological health, and intercultural identity—have been identified as direct consequences of prolonged communication-adaptation experiences in the host society."[71] Chapter 10 explores areas where the firm has responsibility to improve the employee/managerial ability to adapt.

In identifying personal and behavioral specifics that facilitate ICE, however, we cannot lose sight of the whole picture. We must remember the basic principle of contingency management, which is that managers operate in a system of many interacting variables in a

EXHIBIT 4-9   A Communication Model of Cross-cultural Adaptation

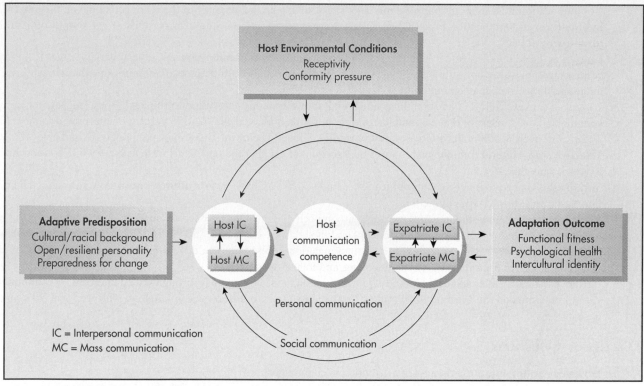

SOURCE: Adapted from Young Yun Kim, *Communication and Cross-Cultural Adaptation* (Clevedon, England: Multilingual Matters, 1988): 79.

dynamic context. Studies show that situational factors—such as the physical environment, time constraints, degree of structure, feelings of boredom or overwork, and anonymity— are strong influences on intercultural communication competence.[72]

It is this interdependence of many variables that makes it difficult for intercultural researchers to isolate and identify factors for success. Although managers try to understand and control up front as many factors as possible that will lead to management effectiveness, often they only find out what works from the results of their decisions.

CONCLUSION

Effective intercultural communication is a vital skill for international managers and domestic managers of multicultural workforces. Because miscommunication is much more likely to occur among people from different countries or racial backgrounds than among those from similar backgrounds, it is important to be alert to how culture is reflected in communication—in particular through the development of cultural sensitivity and an awareness of potential sources of cultural noise in the communication process. A successful international manager is thus attuned to these variables and is flexible enough to adjust his or her communication style to best address the intended receivers— that is, to do it "their way."

Cultural variables and the manner in which culture is communicated underlie the processes of negotiation and decision making. How do people around the world negotiate: What are their expectations and their approach to negotiations? What is the importance of understanding negotiation and decision-making processes in other countries? Chapter 5 addresses these questions and makes suggestions for the international manager to handle these important tasks.

Summary of Key Points

1. Communication is an inherent part of a manager's role, taking up the majority of the manager's time on the job. Effective intercultural communication largely determines the success of international transactions or the output of a culturally diverse workforce.
2. Culture is the foundation of communication, and communication transmits culture. Cultural variables that can affect the communication process by influencing a person's perceptions include attitudes, social organizations, thought patterns, roles, language, nonverbal language, and time.
3. Language conveys cultural understandings and social norms from one generation to the next. Body language, or nonverbal communication, is behavior that communicates without words. It accounts for 65 to 93 percent of interpreted communication.
4. Types of nonverbal communication around the world are kinesic behavior, proxemics, paralanguage, and object language.
5. Effective cross-cultural communication must take account of whether the receiver is from a country with a monochronic or a polychronic time system.
6. Variables related to channels of communication include high- and low-context cultures, fast or slow messages and information flows, and various types of media.
7. In high-context cultures, feelings and messages are implicit and must be accessed through an understanding of the person and the system. In low-context cultures, feelings and thoughts are expressed, and information is more readily available.
8. The effective management of intercultural communication necessitates the development of cultural sensitivity, careful encoding, selective transmission, careful decoding, and follow-up actions.
9. Certain personal abilities and behaviors facilitate adaptation to the host country through skilled intercultural communication.
10. Communication via the Internet must still be localized to adjust to differences in language, culture, local laws, and business models.

Discussion Questions

1. How does culture affect the process of attribution in communication?
2. What is stereotyping? Give some examples. How might people stereotype you? How does a sociotype differ from a stereotype?
3. What is the relationship between language and culture? How is it that people form different countries who speak the same language may still miscommunicate?
4. Give some examples of cultural differences in the interpretation of body language. What is the role of such nonverbal communication in business relationships?
5. Explain the differences between monochronic and polychronic time systems. Use some examples to illustrate their differences and the role of time in intercultural communication.
6. Explain the differences between high- and low-context cultures, giving some examples. What are the differential effects on the communication process?
7. Discuss the role of information systems in a company, how and why they vary from country to country, and the effects of these variations.

Application Exercises

1. Form groups in your class—multicultural groups, if possible. Have each person make notes about his or her perceptions of (1) Mexican-Americans, (2) Native Americans, (3) African-Americans, and (4) Americans of European descent. Discuss your notes and draw conclusions about common stereotypes. Discuss any differences and why stereotyping occurs.
2. Invite some foreign students to your class. Ask them to bring photographs, slides, and so forth of people and events in their native countries. Have them explain the meanings of various nonverbal cues, such as gestures, dress, voice inflections, architecture, and events. Discuss with them any differences between their explanations and the attributions you assigned to those cues.
3. Interview a faculty member or a businessperson who has worked abroad. Ask him or her to identify factors that facilitated or inhibited adaptation to the host environment. Ask whether more preparation could have eased the transition and what, if anything, that person would do differently before another trip.

Experiential Exercise: Script for Juan Perillo and Jean Moore

Scene I: February 15, San Juan, Puerto Rico

JUAN: Welcome back to Puerto Rico, Jean. It is good to have you here in San Juan again. I hope that your trip from Dayton was a smooth one.

JEAN: Thank you, Juan. It's nice to be back here where the sun shines. Fred sends his regards and also asked me to tell you how important it is that we work out a firm production schedule for the next three months. But first, how is your family? All doing well, I hope.

JUAN: My wife is doing very well, but my daughter, Marianna, broke her arm and has to have surgery to repair the bone. We are very worried about that because the surgeon says she may have to have several operations. It is very difficult to think about my poor little daughter in the operating room. She was out playing with some other children when it happened. You know how roughly children sometimes play with each other. It's really amazing that they don't have more injuries. Why, just last week, my son. . . .

JEAN: Of course I'm very sorry to hear about little Marianna, but I'm sure everything will go well with the surgery. Now, shall we start work on the production schedule?

JUAN: Oh, yes, of course, we must get started on the production schedule.

JEAN: Fred and I thought that June 1 would be a good cutoff date for the first phase of the schedule. And we also thought that a hundred A-type computers would be a reasonable goal for that phase. We know that you have some new assemblers whom you are training, and that you've had some problems getting parts from your suppliers in the past few months. But we're sure you have all those problems worked out by now and that you are back to full production capability. So, what do you think? Is a hundred A-type computers produced by June 1 a reasonable goal for your people?

JUAN: (Hesitates a few seconds before replying) You want us to produce one hundred of the newly designed A-type computers by June 1? Will we also be producing our usual number of Z-type computers, too?

JEAN: Oh, yes. Your regular production schedule would remain the same as it's always been. The only difference is that you would be producing the new A-type computers, too. I mean, after all, you have a lot of new employees, and you have all the new manufacturing and assembling equipment that we have in Dayton. So, you're as ready to make the new product as we are.

JUAN: Yes, that's true. We have the new equipment, and we've just hired a lot of new assemblers who will be working on the A-type computer. I guess there's no reason we can't meet the production schedule you and Fred have come up with.

JEAN: Great, great. I'll tell Fred you agree with our decision and will meet the goal of 100 A-type computers by June 1. He'll be delighted to know that you can deliver what he was hoping for. And, of course, Juan, that means that you'll be doing just as well as the Dayton plant.

Scene II: May 1, San Juan, Puerto Rico

JEAN: Hello, Juan. How are things here in Puerto Rico? I'm glad to have the chance to come back and see how things are going.

JUAN: Welcome, Jean. It's good to have you here. How is your family?

JEAN: Oh, they're fine, just fine. You know, Juan, Fred is really excited about that big order we just got from the Defense Department for fifty A-type computers. They want them by June 10, so we will ship them directly to Washington from San Juan as the computers come off your assembly line. Looks like it's a good thing we set your production goal at a 100 A-type computers by June 1, isn't it?

JUAN: Um, yes, that was certainly a good idea.

JEAN: So, tell me, have you had any problems with the new model? How are your new assemblers working out? Do you have any suggestions for changes in the manufacturing specs? How is the new quality control program working with this model? We're always looking for ways to improve, you know, and we appreciate any ideas you can give us.

JUAN: Well, Jean, there is one thing. . . .

JEAN: Yes? What is that?

JUAN: Well, Jean, we have had a few problems with the new assemblers. Three of them have had serious illnesses in their families and have had to take off several days at a time to nurse a sick child or elderly parent. And another one was involved in a car accident and was in the hospital for several days. And you remember my daughter's surgery? Well, her arm didn't mend properly, and we had to take her to Houston for additional consultations and therapy. But, of course, you and Fred knew about that.

JEAN: Yes, we were aware that you had had some personnel problems and that you and your wife had had to go to Houston with Marianna. But what does that have to do with the fifty A-type computers for the Defense Department?

JUAN: Well, Jean, because of all these problems, we have had a few delays in the production schedule. Nothing serious, but we are a little bit behind our schedule.

JEAN: How far behind is "a little bit"? What are you trying to tell me, Juan? Will you have fifty more A-type computers by June 1 to ship to Washington to fill the Defense Department order?

JUAN: Well, I certainly hope we will have that number ready to ship. You know how difficult it can be to predict a precise number for manufacturing, Jean. You probably have many of these same problems in the Dayton plant, don't you?

SOURCE: L. Catlin and T. White, *International Business: Cultural Sourcebook and Case Studies* (Cincinnati, Ohio: South-Western, 1994), used with permission.

Exercise Questions

1. What went wrong for Jean in Puerto Rico? Could this have been avoided? What should she have done differently?
2. Replay the role of Jean and Juan during their conversation, establishing a more constructive communication and management style than Jean did previously.

Internet Resources

Visit the Deresky companion Web site at www.prenhall.com/deresky for this chapter's Internet resources.

Elizabeth Visits GPC's French Subsidiary

Elizabeth Moreno is looking out the window from her business-class seat somewhere over the Indian Ocean on Thai Air en route to Paris's Orly International Airport from the Philippines, where she has just spent a week of meetings and problem solving in a pharmaceutical subsidiary of the Global Pharmaceutical Company (GPC).

GPC has the lion's share of the worldwide market in ethical pharmaceutical products. Ethical drugs are those that can be purchased only through a physician's prescription. In the United States, GPC has research and manufacturing sites in New York, New Jersey, Pennsylvania, and Michigan. The company also has subsidiaries in Canada, Puerto Rico, Australia, the Philippines, Brazil, England, and France. GPC has its administrative headquarters in Pennsylvania.

Because of the geographically dispersed locations of its subsidiaries, GPC's top scientists and key managers log thousands of jet miles a year visiting various offices and plants. Its top specialists and executives regularly engage in multisite real-time video and telephone conferences, and they also use electronic mail, faxes, modems, and traditional mail to keep in touch with key personnel.

Despite these technological advances, face-to-face meetings and on-site consultations are used widely. In the case of the French subsidiary, nothing can take the place of face-to-face consultations. The French manager is suspicious of figures in the balance sheet, of the telephone, of his subordinates, of what he reads in the newspaper, and of what Americans tell him in confidence. In contrast, the American trusts all these (Hill 1994, 60). This is the reason GPC regularly sends its scientists and executives to France.

Elizabeth Moreno is one of the key specialists within GPC. Her expertise in chemical processing is widely known not only within her company but also in the pharmaceutical industry worldwide. She has been working at GPC for more than twelve years since finishing her advanced degree in chemistry from a university in the Midwest. While working for GPC, she has been given more and more responsibilities leading to her current position as vice president of chemical development and processing.

From a hectic visit in the Philippines, her next assignment is to visit the French subsidiary plant for one week to study a problem with shelf-life testing of one of its newest anti-allergy capsules. It seems that the product's active ingredient is degrading sooner than the expiration date. During her stay, she will conduct training for chemists in state-of-the-art techniques for testing and for training local managers in product statistical quality control. These techniques are now currently used in other GPC locations.

To prepare for her foreign assignments, Elizabeth attended a standard three-hour course given by her company's human resource management department on dealing with cross-cultural issues. Moreover, she recalls reading from a book on French management about the impersonal nature of French business relations. This was so much in contrast with what she just has experienced during her visit to the Philippine subsidiary. The French tend to regard authority as residing in the role and not in the person. It is by the power of the position that a French manager gets things done (Hill 1994, 58). With this knowledge, she knows that her expertise and her position as vice president will see her through the technical aspects of the meetings that are lined up for the few days she will be in Paris.

French managers view their work as an intellectual challenge that requires application of individual brainpower. What matters to them is the opportunity to show one's ability to grasp complex issues, analyze problems, manipulate ideas, and evaluate solutions (Hill 1994, 214).

There are a few challenges for Elizabeth on this assignment. She is not fluent in French. Her only exposure to France and the language was a two-week vacation with her husband in Paris a couple of years ago. However, in her highly technical field, the universal language is English. Thus, she believes she will not have much difficulty communicating with the French management to get her assignment successfully completed.

Americans place high value on training and education. In the United States, the field of management has principles that are generally applicable and can be taught and learned. In contrast, the French place more emphasis on the person who can adapt to any situation by virtue of his intellectual quality (Hill 1994, 63). Expertise and intellectual ability are inherent in the individual and cannot be acquired simply through training or education.

It appears that Elizabeth will be encountering very different ways of doing business in France. While she thought about the challenges ahead, her plane landed at Orly International Airport. She whisked through customs and immigration without any delays. No limousine was waiting for her curbside at the arrival. Instead she took the train to downtown Paris and checked into an apartment hotel that was reserved for her in advance of her arrival.

After a week in Paris, she is expected back in her home office to prepare reports to GPC management about her foreign assignments.

CASE QUESTIONS

1. What can Elizabeth Moreno do to establish a position of power in front of French managers to help her accomplish her assignment in five days? Explain.
2. What should Elizabeth know about high-context versus low-context cultures in Europe? Explain.
3. What should Elizabeth include in her report, and what should be the manner in which it is communicated, so that future executives and scientists avoid communications pitfalls? Explain.
4. How can technical language differ from everyday language in corporate communications? Explain.

Case Bibliography

Richard Hill, *Euro-Managers and Martians: The Business Cultures of Europe's Trading Nations* (Brussels: Europublications, Division of Europublic, SA/NV, 1994).

SOURCE: This case was prepared by Edwin J. Portugal, MBA, Ph.D., who teaches multinational management at State University of New York–Potsdam. It is intended to be used as a basis for discussion on the complexity of multicultural management and not to illustrate effective versus ineffective management styles. Copyright © 2004 by Edwin J. Portugal.

CHAPTER 5

Cross-cultural Negotiation and Decision Making

Outline

Opening Profile: Bechtel and GE Benefit from Enron's Failed Negotiations over Dabhol Plant

The Bechtel Group and the General Electric Company (GE), partners of the Enron Corporation in the Dabhol Power Company in India, have bought 65 percent of Dabhol to recoup part of the $1.2 billion they invested in the failed $3 billion venture.

Bechtel and a financing unit of General Electric bought Enron's 65 percent stake in Dabhol for $22 million through a U.S. bankruptcy court in Manhattan, said Jeff Leichtman, a Bechtel spokesman, on Monday. The companies, the two main contractors for the plant, each had a 10 percent stake.

The purchase may help restart the 740-megawatt plant, idle for almost three years, and provide a way for the Indian banks to get back some of the $1.4 billion Enron and its partners borrowed to pay for the project, the companies said.

"The consolidation of foreign equity moves Dabhol closer to restarting," Mr. Leichtman said in a telephone interview from Boston. "It clearly defines who the majority owner is and simplifies things for the purchasers. You no longer have to deal with Enron and the bankruptcy courts."

The dispute over Dabhol—which went bankrupt in May 2001 after a state electricity board stopped paying its bills, saying the cost was too high—continues to deter overseas investment in India's $42 billion power market. A disagreement between local and overseas creditors on how to divide any proceeds has delayed a sale for more than two years; the plant has been placed in court receivership pending the disposal.

The country needs about $200 billion to double generation capacity to 200,000 megawatts in the next decade. As many as ten overseas utilities have quit India, citing red tape and the risk of power sale contracts not being honored.

Bechtel began in September to recover $1.2 billion the companies say they invested in Dabhol. The Overseas Private Investment Corporation, a U.S. agency providing political risk insurance, paid the two companies a total of $57.4 million as damages. "Now that the foreign equity has been consolidated in one place, we can negotiate a fair and equitable settlement and get the plant started," the Bechtel spokesman said. "We are more than willing to sit down and talk to anybody who's interested."

Buyers for Dabhol Power must find a resolution for the legal proceedings as quickly as possible, Mr. Leichtman said. Bidders for Dabhol include Reliance Industries, India's biggest nongovernment company, and a group comprising GAIL (India), British Petroleum (BP), and Tata Power, which last month signed an accord to bid jointly for Dabhol. Tata Power will run the plant, while GAIL, the country's biggest gas supplier, would operate Dabhol's liquefied natural gas import terminal, according to the terms of the accord.

SOURCE: "Bechtel and G.E. Acquire India's Part of Enron Plant," www.nytimes.com, April 13, 2004. Reprinted with permission of The New York Times.

Global managers negotiate with parties in other countries to make specific plans for strategies (exporting, joint ventures, and so forth) and for continuing operations. While the complexities of cross-cultural negotiations among firms around the world present challenge enough, managers also sometimes are faced with negotiating with various governmental agencies. Such a situation is illustrated in the opening profile about Enron's Dabhol plant, where negotiators were faced with years of a shifting political agenda, internal political conflicts between state and national governments, and multiple layers of bureaucratic hurdles, leading to a failed $3 billion venture.

The high-level political negotiations between the United States and China to gain the return of the U.S. military crew from the plane that was forced to land there in April 2001 is another example of complex situations fraught with both political agenda and cultural nuances, such as the need for the Chinese to "save face" by demanding an apology.[1]

Managers must prepare for strategic negotiations. Next the operational details must be negotiated—the staffing of key positions, the sourcing of raw materials or component parts, the repatriating of profits, to name a few. As globalism burgeons, the ability to conduct successful cross-cultural negotiations cannot be overemphasized. Failure to negotiate productively will result in lost potential alliances and lost business at worst, confusion and delays at best.

During the process of negotiation—whether before, during, or after negotiating sessions—all kinds of decisions are made, both explicitly and implicitly. A consideration of cross-cultural negotiations must therefore include the various decision-making processes that occur around the world. Negotiations cannot be conducted without decisions being made.

This chapter examines the processes of negotiation and decision making as they apply to international and domestic cross-cultural contexts. The objective is a better understanding of successful management.

NEGOTIATION

Effecting strategy depends on management's ability to negotiate productively—a skill widely considered one of the most important in international business. In the global arena, cultural differences produce great difficulties in the negotiation process. Ignorance of native bargaining rituals, more than any other single factor, accounts for unimpressive sales efforts.[2] Important differences in the negotiation process from country to country include (1) the amount and type of preparation for a negotiation, (2) the relative emphasis on tasks versus interpersonal relationships, (3) the reliance on general principles rather than specific issues, and (4) the number of people present and the extent of their influence.[3] In every instance, managers must familiarize themselves with the cultural background and underlying motivations of the negotiators—and the tactics and procedures they use—to control the process, make progress, and therefore maximize company goals.

The term **negotiation** describes the process of discussion by which two or more parties aim to reach a mutually acceptable agreement. For long-term positive relations, the goal should be to set up a win–win situation—that is, to bring about a settlement beneficial to all parties concerned. This process, difficult enough when it takes place among people of similar backgrounds, is even more complex in international negotiations because of differences in cultural values, lifestyles, expectations, verbal and nonverbal language, approaches to formal procedures, and problem-solving techniques. The complexity is heightened when negotiating across borders because of the greater number of stakeholders involved. These stakeholders are illustrated in Exhibit 5-1. In preparing for negotiations, it is critical to avoid projective cognitive similarity—that is, the assumption that others perceive, judge, think, and reason in the same way when, in fact, they do not because of differential cultural and practical influences. Instead, astute negotiators empathetically enter into the private world or cultural space of their counterparts, while willingly sharing their own view of the situation.[4]

THE NEGOTIATION PROCESS

The negotiation process comprises five stages, the ordering of which may vary according to the cultural norms; for most people, relationship building is part of a continuous process in any event: (1) preparation, (2) relationship building, (3) the exchange of task-related information, (4) persuasion, and (5) concessions and agreement.[5] Of course, in reality these are seldom distinct stages but rather tend to overlap; negotiators may also temporarily revert to an earlier stage. With that in mind, it is useful to break down the negotiation process into stages to discuss the issues relevant to each stage and what international managers might expect, so that they might more successfully manage this process. These stages are shown in Exhibit 5-2 and discussed in the following sections.

EXHIBIT 5-1   Stakeholders in Cross-cultural Negotiations

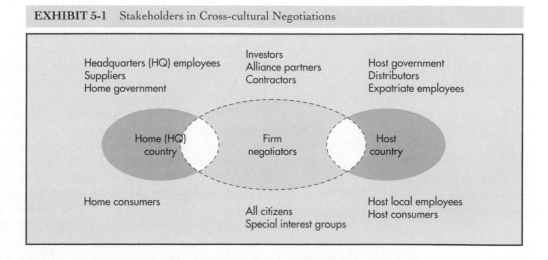

EXHIBIT 5-2   The Negotiation Process

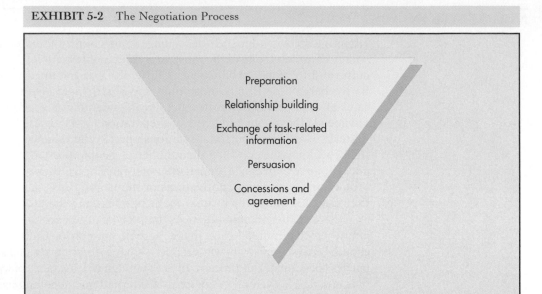

Preparation

Relationship building

Exchange of task-related
information

Persuasion

Concessions and
agreement

Stage One: Preparation

The importance of careful preparation for cross-cultural negotiations cannot be overstated. To the extent that time permits, a distinct advantage can be gained if negotiators familiarize themselves with the entire context and background of their counterparts (no matter where the meetings will take place) in addition to the specific subjects to be negotiated. Because most negotiation problems are caused by differences in culture, language, and environment, hours or days of tactical preparation for negotiation can be wasted if these factors are not carefully considered.[6]

To understand cultural differences in negotiating styles, managers first must understand their own styles and then determine how they differ from the norm in other countries. They can do this by comparing profiles of those perceived to be successful negotiators in different countries. Such profiles reflect the value system, attitudes, and expected behaviors inherent in a given society. Other sections of this chapter describe and compare negotiating styles around the world.

Variables in the Negotiating Process

Adept negotiators do some research to develop a profile of their counterparts so that they know, in most situations, what to expect, how to prepare, and how to react. Exhibit 5-3 shows twelve variables to consider when preparing to negotiate. These variables can, to a great degree, help managers understand the deep-rooted cultural and national motivations and traditional processes underlying negotiations with people from other countries.

After developing thoughtful profiles of the other party or parties, managers can plan for the actual negotiation meetings. Prior to the meetings, they should find out as much as possible about (1) the kinds of demands that might be made, (2) the composition of the "opposing" team, and (3) the relative authority that the members possess. After this, the managers can gear their negotiation strategy specifically to the other side's firm, allocate roles to different team members, decide on concessions, and prepare an alternative action plan in case a negotiated solution cannot be found.[7]

In some situations, however, the entire negotiation process is something people have to learn from scratch. After the splintering of the Soviet Union into fifteen independent republics, managers from the Newmont Mining Corporation of Denver, wishing to form a joint venture to refine gold deposits in Uzbekistan, found themselves at a standstill. Officials in Uzbekistan had never negotiated a business contract and had no one to tell them how to proceed.[8]

Following the preparation and planning stage, which is usually done at the home office, the core of the actual negotiation takes place on-site in the foreign location (or at

---

EXHIBIT 5-3   Variables in the Negotiation Process

1. *Basic conception of negotiation process:* Is it a competitive process or a problem-solving approach?
2. *Negotiator selection criteria:* Is selection based on experience, status, expertise, personal attributes, or some other characteristic?
3. *Significance of type of issues:* Is it specific, such as price, or is the focus on relationships or the format of talks?
4. *Concern with protocol:* What is the importance of procedures, social behaviors, and so forth in the negotiation process?
5. *Complexity of communicative context:* What degree of reliance is placed on nonverbal cues to interpret information?
6. *Nature of persuasive arguments:* How do the parties attempt to influence each other? Do they rely on rational arguments, on accepted tradition, or on emotion?
7. *Role of individuals' aspirations:* Are motivations based on individual, company, or community goals?
8. *Bases of trust:* Is trust based on past experience, intuition, or rules?
9. *Risk-taking propensity:* How much do the parties try to avoid uncertainty in trading information or making a contract?
10. *Value of time:* What is each party's attitude toward time? How fast should negotiations proceed, and what degree of flexibility is there?
11. *Decision-making system:* How does each team reach decisions—by individual determination, by majority opinion, or by group consensus?
12. *Form of satisfactory agreement:* Is agreement based on trust (perhaps just a handshake), the credibility of the parties, commitment, or a legally binding contract?

SOURCE: Adapted from S. E. Weiss and W. Stripp, *Negotiation with Foreign Business Persons: An Introduction for Americans with Propositions on Six Cultures* (New York University Faculty of Business Administration, February 1985).

the manager's home office if the other team has decided to travel there). In some cases, a compromise on the location for negotiations can signal a cooperative strategy, which Weiss calls "Improvise an Approach: Effect Symphony"—a strategy available to negotiators familiar with each other's culture and willing to put negotiation on an equal footing. Weiss gives the following example of this negotiation strategy:

> *For their negotiations over construction of the tunnel under the English Channel, British and French representatives agreed to partition talks and alternate the site between Paris and London. At each site, the negotiators were to use established, local ways, including the language . . . thus punctuating approaches by time and space.[9]*

In this way, each side was put into the context and the script of the other culture about half the time.

The next stage of negotiation—often given short shrift by Westerners—is that of relationship building. In most parts of the world, this stage usually has either taken place already or is concurrent with other preparations.

Stage Two: Relationship Building

Relationship building is the process of getting to know one's contacts in a host country and building mutual trust before embarking on business discussions and transactions. This process is regarded with much more significance in most parts of the world than it is in the United States. U.S. negotiators are, generally speaking, objective about the specific matter at hand and usually want to waste no time in getting down to business and making progress. This approach, well understood in the United States, can be disastrous if the foreign negotiators want to take enough time to build trust and respect as a basis for negotiating contracts. In such cases, American efficiency interferes with the patient development of a mutually trusting relationship—the very cornerstone of an Asian business agreement.[10]

In many countries, such as Mexico and China, personal commitments to individuals, rather than the legal system, form the basis for the enforcement of contracts. Effective negotiators allow plenty of time in their schedules for such relationship building with bargaining partners. This process usually takes the form of social events, tours, and ceremonies, along with much **nontask sounding** *(nemawashi)*—general, polite conversation and informal communication before meetings—while all parties get to know each another. In such cultures, one patiently waits for the other party to start actual business negotiations, aware that relationship building is, in fact, the first phase of negotiations.[11] It is usually recommended that managers new to such scenarios use an intermediary—someone who already has the trust and respect of the foreign managers and who therefore acts as a "relationship bridge." Middle Easterners, in particular, prefer to negotiate through a trusted intermediary, and for them as well, initial meetings are only for the purpose of getting acquainted. Arabs do business with the person, not the company, and therefore mutual trust must be established.

In their bestseller on negotiation, *Getting to Yes,* Fisher and Ury point out the dangers of not preparing well for negotiations:

> *In Persian, the word "compromise" does not have the English meaning of a midway solution which both sides can accept, but only the negative meaning of surrendering one's principles. Also, "mediator" means meddler, someone who is barging in uninvited. In 1980, United Nations Secretary-General Kurt Waldheim flew to Iran to deal with the hostage situation. National Iranian radio and television broadcast in Persian a comment he was to have made upon his arrival in Tehran: "I have come as a mediator to work out a compromise." Less than an hour later, his car was being stoned by angry Iranians.[12]*

As a bridge to the more formal stages of negotiations, such relationship building is followed by posturing—that is, general discussion that sets the tone for the meetings. This phase should result in a spirit of cooperation. To help ensure this result, negotiators must use words like "respect" and "mutual benefit" rather than language that would suggest arrogance, superiority, or urgency.[13]

Stage Three: Exchanging Task-Related Information

In the next stage—exchanging task-related information—each side typically makes a presentation and states its position; a question-and-answer session usually ensues, and alternatives are discussed. From an American perspective, this represents a straightforward, objective, efficient, and understandable stage. However, Copeland and Griggs point out that negotiators from other countries continue to take a more indirect approach at this stage. Mexican negotiators are usually suspicious and indirect, presenting little substantive material and more lengthy, evasive conversation. French negotiators enjoy debate and conflict and will often interrupt presentations to argue about an issue even if it has little relevance to the topic being presented. The Chinese also ask many questions of their counterparts, and they delve specifically and repeatedly into the details at hand; conversely, the Chinese presentations contain only vague and ambiguous material. For instance, after about twenty Boeing officials spent six weeks presenting masses of literature and technical demonstrations to the Chinese, the Chinese said, "Thank you for your introduction."[14]

The Russians also enter negotiations well prepared and well versed in the specific details of the matter being presented. To answer their (or any other side's) questions, it is generally a good idea to bring along someone with expertise to answer any grueling technical inquiries. Russians also put a lot of emphasis on protocol and expect to deal only with top executives.

Adler suggests that negotiators should focus not only on presenting their situation and needs but also on showing an understanding of their opponents' viewpoint. Focusing on the entire situation confronting each party encourages the negotiators to assess a wider range of alternatives for resolution, rather than limiting themselves to their preconceived, static positions. She suggests that to be most effective, negotiators should prepare for meetings by practicing role reversal.[15]

Stage Four: Persuasion

In the next phase of negotiations—persuasion—the hard bargaining starts. Typically, both parties try to persuade the other to accept more of their position and to give up some of their own. Often, some persuasion has already taken place beforehand in social settings and through mutual contacts. In the Far East, details are likely to be worked out ahead of time through the backdoor approach *(houmani)*. For the most part, however, the majority of the persuasion takes place over one or more negotiating sessions. International managers usually find that this process of bargaining and making concessions is fraught with difficulties because of the different uses and interpretations of verbal and nonverbal behaviors. Although variations in such behaviors influence every stage of the negotiation process, they can play a particularly powerful role in persuasion, especially if they are not anticipated.

Studies of negotiating behavior have revealed the use of certain recognizable tactics, which skilled negotiators recognize and use. Exhibit 5-4 shows the results of a study comparing the use of various tactics (promises, threats, and so forth) among Japanese, Americans, and Brazilians. The results indicate that the Japanese and the Americans tend to be more alike in the use of these behaviors, whereas the Japanese and the Brazilians are less alike. For example, the Brazilians use fewer promises and commitments than the Japanese or the Americans (only half as many), but they use commands far more often. The Japanese and the Americans use threats twice as often as the Brazilians, and they use commands only about half as often as the Brazilians. The Brazilians and the Japanese seldom behave similarly.

Other, less savory tactics are sometimes used in international negotiations. Often called "dirty tricks", these tactics, according to Fisher and Ury, include efforts to mislead

EXHIBIT 5-4   Differences among Japanese, American, and Brazilian Verbal Negotiating Behavior

Bargaining Behaviors and Definition	Frequency per Half-Hour Bargaining Session		
	Japanese	American	Brazilian
Promise. A statement in which the source indicated his or her intention to provide the target with a reinforcing consequence that source anticipates target will evaluate as pleasant, positive, or rewarding.	7	8	3
Threat. Same as promise, except that the reinforcing consequences are thought to be noxious, unpleasant, or punishing.	4	4	2
Recommendation. A statement in which the source predicts that a pleasant environmental consequence will occur to the target. Its occurrence is not under the source's control.	7	4	5
Warning. Same as recommendation, except that the consequences are thought to be unpleasant.	2	1	1
Reward. A statement by the source that is thought to create pleasant consequences for the target.	1	2	2
Punishment. Same as reward, except that the consequences are thought to be unpleasant.	1	3	3
Positive normative appeal. A statement in which the source indicates that the target's past, present, or future behavior was or will be in conformity with social norms.	1	1	0
Negative normative appeal. Same as positive normative appeal, except that the target's behavior is in violation of social norms.	3	1	1
Commitment. A statement by the source to the effect that its future bids will not go below or above a certain level.	15	13	8
Self-disclosure. A statement in which the source reveals information about itself.	34	36	39
Question. A statement in which the source asks the target to reveal information about itself.	20	20	22
Command. A statement in which the source suggests that the target perform a certain behavior.	8	6	14

SOURCE: From John L. Graham, "The Influence of Culture on the Process of Business Negotiations in an Exploratory Study," *Journal of International Business Studies* (Spring 1985): 88.

"opponents" deliberately.[16] Some negotiators may give wrong or distorted factual information or use the excuse of ambiguous authority—giving conflicting impressions about who in their party has the power to make a commitment. In the midst of hard bargaining, the prudent international manager will follow up on possibly misleading information before taking action based on trust.

Other rough tactics are designed to put opposing negotiators in a stressful situation physically or psychologically so that their giving in is more likely. These include uncomfortable room temperatures, too-bright lighting, rudeness, interruptions, and other irritations. Specific bargaining pressures include extreme or escalating demands, threats to stop negotiating, calculated delays, and a take-it-or-leave-it attitude. In a survey of eighteen U.S.–Korean joint ventures, for example, U.S. executives reported that the behavior of the Koreans during the course of negotiations was often "abusive," resulting in "shouting matches, desk pounding, and chest beating."[17]

International negotiators must keep in mind, however, that what might seem like dirty tricks to Americans is simply the way other cultures conduct negotiations. In some South American countries, for example, it is common to start negotiations with misleading or false information.

The most subtle behaviors in the negotiation process, and often the most difficult to deal with, are usually the nonverbal messages—the use of voice intonation, facial and body expressions, eye contact, dress, and the timing of the discussions. Nonverbal behaviors are ingrained aspects of culture used by people in their daily lives; they are not specifically changed for the purposes of negotiation. In a comparative study of the nonverbal negotiating behaviors of Japanese, Americans, and Brazilians, Graham assessed the relative frequency of the use of silent periods, conversational overlaps, facial gazing (staring at people's faces), and touching. He found that the Brazilians interrupted conversation about twice as often as the Japanese and the Americans and used much more touching and facial gazing. Needless to say, they scored low on silent periods. The Japanese tended to use more silent periods and interruptions than the Americans but less facial gazing. The Japanese and the Americans evidenced no touching whatsoever, other than handshaking, during a thirty-minute period.[18]

Although persuasion has been discussed as if it were always a distinct stage, it is really the primary purpose underlying all stages of the negotiation process. In particular, persuasion is an integral part of the process of making concessions and arriving at an agreement.

Stage Five: Concessions and Agreement

In the last stage of negotiation—concessions and agreement—tactics vary greatly across cultures. Well-prepared negotiators are aware of various concession strategies and have decided ahead of time what their own concession strategy will be. Familiar with the typical initial positions that various parties are likely to take, they know that the Russians and the Chinese generally open their bargaining with extreme positions, asking for more than they hope to gain, whereas the Swedes usually start with what they are prepared to accept.

Research in the United States indicates that better end results are attained by starting with extreme positions. With this approach, the process of reaching an agreement involves careful timing of the disclosure information and of concessions. Most people who have studied negotiations believe that negotiators should disclose only the information that is necessary at a given point and that they should try to obtain information piece by piece to gradually get the whole picture without giving away their goals or concession strategy. These guidelines will not always work in intercultural negotiations because the American process of addressing issues one at a time, in a linear fashion, is not common in other countries or cultures. Negotiators in the Far East, for example, approach issues in a holistic manner, deciding on the whole deal at the end, rather than making incremental concessions.

Again, at the final stage of agreement and contract, cultural values determine how these agreements will be honored. Whereas Americans take contracts very seriously, Russians often renege on their contracts. The Japanese, on the other hand, consider a formal contract to be somewhat of an insult and a waste of time and money in legal costs, since they prefer to operate on the basis of understanding and social trust.[19]

UNDERSTANDING NEGOTIATION STYLES

Global managers can benefit from studying differences in negotiating behaviors (and the underlying reasons for them), which can help them recognize what is happening in the negotiating process. Exhibit 5-5 shows some examples of differences among North American, Japanese, and Latin American styles. Brazilians, for example, generally have a spontaneous, passionate, and dynamic style. They are very talkative and particularly use the word "no" extensively—more than 40 times per half hour compared with 4.7 times for Americans, and only 1.9 times for the Japanese. They also differ markedly from the Americans and Japanese by their use of extensive physical contact.[20]

The Japanese are typically skillful negotiators. They have spent a great deal more time and effort studying U.S. culture and business practices than Americans have spent studying Japanese practices. A typical example of this contrast was apparent at recent trade negotiations between Japan and the United States in 1994. Charlene Barshefsky—a tough American international lawyer—had never visited Japan before being sent there as a trade negotiator and had little knowledge of its counterparts. But, Mr. Okamatsu, like most Japanese negotiators, was very familiar with America. He had lived with his family in New York for three years and had spent many years handling bilateral trade disputes between the two countries. The different styles of the two negotiators were apparent in the negotiations. Ms. Barshefsky wanted specific import goals. Mr. Okamatsu wanted to talk more about the causes of trade problems rather than set specific targets, which he called the "cooperative approach." Ms. Barshefsky snapped that the approach was nonsense and "would analyze the past to death, with no link to future change."[21]

Such differences in philosophy and style between the two countries reflect ten years of anger and feelings of betrayal in trade negotiations. John Graham, a California professor who has studied international negotiating styles, says that the differences between U.S. and Japanese styles are well illustrated by their respective proverbs: The American believes that "The squeaking wheel gets the grease," and the Japanese say that "The pheasant would not be shot but for its cry."[22] The Japanese are calm, quiet, patient negotiators; they are accustomed to long, detailed negotiating sessions. Whereas Americans

EXHIBIT 5-5   Comparison of Negotiation Styles—Japanese, North American, and Latin American

Japanese	North American	Latin American
Emotional sensitivity highly valued	Emotional sensitivity not highly valued	Emotional sensitivity valued
Hiding of emotions	Dealing straightforwardly or impersonally	Emotionally passionate
Subtle power plays; conciliation	Litigation not so much as conciliation	Great power plays; use of weakness
Loyalty to employer; employer takes care of employees	Lack of commitment to employer; breaking of ties by either if necessary	Loyalty to employer (who is often family)
Face-saving crucial; decisions often on basis of saving someone from embarrassment	Decisions made on a cost-benefit basis; face-saving does not always matter	Face-saving crucial in decision making to preserve honor, dignity
Decision makers openly influenced by special interests	Decision makers influenced by special interests but often not considered ethical	Execution of special interests of decision expected, condoned
Not argumentative; quiet when right	Argumentative when right or wrong, but impersonal	Argumentative when right or wrong; passionate
What is down in writing must be accurate, valid	Great importance given to documentation as evidential proof	Impatient with documentation as obstacle to understanding general principles
Step-by-step approach to decision making	Methodically organized decision making	Impulsive, spontaneous decision making
Good of group is the ultimate aim	Profit motive or good of individual ultimate aim	What is good for group is good for the individual
Cultivate a good emotional social setting for decision making; get to know decision makers	Decision making impersonal; avoid involvements, conflict of interest	Personalism necessary for good decision making

SOURCE: From Pierre Casse, *Training for the Multicultural Manager: A Practical and Cross-cultural Approach to the Management of People* (Washington, D.C.: Society for Intercultural Education, Training, and Research, 1982).

often plunge straight to the matter at hand, the Japanese instead prefer to develop long-term, personal relationships. The Japanese want to get to know those on the other side and will spend some time in nontask sounding.

In negotiations, the Japanese culture of politeness and hiding of emotions can be disconcerting to Americans when they are unable to make straightforward eye contact or when the Japanese maintain smiling faces in serious situations. It is important that Americans understand what is polite and what is offensive to the Japanese—and vice versa. Americans must avoid anything that resembles boasting because the Japanese value humility, and physical contact or touching of any sort must be avoided.[23] Consistent with the culture-based value of maintaining harmony, the Japanese are likely to be evasive or even leave the room rather than give a direct negative answer.[24] Fundamental to Japanese culture is a concern for the welfare of the group; anything that affects one member or part of society affects the others. Thus, the Japanese view decisions carefully in light of long-term consequences; they use objective, analytic thought patterns; and they take time for reflection.[25]

Further insight into negotiating styles around the world can be gained by comparing the North American, Arab, and Russian styles. Basic cultural values often shed light on the way information is presented, whether and how concessions will be made, and the general nature and duration of the relationship.

For North Americans, negotiations are businesslike; their factual appeals are based on what they believe is objective information, presented with the assumption that it is understood by the other side on a logical basis. Arabs use affective appeals based on emotions and subjective feelings. Russians employ axiomatic appeals—that is, their appeals are based on the ideals generally accepted in their society. The Russians are tough negotiators; they stall for time until they unnerve Western negotiators by continuously delaying and haggling. Much of this approach is based on the Russians' different attitude toward time. Because Russians traditionally do not subscribe to the Western belief that "time is money," they are more patient, more determined, more dogged negotiators. They try to keep smiles and other expressions of emotion to a minimum to present a calm exterior.[26]

In contrast to the Russians, Arabs are more interested in long-term relationships and are, therefore, more likely to make concessions. Compared with Westerners, Arabs have a casual approach to deadlines, and frequently the negotiators lack the authority to finalize a deal.[27]

Successful Negotiators Around the World

Following are selected profiles of what it takes to be a successful negotiator, as perceived by people in their home countries. These are profiles of American, Indian, Arab, Swedish, and Italian negotiators, according to Pierre Casse, and give some insight into what to expect from different negotiators and what they expect from others.[28]

American Negotiators
According to Casse, a successful American negotiator acts as follows:

1. Knows when to compromise
2. Takes a firm stand at the beginning of the negotiation
3. Refuses to make concessions beforehand
4. Keeps his or her cards close to his or her chest
5. Accepts compromises only when the negotiation is deadlocked
6. Sets up the general principles and delegates the detail work to associates
7. Keeps a maximum of options open before negotiation
8. Operates in good faith
9. Respects the "opponents"
10. States his or her position as clearly as possible
11. Knows when he or she wishes a negotiation to move on
12. Is fully briefed about the negotiated issues
13. Has a good sense of timing and is consistent
14. Makes the other party reveal his or her position while keeping his or her own position hidden as long as possible
15. Lets the other negotiator come forward first and looks for the best deal

Indian Negotiators

Indians, says Casse, often follow Gandhi's approach to negotiation, which Gandhi called *satyagraha*, "firmness in a good cause." This approach combines strength with the love of truth. The successful Indian negotiator thus acts as follows:

1. Looks for and says the truth
2. Is not afraid of speaking up and has no fears
3. Exercises self-control ("The weapons of the *satyagraha* are within him.")
4. Seeks solutions that will please all the parties involved ("*Satyagraha* aims to exalt both sides.")
5. Respects the other party ("The opponent must be weaned from error by patience and sympathy. Weaned, not crushed; converted, not annihilated.")
6. Neither uses violence nor insults
7. Is ready to change his or her mind and differ with himself or herself at the risk of being seen as inconsistent and unpredictable
8. Puts things into perspective and switches easily from the small picture to the big one
9. Is humble and trusts the opponent
10. Is able to withdraw, use silence, and learn from within
11. Relies on himself or herself, his or her own resources and strengths
12. Appeals to the other party's spiritual identity ("To communicate, the West moves or talks. The East sits, contemplates, suffers.")
13. Is tenacious, patient, and persistent
14. Learns from the opponent and avoids the use of secrets
15. Goes beyond logical reasoning and trusts his or her instinct as well as faith

Arab Negotiators

Many Arab negotiators, following Islamic tradition, use mediators to settle disputes. A successful Arab mediator acts in the following way:

1. Protects all the parties' honor, self-respect, and dignity
2. Avoids direct confrontations between opponents
3. Is respected and trusted by all
4. Does not put the parties involved in a situation where they have to show weakness or admit defeat
5. Has the necessary prestige to be listened to
6. Is creative enough to come up with honorable solutions for all parties
7. Is impartial and can understand the positions of the various parties without leaning toward one or the other
8. Is able to resist any kind of pressure that the opponents could try to exercise on him
9. Uses references to people who are highly respected by the opponents to persuade them to change their minds on some issues ("Do it for the sake of your father.")
10. Can keep secrets and in so doing gains the confidence of the negotiating parties
11. Controls his temper and emotions (or loses it when and where necessary)
12. Can use conferences as mediating devices
13. Knows that the opponents will have problems in carrying out the decisions made during the negotiation
14. Is able to cope with the Arab disregard for time
15. Understands the impact of Islam on the opponents who believe that they possess the truth, follow the Right Path, and are going to "win" because their cause is just

Swedish Negotiators

Swedish negotiators, according to Casse, are:

1. Very quiet and thoughtful
2. Punctual (concerned with time)
3. Extremely polite
4. Straightforward (they get straight down to business)
5. Eager to be productive and efficient

6. Heavy going
7. Down to earth and overcautious
8. Rather flexible
9. Able to and quite good at holding emotions and feelings
10. Slow at reacting to new (unexpected) proposals
11. Informal and familiar
12. Conceited
13. Perfectionist
14. Afraid of confrontations
15. Very private

Italian Negotiators

Italians, says Casse, value a negotiator who acts as follows:

1. Has a sense of drama (acting is a main part of the culture)
2. Does not hide his or her emotions (which are partly sincere and partly feigned)
3. Reads facial expressions and gestures very well
4. Has a feeling for history
5. Does not trust anybody
6. Is concerned about the *bella figura*—the "good impression"—he or she can create among those who watch his or her behavior
7. Believes in the individual's initiatives, not so much in teamwork
8. Is good at being obliging and simpatico at all times
9. Is always on the *qui vive*—the "lookout"
10. Never embraces definite opinions
11. Is able to come up with new ways to immobilize and eventually destroy his or her opponents
12. Handles confrontations of power with subtlety and tact
13. Has a flair for intrigue
14. Knows how to use flattery
15. Can involve other negotiators in complex combinations

Comparing Profiles

Comparing such profiles is useful. Indian negotiators, for example, are humble, patient, respectful of the other parties, and very willing to compromise, compared with Americans, who are firmer about taking stands. An important difference between Arab negotiators and those from most other countries is that the negotiators are mediators, not the parties themselves; hence, direct confrontation is made impossible. Successful Swedish negotiators are conservative and careful, dealing with factual and detailed information. This profile contrasts with Italian negotiators, who are expressive and exuberant but less straightforward than their Swedish counterparts.

MANAGING NEGOTIATION

Skillful global managers must assess many factors when managing negotiations. They must understand the position of the other parties in regard to their goals—whether national or corporate—and whether these goals are represented by principles or specific details. They should have the ability to recognize the relative importance attached to completing the task versus developing interpersonal relationships. Managers also must know the composition of the teams involved, the power allotted to the members, and the extent of the teams' preparation. In addition, they must grasp the significance of personal trust in the relationship. As stated earlier, the culture of the parties involved affects their negotiating styles and behavior and thus the overall process of negotiation. However, whatever the culture, research by Tse, Francis, and Walls has found person-related conflicts to "invite negative, more relation-oriented (versus information-oriented) responses," leading them to conclude that "The software of negotiation—that is, the nature and the appearance of the relationship between the people pursuing common goals—needs to be carefully addressed in the negotiation process.[29]

This is particularly true when representatives of individual-focused cultures (such as the Americans) and group-focused cultures (such as the Chinese) are on opposite sides of the table. Many of these culture-based differences in negotiations came to light in Husted's recent study on Mexican negotiators' perceptions of the reasons for the failure of their negotiations with U.S. teams. (The summary findings are shown in Exhibit 5-6.) However, Husted believes that "many of the perceived differences relate to the typical differences found between high-context and low-context cultures."[30] In other words, the Mexican managers' interpretations were affected by their high-context culture, with the characteristics of an indirect approach, patience in discussing ideas, and maintenance of dignity. Instead, the low-context Americans conveyed an impatient, cold, blunt communicative style. To maintain the outward dignity of their Mexican counterparts, Americans must approach negotiations with Mexicans with patience and tolerance and to refrain from attacking ideas because these attacks may be taken personally.

The relationships among the factors of cross-cultural negotiation discussed in this chapter are illustrated in Exhibit 5-7.

The successful management of intercultural negotiations requires that a manager go beyond a generalized understanding of the issues and variables involved. She or he must (1) gain specific knowledge of the parties in the upcoming meeting, (2) prepare accordingly to adjust to and control the situation, and (3) be innovative.[31]

Research has shown that a problem-solving approach is essential to successful cross-cultural negotiations, whether abroad or in the home office, although the approach works differently in various countries.[32] This problem-solving approach requires that a negotiator treat everyone with respect, avoid making anyone feel uncomfortable, and not criticize or blame the other parties in a personal way that may make someone feel shame—that is, lose face.

EXHIBIT 5-6   Bargaining with the Gringos Mexican Managers' Perceptions of Causes of Failure of Negotiations with Americans

	Very Important (%)	Important (%)	Moderately Important (%)	Total (%)
Problems with U.S. team				
Lack of authority of U.S. team to make decisions	37.0	20.0	15.0	72.0
U.S. team's failure to resolve doubts of Mexican team	34.0	26.0	14.0	74.0
U.S. team's lack of sincerity	41.0	20.0	9.0	70.0
Eigenvalue: 2.9009/Percent of var.: 26.4/Cum. var.: 26.4				
Negotiation process				
Differences in negotiation styles	26.5	28.4	22.5	77.4
U.S. team quoting unreasonable prices	52.5	17.8	8.9	79.2
Mexican lack of knowledge of delivery systems	42.0	19.0	11.0	72.0
Mexican lack of preparation	40.6	21.8	9.9	72.3
Eigenvalue: 2.3577/Percent of var.: 21.4/Cum. var.: 47.8				
Cultural barriers				
Differences in business practices	24.5	29.4	22.5	76.4
Communication barriers	37.3	17.6	12.7	67.6
Eigenvalue: 1.7976/Percent of var.: 16.3/Cum. var.: 64.1				
Language problems	41.2	21.6	5.9	68.7
Eigenvalue: 1.0763/Percent of var.: 9.8/Cum. var.: 73.9				
Price constraints				
Mexican team's inability to lower the price	32.0	22.0	18.0	72.0
Eigenvalue: 1.0433/Percent of var.: 9.5/Cum. var.: 83.4				

SOURCE: Bryan W. Husted, "Bargaining with the Gringos: An Exploratory Study of Negotiations between Mexican and U.S. Firms," *International Executive* 36(5) (September–October 1994): 625–644.

EXHIBIT 5-7 Cross-cultural Negotiation Variables

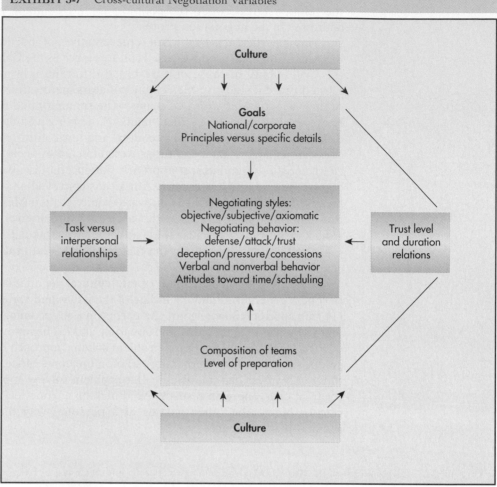

Research by the Huthwaite Research Group reveals how successful negotiators, compared to average negotiators, manage the planning process and their face-to-face behavior. The group found that during the planning process, successful negotiators consider a wider range of options and pay greater attention to areas of common ground. Skillful negotiators also tend to make twice as many comments regarding long-term issues and are more likely to set upper and lower limits regarding specific points. In their face-to-face behavior, skillful negotiators make fewer irritating comments—such as "We're making you a generous offer"—make counterproposals less frequently, and use fewer reasons to back up arguments. In addition, skilled negotiators practice active listening—asking questions, clarifying their understanding of the issues, and summarizing the issues.[33]

Using the Web to Support Negotiations

Modern technology can provide support for the negotiating process, though it can't take the place of the essential face-to-face ingredient in many instances. A growing component for electronic commerce is the development of applications to support the negotiation of contracts and resolution of disputes. As Web applications develop, they may provide support for various phases and dimensions, such as "Multiple issue, multiple party business transactions of a buy–sell nature, international dispute resolution (business disputes, political disputes), internal company negotiations and communications, among others.[34]

Negotiation support systems (NSS) can provide support for the negotiation process in the following ways:

- Increasing the likelihood that an agreement is reached when a zone of agreement exists (solutions that both parties would accept)

- Decreasing the direct and indirect costs of negotiations, such as costs caused by time delays (strikes, violence), and attorneys' fees, among others
- Maximizing the chances for optimal outcomes[35]

One Web-based support system, developed at Carleton University in Ottawa, Canada—called INSPIRE—provides applications for preparing and conducting negotiations and for renegotiating options after a settlement. Users can specify preferences and assess offers; the site also has graphical displays of the negotiation process.[36]

E-Negotiation

Increasingly, the negotiation process is carried out through e-commerce, as more and more e-marketplaces replace middlemen in trading around the world. One example is Samsung's e-Chaebol (see Management Focus: Samsung's e-*Chaebol*).

Management Focus

Samsung's e-*Chaebol*

Korea's Samsung, the trading arm of South Korea's family-run conglomerate, or *chaebol,* is using the Internet to transform its role as a middleman into a global e-marketplace player. Samsung anticipated $7 billion in trades in 2002 from its five online marketplaces, listed as follows, up from $2.8 billion in 2001.[1] Transactions through these trading auctions reduce the need for personal negotiating, which often is problematic from one country to another.

SAMSUNG'S E-MARKETPLACES[2]

FishRound: Online marketplace for frozen fish. Samsung owns 70 percent. Trading fee is 1 percent. FishRound.com provides a full range of services, including consulting, auction, procurement, logistics, financing, and MRO services (ship repair bunkering).

GSX: Trades steel on the spot market. Samsung is one of the majority owners. Trading fee is 0.375 percent.

ChemCross: Trades industrial chemicals in Asia. It is in the refining, petrochemical, and polymer industry. Owned by Samsung and sixty Asian chemical manufacturers. Fee is 0.3 to 0.55 percent.

CareCamp: Korea's top e-marketplace for medical equipment for hospitals and other medical institutions. Samsung owns 50 percent, and 50 percent is owned by hospitals, suppliers, and doctors. Trading fee is between 1 and 3 percent.

Textopia: A textile e-marketplace for buying and selling fiber, yarn, and other raw materials. Composed of five categories: Open Market (for meeting new business partners and exchange and auction services); Private Network (customized for collaborating partners); Functions (for after-contract services: inspection, logistics, insurance, and financing); Information (a guide for business deals); and My Topia (tips for transaction management). Trading fee is less than 1 percent.

[1]www.Samsung.com; *BusinessWeek ebiz*/August 6, 2001.

[2]www.Fishround.com; www.GSX.com; www.Chemcross.com; www.Textopia.com; www.CareCamp.com; *BusinessWeek ebiz*/August 6, 2001.

 ## Comparative Management in Focus

Negotiating with the Chinese

The Chinese think in terms of process that has no culmination. Americans think in terms of concrete solutions to specific problems. . . . The Chinese approach is impersonal, patient and aloof . . . To Americans, Chinese leaders seem polite but aloof and condescending. To the Chinese, Americans appear erratic and somewhat frivolous.

—Henry Kissinger,
Newsweek, May, 2001[37]

The Chinese way of making decisions begins with socialization and initiation of personal guanxi rather than business discussion. The focus is not market research, statistical analysis, facts, PowerPoint presentations, or to-the-point business discussion. My focus must be on fostering guanxi.

—Sunny Zhou, General Manager of Kunming
Lida Wood and Bamboo Products[38]

When Westerners initiate business negotiations with representatives from the People's Republic of China, cultural barriers confront both sides. The negotiation process used by the Chinese—although there are variations among the Cantonese, Shanghainese, and northern Chinese—is mystifying to Westerners. For instance, the Chinese put much greater emphasis than Americans on respect and friendship, on saving face, and on group goals. Long-term goals are more important to the Chinese than the specific current objectives typical of Western negotiators.[39] Even though market forces are starting to have more influence in China, political and economic agendas are still expected to be considered in negotiations. Research by Xinping Shi of 198 managers in Beijing, 185 in Shanghai, and 189 in Guangzhou shows that prevailing economic conditions, political pervasiveness, and "constituent shadow" (the influence that constituents, such as political and state agencies, have on the negotiating parties in China) are key practical factors that, added to cultural factors, make up the context affecting Chinese negotiations. These antecedent factors, when filtered through the specific negotiator's profile, result in various behaviors, processes, and outcomes from those negotiations. Moreover, little difference in those factors was found among the different regions in China. Exhibit 5-8 shows these environmental factors and the relationships among the factors involved in Western–Chinese business negotiation.

Businesspeople report two major areas of conflict in negotiating with the Chinese: (1) the amount of detail the Chinese want about product characteristics, and (2) their apparent insincerity about reaching an agreement. In addition, Chinese negotiators frequently have little authority, frustrating Americans who do have the authority and are ready to conclude a deal.[40] This situation arises because Chinese companies report to the government trade corporations, which are involved in the negotiations and often have a representative on the team. The goals of Chinese negotiators remain primarily within the framework of state planning and political

EXHIBIT 5-8   Influences on Western–Chinese Business Negotiations

ideals. Although China is tending to become more profit-oriented, most deals are still negotiated within the confines of the state budget allocation for that project rather than on the basis of a project's profitability or value. It is crucial, then, to find out which officials—national, provincial, local—have the power to make, and keep, a deal. According to James Broering of Arthur Andersen, who does much business in China, "companies have negotiated with government people for months, only to discover that they were dealing with the wrong people."[41]

Research shows that for the Chinese, the negotiation process is greatly affected by three cultural norms: their ingrained politeness and emotional restraint; their emphasis on social obligations; and their belief in the interconnection of work, family, and friendship. Because of the Chinese preference for emotional restraint and saving face, aggressive or emotional attempts at persuasion in negotiation are likely to fail. Instead, the Chinese tendency to avoid open conflict will more likely result in negative strategies such as discontinuing or withdrawing from negotiation.[42] The concept of face is at the heart of this kind of response—it is essential for foreigners to recognize the role that face behavior plays in negotiations. There are two components of face—*lien* and *mien-tzu*. *Lien* refers to a person's moral character; it is the most important thing defining that person, and without it one cannot function in society. It can only be earned by fulfilling obligations to others. *Mien-tzu* refers to one's reputation or prestige, earned through accomplishments or through bureaucratic or political power.[43] Giving others one's time, gifts, or praise enhances one's own face. In negotiations, it is vital that you do not make it obvious that you have "won" because that means that the other party has "lost" and will lose face. One must, therefore, make token concessions and other attempts to show that respect must be demonstrated, and modesty and control must be maintained; otherwise anyone who feels he or she has "lost face" will not want to deal with you again. The Chinese will later ignore any dealings or incidents that caused them to lose face, maintaining the expected polite behavior out of social consciousness and concern for others. When encountering an embarrassing situation, they will typically smile or laugh in an attempt to save face, responses that are confusing to Western negotiators.[44]

The emphasis on social obligations underlies the strong orientation of the Chinese toward collective goals. Therefore, appeals to individual members of the Chinese negotiating team, rather than appeals to benefit the group as a whole, will probably backfire.[45] The Confucian emphasis on the kinship system and the hierarchy of work, family, and friends explains the Chinese preference for doing business with familiar, trusted people and trusted companies. "Foreign" negotiators, then, should focus on establishing long-term, trusting relationships, even at the expense of some immediate returns.

Deeply ingrained in the Chinese culture is the importance of harmony for the smooth functioning of society. Harmony is based primarily on personal relationships, trust, and ritual. After the Chinese establish a cordial relationship with foreign negotiators, they use this relationship as a basis for the give-and-take of business discussions. This implicit cultural norm is commonly known as *guanxi*, which refers to the intricate, pervasive network of personal relations that every Chinese carefully cultivates. It is the primary means of getting ahead, in the absence of a proper commercial legal system.[46] In other words, *guanxi* establishes obligations to exchange favors in future business activities.[47] Even within the Chinese bureaucracy, *guanxi* prevails over legal interpretations. Although networking is important anywhere to do business, the difference in China is that "*guanxi* networks are not just commercial, but also social, involving the exchange both of favor and affection."[48] Firms that have special *guanxi* connections and give preferential treatment to one another are known as members of a *guanxihu* network.[49] Sunny Zhou, general manager of Kumming Lida Wood and Bamboo Products, states that when he shops for lumber, "The lumber price varies drastically, depending on whether one has strong *guanxi* with the local administrators."[50]

Western managers should thus anticipate extended preliminary visiting (relationship building), in which the Chinese expect to learn more about them and their trustworthiness. The Chinese also use this opportunity to convey their deeply held principles. They attach considerable importance to mutual benefit.[51] The Chinese expect Western firms to sacrifice corporate goals and above-average profits to Chinese national goals and principles, such as meaningful friendship, Chinese national development, and the growth and enhancement of the Chinese people. Misunderstandings occur when Americans show polite acceptance of these general principles without understanding their significance—because they do not have any obvious relationship to American corporate goals, such as profit. Nor do such principles seem relevant to practical decisions on plant locations, employee practices, or sourcing.[52]

Americans often experience two negotiation stages with the Chinese: the technical and the commercial. During the long technical stage, the Chinese want to hammer out every detail of the proposed product specifications and technology. If there are two teams of negotiators, it may be several days before the commercial team is actually called in to deal with aspects of production, marketing, pricing, and so forth. However, the commercial team should sit in on the first stage to become familiar with the Chinese negotiating style.[53] The Chinese negotiating team is usually about twice as large as the Western team; about a third of the time is spent discussing technical specifications, and another third on price negotiations, with the rest devoted to general negotiations and posturing.[54]

The Chinese are among the toughest negotiators in the world. American managers must anticipate various tactics, such as their delaying techniques and their avoidance of direct, specific answers: Both ploys are used to exploit the known impatience of Americans. The Chinese frequently try to put pressure on Americans by "shaming" them, thereby implying that the Americans are trying to renege on the friendship—the basis of the implicit contract. Whereas Westerners come to negotiations with specific and segmented goals and find it easy to compromise, the Chinese are reluctant to negotiate details. They find it difficult to compromise and trade because they have entered negotiations with a broader vision of achieving development goals for China, and they are offended when Westerners don't internalize those goals.[55] Under these circumstances, the Chinese will adopt a rigid posture, and no agreement or contract is final until the negotiated activities have actually been completed.

Patience, respect, and experience are necessary prerequisites for anyone negotiating in China. For the best outcomes, older, more experienced people are more acceptable to the Chinese in cross-cultural negotiations. The Chinese want to deal with the top executive of an American company, under the assumption that the highest officer has attained that position by establishing close personal relationships and trust with colleagues and others outside the organization. Western delegation practices are unfamiliar to them, and they are reluctant to come to an agreement without the presence of the Chinese foreign negotiator.[56] From the Western perspective, confusing jurisdictions of government ministries hamper decisions in negotiations.[57] Americans tend to send specific technical personnel with experience in the task at hand; therefore, they have to take care in selecting the most suitable negotiators. In addition, visiting negotiating teams should realize that the Chinese are probably negotiating with other foreign teams, often at the same time, and will use that setup to play one company's offer against the others. On an interpersonal level, Western negotiators must also realize that, while a handshake is polite, physical contact is not acceptable in Chinese social behavior, nor are personal discussion topics such as one's family. However, it is customary to give and take small gifts as tokens of friendship. Pye offers the following additional tips to foreigners conducting business with the Chinese:[58]

- Practice patience
- Accept prolonged periods of stalemate
- Refrain from exaggerated expectations and discount Chinese rhetoric about future prospects
- Expect the Chinese to try to manipulate by shaming
- Resist the temptation to believe that difficulties may have been caused by one's own mistakes
- Try to understand Chinese cultural traits, but realize that a foreigner cannot practice them better than the Chinese

Managing Conflict Resolution

Much of the negotiation process is fraught with conflict—explicit or implicit—and such conflict can often lead to a standoff, or a lose–lose situation. This is regrettable, not only because of the situation at hand, but also because it probably will shut off future opportunities for deals between the parties. Much of the cause of such conflict can be found in cultural differences between the parties—in their expectations, in their behaviors, and particularly in their communication styles.

As discussed in Chapter 4, much of the difference in communication styles is attributable to whether you belong to a high-context or low-context culture (or somewhere in between, as shown in Exhibit 4-4). In low-context cultures such as that in the United States, conflict is handled directly and explicitly. It is also regarded as separate from the person negotiating—that is, the negotiators draw a distinction between the people involved and the information or opinions they represent. They also tend to negotiate on the basis of factual information and logical analysis. That approach to conflict is called **instrumental oriented**.[59] In high-context cultures, such as in the Middle East, the approach to conflict is **expressive oriented**—that is, the situation is handled indirectly and implicitly, without clear delineation of the situation by the person handling it. Such negotiators do not want to get in a confrontational situation because it is regarded as insulting and would cause a loss of "face," so they tend to use evasion and avoidance if they cannot reach agreement through emotional appeals. Their avoidance and inaction conflict with the expectations of the low- context negotiators who are looking to move ahead with the business at hand and arrive at a solution.

The differences between high- and low-context cultures that often lead to conflict situations are summarized in Exhibit 5-9. Most of these variables were discussed previously in this chapter or in Chapter 4. They overlap because the subjects, culture, and communication

EXHIBIT 5-9   Sources of Conflict between Low-Context and High-Context Cultures

Key Questions	Low-Context Conflict	High-Context Conflict
Why	Analytic, linear logic; instrumental oriented; dichotomy between conflict and conflict parties	Synthetic, spiral logic; expressive oriented; integration of conflict and conflict parties
When	Individualistic oriented; low collective normative expectations; violations of individual expectations create conflict potentials	Group oriented; high collective normative expectations; violations of collective expectations create conflict potentials
What	Revealment; direct, confrontational attitude; action and solution oriented	Concealment; indirect nonconfrontational attitude; "face" and relationship oriented
How	Explicit communication codes; line-logic style: rational-factual rhetoric; open, direct strategies	Implicit communication codes; point-logic style: intuitive-effective rhetoric; ambiguous, indirect strategies

SOURCE: W. Gudykunst, L. Stewart, and S. Ting-Toomey, *Communication, Culture, and Organizational Processes.* Copyright © 1985 by Sage Publications, Inc. Reprinted by permission of Sage Publications, Inc.

are really inseparable and because negotiation differences and conflict situations arise from variables in culture and communication.

The point here is, how can a manager from France, from Japan, or from Brazil, for example, manage conflict situations? The solution, as discussed previously, lies mainly in one's ability to know and understand the people and the situation to be faced. Managers must be prepared by developing an understanding of the cultural contexts in which they will be operating. What are the expectations of the persons with whom they will be negotiating? What kinds of communication styles and negotiating tactics should they expect, and how will they differ from their own? It is important to bear in mind one's own expectations and negotiating style, as well as to be aware of the other parties' expectations. Managers ought to consider in advance what it will take to arrive at a win–win solution. Often it helps to use the services of a host-country adviser or mediator, who may be able to help with early diffusion of a conflict situation.

One contemporary tool in negotiation and decision making that helps to avoid circumstances of conflict is the online B2B marketplace; exchanges, where buyers and sellers negotiate prices, speed up the decision-making and transaction processes (see E-Biz Box: B2B Markets—Fast Negotiations and Transactions).

E-BIZ BOX

B2B Markets: Fast Negotiations and Transactions

More than 80 percent of online downloads are business-to-business (B2B) transactions. B2B e-commerce—in which transactions between businesses are conducted online—offers a number of inherent advantages over traditional commerce. First, it is cheaper to process the nuts and bolts of transactions—purchase orders, proposals, billing statements, fund transfers—when customers are serving themselves online. In addition, large buyers such as manufacturers can find better prices if they set up reverse-bidding systems on the Internet that pit suppliers against each other.

For sellers who participate in these markets, there's a lower comfort level with the customer, but there are opportunities for more flexible pricing—at least in theory. In addition, the Internet helps everyone reach more potential trading partners.

The Internet adds new dynamics to the traditional one-to-one model for business transactions. Many vendors sell directly from their sites—virtually all computer-related companies now provide an online storefront—but more sophisticated virtual marketplaces seek to bring buyers and sellers together in one place. By doing this, they hope to increase pricing efficiencies. Some B2B marketplaces are vertically oriented, seeking to capture a large share of a single industry's transactions. Others are horizontal—offering, for instance, places where small businesses can purchase telephone service, office supplies, and insurance.

These online markets where buyers and sellers negotiate prices are called *exchanges*. They generally use some sort of bidding or reverse-bid system, and prices fluctuate based on demand. These types of exchanges work well with commodity-type goods that are easily definable. Other B2B sites make comparison shopping possible by aggregating catalogs from more than one vendor.

Typically, B2B sites are supported by membership, subscription, or transaction fees, along with revenue from advertisers. Like stock markets, online B2B markets seek to drive volume to their sites to create liquidity and thus efficient pricing.

SOURCE: Adapted from A. Palazzo, *B2B Markets Basics*, www.business.com and www.FT.com, January 28, 2001.

DECISION MAKING

Negotiation actually represents the outcome of a series of small and large decisions. The decisions include those made by each party before actual negotiations start—for example, in determining the position of the company and what fallback proposals it may suggest or accept. The decisions also include incremental decisions, made during the negotiation process, on how to react and proceed, when to concede, and on what to agree or disagree. Negotiation can thus be seen as a series of explicit and implicit decisions, and the subjects of negotiation and decision making become interdependent.

For instance, sometimes just the way a decision is made during the negotiation process can have a profound influence on the outcome, as this example shows:

> *In his first loan negotiation, a banker new to Japan met with seven top Japanese bankers who were seeking a substantial amount of money. After hearing their presentation, the American agreed on the spot. The seven Japanese then conferred among themselves and told the American they would get back to him in a couple of days regarding whether they would accept his offer or not. The American banker learned a lesson he never forgot.[60]*

The Japanese bankers expected the American to negotiate, to take time to think it over, and to consult with colleagues before giving the final decision. His immediate decision made them suspicious, so they decided to reconsider the deal.

There is no doubt that the speed and manner of decision making affect the negotiation process. In addition, how well negotiated agreements are implemented is affected by the speed and manner of decision making. In that regard, it is clear that the effective use of technology is playing an important role, especially when dealing with complex cross-border agreements in which the hundreds of decision makers involved are separated by time and space.

The role of decision making in management, however, goes far beyond the finite occasions of negotiations. It is part of the manager's daily routine—from operational-level, programmed decisions requiring minimal time and effort to those nonprogrammed decisions of far broader scope and importance, such as the decision to enter into a joint venture in a foreign country.

The Influence of Culture on Decision Making

It is crucial for international managers to understand the influence of culture on decision-making styles and processes. Culture affects decision making both through the broader context of the nation's institutional culture, which produces collective patterns of decision making, and through culturally based value systems that affect each individual decision maker's perception or interpretation of a situation.[61]

The extent to which decision making is influenced by culture varies among countries. For example, Hitt, Tyler, and Park have found a "more culturally homogenizing influence on the Korean executives' cognitive models" than on those of U.S. executives, whose individualistic tendencies lead to different decision patterns.[62] The ways that culture influences an executive's decisions can be studied by looking at the variables involved in each stage of the rational decision-making process. These stages are (1) defining the problem, (2) gathering and analyzing relevant data, (3) considering alternative solutions, (4) deciding on the best solution, and (5) implementing the decision.

One of the major cultural variables affecting decision making is whether a country assumes an objective approach or a subjective approach. Whereas the Western approach is based on rationality (managers interpret a situation and consider alternative solutions based on objective information), this approach is not common throughout the world. Latin Americans, among others, are more subjective, basing decisions on emotions.

Another cultural variable that greatly influences the decision-making process is the risk tolerance of those making the decision. Research shows that people from Belgium, Germany, and Austria have a considerably lower tolerance for risk than people from Japan or the Netherlands—whereas American managers have the highest tolerance for risk.[63]

Another important variable in the decision-making process is the manager's perception of the locus of control over outcomes—whether that locus is internal or external. Some managers feel they can plan on certain outcomes because they are in control of events that will direct the future in the desired way. In contrast, other managers believe that such decisions are of no value because they have little control over the future—which lies in the hands of outside forces, such as fate, God, or nature. American managers believe strongly in self-determination and perceive problem situations as something they can control and should change. However, managers in many other countries, Indonesia and Malaysia among them, are resigned to problem situations and do not feel that they can change them. Obviously, these different value systems will result in a great difference in the stages of consideration of alternative actions and choice of a solution, often because certain situations may or may not be viewed as problems in the first place.

Another variable that affects the consideration of alternative solutions is how managers feel about staying with familiar solutions or trying new ones. Many managers, particularly those in Europe, value decisions based on past experiences and tend to emphasize quality. Americans, on the other hand, are more future oriented and look toward new ideas to get them there.

Approaches to Decision Making

In addition to affecting different stages of the decision-making process, value systems influence the overall approach of decision makers from various cultures. The relative level of utilitarianism versus moral idealism in any society affects its overall approach to problems. Generally speaking, utilitarianism strongly guides behavior in the Western world. Research has shown that Canadian executives are more influenced by a short-term, cost–benefit approach to decision making than their Hong Kong counterparts. Canadian managers are considerably more utilitarian than leaders from the People's Republic of China, who approach problems from a standpoint of moral idealism; they consider the problems, alternatives, and solutions from a long-term, societal perspective rather than an individual perspective.[64]

Another important variable in companies' overall approach to decision making is that of autocratic versus participative leadership. In other words, who has the authority to make what kinds of decisions? A country's orientation—whether it is individualistic or collectivist (see Chapter 3)—influences the level at which decisions are made. In many countries with hierarchical cultures—Germany, Turkey, and India, among others—authorization for action has to be passed upward through echelons of management before final decisions can be made. Most employees in these countries simply expect the autocrat—the boss—to do most of the decision making and will not be comfortable otherwise. Even in China, which is a highly collectivist society, employees expect autocratic leadership because their value system presupposes the superior to be automatically the most wise. In comparison, decision-making authority in Sweden is very decentralized. Americans talk a lot about the advisability of such participative leadership, but in practice they are probably near the middle between autocratic and participative management styles.

Arab managers have long traditions of consultative decision making, supported by the Qur'an and the sayings of Muhammad. However, such consultation occurs more on a person-to-person basis than during group meetings and thus diffuses potential opposition.[65] Although business in the Middle East tends to be transacted in a highly personalized manner, the final decisions are made by the top leaders, who feel that they must impose their will for the company to be successful. In comparison, in cultures that emphasize collective harmony, such as Japan, participatory or group decision making predominates, and consensus is important. The best-known example is the bottom-up (rather than top-down) decision-making process used in most Japanese companies, described in more detail in the following section.

One final area of frequent incongruence concerns the relative speed of decision making. A country's culture affects how fast or slow decisions tend to be made. The relative speed may be closely associated with the level of delegation, as just discussed—but not always. The pace at which decisions are made can be very disconcerting for outsiders. North Americans and Europeans pride themselves on being decisive; managers in the Middle East, with a different sense of temporal urgency, associate the importance of the matter at hand with the length of time needed to make a decision. Without knowing this cultural attitude, a hasty American would insult an Egyptian; a quick decision, to the Egyptian, would reflect a low regard for the relationship and the deal.

Exhibit 5-10 illustrates, in summary form, how all the variables just discussed can affect the steps in the decision-making process.

EXHIBIT 5-10   Cultural Variables in the Decision-Making Process

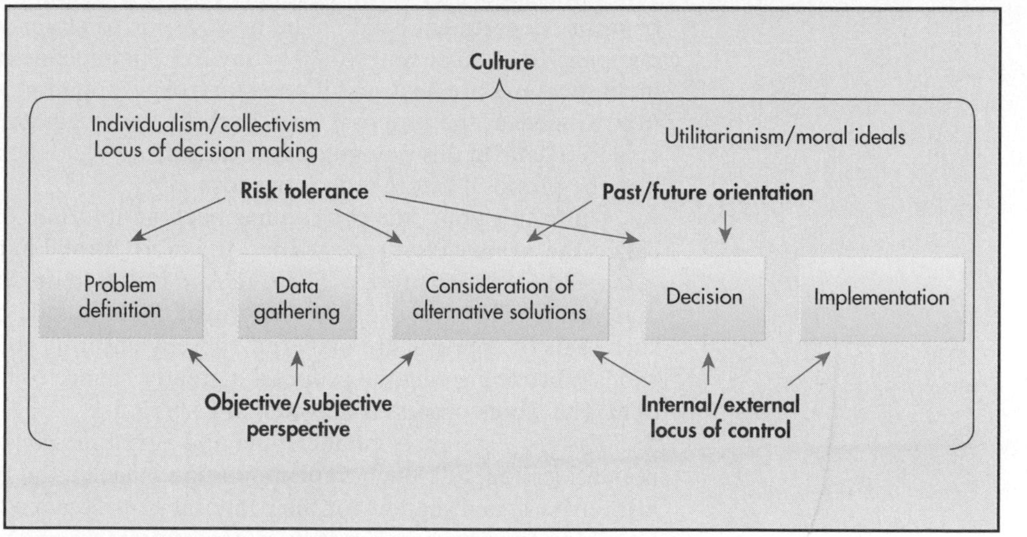

Comparative Management in Focus

Decision Making in Japanese Companies

Japanese companies are involved in joint ventures throughout the world, especially with U.S. companies. The GM–Toyota joint venture agreement process, for example, was the result of more than two years of negotiation and decision making. In this new company and in similar companies, Americans and Japanese are involved in decision making at all levels on a daily basis. The Japanese decision-making process differs greatly not only from the U.S. process but from that of many other countries—especially at the higher levels of their organizations.

An understanding of the Japanese decision-making process—and indeed of many Japanese management practices—requires an understanding of Japanese national culture. Much of the Japanese culture, and therefore the basis of Japanese working relationships, can be explained by the principle of *wa*, meaning "peace and harmony." This principle is one aspect of the value the Japanese attribute to *amae*, meaning "indulgent love," a concept probably originating in the Shinto religion, which focuses on spiritual and physical harmony. *Amae* results in *shinyo*, which refers to the mutual confidence, faith, and honor required for successful business relationships. The principle of *wa* influences the work group, the basic building block of Japanese work and management. The Japanese strongly identify with their work groups, where the emphasis is on cooperation, participative management, consensus problem solving, and decision making based on a patient, long-term perspective. Open expression of conflict is discouraged, and it is of utmost importance to avoid embarrassment or shame—to lose face—as a result of not fulfilling one's obligations. These elements of work culture generally result in a devotion to work, a collective responsibility for decisions and actions, and a high degree of employee productivity. It is this culture of collectivism and shared responsibility that underlies the Japanese *ringi* system of decision making.

In the *ringi* system, the process works from the bottom up. Americans are used to a centralized system, where major decisions are made by upper-level managers in a top-down approach typical of individualistic societies. The Japanese process, however, is dispersed throughout the organization, relying on group consensus.

The *ringi* process is one of gaining approval on a proposal by circulating documents to those concerned throughout the company. It usually comprises four steps: proposal, circulation, approval, and record.[66] Usually, the person who originates the written proposal, which is called a *ringi-sho*, has already worked for some time to gain informal consensus and support for the proposal within the section and then from the department head.[67] The next step is to attain a general consensus in the company from those who would be involved in implementation. To this end, department meetings are held, and if necessary, expert opinion is sought. If more information is needed, the proposal goes back to the originator, who finds and adds the required data. In this way, much time and effort— and the input of many people—go into the proposal before it becomes formal.[68]

Up to this point, the process has been an informal one to gain consensus; it is called the *nemawashi* process. Then the more formal authorization procedure begins, called the *ringi* process. The *ringi-sho* is passed up through successive layers of management for approval—the approval made official by seals. In the end, many such seals of approval are gathered, thereby ensuring collective agreement and responsibility and giving the proposal a greater chance of final approval by the president. The whole process is depicted in Exhibit 5-11.

The *ringi* system is cumbersome and very time-consuming prior to the implementation stage, although implementation is facilitated because of the widespread awareness of and support for the proposal already gained throughout the organization. However, its slow progress is problematic when decisions are time-sensitive. This process is the opposite of the Americans' top-down decisions, which are made quite rapidly and without consultation, but which then take some time to implement because unforeseen practical or support problems often arise.

EXHIBIT 5-11   Decision-Making Procedure in Japanese Companies

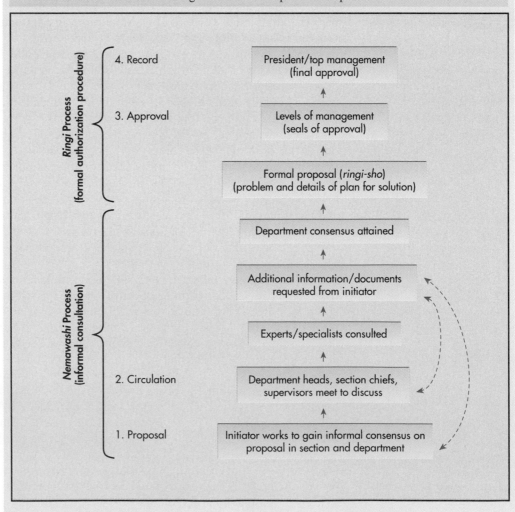

Another interesting comparison is often made regarding the planning horizon (aimed at short- or long-term goals) in decision making between the American and Japanese systems. The Japanese spend considerable time in the early stages of the process defining the issue, considering what the issue is all about, and determining whether there is an actual need for a decision. They are more likely than Americans to consider an issue in relation to the overall goals and strategy of the company. In this manner, they prudently look at the "big picture" and consider alternative solutions, instead of rushing into quick decisions for immediate solutions, as Americans tend to do.[69]

Of course, in a rapidly changing environment, quick decisions are often necessary—to respond to competitors' actions, a political uprising, and so forth—and it is in such contexts that the *ringi* system sometimes falls short because of its slow response rate. The system is, in fact, designed to manage continuity and to avoid uncertainty, which is considered a threat to group cohesiveness.[70]

CONCLUSION

It is clear that competitive positioning and long-term successful operations in a global market require a working knowledge of the decision-making and negotiating processes of managers from different countries. These processes are complex and often interdependent. Although managers may make decisions that do not involve negotiating, they cannot negotiate without making decisions, however small, or they would not be negotiating. In addition, managers must understand the behavioral aspects of these processes to work effectively with people in other countries or with a culturally diverse workforce in their own countries.

With an understanding of the environment and cultural context of international management as background, we move next in Part III to planning and implementing strategy for international and global operations.

Summary of Key Points

1. The ability to negotiate successfully is one of the most important in international business. Managers must prepare for certain cultural variables that influence negotiations, including the relative emphasis on task versus interpersonal relationship, the use of general principles versus specific details, the number of people present, and the extent of their influence.
2. The negotiation process typically progresses through the stages of preparation, relationship building, exchange of task-related information, persuasion, and concessions and agreement. The process of building trusting relationships is a prerequisite to doing business in many parts of the world.
3. Culturally-based differences in verbal and nonverbal negotiation behavior influence the negotiation process at every stage. Such tactics and actions include promises, threats, initial concessions, silent periods, interruptions, facial gazing, and touching; some parties resort to various dirty tricks.
4. The effective management of negotiation requires an understanding of the perspectives, values, and agendas of other parties and the use of a problem-solving approach.
5. Decision making is an important part of the negotiation process, as well as an integral part of a manager's daily routine. Culture affects the decision-making process both through a society's institutions and through individuals' risk tolerance, their objective versus subjective perspectives, their perceptions of the locus of control, and their past versus future orientations.
6. The Internet is used increasingly to support the negotiation of contracts and resolution of disputes. Web sites that provide open auctions take away the personal aspects of negotiations, though those aspects are still essential in many instances.

Discussion Questions

1. Discuss the stages in the negotiation process and how culturally based value systems influence these stages. Specifically, address the following:
   - Explain the role and relative importance of relationship building in different countries.
   - Discuss the various styles and tactics that can be involved in exchanging task-related information.
   - Describe differences in culturally based styles of persuasion.
   - Discuss the kinds of concession strategies a negotiator might anticipate in various countries.

2. Discuss the relative use of nonverbal behaviors, such as silent periods, interruptions, facial gazing, and touching, by people from various cultural backgrounds. How does this behavior affect the negotiation process in a cross-cultural context?

3. Describe what you would expect in negotiations with the Chinese and how you would handle various situations.

4. What are some of the differences in risk tolerance around the world? What is the role of risk propensity in the decision-making process?

5. Explain how objective versus subjective perspectives influences the decision-making process. What role do you think this variable has played in all the negotiations conducted and decisions made by Iraq and the United Nations?

6. Explain differences in culturally based value systems relative to the amount of control a person feels he or she has over future outcomes. How does this belief influence the decision-making process?

Experiential Exercises

Exercise 1: Multicultural Negotiations

Goal

To experience, identify, and appreciate the problems associated with negotiating with people of other cultures.

Instructions

1. Eight student volunteers will participate in the role play. Four represent a Japanese automobile manufacturer, and four represent a U.S. team that has come to sell microchips and other components to the Japanese company. The remainder of the class will observe the negotiations.

2. The eight volunteers will divide into the two groups and then separate into different rooms, if possible. At that point, they will be given instruction sheets. Neither team can have access to the other's instructions. After dividing the roles, the teams should meet for ten to fifteen minutes to develop their negotiation strategies based on their instructions.

3. While the teams are preparing, the room will be set up using a rectangular table with four seats on each side. The Japanese side will have three chairs at the table with one chair set up behind the three. The American side of the table will have four chairs side by side.

4. Following these preparations, the Japanese team will be brought in, so they may greet the Americans when they arrive. At this point, the Americans will be brought in and the role play begins. Time for the negotiations should be twenty to thirty minutes. The rest of the class will act as observers and will be expected to provide feedback during the discussion phase.

5. When the negotiations are completed, the student participants from both sides and the observers will complete their feedback questionnaires. Class discussion of the feedback questions will follow.

Feedback Questions for the Japanese Team

1. What was your biggest frustration during the negotiations?

2. What would you say the goal of the American team was?

3. What role (e.g., decider, influencer, etc.) did each member of the American team play?
   Mr. Jones
   Mr./Ms. Smith
   Mr./Ms. Nelson
   Mr./Ms. Frost

4. How would you rate the success of each of the American team members in identifying your team's needs and appealing to them?
   Mr./Ms. Jones, Vice President and Team Leader
   Mr./Ms. Smith, Manufacturing Engineer
   Mr./ Ms. Nelson, Marketing Analyst
   Mr./Ms. Frost, Account Executive

5. What strategy should the American team have taken?

Feedback Questions for the American Team

1. What was your biggest frustration during the negotiations?

2. What would you say the goal of the Japanese team was?

3. How would you rate the success of each of the American team members?
   Mr. Jones, Vice President and Team Leader
   Mr./Ms. Smith, Manufacturing Engineer
   Mr./Ms. Nelson, Marketing Analyst
   Mr./Ms. Frost, Account Executive

4. What would you say the goal of the American team was?

5. What role (e.g., decider, influencer, etc.) did each member of the Japanese team play?
   Mr. Ozaka
   Mr. Nishimuro
   Mr. Sheno
   Mr. Kawazaka
6. What strategy should the American team have taken?

Feedback Questions for the Observers

1. What was your biggest frustration during the negotiations?
2. What would you say the goal of the Japanese team was?
3. How would you rate the success of each of the American team members?
   Mr./Ms. Jones, Vice President and Team Leader
   Mr./Ms. Smith, Manufacturing Engineer
   Mr./Ms. Nelson, Marketing Analyst
   Mr./Ms. Frost, Account Executive
4. What would you say the goal of the American team was?
5. What role (e.g., decider, influencer, etc.) did each member of the Japanese team play?
   Mr. Ozaka
   Mr. Nishimuro
   Mr. Sheno
   Mr. Kawazaka
6. What strategy should the American team have taken?

Exercise 2: Japanese Decision Making

Time: Two class meetings

Goal

To allow students to experience the process and results of solving a problem or initiating a project using the Japanese decision processes of *nemawashi* and *ringi*.

Preparation

Review Chapter 4 and Chapter 5. In Chapter 5, study Comparative Management in Focus: Decision Making in Japanese Companies.

Note: Instructions for this exercise will be given by your Professor, from the Instructor's Manual.

SOURCE: E. A. Diodati, in C. Harvey and M. J. Allard, *Understanding Diversity* (New York: HarperCollins Publishers, 1995). Used with permission.

Internet Resources

Visit the Deresky companion Web site at www.prenhall.com/deresky for this chapter's Internet resources.

Martinez Construction Company in Germany (Martinez Construction & Konstruktion Dreizehn)

Juan Sanchez glanced out the window of the Boeing jet-liner and admired the countryside below. The overcast skies failed to dampen his enthusiasm for the challenges and opportunities he and his company now faced. Two generations of local services had done little to prepare Martinez Construction for the coming days. Nevertheless, Juan remained confident that once the spirit of cooperation and trust was established, the new German operation would be a success.

Martinez Construction Company

Martinez Construction is a well-established construction company in eastern Spain. Founded in Barcelona in the mid-1940s, its reputation and quality of service ensured growing profits for decades. However, a recent decline in contracts has resulted in a growing awareness of the dependence the business has on local economic conditions. Diego Martinez, president and son of the founder of Martinez Construction, now faces a growing certainty that the survival and continued growth of the family business depend on expansion into the international marketplace.

In Barcelona, Diego had met many German tourists. They seemed to enjoy the warm sunshine of Spain. He also knew that many German companies now conducted business in Spain. Thus, it was natural when his company started thinking globally that they were drawn to the new German states. The recent collapse of communism and subsequent opening of new markets in Eastern Europe provided what seemed like an excellent opportunity for expansion. After all, why shouldn't Martinez Construction take advantage of the cheap labor and raw materials?

More information was needed, however. Martinez Construction representatives contacted banks, commercial departments of foreign consulates, and chambers of commerce, as well as the Investor Services department of the Treuhandanstalt (THA), which was, for a short time, the world's largest holding company. They also depended on accountants, lawyers, consultants, and others to provide advice. After the initial research and discussion of the alternatives with other members of management, Diego has come to the conclusion that the best approach to this venture will be through the acquisition of an existing company from the Treuhandanstalt. This decision was made after concluding that Martinez Construction lacked the resources necessary to risk a greenfield operation. Added to this was the certainty that an alliance with other German companies would not allow Martinez Construction to establish itself as a serious competitor in the international construction market.

Diego chose his brother-in-law and manager of the Barcelona branch of Martinez Construction, Juan Sanchez, to act as the negotiator for the company with THA. Although Juan is unfamiliar with German business practices, Diego feels that Juan's friendly demeanor and expertise in the needs of the company will ensure the establishment of the necessary trust to build a strong cooperative venture with THA.

Juan will be accompanied by Diego's nephew and projected manager of the new German acquisition, Miguel Martinez. Miguel is the youngest and most educated of the Martinez managerial staff. His background includes a business degree from a university in the United States, as well as years of employment in the family business. Although lacking in practical managerial experience, it was largely due to his influence that Diego saw the wisdom and necessity of expanding operations abroad. Miguel's opportunity has fueled his optimism despite the challenges he faces in the management of a foreign subsidiary.

Treuhandanstalt

Because of the collapse of communism in the German Democratic Republic, the two Germanys were finally going to be reunified. The Treuhandanstalt was created in what was the German Democratic Republic. The sole purpose of the THA was to find private buyers for some 13,500 businesses and 15,000 parcels of real estate that had been previously owned by the German Democratic Republic. The government knew that the economy in this sector had to be stimulated quickly. There were hopes that many investors would take advantage of the new markets opening up. However, little thought was given to the immensity of the job. No guidelines were issued, which later led to charges of dubious deals, and limited funds were made available to run the agency.

Therefore, any firm wishing to purchase an existing facility in East Germany had no choice in the matter—they had to deal with the THA. The primary job of the THA was to sell the companies and to match existing companies with buyers. However, this proved to be an almost impossible task because the THA had insufficient or no information about the financial positions of the companies it was supposed to sell. In some cases, it could not ascertain what companies were to be sold.

The firms wishing to purchase properties through the THA were initially evaluated on the basis of financial soundness. Second, they were evaluated on potential employment opportunity. Next, they were measured according to the cost of restructuring to the buyer. The speed of the sale was, however, the most important issue to the THA. The sooner the THA finished its work, the sooner the economy would improve.

Price was the main aspect of the sales negotiations. Other facets of the negotiations involved guaranteeing jobs for present employees and arranging for the upgrade and improvement of the companies. This meant the investment of a great deal of time and money by the buyer because many of the firms had fallen into disrepair. In fact, some were no longer operable in their present state.

Negotiations

The THA finally found what it considered to be a match for Martinez Construction. It was an existing construction firm, Konstruktion Dreizehn, located in Leipzig, Germany. (Leipzig is a city of about 564,000 people located in the eastern part of Germany.)

From the time of his arrival in Germany, Juan felt that he was having a difficult time just getting acquainted with the Germans. He felt pressured by the THA representatives. The Germans were all business. They didn't seem to have time to get to know Juan personally: Rush and urgency to complete the sale were the focus of their approach.

The first meeting was scheduled for 9:00 A.M. Juan and Miguel arrived at 9:15. Juan noticed that the THA representative, Helga Schmidt, seemed quite agitated when they arrived. She didn't even offer them coffee. He wondered what had upset her so much.

When he suggested that they be taken on a tour of the city this morning instead of immediately starting the negotiations, he was reminded of the necessity of proceeding with the negotiations. Even though this displeased Juan, he agreed to start negotiations for the sale.

The Germans presented their proposal to Juan. He was amazed. Every detail was in this contract, and yet the THA had not yet ascertained the financial status and position of the construction firm in Leipzig. For this reason, Juan had expected some sort of flexible agreement. This was especially important since, given the dearth of available financial analysis, there was no way to determine the extent of future problems. Didn't the Germans know this? If the THA was to be trusted, why bother with this type of contract? He told the Germans exactly what his thoughts were on this subject.

Helga was clearly uncomfortable with Juan's emotional outburst. However, she did see his point and decided to compromise by offering a phased contract, which made Juan more comfortable with the situation. However, the Germans felt lost without the technicalities represented in the original contract.

The negotiations proceeded smoothly from this point. The final contract stated that the original price would be reviewed in two years, and the contracted parties would recalculate it based on new and presumably more reliable data concerning the true value of the firm. Although there were problems with the negotiations, one thing did impress Juan about the Germans. He really appreciated the way the negotiations were organized. When there was a question, Helga always knew whom to contact. She also knew what forms, reports, and so on, needed to be sent to which department of the THA. Helga, on the other hand, was very uncomfortable with Juan's relaxed manner. She did, however, value his genuineness and practicality.

Operations

Miguel Martinez arrived tired but excited in Leipzig. The flight provided ample time to consider his actions in the new German subsidiary. After spending a few days setting up household, Miguel met with the three-member management team sent the month before to begin studying the situation. It was the consensus of the team, and they quickly convinced Miguel, that human resources would be crucial to the recovery of the company. The company had employed approximately 350 workers inside the German Democratic Republic (GDR). The THA had reduced the workforce to 100. Miguel and his team estimated that 50 employees would be sufficient. However, it was not long before the parties realized that East Germans did not have the same concept of work, or the same incentives, as did West Germans. Further confirmation of the effect of the workers' place of origin showed in the degree of initiative and responsibility demonstrated by the workers, or the lack thereof. Miguel was frustrated by the unwillingness of some employees to actively participate in the formulation of ideas and implementation of new procedures and policies. More than forty years of communism had taught them to expect all guidance and solutions to come from the top.

Added to the lack of initiative were a fear and distrust of management. These were quickly justified when Miguel's new management team investigated a labor union's report criticizing the previous management's hiring practices and competence.

Six months after Miguel's triumphant arrival, his optimism was fading fast. He had just received the latest report concerning the company's financial position, and it was clear that the figures were far from what Martinez Construction had been led to believe. Strict environmental and employee protection regulations forced large investments in plant modifications. Further, other costly projects that had not been foreseen during the negotiation process required attention. Cash flow problems were beginning to arise, and this threatened the very existence of the company.

Although reevaluation of the contract was specified after two years, Miguel wondered whether immediate action might be necessary. Sitting in his office overlooking the southern complex of the plant, the heavy rain clouds matched the darkness of his mood.

CASE QUESTIONS

1. What was the basis for Martinez Construction's decision to enter the international market? Was it proactive or reactive? Why?
2. Were the Spanish prepared for the problems faced in the negotiations? If not, what might the Spanish have done to better prepare themselves for the negotiations?
3. How did the Spanish interpret the actions of the Germans?
4. Do you think the Germans were aware of the cultural differences that came to the surface during the negotiations?
5. What might the Spanish have done differently to address the concerns of the employees?
6. What are the diverse problems created by the differences between the Spanish and German cultures and between communist and capitalist cultures?

Appendix 1: A Comparison of Spanish and German Democratic Republic Work Styles

Spanish

- Clear goals not common; work under assumption that goals of past will be goals of future
- Hierarchical society with status based on position; line of authority is top-down
- Promotions usually determined by seniority
- Decisions influenced by human factors

German Democratic Republic

- Goals related to politics; what is good for the state (society)
- Everyone is equal; however, superiors expected to provide all solutions
- Lifelong employment common; advancement decisions political
- Decisions influenced by what is good for society as a whole

Appendix 2: Negotiating Styles of the Spanish and Germans

Spanish

- Prefer to establish trust by taking time to get to know counterparts
- Don't attach importance to punctuality
- Discuss things at length
- Raise their voices and interrupt speakers during disagreements

- Make decisions based on general principles and leave details undecided.

Germans

- Keep business and pleasure separate
- Stress the importance of punctuality
- State facts in a concise manner
- Reserved and formal during discussions
- Exhibit a strong concern for details and exacting contracts

Case Bibliography

This case is based in part on a company discussed in the referenced article by R. W. Frederick and Adolfo de la Fuente Rodriguez; those authors do not indicate the name of the company discussed, nor whether it is real or fictional.

Ames, Helen Watley. *Spain Is Different*. ME: Intercultural Press, Inc., 1992, 89–96.

Cote, Kevin. "Germany's White Elephant." *Fortune*, June 28, 1991.

"Farewell, Sweet Treuhand: Privatisation," *Economist,* 333, 7895, December 1994, 82–85.

"Fast and Loose: East German Privatisation," *Economist,* 331, 7861, April 30, 1994, 75–76.

Frederick, Richard W., and Adolfo de la Fuente Rodriguez. "A Spanish Acquisition in Eastern Germany: Culture Shock." *Journal of Management Development* 13, no. 2 (March 1994): 42–49.

Hampden-Turner, Charles. "The Boundaries of Business: The Cross-cultural Quagmire," *Harvard Business Review* (September–October 1991).

Hofstede, G. *Cultures and Organization.* New York: McGraw-Hill, 1991, 200–203.

Kanter, Rosabeth Moss. "Transcending Business Boundaries: 12,000 World Managers View Change," *Harvard Business Review* (May–June 1991): 151–164.

Kanter, Rosabeth Moss, and Richard Ian Corn. "Do Cultural Differences Make a Business Difference?" *Journal of Management Development* 13, no. 2 (1993): 5–23.

Lacher, Michael A. "Creating and Securing Joint Ventures in Central and Eastern Europe: A Western Perspective." *Site Selection* (June 1994): 554–555.

Meschi, Pierre-Xavier, and Alain Roger. "Cultural Context and Social Effectiveness in International Joint Ventures." *Mangement International Review* 34 (1994): 197–215.

Miller, Karen Lowery, Jeff Javetski, and Peggy Simson, "Europe: The Push East." *Business Week,* November 7, 1994.

Mueller, Franc. "Societal Effect, Organizational Effect, and Globalization." *Organizational Studies* 15, no. 3 (1994): 407–428.

Olie, Rene, "Shades of Culture and Institutions in International Mergers." *Organizational Studies* 15, no. 3 (1994): 381–405.

"Recognizing and Heeding Cultural Differences Can Be Key to International Business Success." Compiled by staff, *Business America* (October 1994).

Torpey, John. "Growing Together, Coming Apart: German Society Since Unification." *Social Education* 57, no. 5 ( ): 136–239.

West, Judy F., and Judy C. Nixon. "Cultural Diversity among American and European Business Persons." Paper presented at the annual meeting of the Association of Business Communication International Conference, November 8, 1990.

_____

Case 4 Dell's Dilemma in Brazil: Negotiating at the State Level

In mid-March 1999, Keith Maxwell, Senior Vice President for Worldwide Operations, Dell Computer Corporation, looked out the window of his office at Dell's headquarters in Round Rock, Texas, and pondered the frustrating situation he faced in Brazil, where Dell had decided to locate its first manufacturing plant in Latin America.

In early 1998, Maxwell had led the site selection team that visited five different states in Brazil in order to decide where Dell should locate its manufacturing plant.[1] In June 1998, after the team had confirmed its initial findings and concluded its negotiations, Maxwell had made the final recommendation to Michael Dell: the plant should be built in Brazil's southernmost state, Rio Grande do Sul. By mid-March 1999, Dell had already signed agreements with the local state government on the terms of the investment, the process of hiring local personnel to manage the plant had begun, and construction on the plant itself was scheduled to start soon.

Suddenly, however, the political climate in Rio Grande do Sul had changed. A new governor, Olivio Dutra of the Partido dos Trabalhadores (Workers' Party),[2] had taken office in Rio Grande do Sul on January 1, 1999 and appeared likely to rescind the entire agreement. This was a setback, and Maxwell would have to decide on a course of action to recommend: (1) leave Brazil entirely; (2) move the plant to another state; or (3) try to renegotiate with Governor Dutra.

DELL AND THE BRAZILIAN COMPUTER MARKET

As Maxwell considered the options, he reflected on the events that had led to this situation. Dell had begun the process of selecting a site for its manufacturing plant in Brazil in 1998, after the company had experienced a long period of astonishing growth. Founded in 1984 by Michael Dell in his University of Texas dorm room, by 1999 Dell Computer Corporation had annual revenue of over $23 billion and a market capitalization of $98 billion. In just 15 years, the revenues Dell generated were the second largest in the world for personal computer manufacturers, just behind Compaq, and the company was still one of the fastest growing PC makers in the industry.

Most of Dell's success could be attributed to its revolutionary business approach, which had become known as the Direct Model. Following the Direct Model, Dell shipped its products to its customers directly from the factory, without any intermediary retailers. Dell also set up its supply chain of parts and components using the latest just-in-time (JIT) methods, which allowed the company to maintain minimal inventory. These highly efficient practices enabled Dell not only to get its products to customers faster than its competitors could, but also to reduce its costs substantially. The resulting ability to pass on these savings directly to customers created a tremendous competitive edge that enabled the company to control 25% of the U.S. market for personal computers, and 11% of the market worldwide.[3]

In order to maintain its rapid growth, Dell adopted a strategy of emphasizing international expansion. From its headquarters in Round Rock, Texas, the company expanded its operations to the point that by the late 1990s, it had offices in 34 countries around the world, sales in over 170 countries and territories, and manufacturing facilities in five countries, including Ireland and China. Although the company outsourced some of its manufacturing to contract manufacturers in Mexico, it did not have any manufacturing facilities of its own in Latin America when, in early 1998, it began evaluating possible sites for the construction of its own manufacturing plant in Brazil.

---

[1]The principal members of the initial team, in addition to Maxwell, included Daryl Robertson, Vice President, Dell Latin America; Tom Armstrong, Vice President, Tax and Administration; Kip Thompson, Vice President, Worldwide Facilities Management and Corporate Real Estate; and Charlene Coor, Director of International Tax.

[2]Brazil's Partido dos Trabalhadores (PT), the Workers' Party, is a leftist political party with a socialist ideology.

[3]"IDC Results Show Compaq Finished 1999 as Number One in Worldwide PC Market, But Dell Heads into Millennium Leading in the US," *PR Newswire*, January 24, 2000.

Brazil was a logical place for a manufacturing plant. In the late 1990s, sales of personal computers were growing faster in Latin America than anywhere else in the world, and Brazil, the largest Latin American country with a population of over 170 million, was a very attractive market for the company. Despite the maxi-devaluation of the Brazilian currency, the *real,* in January 1999, Dell had decided to continue with its plans to invest in Brazil as part of its long-term strategy. Dell executives realized that having a plant in Brazil would be essential if the company were to enter the Brazilian market successfully. Although in 1992 the Brazilian government had abandoned its market reserve policy of allowing only domestic manufacturers to make computers in the country, Brazil's protectionist barriers for imports were still high. Moreover, Brazil was a member of Mercado Comun do Sul (Mercosul), the South American customs union that included Argentina, Uruguay, and Paraguay, with Chile and Bolivia as associate members. The benefit of Mercosul was that any company that produced at least 60% of a given product in any of the Mercosul countries would, with some exceptions, be able to export the product to any of the other Mercosul countries at zero tariffs. Clearly, Brazil's Mercosul membership was another plus for putting the plant in Brazil.

Once Dell had selected Brazil, however, the question remained as to exactly where the manufacturing plant would be located. Brazil had a federal system, with 26 separate states—each with its own governor and state legislature, as well as a federal district, and many of these states eagerly sought Dell's investment. Having chosen Brazil as the site for the new manufacturing plant in Latin America, Dell's executives would have still another decision to make.

Maxwell and the others on Dell's site selection team visited five different states in Brazil: São Paulo, Minas Gerais, Rio de Janeiro, Paraná, and Rio Grande do Sul. All of these states essentially met the requirements for levels of education and sufficient numbers of qualified personnel, adequate supply of electrical energy, and quality of telecommunications and transportation infrastructure. The main differences of interest to the Dell team were the special financial incentives each state offered, and the nature of the agency with which the company interacted when making the investment decision.

COMPETITION BETWEEN THE STATES

The Guerra Fiscal

In their exuberance during Brazil's transition to democracy, politicians elected to Brazil's Constituent Assembly approved a constitution in 1988 that gave states considerably more power than before. Among other things, states were authorized to collect state sales taxes, or *Impostos sobre a Circulação de Mercadorias e Serviços* (ICMS). Although the current average for these taxes was 12%, states had some leeway to reduce these taxes in order to attract investment.

In theory, individual states could not change their ICMS tax rates unless all states agreed to do so within the *Conselho Nacional de Política Fazendária* (CONFAZ), the representative body for the states on finance and taxation policy. Nevertheless, from the beginning, states made such changes without CONFAZ approval. Since the early 1990s, the competition between the states to lower their taxes and attract investment had become so fierce that journalists called it the *guerra fiscal,* or taxation war.

Taxation rates mattered to large transnational corporations trying to decide where to invest. Competition among these companies was fierce, and a difference in sales tax meant that companies could offer their products at reduced costs without passing on the tax burden to consumers. Such incentives also compensated for extra costs associated with investing outside of the more industrialized and heavily populated locations of Brazil, especially the state of São Paulo, which traditionally received, by far, the greatest proportion of Brazil's foreign investment. Significantly, São Paulo itself did not offer this particular incentive—it did not need to do so.

But many in Brazil saw this policy as detrimental to the country's overall interests. Critics of the *guerra fiscal* argued that transnational corporations (TNCs) could use it to play one state against another for their own benefit, without concern for the welfare of the country as a whole. Poor Brazilian states, these critics maintained, were in no position to be giving tax concessions to large, wealthy transnational corporations.[4] Supporters of the policy, on the other hand, argued that without such incentives, the TNCs would not invest at all in states far from the more industrialized regions.[5] And as one supporter of the policy put it, "12% [the full taxation rate] of nothing is still nothing."[6]

The incentives Brazil's states could offer to attract foreign investment went beyond reductions in the ICMS. State governments could (and did, in many cases) also offer to provide free land on which to build infrastructure (usually roads or port facilities), and to provide government loans on highly concessional terms, including lengthy grace periods and low interest rates. As with the ICMS tax reductions, these incentives also came under harsh attack from critics. This was the environment that Maxwell and the Dell team had entered when they began their site selection process in Brazil.

---

[4]Talita Moreira, "Business Leaders Praise Responses to Incentives Dispute," *Gazeta Mercantil Invest News,* http://lexis-nexis.com/ universe, January 11, 2000; Denise Neumann et al., "Guerra Fiscal Abala Finanças dos Estados," *Estado do São Paulo,* July 13, 1997, p. 31; and Maria Quadros, "Governors Fail to Find Consensus on Fiscal War," *Gazeta Mercantil Invest News,* http://lexis-nexis.com/ universe, January 28, 2000.
[5]Ricardo Caldeira, "Os Incentivos Fiscal Gera Desenvolvimento," *Gazeta Mercantil,* March 23, 1999, p. 2.
[6]Interview with Ricardo Hinkelman, Former Technical Adviser, SEDAI, Porto Alegre, November 10, 1999.

Financial Incentives and Contrasting Approaches to Investment Promotion

During the site selection process, one of the team's chief concerns had been to investigate the prospects for obtaining financial incentives in each state. Upon actually visiting each state, however, the site selection team's initial and most important contacts were with the agency responsible for investment promotion. The nature of the working relationships Maxwell and the rest of the team established with these agencies also turned out to play a major role in the decision-making process.

Each state in Brazil that the Dell executives visited had a unique approach to promoting foreign investment; and in every state, the investment promotion organization responsible for meeting with the Dell team had a slightly different organizational structure and style. With the sole exception of Pólo-RS, Agência de Desenvolvimento (Pólo), the independent, private, nonprofit investment promotion agency that collaborated with the state government of Rio Grande do Sul, all of the state agencies the Dell executives encountered were government agencies. This made a difference in how these agencies interacted with Dell. While other states such as Minas Gerais offered Dell similar financial incentives, only in Rio Grande do Sul did the Dell executives, working with Pólo as an intermediary, encounter an investment promotion agency that they felt had made a concerted effort to understand Dell's specific needs. In other states, in contrast, Dell executives perceived that the government officials they were dealing with either did not sufficiently understand Dell's unique requirements, or were not sufficiently committed to attracting high-technology investment.

São Paulo, for example, was a state that initially attracted Dell. It had a large pool of skilled labor and, because of its large, relatively prosperous population, it was the principal market for computers in Brazil. São Paulo's sheer market size was the main reason that in the final selection process, two possible sites in the state, one in the city of São Jose dos Campos and the other in Campinas, were ranked high on the list, although still below Rio Grande do Sul.[7] But the Dell site selection team formed a negative impression of São Paulo when harried state government officials appeared to be somewhat indifferent to Dell's specific concerns.[8] Moreover, the state, which already had significant investment, had a policy of not offering special financial incentives.[9]

In Rio de Janeiro, the team encountered a different situation. The head of the Companhia de Desenvolvimento Industrial do Estado do Rio de Janeiro (CODIN), Rio de Janeiro's investment promotion agency, was accustomed to long drawn-out negotiations with automobile firms that sometimes lasted for a year or more. Consequently, he made a very low initial offer for financial incentives to Dell, expecting the company to come back with a counter offer. He was stunned when the Dell executives, accustomed to making decisions on a much speedier basis, never returned.[10]

In Paraná, the state government was not able to offer Dell the same financial incentives that Rio Grande do Sul offered.[11] In addition to that, Maxwell and others on the Dell team also perceived that the state was giving the same sort of presentation to them that it gave to all companies, regardless of the specific sector the company represented.[12]

Other than São Paulo, which was ranked high principally because of the size of its market rather than its investment promotion efforts, only Minas Gerais came close to winning the competition with Rio Grande do Sul for Dell's investment. In Minas, the Dell executives met with state government officials from various agencies, as well as with *técnicos* from the Instituto de Desenvolvimento Industrial de Minas Gerais (INDI).

Created in 1968, INDI had a unique structure. It was financed partly by the Companhia Energética de Minas Gerais (CEMIG), the state energy company—a mixed enterprise, 70% state-owned, 30% private—and partly by the Banco de Desenvolvimento de Minas Gerais (BDMG), the state-owned Minas Gerais Development Bank. While INDI was a government institution, then, the partially private ownership of one of INDI's supporting institutions, CEMIG, gave INDI more flexibility in hiring personnel than it would have had if it were purely a state-owned institution.[13] As a result, at least some of INDI's staff also received salaries that were considerably higher than those working in regular government agencies.[14] In this way, INDI was able to recruit highly qualified staff that specialized in at least six broadly diversified industrial sectors—mining and metallurgy; chemicals and nonchemical materials; industry and tourism; agroindustries; textiles, garments, leather, footwear, furniture, and publishing; and mechanics, electroelectronics and computers—who might otherwise have taken jobs in the private sector.[15]

[7]Interview with Keith Maxwell, Senior Vice President, Dell Computer Corporation, Round Rock, Texas, March 20, 2000.

[8]*Ibid.*

[9]Interview with Jorge Funaro, Chief of Staff, Secretariat of Science, Technology and Economic Development, São Paulo, November 15, 1999.

[10]Interview with Enrique Weber, President of CODIN, Rio de Janeiro, March 13, 2000.

[11]Interviews with Fernando Sicuro, Technical Adviser of State Government of Paraná, and Clemente Simião, Coordinator, Secretariat of Industry, Commerce and Economic Development, State Government of Paraná, Curitiba, Parana, November 23, 1999.

[12]Maxwell, March 20, 2000.

[13]In fact, strictly speaking INDI did not have its own staff because all of INDI's personnel worked either for CEMIG, BDMG, or were outsourced from other agencies, and were technically on loan from these other institutions, Khoury Rolim Dias 2001, 2002.

[14]Interview with Romulo Ronan Fontes, Manager of Technical and Economic Studies Department, INDI, Belo Horizonte, November 26, 1999.

[15]INDI, http://www.indi.mg.gov 2001, January 23, 2002. Clearly, INDI, an older, larger, more established institution with a wider range of investment promotion activities, did not have what Pólo was able to develop in a very short time: a specific focus on attracting high-technology industries.

It is a testament to INDI's effectiveness, members of Dell's site selection team made three separate visits to Minas Gerais to meet with state government officials. The final proposal that INDI prepared was only slightly less favorable than that of Rio Grande do Sul—the state that ultimately won Dell's investment. Minas Gerais was able to offer Dell a 70% reduction in the ICMS tax for 10 years; a loan for R\$20 million (20 million *reais*), with a four-year grace period and a four-year repayment period; and free land for the plant site.[16] But in the end, Dell chose Rio Grande do Sul.

INDI was in some ways a victim of its own success. The agency's past achievements in attracting companies from the mining, steel, and automobile sectors had made such an impact on the state that when the Dell site selection team arrived, they had the impression that this was the primary focus of the government's activities. Historically, of course, Minas Gerais had always had a strong mining sector. (Minas Gerais itself means "General Mines" in Portuguese.) INDI's later success in attracting foreign investment from companies in the heavy capital equipment and automobile sectors further contributed to the state's industrial development. Observing the results of this prior industrialization, however, the Dell executives came away with the impression that Minas Gerais, especially in the vicinity of the Fiat plant and the greater metropolitan region of Belo Horizonte, was a heavy-industry, rust-belt region. This reinforced their sense that the government officials they were dealing with in Minas had grown accustomed to working with the large, capital-intensive, heavy-industry firms that were common in the mining and automobile industries, and would not fully be able to appreciate Dell's specific needs as a fast-paced, just-in-time-oriented, knowledge-intensive company.[17] Fair impression or not, the INDI staff were unable to change this view during the Dell executives' time in Minas Gerais, and it had a strong influence on the company's decision not to invest there.

RIO GRANDE DO SUL, THE ULTIMATE CHOICE

Rio Grande do Sul had not even been on Dell's short list when representatives from Pólo and the state government visited the company in early 1998 and convinced Dell's senior executives that the state deserved a closer look. But by June 1998—less than six months after that initial visit—Maxwell and the team had made the recommendation that Dell should establish a plant in Rio Grande do Sul.

Certainly, Rio Grande do Sul had a lot to offer. It had a well-developed, modern infrastructure; and as the first state to privatize its telecommunications company, its telecommunications infrastructure was among the more efficient in the country. In fact, a quick analysis indicated that, even before factoring in any incentives the state government might offer, lower costs in Rio Grande do Sul for the plant's overall facilities would already compensate for the additional expense associated with shipping computers to customers elsewhere in Brazil.[18] And although customers in São Paulo, for example, would have to wait a day longer to receive their computers from a plant in Rio Grande do Sul than they would if the plant were located in São Paulo itself, previous studies had indicated that this would not be a serious problem.[19]

Security was another factor. In terms of security from hijackings and robbery, the main road from Rio Grande do Sul to São Paulo, Dell's principal market, appeared to be considerably safer than many of the roads within the state of São Paulo itself. In addition, the Dell executives felt personally safe in and around the vicinity of Porto Alegre, Rio Grande do Sul's capital, where the plant would be located. Expatriate executives and suppliers from out of town might not know which areas to avoid in a large, unfamiliar city, but this was not really a serious problem in the greater metropolitan region of Porto Alegre, where the crime rate was relatively low.

Home to a number of well-regarded universities, Rio Grande do Sul had a well-educated population. It was one of the most prosperous of Brazil's states, with a standard of living that some rated as the highest in Brazil. In the end, too, the Rio Grande do Sul state government was able to offer very generous terms: a 75% reduction in the ICMS tax for 12 years, plus a R\$20 million loan (over USD \$16 million at the prevailing exchange rate), with a five-year grace period, to be paid back over a 10-year period.[20]

While offering generous incentives, the state government made sure that Dell would be providing benefits to Rio Grande do Sul as well. In the contract that the government signed with the company, Dell promised to develop joint research and development projects with local universities, such as the Universidade Federal de Rio Grande do Sul (UFRGS) and the Pontifícia Universidade Católica (PUC).[21] In addition to the company's

---

[16]Governo de Minas Gerais, Dell Proposal, Belo Horizonte, 1998.
[17]Maxwell, March 20, 2000.

[18]All computers were to be shipped by truck. This service was to be outsourced to local shipping companies.
[19]Telephone interview with Keith Maxwell, August 4, 2003.
[20]Guilherme Diefenthaeler, "O Dedo da Dell," *Amanha*, November, 1999, p. 39.
[21]Of course, in order to qualify for a tax incentive, the federal government gave to the computer industry known as the Proceso Produtivo Básico (PPB), which included a reduction of up to 50% of corporate income tax, companies such as Dell had to invest 5% of their total revenue in Brazil on research and development (R&D) within the country. At the time, at least 2% of this had to be invested in universities or other government-approved institutions; the rest could be invested inside the company. (Renato Bastos, "Computer Hardware and Peripherals," U.S. Department of Commerce Industry Sector Analysis for Brazil, São Paulo, Brazil, 1998, p. 15.) As a result of these provisions, Dell would have to spend some money in Brazil on R&D in any case. The federal law, however, did not specify where in Brazil this expenditure on R&D would have to be made.

R$128 million investment in its plant (USD $108.5 million), which alone would create beneficial linkage effects in the local economy in its construction and continued operation, Dell also promised to hire 260 direct employees in the first year and 700 employees within five years. If it did not, the contract would be nullified.[22]

These potential benefits help to explain why so many states in Brazil considered Dell's investment to be such a prize, and why Rio Grande do Sul was willing to offer such attractive incentives. Nevertheless, without Pólo's intervention Dell would not even have considered the state. Because Pólo played such an instrumental role in this outcome, further background on the agency itself is in order.

The Creation of Pólo

Pólo originated in the early 1990s within the Federação das Associacoes do Rio Grande do Sul (FEDERASUL), which represented commercial enterprises in the state, and the Federação das Industrias do Rio Grande do Sul (FIERGS), which represented industries. Leaders within these two organizations proposed creating an independent, private agency to promote foreign investment that would be more flexible and nimble than a government entity. Funding for the agency would come from the private sector, but Pólo would work in conjunction with the state government to promote economic development in Rio Grande do Sul by attracting direct foreign investment in the state. Representatives from FEDERASUL and FIERGS presented it to the two candidates for governor in the 1994 election: Olivio Dutra, a socialist from the Partido dos Trabalhadores (PT), and Antonio Britto, a pro-business moderate from the relatively centrist Partido do Movimento Democrático Brasileiro (PMDB). Although holding widely divergent political views, both candidates endorsed the idea, and thus Pólo was formally created in December 1995.

Pólo's founders sought to maintain a connection with the government by allowing the governor a key role in selecting the agency's president. This was done to ensure that the governor would maintain a close working relationship with the agency.[23] Ideally, both the government and the agency would work in concert to attract foreign investment that would contribute to the development of the state. However, this rule was changed in 1999, and the Board of Directors became solely responsible for selecting Pólo's president.[24]

The New High-Technology Emphasis

Antonio Britto, the pro-business moderate, won the 1994 gubernatorial campaign and took office in January 1995. Having campaigned on a promise to promote foreign investment in areas that would bring jobs and economic development to Rio Grande do Sul, Britto was, for the most part, able to follow through with his plans. Using tax and other incentives aggressively, he was able to land large investments.[25] In order to convince General Motors (GM) to establish a plant in the state, for example, Britto had offered substantial reductions in the ICMS state sales tax and generous loans at low interest rates, totalling hundreds of millions of dollars.[26]

José Cesar Martins, who became president of Pólo midway through Britto's administration in 1997, collaborated closely with the state government in an aggressive effort to attract more foreign investment like the GM plant. The agency maintained close contacts with several of what it called its "virtual" representatives: expatriate business people from Rio Grande do Sul working in New York City and San Francisco, who helped the agency by keeping tabs on investment trends and providing advice about how to deal with foreign investors. Martins also made sure that Pólo's staff participated in frequent investment forums and road shows around the world, in order to make contacts with potential investors and persuade them of the merits of investing in Rio Grande do Sul.

On one of these visits, Martins and other representatives from Pólo accompanied Governor Britto himself, as well as Nelson Proença, head of the Secretaria do Desenvolvimento e dos Assuntos Internacionais (SEDAI)—the state agency charged with attracting foreign investment to Rio Grande do Sul—to New York City for a series of meetings with potential investors. Marcelo Cabral, U.S. Managing Director for Banco Fator (a Brazilian investment bank) in New York City and one of Pólo's virtual agents in the U.S., had a substantial role in arranging this event.

A former equity analyst for Morgan Stanley, Cabral had extensive experience dealing with U.S. institutional investors who invested in Latin America, such as Scudder and Alliance Capital, and knew something about what made them tick. As an informal (virtual) advisor to Pólo, he explained to Martins that such investors would want to hear only briefly from the Governor and from Proença before speaking directly with managers of local companies looking for investment capital. To Cabral's surprise, Martins, a businessman himself, understood immediately and followed his suggestion.[27]

[22]"Alvorada Instala Pólo Tecnológico Com A Dell," *Jornal do Comércio,* August 21, 1998, p. 8; and Paulo Ricardo Fontoura, "Empresa Receberá Mais de 25 Anos de Incentivos Fiscais," *Gazeta Mercantil* August 26, 1998, p. 4.
[23]Interview with Telmo Magadan, former President of Pólo, Porto Alegre, December 17, 1999.
[24]Pólo-RS, Agência de Desenvolvimento, http://www.polors.com.br, January 11, 2000.

[25]"Portas Abertas Para Novos Investimentos," *Zero Hora,* December 30, 1998, p. 11.
[26]Darcy Oliveira, "A Qualquer Custo," *Istoé,* April 14, 1997, pp. 34–6.
[27]Interviews with Marcelo Cabral, Former Managing Director of Banco Fator, Porto Alegre, December 17, 1999 and José Cesar Martins, former president of Polo, Porto Alegre, November 11, 1999 and December 15, 1999.

At the meeting, one of the investors that Cabral had invited argued that Rio Grande do Sul should seek to attract high-technology companies. Although Governor Britto was at first resistant to this idea, Nelson Proença, who had been an executive for IBM in Brazil for 10 years before working in the Britto government, was intrigued by this possibility. He reasoned that focusing on high-technology investment made a lot of sense given Rio Grande do Sul's unique characteristics: the large number of universities in the state already offering degrees in Computer Science and Electrical Engineering, and the overall high levels of education in the state's population as a whole.[28]

José Cesar Martins also thought the idea was worth pursuing. After discussing it further with Proença, Martins asked Cabral to help Pólo find a consultant in the area of high technology. From his extensive contacts in the financial community, Cabral knew the person to call was Duane Kirkpatrick, head of international operations for Robertson Stephens in San Francisco, one of the leading investment banks in the world in financing for high-technology businesses. Kirkpatrick agreed to serve as an outside consultant to Pólo to assess Rio Grande do Sul's prospects for attracting investment from high-technology companies.

After an extended visit to Rio Grande do Sul, Kirkpatrick came to the conclusion that high-technology investment would provide the state with high-wage jobs, in addition to linkages to the local economy. He also provided a number of suggestions about how Pólo and the state government of Rio Grande do Sul could attract such firms. Impressed, Pólo—in collaboration with Nelson Proença and Governor Britto—decided to focus future investment promotion efforts in this area.[29]

Rio Grande do Sul Makes the Short List: An Exchange of Visits

As part of the new strategy, in February 1998, José Cesar Martins and a number of representatives from Pólo flew to San Francisco to attend a symposium for high-technology industries sponsored by Robertson Stephens bank. By this time, Pólo, with the help of Kirkpatrick and its virtual agents at Banco Fator (Marcelo Cabral and Dennis Rodriques), had already identified a list of high-technology companies that it would like to attract to Rio Grande do Sul. One of these was Dell Computer Corporation.

During the conference, Marcelo Cabral came upon an article in *América Económica* magazine about Dell's interest in building a manufacturing plant in Brazil, and he showed it to Martins. Demonstrating just how quick and flexible Pólo could be, Martins and his staff immediately left the conference, went back to their hotel and

put in a call to Dell. When they got through to Tom Armstrong, Dell's Vice President of Tax and Administration, Armstrong told him that the company's preliminary site selection team, reporting to Keith Maxwell, had already been to Brazil three times and was closing its short list of potential sites in Brazil. "You are going to lose a big opportunity," Armstrong said. Martins protested, "But we are fast!" Martins told Armstrong that he, his staff, and Nelson Proença (who was in New York at the time) could be at Dell's headquarters the next day. They packed up, left the hotel, and were on a plane to Texas that night.

At Dell headquarters, the group was to be received by some of Dell's senior executives, including Daryl Robertson, Vice President of Dell Latin America, Tom Armstrong, and Keith Maxwell. But before the meeting at which Proença and Martins would make their pitch to Dell, they were given a tour of Dell's facilities and manufacturing plant in Round Rock. During this tour, something fortuitous happened. One of the workers in the plant, a skilled technician, happened to be Brazilian. The group stopped briefly to speak with him in Portuguese.

"I'll tell you how to win the hearts of Dell management," he told José Cesar Martins. "Tell them that Pólo is like the Irish Development Authority."[30] He explained that Dell's executives had had an excellent experience working with that organization. The Irish Development Authority (IDA) was Ireland's investment promotion agency. Dell executives had returned from a site selection trip to Ireland raving about how professional and helpful the IDA had been. Dell's experience with the IDA was an important factor in its decision to build a plant in Ireland.

Significantly, although Pólo had not consciously modelled itself after the IDA, it had many of the same characteristics. Pólo was entirely private, but worked in close collaboration with the government. It also had a targeted investment promotion strategy: it selected specific industries, and then focused on attracting investment from specific companies in those industries. Similarly, IDA's targeted investment promotion strategy allowed it to research an industry and specific companies thoroughly to anticipate any questions that site selection teams might have and address questions, concerns, or potential problems in advance, before the team even raised them. This is what made the organization so effective.

In its effort to focus on high-technology companies, Pólo clearly was pursuing a strategy similar to IDA's. In the meeting with Dell's senior management, then, José Cesar Martins did emphasize that Pólo was like the IDA. He noticed that this comment definitely caught their attention. The Dell executives listened attentively to presentations from Proença and Martins, and asked a number of penetrating questions about Rio Grande do

[28]Interview with Nelson Proença, Congressman, Chamber of Deputies, National Congress of Brazil, Brasília, December 5, 1999.
[29]Interviews with José Cesar Martins, November 11, 1999 and December 15, 1999; and Nelson Proença, December 5, 1999.

[30]Martins, November 11, 1999, and December 15, 1999.

Sul's level of education, rules regarding unions, and infrastructure. The Dell executives told the visitors that members of the site selection team had already visited São Paulo, Paraná, and Minas Gerais, but would like to return to Brazil to visit Rio Grande do Sul.

The site selection team came to Rio Grande do Sul sooner than expected, only about a week after that first meeting. Nevertheless, with only a short advance notice of the visit, Pólo called upon all its speed and agility. Notified over the weekend that the Dell executives were arriving Monday, Martins immediately called his staff and explained that they would have to make some urgent preparations for the meeting: charts would have to be prepared, statistics ready; in short, everything that would be relevant to Dell's concerns. Martins also called Proença, who convinced the governor to cancel meetings that Monday in order to give a presentation to the visiting Dell team. Thinking ahead, Martins made sure to hold the Monday meeting with Dell in a hotel, rather than in Pólo's offices, in order to avoid unwanted press attention at this delicate stage of the negotiations process.

It helped Pólo's case considerably that Martins was able to use his contacts in the business community to arrange private interviews for the Dell team with important business leaders in the state. These included high-level executives from three local companies: Gerdau, a steel conglomerate; Ipiranga, a gasoline distribution firm; and Rede Brasil Sul de Comunicações (RBS), a media company. Also present was one U.S. multinational, Coca-Cola, with which everyone on Dell's team would be familiar. A businessman himself, Martins was sensitive to the concerns of business executives. He knew that the Dell team would want to talk privately with local business executives in order to gain a perspective that was independent of Pólo and the state government officials.

The Pólo officials also made sure, on the first night the Dell executives were in town, to take them to visit a very popular local microbrewery called Dado Bier. They knew that the ambience of this popular local restaurant and bar would make a favorable impression on the Dell executives, and it did. To the visitors from Dell, the obviously well-educated, high-energy young clientele at Dado Bier seemed very similar to the kind of crowd that frequented such places in Austin, Texas.[31] This seemed to be just another indication that Dell would be able to find the kinds of employees it needed in Rio Grande do Sul. In addition to executives, engineers, and technicians, Dell's new plant in Brazil (which would also become its headquarters there) would need a large staff of personable, articulate, and technically proficient employees to take orders and handle technical questions over the telephone.

All of Pólo's quick, highly focused preparations worked. After listening to the presentations, speaking privately with business executives already in the state, and touring greater Porto Alegre for possible manufacturing

sites, the Dell team said that they were interested.[32] They would send more teams later to examine potential sites more carefully, to ask additional questions, and to negotiate financial incentives. The Dell executives made clear that they would continue to negotiate with other states, but that they had decided that Rio Grande do Sul was definitely one of the leading candidates. To that extent, then, Pólo had been successful. Rio Grande do Sul would now just have to win against the other competing states.

In the end, of course, this was what happened. Tom Armstrong and Charlene Coor, as well as others at Dell whose job it was to confirm the site selection team's initial findings, made more visits and continued negotiations. Ultimately, determined to win high-technology investment for the state, the Britto government offered Dell the best terms for its investment. Less than six months after beginning negotiations with Pólo and the state government, Maxwell recommended to Michael Dell that the company should build its manufacturing plant in Rio Grande do Sul.

THE CHANGE IN GOVERNMENT

Michael Dell agreed with this recommendation, and the company's plans to build its plant finally appeared to be set. But then the time came for another round of gubernatorial elections in 1998. Unfortunately, Britto's challenger—Olivio Dutra—once again, did not approve of the deal that Britto had negotiated with Dell. A member of Brazil's socialist Partido dos Trabalhadores, the Workers' Party, Dutra was against the government's granting of benefits to foreign transnational corporations. One of the main charges he had raised against Britto in his last campaign for governor was that "excessive" concessions granted to foreign transnational corporations would have to stop.

Dutra had served as mayor of Porto Alegre, where both he and the PT had a reputation for honest and effective government. Moreover, the Workers' Party was popular in 1998 as Brazil's financial crisis deepened and the federal government attempted to solve it with higher interest rates and other austerity measures. Perhaps not too surprisingly, then, Dutra won the 1998 election.

Since during his campaign Dutra had talked so much about the excessive benefits given to TNCs, once he was in office he had to take action. During the first several weeks, he argued that the tax incentives granted to Dell, and also to Ford, which planned to build a multi-million dollar plant in the state and had been offered millions in incentives, would have to be renegotiated.[33]

[31]Telephone Interview with Keith Maxwell, August 4, 2003.

[32]Interviews with Miguelangelo Azário, Former Investment Analyst, Pólo, November 19, 1999, and November 1, 2001; Alex Martins, Former Director of Investments, Pólo, December 16, 1999, and Maxwell, March 20, 2000.
[33]Rosane de Oliveira, "A Opção e Seu Risco," *Zero Hora,* March 22, 1999, p. 10.

Ford's attempts to negotiate with Dutra were futile. The new governor held fast to his position regarding the incentives by suspending the payment of loans the Britto government had promised the company.[34] Realizing that other states would offer the same incentives, and with minimal capital sunk into the project, Ford investigated its opportunities elsewhere. The state government of Bahia was quick to offer incentives identical to those the Britto administration had offered. Additionally, by locating its plant in Bahia, Ford would receive special incentives from the federal government for automobile manufacturers investing in the poorer northeastern states of Brazil.[35]

It helped Bahia's case considerably, of course, that the federal government was more than willing to intervene to make Bahia an attractive alternative to Rio Grande do Sul. Antonio Carlos Magalhães (ACM), President of the Brazilian Senate at the time, was an enormously influential politician from Bahia who was a key member of President Cardoso's governing coalition. It was ACM who pushed through the Congress a modification of the legislation on incentives for manufacturing automobiles in the northeast, so that Ford could still take advantage of it—even though the

deadline for additional companies to do this had passed.[36] The federal government even approved additional incentives in order to make up for the extra costs Ford would face by putting its plant in Bahia rather than the more conveniently located Rio Grande do Sul. It was also significant that Brazil's national development bank, Banco Nacional de Desenvolvimento Económico e Social (BNDES), provided a low interest loan of over US$300 million to Ford, more than it had planned to give for Ford's investment in Rio Grande do Sul. Again, the justification was that the additional amount was needed to make up for the extra costs associated with locating the plant in Bahia.[37] Realizing that Ford was now likely to withdraw from its plan to invest in Rio Grande do Sul, Dutra tried to negotiate with the company. But he was too late. Ford had already made its decision, and soon signed a contract with the Bahian state government.

The loss of Ford's investment was politically disastrous for Dutra. Residents of the town where the plant was to have been located protested.[38] The press lambasted the governor. And, of course, the political opposition had a field day lamenting the jobs that had been lost.

[34]Peter Fritsch, "Ford and GM Clash with Brazilian State—Dispute Over Incentives, Tax Breaks May Hurt Investment," *Wall Street Journal,* April 9, 1999, p. A11.
[35]Nelson Silveira, "Ford Promove Festa Política na Bahia," *Jornal do Brasil,* June 29, 1999, p. 16.

[36]Denise Madueño, "Governo Muda Lei Para Beneficiar Ford," *Folha de São Paulo,* June 30, 1999, p. 1.
[37]Denise Chrispim Marin, "Receita e Ford Já Negociam Incentivos à Fábrica da BA," *Folha de São Paulo,* July 14, 1999, p. 1.
[38]"Guiaba, De Luto, Grita 'Fica, Fica'; Prefeito Chora," *Folha de São Paulo,* April 30, 1999, p. 5.

APPENDIX 1   Brazilian States

APPENDIX 2 Principal Site Options

	Rio Grande do Sul	Minas Gerais	São Paulo
General			
Population	10.2 Million	17.8 Million	37 Million
Area	281,749 Sq. km	586,528 Sq. km	1,522,000 Sq. km
Demographic density	36.1 inhabitants / Sq. km	30.5 inhabitants / Sq. km	149.2 inhabitants / Sq. km
Capital (population)	Porto Alegre (1.3 M)	Belo Horizonte (2.2M)	São Paulo (10.4M)
Economic Active population	53.5%	49.7%	47.6%
Life expectancy	71.7 years	70.4 years	70 years
Population Annual Growth	1.2%	1.4%	1.8%
Population distribution	Urban: 81.6%; Rural: 18.4%	Urban: 82%; Rural: 18%	Urban: 93.4%; Rural: 6.6%
Economic Indicators			
Total GDP	US$41.7 Billion	US$51.9 Billion	US$188.3 Billion
GDP per capita	US$ 4130	US$ 2928	US$ 5148
Commercial Balance	+ US$2.8 M	+ US$3.8 M	+ US$253 M
Principal Industries	Tobacco, Chemicals, Automobiles, Steel, Footwear, Foodstuffs	Metallurgy, General Engineering, Agribusiness, Minerals, Automobiles	Metallurgy, Automobiles, Foodstuffs, Engineering, Electronics
Infrastructure			
Homes with fixed telephone lines	67.9%	57.5%	77.9%
Paved roads	10,332 km	19,234 km	26,377 km
Incentives			
ICMS	75% reduction for 12 years	70% reduction for 10 years	N/A
Free land	no	Free land for plant site	N/A
Loan Agreements			
Amount	R$ 20 Million	R$ 20 Million	N/A
Grace period	5 year	4 year	N/A
Repayment period	10 year program	4 year program	N/A
Nature of Investment Agency	Pólo	INDI	Secretaria da Ciência e Tecnologia (SCT)
	Private, nonprofit agency	70% state-owned; 30% private	State institution

SOURCE: Instituto Brasileiro de Geografia e Estatística (IBGE).

Nevertheless, Dutra had made his views very clear. It was at this point, by mid-March 1999, that Maxwell realized something had to be done.

DELL'S OPTIONS

Maxwell considered his options again:

1. **Dell could simply leave Brazil altogether.** After all, the country had just experienced a massive devaluation in January 1999. Dell had continued with its plans in the immediate aftermath of the devaluation, demonstrating its faith in Brazil's long-terms prospects. But the country clearly had a significant degree of economic volatility, and even a fair amount of political volatility, or at least policy uncertainty, as Governor Dutra's recent actions indicated.

2. **Dell could stay in Brazil but go to another state, such as Ford had done in Bahia.** Certainly, the other states on the list that the site selection team had considered offered some interesting possibilities. Bahia would not be an option for Dell, but Minas Gerais might be. Minas met Dell's basic selection criteria and had offered an incentives package that was very similar to what Dell had received in Rio Grande do Sul.

   Minas Gerais had other benefits also. It did not have the same level of partisan differences, at least with regard to attracting foreign direct investment, that Rio Grande do Sul seemed currently to be experiencing. INDI, the state government's investment promotion agency, had seemed interested in working with Dell and knowledgeable about Dell's needs, if not quite to the same extent that Pólo had been. Perhaps the impression that members of the site selection team had—that Minas Gerais was too oriented toward the mining and automobile industries—had been misleading. After all, that did not mean that the state could not also develop a niche in high-technology investment as well.

   Dell had not yet begun construction on the plant in Rio Grande do Sul. As of yet, it really had no sunk costs that would make it difficult to leave the state and go elsewhere. Going to Minas was definitely still a possibility.

3. **Dell could stay put and try to negotiate with the new governor.** Fernando Loureiro was a talented Brazilian executive whom Dell had already hired to serve as its new Corporate Affairs Director in Brazil. He proposed that Dell could attempt to negotiate with the governor by showing how keeping Dell in the state could help him, or at least would not be inconsistent with his own goals and agenda.

   Loureiro's idea was that Dell executives could reason with the new governor by pointing out the harmony between the governor's objectives and Dell's. After all, Loureiro's argument went, Dell was a very different company from Ford. Unlike an automobile company, Dell did not manufacture something that damaged the environment; it manufactured computers. Computers provided people with access to the Internet. The Internet provided even people in poor slum areas access to information. This had a democratizing effect on society. Giving people everywhere access to information in this way could potentially create the conditions for a more just and egalitarian social order. Thus, Dell's goal to provide people with computers was in harmony with the governor's goal of working to create a more just and egalitarian society!

This last option seemed somewhat dubious to Maxwell. But, it was true that the governor had suffered a major political blow when Ford left. It would be very bad for him indeed if another major U.S. company decided to move to another state.

With such logic, perhaps the governor could be persuaded to let Dell keep all of its incentives. Loureiro had suggested this might be possible, provided that Dell offered to donate some computers to poor areas as a gesture of goodwill.

Should Dell take a chance on this last option or follow one of the others? Maxwell realized that there were risks either way. But he would be the one making the final recommendation to Michael Dell, and the decision would have to be made quickly.

THUNDERBIRD
THE GARVIN SCHOOL OF INTERNATIONAL MANAGEMENT

Case 5   General Motors and AvtoVAZ of Russia

To compete on technology, you have to spend on it, but we have nothing to spend. Were there a normal economic situation in the country, people wouldn't be buying these cars.

VLADIMIR KADANNIKOV,
Chairman, AvtoVAZ of Russia.

There are 42 defects in the average new car from AvtoVAZ, Russia's biggest carmaker. And that counts as the good news. When the firm introduced a new model last year, a compact salon called the VAZ-2110, each car came with 92 defects—all the fun of the space station Mir, as it were, without leaving the ground.

"MIR ON EARTH,"
The Economist, August 21, 1997.

In June 2001, David Herman, President of General Motors (GM) Russia, and his team arrived in Togliatti, Russia for joint venture negotiations between GM and OAO AvtoVAZ, the largest automobile producer in Russia. GM and AvtoVAZ had originally signed a memorandum of understanding (MOU)—a non-binding commitment—on March 3, 1999 to pursue a joint venture in Russia. Now, nearly two years later, Herman had finally received GM's approval to negotiate the detailed structure of the joint venture (JV) with AvtoVAZ to produce and sell Chevrolets in the Russian market.

The Russian car market was expected to account for a significant share of global growth over the next decade. Herman was increasingly convinced that if GM did not move decisively and soon, the market opportunity would be lost to other automakers. Ford, for example, was proceeding with a substantial JV in Russia and was scheduled to begin producing the Ford Focus in late 2002 (it was already importing car kits). Fiat of Italy was already in the construction phases of a plant to build 15,000 Fiat Palios per year beginning in late 2002. Daewoo of Korea had started assembly of compact sedan kits in 1998 and were currently selling 15,000 cars a year.

However, Herman also knew that doing business in Russia presented many challenges. The Russian economy, although recovering from the 1998 collapse, remained weak, uncertain, and subject to confusing tax laws and government rules. The Russian car industry seemed to reel from one crisis to another. The second largest automobile producer, GAZ, had been the victim of an unexpected hostile takeover only three months ago. GAZ's troubles had contributed to GM's fears over the actual ownership of AvtoVAZ itself. In addition, AvtoVAZ had been the subject of an aggressive income tax evasion case by Russian tax authorities in the summer of 2000. Finally, from a manufacturing point of view, AvtoVAZ was far from world class. AvtoVAZ averaged 320 man-hours to build a car, a stark comparison against the 28 hours typical of Western Europe and 17 hours in Japan.

Further complicating the situation was a lack of consensus within different parts of GM about the Russian JV. GM headquarters in Detroit had told Herman to find a third party to share the risk and the investment of a Russian JV. Within Adam Opel, GM's European division, there were questions about the scope and timing of Opel's

role. Prior to becoming GM's vice president for the former Soviet Union, Herman had been chairman of Adam Opel. Now, Herman needed Opel's support for the Russian JV and had to convince his former colleagues that the time was right to enter Russia. As he prepared for the upcoming negotiations, Herman knew there were many more battles to be fought, both within GM and in Russia.

GENERAL MOTORS CORPORATION

General Motors Corporation (U.S.), founded in 1908, was the largest automobile manufacturer in the world. GM employed more than 388,000 people, operated 260 subsidiaries, affiliates, and joint ventures, managed operations in more than 50 countries, and closed the year 2000 with $160 billion in sales and $4.4 billion in profits.

John F. "Jack" Smith had been appointed Chairman of GM's Board of Directors in January 1996, after spending the previous five years as President and Chief Executive Officer. Taking Jack Smith's place as President and CEO was G. Richard "Rick" Wagoner, Jr., previously the director of strategic and operational leadership within GM. GM's International Operations were divided into GM Europe, GM Asia Pacific, and GM Latin America, Africa, Middle-East. GM Europe, headquartered in Zurich, Switzerland, provided oversight for GM's various European operations including Opel of Germany and the new initiatives in Russia.

Although the largest automobile manufacturer in the world, GM's market share had been shrinking. By the end of 2000, GM's global market share (in units) was 13.6%, with the Ford group closing quickly with a 11.9% share, and Volkswagen a close third at 11.5%. Emerging markets, like that of Russia, represented so-called "white territories" which were still unclaimed and uncertain markets for the traditional Western automakers.

THE RUSSIAN AUTOMOBILE INDUSTRY

The Russian auto industry lagged far behind that of the Western European, North American, or Japanese industries. Although the Russian government had made it a clear priority to aid in the industry's modernization and development, inadequate capital, poor infrastructure, and deep-seated mismanagement and corruption resulted in outdated, unreliable, and unsafe automobiles.

Nevertheless, the industry was considered promising because of the continuing gap between Russian market demand and supply and because of expected future growth in demand. As illustrated in Exhibit C5-1, between

EXHIBIT C5-1 The Russian Automobile Industry, 1991–2000 (units)

Russian Production	1991	1992	1993	1994	1995	1996	1997	1998	1999
AvtoVAZ	677,280	676,857	660,275	530,876	609,025	684,241	748,826	605,728	717,660
GAZ	69,000	69,001	105,654	118,159	118,673	124,284	124,339	125,398	125,486
AvtoUAZ	52,491	54,317	57,604	53,178	44,880	33,701	51,411	37,932	38,686
Moskovich	104,801	101,870	95,801	67,868	40,600	2,929	20,599	38,320	30,112
KamAZ	3,114	4,483	5,190	6,118	8,638	8,935	19,933	19,102	28,004
IzhMash	123,100	56,500	31,314	21,718	12,778	9,146	5,544	5,079	4,756
DonInvest	0	0	0	0	321	4,062	13,225	4,988	9,395
Other	14	14	6	7	1	41	3,932	3,061	1,307
Total	1,029,800	963,042	955,844	797,924	834,916	867,339	985,809	839,608	955,406
Percent change	−6.6%	−6.5%	−0.7%	−16.5%	4.6%	3.9%	13.7%	−14.8%	13.8%
Russian Exports	411,172	248,032	533,452	143,814	181,487	144,774	120,551	67,913	107,701
Percent of production	39.9%	25.8%	55.8%	18.0%	21.7%	16.7%	12.2%	8.1%	11.3%
Imports into Russia	26,649	43,477	405,061	97,400	69,214	54,625	42,974	62,718	55,701
Percent of sales	4.1%	5.7%	49.0%	13.0%	9.6%	7.0%	4.7%	7.5%	6.2%
Auto Sales in Russia	645,277	758,487	827,453	751,510	722,643	777,190	908,232	834,413	903,406
Percent growth		17.5%	9.1%	−9.2%	−3.8%	7.5%	16.9%	−8.1%	8.3%

SOURCE: www.just-auto.com, February 2001.

1991 and 1993 purchases of cars in Russia had grown dramatically. But, this growth had been at the expense of domestic producers, as imports had garnered most of the increase in sales, largely because of a reduction in automobile import duties. With the reduction of import duties in 1993, imports surged to 49% of sales and Russian production hit the lowest level of the decade. Domestic producers reacted by increasing their focus on export sales, largely to former Commonwealth of Independent States (CIS) countries. Exports ranged between 18% and 56% of all production during the 1991–95 period.

With the reimposition of import duties in 1994, the import share of the Russian marketplace returned to a level of about 7–10%. Domestic production began growing again and fewer Russian-made cars were exported. Unfortunately, just as domestic producers were nearly back to early-1990s production levels, the 1998 financial crisis sent the Russian economy and auto industry into a tailspin. Domestic production of automobiles fell nearly 15% in 1998. Auto sales in Russia as a whole fell 8%. The industry, however, experienced a strong resurgence in 1999 and 2000.

Russian auto manufacturing was highly concentrated, with AvtoVAZ holding a 65% market share in 2000, followed by GAZ with 13%, and an assorted collection of what could be called "boutique producers."[1] Although foreign producers accounted for less than 2% of all auto manufacturing in Russia in 2000, estimates of the influx of used foreign-made cars were upwards of 350,000 units in 2000 alone.

Although much had changed in Russia in the 1990s, much had also remained the same. In the Russian automobile market, demand greatly exceeded supply. Russians without the right political connections had to wait years for their cars. Cars were still rare, spare parts still difficult to find, and crime still rampant. It was still not unusual to remove windshield wipers for safekeeping from cars parked on major city streets. Cars had to be paid for in cash, as dealer financing was essentially unheard of as a result of the inability of the Russian financial and banking sector to perform adequate credit checks on individuals or institutions. And once paid for, most Russian-made new cars were full of defects to the point that repair was often required before a new car could be driven.

AVTOVAZ

It's mind-blowingly huge. The assembly line goes on for a mile and a quarter. Workstation after workstation. No modules being slapped in. It's piece by piece. The hammering is incessant. Hammering the gaskets in, hammering the doors down, hammering the bumpers. On the engine line a man seems to be screwing in pistons by hand and whopping them with a hammer. If there's a robot on the line, we didn't see it. Forget statistical process control.

"Would You Want to Drive a Lada?"
Forbes, August 26, 1996.

AvtoVAZ, originally called VAZ for Volzhsky Avtomobilny Zavod (Volga Auto Factory), was headquartered approximately 1,000 kilometers southeast of Moscow in Togliatti, a town named after an Italian communist. The original auto manufacturing facility was a JV (in effect,

---

[1]Other Russian auto manufacturers included KAMAZ, Roslada, SeAZ, IzhMash, and DonInvest.

a pure turn-key operation) with Fiat of Italy. The original contract, signed in 1966, resulted in the first cars produced in 1970. The cars produced at the factory were distributed under the *Lada* and *Zhiguli* brands and for the next 20 years became virtually the only car the average Russian could purchase.

AvtoVAZ employed more than 250,000 people in 1999 (who were paid an average of $333 per month), and produced 677,700 cars, $1.9 billion in sales, and $458 million in gross profits. However, the company had a pretax loss of $123 million. AvtoVAZ was publicly listed on the Moscow Stock Exchange. The Togliatti auto plant, with an estimated capacity of 750,000 vehicles per year, was the largest single automobile assembly facility in the world. It had reached full capacity in 2000. But the company developed only one new car in the 1990s and had spent an estimated $2 billion doing so.

In the early 1990s, following the era of Perestroika and the introduction of economic reforms, AvtoVAZ began upgrading its technology and increasing its prices. As prices skyrocketed, Russians quickly switched to comparably-priced imports of higher quality. As a result, AvtoVAZ suffered continual decreases in market share throughout the 1990s (see Exhibit C5-1), although it still dominated all other Russian manufacturers.

The financial crisis of August 1998 had actually bolstered AvtoVAZ's market position, with the fall of the rouble from Rbl 11/$ to over Rbl 25/$. Imports were now prohibitively expensive for most Russians.

> *It's cynical to say, but in the case of a devaluation, the situation at AvtoVAZ would be better. There would be a different effectiveness of export sales, and demand would be different. Seeing that money is losing value, people would buy durable goods in the hopes of saving at least something.*
>
> VLADIMIR KADANNIKOV,
> *Chairman of the Board, AvtoVAZ, May 1998*

In recent years, AvtoVAZ senior management had been discussing the development of a more modern car that could be exported to developed countries. This car, called the Kalina, would require an investment of as much as $850 million. AvtoVAZ Chairman Vladimir Kadannikov had stated publicly that he hoped commercial production of the Kalina could begin by 2004. He had also indicated that he was receptive to the Kalina being produced in a joint venture with an outsider automaker.

AvtoVAZ also suffered from tax problems and was called a "tax deadbeat" by the Russian press. In July 2000 the Russian Tax Police accused AvtoVAZ of tax fraud. The accusations centered on alleged under-reporting of automobile production by falsifying vehicle identification numbers (VINs), the basis for the state's assessment of taxes. The opening of the criminal case coincided with warnings from the Kremlin that the new administration of President Vladimir Putin would not tolerate continued industry profiteering and manipulation from the country's *oligarchs,* individuals who had profited greatly from Russia's difficult transition to market capitalism. AvtoVAZ denied the charges and less than one month later, the case was thrown out by the chief prosecutor for tax evasion. A spokesman for the prosecutor's office stated that investigators had found no basis for the allegations against AvtoVAZ executives.

AvtoVAZ Ownership. One of the primary deterrents to foreign investment in Russia had been the relatively lax legal and regulatory structure for corporate governance. Identifying the owners of most major Russian companies was extremely difficult.

Although the exact ownership of AvtoVAZ remained unclear, two different management groups controlled the majority of AvtoVAZ shares. One group, the All-Russian Automobile Alliance (AVVA) was based in Moscow and led by Mr. Yuri Zektser. AVVA held 32.35% of total shares. A second group, the Automobile Finance Corporation (AFC), owned 19.19%. Two other groups, OAO Russ-Invest and ZAO Depository Center, owned 5.45% and 5.05%, respectively. The remainder of the shares were widely held. AvtoVAZ itself held an 80.8% interest in AVVA (see Exhibit C5-2 for an overview of the complex relationships surrounding AvtoVAZ). AVVA itself was in some way influenced, controlled, or owned in part by one of the most high profile oligarchs in Russia, Boris Berezovsky.

In 1989, prior to the implementation of President Boris Yelstin's economic reforms, Boris Berezovsky, a mathematician and management-systems consultant to AvtoVAZ, persuaded Vladimir Kadannikov to cooperate in a new car distribution system. Berezovsky formed an automobile dealer network, LogoVAZ that was supplied with AvtoVAZ vehicles on consignment. LogoVAZ did not pay for the cars it distributed (termed "re-export" by Berezovsky) until a date significantly after his dealer network sold the cars and received payment themselves. The arrangement proved disastrous for AvtoVAZ and incredibly profitable for Berezovsky. In the years that followed, hyperinflation raged in Russia, and Berezovsky was able to run his expanding network of businesses with AvtoVAZ's cash flow. (Mr. Berezovsky has admitted to the arrangement, and its financial benefits to him. He has also pointed out, correctly, that under Russian law he has not broken any laws.) LogoVAZ was also one of the largest auto importers in Russia.

In 1994, the Russian government began privatizing many state-owned companies, including AvtoVAZ. Boris Berezovsky, Vladimir Kadannikov, and Alexander Voloshin, recently appointed Chief of Staff for Russian President Vladimir Putin, then formed AVVA. The stated purpose of AVVA was to begin building a strong dealer network for the automobile industry in Russia. AVVA quickly acquired its 32.35% interest in AvtoVAZ, in

EXHIBIT C5-2   AvtoVAZ's Web of Influence and Ownership

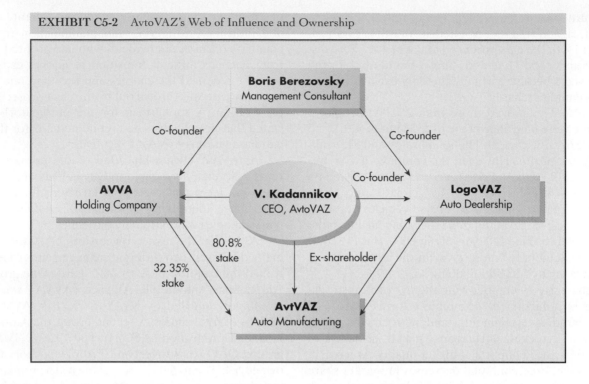

addition to many other enterprises. AVVA frequently represented AvtoVAZ's significant international interests around the world.

By 2000, Berezovsky purportedly no longer had formal relations with AVVA, but many observers believed he continued to have a number of informal lines of influence. In December 2000, AVVA surprised many analysts by announcing that it was amending its charter to change its status from an *investment fund* to a *holding company*. Auto analysts speculated that AVVA was positioning itself to run AvtoVAZ, which had reorganized into divisions (car production, marketing and sales, research and development).

Share ownership anxiety had intensified in November 2000 when the second largest automobile manufacturer in Russia, GAZ, had been the victim of a hostile takeover. Beginning in August 2000, Sibirsky Alyuminiy (SibAl) started accumulating shares in GAZ until reaching the 25% plus one share threshold necessary for veto power under Russian law. The exact amount of SibAl ownership in GAZ, however, was unknown, even to GAZ. Current regulations required only the disclosure of the identity and stake of stockholders of 5% equity stake or more. Only direct investors were actually named, and those named were frequently only agents operating on behalf of the true owners. Adding to the confusion was the fact that frequently the "nominees" named represented multiple groups of ultimate owners. The inadequacy of information about ownership in Russia was demonstrated by GAZ's inability to actually confirm whether SibAl did indeed have a 25% ownership position.

Rumors surfaced immediately that AvtoVAZ could be next, and the threat could arise from the Samara Window Company (abbreviated as SOK), AvtoVAZ's largest single supplier. Many industry players, however, viewed this as highly unlikely.

> *Besides Kadannikov, the brass at AvtoVAZ tend to keep a low profile, but they still rank among Russia's elite executives, and they are independent," said an official of a foreign supplier in Russia. "SOK may be powerful with AvtoVAZ, and AvtoVAZ may find SOK highly useful, but I doubt SOK ever could impact AvtoVAZ strategy, and I think SOK ultimately plays by rules set by AvtoVAZ.*
>
> "Domino Theory: AvtoVAZ following GAZ falling to new owner?", just-auto.com, December 12, 2000.

Management of AvtoVAZ also felt they had an additional takeover defense, which strangely enough, arose from their history of not paying corporate taxes. In 1997, as part of a settlement with Russian tax authorities on $2.4 billion in back-taxes, AvtoVAZ gave the Russian tax authorities the right to 50% plus one share of AvtoVAZ if the firm failed—in the future—to make its tax payments. AvtoVAZ management now viewed this as their own version of a poison pill. If the target of a hostile takeover, management could stop paying taxes and the Russian government would take management control, defeating the hostile takeover.[2]

---

[2]The Russian government was not, however, anxious for this series of events to unfold. It would also mean that AvtoVAZ would be entering an 18-month period in which it paid no taxes whatever to the government if the option were exercised by the Tax Police.

EXHIBIT C5-3   AvtoVAZ Suppliers Owned or Controlled by SOK

Supplier	Location	Parts
Avtopribor	Vladimir	clusters for instrument panels, gauges, speedometers
Avtosvet	Kirzhach	connectors, exterior and interior lights, reflectors, signals
DAAZ	Dimitrovgrad	electronics, lights, moldings, wheels
Osvar	Vyazniki	exterior and interior lights, reflectors, signals, warning lights
Plastik	Syzran	foam, plastics, sealants
Syzranselmash	Syzran	chemicals, headliners, sun visors, window lifters

SOURCE: just-auto.com

AvtoVAZ Suppliers. Unlike many former Communist enterprises, AvtoVAZ was not vertically integrated. The company depended on a variety of suppliers for components and subassemblies and an assortment of retail distributors. It had little control over its suppliers, and was prohibited by law from retail distribution. In recent years, AvtoVAZ' supplier base had been continually consolidated. The three biggest suppliers to AvtoVAZ were DAAZ, Plastik, and Avtopribor (see Exhibit C5-3), all of which had been purchased by SOK in the preceding years. *Sok* in Russian means "juice," but in the auto sector in Russia, the English-language joke was that SOK was SOKing-up the supplier industry.

Starting from a relatively small base, SOK had grown from a small glass window factory to a diversified enterprise of roughly $2 billion sales in 1999, with businesses that included bottled water, building construction, medical equipment, plastic parts and windows, and most recently, AvtoVAZ' largest supplier and retailer. Although SOK officially purchased only 8,000 cars per year for distribution from AvtoVAZ, it was purportedly selling over 40,000 cars per year. The difference was rumored to be cars assembled by SOK from kits exchanged with AvtoVAZ. AvtoVAZ, often short of cash, frequently paid taxes, suppliers, and management in cars.

Dealerships and Distribution. In the early 1990s hundreds of trading companies were formed around the company. Most trading companies would exchange parts and inputs for cars, straight from the factory, at prices 20% to 30% below market value. The trading companies then sold the cars themselves, capturing significant profit, while AvtoVAZ waited months for payment of any kind from the trading companies. The practice continued unabated in 1996 and 1997 because most of the trading companies were owned and operated by AvtoVAZ managers. Russian law did not prevent management from pursuing private interests related to their own enterprises. Despite these issues, AvtoVAZ dealers across the country made up the only truly national distribution network for cars in Russia. The existence of a dealer network was viewed very positively by GM because building a dealer network from scratch was enormously difficult.

Crime was also prevalent on the factory floor. Mobsters purportedly would enter the AvtoVAZ factory and take cars directly from the production lines at gunpoint. Buyers or distributors were charged $100 at the AvtoVAZ factory gates for protection. To quote one automobile distributor, "They were bandits. Nevertheless, they provided a service." By the fall of 1997 the intrusion of organized crime became so rampant that Kadannikov used Russian troops to clear the plant of thugs.

International activities. AvtoVAZ was actually a multinational company, with significant international operations in addition to significant export sales.

As illustrated in Exhibit C5-4, in 1991 AvtoVAZ was exporting over 125,000 cars per year to the countries of the Soviet state. With the deconstruction of the old Soviet Union, sales plummeted to the now CIS countries as a result of the proliferation of weak currencies from country to country, as well as the imposition of new import duties

EXHIBIT C5-4   AvtoVAZ Exports

	1991	1992	1993	1994	1995	1996	1997	1998	1999
Baltic countries	8,392	3,895	3,325	590	8,832	2,648	1,101	716	487
CIS countries	126,440	42,900	19,644	4,491	1,601	1,074	962	108	331
Elsewhere	269,936	271,763	280,593	196,696	175,161	129,957	94,303	68,689	49,957
Total exports	404,768	318,558	303,562	201,777	185,594	133,679	96,366	69,513	50,775
Total sales	674,884	673,821	656,403	528,845	607,279	680,965	736,000	599,829	677,669
Export percentage	60%	47%	46%	38%	31%	20%	13%	12%	7%

SOURCE: just-auto.com

EXHIBIT C5-5 Foreign Auto Producers in Russia

Foreign Manufacturer	Russian Partner	Auto Model	Target Price Range	Capacity per year	Expected Startup
Daewoo (Korea)	Doninvest	Compact	$6,000–$8,000	20,000	1998
BMW (Germany)	Avtotor	523, 528	$36,000–$53,000	10,000	2000
Renault (France)	City of Moscow	Megane	$8,500–$13,500	100,000	1998
Ford (USA)	Bankirsky Dom	Focus	$13,000–$15,000	25,000	2002
Fiat (Italy)	GAZ	Palio, Siena	$7,000–$10,000	15,000	2002
GM (USA)	AvtoVAZ	Niva, T3000	$7,500–$10,000	75,000	2002

at every border to Russia of 30% or more.[3] In the late 1990s, sales were essentially zero. Similarly, sales in the Baltic countries of Latvia, Lithuania, and Estonia had also essentially disappeared.

Brazil has been the site of substantial AvtoVAZ activity in the past decade, with starts and stops. AvtoVAZ had originally flooded the Brazilian market in 1990 with imports when the government of Brazil had opened it to imports. Despite 85% import duties, deeply discounted Ladas and Nivas sold well. However, in 1995, the Brazilian government excluded AvtoVAZ from a list of select international manufacturers which would be allowed much lower import duties. AvtoVAZ then withdrew from the Brazilian market. In November of 2000, AvtoVAZ concluded the negotiation of an agreement with a Brazilian entrepreneur, Carlos de Moraes, for his company, Abeiva Car Imports, to begin assembly of Nivas in 2001. The target price, 17,000 Brazilian *reais*, about $8,900, would hopefully make them affordable for Brazilian farmers.

In the past decade, AvtoVAZ has exported to a variety of European countries as well, including Germany, Portugal, Spain, the United Kingdom, and Greece. These sales have typically been small special-order models of the Niva (diesel engines, Peugeot gas engines, etc.). Continued issues surrounding quality and reliability, however, had pushed the company toward an emerging market strategy. It was hoped that low-income markets such as Egypt, Ecuador, and Uruguay would reignite the export potential of the company. GM's strategy was based on extreme low prices to successfully penetrate local markets.

FOREIGN ENTRY INTO RUSSIA

GM interest in Russia extended back to the 1970s when Opel had proposed shipping car kits to Moscow for assembly. The plan foundered because of GM concerns about quality control. In 1991, GM renewed its interest in Russia, once again opening talks with a number of

potential JV partners. But after more than a decade, few deals had materialized.

In December 1996 GM opened a plant in Elabuga, Tatarstan, in a JV with Yelaz to assemble Chevrolet Blazers from imported kits (complete knockdown kits or CKDs). The original plan had been to ramp up production volumes rapidly to 50,000 units a year, but the operation struggled. One problem was the product; the Blazers were 2-wheel drive with 2.2 liter engines. The Russian consumer wanted the 4-wheel-drive version widely sold in the United States, typically powered by a 3-liter engine. A second problem was the origin of the kits. The CKDs were imported from Brazil and most Russians did not have a high degree of respect for Brazilian products.

In September 1998 operations were suspended as a result of the Russian financial crisis. Only 3,600 units had been assembled. An attempt was made to restart assembly operations in 1999, this time assembling Opel Vectras, but when it became apparent that the market for a vehicle costing $20,000 would not succeed in the needed volumes, the JV's assembly operations were closed. GM still had over 200 Blazers in inventory in January 2001 and was attempting to close out the last vestiges of the operation.

There were a number of foreign automobile producers in various stages of entry into the Russian marketplace, as summarized in Exhibit C5-5. Daewoo of Korea, which had made major volume achievements in a number of former Eastern Block countries such as Poland, had begun assembly of compact sedan kits in 1998, and had quickly reached a sales level in Russia of 15,000 units in 1999. Similarly, Renault of France had followed the kit assembly entry strategy with the Renault Megane in 1998, but had only assembled and sold 1,100 units by end of year 1999.

Others, like Ford Motor Company of the United States, had announced JVs with Russian manufacturers to actually build automobiles in Russia. The Ford Focus, priced on the relatively high side at $13,000 to $15,000, was planned for a production launch in late 2002. The facility plan was to produce 25,000 cars per year. The Russian government had given its blessing to the venture by allowing the elimination of import duties on imported inputs as long as the local content of the Focus reached 50% within five years of startup (2007 under current plans). Ford was already importing the Focus to begin building a market, but in the early months of 2001, sales were sluggish.

---

[3]AvtoVAZ did attempt to restart CIS sales in 1997 with the introduction of hard-currency contracts. The governments of Uzbekistan, Byelorussia, and Ukraine, however, forbid residents from converting local currency into hard currency for the purpose of purchasing automobiles (in two cases, specifically the product of AvtoVAZ). AvtoVAZ accused the authorities in these countries of working in conjunction with Daewoo of Korea, who had production facilities in Uzbekistan and the Ukraine, of working to shut them out.

Fiat of Italy was potentially the most formidable competitor. Fiat planned to introduce the Fiat Palio and Fiat Siena into the Russian marketplace through a JV with GAZ in 2002. Although the planned capacity of the plant was only 15,000 cars per year, the Fiat Palio was considered by many auto experts as the right product for the market. The critical question was whether Fiat could deliver the Palio to the market at a low enough price. In its negotiations with the Russian government, Fiat announced its intentions to make the Palio a true Russian-made automobile which would quickly rise to over 70% in local content. If Fiat could indeed achieve this, and there were many who believed that if anyone could it was Fiat, then this would be the true competitive benchmark.

RENEWED INTEREST

For most Russians, price was paramount. The average income levels in Russia prevented automobile pricing at Western levels. As seen in Exhibit C5-6, prices over the past few years had dropped as a result of the 1998 financial crisis. For 2001, analysts estimated that almost the entire market in Russia was for cars priced below $10,000. Given that the average Russian's salary was about $100 per month, cars remained out of reach for the average Russian.

In a September 2000 interview, David Herman summarized GM's viewpoint on pricing and positioning:

> We could not make an interesting volume with a base price above $10,000. Such a vehicle would feature few specifications—ABS [anti-lock braking systems] and airbags plus a 1.6-liter 16-valve engine. But, if the car costs $12,000, it is only $2,000 less than certain foreign imports, and this gap may be too small to generate enough sales to justify a factory. We knew we could make a vehicle cheaper with AvtoVAZ, but we need to ensure the price advantage of T3000 imports over competitive models is closer to $7,000 than $2,000.[4]

GM had originally considered the traditional emerging market approach of building complete cars in existing plants and then disassembling them by removing bumpers, wheels, and other separable parts, shipping the disassembled "kit" into Russia, and reassembling with local labor. The disassembly/assembly process allowed the automobile to be considered domestically produced by Russian authorities, thereby avoiding prohibitive import duties. The market assessment group at GM, however, believed that Russian buyers (as opposed to customs officials) would see through the ruse and consider the cars high-quality imports. But marketing research indicated the opposite: Russians did not want to buy cars reassembled by Russians. The only way they would purchase a Russian-made automobile was if it was extremely cheap, like the majority of the existing AvtoVAZ and GAZ product lines, which retailed for as little as $3,000 per car. GM, realizing that it could not deliver the reassembled Opel to the Russian marketplace for less than $15,000 per car, dropped the kit proposal.

GM's marketing research unveiled an additional critical element. Russians would gladly pay an additional $1,000 to $1,500 per car if it had a *Chevrolet* label or badge on it. This piece of research resulted in the original proposal that David Herman and his staff had been pursuing since early 1999: a two-stage JV investment with AvtoVAZ that would allow GM to both reach price targets and position the firm for expected market growth. In the first stage, GM would co-produce a four-wheel-drive sport utility vehicle named the Lada Niva II (VAZ-2123). The target price was $7500 and plant capacity was to be 90,000 cars. The Niva II would be largely Russian-engineered and, therefore GM would avoid many of the development costs associated with the introduction of a totally new vehicle. The Lada Niva I had originally been introduced in 1977 and updated in new models in 1990 and again in 1996. It had been a successful line for AvtoVAZ, averaging 70,000 units per year throughout the 1990s.[5] Since the Niva II was largely Russian-engineered, GM would bring capital and name to the venture. Because the Niva II supplier base was in place and component costs already established, GM would not have to deal with issues of local content compliance. In other parts of the world, such as China, local content requirements meant that multinational firms were often forced to source parts from technically unqualified suppliers unfamiliar with the demands of world standard competitive sourcing. As well, existing Niva II suppliers would likely appreciate becoming GM suppliers because they would get paid on time and possibly receive technical support and advances for new tools.

The second stage of the project would be the construction of a new factory to produce 30,000 Opel Astras (T3000) for the Russian market. Herman's proposal was for AvtoVAZ to use a basic Opel AG vehicle platform as a pre-engineering starting point. Pre-engineering represented about 30% of the development cost of a vehicle. The remaining 70% would be developed by AvtoVAZ's 10,000 engineers and technicians who worked at a much lower cost than Opel's

EXHIBIT C5-6 Russian Auto Market Shares by Price

Price Range	1998		1999	
	Seg	Cum	Seg	Cum
Below $5,000	3%	3%	85%	85%
$5,001–$10,000	65%	68%	12%	97%
$10,001–$15,000	15%	83%	1%	98%
Above $15,000	17%	100%	2%	100%

SOURCE: General Motors.
Seg=segment, cum=cumulative.

[4]"Exclusive Interview: David Herman on GM's Strategy for Russia," just-auto.com, September 2000.

[5]One of the primary reasons for the success of the Niva was the poor state of Russian roads. The four-wheel-drive Niva handled the potholed road infrastructure with relative ease.

engineers in Germany. Herman's Russian Group estimated that even if GM and AvtoVAZ used AvtoVAZ's factory to build the existing Opel Astra from mostly imported parts and kits from Germany, the resulting price tag would have to fall to between $12,500 and $14,000 per car. This was still considered too expensive for substantial economic volumes. Using the Russian engineering approach, the car would be cheaper, but still fall at the higher end of the spectrum, retailing at about $10,000 per car. As seen in Exhibit C5-5, this would still put the higher-priced Chevrolet in the lower end of the foreign-made market.

By no means was there consensus within GM and Opel about the viability of the proposed JV. One concern was that as a result of the cash shortage at AvtoVAZ and the slow rate of negotiation progress, in order to build test-models of the new Niva, AvtoVAZ had to use 60% of the old Niva's parts. Although many of the consumers that tested the Niva II ranked it above all other Russian-built cars, the car was rough riding and noisy by Western standards. One Opel engineer from Germany who safety-tested the Niva II and evaluated its performance declared it "a real car, if primitive." Heidi McCormack, General Director for GM's Russian operations believed that with some minor engineering adjustments, better materials for the interior construction, and a new factory built and operated by GM, the quality of the Niva II would be "acceptable."

GM management was pleased AvtoVAZ appeared willing to contribute the rejuvenated Niva to the JV. "That's their brand new baby," said McCormack. "It's been shown in auto shows. And here's GM, typical big multinational, saying, 'Just give us your best product.'"[6] But in the end, AvtoVAZ's limited access to capital was the driver. Without GM, AvtoVAZ would probably take five years to get the Niva II to market; with GM the time could be cut in half.

NEGOTIATIONS

Negotiations between AvtoVAZ and GM had taken a number of twists and turns over the years, involving every possible dimension of the project. The JV's *market strategy, scope, timing, financing,* and *structure* were all under continual debate. GM's team was led by David Herman.

Herman had been appointed Vice President of General Motors Corporation for the former Soviet Union in 1998. Starting with General Motors Treasury as an attorney in 1973, Herman had extensive international experience, including three years as GM's Manager of Sales Development in the USSR (1976–79), and other Managing Director positions in Spain (1979–82), Chile (1982–84), and Belgium (1986–1988). These were followed by Chief Executive positions for GM (Europe) in Switzerland and Saab Automobile. From 1992 to 1998, Herman had been Chairman and

Managing Director of Adam Opel in Germany. Although Herman's new appointment as head of GM's market initiatives in Russia was described by the press as a Siberian exile, Herman actually requested the position in 1997. Herman's parents were Belorussian and he had studied Russian at Harvard. In addition to Russian and English, he was also fluent in German and Spanish.

Market Strategy. Back in Detroit, the JV proposal continued to run into significant opposition. GM President Rick Wagoner continued to question whether the Russian market could actually afford the Opel-based second car, the Opel T3000. Wagoner wondered whether the second phase of the project should not be cut, making the Niva the single product which the JV would produce. This could potentially reduce GM's investment to $100 million.

A further point of debate concerned export sales. As a result of the 1998 financial crisis in Russia, a number of people inside both GM and AvtoVAZ pushed for a JV which would produce a car designed for both Russian sales and export sales. After 1998 the weaker Russian *rouble* meant that Russian exports were more competitive. If the product quality was competitive for the targeted markets, there was a belief that Russian cars could be profitably exported. As a result, Herman expanded his activities to include export market development. The working proposal now assumed that one-third of all the Chevrolet Nivas produced would be exported. The domestic market continued to be protected with a 30% import duty against foreign-made automobiles, both new and used.

Herman brought AvtoVAZ senior management to the Detroit auto show in the spring of 2000 to meet with GM President Rick Wagoner and Vice Chairman Harry Pearce. The meetings went well. In March 2000, however, GM announced an alliance with Fiat. A key element of the alliance involved GM acquiring 20% of Fiat's automotive business. GM paid $2.4 billion using GM common stock for the 20% stake, which resulted in Fiat owning 5.1% of GM. In June 2000, GM and Fiat submitted a joint bid for Daewoo, which was part of the bankrupt Daewoo *chaebol*. The bid was rejected. Herman returned to Russia, once again slowing negotiations until any possible overlap between GM and Fiat ambitions in Russia were resolved.

Timing. In the summer of 1999, AvtoVAZ had formally announced the creation of a JV with General Motors to produce Opel Astras and the Chevrolet Niva. However, this announcement was not confirmed by GM. Later in 1999, GM's European management, primarily via the Opel division, lobbied heavily within GM to postpone the proposed Chevrolet Niva launch until 2004 to allow a longer period of economic recovery in Russia. Upon learning of this, Kadannikov reportedly told GM to "keep its money," that AvtoVAZ would launch the new Niva on its own. The two sides were able to agree on a tentative 2003 launch date.

Financing. In May 2000 Herman's presentation of the JV proposal to Wagoner and Pearce in Detroit hit another

[6]Gregory L. White, "Off Road: How the Chevy Name Landed an SUV Using Russian Technology," *Wall Street Journal,* February 20, 2001.

roadblock: the proposed $250 million investment was considered "too large and too risky for a market as risky as Russia—with a partner as slippery as AvtoVAZ."[7] Wagoner instructed Herman to find a third party to share the capital investment and the risk, as GM would not risk more than $100 million itself. Within three months Herman found a third party—the European Bank for Reconstruction and Development (EBRD). EBRD was willing to provide debt and equity. It would lend $93 million to the venture and invest an additional $40 million for an equity stake of 17%.[8]

The European Bank for Reconstruction and Development was established in 1991 with the express purpose of fostering the transition to open market-oriented economies and promoting private and entrepreneurial ventures in Eastern Europe and the Commonwealth of Independent States (CIS). As a catalyst of change the Bank seeks to co-finance with firms that are providing foreign direct investment (FDI) in these countries in order to help mobilize domestic capital and reduce the risks associated with FDI. Recent economic reforms and the perceived stability of President Putin's government had convinced the EBRD's senior management that conditions were right.

GM management knew that $332 million would be insufficient to build a state-of-the-art manufacturing facility. However, given that AvtoVAZ contributions would include the design, land, and production equipment, $332 million was believed to be sufficient to launch the new Niva. The planned facility would include a car body paint shop, assembly facilities, and testing areas. AvtoVAZ would supply the JV with the car body, engine and transmission, chassis units, interior components, and electrical system.

Structure. A continuing point of contention was where the profits of the JV would be created. For example, AvtoVAZ had consistently quoted a price for cement for the proposed plant which was thought to be about 10 times what GM would customarily pay in Germany. Then, just prior to the venture's going before the GM Board for preliminary approval for continued negotiations, AvtoVAZ made a new and surprising demand that GM increase the price the JV would pay AvtoVAZ for Niva parts by 25%. (Vladimir Kadannikov demanded to know where the profits would be, "in the price of the parts each side supplied to the joint venture or in the venture itself?").[9] When Herman warned them this would scuttle the deal, AvtoVAZ backed-off. After heated debate, the two parties now agreed that they would not try to profit from the sale of components to the JV.

The structure for the management team and specific allocation of managerial responsibilities had yet to be determined. Although both sides expected to be actively involved in day-to-day management, GM had already made it clear that management control of the JV was a priority for going forward. GM also wanted to minimize the number of expatriate managers assigned to the venture. AvtoVAZ saw the JV as an opportunity for its managers to gain valuable experience and expected to have significant purchasing, assembly, and marketing responsibilities. AvtoVAZ expected GM to develop and support an organizational structure that ensured technology transfer to the JV. AvtoVAZ knew that in China GM had created a technical design center as a separate JV with its Chinese partner. The specific details as to how GM might be compensated for technology transfer to Russia remained unclear. Finally, the issue of who would control the final documentation for the JV agreement had yet to be agreed.

The JV would be located on the edge of the massive AvtoVAZ complex in Togliatti. It would utilize one factory building which was partially finished and previously abandoned. The building already housed much equipment in various operational states, including expensive plastic molding and cutting tools imported from Germany in the early 1990s which AvtoVAZ had been unable to operate effectively but could not resell.

Progress. Again, primarily out of frustration with the pace of negotiations, AvtoVAZ announced in January 2001 that it would begin small scale production of an SUV under its own Lada brand. Herman once again was able to intervene. Herman promised GM's Board that AvtoVAZ would actually build no more than a few dozen of the SUVs "for show." The two sides also continued to debate whether AvtoVAZ would be allowed to sell the prototypes of the new Niva that AvtoVAZ planned to build (approximately 500). GM was adamant, according to long-standing policy, that these should not find their way to the marketplace. AvtoVAZ countered that this was routine for Russian manufacturers and served as a type of "test fleet."

Finally, on February 6, 2001, Herman presented the current proposal to GM's board in Detroit. After heated debate, the board approved the proposal. The possibility of entering a large and developing market, with shared risk and investment, was a rare opportunity to get in early and develop a new local market. According to Rick Wagoner, "Russia's going to be a very big market."

We'll sell it in former Soviet Union, and eventually export it and because of the cost of material and labor in Russia, we should reach a price point which gives us a decent volume. That will give us a chance to get a network and get started with suppliers and other partners in Russia in a way which I hope will make us amongst the leaders.[10]

[7]*Wall Street Journal,* February 20, 2001.
[8]The willingness of EBRD to invest was a bit surprising given that two of its previous investments with Russian automakers, GAZ and KamAZ, had resulted in defaults on EBRD credits. A third venture in which EBRD was still a partner (20% equity), Nizhegorod Motors, a JV between Fiat and GAZ, had delayed its car launch from late 1998 to the first half of 2002.
[9]*Wall Street Journal,* February 21, 2001.
[10]"David Herman on GM's Strategy for Russia," just-auto.com, September 2000.

David Herman had gained the approval of the General Motors Board to pursue and complete negotiations with AvtoVAZ. The negotiations themselves, however, represented an enormous undertaking, and both GM and AvtoVAZ had many issues yet to be resolved. The two sides at the negotiating table in June included David Herman and Heidi McCormack of GM Russia and Vladimir Kadannikov and Alexei Nikolaev representing AvtoVAZ.

APPENDIX 1   OAO AvtoVAZ Profit and Loss Statement, 1996–1999

(Thousands of roubles)	1996	1997	1998	Jan–Oct 1999
Net sales less VAT	23,697,167	26,255,183	9,533,172	33,834,987
Less cost of goods sold	(18,557,369)	(21,552,999)	(7,650,161)	(25,998,011)
Gross profits	5,139,798	4,702,184	1,883,011	7,836,976
Gross margin	21.7 %	17.9 %	19.8 %	23.2 %
Less sales & marketing expenses	(638,739)	(497,540)	(168,381)	(603,170)
Operating income	4,501,059	4,204,644	1,714,630	7,233,806
Operating margin	19.0 %	16.0 %	18.0 %	21.4 %
Interest	—	—	—	—
Dividend income	3,366	3,392	159	8,749
Income on asset disposal	3,084,203	23,052,035	2,516,466	4,115,346
Loss on asset disposal	(3,935,990)	(21,718,864)	(3,430,751)	(5,716,732)
Income from core business	3,652,638	5,541,207	800,504	5,641,169
Non-operating income	400,185	372,340	69,415	252,713
Non-operating expenses	(1,136,225)	(1,033,305)	(299,123)	(1,124,448)
Income for period	2,916,598	4,880,242	570,796	4,769,434
Less income tax	(682,556)	(1,166,911)	77,268	(1,112,039)
Disallowable expenses	(409,906)	(7,069,333)	(251,574)	(1,674,947)
Net income	1,824,136	(3,356,002)	396,490	1,982,448
Return on sales (ROS)	7.7 %	−12.8 %	4.2 %	5.9 %
In U.S. dollars				
Exchange rate (roubles/US$)	5.6	6.0	9.7	24.6
Net sales	$ 4,231,636,964	$ 4,375,863,833	$ 982,801,237	$ 1,375,405,976
Gross profits	917,821,071	783,697,333	194,124,845	318,576,260
Income from core business	652,256,786	923,534,500	82,526,186	229,315,813
Income for period	520,821,071	813,373,667	58,844,948	193,879,431
Net income	325,738,571	(559,333,667)	40,875,258	80,587,317

SOURCE: AvtoVAZ.

APPENDIX 2   AvtoVAZ Product Prices by City (February 2001, in roubles)

Code	Model	Type	Tolyatti	Moscow	St. Petersburg
21060	Lada Classic	1976 sedan	84,100	86,500	90,100
2107	Lada Classic	1982 sedan	86,700	91,700	94,400
21083	Lada Samara	1985 3-door hatch	111,900	117,500	115,800
21093	Lada Samara	1987 5-door hatch	112,200	119,700	115,800
21099	Lada Samara	1990 sedan	122,500	132,000	132,600
21102	Lada 2110	1996 sedan	146,500	150,700	151,700
21103	Lada 2110	1997 station wagon	161,100	164,800	162,300
21110	Lada 2110	1999 5-door hatch	157,200	161,900	168,900
2112	Lada Samara II	2001 3-door hatch	167,300	168,600	168,300
2115	Lada Samara II	1997 sedan	143,000	153,700	149,600
21213	Lada Niva	1997 SUV	103,500	111,300	111,100
Average (roubles)			126,909	132,582	123,582
Exchange rate (roubles/US$)			30.00	30.00	30.00
Average (US$)			$4,230	$4,419	$4,111

SOURCE: AvtoVAZ.

APPENDIX 3   Russian Demographics and Economics, 1993–2005

Indicator	1993	1994	1995	Actual 1996	1997	1998	1999
Real GDP growth (%)	−8.7%	−12.7%	−4.1%	−3.5%	−0.8%	−4.9%	3.2%
GDP per capita (US$)	1,135	1,868	2,348	2,910	3,056	1,900	1,260
Consumer price index (%chg)	875%	308%	198%	48%	15%	28%	86%
External debt (bill US$)	112.7	119.9	120.4	125.0	123.5	183.6	174.3
Foreign direct investment (bill US$)	N/A	0.5	0.7	0.7	3.8	1.7	0.8
Population (millions)	148.2	148.0	148.1	147.7	147.1	146.5	146.0
Unemployment rate (%)	5.3%	7.0%	8.3%	9.3%	10.8%	11.9%	12.5%
Wages (US$/hour)						0.63	0.36
Exchange rate (roubles/US$)	1.2	3.6	4.6	5.6	6.0	9.7	24.6

Indicator	2000	2001	Estimates 2002	2003	2004	2005
Real GDP growth (%)	5.8%	3.5%	4.0%	4.0%	4.5%	4.2%
GDP per capita (US$)	1,560	1,760	1,970	2,170	2,390	2,610
Consumer price index (%chg)	21%	17%	14%	12%	11%	8%
External debt (bill US$)	160.6	171.2	176.8	182.8	186.2	188.8
Foreign direct investment (bill US$)	2.0	4.0	5.7	6.5	6.5	6.5
Population (millions)	145.4	145.1	144.8	144.5	144.2	143.2
Unemployment rate (%)	10.8%	10.1%	10.1%	9.8%	9.2%	9.1%
Wages (US$/hour)	0.44	0.52	0.60	0.70	0.80	0.90
Exchange rate (roubles/US$)	28.4	30.5	32.0	33.5	35.0	36.0

SOURCE: Economist Intelligence Unit, February 2001.

APPENDIX 4   Foreign Automobile Manufacturers & Russian Partners in Russia

Manufacturer/ Partner	Price Range Model	Low	High	Capacity per year	Startup
Daewoo Doninvest	Compact sedan	$6,000	$8,000	20,000	1998 Assembly
BMW Group ZAO Avtotor	523 & 528 models	$36,450	$53,010	10,000	2000 Assembly
Renault City of Moscow	Clio Symbol Megane	$8,500 $13,500	$9,000 $16,000	100,000 3,000	1998 Assembly 2002 Assembly
Ford Motor Co ZAO Bankirsky Dom	Focus to >50% local in 5 yrs	$13,000	$15,000	25,000	2002 Staged
Fiat SpA OAO Gaz	Palio Siena	$9,000 $10,000	$10,000 $11,000	10,000 5,000	2002 Production
General Motors OAO AvtoVAZ	New Niva Astra T3000	$7,500 $10,000	$10,000 $12,000	75,000	2002 Production

SOURCE: Compiled by authors.

APPENDIX 5   Russian Automobile Sales Forecasts by Scenario, 2000–2008 (millions)

Scenario	2000	2001	2002	2003	2004	2005	2006	2007	2008
Optimistic	1.317	1.387	1.439	1.498	1.538	1.560	1.615	1.650	1.710
Moderate	1.045	1.131	1.232	1.288	1.315	1.368	1.483	1.500	1.570
Pessimistic	1.017	1.090	1.099	1.125	1.145	1.153	1.174	1.191	1.135

SOURCE: www.just-auto.com, September 2000.
Average annual growth rates by scenario: 3.3%, 5.2%, and 1.4%, respectively.

The EBRD proposes to provide financing for the construction and operation of a factory to manufacture and assemble up to 75,000 Niva vehicles in Togliatti, Russia.

Operation Status: Signed **Board Review Date:** 28 March 2000

Business Sector: Motor vehicle manufacturing **Portfolio Classification:** Private sector

The Client: General Motors—AvtoVAZ Joint Venture is a closed joint-stock company to be created under Russian law specifically for the purpose of carrying out the project. Once the investment is complete, AvtoVAZ (VAZ) and General Motors (GM) will hold an equal share in the venture. GM is currently the world's top automotive manufacturer with production facilities in 50 countries and 388,000 employees worldwide. VAZ is the largest producer of vehicles in Russia, having sold approximately 705,500 (over 70 percent of the Russian new car market) in 2000.

Proposed EBRD Finance: The EBRD proposes to provide up to 41 percent of the financing of the venture in a combination of a loan of US$100 million (108 million) and an equity investment of US$40 million (43 million). The loan includes interest during the construction phase. Up to US$38 million of the loan may be syndicated after signing to reduce EBRD exposure.

Total Project Cost: US$338 million (365 million)

Project Objectives: The construction and operation of a factory to manufacture and assemble up to 75,000 Niva vehicles per annum in Togliatti, Russia.

Expected Transition Impact: The transition impact potential of this transaction stems primarily from the demonstration effects associated with the entrance of a major Western strategic investor into the Russian automotive market. The fact that this investment has two well-known partners who are investing equally in the joint venture adds both to the visibility and the potential of the project. This complex project is one of the largest examples of foreign direct investment in post-crisis Russia in a period when many foreign investors are still adopting a wait and see approach. The use of Russian design and engineering skills together with the introduction of Western technologies, methods and processes and the related development of skills are further key sources of positive demonstration effect, especially given the huge modernisation needs of the Russian automotive sector. Other suppliers and client companies will also benefit from technological links or training programmes with the joint venture.

Environmental Impact: The project was screened B/1, requiring an audit of the existing facility and an analysis of the impact associated with the joint venture (JV). While typical environmental issues associated with heavy manufacturing are present at the main AvtoVAZ facility, there have been no prior operations at the site of the proposed JV. Potential liabilities arising from historic soil and ground water pollution were addressed as part of the due diligence, and no significant levels of contamination have been identified. The engine for the new Niva will meet Euro II (Russian market) and Euro IV (European market) standards for vehicle emissions. All vehicles will be fitted with catalytic converters. Safety standards for all vehicles will meet EU and GM standards in full. On formation, the JV will adopt GM management and operations systems and GM corporate practices for all aspects of environment, health and safety and will be in compliance with all applicable EU and best international environmental standards.

SOURCE: http://www.ebrd.com/english/opera/psd/psd2001/483gm.htm.

Case 6 TelSys International: A Marriage of Two Cultures (Case or Negotiation Simulation)

FINAL NEGOTIATIONS IN KUALA LUMPUR

James R. Chesney, a veteran engineer and former head of the Microelectronic Systems Branch at NASA's Goddard Space Flight Center, allowed his gaze to drift away from the negotiating table toward the view of skyscrapers and blue sky visible through the tall windows on the opposite wall. He smiled faintly, realizing that this was the most he had seen of Kuala Lumpur in the three days he had been there. Since then, Chesney and his colleagues had been chauffeured back and forth from their suite at the Hilton. Each day they had encountered intense negotiations over the terms of the pending agreement with the Malaysian Venture Capital Group (VCG). Negotiations revolved around the creation of a new venture, TelSys International, Inc. (TelSys).

Only if Chesney could secure the financing he needed would TelSys be able to produce and market high-quality satellite ground station communications equipment based on his patented designs. While the company's initial customer base would revolve around the world's space agencies and major satellite providers, Chesney knew that there was a huge potential commercial market for TelSys's products as well. So far the negotiations were promising, and the parties were moving toward an arrangement that would allow Chesney to fulfill his dream.

Major concerns were being addressed during the Kuala Lumpur meetings in August 1995. One thorny issue had been settled. As a financial investment firm, each of VCG's holdings had to be in a company that was publicly traded in order that the investment remained liquid. While both VCG and TelSys would have preferred a U.S. stock exchange listing, this was not possible, given the new venture's fledgling status. TelSys was unable to meet the market listing requirements of either the New York Stock Exchange or NASDAQ, so an acceptable solution had been reached to utilize a Canadian Stock Exchange instead. TelSys would become a wholly owned subsidiary of International Technology Contours Incorporated (ITC), a Canadian firm that was already listed on the Toronto Stock Exchange. A major advantage of listing through ITC was that the firm would save underwriting fees and other expenses associated with an initial public offering. However, other critical issues were yet to be resolved in these final days of negotiations:

1. Determination of the equity split between Chesney's management group and VCG
2. Decisions regarding leadership of (a) the ITC holding company in Canada; (b) TelSys International; and (c) the ITC Board of Directors
3. Composition and size of the ITC Board of Directors
4. Decisions regarding technology sharing between Chesney and his Malaysian partners

On this fateful day in Kuala Lumpur, Gary Baker, president of ITC, sat on Chesney's right. Chesney's other advisers during the negotiation were Bruce Montgomery (TelSys vice president of Operations, formerly part of the senior management group with Fairchild), and Peter Campisi (TelSys vice president of Finance, formerly Chief Financial Officer of DavCo Restaurants, Inc.).

THE TENSION BUILDS

Chesney's gaze focused on his VCG counterparts. Less than a year ago, he could not have imagined this scene. The potential saviors of his high-tech venture represented an Islamic banking and finance group. He studied the Malaysian team that faced him: Dr. Nik Bashshâr Ahmad abu Munîr, president and CEO of VCG; Drs. Kalîl 'Abd Al Wâhid and Rafîq Ibn Tammân (both vice presidents of VCG); Mr. Is hâq 'Abd Al 'Aliyy bin Ahmad (managing director of VCG Investments, Inc, the North American subsidiary located in Connecticut); Ms. Azîzah Hasnâ' Sâlih (financial controller in *purdah*, following the Islamic tradition of wearing veils), and Mr. Yûsuf Sulaymân, (director of Finance). (See Exhibit C6-1, Profiles of Negotiating Team Members.)

Time was running out. Dr. Nik had arranged for a press conference in the Hilton Hotel Ballroom in two hours to announce the agreement. Chesney still had to return to his hotel and change. Significant conditions of the deal were not yet settled. He turned his attention to the discussion. Fortunately, all members of VCG's negotiating team were fluent in English, so an interpreter was not necessary. Yûsuf Sulaymân, director of Finance, was speaking with an insistent tone. (Sulaymân was responsible for due diligence investigations, and Chesney's group had begun to refer to him among themselves as VCG's "devil's advocate," since he frequently raised questions regarding the feasibility of this undertaking.) Sulaymân was insisting that the venture would not qualify for listing on the Toronto Stock Exchange. "The Exchange regulations will not allow us to increase the total number of shares materially above the number authorized when ITC first listed," Sulaymân declared.

Sulaymân had been a difficult negotiator throughout the process. It appeared that he was out to create obstacles to the deal. Baker responded that there would be "no problem" with the listing. Chesney eased back into his chair and reflected on all the stories he had been told before leaving the states—stories about Americans going to Asia to sign deals, only to find themselves squeezed under tight time constraints. Chesney especially remembered all those back home who had warned him: "Be careful. You are dealing with some of the shrewdest deal makers in the world." (See Exhibit C6-2, Malaysian Culture: Negotiating Strategies.)

Chesney was having serious doubts about the wisdom of proceeding. Dr. Nik could tell from the look on Chesney's face that he was running out of patience. At that moment, Dr. Nik interceded to assure Sulaymân that any problems associated with the Canadian listing could be overcome. Chesney breathed a sigh of relief and glanced down at the 20-word speech in Malay that he was expected to deliver at the upcoming press conference. The minister of Entrepreneurial Development would be there, as well as representatives of the Canadian and U.S. embassies. This deal had appeared so much easier to consummate when he first met Dr. Nik in the comforts of his Columbia, Maryland, office.

TWO VISIONARIES MEET

Dr. Nik Bashshâr Ahmad abu Munîr, president and CEO of VCG, met James R. Chesney in July 1995, during Dr. Nik's first visit to Columbia, Maryland. The visit came as no surprise. Teams of VCG executives had been paying visits to TelSys over a period of months since February. "They came in waves," remarked Montgomery, a member of the entrepreneurial team pulled together by Chesney. "There were operations guys, technology and engineering specialists, financial experts. They didn't tell us who was whom; it always took us a while to figure it out."

James R. Chesney
President
TelSys International

Mr. Chesney, 51, is the founder and president of TelSys International. He retired in 1994 from NASA as a branch head-level manager (GM-15) with over 20 years of professional experience at the Goddard Space Flight Center (GSFC).

At NASA, Mr. Chesney began in 1985 to create the technical team that provided many of the founding employees for TelSys International. With a limited budget, he recruited top engineers, developed a nationally respected organization, and produced the world's leading-edge space telemetry data processing systems and components. He directed the team's efforts to design, develop, and deploy advanced data system architectures and components needed to support NASA's future missions, including such missions as the Earth Observing System (EOS), Gamma Ray Observatory (GRO), and the Space Station Program. His personal success is reflected in the recognized excellence of these systems and components, and their informal identification generally within the industry as "Chesney's systems or components." His other innovations include NASA's first flight application of a commercial VLSI gate array, in 1980.

Mr. Chesney holds a BSEE from Johns Hopkins University and is a member of the ETA KAPPA NU National Electrical Engineering Honor Society. He has written, published, and presented many articles on space telemetry architectures and components and has received numerous awards including NASA's GSFC Exceptional Achievement Award and NASA's Exceptional Engineering Achievement Medal.

Bruce G. Montgomery
Vice President of Operations
TelSys International

Mr. Montgomery has 23 years of engineering, manufacturing, and general management experience in high-technology and aerospace industries. He previously was with Fairchild Space and Defense for 14 years, the last 8 as a founder and general manager of a division that grew to 200 employees. Earlier, Mr. Montgomery worked for the management consulting firm Booz Allen & Hamilton; he began his career at the Jet Propulsion Laboratory.

Mr. Montgomery has a B.S. in Science and Engineering from the California Institute of Technology; an M.S. in Civil Engineering from California State University at Los Angeles; and an MBA from the Graduate School of Industrial Administration at Carnegie Mellon University. He is a director of the nonprofit Maryland Space Business Roundtable and a registered Professional Engineer in the State of Maryland.

Nik Bashshâr Ahmad abu Munîr
President and CEO
Venture Capital Group

Dr. Nik Bashshâr Ahmad abu Munîr, founder of VCG, obtained his Master's degree in Actuarial Science and his Ph.D. in Finance from a U.S. university. He has vast experience in international fund management, having been deeply involved in the major capital markets of the world, especially the New York Stock Exchange and the Kuala Lumpur Stock Exchange. His specialty is investment analysis and strategy, and he is responsible for developing the investment analysis and strategy of VCG, which has been successful in both the U.S. and Malaysian markets over the years. As the chief executive officer, he oversees the overall investment strategy for VCG and is involved in development of financial and investment instruments, as well as systems development for the financial institutions under the VCG.

Given his exposure and experience in international business Dr. Nik also leads VCG in its international business ventures and exercises.

Kalîl 'Abd Al Wâhid
Vice President
Venture Capital Group

Dr. Kalîl 'Abd Al Wâhid graduated with a B.Eng. (Honors) in Electrical Engineering and an M.Eng. in Microwave Communications Engineering from a university in the United Kingdom in 1979 and 1981, respectively. He joined Universiti Kebangsaan Malaysia as a tutor in 1979 and was appointed a lecturer in 1981. In 1984, Dr. Kalîl took a leave of absence to pursue his doctoral degree (funded by the U.S. Office of Naval Research) and graduated with a Ph.D. in Electrical Engineering from a U.S. university.

He was promoted to associate professor in the mid-1990s and shortly thereafter became head of the Electrical, Electronics and Systems Engineering Department, Universiti Kebangsaan Malaysia. Dr. Kalîl is a registered professional engineer with the Board of Engineers Malaysia. He is also a senior member of the Institute of Electrical and Electronics Engineers and a member of the Institute of Engineers Malaysia.

Rafîq Ibn Tammân
Vice President
Venture Capital Group

Dr. Rafîq Ibn Tammân obtained his Ph.D. in Taxation from a university in the United Kingdom. He is a member of the Malaysian Institute of Accountants, and his in-depth experience of the financial sector encompasses over 20 years of professional service. Dr. Rafîq has served on the Boards of Directors of several prominent companies in Malaysia and currently sits on the Board of BIMB Unit Trust Sdn Bhd and other institutions. He has been consultant and adviser to the Ministry of Finance, Malaysia, as well as to the Economic Planning Unit (EPU) of the Prime Minister's Department. His major roles are giving advice on tax matters, leading the advisory and research activities of the group, and aiding in the development of new ventures and financial institutions.

Is hâq 'Abd Al 'Aliyy bin Ahmad
Managing Director
VCG Investments, Inc.

Mr. Is hâq is among the founding members of a pioneering Islamic investment management company in North America. He possesses qualifications in the area of security analysis and fund management from the New York Society of Security Analysis and is a chartered financial analyst candidate. He is a member of a number of professional bodies, including the Association of Investment Management & Research (AIMS).

Azîzah Hasnâ' Sâlih
Financial Controller
Venture Capital Group

Ms. Azîzah Hasnâ' Sâlih is a member of the Australian Society of Certified Public Accountants as well as the Malaysian Institute of Accountants. Graduating in 1981 with a Bachelor of Economics majoring in Accountancy, she began her career as credit officer with Sabah Bank, a Malaysian commercial bank. Her banking experience of nine years spanned all areas from Credit to Finance and Money Market Operations. Ms. Azîzah joined American Express (M) Sdn Bhd in 1990 as manager of Accounting & Financial Control, where she gained valuable experience in the requirements of international financial reporting.

*Please note: Profiles for a majority of negotiating team members are included. Several are not available.

EXHIBIT C6-2   Malaysian Culture: Negotiating Strategies

With Malaysian Partners	Negotiation Tactics
■ Indicate your willingness to "give and take." Remember, the person who compromises is the most respected and usually receives more than anticipated in negotiations. ■ An American meeting a Bumiputra should try at all times to treat that person with great respect. Err on the side of formality until your relationship develops. (A literal translation of Bumiputra is "son of the soil" and refers to the indigenous Malay, the largest ethnic group in Malaysia.) ■ Get them "on board" the project so that they are truly part of the team, not perceived as the "opposition." ■ Ensure that they fully understand the proposed operations.	■ Build solid relationships, but keep them at a formal level. ■ Be patient; look at issues from both Malaysian and your own corporate points of view, and work to build solutions of mutual benefit. ■ Avoid confrontation and remember the importance of saving face. Never embarrass them, or back them into a corner during negotiations. If you do, you will never have a chance to get the answer or approval that you seek. Do not be averse to asking them their opinion as to how to best address a particular issue. Their answer will provide the opportunity for you to determine how they would address the matter, enable you to develop a "middle ground" position if necessary, and most importantly, learn their thought processes. ■ After proposal submission, meet as regularly as possible with your counterparts to ensure they understand the project as well as the benefits to Malaysia and the end users. ■ Avoid industry jargon.
With the Government ■ Make certain that you are represented by a senior Malaysian executive. ■ Use Malaysian partners to promote the project outside formal meetings.	**Resolving Issues** ■ The Malaysian way is to resolve by discussion and consensus. ■ The court system is rarely used. ■ Avoid trying to promote the "American Way" of doing things.
On Technical/Product Issues ■ Include senior technical executives on your team.	

SOURCE: By Alan J. Wood, of Malwood Global, Inc. This exhibit is provided by Malwood Global, Inc. and Intercultural Communications, Inc. Both companies agree to share with NACRA the right to reproduce the material in this exhibit for a commercially available textbook, and for the Case Research Journal. Intercultural Communications, Inc.
Alden T. Leavenworth, Executive Director
Malwood Global, Inc.

Both Dr. Nik and Chesney viewed the July 1995 encounter as the most significant in determining whether VCG's investment could represent a "win-win" situation for both parties. During this visit to Columbia, Dr. Nik, and the VCG executives who accompanied him, carefully reviewed the TelSys business plan. VCG's reaction to the plan was enthusiastic, and Dr. Nik made it clear to Chesney that VCG was very interested in exploring investment opportunities in the TelSys start-up.

VCG did have the venture capital Chesney desperately needed to commercialize what he called a Functional Components Architecture that could process data received from space. With VCG's venture capital, TelSys could become a world leader in telemetry for remote sensing satellite communications (a $50 million to $100 million/year business). TelSys technology systems could perform both traditional telemetry processing and the bridging and switching functions that interconnect local area and wide area terrestrial networks to space-ground and air-ground communications networks. Although TelSys products and technology were developed for satellite telemetry applications, the inherent ability of the equipment to process high rate streams of multimedia data (voice, image, video, and text) makes these products ideal for interconnecting broadband networks using commercial communications satellites. Chesney was enthusiastic about TelSys's abilities to cash in on a

multibillion-dollar business if the company's technologies were adapted to the needs of other industries, such as telecommunication applications. (See Exhibit C6-3 for the TelSys International Technology Proposal.)

Dr. Nik and Chesney discussed their visions of the future for TelSys. With a shared goal of TelSys as a billion dollar company, the men turned their attention to a discussion of *how* this would be accomplished. Dr. Nik assured Chesney that VCG, in the role of venture capitalist, was not out to run TelSys. This was very good news to Chesney. VCG's investors were interested in the liquidity of their investments, so a deal would need to be struck that allowed TelSys stock to be publicly traded.

Of course, both agreed that as the company grew to serve emerging market demands, starting with those in Asia, there would be a need for a local presence. Dr. Nik was interested in establishing a subsidiary of TelSys in Kuala Lumpur for sales and engineering support and for maintenance contracts. A requirement of any agreement would be a training component for young Malaysian engineers to serve on internships in the United States, and then to be transferred to Malaysia. In this way, Dr. Nik would be building indigenous capabilities in the telecommunications field. He knew of a U.S. visa program that would allow foreign engineers to enter the United States for this type of training. Both Dr. Nik and Chesney left their first

EXHIBIT C6-3 Proposal for Telsys International Technology

Overview

TelSys International will offer the technology systems and professional experience required to become a world leader in telemetry and satellite communications. TelSys will design, manufacture, market, and support satellite telecommunications products. TelSys's systems will perform traditional telemetry processing, bridging and switching functions required to seamlessly interconnect local area and wide area terrestrial networks to space–ground or air–ground communications networks.

TelSys's commercial off-the-shelf (COTS) technology will reduce the cost and complexity of accessing and processing satellite data for remote sensing and telecommunications applications. TelSys's reconfigurable systems technology, a new paradigm in communications, will extend object-oriented programming to hardware as well as software. This technology will break price/performance expectations for communications equipment and will set new benchmarks for flexibility, upgradability, and time to market.

TelSys Products

TelSys's family of products will span a broad range of functional and performance capabilities. Products could easily be tailored to meet customer requirements by configuring different sets of standard family components. This will be accomplished using product architecture featuring technologies such as parallel pipelined processing, dynamically reconfigurable computing, object-oriented hardware, as well as software and expert systems. TelSys will leverage these technologies by supporting a library of canned configurations for many satellites. Further, standard product capabilities could be easily augmented to address unique telemetry processing requirements or to perform functions such as decompression, decryption, or image processing.

All TelSys products will conform to open systems network standards for seamless integration into distributed computing environments. From a user's perspective, accessing data from satellites will appear to be similar to accessing data from the Internet. TelSys's state-of-the-art network management application software will allow users to remotely control, operate, and monitor the multimission TelSys system, as well as other ground station equipment via a graphical user interface. From a network management perspective, conformance to network management protocols will allow TelSys systems to become an extension of local and wide area networks.

Professional Experience

TelSys's expertise will be based on over 150 man-years of engineering experience with data systems technology supporting both traditional and sophisticated telemetry formats. A leading example is the Consultative Committee for Space Data Systems (CCSDS) protocol, a packet-based communications protocol for satellite data links, used by most of the world's space agencies including NASA, the United States Department of Defense, the European Space Agency (ESA), and the Japanese National Space Development Agency (NASDA). TelSys systems will support space program requirements such as the International Space Station, NASA's Mission to Planet Earth, and the Jet Propulsion Laboratory's Deep Space Network.

---

meeting convinced that they clearly understood each other's motives and requirements. Any difficulty that would arise could be worked out.

HISTORY OF TELSYS

In 1985, NASA's Goddard Space Flight Center had asked Chesney to create a new research unit. Chesney's unit grew into the Microelectronic Systems Branch, complete with prototyping, manufacturing, testing, training, and even marketing functions. Under Chesney's guidance, advanced telemetry data systems were developed that would allow the next generation of satellites to transmit space data back to Earth at the rate of "one Library of Congress" per week. The Microelectronic Systems Branch grew to an 80-person, multimillion-dollar "company within NASA" that built more than 150 high-performance, low-cost systems for NASA and its contractors.

By 1992, Chesney had field-tested a ground system design using what he termed a Functional Components Architecture that could process data received from space at 20 megabits per second. At NASA's 1992 "spin-off" conference, designed to transfer public sector technologies to the private sector, Chesney's design was featured. More than 40 companies expressed an interest in commercializing the technology. Chesney became convinced that the market for space data was about to explode. So, with the encouragement of NASA's senior management, he announced his intentions in 1993 to "spin off" the technology to the private sector. Chesney had the expertise required to develop the technical aspects of his business plan, but he knew he would need assistance in developing the financial plan. It was at this juncture that he contacted Montgomery, whom he had known through his work with Fairchild Space and Defense. Montgomery had years of experience in the aerospace industry, as well as the business background that

Chesney lacked. With Montgomery's help, Chesney developed a business plan for TelSys and began looking for venture capital to underwrite this process.

Chesney knew exactly what would be required: 20 engineers and 10 to 15 businesspeople would need to be on board in order for his dream to become a reality. These human resource requirements could easily be met, provided that Chesney could secure the venture capital to pay their salaries. Chesney was a charismatic leader, sometimes called a "driven, strategic visionary." Engineers from Goddard who had worked under his leadership were ready to abandon their secure jobs for the opportunity to work for him in the private sector. This was "his baby," and they were part of "his family."

Chesney's financial requirements were far more difficult to satisfy. In addition to the $2 million in funds required to hire qualified professionals, Chesney estimated that at least $4 million would be needed to set up a specialized, high-tech manufacturing facility, with an additional $1 million for hardware. All totaled, he would require at least $7 million in investment capital. This was a large request of the venture capital community, given that Chesney wanted to be retained as the firm's president (he had no industry experience), and there was as yet no proven commercial product.

Chesney realized that venture capital firms were becoming more sophisticated and their motivations more varied. Some venture capital firms were most interested in developing businesses and viewed their involvement as a "window on technology," allowing them to access technologies that could be applied profitably to the firm's own operations. Other venture capital firms focused on providing financing and generating high rates of return for their clients. Rates of return in the range of 15 to 30 percent were not uncommon.

Over the many months that Chesney and Montgomery courted U.S. venture capitalists, it became clear that they faced two major stumbling blocks. The first had to do with the issue of control over operations. Chesney was adamant that he should maintain management control. However, he soon learned that venture capitalists would frequently take over 40 to 60 percent of the equity shares of a firm in which they had invested, and in a majority of these cases the venture capitalists would insist on replacing top leadership with their own managers. In public offerings, the original owners were frequently left with as little as 5 to 20 percent of the stock. This arrangement was unacceptable to Chesney.

The second major stumbling block in attracting U.S. venture capitalists was their lack of understanding of satellite telecommunication technology and the potential size of future markets for these systems. Many of the venture capitalists viewed this as a risky scheme. From Chesney's point of view, since the technology and a substantial customer base were already developed through Goddard's Microelectronics Systems Branch, this venture was a "safe bet." He believed that venture capitalists had

"hearts of ice." They were most interested in financial forecasts, market projections, and quantitative "number crunching." Chesney learned this the hard way. After retiring from NASA in 1994, he spent the majority of his time seeking venture capital for TelSys. The only success that Chesney had was during a trip to the United Kingdom, where Chesney and Montgomery made a presentation to a group of British investors. A number of these individuals expressed interest in becoming shareholders, provided they could be assured that the total amount of venture capital secured was adequate to meet TelSys needs. In other words, if Chesney and Montgomery could find at least $7 million from other sources, the British investors would come on board as well. "Venture capitalists are like frogs, and when you are looking for money, you've got to kiss a lot of them. . . and some pretty ugly ones," according to Montgomery.

During the summer of 1994, Chesney was introduced to Gary Baker, the president of a Canadian firm, International Technology Contours (ITC), located in Vancouver. ITC was comprised of two subsidiaries engaged in appliance distribution and kitchen retailing. Baker admitted to Chesney that the company's traditional revenue base was shrinking rapidly. Baker had decided that ITC would have to move into new business areas if the company were to survive. Baker offered to serve as Chesney's "broker" with VCG, a venture company based in Kuala Lumpur. Baker had a plan that he thought would satisfy both Chesney's need for capital and Dr. Nik's requirement of liquidity for VCG's foreign investments. Baker explained that he would suggest to Dr. Nik that ITC serve as a Canadian holding company for TelSys, which could be set up as its U.S. subsidiary. This was a "win-win-win" situation according to Baker.

HISTORY OF THE VENTURE CAPITAL GROUP

During the period 1982–1992, Dr. Nik Bashshâr Ahmad abu Munîr earned his graduate degrees (Master's in Actuarial Science and Ph.D. in Finance) in the United States and returned to Malaysia with his family. He had a mission: to become a leader of the Islamic financial services industry. Given his early achievements, this goal was within reach. Dr. Nik had become a multimillionaire during his sojourn in the United States, balancing his studies with "savvy financial forays" into the stock market, setting up an asset management company that began with an investment of $5,000 (U.S.). The company's investments were *Syariah*-based, that is, in keeping with the Islamic principle that business activities must be founded on allowable profit-making, not interest-earning operations.[1]

---

[1] According to the *Syariah* principles of Islamic investment and financing, interest-earning instruments are not permitted; rather, business activities emphasize profit and risk-sharing on selected projects. Islamic financial instruments do include such products as *Al Bai Bithaman Ajil*, "cost plus financing," and *Al-Ijarah*, "lease financing".

Dr. Nik returned to Kuala Lumpur with $12 million (U.S.) on which to build VCG's foundation. He became VCG's president and CEO, strongly believing that his company could *do good while doing well.* "These two goals are mutually inclusive," he said. "It is the creation of wealth that makes it possible to do good works." By the time Chesney first heard of VCG, it was an investment holding company with over $360 million (U.S.) in managed funds, focused on four sectors: (1) banking and financial investment; (2) property development and investment; (3) international business and trading; and (4) information technology.

Dr. Nik was determined to make a substantial contribution to the development of his country and other developing regions. This goal was in keeping with the Malaysian prime minister's "Vision 2020," which was to see Malaysia as a fully developed country by that time. Dr. Nik was convinced that the telecommunications industry would be the "rising star" of the fast-emerging economies of Asia, so that being a leader in this sector would allow him to take the type of leadership position he wanted. But he was waiting for the right opportunity to stake his claim. He brought Dr. Kalîl 'Abd Al Wâhid on board to assist him in evaluating potential investments in this area. Dr. Kalîl, formerly head of the Electrical, Electronics and Systems Engineering Department at the University of Malaysia, had received his Ph.D. in Electrical Engineering from Penn State.

THE COURTSHIP

In February and March 1995, VCG executives made their first exploratory trips to visit Chesney in Maryland, on the advice of Baker from ITC. Dr. Kalîl, vice president of VCG, was accompanied by Is hâq 'Abd Al 'Aliyy bin Ahmad, managing director of VCG, Inc. (the North American subsidiary located in Stamford, Connecticut). Is hâq and Kalîl liked what they saw: (1) a technology leader in the critical area of space data communications; (2) a small but cohesive group of engineering talent who believed in the technology; and (3) a sense that they could build a business relationship with Chesney that would be based on trust. (In fact, they remarked that TelSys was "almost too open, to the point of naivete.") Clearly, this was a small, emerging company that had not yet become hardened by the business world.

Chesney appreciated Dr. Kalîl's in-depth knowledge of satellite communications technology. Kalîl's understanding of the field and its market potential represented a marked contrast to the situation Chesney had faced when trying to sell the TelSys business plan to U.S. venture capital firms. Also, Kalîl assured Chesney that VCG was not interested in running TelSys operations. VCG would agree to Chesney's continued leadership of the firm's day-to-day operations. Finally,

Chesney and Montgomery believed they had found a venture capital partner with whom they could work. Kalîl's message appeared to overcome the two major stumbling blocks TelSys had faced in attempting to secure funds from the U.S. venture community.

In April 1995, Dr. Rafîq Ibn Tammân, vice president of VCG and the person in charge of new ventures, arrived in Columbia, Maryland. Rafîq, with his stern countenance and severe manners, emanated an ominous aura. Within just a few days, however, Chesney learned that Rafîq loved to laugh and share good times. They were completely at ease with each other by the end of the first week. Rafîq became actively involved with Baker and Chesney, working to structure a deal that everyone would like. With this groundwork completed, the July 1995 meeting between Dr. Nik and Chesney laid the cornerstone for a contractual agreement. At that meeting, Dr. Nik had invited Chesney to Kuala Lumpur for the final negotiating session, scheduled for August 1995.

NEGOTIATIONS IN THE FINAL HOUR: AUGUST 15, 1995

As negotiations intensified in Kuala Lumpur, Chesney was surprised to learn that the VCG team was offering to invest up to $10.4 million. Before this final phase of negotiations had begun, Chesney understood that VCG's upper limit was closer to $7 million. By August 15, TelSys and VCG negotiators had agreed to the issuance of 43,711,944 total shares in the Canadian company, ITC, which would serve as a holding company for TelSys International in the United States. This approach seemed reasonable, since ITC was already listed on the Toronto Stock Exchange, and VCG insisted that shares in the new company must be publicly traded. Shares would be issued at $0.52 per share. Of the total shares, several British institutions that had been approached prior to the VCG negotiations would receive 1,800,000 shares for an investment of $936,000. Current ITC shareholders (primarily Baker) would receive 8,761,994 shares. Exhibit C6-4 summarizes areas of agreement as well as the issues yet to be determined.

Resolved Equity and Capital Investment Issues

- ITC will become the holding company for TelSys International.
- ITC will serve only as a holding company. All technological and manufacturing operations will be conducted by TelSys, its U.S. subsidiary.
- ITC's appliance distribution and kitchen retailing businesses will cease.
- Prior to the proposed deal with VCG, ITC had 8,761,994 shares outstanding, and these will continue to be held by ITC's shareholders.
- British investors, who had shown an interest in TelSys prior to the time VCG appeared on the scene,

EXHIBIT C6-4   ITC and TelSys International

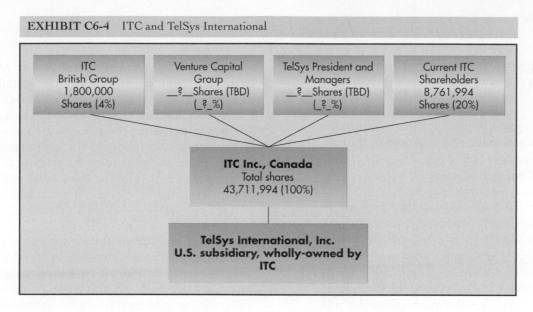

will be issued 1,800,000 shares of stock for their investment of $936,000.

- New shares of ITC will be issued at $0.52 per share. VCG is prepared to invest up to $10,400,000 in ITC.

Outstanding Equity and Managerial Issues

- What percentage of ITC stock will Chesney's group hold?
- What percentage of ITC stock will VCG hold?
- What will be the composition and size of ITC's Board of Directors?
- Who will be named chairman of the Board of ITC?
- Who will be named president of ITC?
- Who will be named president of TelSys International?

Chesney knew the final hour of negotiations was at hand. Dr. Nik and he had come too far in this relationship to retreat—or had they? Finally, after many long months seeking financial backing, Chesney knew he was in a position to obtain the investment capital he needed, although from an entirely unexpected source. His spirits were high, but he could not dismiss some nagging doubts in the back of his mind:

1. Would he be able to maintain control over his "baby"?
2. Was VCG truly interested in a long-term relationship or short-term gains? (After all, as a financial investment firm, VCG was very concerned about the liquidity of their investments.)
3. Was VCG interested in sustaining his business in the United States, or transplanting it back to Malaysia?

4. Finally, what did he really know about his potential partners who came from an entirely different culture from his own?

Chesney asked for a half hour in which to confer with his advisers, Montgomery and Campisi. Dr. Nik and his associates appeared to welcome this development. Chesney realized there was very little time left before the scheduled press conference. The pressure was on. He believed this might be his last chance to secure the venture capital he needed; his own investment funds were nearly depleted. He had to consider his responsibilities to Montgomery and Campisi as well. To this point, both men had invested their time in TelSys without any compensation. As the three Americans left the meeting, they promised to return shortly for the "final" negotiation session.

SOURCE: By Christine S. Nielsen, University of Baltimore; Bruce G. Montgomery, Synotinics LLC; Matthew R. Leavenworth, Saltmine LLC; and Geoffrey N. Walter, Meat and Livestock Australia Ltd. Reprinted by permission from the *Case Research Journal.* Copyright © Christine S. Nielsen, Bruce G. Montgomery, Matthew R. Leavenworth, and Geoffrey N. Walter, and the North American Case Research Association. All rights reserved.

This case was prepared as the basis of class discussion rather than to illustrate effective or ineffective handling of a management situation. The company name TelSys International was used during early stages of Chesney's search for venture capital. All individuals and events in the case are real. The history has been abbreviated in order to fit a case format. Certain names have been disguised. The authors express their gratitude for the graduate research assistance of Asaf Cohen for his research into the world of venture capitalists, and his design of the exhibit "ITC and TelSys International." Our thanks to Rhoda Lee for her research into Malaysian customs. We gratefully acknowledge the valuable support of Kathy Webb in document assembly and integration. The authors' appreciate the thorough review of this case by the *CRJ* reviewers. Their advice led to significant improvements in this revision.

Case 7   Guanxi in Jeopardy

JOINT VENTURE NEGOTIATIONS IN CHINA[1]

"Nothing like this has ever happened before. A nation with a fifth of the world's population has a bad 500 years. It is humiliated by barbarians; it lacerates itself; it sinks from torpor to anarchy. And then, in the space of a few decades, it steps forward. Its economy grows at a rate for which the word miraculous seems too modest. Its culture shows a new vitality. Its armed forces modernize. And the rest of the world watches, impressed and nervous at the same time, wondering if the new giant still seethes with resentment about the half millennium in which it was slighted."

—Kenneth Auchincloss, Newsweek[2]

INTRODUCTION

Tom Sherman was deeply perplexed as he studied the translation of a cover story from yesterday's edition of the *Beijing Daily,* the only local English newspaper. The article, titled "Motosuzhou/Electrowide, Inc.: *Guanxi* in Jeopardy," had taken him by surprise. Tom has always known that efforts in securing a joint venture with Motosuzhou, a local Chinese manufacturer, would need an enormous amount of diligence and persistence, which he thought that he and his appointed team members were portraying to their Chinese counterparts. The many sleepless nights Tom and his team worked together in planning the next day's negotiation strategies based on events that transpired with Motosuzhou the day before, coupled with the frustrations of living in a strange place and trying to cope with stark living accommodations, had ultimately accentuated the frustrations of the team.

"Why can't Motosuzhou comply with our objectives?" Tom repeatedly asked himself. The success in securing the joint venture would be a symbolic victory for a man who dedicated this entire career to Electrowide, Inc. Tom could retire from the company knowing that his last "hoorah" might have opened the door to new global opportunities for Electrowide, Inc. After all, China was becoming an enormous window of global opportunity especially for Western firms. Several of the company's competitors were already operational in Malaysia and Hong Kong. In order to compete successfully in today's globally expanding economy, Electrowide realized it needed to quickly serve markets and that the best way to do this was to locate production in Asia. As it appeared, however, Tom was in jeopardy of returning to the United States without the joint venture agreement necessary for Electrowide's entry into the People's Republic of China.

ELECTROWIDE, INC.

Electrowide is a $5B manufacturer of a broad range of automotive electronics products. In an effort to become more proactive in today's ever increasing competitive automotive electronics market, the company is undergoing a massive structural overhaul, streamlining many of its operations and flattening levels of organizational hierarchy. The purpose of this restructuring is to grant more autonomy to the company's various product line departments with respect to operation and business planning decisions so that eventually each will be responsible for its own profit and loss statements. One of the company's key strategic objectives is to become a major, aggressive player in Asia. This is considered a major change in the company's strategic direction. As part of this rapid expansion effort, Electrowide officially opened a regional design center in Tokyo. The center has world-class engineering capabilities that enable Electrowide to develop original designs at this site. The company employs about 15,000 people in the United States and is aggressively pursuing a policy of increasing its overseas workforce.

Electrowide is looking to find an Asian partner to help manufacture and sell engine management systems that run emission-control, fuel nozzle, and ignition systems for Chinese-made vehicles. Output would be initially sold to the Chinese market with plans to export later. It is projected that the company's first manufacturing JV in China will result in at least $3M in sales its first year. The company also estimates that the JV will have a cooperative life of ten years. The company believes that the facility that its partner can provide will play a major role not only in rapidly promoting Electrowide's business growth, but in providing product development expertise in the region. According to Mike Strong, CEO, "A good part of our growth is going to come from finding the right partners in Asia."

MOTOSUZHOU

Motosuzhou is an enterprise of the Beijing municipal government, from where it takes ultimate direction. Structurally, the company is a top-heavy hierarchy with a deputy director overseeing daily operations and various supervisors in charge of functional units (see Exhibit C7-1.)

---

[1]The concept of *guanxi* requires immediate explanation. It is pronounced as *Guaan-ji* and refers to the special relationship two people develop or already have with each other. Pye (1982: 101) describes it as "friendship with implications of a continual exchange of favors, and the relationship is continuously bound by these exchanges."
[2]Kenneth Auchincloss, "Friend or Foe," *Newsweek,* April 1, 1996, 32.

EXHIBIT C7-1   Motosuzhou Organizational Chart

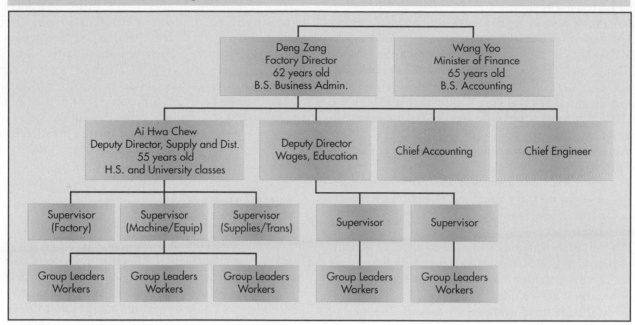

Motosuzhou Team

Decision making is top-down in nature. Approvals for RFCs (Request for Change) must follow a precise, government-audited procedure. Consequently, some decisions take several months to be approved. However, as part of modest experiments in Beijing, the company is on a selected, government-approved list along with 1,000 other companies that enable it to run its own operations free from government interference. Motosuzhou is a small company, operational since 1962. Its labor force is comprised mainly of rural employees, mostly Han Chinese. Although the company's strength is in achieving economies of scale in assembly-line manufacturing of engine control subassemblies, competition in the local market is growing.

The company's objective in teaming with a foreign enterprise is to develop a long-lasting relationship that will work in harmony with local government policies, as well as to gradually acquire technology through transfer by importing equipment and designs and adapt them to the automotive industry in China. The company's facilities and operations are such that to be inundated with new and improved technology techniques too quickly would prove devastating. Certainly, Motosuzhou does not want to fail in the eyes of the government or the community. Electrowide appeared to be keenly interested in Motosuzhou because of the American company's technical proficiency in its design of automotive subsystems. Acquisition of such knowledge would give Motosuzhou a competitive edge in the industry. Also, Motosuzhou would rely on Electrowide for financing most of the cost incurred in establishing the venture. The company is currently on a mission to educate its workforce by providing after-hour English language studies at a local university.

Deng Zang is 62 years old, with a B.S. in Business Administration earned from a local evening university. Deng is factory director, a position he has held for ten years. He speaks English poorly.

Ai Hwa Chew is 55 years old, a high school graduate with an accumulation of post-high school classes taken at the factory-run university. Ai Hwa was considered a member of the "delayed generation," that is, one who lost educational opportunities during the Cultural Revolution. His English is very poor, and he relies heavily on an interpreter or one of his managers when English translation is needed. Overall, Ai Hwa is considered a very serious, diligent, and competent deputy director of Supply and Distribution. He is well respected in the company.

Wang Yoo. Wang Yoo is 65 years old, with a B.S. in Accounting from Beijing University and is relatively fluent in English. He has served as the Minister of Finance for 15 years. He is a cousin of Deng Zang.

CHINA: CURRENT BUSINESS ASSESSMENT

China is presently on a course of economic liberalization. It is a country that is increasingly worried about anarchy. Gradually, more and more power is filtering to the provinces and localities. Rich coastal cities such as Shanghai and Guangzhou operate freely. City leaders establish their own economic targets, court foreign investors, and even raise internal trade barriers against the products of other parts of China. The huge rural populations is leaving its ancestral villages for coastal cities, trying to find jobs in the new, growing economy. Chinese cities, in contrast to those in many developing countries, contain high proportions of workers in factories and offices and a low proportion of workers in the service sector. During the "Deng" (i.e., Deng Xiaoping, former premier of the People's Republic) years, from 1978 to 1994, China's real growth rose an average of 9 percent a year. It is predicted that by the year 2025, China's economy will be by far the largest in the world, 1.5 times the size of the U.S. economy.[3]

American firms agree that China has never been an easy place to conduct business. Many foreign investments do not succeed financially. The costs of entering the Chinese market are climbing steeply. Tax preferences for foreign investors have been scaled back. The central government is becoming more restrictive with the JVs that provincial officials used to approve quickly. The Chinese are growing tougher in their bargaining stance. There are tighter limits on certain industries such as utilities and oil refining. One wonders if this will spread to the manufacturing sector as well. The foreign impression is that the Chinese act as if they are in the "driver's seat." As China grows economically, it openly scoffs at the global rules for international trade. The government still controls decisions on imports. Furthermore, contracts in Chinese courts are not enforceable. In the courts' eyes, China is a poor country that should not be held to the same standards as wealthy nations.

With respect to education, it was predicted that by the mid-1990s, 5 percent of its workers and staff in coastal areas, inland cities, and moderately developed areas would have a college education, building a solid intellectual foundation for China. Furthermore, it is anticipated that university entrants will increase by the year 2000. Because only a small percentage of graduates are admitted to universities, China has found alternative ways of meeting demand for education. Schools have been established by government departments and businesses, and in the case of China's factories, workers' colleges exist internally, providing part-time classes. Acquiring literacy is still a problem, particularly among the rural population. The difficulty of mastering written Chinese makes raising the literacy rate particularly difficult. This creates problems in the workplace. An overview of the labor force reveals that males account for slightly more than half of the workforce and occupy the great majority of leadership positions. Though traditional Chinese society is male-centered, on the whole women are better off than their counterparts decades ago.

However, discrimination still exists in hiring for urban jobs, with women offered lower wages and benefits than their male counterparts. In the mid-1980s, less than 40 percent of the labor force had more than a primary education. Skilled workers, engineers, and managerial personnel are still in short supply. Yet China

ranks second to the United States as a host country for foreign investment. However, U.S. firms must forge alliances based on common interests to ensure effective market entry. If the Chinese leaders are threatened and demeaned as is the case when the United States denounces China's MFN (Most Favored Nation) status, China will surely behave in an increasingly disruptive fashion. However, if U.S. firms reach out to the Chinese, the prospects for mutual growth will be somewhat brighter. With China's vast need for the investment and technology that America has to offer, it should not be difficult to gain China's cooperation.

STAGE OF EVENTS

Recently at Electrowide, all employees received an announcement pertaining to structural redesign stemming from a year's worth of BPE (Business Process Engineering) initiatives. The establishment of various councils would eventually assume the majority of decision making within the corporation (see Exhibit C7-2). Although specific personnel were not yet appointed to each process council, roles and responsibilities in addition to process definitions were established (see Exhibit C7-3). Most of the councils, however, including SMC (Strategy Management Council), were not operational. Electrowide had plans to empower the SMC with responsibilities for establishing processes and guidelines for exploring and establishing acquisitions and joint venture particularly focusing on overseas opportunities. At the same time, the corporation was on another aggressive transformation mission: to seek global pursuits at a rapidly expanding rate in order to become a $10 billion international enterprise by the year 2000. In consideration of a study that Electrowide conducted several months ago, China was strongly favored as a revenue gateway for the corporation. Tom was not appointed to

---

EXHIBIT C7-2   Electrowide Restructuring: Establishment of Councils

Process Councils' Definitions

Strategy Management Council: To develop Electrowide's mission, vision, values, and short-term/long-term strategic direction.

Operations Strategy Council: To lead operations transition from a product focus to a process-focused organization with common operating processes and practices.

Product Technology Council: To drive implementation of product line planning, program teams, re-use and technology centers, and to decide Electrowide's strategic enabling technologies.

Information Technology Council: To direct information technology prioritization, policy, alignment, and worldwide infrastructure.

People Process Council: To establish guidelines for selecting, developing, evaluating, and rewarding people to develop a global workforce with the necessary skill sets for Electrowide.

---

[3]Robert J. Samuelson, "The Big Game," *Newsweek,* April 1, 1996, 37.
[4] Ibid., 90.

EXHIBIT C7-3   Councils' Roles and Responsibilities

Strategy Management Council

- Set policy, direction, strategy, and pace for the corporate strategy management business processes and ensure alignment with corporate objectives.
- Manage the corporate portfolio based on strategic direction; for example, the SMC determines core competencies, makes portfolio decisions, and commissions the Ventures Council to fill gaps in core competencies.
- Balanced scorecard metrics: revenue, earnings before tax margin, net asset turnover x.

Operations Council

- Develop operations strategy, for example, operations planning, quality systems, facilities, integrated supply management.
- Develop the global labor strategy.
- Lead transition from product focus to common process focus.
- Balanced scorecard metrics: best practices of an electronics company, delivery on time.

Information Council

- Set priority for infrastructure development.
- Approve information technology infrastructure projects and overall IT spending.

People Council

- Establish the strategy for right sizing, re-deployment, and re-skilling of the global workforce.
- Establish the framework for global labor strategy implementation.
- Balanced scorecard metrics: employee satisfaction index.

EXHIBIT C7-4   Request for Approval by the Executive Committee

Electrowide, Inc.	
Recommended Action:	Authorize Electrowide, Inc., to establish a joint venture with Motosuzhou.
Recommended By:	Mike Strongarm, CEO
Performance Responsibility:	Tom Sherman

Objective: To establish a joint venture between Electrowide and Motosuzhou of China to conduct manufacturing operations in China.

Electrowide, Inc., seeks to establish a joint venture entity in the Suzhou Township, Guangzhou Province, China. This request is only for the establishment of the entity. In the event that the Executive Committee does not approve this project, the newly established joint venture can be dissolved at minimal legal cost. This proposal consists of providing detailed designs, financial, and technical clout necessary to commercialize the joint venture's technology. Manufacturing cost savings will be realized through low labor costs in China. Long-term objectives will include expanding the manufacturing capabilities to include additional automotive electronic product for both export and for sale to domestic Chinese vehicle manufactures.

The Chinese government announced plans to withdraw the tax and tariff exemption for imports of capital equipment by foreign-invested companies.

We request that the Executive Committee ratify and confirm the establishment of the joint venture in order to conduct manufacturing operations in China.

Date: 9/10/95

Approval Recommended: Mike Strongarm, CEO
                                         Electrowide, Inc.

_____
Doyle P. Cunningham, Director of Taxes

_____
Bart C. Chang
Sr. Vice President Marketing and President, Electrowide, Inc.

_____
Suzanne A. Jenkins
Corporate Vice President and Controller

sit on any of the newly established councils. However, considering his decades of experience in managing manufacturing operations at Electrowide, and having developed strong bonds to several top corporate executives, he was selected to lead a team to China which was commissioned to pursue a JV with Motosuzhou (see Exhibit C7-4).

Tom was assigned a two-person team to carry out this mandate but was not consulted as to its composition. He was 55 years old, with a B.S. in Mechanical Engineering from the University of Michigan. He was considered highly technical and knowledgeable about industrial operation and manufacturing techniques. His career has spanned 32 years with Electrowide. He has held various technical management positions within the company and is currently manager of Materials Resource Management, overseeing production inventory for North American Operations. His only international experience was participating in a technology transfer symposium in Canada two years ago. He plans to retire at the end of the year.

Tom requested the personnel files of his two team members. He noted that **Barb Morgan** was 42 years old and had a joint B.S. in Psychology and Computer Science

from Johns Hopkins University in Baltimore. Barb had begun her career at Electrowide three years ago as a contractor but was hired as a permanent employee upon completion of her first year. Barb's most recent assignment in the company was project manager for an acquisition venture in Sweden. She spoke conversational Chinese as well as fluent French. Apparently, her current assignment was near completion, and she wanted to continue seeking overseas assignments partly as a means of trying to cope with her recent divorce.

Mark Porter's current assignment in Corporate Business Planning was also coming to an end, and he was eager to do some international work. He was 31 years old and had a B.S. in Finance from the University of Pennsylvania and an MBA from Duke University. He was apparently a "fast-tracker" at Electrowide, rotating among various organizational functions every 1.5 years, and had been employed with the company six years. His most recent position was that of business analyst responsible for relaying backlog data to Corporate Finance and Shareholder's Relations. According to his file, he is a type-A personality and a self-starter, focusing on excelling no matter what the cost or sacrifice.

Tom also noted that, as part of the study, Motosuzhou was investigated along with several other possible Eastern Asian partners. Such parameters as the partner's physical location in the country, the size of its labor force, and the strength of the resources that could enhance as well as reduce operational costs for Electrowide were examined. In addition, the company was dependent on finding a local manufacturing company with a strong, established network that could readily market products produced under the JV without additional expense in the effort. Furthermore, finding a local company with ties to government officials was thought to be of benefit. Early warnings about any impending government policy changes that might impact operations within the JV would be advantageous. Above all, management wanted to ensure that its corporate objectives would be achieved upon establishment of the JV. Motosuzhou seemed to fit most closely to the criteria identified in the study.

Tom envisioned that he and the rest of the team would spend the majority of their first several weeks with Motosuzhou discussing the specific details of the proposed JV. Instead, their counterparts were keenly interested in learning about their visitors' personal lives, their interests, the size of their families, and the like. Usually, the days were spent touring the city and surrounding countryside, while long hours were spent at night engaging in elaborate dinner get-togethers and nightlife entertainment. Mark never showed much interest or appreciation of the scenery. His thoughts were usually preoccupied with how to steer the course of the next day's discussions on the details of the proposed JV. He was not one for small talk. Barb was quite affable with her Chinese hosts initially. She particularly enjoyed experiencing a night of *quyi,* for which the Motosuzhou team generously paid admission. Yet, her enthusiasm diminished when she took notice that Ai Hwa and this constituents tended not to include her in conversation but rather directed their discussions and eye contact to Barb's male counterparts. One night in particular stood out in Tom's mind. As Ai Hwa Chew was making toasts to his guests thanking them for their interests in his company, he presented Tom with a sterling silver tea set. Tom felt a bit uncomfortable accepting such an expensive gift

and even tried to tactfully refuse it. However, Ai Hwa stubbornly refused Tom's insistence. Tom thought that he detected irritation in Hwa's voice but decided not to apologize and prolong the uncomfortable silence that punctuated the room.

By the fourth week, Tom and his team were growing a bit restless. Habitually, they left telephone messages with Ai Hwa's secretary requesting to meet with him and his constituents. Tom even went as far as to establish specific days and times for these proposed discussions. Nothing constructive with respect to these transpired during that week. Tom's patience grew thin as he tried to force smile after smile during long dinner extravaganzas where conversation continued to remain light and disassociated from any issues pertaining to work. Mark was growing extremely impatient, and he frequently excused himself early from get-togethers, or, on occasion, refrained from attending altogether.

A change in routine finally occurred during the fifth week. Deng Zang felt the proper time had materialized when issues concerning the JV should be approached with Electrowide. He commissioned Ai Hwa to put together a formal written invitation that was subsequently hand-delivered to the hotel early in the week. Tom and his team were invited to an arranged meeting to be conducted in Ai Hwa Chew's office the morning following receipt of the letter. Although no agenda was distributed and the time and location for the meeting were changed at 11 P.M. the night before, the team managed to regain their composure in anticipation of cooperative dialogue with their potential partners. Tom had been instructed by executive staff to remain firm in its' pursuit of negotiating specific roles and responsibilities that each party would assume under the JV. Electrowide was to provide and control design, financial, and technical clout necessary to commercialize the JV's technology. Conversely, Electrowide wanted Motosuzhou to provide the manufacturing plant facility, marketing functions utilizing a local sales force, as well as provide the majority of the technical labor force. Furthermore, Electrowide thought it was in its best interest to allow Motosuzhou to continue in its current managerial capacity inasmuch as Electrowide lacked the personnel proficient in Chinese. Moreover, Electrowide planned to hold a 51 percent stake in the venture, with Motosuzhou taking a 39 percent portion, and the remainder to go to the Beijing Municipal government.

Meetings continued throughout the week. Although Mark would have preferred to continue doing research in his hotel room, Tom insisted that his attendance at the meetings was crucial. As the meetings progressed, the American team's overall assessment of whether the objectives of most of their concessions were going to be met was favorable. Barb was instructed not to vocally participate in negotiations, but her keen eye played an important role. She recorded conversations at each meeting and noticed that affirmative nodding by the

Chinese counterparts was apparent. Tom's team interpreted this as a sign that concessions outlined by the Electrowide team would be easily confirmed. Barb also noticed, however, that the Chinese team rarely posed specific questions about the details of the JV. The inference was that the Motosuzhou team understood the concessions and, therefore, had no concerns. The interpreter that Motosuzhou provided to the team continually assuaged any doubts about failing progress. This constant reminder renewed the team's faith that Motosuzhou was a compatible fit with Electrowide.

In about the eighth week, however, positive attitudes on the part of Tom and his team began to wane. From the start, HQ promised Tom that his maximum required length of stay would not exceed two months as the company planned at most six weeks to secure agreement for the JV. Tom would certainly miss his daughter's college graduation if negotiations persisted much longer. In addition, Barb, who was a member of the Information Technology Council, was "burning the candle at both ends" as she feverishly worked on several assignments faxed to her from HQ. Mark had contracted the Asian flu and was miserably trying to battle its nasty symptoms while trying to play Tom's right-hand man. Moreover, War Games with Taiwan were growing intense, the threat of which strengthened the team's desire to repatriate as soon as possible. Ai Hwa Chew and his aides were behaving less passively. Questions particular to the concessions proposed by Electrowide were now being raised. Motosuzhou had its own objectives to pursue as commissioned by the minister of Finance, Wang Yoo. Motosuzhou knew it was in its best interest to comply with government mandates; otherwise, the company risked losing its position on the list of free-enterprise entities. Ai Hwa was skeptical about Electrowide's concessions. His assessment was the Electrowide really wanted to gain greater control for itself in the local Asian market. Nowhere in the objective statement as documented on the "Request for Approval" were marketing concessions addressed or implied. One concession Motosuzhou was adamant in winning was control of financial operations of the JV. Moreover, the Chinese company insisted that any profits earned under the JV could be invested only in China, the currency remaining in *yuan*.

Although this was a crucial point for them, Motosuzhou focused on softer issues initially. For example, Motosuzhou requested that training, consulting, and warranties would be provided to them free of charge. Ai Hwa Chew kept reminding the American team that such provisions were considered free goods in their Chinese system, and hence were perceived as indications of one's sincerity and good will. In addition, Ai Hwa Chew pointed out inconsistencies between the partner's accounting systems which created disagreement regarding allocation of manufacturing costs. Tom was alarmed, for his assessment of Motosuzhou's accounting policies was that they were in complete disarray and that the Chinese

firm's management would greatly appreciate it if this function was handled by Electrowide. No formal auditing records had been kept. Ai Hwa Chew kept assuring Tom that Wang Yoo could provide auditing documentation that the state agency kept on file on all its state-run operations. However, Tom's direct request to the top Finance representative at the Ministry for copies of accounting records fell on deaf ears. Tom knew that he could not allow accounting practices to continue as they were because they would result in the reduction of Electrowide's operating margins, an outcome that violated one of Electrowide's ultimate objectives for establishing a JV. HQ also instructed Tom to remain firm on providing training instructors and training materials. However, training costs were to be a necessary expense of Motosuzhou.

To drive a further wedge in objectives, Ai Hwa Chew made it very clear that he was not comfortable continuing management practices as they currently operated. He stressed the need for more harmony in all aspects of the negotiations and JV operations. At the same time, the Executive Committee at Electrowide was enmeshed in activities to finalize formulation, appointments, and operations of each of the council organizations. Consequently, Tom found it increasingly difficult to relay concerns and seek support and approval for changes requested. In addition, the time difference made it difficult for Tom to directly communicate issues to HQ on a timely basis. Delays were not part of Electrowide's plan in securing the JV.

Tom and his team decided to take matters into their own hands. While Ai Hwa called for a few days' reprieve to honor the Chinese Winter holiday, the Electrowide team took advantage of the free days. Unknown to their potential partners, the American team sought the counsel of an American law firm located in Beijing. To circumvent the likelihood of any future misunderstandings between the two parties, Tom instructed the attorney to structure a very formal extensive contract to address every conceivable contingency.

The next morning, over breakfast, as Tom and his team were reviewing their plan of action on how to best present the contract to Ai Hwa Chew, the hotel concierge presented Tom with a Western Union telegram. Tom scanned the contents, shared the information with his team, and then tossed the telegram in the trash, thinking little of its effect on the day's negotiation activities. "Today," Tom assuredly thought, "I feel we're going to come to final agreement." As the telegram started to unfurl in the trash, its contents exposed the following: "Trade Representative Mickey Kantor was quoted as bashing Beijing over MFN status on account of China violating intellectual property issues."

Tom wanted to waste little time in presenting the contract to his counterpart. He was anxious to solidify the deal. Almost immediately upon entering Ai Hwa Chew's office, Tom handed over the legal document, which was written entirely in English. As the interpreter read the contract, Ai Hwa's grew dim and his face flushed. While only one-third of the way into listening to the concessions, Ai Hwa motioned Tom and his party to the door of his office. Once outside the office, Tom and his team were quite confused. Shortly, thereafter, Ai Hwa's secretary notified the group that the day's negotiation meetings were canceled. Tom and his team left

feeling a bit confused but thought that perhaps Ai Hwa needed some time alone to review the contents of the contract. Unknown to Tom, Ai Hwa was drafting a letter to the Minister of Finance requesting to meet with him. The tone of the letter was rather urgent.

The next morning, Tom spotted the article in the *Beijing Daily*. He was disappointed and at a loss as to how to make reparations.

CASE QUESTIONS

1. What are the main characteristics of Chinese culture? How do they differ from the predominant characteristics of U.S. culture? How do these differences relate to the negotiation process?
2. What are the criteria that should be used in selecting a joint venture partner? Have those criteria been met in this situation? Why, or why not?
3. Evaluate the composition of Electrowide's team and of Motosuzhou's team. Did each of the companies make appropriate choices for this negotiation? Give reasons for your answer.
4. Should Barb Morgan have been on the negotiating team? Evaluate and give your reasons.
5. What should Tom Sherman do?

APPENDIX 1: KEY ASPECTS OF CHINESE CULTURE AS THEY RELATE TO NEGOTIATIONS[5]

Guanxi: **The Value of an Ongoing Relationship**

Guanxi is the word that describes the intricate, pervasive network of personal relations that every Chinese cultivates with energy, subtlety and imagination. *Guanxi* is the currency of getting things done and getting ahead in Chinese society. *Guanxi* is a relationship between two people containing implicit mutual obligation, assurances, and intimacy, and is the perceived value of an ongoing relationship and its future possibilities that typically govern Chinese attitudes toward long-term business. If a relationship of trust and mutual benefit is developed, an excellent foundation will be built for future business with the Chinese. Guanxi ties are also helpful in dealing with the Chinese bureaucracy as personal interpretations are used in lieu of legal interpretations.

Because of cultural differences and language barriers, visitors to China are not in a position to cultivate *guanxi* with the depth possible between two Chinese. Regardless, *guanxi* is an important aspect of interrelations in China and deserves attention so that good

friendly relations may be developed. These connections are essential to getting things accomplished.[6]

FORMAL AND INFORMAL RELATIONS

At present, it is likely that the majority of social contracts foreigners have with the Chinese are on a more formal than informal level. Informality in China relates not to social pretension or artifice but to the concept of face. Great attention is paid to observance of formal, or social behavior and attendant norms. The social level is the level of form and proper etiquette where face is far more important than fact. It is considered both gauche and rude to allow one's personal feelings and opinions to surface here to the detriment of the social ambience. It is much more important to compliment a person or to avoid an embarrassing or sensitive subject than to express an honest opinion if honesty is at the expense of another's feelings. Directness, honesty, and individualism that run counter to social conventions and basic politeness have no place on the social level; emotions and private relationships tend to be kept private in Chinese society.

CHINESE ETIQUETTE FOR SOCIAL FUNCTIONS

Ceremonies and rules of ceremony have traditionally held a place of great importance in Chinese culture. Confucianism perpetuated and strengthened these traditions by providing the public with an identity, mask, or persona with which a person is best equipped to deal with the world with a minimum of friction. Confucianism consists of broad rules of conduct evolved to aid and guide interpersonal relations. Confucius assembled all the details of etiquette practiced at the courts of the feudal lords during the period c. 551–479 B.C. These rules of etiquette are called the *li* and have long since become a complete way of life for the Chinese.

---

[7]This appendix is very largely drawn from James A. Brunner's case, "Buckeye Glass Co. in China," in *International Management: A Cross-Cultural and Functional Perspective* by Kamal Fatehi (Upper Saddle River, NJ: Prentice Hall).

[8]An extremely useful new article that extends this analysis of *guanxi* is "Achieving Business Success in Confucian Societies: The Importance of Guanxi (Connections)" by Irene Y. M. Yeung and Rosalie Tung, *Organizational Dynamics* (Autumn 1996): 54–65. The article is accompanied by an excellent bibliography.

The *li* may appear overly formalistic to Westerners at first glance. Upon closer inspection, it is apparent that the rules of etiquette play a very important role in regulating interpersonal relations. Some basic rules of behavior are as follows:

- A host should always escort a guest out to his car or other mode of transportation and watch until the guest is out of sight.
- Physical expression is minimal by Western standards. A handshake is polite, but backslapping and other enthusiastic grasping is a source of embarrassment.
- At culture functions and other performances, audience approval of performers is often subdued by American standards. Although the accepted manner of expressing approval varies between functions and age groups, applause is often polite rather than roaring and bravo-like cheers.
- A person should keep control over his temper at all times.
- One should avoid blunt, direct, or abrupt discussion, particularly when the subject is awkward; delicate hints are often used to broach such a topic.
- It is a sign of respect to allow another to take the seat of honor (left of host) or to be asked to proceed through a door first.
- The serving of tea often signals the end of an interview or meeting. However, it is also served during extended meetings to quench the thirst of the negotiators.

SMILING AND LAUGHTER

Laughter and smiling in Chinese culture represent the universal reaction to pleasure and humor. They are also a common response to negative occurrences, such as death and other misfortunes. When embarrassed or in the wrong, the Chinese frequently respond with laughter or smiling, which will persist if another person continues to speak of an embarrassing topic or does not ignore the wrong. Westerners are often confused and shocked by this behavior, which is alien to them. It is important to remember that smiling and laughter in the previously discussed situations are not exhibitions of glee, but rather are a part of the concept of face when used in response to a negative or unpleasant situation. (L. Pye, *Chinese Negotiating Style* (Cambridge, MA: Oelgeschlager, Gunn and Hain, 1982), 101.

SOURCE: This case was prepared by John Stanbury, Assistant Professor of International Business Studies at Indian University, Kokomo, with the considerable assistance of Carole Pelteson and Duwayne Cox, MBA students. The views represented here are those of the case authors and do not necessarily reflect the views of the Society for Case Research. Authors' views are based on their own professional judgments.

The names of the organization and individuals' names and the events described in this case have been disguised to preserve anonymity.

Presented to and accepted by the Society for Case Research. All rights reserved to the authors and SCR. Copyright 1996.

Case 8   Moto: Coming to America

Moto arrived in Chicago in the middle of winter, unprepared for the raw wind that swept off the lake. The first day he bought a new coat and fur-lined boots. He was cheered by a helpful salesgirl who smiled as she packed his lined raincoat into a box. Americans were nice, Moto decided. He was not worried about his assignment in America. The land had been purchased, and Moto's responsibility was to hire a contracting company and check on the pricing details. The job seemed straightforward.

Moto's firm, KKD, an auto parts supplier, had spent a year and a half researching U.S. building contractors. Allmack had the best record in terms of timely delivery and liaisons with good architects and the best suppliers of raw materials. That night Moto called Mr. Crowell of Allmack, who confirmed the appointment for the next morning. His tone was amiable.

Moto arrived at the Allmack office at nine sharp. He had brought a set of *kokeshi* dolls for Crowell. The dolls, which his wife had spent a good part of a day picking out, were made from a special maple in the mountains near his family home in Niigata. He would explain that to Crowell later, when they knew each other. Crowell also came from a hilly, snowy place, which was called Vermont.

When the secretary ushered him in, Crowell stood immediately and rounded the desk with an outstretched hand. Squeezing Moto's hand, he roared, "How are you? Long trip from Tokyo. Please sit down, please."

Moto smiled. He reached in his jacket for his card. By the time he presented it, Crowell was back on the other side of the desk. "My card," Moto said seriously.

"Yes, yes," Crowell answered. He put Moto's card in his pocket without a glance.

Moto stared at the floor. This couldn't be happening, he thought. Everything was on that card: KKD, Moto, Michio, Project Director. KKD meant University of Tokyo and years of hard work to earn a high recommendation from Dr. Iwasa's laboratory. Crowell had simply put it away.

"Here." Crowell handed Moto his card.

"Oh, John Crowell, Allmack, President," Moto read aloud, slowly trying to recover his equilibrium. "Allmack is famous in Japan."

"You know me," Crowell replied and grinned. "All those faxes. Pleased to meet you, Moto. I have a good feeling about this deal."

Moto smiled and laid Crowell's card on the table in front of him.

"KKD is pleased to do business with Allmack," Moto spoke slowly. He was proud of his English. Not only had he been a top English student in high school and university, but he had also studied English in a *juku* (an after-school class) for five years. As soon as he received this assignment, he took an intensive six-week course taught by Ms. Black, an American, who also instructed him in U.S. history and customs.

Crowell looked impatient. Moto tried to think of Ms. Black's etiquette lessons as he continued talking about KKD and Allmack's history. "We are the best in the business," Crowell interrupted. "Ask anyone. We build the biggest and best shopping malls in the country."

Moto hesitated. He knew Allmack's record—that's why he was in the room. Surely Crowell knew that. The box of *kokeshi* dolls pressed against his knees. Maybe he should give the gift now. No, he thought, Crowell was still talking about Allmack's achievements. Now Crowell had switched to his own achievements. Moto felt desperate.

"You'll have to come to my house," Crowell continued. "I live in a fantastic house. I had an architect from California build it. He builds for all the stars, and for me." Crowell chuckled. "Built it for my wife. She's the best wife, the very best. I call her my little sweetheart. Gave the wife the house on her birthday. Took her right up to the front door and carried her inside."

Moto shifted his weight. Perhaps if he were quiet, Crowell would change the subject. Then they could pretend the conversation never happened. "Moto-san, what's your first name? Here, we like to be on a first-name basis."

"Michio," Moto whispered.

"Michio-san, you won't get a better price than from me. You can go down the block to Zimmer or Casey, but you got the best deal right here."

"I brought you a present," Moto said, handing him the box of *kokeshi* dolls.

"Thanks," Crowell answered. He looked genuinely pleased as he tore open the paper. Moto looked away while Crowell picked up a *kokeshi* doll in each hand. "They look like Russian dolls. Hey, thanks a lot, my daughter will love them."

Moto pretended that he hadn't heard. I'll help by ignoring him, Moto thought, deeply embarrassed.

Crowell pushed the *kokeshi* dolls aside and pressed a buzzer. "Send George in," he said.

The door opened and a tall, heavyset man with a dark crew cut stepped inside the room.

"George Kubushevsky, this is Moto-san, Michio. . . ."

"How do you do?" Kubushevsky's handshake was firm.

Moto took out his card.

"Thanks," Kubushevsky said. "Never carry those." He laughed and hooked his thumbs in his belt buckle. Moto nodded. He was curious. Kubushevsky must be a Jewish name—or was it Polish, or maybe even German? In Japan he'd read books about all three groups. He looked at Kubushevsky's bone structure. It was impossible to tell. He was too fat.

"George, make sure you show Michio everything. We want him to see all the suppliers, meet the right people, you understand?"

"Sure." George grinned and left the room.

Moto turned to Crowell. "Is he a real American?" Moto asked.

"A real American? What's that?"

Moto flushed. "Is he first generation?" Moto finished lamely. He remembered reading that Jews, Lebanese, and Armenians were often first generation.

"How do I know? He's just Kubushevsky."

During the next few weeks Moto saw a great deal of Kubushevsky. Each morning he was picked up at nine and taken to a round of suppliers. Kubushevsky gave him a rundown on each supplier before they met. He was amiable and polite, but never really intimate. Moto's response was also to be polite. Once he suggested that they go drinking after work, but Kubushevsky flatly refused, saying that he had to work early the next morning. Moto sighed, remembering briefly his favorite bar and his favorite hostess in Tokyo. Yuko-san must be nearly fifty now, he thought affectionately. She could make him laugh. He wished he were barhopping with his colleagues from his *ringi* group at KKD. Moto regretted that he had not brought more *kokeshi* dolls, since Kubushevsky had not seemed delighted with the present of the KKD pen.

One morning they were driving to a cement outlet.

"George."

"Yes, Michio-san."

Moto paused. He still found it difficult to call Kubushevsky by his first name. "Do you think I could have some papers?"

"What kind of papers?" Kubushevsky's voice was friendly. Unlike Crowell, he kept an even tone. Moto liked that.

"I need papers on the past sales of these people."

"We're the best."

"I need records for the past five years on the cement place we are going to visit."

"I told you, Michio-san, I'm taking you to the best! What do you want?"

"I need some records."

"Trust me, I know what I'm doing."

Moto was silent. He didn't know what to say. What did trust have to do with anything? His *ringi* group in Tokyo needed documentation so they could discuss the issues and be involved in the decisions. If the decision to go with one supplier or the other was correct, that should be reflected in the figures.

"Just look at what's going on now," George said. "Charts for the last five years, that's history."

Moto remained silent. George pressed his foot to the gas. The car passed one truck, and then another. Moto looked nervously at the climbing speedometer. Suddenly Kubushevsky whistled and released his foot. "Alright, Michio-san, I'll get you the damned figures."

"Thanks," Moto said softly.

"After we see the cement people, let's go for a drink."

Moto looked uneasily at the soft red lightbulb that lit the bar. He sipped his beer and ate a few peanuts. Kubushevsky was staring at a tall blonde at the other end of the bar. She seemed to notice him also. Her fingers moved across the rim of the glass.

"George," Moto said gently. "Where are you from, George?"

"Here and there," Kubushevsky said idly, still eyeing the blonde.

Moto laughed. "Here and there."

Kubushevsky nodded. "Here and there," he repeated.

"You Americans," Moto said. "You must have a home."

"No home, Michio-san."

The blonde slid her drink down the bar and slipped into the next seat. Kubushevsky turned more toward her.

Moto felt desperate. Last week Crowell had also acted rudely. When Imai, KKD's vice president, was visiting from Japan, Crowell had dropped them both off at a golf course. What was the point?

He drained his beer. Immediately the familiar warmth of the alcohol made him buoyant. "George," he said intimately. "You need a wife. You need a wife like Crowell has."

Kubushevsky turned slowly on his seat. He stared hard at Moto. "You need a muzzle," he said quietly.

"You need a wife," Moto repeated. He had Kubushevsky's full attention now. He poured Kubushevsky another beer. "Drink," he commanded.

Kubushevsky drank. In fact they both drank. Then suddenly Kubushevsky's voice changed. He put his arm around Moto and purred in his ear. "Let me tell you a secret, Moto-san. Crowell's wife is a dog. Crowell is a dog. I'm going to leave Allmack, just as soon as possible. Want to join me, Michio-san?"

Moto's insides froze. Leave Crowell. What was Kubushevsky talking about? He was just getting to know him. They were a team. All those hours in the car together, all those hours staring at cornfields and concrete. What was Kubushevsky talking about? Did Crowell know? What was Kubushevsky insinuating about joining him? "You're drunk, George."

"I know."

"You're very drunk."

"I know."

Moto smiled. The blonde got restless and left the bar. Kubushevsky didn't seem to notice. For the rest of the night he talked about his first wife and his two children, whom he barely saw. He spoke of his job at Allmack and his hopes for a better job in California. They sat at a low table. Moto spoke of his children and distant wife. It felt good to talk, almost as good as having Yuko next to him.

As they left the bar, Kubushevsky leaned heavily on him. They peed against a stone wall before getting in the car. All the way home Kubushevsky sang a song about a folk here named Davy Crockett, who "killed himself a bear when he was only three." Moto sang a song from Niigata about the beauty of the snow on the rooftops in winter. Kubushevsky hummed along.

They worked as a team for the next four months. Kubushevsky provided whatever detailed documentation Moto asked for. They went drinking a lot. Sometimes they both felt a little sad, sometimes happy, but Moto mostly felt entirely comfortable. Kubushevsky introduced him to Porter, a large, good-natured man in the steel business who liked to hunt and cook gourmet food, to Andrews, a tiny man who danced the polka as if it were a waltz and to many others.

Just before the closing, Kubushevsky took him to a bar and told him of a job offer in California. He had tears in his eyes and hugged Moto good-bye. Moto had long since accepted the fact that Kubushevsky would leave.

Two weeks later Moto looked around the conference room at Allmack. Ishii, KKD's president, and Imai had flown in from Tokyo for the signing of the contract for the shopping mall, the culmination of three years of research and months of negotiation. John Crowell stood by his lawyer, Sue Smith. Sue had been on her feet for five hours. Mike Apple, Moto's lawyer, slammed his fist on the table and pointed at the item in question. The lawyers argued a timing detail that Moto was sure had been worked out weeks before. Moto glanced nervously at Ishii and Imai. Ishii's eyes were closed. Imai stared at the table.

Moto shifted uneasily in his seat. Sue was smarter than Mike, he thought. Perhaps a female lawyer wouldn't have been so terrible. While it was not unusual to see females in professional positions in Japan, this was America. Tokyo might have understood. After all, this was America, he repeated to himself. Internationalization required some adjustment. A year ago he would have had total loss of face if confronted with this prolonged, argumentative closing. Today he did not care. He could not explain to Tokyo all he'd learned in that time, all the friends he'd made. When he tried to communicate about business in America, the home office sent him terse notes by fax.

Now the lawyers stood back. President Ishii opened his eyes. Crowell handed a pen to Ishii. They signed the document together. The lawyers smiled. Sue Smith looked satisfied. She should be pleased, Moto thought. Her extensive preparation for the case made him realize again that the Japanese stereotype of the "lazy" American was false. Sue's knowledge of the case was perfect in all details. I'll have to use her next time, Moto thought. She's the smart one. Yes, he thought, his friend Kubushevsky had taught him many things. Suddenly he felt Kubushevsky's large presence. Moto lowered his head in gratitude.

CASE QUESTIONS

1. What was Moto's purpose and agenda for the first meeting with Crowell? How does he try to implement his agenda?

2. What happened to introduce *noise* in the communication from Moto to Crowell, and then from Crowell to Moto?

3. What was the significance of the dolls? What went wrong?

4. Why did Crowell's remarks about Allmack threaten a loss of face from Moto's perspective?

5. How did Moto feel about Kubushevsky's behavior early on? How did their relationship change?

SOURCE: Patricia Cercik, *On Track with the Japanese, 1992 (New York: Kodansha International, 114 Fifth Ave.,* NY, NY, 10011) *(OR Kudanske America).*

CHAPTER
6
Formulating Strategy

Outline

Opening Profile: Mexican Cement Maker with a Worldview

MONTERREY, Mexico—Lorenzo Zambrano seems to be one of the few global chief executives not rushing into China—at least not yet.

Such caution is uncharacteristic for Mr. Zambrano, the man who built Cemex of Mexico into the world's third-largest cement company by snapping up companies from Colombia to Egypt, and on to Indonesia. But the Chinese market, he says, is unattractive.

"The industry isn't profitable there," he said, citing governmental factors like informal price controls and a tax system that he says is designed to suck up profits.

Since 1985, when Mr. Zambrano became chief executive of the company his grandfather founded, he has turned Cemex from a provincial cement company into the country's first home grown multinational, with operations in thirty countries on five continents. His first major foray abroad came in 1992 when he bought two Spanish cement companies, saddling Cemex with debt that analysts said would sink the company.

Mr. Zambrano, who recently turned sixty, dismisses Wall Street's concern about Cemex's debt, calling analysts "napkin scribblers." He has continued to borrow to expand.

He borrowed to buy the Houston-based cement maker, Southdown, for $2.6 billion in 2001, a deal that made Cemex the largest cement producer in the United States but increased the company's debt to $6 billion, an amount nearly equal to Cemex's annual sales. By the end of last year, the debt dropped to $5.6 billion, or four-fifths of annual sales of $7.16 billion, sales that represented a 9 percent rise from the previous year as the company benefited from the economic recovery in America and Mexico.

A dapper man with a big appetite for risk and the courtly manners of his Spanish forebears, Mr. Zambrano learned the cement business from the ground up. He arrived at Cemex with a Stanford M.B.A. degree and was promptly sent off to distant plants, including one built on a clay pit that is known as the company's Siberia. There, he fired half the staff and pushed through a year's worth of production in six months.

After eighteen years of toiling in the hinterlands, his performance, along with his family's large—but undisclosed—stake, got him the top job, though he did have to win over some dissenting board members.

He pumped the company's spare cash into the local stock market, without telling the board. "Once I had made $80 million, I could tell them," Mr. Zambrano said with a grin during an interview at his glass and steel headquarters here in this northern industrial city.

He used the earnings to buy two Mexican cement companies, almost doubling Cemex's size and setting the stage for global expansion. He also narrowly refocused the company on cement, dumping stakes in hotels and chemicals, and turned to a pet obsession that was to become part of the company's image: high-tech gadgetry and innovation.

His growth strategy has been to acquire, follow that with a period of calm in which the acquired entity is integrated and the debt starts to be paid off, and follow that by a lunge into a new market.

Right now, "Cemex is doing a lot of housekeeping," said Carlos Perezalonso, an analyst at BBVA–Bancomer in Mexico City. "The market is grateful it isn't taking risks in a time of uncertainty."

It has been Mr. Zambrano's expansion into regions that other Mexican companies will not touch that has set Cemex apart. Cemex, Mr. Zambrano said, must either grow or be swallowed up in a globalizing economy and a consolidating industry.

The expansion does not always go smoothly.

"The company has a tendency to reach far beyond its home base, which is not an easy thing," said Arjun Divecha, an equity manager at the GMO Emerging Markets Fund based in Berkeley, California, which invests in Cemex.

Cemex's most pressing problem at the moment is in Indonesia. Local protests over foreign ownership have led the Indonesian government to renege on an agreement to sell control of the cement maker, PT Semen Gresik, to Cemex; Cemex has already spent $300 million for a 25 percent stake.

This stumble has made Cemex more cautious, Mr. Zambrano admitted. Still, he loves a good challenge, as his hobby of racing his 1950s Ferraris shows. "Modern cars lack character," Mr. Zambrano said. "I have very fast modern cars, but anyone can drive them. A housewife could drive them." Outside the racetrack and a fondness for contemporary Mexican art, Mr. Zambrano, a bachelor, admits Cemex is his life. And, though technology bores him in a car, he likes it in his company.

When he took over in 1985, he installed expensive satellite equipment to give him an instant picture of how all the plants were doing. "When Lorenzo calls, if the plant manager doesn't know what is going on, well, that's not good," said Héctor Medina, the company's planning and strategy director.

More recently, technology helped Mr. Zambrano win over his new American employees at Southdown. "They were very nervous, a lot of the gringos at the facilities, but they've adjusted," said Steven Prokopy, editor of *Cement Americas,* a Chicago-based trade journal. "What they like is that Cemex has money to spend on upgrades and technology."

Cemex's search for an edge has kept it ahead of competitors, said James L. Heskett, a Harvard Business School professor. The company, he said, has a novel approach to customer service in an industry known more for its sweat-stained engineers. For instance, it studied the 911 dispatcher's office in Houston and then set up a similar system to provide more flexible delivery. The result was less wasted cement and better service to customers, enabling Cemex to charge them more.

Other innovations include a program that lets Mexican migrants in the United States pay for cement that their relatives back home can pick up at a store near them and use to build houses.

Mr. Zambrano, a billionaire, is also frugal. Until recently, he lived in an apartment so small he had to store valuable works of art in boxes. And, when his company buys a company, the first thing it does is cut costs.

One new way to do so came from the purchase of one of the Spanish companies, Valenciana, whose engineers had developed a way to burn petroleum coke, a cheap waste product. Mr. Zambrano converted other Cemex plants to petroleum coke and was able to save on energy, a component that accounts for 40 percent of the cost of making cement, the company said.

Despite the global expansion, the home market, where Cemex has a 55 percent share, is still its most important. Mexico contributed 70 percent of the company's profits last year, though it accounted for just 37 percent of sales.

Such figures have brought media reports of price gouging. And, a bag of cement in Harlingen, Texas, for instance, in the more competitive United States market, does cost 22 percent less than a bag just across the border in Matamoros. Cemex executives say that in Mexico a higher proportion of cement is sold to individual home builders in sacks, a retail operation with higher margins.

The Mexican competition authorities have said they see nothing wrong with Cemex's pricing policies. Other cement companies also do well in Latin America. Holcim. of Switzerland, the world's largest, has a profit margin of 27 percent in Latin America but just 15.3 percent overall. The margin for No. 2, the Paris-based Lafarge S.A., is 39.4 percent in Latin America but only 14.2 percent overall.

Mr. Zambrano bristles, at the criticism that his company, engages in price gouging in his own country, and he would clearly rather talk about other things.

Like China? Or maybe India? "We're prepared if there is an opportunity," Mr. Zambrano said with a grin.

SOURCE: www.nytimes.com, April 15, 2004. Copyright 2004 The New York Times Company, reprinted with permission.

As the opening profile on Cemex illustrates, companies around the world are spending increasing amounts of money and time on global expansion in search of profitable new markets, acquisitions, and alliances—but are often spending those resources on very different strategies. Experts predict that those companies with operations in major overseas markets (North America, Europe, and Asia) are far more likely to prosper in the twenty-first century than those without such operations. [1]Because these new international opportunities are far more complex than those in domestic markets, managers must plan carefully—that is, strategically—to benefit from them. As evident in the Cemex case, Mr. Zambrano is wary about expanding into politically risky areas or those countries where he finds government practices to be prohibitive, but is opportunistic about expanding in other regions.

The process by which a firm's managers evaluate the future prospects of the firm and decide on appropriate strategies to achieve long-term objectives is called **strategic planning**. The basic means by which the company competes—its choice of business or businesses in which to operate and the ways in which it differentiates itself from its competitors—is its **strategy**. Almost all successful companies engage in long-range strategic planning, and those with a global orientation position themselves to take full advantage of worldwide trends and opportunities. Multinational corporations (MNCs), in particular, report that strategic planning is essential to contend with increasing global competition and to coordinate their far-flung operations.

In reality, however, that rational strategic planning is often tempered, or changed at some point, by a more incremental, sometimes messy, process of strategic decision making by some managers. When a new CEO is hired, for example, she will often call for a radical change in strategy. That is why new leaders are very carefully chosen, on the basis of what they are expected to do. So, although the rational strategic planning process is presented in this text because it is usually the ideal, inclusive, method of determining long-term plans, managers must remember that, throughout, people are making decisions and their own personal judgments, experiences, and motivations will shape the ultimate strategic direction.

REASONS FOR GOING INTERNATIONAL

"AOL Europe is emerging as an upbeat counterpoint to AOL's sagging business in the United States. Partly a matter of timing, as Europe follows the United States online ... but also reflecting differences in strategy and execution. AOL Europe lobbied hard ... to establish rules guaranteeing AOL Europe equal access to telecommunications networks."

www.nytimes.com,
September 8, 2003[2]

As illustrated by the AOL experience cited, companies "go international" for different reasons, some reactive (or defensive) and some proactive (or aggressive). The threat of their own decreased competitiveness is the overriding reason many large companies adopt a strategy of aggressive globalization. To remain competitive, these companies want to move fast to build strong positions in key world markets with products tailored to the common needs of 650 million customers in Europe, Latin America, and Japan. Building on their past success, companies such as IBM and Digital Equipment are plowing profits back into operations overseas. Europe is now attracting much new investment capital because of both the European Union (EU) and the opening of extensive new markets in Eastern Europe.

Reactive Reasons

Globalization of Competitors
One of the most common reactive reasons that prompt a company to go overseas is global competition. If left unchallenged, competitors who already have overseas operations or investments may get so entrenched in foreign markets that it becomes difficult for other companies to enter at a later time. In addition, the lower costs and market power available to these competitors operating globally may also give them an advantage domestically.

Trade Barriers
Restrictive trade barriers are another reactive reason that companies often switch from exporting to overseas manufacturing. Barriers such as tariffs, quotas, buy-local policies, and other restrictive trade practices can make exports to foreign markets too expensive and too impractical to be competitive. Many firms, for example, want to gain a foothold in Europe—to be regarded as insiders—to counteract trade barriers and restrictions on non–European Union (EU) firms (discussed further in the Comparative Management in Focus: Strategic Planning for the EU Market in this chapter). In part, this fear of "Fortress Europe" is caused by actions such as the EU's block exemption for the franchise industry. This exemption prohibits a franchisor, say McDonald's, from contracting with a single company, say Coca-Cola, to supply all its franchisees, as it does in the United States.

Regulations and Restrictions
Similarly, regulations and restrictions by a firm's home government may become so expensive that companies will seek out less restrictive foreign operating environments. Avoiding such regulations prompted U.S. pharmaceutical maker SmithKline and Britain's Beecham to merge. Both thereby guaranteed that they would avoid licensing and regulatory

hassles in their largest markets: Western Europe and the United States. The merged company is now an insider in both Europe and America.[3]

Customer Demands

Operations in foreign countries frequently start as a response to customer demands or as a solution to logistical problems. Certain foreign customers, for example, may demand that their supplying company operate in their local region so that they have better control over their supplies, forcing the supplier to comply or lose the business. McDonald's is one company that asks its domestic suppliers to follow it to foreign ventures. Meat supplier OSI Industries does just that, with joint ventures in seventeen countries, such as Bavaria, so that it can work with local companies making McDonald's hamburgers.[4]

Proactive Reasons

From rain forests to remote Chinese villages, the queen of cosmetics (Avon) is cleaning up across the globe.[5] China is our single biggest growth opportunity.

[Now] we have beauty boutiques, with 5,000 store representatives in every province including Tibet. A corollary on the [WTO] bill said that China would reestablish the legitimacy of direct selling in the marketplace. It could be in the next couple of years.

SUSAN KROPF, PRESIDENT, AVON PRODUCTS,
January 12, 2004[6]

Economies of Scale

Careful, long-term strategic planning encourages firms to go international for proactive reasons. One pressing reason for many large firms to expand overseas is to seek economies of scale—that is, to achieve world-scale volume to make the fullest use of modern capital-intensive manufacturing equipment and to amortize staggering research and development costs when facing brief product life cycles.[7] Otis Elevator, for example, developed the Elevonic 411 by means of six research centers in five countries. This international cooperation saved more than $10 million in design costs and cut the development cycle from four years to two. Economies of scale in production are achieved when higher levels of output spread fixed costs over more units, thus lowering the per-unit cost. Gerrit Jeelof, of Holland's Philips Group, contends that "only with a global market can a company afford the large development costs necessary to keep up with advancing technology."[8]

Growth Opportunities

Companies in mature markets in developed countries experience a growth imperative to look for new opportunities in emerging markets. When expansion opportunities become limited at home, firms such as McDonald's are often driven to seek expansion through new international markets. A mature product or service with restricted growth in its domestic market often has "new life" in another country, where it will be at an earlier stage of its life cycle.[9] Avon Products, for example, has seen a decline in its U.S. market since its traditional sales and marketing strategy of "Avon Calling" (house-to-house sales) now meets with empty houses, due to the spiraling number of women who now work outside the home. To make up for this loss, Avon pushed overseas to twenty-six emerging markets, such as Mexico, Poland, China, India, South Africa, and Vietnam. In Brazil, for instance, Josina Reis Teixeira carries her sample kit to the wooden shacks in the tiny village of Registro, just outside of São Paulo. In some markets, Avon adapts to cultural influences, such as in China, where consumers are suspicious of door-to-door salespeople. There, Avon sets up showrooms (beauty boutiques) in its branch offices in major cities so that women can consult cosmeticians and sample products.[10]

In addition, new markets abroad provide a place to invest surplus profits as well as employ underutilized resources in management, technology, and machinery. When entirely new markets open up, such as in Eastern Europe, both experienced firms and those new to international competition usually rush to take advantage of awaiting opportunities. Such was the case with the proactive stance that Unisys took in preparing for and jumping on the newly opened market opportunity in Vietnam.

Resource Access and Cost Savings

Resource access and cost savings entice many companies to operate from overseas bases. The availability of raw materials and other resources offers both greater control over inputs and lower transportation costs. Lower labor costs (for production, service, and technical personnel), another major consideration, lead to lower unit costs and have proved a vital ingredient to competitiveness for many companies.

Sometimes just the prospect of shifting production overseas improves competitiveness at home. When Xerox Corporation started moving copier rebuilding operations to Mexico, the union agreed to needed changes in work style and productivity to keep the jobs at home.[11] Lower operational costs in other areas—power, transportation, and financing—frequently prove attractive. Trinidad, for example, offers abundant inexpensive energy, a skilled and well-educated workforce with labor rates at about one-fourth of U.S. levels, and government incentives for export-oriented ventures that generate foreign exchange.[12]

Incentives

Governments in countries such as Poland seeking new infusions of capital, technology, and know-how willingly provide incentives—tax exemptions, tax holidays, subsidies, loans, and the use of property.[13] Because they both decrease risk and increase profits, these incentives are attractive to foreign companies. One study surveyed 103 experienced managers concerning the relative attractiveness of various incentives for expansion into the Caribbean region (primarily Mexico, Venezuela, Colombia, Dominican Republic, and Guatemala). The results indicate the opinion of those managers about which incentives are most important; however, the most desirable mix would depend on the nature of the particular company and its operations. The first two issues reflect managers' concerns about limiting foreign exchange risk, where restrictions often change overnight and limit the ability of the firm to repatriate profits. Other concerns are those of political instability in countries such as Haiti and Nicaragua, and the possibility of expropriation, and those of tax concessions.[14]

STRATEGIC FORMULATION PROCESS

Typically, the strategic formulation process is necessary both at the headquarters of the corporation and at each of the subsidiaries. One study reported, for example, that 70 percent of fifty-six U.S. MNC subsidiaries in Latin America and the Far East operated on planning cycles of five or more years.[15]

The global strategic formulation process, as part of overall corporate strategic management, parallels the process followed in domestic companies. However, the variables, and therefore the process itself, are far more complex because of the greater difficulty in gaining accurate and timely information, the diversity of geographic locations, and the differences in political, legal, cultural, market, and financial processes. These factors introduce a greater level of risk in strategic decisions. However, for firms that have not yet engaged in international operations (as well as for those that do), an ongoing strategic planning process with a global orientation identifies potential opportunities for (1) appropriate market expansion, (2) increased profitability, and (3) new ventures by which the firm can exploit its strategic advantages. Even in the absence of immediate opportunities, monitoring the global environment for trends and competition is important for domestic planning.

The strategic formulation process is part of the strategic management process in which most firms engage, either formally or informally. The planning modes range from a proactive, long-range format to a reactive, more seat-of-the-pants method, whereby the day-by-day decisions of key managers, in particular owner-managers, accumulate to what can be discerned retroactively as the new strategic direction.[16] The stages in the strategic management process are shown in Exhibit 6-1. In reality, these stages seldom follow such a linear format. Rather, the process is continuous and intertwined, with data and results from earlier stages providing information for the next stage.

EXHIBIT 6-1   The Strategic Management Process

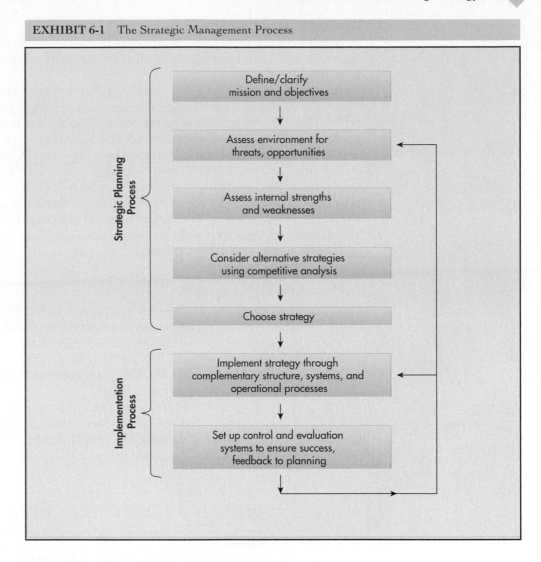

The first phase of the strategic management process—the *planning phase*—starts with the company establishing (or clarifying) its mission and its overall objectives. The next two steps comprise an assessment of the external environment that the firm faces in the future and an analysis of the firm's relative capabilities to deal successfully with that environment. Strategic alternatives are then considered, and plans are made based on the strategic choice. These five steps constitute the planning phase, which will be further explained in this chapter.

The second part of the strategic management process is the *implementation phase.* Successful implementation requires the establishment of the structure, systems, and processes suitable to make the strategy work. These variables, as well as functional-level strategies are explored in detail in the remaining chapters on organizing, leading, and staffing. At this point, however, it is important to note that the strategic planning process by itself does not change the posture of the firm until the plans are implemented. In addition, feedback from the interim and long-term results of such implementation, along with continuous environmental monitoring, flows directly back into the planning process.

STEPS IN DEVELOPING INTERNATIONAL AND GLOBAL STRATEGIES

In the planning phase of strategic management—strategic formulation—managers need to carefully evaluate dynamic factors, as described in the stages that follow. However, as discussed earlier, managers seldom consecutively move through these phases; rather, changing events and variables prompt them to combine and reconsider their evaluations on an ongoing basis.

Mission and Objectives

The *mission* of an organization is its overall *raison d'être* or the function it performs in society. This mission charts the direction of the company and provides a basis for strategic decision making.

A company's overall *objectives* flow from its mission, and both guide the formulation of international corporate strategy. Because we are focusing on issues of international strategy, we will assume that one of the overall objectives of the corporation is some form of international operation (or expansion). The objectives of the firm's international affiliates should also be part of the global corporate objectives. A firm's global objectives usually fall into the areas of marketing, profitability, finance, production, and research and development, among others, as shown in Exhibit 6-2. Goals for market volume and for profitability are usually set higher for international than for domestic operations because of the greater risk involved. In addition, financial objectives on the global level must take into account differing tax regulations in various countries and how to minimize overall losses from exchange rate fluctuations.

Environmental Assessment

After clarifying the corporate mission and objectives, the first major step in weighing international strategic options is the **environmental assessment**. This assessment includes environmental scanning and continuous monitoring to keep abreast of variables around the world that are pertinent to the firm and that have the potential to shape its future by posing new opportunities (or threats). Firms must adapt to their environment to survive. The focus of strategic planning is how to adapt.

The process of gathering information and forecasting relevant trends, competitive actions, and circumstances that will affect operations in geographic areas of potential interest is called **environmental scanning**. This activity should be conducted on three levels—global, regional, and national (discussed in detail later in this chapter). Scanning

---

EXHIBIT 6-2   Global Corporate Objectives

Marketing
Total company market share—worldwide, regional, national
Annual percentage sales growth
Annual percentage market share growth
Coordination of regional markets for economies of scale

Production
Relative foreign versus domestic production volume
Economies of scale through global production integration
Quality and cost control
Introduction of cost-efficient production methods

Finance
Effective financing of overseas subsidiaries or allies
Taxation—globally minimizing tax burden
Optimum capital structure
Foreign-exchange management

Profitability
Long-term profit growth
Return on investment, equity, and assets
Annual rate of profit growth

Research and Development
Develop new products with global patents
Develop proprietary production technologies
Worldwide research and development labs

should focus on the future interests of the firm and should cover the following major variables (as discussed by Phatak[17] and others):

- *Political instability.* This variable represents a volatile and uncontrollable risk to the multinational corporation, as illustrated by the upheaval in the Middle East in recent years. MNCs must carefully assess such risk because it may result in a loss of profitability or even ownership.[18]
- *Currency instability.* This variable represents another risk; inflation and fluctuations in the exchange rates of currencies can dramatically affect profitability when operating overseas. For example, both foreign and local firms got a painful reminder of this risk when Mexico devalued its peso in 1998 and the currency collapsed in Indonesia, and in 2002 Argentina was suffering the same problems.
- *Nationalism.* This variable, representing the home government's goals for independence and economic improvement, often influences foreign companies. The home government may impose restrictive policies—import controls, equity requirements, local content requirements, limitations on the repatriation of profits, and so forth. Japan, for example, protects its home markets with these kinds of restrictive policies. Other forms of nationalism may be exerted through the following: (1) pressure from national governments—exemplified by the United States putting pressure on Japan to curtail unfair competition; (2) lax patent and trademark protection laws, such as those in China in recent years, which erode a firm's proprietary technology through insufficient protection; and (3) the suitability of infrastructure, such as roads and telecommunications.
- *International competition.* Conducting a global competitor analysis is perhaps the most important task in environmental assessment and strategy formulation. The first step in analyzing the competition is to assess the relevant industry structures as they influence the competitive arena in the particular country (or region) being considered. For example, will the infrastructure support new companies in that industry? Is there room for additional competition? What is the relative supply and demand for the proposed product or service? The ultimate profit potential in the industry in that location will be determined by these kinds of factors.[19]
- *Environmental Scanning.* Managers must also specifically assess their current competitors—global and local—for the proposed market. They must ask some important questions: What are our competitors' positions, their goals and strategies, and their strengths and weaknesses, relative to those of our firm? What are the likely competitor reactions to our strategic moves? Managers should compare their company with potential international competitors; in fact, it is useful to draw up a competitive position matrix for each potential international market. For example, Exhibit 6-3 analyzes a U.S. specialty seafood firm's competitive profile in Malaysia.[20]

The U.S. firm in Exhibit 6-3 has advantages in financial capability, future growth of resources, and sustainability but a disadvantage in quickness. It also is at a disadvantage

EXHIBIT 6-3 Global Competitor Analysis

Comparison Criteria	A (U.S. MNC)	B (Korean MNC)	C (Local Malaysian Firm)	D (Japanese MNC)	E (Local Malaysian Firm)
Marketing capability	0	0	0	0	—
Manufacturing capability	0	+	0	0	0
R & D capability	0	0	0	—	0
HRM capability	0	0	0	0	0
Financial capability	+	—	0	0	—
Future growth of resources	+	0	—	0	—
Quickness	—	0	+	—	0
Flexibility/adaptability	0	+	+	0	0
Sustainability	+	0	0	0	—

Key:
+ = firm is better relative to competition.
0 = firm is same as competition.
— = firm is poorer relative to competition.

SOURCE: Diane J. Garsombke, "International Competitor Analysis." *Planning Review* 17, no. 3 (May–June 1989): 42–47.

compared to the Korean MNC in important factors such as manufacturing capability and flexibility and adaptability. Because the other firms seem to have little **comparative advantage**, the major competitor is likely to be the Korean firm. At this point, then, the U.S. firm can focus in more detail on assessing the Korean firm's relative strengths and weaknesses.

The firm can also choose varying levels of environmental scanning. To reduce risk and investment, many firms take on the role of the "follower," meaning that they limit their own investigations. Instead, they simply watch their competitors' moves and go where they go, assuming that the competitors have done their homework. Other firms go to considerable lengths to carefully gather data and examine options in the global arena.

Ideally, the firm should conduct global environmental analysis on three different levels: multinational, regional, and national. Analysis on the multinational level provides a broad assessment of significant worldwide trends—through identification, forecasting, and monitoring activities. These trends would include the political and economic developments of nations around the world, as well as global technological progress. From this information, managers can choose certain appropriate regions of the world to consider further.

Next, at the regional level, the analysis focuses in more detail on critical environmental factors to identify opportunities (and risks) for marketing the company's products, services, or technology. For example, one such regional location ripe for investigation by a firm seeking new markets is the EU.

Having zeroed in on one or more regions, the firm must, as its next step, analyze at the national level. Such an analysis explores in depth specific countries within the desired region for economic, legal, political, and cultural factors significant to the company. For example, the analysis could focus on the size and nature of the market, along with any possible operational problems, to consider how best to enter the market. In many volatile countries, continuous monitoring of such environmental factors is a vital part of ongoing strategic planning. In Peru in 1988, inflation had soared to 2,000 percent, and leftist terrorists were kidnapping or murdering business leaders. Although key managers fled and many multinational companies pulled out of Peru, Procter & Gamble remained to take advantage of a potentially large market share when competitors left. "Everybody should be dying to come here—you couldn't go to a better business school [than what you learn by managing here]," said Susana Elesperu de Freitas, the thirty-four-year-old Peruvian manager of Procter & Gamble's subsidiary, who was flanked by armed bodyguards wherever she went.[21] Since then, Procter & Gamble, a consumer-products company, has expanded and is now a major force in Peru.

This process of environmental scanning, from the broad global level down to the local specifics of entry planning, is illustrated in Exhibit 6-4. The first broad scan of all potential world markets results in the firm being able to eliminate from its list those markets that are closed or insignificant or do not have reasonable entry conditions. The second scan of remaining regions, and then countries, is done in greater detail—perhaps eliminating some countries based on political instability, for example. Remaining countries are then assessed for competitor strengths, suitability of products, and so on. This analysis leads to serious entry planning in selected countries; managers start to work on operational plans, such as negotiations and legal arrangements.

Sources of Environmental Information

The success of environmental scanning depends on the ability of managers to take an international perspective and to ensure that their *sources of information and business intelligence* are global. A variety of public resources are available to provide information. In the United States alone, more than 2,000 business information services are available on computer databases tailored to specific industries and regions. Other resources include corporate "clipping" services and information packages. However, internal sources of information are usually preferable—especially alert field personnel who, with firsthand observations, can provide up-to-date and relevant information for the firm. Extensively using its own internal resources, Mitsubishi Trading Company employs worldwide more than 60,000 market analysts, whose job it is to gather, analyze, and feed market information to the parent company.[22] Internal sources of information help to

EXHIBIT 6-4   Global Environmental Scanning Process

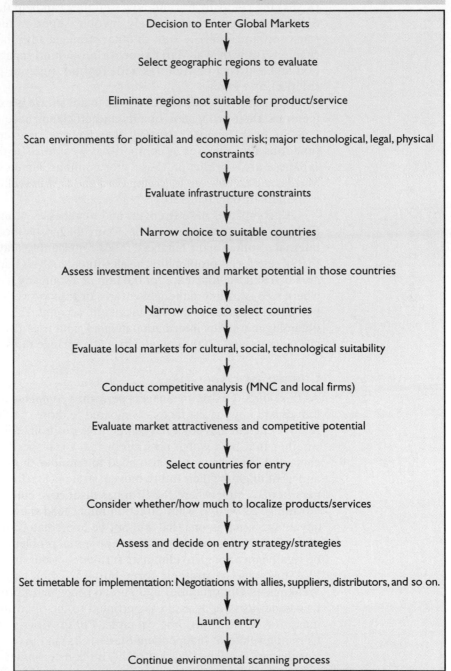

Decision to Enter Global Markets → Select geographic regions to evaluate → Eliminate regions not suitable for product/service → Scan environments for political and economic risk; major technological, legal, physical constraints → Evaluate infrastructure constraints → Narrow choice to suitable countries → Assess investment incentives and market potential in those countries → Narrow choice to select countries → Evaluate local markets for cultural, social, technological suitability → Conduct competitive analysis (MNC and local firms) → Evaluate market attractiveness and competitive potential → Select countries for entry → Consider whether/how much to localize products/services → Assess and decide on entry strategy/strategies → Set timetable for implementation: Negotiations with allies, suppliers, distributors, and so on. → Launch entry → Continue environmental scanning process

eliminate unreliable information from secondary sources, particularly in developing countries. As Garsombke points out, the "official" data from such countries can be misleading: "Census data can be tampered with by government officials for propaganda purposes or it may be restricted.... In South Korea, for instance, even official figures can be conflicting depending on the source."[23]

Internal Analysis

After the environmental assessment, the second major step in weighing international strategic options is the **internal analysis**. This analysis determines which areas of the firm's operations represent strengths or weaknesses (currently or potentially) compared to competitors, so that the firm may use that information to its strategic advantage.

The internal analysis focuses on the company's resources and operations and on global synergies. The strengths and weaknesses of the firm's financial and managerial expertise and functional capabilities are evaluated to determine what key success factors (KSFs) the company has and how well they can help the firm exploit foreign opportunities. Those factors increasingly involve superior technological capability (as with Microsoft and Intel), as well as other strategic advantages such as effective distribution channels (as with Wal-Mart), superior promotion capabilities (Disney), low-cost production and sourcing position (as with Toyota), superior patent and new product pipeline (Merck), and so on.

Using such operational strengths to advantage is exemplified by Japanese car manufacturers: their production quality and efficiency have catapulted them into world markets. As to their global strategy, they have recognized that their sales and marketing functions have proven a competitive weakness in the European car wars, and the Japanese are working on these shortcomings. Japanese automakers—Toyota, Honda, Mazda, and so on—are following Ford and GM in seeking to become more sophisticated marketers throughout Europe.[24]

All companies have strengths and weaknesses. Management's challenge is to identify both and take appropriate action. Many diagnostic tools are available for conducting an internal resource audit. Financial ratios, for example, may reveal an inefficient use of assets that is restricting profitability; a sales-force analysis may reveal that the sales force is an area of distinct competence for the firm. If a company is conducting this audit to determine whether to start international ventures or to improve its ongoing operations abroad, certain operational issues must be taken into account. These issues include (1) the difficulty of obtaining marketing information in many countries, (2) the often poorly developed financial markets, and (3) the complexities of exchange rates and government controls.

Competitive Analysis

At this point, the firm's managers perform a *competitive analysis* to assess the firm's capabilities and key success factors compared to those of its competitors. They must judge the relative current and potential competitive position of firms in that market and location—whether that be a global position or that for a specific country or region. Like a chess game, the firm's managers also need to consider the strategic intent of competing firms and what might be their future moves (strategies). This process enables the strategic planners to determine where the firm has **distinctive competencies** that will give it strategic advantage as well as what direction might lead the firm into a sustainable competitive advantage—that is, one that will not be immediately eroded by emulation. The result of this process will also help to identify potential problems that can be corrected or that may be significant enough to eliminate further consideration of certain strategies.[25]

This stage of strategic formulation is often called a **SWOT analysis** (Strengths, Weaknesses, Opportunities, and Threats), in which a firm's capabilities relative to those of its competitors are assessed as pertinent to the opportunities and threats in the environment for those firms. For example, Philip Morris (PM) considered entry into the Commonwealth of Independent States (CIS) in the early 1990s. The attraction, of course, was the newly opened market of 290 million consumers. Of these, 70 million were smokers and would provide an immediate target market for Philip Morris's cigarette brands. In addition, all 290 million would be a vast potential market for PM's Kraft and General Foods subsidiaries. The next step would be an in-depth assessment of the local and foreign competitors in the region, such as RJR Nabisco.

After its analysis, Philip Morris concluded that the Russian commonwealth presented an attractive opportunity, particularly if the firm could establish a market foothold before RJR Nabisco followed suit. In hindsight, however, Philip Morris might have done some more homework and added other threats to this matrix. After the company set up kiosks to sell packs of Marlboros to people in St. Petersburg in 1992, those booths were blown up overnight—a signal that Russian cigarette distributors didn't want any outside competitors on their turf. Philip Morris subsequently got out of the distribution business. It is also worth noting that, in September 1998, RJR withdrew all operations from Russia as a result of that country's economic problems, after investing about $520 million. The company was among many suffering major losses in Russia's economic collapse in 1998, when the inflation rate reached 84.3 percent by the end of 1999.[26]

Most companies develop their strategies around key strengths, or **core competencies**. Core competencies represent important corporate resources because, as Prahalad and Hamel explain, they are the "collective learning in the organization, especially how to coordinate diverse production skills and integrate multiple streams of technologies."[27] Core competencies—like Sony's capacity to miniaturize and Philips's optical-media expertise—are usually difficult for competitors to imitate and represent a major focus for strategic development at the corporate level.[28] Canon, for example, has used its core competency in optics to its competitive advantage throughout its diverse businesses: cameras, copiers, and semiconductor lithographic equipment.

Managers must also assess their firm's weaknesses. A company already on shaky ground financially, for example, will not be able to consider an acquisition strategy, or perhaps any growth strategy. Of course, the subjective perceptions, motivations, capabilities, and goals of the managers involved in such diagnoses frequently cloud the decision-making process. The result is that because of poor judgment by key players sometimes firms embark on strategies that were contraindicated by objective information.

Global and International Strategic Alternatives

The fourth major step in the strategic planning process involves considering the advantages (and disadvantages) of various strategic alternatives in light of the competitive analysis. While weighing alternatives, managers must take into account the goals of their firms and the competitive status of other firms in the industry.

Depending on the size of the firm, a firm must consider two levels of strategic alternatives. The first level, *global strategic alternatives* (applicable primarily to MNCs), determines what overall approach to the global marketplace a firm wishes to take. The second level, *entry strategy alternatives,* applies to firms of any size; these alternatives determine what specific entry strategy is appropriate for each country in which the firm plans to operate. Entry strategy alternatives are discussed in a later section. The two main global strategic approaches to world markets—globalization and regionalization—are presented in the following subsections.

Approaches to World Markets

Globalization

In the last decade, increasing competitive pressures have forced businesses to consider global strategies—to treat the world as an undifferentiated worldwide marketplace. Such strategies are now loosely referred to as **globalization**—a term that refers to the establishment of worldwide operations and the development of standardized products and marketing. Many, analysts, like Porter, have argued that globalization is a competitive imperative for firms in global industries: "In a global industry, a firm must, in some way, integrate its activities on a worldwide basis to capture the linkages among countries. This includes, but requires more than, transferring intangible assets among countries."[29] The rationale behind globalization is to compete by establishing worldwide economies of scale, offshore manufacturing, and international cash flows. The term *globalization,* therefore, is as applicable to organizational structure as it is to strategy. (Organizational structure is discussed further in Chapter 8.)

The pressures to globalize include (1) increasing competitive clout resulting from regional trading blocs; (2) declining tariffs, which encourage trading across borders and open up new markets; and (3) the information technology explosion, which makes the coordination of far-flung operations easier and also increases the commonality of consumer tastes.[30] Use of Web sites has allowed entrepreneurs, as well as established companies, to go global almost instantaneously through e-commerce—either B2B or B2C.[31] Examples are Yahoo!, Lands' End, and the ill-fated E-Toys, which met its demise in 2001. In addition, the success of Japanese companies with global strategies has set the competitive standard in many industries—most visibly in the automobile industry. Other companies, such as Caterpillar, ICI, and Sony, have fared well with global strategies.

One of the quickest and cheapest ways to develop a global strategy is through strategic alliances. Many firms are trying to go global faster by forming alliances with rivals, suppliers, and customers. The rapidly developing information technologies are spawning cross-national business alliances from short-term virtual corporations to long-term strategic partnerships.[32] (Strategic alliances are discussed further in Chapter 7.)

Globalization is inherently more vulnerable to environmental risk, however, than a regionalization strategy. Global organizations are difficult to manage because doing so requires the coordination of broadly divergent national cultures. It also means, say Morrison, Ricks, and Roth, that firms must lose some of their original identity—they must "denationalize operations and replace home-country loyalties with a system of common corporate values and loyalties."[33] In other words, the globalization strategy necessarily treats all countries similarly, regardless of their differences in cultures and systems. Problems often result, such as a lack of local flexibility and responsiveness and a neglect of the need for differentiated products. In some recent research into how U.S. companies compete, Morrison et al. discovered that many companies are finding that "globalization is no panacea, and, in fact, global imperatives are being eclipsed by an upsurge in regional pressures."[34] These researchers claim that many companies now feel that regionalization is a more manageable and less risky approach, one that allows them to capitalize on local competencies as long as the parent organization and each subsidiary retain a flexible approach to each other.

Regionalization

For those firms in multidomestic industries—those industries in which competitiveness is determined on a country-by-country basis rather than a global basis—regional strategies are more appropriate than globalization.[35] The **regionalization strategy (multidomestic (or multi-local) strategy)** is one in which local markets are linked together within a region, allowing more local responsiveness and specialization. Top managers within each region decide on their own investment locations, product mixes, and competitive positioning; in other words, they run their subsidiaries as quasi-independent organizations.

Since there are pressures to globalize—such as the need for economies of scale to compete on cost—there are opposing pressures to regionalize, especially for newly developed economies (NDEs) and less developed countries (LDCs). These localization pressures include unique consumer preferences resulting from cultural or national differences (perhaps something as simple as right-hand-drive cars for Japan), domestic subsidies, and new production technologies that facilitate product variation for less cost than before.[36] By "acting local," firms can focus individually in each country or region on the local market needs for product or service characteristics, distribution, customer support, and so on.

As with any management function, the strategic choice as to where a company should position itself along the globalization–regionalization continuum is contingent on the nature of the industry, the type of company, the company's goals and strengths (or weaknesses), and the nature of its subsidiaries, among many factors. In addition, each company's strategic approach should be unique in adapting to its own environment. Many firms may try to "Go Global, Act Local" to trade off the best advantages of each strategy. Matsushita is one firm with considerable expertise at being a "GLOCAL" firm (GLObal, LoCAL). Matsushita has more than 150 production and research-and-development (R&D) bases in thirty-eight countries. In Malaysia, for example, where Matsushita employs 23,500 people in its thirteen subsidiaries, the company diligently follows its policy of trying to keep the expatriate headcount down and train local managers—only 230 employees there are Japanese. Other Matsushita local policies are to develop local R&D to tailor products to markets, to let plants set their own rules, and to be a good corporate citizen in every country.[37] Another global company that works hard to act local in certain markets, such as India, is illustrated in the accompanying Management Focus: Whirlpool India's Whitemagic Blends with Local Culture and Traditions.

Global Integrative Strategies

Many MNCs have developed their global operations to the point of being fully integrated—often both vertically and horizontally, including suppliers, productive facilities, marketing and distribution outlets, and contractors around the world. Dell, for example, is a globally integrated company, with worldwide sourcing and a fully

---

Management Focus

Whirlpool India's Whitemagic Blends with Local Culture and Traditions

Whirlpool India launched "Whitemagic Hotwash"—a fully automatic top-loading washing machine—in Kerala. The machine, priced at Rs 19,000, was specially designed for the Indian market.[1] After more than a year of research into the values of Indian people, especially homemakers, Whirlpool concluded that hygiene and purity were matters of intense pride for Indians, and so it was very important to them to have very white clothes for their families.[2] However, after a number of washes in local water in their existing washing machines, their clothes became dull. So Whirlpool designed the "Whitemagic," which has a hot wash option with a super white cycle for special attention to white clothes.[3] A typical advertisement for the machine shows someone in very white clothes, with others in the background in more dull-looking clothes.

These are just some of the ways Whirlpool tries to "act local" while "going global," especially in emerging markets, where it is trying to establish a foothold in anticipation of high growth levels. Offering incentives to the thousands of Indian retailers to get them to stock Whirlpool products and using local contractors who speak the eighteen main languages used in India are other tactics it uses to fall in with the local distribution system.[4] The contractors collect payments in cash and deliver the appliances by whatever means works in that area, which may be by bicycle or by oxcart.

Early cooperation with local partners and focusing on local cultures are lessons that Whirlpool learned the hard way after having to shut down two of the four appliance plants it had built in China. Now Whirpool's global strategy is to design basic models of appliances with about 70 percent common parts, leaving the remaining 30 percent to be localized to the needs of the particular market.[5] It looks like they are on to a winning combination: Whirlpool's sales in India have jumped by 80 percent and are expected to reach $200 million for 2001.[6]

[1] "India: Whirlpool's Whitemagic Hits Kerala Market," *Business Line,* November 10, 2000.

[2] P. Engardio and C. Frazier, Smart Globalization," Business Week, August 27, 2001.

[3] www.Whirlpool.com; www.WhirlpoolIndia.com.

[4] Engardio and Frazier.

[5] Ibid.

[6] Ibid.

---

integrated production and marketing system. It has factories in Ireland, Malaysia, and Texas, and it has an assembly and delivery system from forty-seven locations around the world. At the same time, it has extreme flexibility. Since Dell builds computers to each order, it carries very little inventory and, therefore, can change its operations at a moment's notice.

Although some companies move very quickly to the stage of global integration—often through merger or acquisition—many companies evolve into multinational corporations by going through the entry strategies in stages, taking varying lengths of time between stages. Typically, a company starts with simple exporting, moves to large-scale exporting with sales branches abroad (or perhaps begins licensing), then proceeds to assembly abroad (either by itself or through contract manufacturing), and eventually evolves to full production abroad with its own subsidiaries. Finally, the MNC will undertake the global integration of its foreign subsidiaries, setting up cooperative activities among them to achieve economies of scale. By this point, the MNC has usually adopted a geocentric orientation, viewing opportunities and entry strategies in the context of an interrelated global market instead of regional or national markets. In this way, alternative entry strategies are viewed on an overall portfolio basis to take maximum advantage of potential synergies and leverage arising from operations in multi-country markets.[38]

Exhibit 6-5 illustrates the integrated, concurrent strategies used in the global network of the Helicopter Division of France's Société Nationale Industrielle Aerospatiale. The corporation employs a complex pattern of entry strategies and alliances among plants around the world, involving exporting, licensing, joint ventures, importing, and subassembly and maintenance facilities.[39] For example, the company has joint ventures with Brazil and Singapore and also exports parts to those countries for assembly; it licenses certain models to India and Yugoslavia and also exports to them; and it exports rotors and airframes to the United States, which, in turn, direct markets to Canada and Mexico and maintains spares and maintenance facilities for operations in those countries.

EXHIBIT 6-5   Network of Entry Strategies: French Helicopter Company

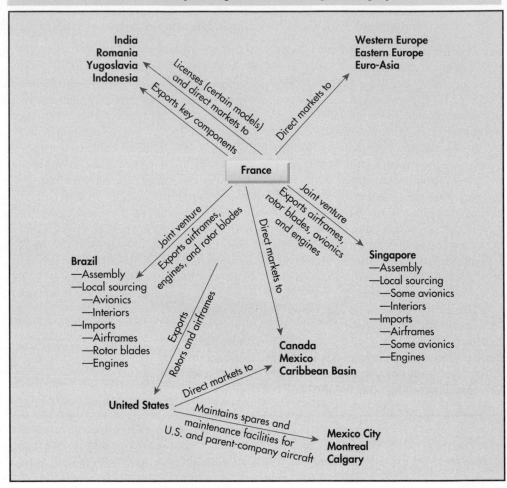

SOURCE: Adapted from R. Grosse and D. Kujawa, *International Business* (Homewood, IL: Irwin, 1988), 372.

Using E-Business for Global Expansion

Companies of all sizes are increasingly looking to the Internet as a means of expanding their global operations. However, the Internet is not just about e-business:

> *The real story is the profound impact this medium will have on corporate strategy, organization and business models. Our research reveals that the Internet is driving global marketplace transformation and paradigm shift in how companies get things done, how they compete and how they serve their customers.*

> WWW.IBM.COM,
> *April 10, 2001*[40]

While the benefits of e-business are many, including rapid entrance into new geographic markets (see Exhibit 6-6), less touted are the many challenges inherent in a global B2B or B2C strategy. These include cultural differences and varying business models, governmental wrangling and border conflicts, in particular the question over which country has jurisdiction and responsibility over disputes regarding cross-border electronic transactions.[41] Potential problem areas that managers must assess in their global environmental analysis include conflicting consumer protection, intellectual property and tax laws, increasing isolationism even among democracies, language barriers, and a lack of tech-savvy legislators worldwide.[42]

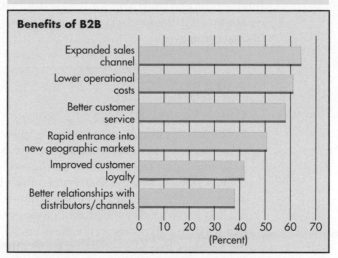

EXHIBIT 6-6   Benefits of B2B

SOURCE: Data from IDC Internet executive Advisory Council
Surveys, 2001.

Savvy global managers will realize that e-business cannot be regarded as just an extension of current businesses. It is a whole new industry in itself, complete with a different pool of competitors and entirely new sets of environmental issues. A reassessment of the environmental forces in the newly configured industry, using Michael Porter's five forces analytical model, should take account of shifts in the relative bargaining power of buyers and suppliers, the level of threat of new competitors, existing and potential substitutes, as well as a present and anticipated competitor analysis.[43] The level of e-competition will be determined by how transparent and imitable the company's business model is for its product or service as observed on its Web site.

It is clear that a competitive global B2B or B2C strategy must offer a technology solution that goes beyond basic transaction or listing service capabilities.[44] To assess the potential competitive position of the company, managers must ask themselves the following:

- Does the exchange provide a technology solution that helps industry trading partners to do business more efficiently?
- Is the exchange known to be among the top three to five within its vertical industry?
- Does the exchange offer industry-specific technology and expertise that gives it an advantage over generic exchange-builders?[45]

There is no doubt that the global e-business competitive arena is a challenging one, both strategically and technologically. But many companies around the world are plunging in, fearing that they will be left behind in this fast-developing global e-marketplace. Included are Fuji Xerox, which has formed a new e-marketplace with NEC and other leading e-commerce players, including Simitomo, Hewlett Packard Japan, Ltd., Sumisho Computer Systems, and U.S. software developer Ariba. Their site, PLEOMART (plenty of markets) is a B2B marketplace for companies to buy and sell, on the Internet, office equipment and supplies, parts, and related solutions services such as consultation, finance, and logistics services.[46] In Melbourne, Australia, the Broken Hill Proprietary Company. (BHP), which specializes in natural resources and regional steel for the global market, has launched its own one-stop global e-marketplace. The site provides logistics, sample products, and supply procurements to e-business producer marketplaces. Recently, BHP has conducted a series of Internet-based "reverse" auctions, where suppliers agree on starting prices and then bid against each other to lower prices for ferroalloys. BHP's Francis Egan, vice president for Global Supply, reports that BHP already spends about $10 billion annually on goods and services online. He says that "online auctions allow us to move readily, aggregate our buying power and leverage greater savings . . . they also provide economies of scale and promote greater efficiency in the supply function itself."[47]

For companies like eBay, e-business is their business—services are provided over the Internet for end users and for businesses. With a unique business model, and as a young company, eBay has embarked on a global e-strategy, as described in the E-Biz Box: eBay's Global Strategy.

E-BIZ BOX

eBay's Global Strategy

Becoming the world's premier marketplace for millions of businesses is eBay's plan. The company is positioning itself to be global and giant: part international swap meet, part clearinghouse for the world's manufacturers and retailers. To become a global colossus, eBay is pursuing a fairly simple, three-pronged strategy. It's evangelizing the wonders of eBay around the world. It's starting to get non-U.S. auction goers used to the idea of paying over its PayPal electronic payment system, and it's doing all this as it is beefing up the U.S. site by adding new categories and big partners, like Sears, Sharper Image, IBM, and Disney, which all unload excess inventory via eBay.

The company touts itself as the world's online marketplace. Founded in 1995, eBay created a powerful platform for the sale of goods and services. On any given day, millions of items across thousands of categories are for sale on eBay. The company's Web presence enables trade on a local, national, and international basis with customized sites in markets around the world.

Most people know eBay as B2C (consumer e-commerce), but the company is also a business-to-business site (B2B). Its eBay Business Marketplace is located at www.ebaybusiness.com. That site brings together all business-related listings on eBay into one destination, offering products and services through "Vertical Industry Marketplaces" for various industries.

The global reach of eBay includes a presence in twenty-seven markets around the world. Its portfolio of international business includes its top three international sites: eBay Germany, eBay United Kingdom, and Internet Auction in Korea. In June, 2004, eBay announced a $50 million acquisition of Indian auctioneer Baazee.com, India's most popular online shopping site. However, as in China, few people own computers. In India there are cyber cafes where people can browse the Internet, but few have credit cards, and there is also considerable distrust of e-commerce transactions. So, while eBay's executives attribute their increased earnings to a surge in international sales and are optimistic for their fledgling operations in China, India, and other international markets, others are not so optimistic. Among the concerns are the increased exposure of the company to currency swings worldwide, and seasonality in Europe, where holidays in the summer severely limit e-commerce.

SOURCES: "Ebay Earnings Beat Analysts' Estimates," www.nytimes.com, July 21, 2004; "Companies to Watch," *Fortune*, February 23, 2004; "eBay Launches eBay Business to Serve Its Growing Community of Business Buyers," www.ebay.com, January 28, 2002; "Tech Comes Out Swinging," www.businessweek.com, August 25, 2003.

E-global or E-local?

Although the Internet is a global medium, the company is still faced with the same set of decisions regarding how much its products or services can be "globalized" or how much they must be "localized" to national or regional markets. Local cultural expectations, differences in privacy laws, government regulations, taxes, and payment infrastructure are just a few of the complexities encountered in trying to "globalize" e-commerce. Further complications arise because the local physical infrastructure must support e-businesses that require the transportation of actual goods for distribution to other businesses in the supply chain, or to end users. In those instances, adding e-commerce to an existing "old-economy" business in those international markets is likely to be more successful than starting an e-business from scratch without the supply and distribution channels already in place. However, many technology consulting firms, such as NextLinx, provide software solutions and tools to penetrate global markets, extend their supply chains, and enable new buyer and seller relationships around the globe.

Going global with e-business, as Yahoo! has done, necessitates a coordinated effort in a number of regions around the world at the same time to gain a foothold and to grab new markets before competitors do. Certain conditions dictate the advisability of going e-global:

> *The global beachhead strategy makes sense when trade is global in scope; when the business does not involve delivering orders; and when the business model can be hijacked relatively easily by local competitors.[48]*

This strategy would work well for global B2B markets in steel, plastics, and electronic components.

The e-local, or regional strategic, approach is suited to consumer retailing and financial services, for example. Amazon and eBay have started their regional approach in Western Europe. Again, certain conditions would make this strategy more advisable:

> *[The e-local/regional approach] is preferable under three conditions: when production and consumption are regional rather than global in scope; when customer behavior and market structures differ across regions but are relatively similar within a region; and when supply-chain management is very important to success.[49]*

The selection of which region or regions to target depends on the same factors of local market dynamics and industry variables as previously discussed in this chapter. However, for e-businesses, additional variables must also be considered, such as the rate of Internet penetration and the level of development of the local telecommunications infrastructure.

Entry Strategy Alternatives

For a multinational corporation (or a company considering entry into the international arena), a more specific set of strategic alternatives, often varying by targeted country, focuses on different ways to enter a foreign market. Managers need to consider how potential new markets may best be served by their company in light of the risks and the critical environmental factors associated with their entry strategies. The following sections examine the various entry and ownership strategies available to firms, including exporting, licensing, franchising, contract manufacturing, turnkey operations, management contracts, joint ventures, and fully owned subsidiaries set up by the firm. These alternatives are not mutually exclusive; several may be employed at the same time. They are addressed in order of ascending risk.

Exporting

Exporting is a relatively low-risk way to begin international expansion or to test out an overseas market. Little investment is involved, and fast withdrawal is relatively easy. Small firms seldom go beyond this stage, and large firms use this avenue for many of their products. Because of their comparative lack of capital resources and marketing clout, exporting is the primary entry strategy used by small businesses to compete on an international level. Jordan Toothbrush, for example, a small company with one plant in Norway and with limited resources, is dependent on good distributors. Since Jordan exports around the world, the company recognizes the importance of maintaining good distributor relations. A recent survey by Dun and Bradstreet showed that more than half of small to medium-sized businesses anticipate growth in their export sales in the next few years.[50]

An experienced firm may want to handle its exporting functions by appointing a manager or establishing an export department. Alternatively, an export management company (EMC) may be retained to take over some or all exporting functions, including dealing with host-country regulations, tariffs, duties, documentation, letters of credit, currency conversion, and so forth. Frequently, it pays to hire a specialist for a given host country.

Certain decisions need special care when managers are setting up an exporting system, particularly the choice of distributor. Many countries have regulations that make it very hard to remove a distributor who proves inefficient. Other critical environmental factors include export-import tariffs and quotas, freight costs, and distance from supplier countries.

Licensing

An international **licensing** agreement grants the rights to a firm in the host country to either produce or sell a product, or both. This agreement involves the transfer of rights to patents, trademarks, or technology for a specified period of time in return for a fee paid by the licensee. Anheuser-Busch, for instance, has granted licenses to produce and market Budweiser beer in England, Japan, Australia, and Israel, among other countries. Many food manufacturing MNCs license their products overseas, often under the names of local firms, and products like those of Nike and Disney can be seen around the world under various licensing agreements. Like exporting, licensing is also a relatively low-risk strategy because it requires little investment, and it can be a very useful option in countries where market entry by other means is constrained by regulations or profit-repatriation restrictions.

Licensing is especially suitable for the mature phase of a product's life cycle, when competition is intense, margins decline, and production is relatively standardized.[51] It is also useful for firms with rapidly changing technologies, for those with many diverse product lines, and for small firms with few financial and managerial resources for direct investment abroad. A clear advantage of licensing is that it avoids the tariffs and quotas usually imposed on exports. The most common disadvantage is the licensor's lack of control over the licensee's activities and performance.

Critical environmental factors to consider in licensing are whether sufficient patent and trademark protection is available in the host country, the track record and quality of the licensee, the risk that the licensee may develop its competence to become a direct competitor, the licensee's market territory, and legal limits on the royalty rate structure in the host country.[52]

Franchising

Similar to licensing, **franchising** involves relatively little risk. The franchisor licenses its trademark, products and services, and operating principles to the franchisee for an initial fee and ongoing royalties. Franchises are well known in the domestic fast-food industry; McDonald's, for example, operates primarily on this basis. For a large up-front fee and considerable royalty payments, the franchisee gets the benefit of McDonald's reputation, existing clientele, marketing clout, and management expertise. The "Big M" is well recognized internationally, as are many other fast-food and hotel franchises, such as Holiday Inn. A critical consideration for the franchisor's management is quality control, which becomes more difficult with greater geographic dispersion.

Franchising can be an ideal strategy for small businesses because outlets require little investment in capital or human resources. Through franchising, an entrepreneur can use the resources of franchisees to expand; most of today's large franchises started out with this strategy. An entrepreneur can also use franchisees to enter a new business. Higher costs in entry fees and royalties are offset by the lower risk of an established product, trademark, and customer base, as well as the benefit of the franchisor's experience and techniques.[53]

Contract Manufacturing

A common means of using cheaper labor overseas is **contract manufacturing**, which involves contracting for the production of finished goods or component parts. These goods or components are then imported to the home country, or to other countries, for assembly or sale. Alternatively, they may be sold in the host country. If managers can ensure the reliability and quality of the local contractor and work out adequate means of capital repatriation, this strategy can be a desirable means of quick entry into a country with a low capital investment and none of the problems of local ownership. Firms like Nike use contract manufacturing around the world.

Service Sector Outsourcing

An increasing number of firms are **outsourcing** "white collar" jobs overseas in an attempt to reduce their overall costs. Often they enter overseas markets by setting up local offices, research laboratories, call centers, and so on, in order to utilize the highly skilled but lower-wage "human capital" that is available in countries such as India, the Philippines, and China, as well as the ability to offer global, round-the-clock service from different time zones. Some examples include the following:

General Electric: 20,000 in India in 2004; big China R&D center: services in finance, IT support, R&D for medical, lighting, aircraft

Accenture: 5,000 in the Philippines in 2004; accounting, software, back-office work

Oracle: Doubling India staff to 4,000; software design, customer support, accounting

Conseco: 1,700 in India, 3 more centers planned; Insurance claimprocessing[54]

In turn, both Indian and American IT service providers are opening offices in Hungary, Poland, and the Czech Republic to take advantage of the German and English-speaking workforce for European clients. Overall, India, in particular, is benefiting from outsourced service sector jobs—in particular, high-tech work. In Bangalore alone, companies like Intel, IBM, HP, AOL, Yahoo!, and Motorola are employing 109,500 knowledge workers in chip design, software, call centers, IT consulting, tax processing, and so on, at about 20 percent of the wages typically paid in the United States.[55]

Whether the firms outsource (or "offshore") white-collar or blue-collar jobs, they must consider strategic aspects of that decision beyond immediate cost savings. According to Hewitt Associates, a global human resources consulting firm, the "global sourcing" strategy utilized by the firms it surveyed was often short-sighted:

> *Although cost reduction is the primary driver, less than half of companies analyze the tax environments of considered countries, only three-fourths measure the impact on supply chain costs, and only 34 percent assess the cost of plant or office shutdown.*[56]

Turnkey Operations

In a so-called **turnkey operation**, a company designs and constructs a facility abroad (such as a dam or chemical plant), trains local personnel, and then turns the key over to local management—for a fee, of course. The Italian company Fiat, for example, constructed an automobile plant in the former Soviet Union under a turnkey agreement. Critical factors for success are the availability of local supplies and labor, reliable infrastructure, and an acceptable means of repatriating profits. There may also be a critical risk exposure if the turnkey contract is with the host government, which is often the case. This situation exposes the company to risks such as contract revocation and the rescission of bank guarantees.

Management Contracts

A **management contract** gives a foreign company the rights to manage the daily operations of a business but not to make decisions regarding ownership, financing, or strategic and policy changes. Usually, management contracts are enacted in combination with other agreements, such as joint ventures. By itself, a management contract is a relatively low-risk entry strategy, but it is likely to be short term and to provide limited income unless it leads to another more permanent position in the market.[57]

International Joint Ventures

At a much higher level of investment and risk (though usually less risky than a wholly owned plant), joint ventures present considerable opportunities unattainable through other strategies. A joint venture involves an agreement by two or more companies to produce a product or service together. In an **international joint venture (IJV)**, ownership is shared, typically by an MNC and a local partner, through agreed-upon proportions of equity. This strategy facilitates an MNC's rapid entry into new markets by means of an already established partner who has local contacts and familiarity with local operations. IJVs are a common strategy for corporate growth around the world. They also are a means to overcome trade barriers, to achieve significant economies of scale for development of a strong competitive position, to secure access to additional raw materials, to acquire managerial and technological skills, and to spread the risk associated with operating in a foreign environment.[58] Not surprisingly, larger companies are more inclined to take a high-equity stake in an IJV, to engage in global industries, and to be less vulnerable to the risk conditions in the host country.[59] The joint venture reduces the risks of expropriation and harassment by the host country. Indeed, it may be the only means of entry into certain countries, like Mexico and Japan, that stipulate proportions of local ownership and local participation.

In recent years, IJVs have made up about 20 percent of direct investments by MNCs in other countries, including such deals as the robotics venture between Fujitsu and General Electric and the fiber-optic venture between Siemens AG and Corning Glass Works. Many companies have set up joint ventures with European companies to gain the status of an "insider" in the European Common Market. Most of these alliances are not just tools of convenience but are important—perhaps critical—means to compete in the global arena.[60] To compete globally, firms have to incur, and defray, immense fixed costs—and they need partners to help them in this effort.[61]

Sometimes countries themselves need such alliances to improve economic conditions: the Russian Federation has recently opened its doors to joint ventures, seeking an infusion of capital and management expertise. IJVs are one of the many forms of strategic global alliances that are further discussed in the next chapter.

In a joint venture, the level of relative ownership and specific contributions must be worked out by the partners. The partners must share management and decision making for a successful alliance. The company seeking such a venture must maintain sufficient control, however, because without adequate control, the company's managers may be unable to implement their desired strategies. Initial partner selection and the development of a mutually beneficial working agreement are, therefore, critical to the success of a joint venture. In addition, managers must ascertain that there will be enough of a "fit" between the partners' objectives, strategies, and resources—financial, human, and technological—to make the venture work. Unfortunately, too often the need for preparation and cooperation is given insufficient attention, resulting in many such marriages ending in divorce. About 60 percent of IJVs fail, usually because of ineffective managerial decisions regarding the type of IJV, its scope, duration, and administration, as well as careless partner selection.[62] The list of cross-cultural disappointments is getting longer—for example, the recent DaimlerChrysler problems, including breakups with its partner in Japan, Mitsubishi Motors (MMC), and crisis talks in May 2004 with its South Korean partner, Hyundai, leaving DaimlerChrysler's global plan unraveling. Previous deals, such as that between Fiat–Nissan have, according to *Business Week,* "produced as much rancor as rewards."[63] After years of arguments, GM pulled out of its operations with Korea's Daewoo Motors, citing insufficient care given to their relationship.

Fully Owned Subsidiaries

In countries where a **fully owned subsidiary** is permitted, an MNC wishing total control of its operations can start its own product or service business from scratch, or it may acquire an existing firm in the host country. Philip Morris acquired the Swiss food firm Jacobs Suchard to gain an early inside track in the European Common Market and to continue its diversification away from its aging tobacco business. With this move, PM became the second U.S. company, after Mars, to ensure itself a place in Europe's food industry. Such acquisitions by MNCs allow rapid entry into a market with established products and distribution networks and provide a level of acceptability not likely to be given to a "foreign" firm.

These advantages somewhat offset the greater level of risk stemming from larger capital investments, compared with other entry strategies.

At the highest level of risk is the strategy of starting a business from scratch in the host country—that is, establishing a new wholly owned foreign manufacturing or service company or subsidiary with products aimed at the local market or targeted for export. Japanese automobile manufacturers, such as Honda, Nissan, and Toyota, have successfully used this strategy in the United States to get around U.S. import quotas.

This strategy exposes the company to the full range of risk, to the extent of its investment in the host country. As evidenced by events in South Africa and China, political instability can be devastating to a wholly owned foreign subsidiary. Add to this risk a number of other critical environmental factors—local attitudes toward foreign ownership, currency stability and repatriation, the threat of expropriation and nationalism—and you have a high-risk entry strategy that must be carefully evaluated and monitored. There are advantages to this strategy, however, such as full control over decision making and efficiency, as well as the ability to integrate operations with overall companywide strategy.

Exhibit 6-7 summarizes the advantages and critical success factors of these entry strategies, which must be taken into account when selecting one or a combination of strategies depending on the location, the environmental factors and competitive analysis, and the overall strategy with which the company approaches world markets.

Complex situational factors face the international manager as she or he considers strategic approaches to world markets, along with which entry strategies might be appropriate, as illustrated in Comparative Management in Focus: Strategic Planning for the EU Market.

EXHIBIT 6-7 International Entry Strategies: Advantages and Critical Success Factors

Strategy	Advantages	Critical Success Factors
Exporting	Low risk No long-term assets Easy market access and exit	Choice of distributor Transportation costs Tariffs and quotas
Licensing	No asset ownership risk Fast market access Avoids regulations and tariffs	Quality and trustworthiness of licensee Appropriability of intellectual property Host-country royalty limits
Franchising	Little investment or risk Fast market access Small business expansion	Quality control of franchisee and franchise operations
Contract manufacturing	Limited cost and risk Short-term commitment	Reliability and quality of local contractor Operational control and human rights issues
Turnkey operations	Revenue from skills and technology where FDI restricted	Reliable infrastructure Sufficient local supplies and labor Repatriable profits Reliability of any government partner
Management contracts	Low-risk access to further strategies	Opportunity to gain longer-term position
Joint ventures	Insider access to markets Share costs and risk Leverage partner's skill base technology, local contacts	Strategic fit and complementarity of partner, markets, products Ability to protect technology Competitive advantage Ability to share control Cultural adaptability of partners
Wholly owned subsidiaries	Realize all revenues and control Global economies of scale Strategic coordination Protect technology and skill base Acquisition provides rapid market entry into established market	Ability to assess and control economic, political, and currency risk Ability to get local acceptance Repatriability of profits

Comparative Management in Focus

Strategic Planning for the EU Market

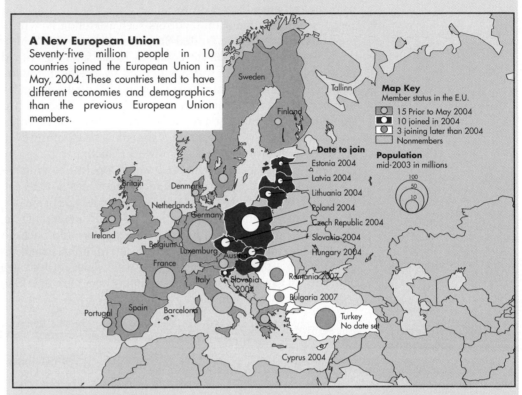

A New European Union
Seventy-five million people in 10 countries joined the European Union in May, 2004. These countries tend to have different economies and demographics than the previous European Union members.

Map 6-1   New European Union

SOURCE: *New York Times*, March 10, 2004, reprinted with permission. Copyright © The New York Times.

> *Multinationals are well placed to benefit from enlargement (inclusion of the ex-communist states) because they have the greatest access to capital, technology and skills. Local entrepreneurs have flair but often lack the funds to grow. Only a handful of locally owned groups—such as Mol, the Hungarian oil group, or CEZ, the Czech electricity company—are big enough to invest abroad.*
>
> FINANCIAL TIMES,
> *April 27, 2004*[64]

> *If you're investing in Hungary or Poland, you get access to the lower costs they offer, compared with, say, Germany or France or Britain. At the same time, if you're producing in Poland, you have an ability to move your goods and services around within the European Union.*
>
> MARK AMBLER,
> *PriceWaterhouseCoopers, London*[65]

> *Business units [in Europe] still tend to focus on individual countries, and managerial practices still follow long-standing national patterns.*
>
> FRANCESCO CAIO,
> *CEO Merloni Elettrodomestici, Fabriano, Italy*[66]

The addition of the eight Central and Eastern Europe (CEE) countries (the Czech Republic, Estonia, Hungary, Latvia, Lithuania, Poland, the Slovak Republic, and Slovenia), as well as Malta and Cyprus, to the EU in May 2004 makes it a twenty-five-nation unified market of more than 400 million people. This expanded EU provides great business opportunities, in particular for small and medium-sized enterprises

(SMEs), to gain access to the EU market by taking advantage of the lower costs in the CEE compared to the rest of the EU, cheaper wages, lower corporate taxes, and educated workforces. Those countries have strengthened their economies in order to meet EU accession requirements, including privatizing state-run businesses, improving the infrastructure, and revamping their finance and banking systems.[67]

For firms within Europe, the euro eliminates currency risk, and so "Pan European thinking becomes not only practicable but essential."[68] The success of companies within Europe, then, depends on their efficiency in streamlining and consolidating their processes and in integrating product and marketing plans across Europe. The challenge is to balance the national and the continental view because a common currency does not bring about cultural or linguistic union.[69]

Clearly, both European and non-European companies must reconsider their European, and indeed global, strategies now that the enlarged EU has become a reality, complete with a common currency, the euro. "Foreign" managers, for example, need to develop an action program to ensure that their products have continued access to the EU and to adapt their marketing efforts to encompass the whole EU. The latter task is difficult, if not impossible, however, because the "citizen of Europe" is a myth; national cultures and tastes cannot be homogenized. With many different languages and distinctive national customs and cultures, companies trying to sell in Europe must thread their way through a maze of varying national preferences. These and other challenges lie ahead, along with numerous opportunities.

UPS is one of many firms experiencing this double-edged sword. Its managers realize that Europe is still virgin territory for service companies, and they expect revenue to grow by 15 percent a year there. However, UPS has run into many conflicts, both practical and cultural. Some of the surprises "Big Brown" experienced as it put its brown uniforms on 25,000 Europeans and sprayed brown paint on 10,000 delivery trucks around Europe include the following:

> *Indignation in France, when drivers were told they couldn't have wine with lunch; protests in Britain, when drivers' dogs were banned from delivery trucks; dismay in Spain, when it was found that the brown UPS trucks resembled the local hearses; and shock in Germany, when brown shirts were required for the first time since 1945.*[70]

Meanwhile, adventurous European businesses are spreading their wings across neighboring countries as they realize that open markets can offer as much growth and profitability as does protectionism—probably more. The Dutch willingness to surrender KLM to a holding company based in Paris is driven not only by the logic of European integration, but also by the promise of a long-overdue deregulation of the trans-Atlantic market.[71]

In one of Europe's biggest mergers, the Zeneca Group P.L.C. of Britain acquired Astra A.B., of Sweden. The resulting pharmaceutical giant was deemed necessary to fund new drug research and to compete in a market dominated by U.S. corporations. Early European mergers were dominated by British companies. But now that Continental European companies will have their shares denominated in euros, there will likely be more cross-border deals among those countries because they will be free of currency-exchange problems.[72]

Companies within the EU are gaining great advantages by competing in a continental-scale market and thereby avoiding duplication of administrative procedures, production, marketing, and distribution. The Italian company Benneton Group SPA is one such company—competing by being technologically efficient. For insiders, a single EU internal market means greater efficiencies and greater economic growth through economies of scale and the removal of barriers, with the consequent lowering of unit costs.

Companies based outside the EU enjoy the same advantages if they have a subsidiary in at least one member state, but they sometimes feel discrimination simply because they are outside what, for the member states, is a domestic market. In other words, the EU has a protectionist wall—of tariffs, quotas, local content laws, and competitive tactics—to keep out the United States and Japan. However, the EU has also created opportunities for nonmembers. Many companies, especially MNCs, start from a better position than some firms based inside the community because of (1) their superior competitiveness and research and development, (2) an existing foothold in the market, and (3) reduced operating expenses (one subsidiary for the whole EU instead of several). But European harmonized standards, while seeking to eliminate trade barriers within Europe, serve to limit access to EU markets by outside companies through the standardized specifications of products allowed to be sold in Europe. The harmonization laws set minimum standards for exports and imports that are EU-wide. However, those standards also frequently hinder European companies from efficient sourcing of raw materials or component parts from "foreign" companies.

Opinions differ about the long-term impact on U.S. firms: The EU could unify its markets, adversely affecting some U.S. industries; market access could be reduced; and demands for reciprocal market access in the United States might ensue. In November 2003, for example, when President Bush imposed tariffs on steel imports, the WTO ruled that the tariffs were illegal and authorized European and Asian nations to impose retaliatory tariffs against the United states. Not long after, President Bush was forced to reverse himself and lift the tariffs.[73]

Others feel that the new single market provides little threat to and considerable opportunity for Americans. Many U.S. firms (in anticipation of protectionism) have invested in Europe since the beginning of the Common Market in 1958, and they now feel satisfied with their current positions. Indeed, U.S. companies (GE, Dow, 3M, Hewlett-Packard) that already have well-established European presences enjoy the same free flow of goods, services, capital, and people as Europeans. It is clear, though, that the EU Competition Commissioner, is keeping a keen eye on any anticompetitive tactics from abroad. In fact, in March 2004, the EU Commission ordered Microsoft to "discontinue abuses of its dominant market position."[74]

Those "foreign" companies not yet established in Europe must examine the EU internal market to decide on their most effective "European strategy." Many firms are opting for joint ventures with European partners, sacrificing their usual preference of 100 percent ownership (or majority control) to extend operations around Europe. This strategy also opens doors to markets dominated by public procurement, as with the AT&T–Philips venture to produce telecommunications equipment. But for a number of firms—both foreign and European—operating in Western Europe, at least, has become cost prohibitive. The average Western European earns more, works fewer hours, takes longer vacations, and receives more social entitlements and job protection than workers in Asia and North America. European MNCs have the highest labor and taxation costs among the TRIAD nations.[75] Siemens AG of Germany, for example, shifted almost all its semiconductor assembly work from its plants in Germany—where it was not permitted to operate around the clock or on weekends—to a plant in Singapore, where it operates twenty-four hours a day, 365 days a year, and pays $4.40 an hour for workers.[76]

Suzuki, Toyota, Nissan, and other Japanese companies are also experiencing the dilemma of operating in Europe. They are reluctant to freely pour yen into Europe, but they want to keep a foothold in the market. Suzuki, for example, found that in its Spanish plant it took five times the number of workers and cost 46 percent more to produce a Suzuki Samurai than in its Japanese plants.

Strategic Choice

The strategic choice of one or more of the entry strategies will depend on (1) a critical evaluation of the advantages (and disadvantages) of each in relation to the firm's capabilities, (2) the critical environmental factors, and (3) the contribution that each choice would make to the overall mission and objectives of the company. Exhibit 6-7 summarized the advantages and the critical success factors for each entry strategy discussed. However, when it comes down to a choice of entry strategy or strategies for a particular company, more specific factors relating to that firm's situation must be taken into account. These include factors relating to the firm itself, the industry in which it operates, location factors, and venture-specific factors, as summarized in Exhibit 6-8.

After consideration of the factors for the firm as shown in Exhibit 6-8, as well as what is available and legal in the desired location, some entry strategies will no doubt fall out of the feasibility zone. With those options remaining, then, strategic planners need to decide which factors are more important to the firm than others. One method is to develop a weighted assessment to compare the overall impact of factors such as those in Exhibit 6-7, relative to the industry, the location, and the specific venture—on each entry strategy. Specific evaluation ratings, of course, would depend on the country conditions at a given point in time, the nature of the industry, and the focal company.

Based on a study of more than 10,000 foreign entry activities into China between 1979 and 1998, Pan and Tse concluded that managers tend to follow a hierarchy of decision-sequence in choosing an entry mode. As depicted in Exhibit 6-9, managers first decide between equity-based and nonequity based. Then, equity modes are split into wholly owned operations and equity joint ventures (EJVs); nonequity modes are divided into contractual agreements and export. Pan and Tse found that the location choice—specifically the level of country risk—was the primary influence factor at the level of deciding between equity and nonequity modes. Host-country government incentives also encouraged the choice of equity mode.[77]

EXHIBIT 6-8   Factors Affecting Choice of International Entry Mode

Factor Category	Examples
Firm factors	International experience
	Core competencies
	Core capabilities
	National culture of home country
	Corporate culture
	Firm strategy, goals, and motivation
Industry factors	Industry globalization
	Industry growth rate
	Technical intensity of industry
Location factors	Extent of scale and location economies
	Country risk
	Cultural distance
	Knowledge of local market
	Potential of local market
	Competition in local market
Venture-specific factors	Value of firm—assets risked in foreign location
	Extent to which know-how involved in venture is informal (tacit)
	Costs of making or enforcing contracts with local partners
	Size of planned foreign venture
	Intent to conduct research and development with local partners

SOURCE: Excerpted and adapted from International Management—Concepts and Cases by A. V. Phatak, pp. 270–275. Copyright © 1997 South-Western College Publishing, Cincinnati, Ohio, a division of International Thomson Publishing Inc.

EXHIBIT 6-9 A Hierarchical Model of Choice of Entry Modes

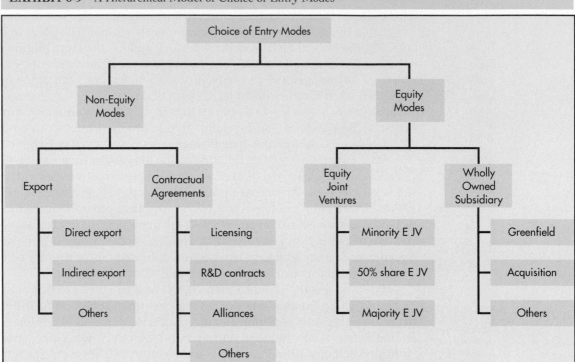

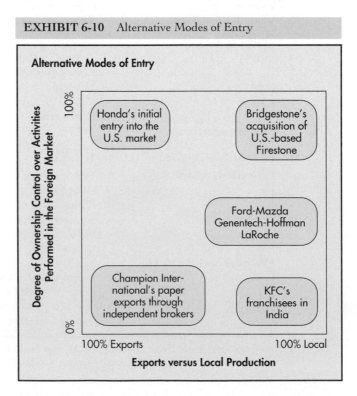

SOURCE: Yigang Pan and David K. Tse, "The Hierarchical Model of Market Entry Modes," *Journal of International Business Studies*, 31, no. 4 (4th Quarter 2000): 535–554.

Gupta and Govindarajan also propose a hierarchy of decision factors but consider two initial choice levels. The first is the extent to which the firm will export or produce locally; the second is the extent of ownership control over activities that will be performed locally in the target market.[78] As shown in Exhibit 6-10, there is an array of choice combinations

EXHIBIT 6-10 Alternative Modes of Entry

SOURCE: Anil K. Gupta and Vijay Gorindarajan, "Managing Global Expansion: A Conceptual Framework," *Business Horizons*, March/April 2000, pp. 45–54.

within those two dimensions. Gupta and Govindarajan point out that, among the many factors to take into account, alliance-based entry modes are more suitable under the following conditions:

- Physical, linguistic, and cultural distance between the home and host countries is high.
- The subsidiary would have low operational integration with the rest of the multinational operations.
- The risk of asymmetric learning by the partner is low.
- The company is short of capital.
- Government regulations require local equity participation.[79]

The choice of entry strategy for McDonald's, for example, varies around the world according to the prevailing conditions in each country. With its 4,700 foreign stores, McDonald's is, according to Fortune, "a virtual blueprint for taking a service organization global."[80] CEO Mike Quinlan notes that, in Europe, the company prefers wholly owned subsidiaries, since European markets are similar to those in the United States and can be run similarly. Those subsidiaries in the United States both operate company-owned stores and license out franchises. Approximately 70 percent of McDonald's stores around the world are franchised. In Asia, joint ventures are preferred so as to take advantage of partners' contacts and local expertise, and their ability to negotiate with bureaucracies such as the Chinese government. Headed by billionaire Den Fujita, McDonald's has more than 1,000 stores in Japan; in China it had 23 stores in 1994, with more planned, in spite of conflicts with the Chinese government, such as when it made McDonald's move from its leased Tiananmen Square restaurant. In other markets, such as in Saudi Arabia, McDonald's prefers to limit its equity risk by licensing the name—adding strict quality standards—and keeping an option to buy later. Some of McDonald's implementation policies are presented in Chapter 7.

Timing Entry and Scheduling Expansions

As with McDonald's, international strategic formulation requires a long-term perspective. Entry strategies, therefore, need to be conceived as part of a well-designed, overall plan. In the past, many companies have decided on a particular means of entry that seemed appropriate at the time, only to find later that it was shortsighted. For instance, if a company initially chooses to license a host-country company to produce a product, then later decides that the market is large enough to warrant its own production facility, this new strategy will no longer be feasible because the local host-country company already owns the rights.[81]

The Influence of Culture on Strategic Choice

In addition, strategic choices at various levels often are influenced by cultural factors, such as a long-term versus a short-term perspective. Hofstede found that most people in such countries as China and Japan generally had a longer-term horizon than those in Canada and the United States.[82] Whereas Americans, then, might make strategic choices with a heavy emphasis on short-term profits, the Japanese are known to be more patient in sacrificing short-term results in order to build for the future with investment, research and development, and market share.

Risk orientation was also found to explain the choice between equity and nonequity modes.[83] Risk orientation relates to Hofstede's uncertainty avoidance dimension.[84] Firms from countries where, generally speaking, people tend to avoid uncertainty (for example, Latin American and African countries) tend to prefer nonequity entry modes to minimize exposure to risk. Managers from firms from low-uncertainty avoidance countries are more willing to take risks and are, therefore, more likely to adopt equity entry modes.[85]

Choice of equity versus nonequity mode has also been found to be related to level of power distance. According to Hofstede, a high power-distance country (such as Arab countries and Japan) is one where people observe interpersonal inequality and hierarchy.[86] Pan and Tse found that firms from countries tending toward high power distance are more likely to use equity modes of entry abroad.[87]

These are but a few of the examples of the relationships between culture and the choices that are made in the strategic planning and implementation phase. They serve to remind us that it is people who make those decisions and that the ways people think, feel, and act are based on their ingrained societal culture. People bring that context to work, and it influences their propensity toward or against certain types of decisions.

CONCLUSION

The process of strategic formulation for global competitiveness is a daunting task in the volatile international arena and is further complicated by the difficulties involved in acquiring timely and credible information. However, early insight into global developments provides a critical advantage in positioning a firm for future success.

When an entry strategy is selected, the international manager focuses on translating strategic plans into actual operations. Often this involves strategic alliances; always it involves functional level activities for **strategic implementation**. These subjects are covered in Chapter 7.

Summary of Key Points

1. Companies "go international" for many reasons, including reactive ones, such as international competition, trade barriers, and customer demands. Proactive reasons include seeking economies of scale, new international markets, resource access, cost savings, and local incentives.

2. International expansion and the resulting realization of a firm's strategy are the product of both rational planning and responding to emergent opportunities.

3. The steps in the rational planning process for developing an international corporate strategy comprise defining the mission and objectives of the firm, scanning the environment for threats and opportunities, assessing the internal strengths and weaknesses of the firm, considering alternative international entry strategies, and deciding on strategy. The strategic management process is completed by putting into place the operational plans necessary to implement the strategy and then setting up control and evaluation procedures.

4. Competitive analysis is an assessment of how a firm's strengths and weaknesses vis-à-vis those of its competitors affect the opportunities and threats in the international environment. Such assessment allows the firm to determine where the company has distinctive competences that will give it strategic advantage or where problem areas exist.

5. Corporate-level strategic approaches to international competitiveness include globalization and regionalization. Many MNCs have developed to the point of using an integrative global strategy. Entry and ownership strategies are exporting, licensing, franchising, contract manufacturing, outsourcing services, turnkey operations, management contracts, joint ventures, and fully owned subsidiaries. Critical environmental and operational factors for implementation must be taken into account.

6. Companies of all sizes are increasingly looking to the Internet as a means of expanding their global operations, but localizing Internet operations is complex.

Discussion Questions

1. Discuss why companies "go international," giving specific reactive and proactive reasons.

2. Discuss the ways in which managers arrive at new strategic directions—formal and informal. Which is the best?

3. Explain the process of environmental assessment. What are the major international variables to consider in the scanning process? Discuss the levels of environmental monitoring that should be conducted. How well do you think managers conduct environmental assessment?

4. How can managers assess the potential relative competitive position of their firm in order to decide on new strategic directions?

5. Discuss the relative advantages of globalization versus regionalization.

6. What are the relative merits of the entry strategies discussed in this chapter? What is their role in an integrative global strategy?

7. Discuss the considerations in strategic choice, including the typical stages of the MNC and the need for a long-term global perspective.

Application Exercises

1. Choose a company in the microcomputer industry or a chain in the fast-food industry. In small groups, conduct a multilevel environmental analysis, describing the major variables involved, the relative impact of specific threats and opportunities, and the critical environmental factors to be considered. The group findings can then be presented to the class, allowing a specific time period for each group so that comparison and debate of different group perspectives can follow. Be prepared to state what regions or specific countries you are interested in and give your rationale.

2. In small groups, discuss among yourselves and then debate with the other groups the relative merits of the alternative entry strategies for the company and countries you chose in question 1. You should be able to make a specific choice and defend that decision.

3. For this exercise, research (individually or in small groups) a company with international operations and find out the kinds of entry strategies the firm has used. Present the information you find, in writing or verbally to the class, describing the nature of the company's international operations, its motivations, its entry strategies, the kinds of implementation problems the firm has run into, and how those problems have been dealt with.

Experiential Exercise

In groups of four, develop a strategic analysis for a type of company that is considering entry into Russia. Which entry strategies seem most appropriate? Share your results with the class.

Internet Resources

Visit the Deresky companion Web site at www.prenhall.com/Deresky for this chapter's Internet resources.

Vodafone U.K. in 2004–2005 — Changing Competition and Global Strategies

Vodafone is a UK-based wireless company that was founded in 1985 after a spin-off from Racal Electronics Group. Since its inception, Vodafone has transformed itself from an unknown wireless company into one of the largest mobile telecommunications and network companies in the world. In 1986, Vodafone had 63,000 customers in the UK. By the end of December 2003, the company had over 130 million customers and was the industry's truly global brand having operations in 26 countries. The company was led by its entrepreneur, CEO Sir Christopher Gent. Unlike other wireless operators, Sir Gent sought an aggressive global expansion since the wireless business was booming in global markets.[1] In 1993, Vodafone Group International was formed to enter into international markets. It is interesting to note that by 2000, the company had acquired some high-profile wireless companies that included AirTouch (US), Mannesmann (Germany), and Omnitel Pronto Italia. In 1999, Vodafone became even more famous for its hostile takeover of Germany's Mannesmann, paying $180 billion for the acquisition. In North America, Vodafone owns 44.3 percent of Verizon, the second largest wireless company in the U.S.

In 2003, Vodafone Group's revenues surpassed $47.9 billion although the company showed a loss $15.5 billion because of its acquisitions and restructuring. In 2004, Vodafone's market capitalization stood at $174.6 billion and was ranked third in market value in the UK.[2]

Previously in 2001, Vodafone's market value surpassed $227.15 billion. In the late nineties, Vodafone made a multitude of overseas acquisitions that made the company one of the largest wireless companies in the world. The company offers mobile services such as Vodafone live, mobile connect card, and mobile office.[3] Like Japan's NTT DoCoMo, Vodafone offers one of the best wireless technologies and is a competitive player in the global wireless industry. In its growth stage, the company immensely benefited from its first-mover advantage, unique technology, and an entrepreneurial culture. In addition, Vodafone's marvelous growth was the result of its niche-oriented strategies, global demographics, and strong business and consumer demand. In 2001, Vodafone's market share was evident from the fact that at the global level, 25 percent of global wireless consumers used the company's networks or its affiliated companies.[4]

Developments in 2004

In January 2004, AT&T Wireless, with a market value of $22 billion, was placed for a possible merger or an acquisition. Many global companies such as NTT DoCoMo, Nextel, Cingular, and Vodafone showed interest in AT&T wireless. During the bidding process, AT&T Wireless' shares rose 15 percent. Vodafone was part of the bidding process for AT&T Wireless and made an offer of $14.50 per share. Vodafone's strong interest in AT&T Wireless was attributed to its lack of visibility in North America although the company maintained a 43 percent stake in Verizon. Eventually, Cingular ended up acquiring AT&T Wireless for $41 billion. Losing AT&T Wireless and having no visibility in North America was a setback for Vodafone.

As of 2004, Vodafone's global strategy continues to be shaky and weak since the company lost its bid for Cingular. Since its inception, Vodafone's major global strategy was to seek majority ownership in its global markets that brought control and maneuverability. In 2004, Vodafone maintained a majority ownership in ten countries and minority stake in 14 markets. In addition, the company had business partners in 11 countries. During Gent's tenure, Vodafone expanded worldwide by seeking acquisitions worth $72 billion although the company lost $45 billion because of stagnant markets and the Internet bubble. In July 2003, Sir Gent resigned from the company and Arun Sarin was made the new CEO of Vodafone. Sarin previously worked for AirTouch, another wireless operator from the U.S. The board selected Sarin because of his earlier experience with Vodafone as a non-executive director. Critics claim that Sir Gent left the company in poor financial health because of a massive global expansion.[5]

Market Expansion, Industry Problems and Global Strategies

In today's competitive world, companies need well defined global strategies. No two markets are same. Changes may be needed in a company's operations to standardize and adapt to local conditions.[6] The global mobile telephone industry is a $340 billion industry. In the last five years, the industry has been growing at a fast pace in North America and other parts of the world. Like other global players in this industry, Vodafone is uniquely positioned to benefit from the growing consumer demand. On the other hand,

SOURCE: Prepared exclusively for this book by Syed Tariq Anwar, Professor, West Texas A&M University. Copyright © 2004 by Syed Tariq Anwar

*The material in this case is intended to be used as a basis for classroom/academic discussion rather than to illustrate either effective or ineffective handling of a managerial situation or business practices.

the company faces problems that may delay its growth in the coming years. Some of the problems are as follows:[7]

1. Unlike other global and national players, Vodafone lacks visibility in North America. As mentioned earlier, Vodafone was unsuccessful in acquiring AT&T Wireless and lost to Cingular in the bidding process although the company continues to keep its low-profile 43 percent stake in Verizon.

2. Vodafone's aggressive expansion in the European and other markets has brought debt and other growth and logistical problems.

3. Since 2002, Vodafone's shares have gone down because of the changes in its management structure. The company's investment in the area of 3G (third generation) has been a drag on the company although Vodafone plans on introducing this technology in the autumn of 2004.

4. Global wireless markets have become highly competitive and may saturate in the developed world unless companies introduce new technologies.[8]

5. With the arrival of its new CEO in 2003, Vodafone is expected to revive its global ambitions although immediate growth in 2004/2005 may not be possible since it failed to acquire Cingular. The company's early-mover knowledge in global markets and reliable product lines are its strong asset in Europe, Asia and Latin America.

6. The wireless industry and its affiliated Web-based markets at the global level is a complex area that is hindered by national regulatory barriers and country-specific standards. Vodafone and other wireless operators may face these hurdles when seeking future acquisitions and global expansion.[9]

7. Some analysts feel that Vodafone's high profile global expansion may have backfired the company since it drew so much publicity, especially in Europe after Mannesmann's acquisition.

8. Since 1998, Vodafone has not been able to establish a strong market share in Japan because of NTT DoCoMo which is a successful wireless company and commands a strong brand loyalty in Japan.

Developments in 2004/2005

As of April 2004, Vodafone is in a strong position to seek global expansion and introduce its 3G technology and

TABLE 1   Vodafone's Equity Interests and Operations (as of 2004)

	Customers ('000s)	Ownership Status
A. Ownership Stake of 50 Percent or More:		
Belgium	1,067	A
France	5,931	A
Germany	23,780	S
Poland	949	A
Romania	537	A
Switzerland	3,635	A
Kenya	303	A
South Africa	2,756	A
Japan	10,140	S
China	4,048	I
B. Ownership Stake of Less than 50 Percent:		
Albania	393	S
Australia	2,627	S
Greece	2,373	S
Hungary	1,061	S
Ireland	1,803	S
Italy	15,345	S
Malta	158	S
Netherlands	3,312	S
Portugal	3,243	S
Spain	9,399	S
Sweden	1,368	S
Great Britain	13,483	N/A
Egypt	1,729	S
U.S.	15,960	A
C. Local Partners and Affiliates in:		
Austria, Croatia, Denmark, Estonia, Finland, Iceland, Lithuania, Slovenia, Bahrain, Kuwait and Luxembourg		

SOURCE: *Financial Times.* (2003), "Brand is a Big Issue: When People Think Mobile Products and Services, we Want them to go to Vodafone," (December 22), p. 9; *The Wall Street Journal.* (2004), "Vodafone Affirms Ties to Verizon", (February 18), p. A10.

Notes: A: Associate; S: Subsidiary; I: Investment; NA: Not Applicable.

other mobile services. To survive and expand in one of the fiercest markets, the following changes may be expected from the company:

A. *Global Acquisitions and Alliances*: Today's Vodafone is more comfortable in making alliances and joint ventures. Previously, the company made alliances in many markets (see Table 1). Currently, Vodafone has 43 percent equity in Verizon that is a good, but low profile entry into the U.S. market.

B. *Issues of 3rd Generation Wireless Technology*: Vodafone plans on introducing its 3G technology in 2004. This move may act as an added value to the company since new products are becoming extremely important in the wireless sector.

C. *Changing Competition, New Products and Global Markets*: As expected, in North America, Europe and Japan, Vodafone has faced a heightened competition because of established players such as NTT DoCoMo, Cingular, Sprint, Deutsche Telecom, and France Telecom. For this reason, Vodafone is expected to centralize its new product development process and coordinate its far-flung operations in an efficient manner. During the tenure of Sir Gent, the company sought so many acquisitions that it lost control of the business model. The new CEO intends to put more emphasis on the company brand by coordinating its global strategies.[10]

In conclusion, Vodafone is a classic mobile phone company because of its unique history, aggressive acquisitions, and worldwide growth. Right from its inception, the company has been the first-mover in many markets. Vodafone's future expansion and global strategy has been affected by the dot-com bubble but continues to accumulate a strong share in the wireless industry. In the coming years, Vodafone will continue to play a major role in the wireless industry along with other players. *The Economist* correctly commented on Vodafone CEO's future global plans:

> *"Losing AT&T Wireless was a setback for the Vodafone chief. But he sees business as long game—. In simple terms, that means concentrating on wireless broadband; capturing new markets; launching 3G phones; and branding Vodafone, in his words, as the Coke or McDonald's of the mobile industry."*[11]

CASE QUESTIONS

1. What are your views of Vodafone's position in the global mobile phone industry?
2. Analyze and evaluate Vodafone's market niche with a SWOT (strengths, weaknesses, opportunities and threats) analysis.
3. What specific global strategies does Vodafone need to undertake in the next three years to be one of the key players in the wireless industry?
4. Compare and contrast Vodafone and other major wireless companies from Europe, North America and Asia regarding their global strategies, expansion, and new products.

ENDNOTES

[1] Merriden, Trevor. (2003), *Rollercoaster: The Turbulent Life and Times of Vodafone and Chris Gent,* Oxford, UK: Capstone Publishing, Ltd.

[2] *Forbes.* (2004), "*Forbes* 2000: The World's Leading Companies", (April 12), pp. 145–224.

[3] See: *Vodafone Group Plc.* (2004), www.vodafone.com.

[4] For detail, see: Anwar, Syed T. (2002), "NTT DoCoMo and M-Commerce: A Case Study in Market Expansion and Global Strategy," *Thunderbird International Business Review,* Vol. 44, No. 1, pp. 139–164; Anwar, Syed T. (2003), "Vodafone and the wireless industry: A case in market expansion and global strategy," *Journal of Business and Industrial Marketing,* Vol. 18, No. 3, pp. 270–286; also see: Kodama, Mitsuru. (2003), "Strategic community-based theory of firms: Case Study of NTT DoCoMo," *Journal of High Technology Management Research,* Vol. 14, pp. 307–330.

[5] For detail, see: *The Economist.* (2003), "Face value: A new voice at Vodafone," (August 2), p. 60; *The Economist.* (2003), "Beyond the bubble: A survey of telecoms," (October 11), pp. 1–22; *The Economist.* (2004), "Vodafone's dilemma," (November 27), pp. 74; *Financial Times.* (2003), "'Brand is a big issue: When people think mobile products and services, we want them to go to Vodafone'" (December 22), p. 9; *Financial Times.* (2004), "A shrewd operator," (February 21/22), p. 7; *The Wall Street Journal.* (2004), Big-name mergers won't ease crowding in cellphone industry," (February 13), pp. A1&A5; *The Wall Street Journal.* (2004), "Cingular deal will reshape industry," (February 18), pp. A1&A11; *The Wall Street Journal.* (2004), Vodafone affirms ties to Verizon," (February 18), p. A10; *The Wall Street Journal.* (2004), "Vodafone holds on in the U.S.," February 25, p. B2.

[6] For more discussion, see: Yip, G. S. (2003). *Total Global Strategy II,* New York: Prentice Hall; Also see: Moore, K. and Rugman, A. (2002), Don't Think Global - Think Regional, *Strategy & Business,* IIIrd quarter <www.strategy-business.com>; Rugman, A. (2001). *The End of Globalization,* New York: AMACOM; *MIT Sloan Management Review.* (2003), The Myth of Globalization? Winter, p. 11.

[7] Anwar, S. T. (2002, 2003), op. cit.

[8] *Standard & Poor's Industry Surveys.* Op. cit.

[9] For more discussion, see: *The Economist.* (2003), "Spread Betting", (June 21), pp. 22–24; *The Economist,* (2003), "Beyond the Bubble: A Survey of Telecoms," (October 11), pp. 1–22; *The Wall Street Journal.* (2004), China Will Keep Pursuing Digital Standards," (April 23), pp. B1&B2.

[10] *The Economist.* (2004), "Vodafone's Dilemma," (November 27), p. 74.

[11] *Financial Times.* (2004), "A Shrewd Operator," (February 21/22), p. 7.

CHAPTER 7

Global Alliances and Strategy Implementation

Outline

Opening Profile: France's Thomson and China's TCL to Join TV Units

PARIS, Nov. 3, 2003—If you can't beat them, join them.

Applying this adage, the French electronics company, Thomson, which sells appliances under the RCA brand in the United States, said in November that it would combine its television and DVD businesses with those of TCL International Holdings of China to form what would become the world's biggest maker of TV sets. The combined companies would make 18 million sets a year and generate annual revenue of $3 billion.

Under the agreement, Thomson would own 33 percent of the combined company, to be known as TCL-Thomson Electronics, and TCL would own the remaining 67 percent. Thomson would have the option to exchange its shares within 18 months for an undisclosed stake in TCL International, which would then own all of TCL-Thomson Electronics.

For Thomson, formerly known as *Thomson Multimedia*, the deal offers a way to resolve problems at its consumer electronics business, which has been unprofitable. In the first half of 2003 its consumer products, like televisions and DVD players, had a net loss of 81 million euros ($92.7 million).

To reverse the loss, Charles Dehelly, who took over as Thomson's chief executive, announced 1,200 job cuts in the United States, closing factories in Indiana and Ohio, to shift production to China.

For TCL, the second-largest television maker in China after the Sichuan Changhong Electric Company, the deal would provide a stepping stone into global markets, particularly Europe and the United States. TCL is based in Guangdong Province in China.

The chairman of TCL, Li Dongsheng, said the deal "fulfills our objective of being one of the top five players in multimedia electronics devices in the global marketplace."

The deal is the latest in a series of steps that has linked TCL more closely with Europe. TCL makes television sets for Royal Philips Electronics of the Netherlands and last year acquired the assets of a failed German maker of electronic goods, Schneider Technologies.

But the deal also gives TCL a foothold in the United States, where Thomson has about 18 percent of the market for television sets. The combined company would use the RCA brand in North America, the TCL brand in Asia, and Thomson in Europe.

The deal reflects the growing power of Chinese products in the European market.

For years, European corporations resisted more stubbornly than their American counterparts the influx of Asian products. Indeed, Thomson was largely established at the government's instigation to form a bridgehead against the Japanese invasion of the 1980's. Then, its chairman, Alain Gomez, a cigar-smoking former paratrooper, acquired, with the blessing of French politicians, television manufacturing assets around the world, including the consumer electronics business of *General Electric* in the United States, with its RCA subsidiary.

But competition in the European electronics market and the growing technical proficiency of Chinese products have forced companies like Thomson to make arrangements or face going under.

China's entry into the World Trade Organization, which has opened previously restricted markets in Europe and North America, has lent a sense of urgency to the situation. Thomson's chief financial officer, Julian Waldron, said in a conference call that Thomson had "already begun a major restructuring program of our consumer activities, and have announced charges the program will entail."

Indeed, the deal is tantamount to Thomson's exit from television manufacturing for all but the most technologically sophisticated models. Mr. Waldron said the deal with TCL would entail no new charges, and would enhance Thomson's 2004 results.

Thomson said it would hold on to a factory in Angers, in the west of France, where it would focus on developing and manufacturing newer display technologies, like plasma screens and flat screens with liquid crystal displays.

Investors cheered the deal, which had been expected. In Hong Kong, where TCL is traded, its shares gained almost 30 percent last week in anticipation of the deal. Shares in Thomson were up slightly in Paris, closing at 18.21 euros. The shares have gained almost 12 percent so far this year.

To offset the loss of TV manufacturing, Mr. Dehelly has been pushing Thomson into new services and technologies, like television studio equipment and devices and software for editing and handling images.

But some commentators questioned the wisdom of Thomson's exit. "Tomorrow or the day after, the Chinese competition will be found in those sectors, too," Le Monde said in a commentary. "Will Thomson have held onto enough of its knowledge and technical mastery to face it?"

Both Thomson and TCL make traditional television sets with cathode ray tubes, though these are expected to be replaced over the next decade by newer display technologies.

SOURCE: NYTimes.com, November 6, 2003, reprinted with permission.

STRATEGIC ALLIANCES

*It is no longer an era in which a single company can dominate any technology
or business by itself. The technology has become so advanced, and the markets
so complex, that you simply can't expect to be the best at the whole process
any longer.*

FUMIO SATO,
CEO, Toshiba Electronics[1]

Strategic alliances are partnerships between two or more firms that decide they can better pursue their mutual goals by combining their resources—financial, managerial, technological—as well as their existing distinctive competitive advantages. Alliances—often called *cooperative strategies*—are transition mechanisms that propel the partners' strategies forward in a turbulent environment faster than would be possible for each company alone.[2] Alliances typically fall under one of three categories: joint ventures, equity strategic alliances, and non-equity strategic alliances.[3]

Joint Ventures

Two or more companies create an independent company in a joint venture (JV). An example is the Nuumi Corporation, created as a joint venture between Toyota and General Motors, which gave GM access to Toyota's manufacturing expertise and provided Toyota with a manufacturing base in the United States.

Equity Strategic Alliances

Two or more partners have different relative ownership shares (equity percentages) in the new venture in an equity strategic alliance. As do most global manufacturers, Toyota has equity alliances with suppliers, subassemblers, and distributors; most of these are part of Toyota's network of internal family and financial links. Recently, GM's expansion strategy has comprised taking minority stakes in other companies around the world:

*GM executives tick off a list of benefits of their alliances: purchasing savings
from extra scale; diesel engines from Isuzu and Fiat; the new Saab; Suzuki's
recent agreement to sell Chevrolets in Japan; and the Agila small MPV, sold in
Europe as an Opel, but designed by Suzuki.*

FINANCIAL TIMES,
February 2, 2004[4]

GM's expansions strategy has been unique in the automotive industry, driven by skepticism about the benefits of big mergers, and no doubt reinforced by the problems resulting from the DaimlerChrysler merger.

A further example of equity strategic alliances is discussed in this chapter's opening profile, whereby France's Thomson owns 33 percent of the combined company, TCL-Thomson Electronics, and China's TCL owns the remaining 67 percent.[5]

Non-equity Strategic Alliances

Agreements are carried out through contract rather than ownership sharing in a non-equity strategic alliance. Such contracts are often with a firm's suppliers, distributors, or manufacturers, or they may be for purposes of marketing and information sharing, such as with many airline partnerships.

Global Strategic Alliances

Working partnerships between companies (often more than two) across national boundaries and increasingly across industries are referred to as global strategic alliances. A glance at the global airline industry, for example, tells us that global alliances have become a mainstay of competitive strategy:

*Not one airline is competing alone; each major U.S. carrier has established
strategic links with non-U.S. companies. Delta is linked with Swissair, Sabena, and
Austrian; American with British Airways, U.S. Airways, JAL, and Qantas;*

Northwest with Continental, KLM (which merged with Air France in 2003), and Alitalia; and United with SAS, Lufthansa, Air Canada, Thai, South African Airways, Varig, Singapore, Air New Zealand, and Ansett Australia.[6]

Alliances are also sometimes formed between a company and a foreign government, or among companies and governments. The European Airbus Industrie consortium comprises France's Aerospatiale and Germany's Daimler–Benz Aerospace, each with 37.9 percent of the business; British Aerospace has 20 percent, and Spain's Construcciones Aeronauticas has 4.2 percent.

Alliances may comprise full global partnerships, which are often joint ventures in which two or more companies, while retaining their national identities, develop a common, long-term strategy aimed at world leadership. Whereas such alliances have a broad agenda, others are formed for a narrow and specific function, including production, marketing, research and development, or financing. More recently, these have included electronic alliances, such as Covisint, which is redefining the entire system of car production and distribution through a common electronic marketplace (featured in E-Biz Box).

E-BIZ BOX

Covisint, LLC

Covisint is an e-business exchange developed by DaimlerChrysler AG, Ford, General Motors, Nissan, and Renault to meet the needs of the automotive industry. It is a multimember joint venture with those companies, and Commerce One and Oracle

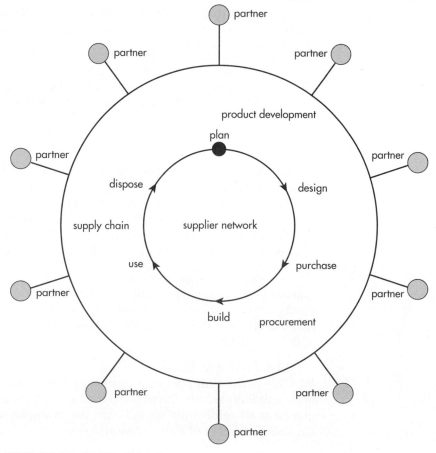

FIGURE 1. Covisint Overview

are members. Covisint provides original equipment manufacturers (OEMs) and suppliers the ability to reduce costs and bring efficiencies to their business operations. Covisint has headquarters in Amsterdam, Tokyo, and Southfield, Michigan.

Covisint has more than 250 customers on two continents engaged in activities on the exchange, including catalogs, auctions, quote management, and collaborative design. Its current product and service offerings are focused on procurement, supply chain, and product development solutions. The purpose of Covisint is to harness the power of Internet technology to create visibility within a company's supply chain—transforming the linear chain into a far more productive and efficient networked model. Furthermore, the company delivers build-to-order capability with proven, scalable, and secure technologies that reinforce customers' individual competitiveness. Internet technology speeds the flow of material through the supply chain, increases responses to consumer demand, and delivers new products to market faster than ever. Figure 1 presents an overview of Covisint's functions.

Four Japanese car manufacturers—Toyota, Mazda, Honda, and Mitsubishi Motors—are also planning to join the Covisint global automotive online exchange, whereas European-owned firms have been more reluctant to commit to Covisint. PSA Peugeot has already joined Covisint.* Covisint expects to generate $300 billion in car sales and save manufacturers up to $263 per car by 2005 as well as reduce delivery periods to a few days and give buyers the opportunity for customized car orders.**

*www.e4engineering.com, January 4, 2001.

**www.businessweek.com, October 14, 2000.

SOURCE: www.covisint.com, September 28, 2001.

Global and Cross-Border Alliances: Motivations and Benefits

1.   To avoid import barriers, licensing requirements, and other protectionist legislation. Japanese automotive manufacturers, for example, use alliances such as the GM–Toyota venture, or subsidiaries, to produce cars in the United States so as to avoid import quotas.

2.   To share the costs and risks of the research and development of new products and processes.   In the semiconductor industry, for example, where each new generation of memory chips is estimated to cost more than $1 billion to develop, those costs and the rapid technological evolution typically require the resources of more than one, or even two, firms. Intel, for example, has alliances with Samsung and NMB Semiconductor for technology (DRAM) development; Sun Microsystems has partners for its technology(RISC), including N. V. Philips, Fujitsu, and Texas Instruments. Toshiba, Japan's third largest electronics company, has more than two dozen major joint ventures and strategic alliances around the world, including partners such as Olivetti, Rhone-Poulenc, GEC Alstholm in Europe, LSI Logic in Canada, and Samsung in Korea. Fumio Sato, Toshiba's CEO, recognized long ago that a global strategy for a high-tech electronics company such as his necessitated joint ventures and strategic alliances.

3.   To gain access to specific markets, such as the EU, where regulations favor domestic companies.

> *Europe has taken 63 percent of the world's $292 billion worth of private equity mergers and acquisitions over the past four years—nearly twice that of the United States.*
>
> FINANCIAL TIMES,
> *November 17, 2003*[7]

Firms around the world are forming strategic alliances with European companies to bolster their chances of competing in the European Union (EU) and to gain access to markets in Eastern European countries as they open up to world business. The EU's new law, passed in November 2003, was intended to increase the opportunities for cross-border mergers and takeovers, for companies both within and outside of the EU.[8] U.S. companies protested that the law did not go far enough to open up a "fortress Europe," because hostile bids would be more difficult to pursue.[9] However, seven of the ten largest deals that Citigroup completed around the world in 2003, for example, were in Europe—including the $2 billion acquisition of British tavern chain Pubmaster.[10] Chun Joo Bum, chief executive of the Daewoo Electronics unit, acknowledges that he is seeking local partners in Europe for two reasons: (1) to provide sorely needed capital (a problem amid Asia's economic woes) and (2) to help Daewoo navigate Europe's still disparate markets, saying "I need to localize our management. It is not one market."[11]

Market entry into some countries may only be attained through alliances—typically joint ventures. South Korea, for example, has a limit of 18 percent on foreign investment in South Korean firms.

4. To reduce political risk while making inroads into a new market.

> *Carefully orchestrated partnerships with governments and other business groups are crucial to the [Disney] entertainment group's thrust into China and the rest of south-east Asia.*
>
> BOB IGER,
> *President and COO, Walt Disney[12]*

Hong Kong Disneyland is jointly owned by the Chinese government, which owns a 57 percent stake. Beijing is especially interested in promoting tourism through the venture, and in the new employment for the 5,000 workers Disney will employ directly, as well as the estimated 18,000 in related services.[13] Maytag Corporation, also determined to stay on the right side of the restrictive Chinese government while gaining market access, formed a joint venture with RSD, the Chinese appliance maker, to manufacture and market washing machines and refrigerators. Maytag also invested large amounts in jointly owned refrigeration products facilities to help RSD get into that market. Coca-Cola—a global player with large-scale alliances—is not beyond using some very small-scale alliances to be "political" in China. The company uses senior citizens in the party's neighborhood committees to sell Coke locally.

5. To gain rapid entry into a new or consolidating industry and to take advantage of synergies.

> *Disney now has 3.5m subscribers for content services, offered through Japan's largest mobile operators.*
>
> STEVE WADSWORTH,
> *President, Internet Division, Walt Disney[14]*

Technology is rapidly providing the means for the overlapping and merging of traditional industries such as entertainment, computers, and telecommunications in new digital-based systems, creating an information superhighway. Disney's business model of cellular partnerships and content sales, for example, created Disney mobile operations in Hong Kong, Taiwan, South Korea, Singapore and the Philippines.[15] The company uses joint venture partners such as the Hong Kong government, or licensees and distributors, such as Oriental Land and NTT DoCoMo.[16]

In many cases, technological developments are necessitating strategic alliances across industries in order for companies to gain rapid entry into areas in which they have no expertise or manufacturing capabilities. Competition is so fierce that they cannot wait to develop those resources alone. Many of these objectives, such as access to new technology and to new markets, are evident in AT&T's network of alliances around the world, as shown in Exhibit 7-1. Agreements with Japan's NEC, for example, give AT&T access to new semiconductor and chip-making technologies, helping it learn how to better integrate computers with communications. Another joint venture with Zenith Electronics will allow AT&T to co-develop the next generation of high-definition television (HDTV).[17]

Challenges in Implementing Global Alliances

> *Five years after Daimler-Benz acquired Chrysler to create DaimlerChrysler AG,. . . . DaimlerChrysler has become a German company and the struggling Chrysler division is run by executives dispatched from DaimlerChrysler's corporate headquarters in Stuttgart.*
>
> KIRK KERKORIAN,
> *November 28, 2003[18]*

EXHIBIT 7-1   AT&T's Alliance Strategy

Partner	Technology	Intent
NEC	Customized chips, computer-design tools	Learn new core technologies from NEC; sales position in Japan
	Mobile phones	Penetrate cellular phone markets; compatible standards
Mitsubishi	SRAM and gallium–arsenide chips	Increase sales in Japan; learn new semiconductor technologies
Italtel	Telecommunications	Expand beachhead in Europe
N.V. Philips	Circuit boards	Market and technology access; purchased 1990
Lucky-Gold Star	Fiber optics, telecommunications, circuits	Entry into Asian markets; technology-sharing agreement
Telefonics	Telecommunications and integrated circuits	Expand European production and marketing
Zenith Technology	High-definition television	Apply and learn digital compression
Intel	Personal computer networks and integrated circuits	Share manufacturing technology and capacity
		Develop UNIX computer operating system for local area networks
Hoya	Photomasks and semiconductor equipment	Develop ion-beam masks and mask design software in Japan and the United States
Mannesmann	Microwave radio gear and cellular phone technology	Serve as OEM supplier to German firm
Go Corp.	Pen-based computers and wireless networks	Set industry standards for telecommunications power and range
Olivetti	Personal computers	Failed in 1988
Eo Corp.	Personal communicator devices	Create new handheld computers
Matsushita	Microprocessors	Encourage new technology standards for Hobbit-based systems
NEC & Toshiba McCaw Cellular	Cellular telephones	Secure downstream market in the United States

SOURCE: D. Lei, "Offensive and Defensive Uses of Alliances," in Heidi Vernon-Wortzel and L. H. Wortzel, *Strategic Management in a Global Economy,* 3rd ed. (New York: John Wiley & Sons, 1997).

> *Daimler is in crisis talks with Hyundai, its South Korean partner, in a move that could see the German company left with no presence in the Asian car market (having abandoned its partner in Japan, Mitsubishi Motors (MMC)), and an increasingly tattered global strategy.*
>
> FINANCIAL TIMES,
> *April 27, 2004[19]*

Effective global alliances are usually tediously slow in the making but can be among the best mechanisms to implement strategies in global markets. In a highly competitive environment, alliances present a faster and less risky route to globalization. It is extremely complex to fashion such linkages, however, especially where many interconnecting systems are involved, forming intricate networks. Many alliances fail or end up in a takeover in which one partner swallows the other. McKinsey & Company, a consulting firm, surveyed 150 companies that had been in alliances and found that 75 percent of them had been taken over by Japanese partners. Problems with shared ownership, the integration of vastly different structures and systems, the distribution of power between the companies involved, and conflicts in their relative locus of decision making and control are but a few of the organizational issues that must be worked out. All these problems, as well as cultural differences, contributed to the declining situation of the DaimlerChrysler–AG alliance. The synergies expected from the alliance have proven elusive, and, as of 2004, Chrysler's losses were mounting, to the point that Kirk Kerkorian, largest shareholder of the premerger Chrysler, brought DaimlerChrysler to court. He contended that the 1998 transaction had been misrepresented as a "merger of equals", but that Juergen Schrempp, the German chairman and CEO of DaimlerChrysler, intended the deal to be a takeover, not a merger.[20] Now DaimlerChrysler is essentially a holding company run from Stuttgart that oversees separate business units, which share few products.

Often, the form of governance chosen for multinational firm alliances greatly influences their success, particularly in technologically intense fields such as pharmaceuticals, computers, and semiconductors. In a study of 153 new alliances, researchers found that the choice of the means of governance—whether a contractual agreement or a joint venture—depended on a desire to control information about proprietary technology.[21] Thus, joint ventures are often the chosen form for such alliances because they provide greater control and coordination in high-technology industries.

Cross-border partnerships, in particular, often become a "race to learn"—with the faster learner later dominating the alliance and rewriting its terms. In a real sense, an alliance becomes a new form of competition. In fact, according to researcher David Lei,

> *Perhaps the single greatest impediment managers face when seeking to learn or renew sources of competitive advantage is to realize that co-operation can represent another form of unintended competition, particularly to shape and apply new skills to future products and businesses.*[22]

All too often, cross-border allies have difficulty collaborating effectively, especially in competitively sensitive areas; this creates mistrust and secrecy, which then undermine the purpose of the alliance. The difficulty that they are dealing with is the dual nature of strategic alliances—the benefits of cooperation versus the dangers of introducing new competition through sharing their knowledge and technological skills about their mutual product or the manufacturing process. Managers may fear that they will lose the competitive advantage of the firm's proprietary technology or the specific skills that their personnel possess. One example of a situation of potential loss of proprietary technology affecting entire industries became apparent in January 2004 when China announced that foreign computer and chip makers selling various wireless devices there would have to use Chinese encryption software and co-produce their products with Chinese companies from a designated list.[23]

> *Foreign computer makers, led by American companies, have protested the decision. In addition to their concern about the separate standard, foreign companies are worried about the possible loss of intellectual property if they are forced to work with Chinese companies that have the potential to become competitors.*
>
> *The concern is about products such as DVD players; about half of the world's DVD players are now made in China. If China develops its own technical standards for the next generation of DVDs, it would be avoiding royalty payments to patent-holding corporations in Japan, Europe, and the United States, and in doing so fractures the world market.24*

The cumulative learning that a partner attains through the alliance could potentially be applied to other products or even other industries that are beyond the scope of the alliance, and therefore would hold no benefit to the partner holding the original knowledge.[25] As noted by Lei, the Japanese have far overtaken their U.S. allies in developing and applying new technologies to other uses. Examples are in the power equipment industry (e.g., Westinghouse–Mitsubishi), the office equipment industry (Kodak–Canon), and the consumer electronics industry (General Electric–Samsung). Some of the trade-offs of the duality of cross-border ventures are shown in Exhibit 7-2.

The enticing benefits of cross-border alliances often mask the many pitfalls involved. In addition to potential loss of technology and knowledge or skill base, other areas of incompatibility often arise, such as conflicting strategic goals and objectives, cultural clashes, and disputes over management and control systems. Sometimes it takes a while for such problems to evidence themselves, particularly if insufficient homework has been done in meetings between the two sides to work out the implementation

EXHIBIT 7-2   The Dual Role of Strategic Alliances

Cooperative	Competitive
Economies of scale in tangible assets (e.g., plant and equipment).	Opportunity to learn new intangible skills from partner, often tacit or organization embedded.
Upstream–downstream division of labor among partners.	Accelerate diffusion of industry standards and new technologies to erect barriers to entry.
Fill out product line with components or end products provided by supplier.	Deny technological and learning initiative to partner via outsourcing and long-term supply arrangements.
Limit investment risk when entering new markets or uncertain technological fields via shared resources.	Encircle existing competitors and preempt the rise of new competitors with alliance partners in "proxy wars" to control market access, distribution, and access to new technologies.
Create a "critical mass' to learn and develop new technologies to protect domestic, strategic industries.	Form clusters of learning among suppliers and related firms to avoid or reduce foreign dependence for critical inputs and skills.
Assist short-term corporate restructurings by lowering exit barriers in mature or declining industries.	Alliances serve as experiential platforms to "demature" and transform existing mature industries via new components, technologies, or skills to enhance the value of future growth options.

SOURCE: David Lei, "Offensive and Defensive Uses of Alliances," in Heidi Vernon-Wortzel and L. H. Wortzel, *Strategic Management in Global Economy,* 3rd ed. (New York: John Wiley & Sons, 1997).

details. The alliance between KLM Royal Dutch Airlines and Northwest Airlines linking their hubs in Detroit and Amsterdam, for example, resulted in a bitter feud among the top officials of both companies over methods of running an airline business—the European way or the American way—and over cultural differences between the companies, as well as a power struggle at the top over who should call the shots.[26]

Guidelines for Successful Alliances

Many difficulties arise in cross-border alliances in melding the national and corporate cultures of the parties, in overcoming language and communication barriers, and in building trust between the parties over how to share proprietary assets and management processes. Some basic guidelines, as follow, will help to minimize potential problems. However, nothing is as important as having a long "courtship" with a potential partner to establish compatibility strategically and interpersonally and set up a "prenuptial" plan with the prospective partner. Even setting up some pilot programs on a short-term basis for some of the planned combined activities can highlight areas that may become problematic.

1. Choose a partner with compatible strategic goals and objectives and with whom the alliance will result in synergies through the combined markets, technologies, and management cadre.
2. Seek alliances where complementary skills, products, and markets will result. If each partner brings distinctive skills and assets to the venture, there will be reduced potential for direct competition in end products and markets. In addition, each partner will begin the alliance in a balanced relationship.[27]
3. Work out with the partner how you will each deal with proprietary technology or competitively sensitive information—what will be shared and what will not, and how shared technology will be handled. Trust is an essential ingredient of an alliance, particularly in these areas; but this must be backed up by contractual agreements.
4. Recognize that most alliances last only a few years and will probably break up once a partner feels it has incorporated the skills and information it needs to go it alone. With this in mind, managers need to "learn thoroughly and rapidly about a partner's technology and management: transfer valuable ideas and practices promptly into one's own operations."[28]

Some of the opportunities and complexities in cross-border alliances are illustrated in the following Comparative Management in Focus box on joint ventures in the Russian Federation. Such alliances are further complicated by the different history of the two parties' economic systems and the resulting business practices.

Comparative Management in Focus

Joint Ventures in the Russian Federation

Map 7-1

We are in Russia for the long term. We still have confidence in the government of Russia. . . . Russia is a country in transition. The question is what direction is the transition going?

LORD JOHN BROWNE,
Chief Executive, British Petroleum, November 2003[29]

An improved climate in Russia in 2004 encouraged foreign companies to consider investing in international joint ventures (IJVs) there. With President Putin's improved fiscal management policies, Russia was regarded as more politically stable. New land, as well as new legal and labor laws, along with a more stable rouble, an underexploited natural resource potential, and a skilled, educated population of 145 million, make it an attractive market.[30] Those already taking advantage of those opportunities include 35,000 Western companies that have set up shop in Moscow alone and more than 20,000 joint ventures in Russia. Of those IJVs, 2,800 are U.S.–Russian. They include Caterpillar, IBM, GE, Ford, Hewlett-Packard, Pepsi-Co., Eastman Kodak, and AT&T, as well as thousands of smaller IJVs—primarily in software, hotels, and heavy industrial production. Many, like Bell Labs, are involved in research and development, taking advantage of the Russians' high-level education and technical capabilities. Oil companies in Russia, for example, are ready to sell a minority stake to foreigners to lessen their costs and add technical expertise. In 2004, however, considerable trouble continued to brew in the industry after President Putin jailed Mikhail Khodorkovsky when he tried to sell a major stake in his giant oil company, Yukos Oil (which he had purchased during the loans-for-shares privatization in 1995), to ExxonMobil. This was said to result from the failure to consult the Kremlin about a venture that would allow a foreign company substantial control over a strategic Russian resource.[31] Others felt it was a politically motivated move. However, it highlighted the risk of government interference in business ventures and was regarded as a test of the post-Soviet society's tumultuous encounter with capitalism. [32] As of July 2004, Khodorkovsky was in jail on charges of tax fraud, embezzlement, and other crimes, although Yukos had offered to pay $8 billion in back taxes, most of which was owned by Khodorkovsky. Yukos' executives claim that it is not about taxes, but rather that the government is trying to claim ownership of the oil company. The Russian authorities' announcement of an enforced sale of Yukos' main subsidiary provides a warning to potential foreign investors about whether their property rights would be honored. [33]

> *Powerful regional governors, aggressive commercial partners and competitors, substantial bureaucracy and corruption, and a shaky legal system subject to widespread abuse impose a heavy burden for those operating daily on the ground.[34]*

Clearly, there are still considerable roadblocks to successful IJVs in the Russian Federation. The overriding concern continues to be the possibility of a repeat of the 1998 economic collapse with the devalued ruble, the lack of debt and equity capital, and the nonconvertibility of currency, resulting in companies such as RJR Nabisco, withdrawing altogether. Most potential alliances were put on hold by Western companies. As a result of the economic problems, many Russian companies benefited by reinforcing their market positions, with some strong local players gaining a foothold, such as Will-Bill-Dann, which produces dairy products, canned vegetables, and juices.[35] Nevertheless, companies such as BP (British Petroleum) are positioning their companies for the long term. BP and Russia's TNK are launching a joint venture (TNK–BP Limited), creating the third-largest oil producer in Russia, with BP investing 5.65 billion euros in the venture, the largest investment by a foreign company in Russia.[36] The new holding creates Russia's largest multinational company. Investors noted of BP Chief Executive Sir John Browne, "He's got there early and he's shut the door on a lot of his Western peers. It's a risky deal, but oil always seems to be in risky parts of the world."[37]

Foreign companies in other industries have plans to enter or expand their operations in Russia. General Motors, for example, plans to make 25,000 Astra cars and 70,000 Nivas a year by 2005 as a joint venture with local carmaker AvtoVAZ in the southern Russian town of Togliatti. The quality of local supplies has been a problem, however, so GM hopes to attract its existing suppliers from the West into Russia.[38]

Most large global companies—accustomed to economic upheavals in Russia— have stuck to their long-term plans.[39] Gillette, for example, which has had a joint venture with Leninets, forming Petersburg Products International (PPI), since 1990, is one that stayed and continues its commitment there. But it was not without its problems during the difficult 1998–1999 period. The effective distribution systems it had painstakingly built up collapsed, as the partners' wholesalers and retailers ran out of money and stopped their orders.

> *Overnight, the ability to invoice and receive payment disappeared. So Gillette had to rebuild the distribution system and develop financial support for its suppliers, offering them credit to be paid upon their next orders.[40]*

Gillette now employs more than 500 people throughout Russia and has built another $40 million razor blade manufacturing plant near St. Petersburg. Other Western companies are trying to move into locally based production in order to cut down on the expenses of a lot of expatriate staff:

> *Danone, the French dairy group, opened its second Russian factory in 2000; Merloni, the Italian fridge manufacturer, bought Stinol, a local competitor with which it already had links; and in 2001, the Greek-based Chipita acquired a bakery in St. Petersburg.[41]*

Western companies willing to take the risk can pick up assets very cheaply because of the Russian need for hard currency, capital, new technology, and management skills.[42] Foreigners may now own 100 percent of a venture, although to get office space, supplies, and other essentials, it is often necessary to have the local partner own at least half. All registered citizens may now own and operate a business, and the governments in most parts of the Russian Federation are encouraging the privatization of businesses in order to move rapidly to a market economy—and to stave off economic disaster.

Exhibit 7-3 shows the joint venture relationship between a U.S. firm and a firm in the Russian Federation, the different goals that they bring to the venture, and the barriers caused by their different operating environments.[43]

The following are some suggestions that may help foreign companies minimize the risk of IJVs in the Russian Federation:

1. **Choose the Right Partner.** The primary reason for IJV failure is a poor match between partners—because of lack of compatible goals or strategy, because the Russian partner company is unreliable, or because it lacks the necessary licenses to either produce a product or to export it, or to be involved in development of natural resources. Check with regional government offices about whether the prospective partner has the requisite licenses, appropriate registrations, and reliable bank backing and history. Also check on the status of future rights to assets that were previously under the control of the state, such as those for property or natural resources, or such as a reserve of shareholdings for future privatization voucher holders.

   The choice of a Russian partner can make or break a venture. A local partner may come with risks: You could end up inheriting his *krysha*, or laundering money (*krysha* is the Russian term for paying for "protection").[44]

   Businesspeople must realize that there are established procedures for getting out of disputes with partners and that those procedures take place outside of the court system.

EXHIBIT 7-3   U.S. Firm–Russian Federation Firm Joint Venture

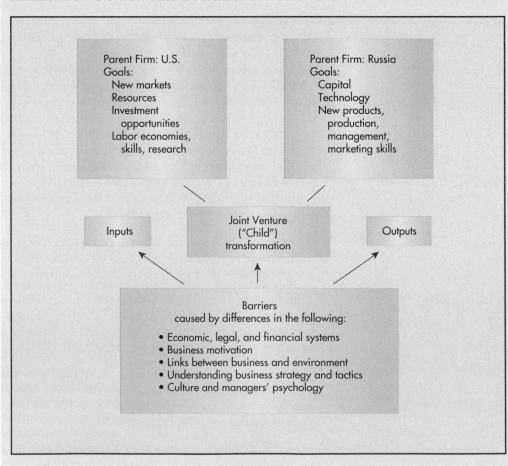

In Russia a handshake is more binding than a 100-page legal document, so disputes are best solved quietly—often through the mediation of *kryshas*. Paul Tatum, U.S. hotel developer, ignored those procedures to his peril. When he took on his fight for control of the Radisson Slavyanskaya Hotel in 1997, he was gunned down in front of his two bodyguards.

2. **Find the Right Local General Manager.**   In a survey of thirty-three successful joint ventures, Lawrence and Vlachoutsicos found that delegating to the right Russian (or Ukrainian, etc.) executive is the secret to success for an IJV because that manager is familiar with the local networks and ministries, the suppliers and markets, and the maze of regulatory issues involved.[45] In addition, local managers are part of the culture of the Russian *mir*, or collective. This involves direct bonds of loyalty between managers and employees, hands-on management practices, and wide consultation but top-down final decision making.

3. **Choose the Right Location.**   The political risk of investments in Russia decreases from south to north and west to east, according to the consultant Vladimir Kvint. Because most people in Siberia have stayed far away from communism and the centers of power and political turmoil in the European parts of Russia, investments there and along the Pacific Coast are more reliable. These areas also have considerable natural resources available. Now that regional leaders have more autonomy, and some have set up economic zones with tax privileges, Kvint recommends that IJVs branch out, away from Moscow to those areas, and to the Russian Far East, where many Japanese IJVs have set up.

4. **Control the IJV.**   The venture's best chance of success is to be vertically integrated to retain control of supplies and access to customers. McDonald's, for example, controlled these elements as well as the quality of its inputs for its Russian restaurants by setting up its own farms for potatoes and beef.

STRATEGIC IMPLEMENTATION

Implementation McDonald's Style

- Form paradigm-busting arrangements with suppliers.
- Know a country's culture before you hit the beach.
- Hire locals whenever possible.
- Maximize autonomy.
- Tweak the standard menu only slightly from place to place.
- Keep pricing low to build market share. Profits will follow when economies of scale kick in.[46]

Decisions regarding global alliances and entry strategies must now be put into motion with the next stage of planning: strategic implementation. Implementation plans are detailed and pervade the entire organization because they entail setting up overall policies, administrative responsibilities, and schedules throughout the organization to enact the selected strategy and to make sure it works. In the case of a merger or IJV, this process requires compromising and blending procedures among two or more companies and is extremely complex. The importance of the implementation phase of the strategic management process cannot be overemphasized. Until they are put into operation, strategic plans remain abstract ideas: verbal or printed proposals that have no effect on the organization.

Successful implementation requires the orchestration of many variables into a cohesive system that complements the desired strategy—that is, a *system of fits* that will facilitate the actual working of the strategic plan. In this way, the structure, systems, and processes of the firm are coordinated and set into motion by a system of management by objectives (MBO), with the primary objective being the fulfillment of strategy. Managers must review the organizational structure and, if necessary, change it to facilitate the administration of the strategy and to coordinate activities in a particular location with headquarters (as discussed further in Chapter 8). In addition to ensuring the strategy–structure fit, managers must allocate resources to make the strategy work, budgeting money, facilities, equipment, people, and other support. Increasingly, that support necessitates a unified technology infrastructure in order to coordinate diverse businesses around the world and to satisfy the need for current gnd reliable information. An efficient technology infrastructure can provide a strategic advantage in a globally competitive environment.

Jack Welch, while CEO of General Electric (he retired in late 2001), used to refer to his e-commerce initiative, saying, "It will change relationships with suppliers. Within 18 months, all our suppliers will supply us on the Internet, or they won't do business with us."[47]

An overarching factor affecting all the other variables necessary for successful implementation is that of leadership; it is people, after all, who make things happen. The firm's leaders must skillfully guide employees and processes in the desired direction. Managers with different combinations of experience, education, abilities, and personality tend to be more suited to implementing certain strategies.[48] In an equity-sharing alliance, sorting out which top managers in each company will be in which position is a sensitive matter. Who in which company will be CEO is usually worked out as part of the initial deal in alliance agreements. This problem seems to be frequently settled these days by setting up joint CEOs, one from each company. Setting monitoring systems into place to control activities and ensure success completes, but does not end, the strategic management process. Rather, it is a continuous process, using feedback to reevaluate strategy for needed modifications and for updating and recycling plans. Of particular note here we should consider what is involved in effective management of international joint ventures, since they are such a common form of global alliance, and yet they are fraught with implementation challenges.

Managing Performance in International Joint Ventures

Much of the world's international business activity involves international joint ventures (IJVs), in which at least one parent is headquartered outside the venture's country of operation. IJVs require unique controls. Ignoring these specific control requisites can limit the parent company's ability to efficiently use its resources, coordinate its activities, and implement its strategy.[49]

The term **IJV control** can be defined, according to Schaan, as "the process through which a parent company ensures that the way a joint venture is managed conforms to its own interest."[50] Most of a firm's objectives can be achieved by careful attention to control features at the outset of the joint venture, such as the choice of a partner, the establishment of a strategic fit, and the design of the IJV organization.

The most important single factor determining IJV success or failure is the choice of a partner. Most problems with IJVs involve the local partner, especially in less developed countries. In spite of this fact, many firms rush the process of partner selection because they are anxious to "get on the bandwagon" in an attractive market.[51] In this process, it is vital to establish whether the partners' strategic goals are compatible (see Chapter 6). The strategic context and the competitive environment of the proposed IJV and the parent firm will determine the relative importance of the criteria used to select a partner.[52] IJV performance is also a function of the general fit between the international strategies of the parents, the IJV strategy, and the specific performance goals that the parents adopt.[53] Research has shown that, to facilitate this fit, the partner selection process must determine the specific task-related skills and resources needed from a partner, as well as the relative priority of those needs.[54] To do this, managers must analyze their own firms and pinpoint any areas of weakness in task-related skills and resources that can be overcome with the help of the IJV partner.

Organizational design is another major mechanism for factoring in a means of control when an IJV is started. Beamish et al. discuss the important issue of the strategic freedom of an IJV. This refers to the relative amount of decision-making power that a joint venture will have, compared with the parents, in choosing suppliers, product lines, customers, and so on.[55] It is also crucial to consider beforehand the relative management roles each parent will play in the IJV because such decisions result in varying levels of control for different parties. An IJV is usually easier to manage if one parent plays a dominant role and has more decision-making responsibility than the other in daily operations. Alternatively, it is easier to manage an IJV if the local general manager has considerable management control, keeping both parents out of most of the daily operations.[56]

International joint ventures are like a marriage: The more issues that can be settled before the merger, the less likely it will be to break up. Control over the stability and success of the IJV can be largely built into the initial agreement between the partners. The contract can specify who has what responsibilities and rights in a variety of circumstances, such as the contractual links of the IJV with the parents, the capitalization, and the rights and obligations regarding intellectual property. Of course, we cannot assume equal ownership of the IJV partners; where ownership is unequal, the partners will claim control and staffing choices proportionate to the ownership share. The choice of the IJV general manager, in particular, will influence the relative allocation of control because that person is responsible for running the IJV and for coordinating relationships with each of the parents.[57]

Where ownership is divided among several partners, the parents are more likely to delegate the daily operations of the IJV to the local IJV management—a move that resolves many potential disputes. In addition, the increased autonomy of the IJV tends to reduce many common human resource problems: staffing friction, blocked communication, and blurred organizational culture, to name a few, which all result from the conflicting goals and working practices of the parent companies.[58] Regardless of the number of parents, one way to avoid such potential problem situations is to provide special training to managers about the unique nature and problems of IJVs.[59]

Various studies reveal three complementary and interdependent dimensions of IJV control: (1) *the focus of IJV control*—the scope of activities over which parents exercise control; (2) the *extent, or degree, of IJV control achieved by the parents;* and (3) the *mechanisms of IJV control used by the parents.*[60]

We can conclude from two research studies—Geringer's study of ninety developed-country IJVs and Schaan and Beamish's study of ten IJVs in Mexico—that parent companies tend to focus their efforts on a selected set of activities that they consider important to their strategic goals, rather than monitoring all activities.[61] Schaan also found a considerable range of mechanisms for control used by the parent firms in his study, including indirect mechanisms such as parent organizational and reporting structure, staffing policies, and close coordination with the IJV general manager (GM). Monitoring the GM typically includes indirect means, perhaps bonuses and career opportunities, and direct mechanisms, such as requiring executive committee approval for specific decisions and budgets. These studies show that a variety of mechanisms are available to parent companies to monitor and guide IJV performance.

The extent of control exercised over an IJV by its parent companies seems to be primarily determined by the decision-making autonomy that the parents delegate to the IJV management—which is largely dependent on staffing choices for the top IJV positions and thus on how much confidence the partners have in these managers. In addition, if top managers of the IJV are from the headquarters of each party, the compatibility of the managers will depend on how similar their national cultures are this is because there are many areas of control decisions where agreement will be more likely between those of similar cultural backgrounds.[62]

Knowledge Management in IJVs

Managing the performance of an IJV for the long term, as well as adding value to the parent companies, necessitates managing the knowledge flows within the IJV network..

Knowledge management is "the conscious and active management of creating, disseminating, evolving, and applying knowledge to strategic ends."[63] Research on eight IJVs by Berdrow and Lane led them to define these processes as follows and as shown in Exhibit 7-4.

1. **transfer:** managing the flow of existing knowledge between parents and from the parents to the IJV
2. **transformation:** managing the transformation and creation of knowledge within the IJV through its independent activities
3. **harvest:** managing the flow of transformed and newly created knowledge from the IJV back to the parents.[64]

In particular, the sharing and development of technology among IJV partners provides the opportunity for knowledge transfer among those individuals who have internalized that

EXHIBIT 7-4   Knowledge Management in IJVs

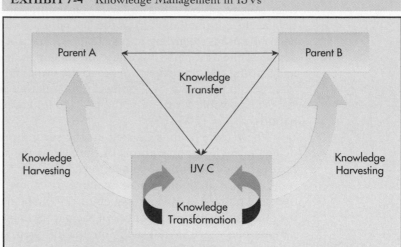

Note: Knowledge transfer usually follows the paths AB and/or BA and BC. Harvesting follows the paths CA and CB.

SOURCE: I. Berdrow and H. W. Lane, "*International Joint Ventures: Creating Value Through Successful Knowledge Management,*" Journal of World Business, Vol. 38, 1, February 2003, pp. 15–30.

information, beyond any tangible assets; the challenge is to develop and harvest that information to benefit the parents through complementary synergies. Those IJVs that were successful in meeting that challenge were found to have personal involvement by the principals of the parent company in shared goals, in the activities and decisions being made, and in encouraging joint learning and coaching.[65]

The many activities and issues involved in strategic implementation—such as negotiating, organizing, staffing, leading, communicating, and controlling—are the subjects of other chapters in this book. Elsewhere we include discussion of the many variables involved in strategic implementation that are specific to a particular country or region, such as goals, infrastructure, laws, technology, ways of doing business, people, and culture. In the following sections, the focus is on three pervasive influences on strategy implementation: government policy, societal culture, and the Internet.

Government Influences on Strategic Implementation

Host governments influence, in many areas, the strategic choices and implementations of foreign firms. The profitability of those firms is greatly influenced, for example, by the level of taxation in the host country and by any restrictions on profit repatriation. Other important influences are government policies on ownership by foreign firms, on labor union rules, on hiring and remuneration practices, on patent and copyright protection, and so on. For the most part, however, if the corporation's managers have done their groundwork, all these factors are known beforehand and are part of the location and entry strategy decisions. However, what hurts managers is to set up shop in a host country and then have major economic or governmental policy changes after they have made a considerable investment.

Unpredictable changes in governmental regulations can be a death knell to businesses operating abroad. Although this occurs in many countries, one country that is often the subject of concern for foreign firms is China. In a survey of European investment in China, for example, 54 percent of companies questioned said their performance in China was worse than they had anticipated.[66] Caterpillar was one of the companies with rapid market growth in producing diesel engines in China in the early 1990s—construction was booming and foreign investment was flooding in. But in 1993, China—afraid that foreign investment was causing inflation—revoked tax breaks and restricted foreign investment. The tables turned on Caterpillar after that because there was not enough domestic demand for their products. While China contends it is more committed to a market economy since it joined the W.T.O. in November 2001, history shows that foreign firms need to be cautious about entering China.

Political change, in itself, can, of course, bring about sudden change in strategic implementation of alliances of foreign firms with host-country projects. This was evident in May

1998 when President Suharto of Indonesia was ousted following economic problems and currency devaluation. The new government began reviewing and canceling some of the business deals linked with the Suharto family, including two water-supply privatization projects with foreign firms—Britain's Thames Water PLC and France's Suez Lyonnaise des Eaux SA. The Suharto family had developed a considerable fortune from licensing deals, monopolies, government "contracts," and protection from taxes.[67] Alliances with the family were often the only way to gain entry for foreign companies.

Cultural Influences on Strategic Implementation

When managers are responsible for implementing alliances among partners from diverse institutional environments, such as transition and established market economies, they are faced with the critical challenge of reconciling conflicting values, practices, and systems. Research by Danis, published in 2003, shows those important differences among Hungarian managers and Western expatriates (see Exhibit 7-5).[68] Such advance knowledge can provide expatriate managers with valuable information to help them in successful local operations.

In other situations, the culture variable is often overlooked when deciding on entry strategies and alliances, particularly when we perceive the target country to be familiar to us and similar to our own. However, cultural differences can have a subtle and often negative effect.

Since many of Europe's largest MNCs—including Nestlé, Electrolux, Grand Metropolitan, and Rhone-Poulenc—experience increasing proportions of their revenues from their positions in the United States, and employ more than 2.9 million Americans, they have decided to shift the headquarters of some product lines to the United States. As they have done so, however, there is growing evidence that managing in the United States is not as easy as they anticipated it would be because of their perceived familiarity with the culture. Rosenzweig documents some reflections of European managers on their experiences of managing U.S. affiliates. Generally, he has found that European managers appreciate that Americans are pragmatic, open, forthright, and innovative. However, they also say that the tendency of Americans to be informal and individualistic means that their need for independence and autonomy on the job causes problems in their relationship with the head office Europeans. Americans simply do not take well to directives from

---

EXHIBIT 7-5   Key Differences in Managerial Values, Practices, and Systems among Hungarian Managers and Western Expatriates

Western	Hungarian	Perceived source of difference[*]
Key differences in values		
Extensive use of espoused values	Relative absence of espoused values	Systemic legacy
Focus on core competencies	Focus on empire building	Systemic legacy
Focus on a broad set of stakeholders	Focus on a narrow set of stakeholders	Systemic legacy
Market mentality	Production/volume mentality	Systemic legacy
Professional relationships	Personal relationships	Systemic legacy
Living to work	Working to live	Cultural and systemic legacy
Key differences in practices		
Team orientation/play by the rules	Individual orientation/beat the system	Cultural and systemic legacy
Consensual management style	Autocratic management style	Systemic legacy
High information/knowledge sharing	Low information/knowledge sharing	Systemic legacy
Plan for the future mentality	Survival mentality	Recent economic events
Key differences in managerial systems		
Market-driven technology	Volume-driven technology	Systemic legacy
Small, flat structures	Large, hierarchical structures	Systemic legacy
Formal, strategic HR systems	Informal, administrative HR systems	Systemic legacy
Transparent information systems	Opaque information systems	Systemic legacy

[*]Consensus of Hungarian and Western respondents.

SOURCE: Reprinted from *Journal of World Business*, August 2003, vol. 38, No 3. W.M. Danis, "Differences in Values, Practices, and Systems among Hungarian Managers and Western Expatriates: An Organizing Framework and Typology," p. 224–244; with permission from Elsevier © 2003.

a foreign-based headquarters. Rosenzweig presents some comments from French managers on their activities in the United States:

French Managers Comment on Their Activities in the United States:

- "Americans see themselves as the world's leading country, and it's not easy for them to accept having a European in charge."
- "It is difficult for Americans to develop a world perspective. It's hard for them to see that what may optimize the worldwide position may not optimize the U.S. activities."
- "The horizon of Americans often goes only as far as the U.S. border. As a result, Americans often don't give equal importance to a foreign customer. If a foreign customer has a special need, the response is sometimes: 'It works here, why do they need it to be different?'"
- "It might be said that Americans are the least international of all people, because their home market is so big."[69]

Other European firms have had more successful strategic implementation in their U.S. plants by adapting to U.S. culture and management styles. When Mercedes-Benz of Germany launched its plant in Tuscaloosa, Alabama, U.S. workers and German "trainers" had doubts. Lynn Snow, who works on the door line of the Alabama plant, was skeptical whether the Germans and the Americans would mesh well. Now she proudly asserts that they work together, determined to build a quality vehicle. As Jurgen Schrempp, CEO of Mercedes's parent, Daimler-Benz (now part of DaimlerChrysler), observed, "'Made in Germany'—we have to change that to 'Made by Mercedes,' and never mind where they are assembled."[70]

The German trainers recognized that the whole concept of building a Mercedes quality car had to be taught to the U.S. workers in a way that would appeal to them. They abandoned the typically German strict hierarchy and instead designed a plant in which any worker could stop the assembly line to correct manufacturing problems. In addition, taking their cue from Japanese rivals, they formed the workers into teams that met every day with the trainers to problem solve. Out the window went formal offices and uniforms, replaced by casual shirts with personal names on the pocket. To add to the collegiality, get-togethers for a beer after work became common. "The most important thing is to bring together the two cultures," says Andreas Renschler, who has guided the M-Class since it began in 1993. "You have to generate a kind of ownership of the plant."[71] The local community has also embraced the mutual goals, often having beer fests and including German-language stations on local cable TV.

The impact of cultural differences in management style and expectations is perhaps most noticeable and important when implementing international joint ventures. The complexity of a joint venture requires that managers from each party learn to compromise to create a compatible and productive working environment, particularly when operations are integrated.

Cultural impacts on strategic implementation are often even more pronounced in the service sector, because of many added variables, especially direct contact with the consumer. Wal-Mart's strategy in Akabane, Japan, was to take a local partner to give it a better chance to adapt to the culture and business practices (see Management Focus: Wal-Mart Takes Local Partner to Adapt in Japan).

Management Focus

Wal-Mart Takes a Local Partner to Adapt in Japan

Akabane, Japan

It's 8:15 on a Friday morning in December 2003 and about fifty managers of the Seiyu supermarket chain are assembled on the second floor of their headquarters here, thirty minutes from downtown Tokyo. Surrounded by signs listing hot products, new promotions, and performance rates, many of the chiefs have already been at work for an hour.

Powered by coffee, tea and Diet Coke, they begin their daily pledge of allegiance, just as their counterparts do in Bentonville, Arkansas home of *Wal-Mart Stores*, which owns 38 percent of Seiyu.

"Give me an S!" a Japanese boss shouts.

"S!" comes the reply.

And so on, until the group spells "S-E-I-Y-U."

"Who's No. 1?" he asks.

"Customers!" they reply, punching the air with their fists.

The routine is one of the small ways in which Wal-Mart is revamping the struggling Seiyu, Japan's fourth-largest retailer. Unlike Toys "R" Us, Costco and other outside rivals that opened their own stores here, Wal-Mart has spent $513 million for a chunk of Seiyu, whose name still adorns its 400 stores.

The logic is simple: By working through a local partner, Wal-Mart is hoping that it can better navigate Japan's serpentine and costly network of suppliers, which has long frustrated other foreign investors. The company also avoids having to build stores and can take advantage of Seiyu's well-recognized brand.

But as it dips its toes into Japan, the world's second-largest economy, mighty Wal-Mart is confronting something it seldom encounters: skeptics who doubt that it can succeed. The retail market here is dominated by powerful manufacturers and wholesalers whose high prices have made the country an inhospitable place for foreign discounters. And Japanese consumers are famously finicky—as other American retailers who have simply imported goods with little regard for local tastes have learned the hard way.

Further complicating matters, Wal-Mart must repair a chain whose sales peaked a decade ago. Seiyu, which also sells housewares, appliances and general merchandise, has a debt-to-capital ratio that is more than twice the industry average in Japan. In the half-year that ended in August, the retailer lost 8.4 billion yen ($77 million) as sales slipped 3.9 percent from the period a year earlier. The company expects to lose 10 billion yen for the full year.

To Wal-Mart, though, Seiyu is a risk worth taking. Japan's dense supplier network and expensive labor and land give the American discounter a chance to cut costs and bolster profitability. The company's "everyday low prices" may also prove a hit with the increasingly bargain-conscious Japanese consumer, analysts said.

The company is also teaching Seiyu's employees to sell the Wal-Mart way. That means using data to analyze sales, not just following store managers' hunches. To reinforce the lesson, Wal-Mart is putting store managers through week-long training sessions and has flown hundreds of Seiyu workers to Arkansas.

"Japanese might think what we're doing is very tough, but they have to realize that this is the world standard," said Seiyu's chief executive, Masao Kiuchi, who, like many Wal-Mart managers, arrived at the morning meeting in an informal open shirt and no jacket.

After Mr. Kiuchi wrapped up the meeting, dozens of managers headed back to their desks to pore over spreadsheets on their laptop computers. Seiyu pools data from all of its stores so that everyone from clerks to suppliers can see what is on the shelves, what is selling, and when.

The data also makes it easier for Seiyu to order only what it needs and to pool those orders for volume discounts. Suppliers, too, can anticipate what Seiyu wants, planning their production and shipments accordingly and cutting the prices they charge. Wal-Mart hopes to use the savings to reduce Seiyu's prices.

Bowing to local tastes, Wal-Mart has also installed a small fish market, where workers slice slabs of tuna for customers. Nearby, baskets of vegetables and fruit sit on casters so workers can roll them into and out of the storeroom instead of unloading boxes in the aisles.

The new layout appears to be a hit with customers. Food sales and traffic have risen 50 percent since the store was remodeled in June, taking business from three major supermarkets nearby.

Satisfying local tastes is just one hurdle. While mothers with children strolled through the aisles, several men in blue suits—managers from rival stores, Mr. Funakoshi said—were snapping pictures of the store with their camera phones.

The corporate spies are symbolic of Japan's competitive retail market and the battle that Wal-Mart faces with rivals that have tried to replicate its no-frills pitch. Japan's two largest chains, Ito-Yokado and Aeon, have also had some success using their size to pressure suppliers to cut their prices.

Wal-Mart executives are aware of the challenge from incumbents like Aeon, whose sales are three times larger than Seiyu's. But they say that Japanese rivals cannot mimic the low-cost ethic that pervades Wal-Mart's ranks.

The company has dispatched fifty managers from Bentonville to teach Seiyu managers the Wal-Mart way. Workers also get a heavy dose of "culture training" to teach them to be more outspoken, upbeat, and goal-oriented. During weeklong sessions, managers were forced to dance in front of the class if they broke the rules—showing up late, for example, or forgetting to turn off cell phone ringers. The tactics apparently helped the normally wary Japanese relax, and several students in one session cried when their trainers returned to the United States.

The Japanese, though, have a tough time adapting to the Wal-Mart practice of continually praising co-workers. Backslapping compliments are rare in a country where workers are taught to be humble and bosses often command respect through intimidation.

At the morning meeting, one sales manager reported brisk sales of Beaujolais nouveau and received a hearty round of applause. Minutes later, smaller groups of Japanese sat in near silence as their bosses held sway.

Like workers at most Japanese companies, Seiyu employees also have difficulty questioning their bosses, particularly foreign managers who often speak through translators. "People cannot even say what they want to their supervisor, let alone jump ahead to the next manager," said Tamae Kobayashi, who is in charge of the human resources group that trains Seiyu employees. Wal-Mart appears confident, though, that the Japanese workers are getting its message.

Wal-Mart acknowledges that such threats exist, but it says its decision to enter Japan through a local partner is the right one, even if it requires more subtlety and patience than simply using its huge size and muscle to go it alone.

"People ask when we'll be done," Mr. McAllister said. "But it's going to take hundreds of little things."

In China, too, strategic implementation necessitates an understanding of the pervasive cultural practice of *guanxi* in business dealings. Discussed in previous chapters, *guanxi* refers to the relationship networks that "bind millions of Chinese firms into social and business webs, largely dictating their success."[72] Tapping into this system of reciprocal social obligation is essential to get permits, information, assistance to access material and financial resources, and tax considerations. Nothing gets done without these direct or indirect connections. In fact, a new term has arisen—**guanxihu**, which refers to a bond between specially connected firms that generates preferential treatment to members of the network. Without *guanxi*, even implementing a strategy of withdrawal is difficult. Joint ventures can get hard to dissolve and as bitter as an acrimonious divorce. Problems include the forfeiture of assets and the inability to gain market access through future joint venture partners—all experienced by Audi, Chrysler, and Daimler-Benz. For example:

> *Audi's decision to terminate its joint venture prompted its Chinese partner, First Automobile Works, to expropriate its car design and manufacturing processes. The result was an enormously successful, unauthorized Audi clone, with a Chrysler engine and a First Automobile Works nameplate.*[73]

E-commerce Impact on Strategy Implementation

> *With subsidiaries, suppliers, distributors, manufacturing facilities, carriers, brokers and customers all over the globe, global trade is complicated and fragmented. Shipments cross borders multiple times a day. Are they compliant with all the latest trade regulations? Are they consistently classified for each country? Can you give your buyers, customers and service providers the latest information, on demand?*[74]

As indicated in this quote, global trade is extremely complicated. Deciding on a global strategy is one thing; implementing it through all the necessary parties and intermediaries around the world presents a whole new level of complexity. Because of that complexity, many firms decide to implement their global e-commerce strategy by outsourcing the necessary tasks to **e-commerce enablers**, companies that specialize in providing the technology to organize transactions and follow through with the regulatory requirements. These specialists can help companies sort through the maze of different taxes, duties, language translations, and so on specific to each country. Such services allow small and medium-sized companies to go global without the internal capabilities to carry out global e-commerce functions. One of these specialist e-commerce enablers is NextLinx (see Management Focus: NextLinx Enables Global Strategy Implementation), which applies technology to the wide range of services it provides for strategic implementation.

Management Focus

NextLinx Enables Global Strategy Implementation

NextLinx's Trade Collaborator has everything needed to automate, streamline, and manage an entire global trade operation. A Web-based environment, it enables all trading partners to collaborate in a single online location, using the same information and processes.

Trade Collaborator, a unique and flexible product suite, simplifies and speeds global trade. It helps companies pay accurate customs charges and reduce their risk of noncompliance. Transaction efficiency will improve and cycle times will be reduced. Plus, NextLinx enables companies to:

- **Calculate accurate landed costs**—Calculate the total cost of delivered products, imports, materials, or components, including customs duties, taxes, other governmental charges, and freight.
- **Automate imports/exports**—Whether buying or selling, Trade Collaborator gives you everything you need to import and export—from classifying products to screening orders to generating the appropriate documentation and creating the right information for a customs entry.
- **Comply with NAFTA 2001**—Take advantage of lower tariffs and reduced compliance costs by getting everything you need to qualify for preferred trading status, generate documentation, and certify compliance.
- **Gain visibility into your shipments**—Rate and book shipments as well as gain crucial visibility into your supply chain so you can track and trace shipments.

POWERED BY GLOBAL KNOWLEDGE

This is the most comprehensive and up-to-date database of trade rules and regulations in the market today, so you'll always have the most current and complete information available, without having to maintain it yourself. We give it to you automatically!

SCALABLE, FLEXIBLE, AND PACKAGED TO MEET YOUR BUSINESS NEEDS

At NextLinx, we understand that no two global corporations are the same. That's why we give you multiple options for integrating Trade Collaborator into your organization.

- **Trade Export**—Export intelligently, increase compliance, reduce costs, and maximize efforts. Manage your orders from order to delivery: screen your products and customers, determine licenses, manage letters of credit, generate documents, and archive everything.
- **Trade Agreements**—Utilize trade agreements to their fullest, saving your company millions. Track inventory down to the line item, from country of origin through delivery and qualify your products for preferential tariffs.
- **Trade Import**—Import the products and goods that are critical to your operations with maximum efficiency and compliance. Maintain all information regarding your imports, screen shipments, control all required documentation and manage your trading partners.
- **Trade Fusion**—Trade Fusion offers you access to the most up-to-date trade information available and intelligent tools that will enable your Web site visitors to legally trade from any location around the world.

SOURCE: www.NextLinx.com, September 10, 2001.

CONCLUSION

Cross-border strategic alliances are becoming increasingly common as innovative companies seek rapid entry into foreign markets and as they try to reduce the risks of going it alone in complex environments. Those companies that do well are those that do their groundwork and pick complementary strategic partners. Too many, however, get "divorced" because "the devil is in the details"—which is what happens when "a marriage made in heaven" runs into unanticipated problems during actual strategic implementation.

Summary of Key Points

1. Strategic alliances are partnerships with other companies for specific reasons. Cross-border, or global, strategic alliances are working partnerships between companies (often more than two) across national boundaries and increasingly across industries.
2. Cross-border alliances are formed for many reasons, including market expansion, cost- and technology-sharing, avoiding protectionist legislation, and taking advantage of synergies.

3. Technological advances and the resulting blending of industries, such as those in the telecommunications and entertainment industries, are factors prompting cross-industry alliances.

4. Alliances may be short or long term; they may be full global partnerships, or they may be for more narrow and specific functions such as research and development sharing.

5. Alliances often run into trouble in the strategic implementation phase. Problems include loss of technology and knowledge skill-base to the other partner, conflicting strategic goals and objectives, cultural clashes, and disputes over management and control systems.

6. Successful alliances require compatible partners with complementary skills, products, and markets. Extensive preparation is necessary to work out how to share management control and technology and to understand each other's culture.

7. Strategic implementation—also called *functional level strategies*—is the process of setting up overall policies, administrative responsibilities, and schedules throughout the organization. Successful implementation results from setting up the structure, systems, and processes of the firm, as well as the functional activities that create a *system of fits* with the desired strategy.

8. Differences in national culture and changes in the political arena or in government regulations often have unanticipated effects on strategic implementation.

9. Strategic implementation of global trade is increasingly being facilitated by e-commerce enablers—companies that specialize in providing the software and Internet technology for complying with the specific regulations, taxes, shipping logistics, translations, and so on for each country with which their clients do business.

Discussion Questions

1. Discuss the reasons that companies embark on cross-border strategic alliances. What other motivations may prompt such alliances?

2. Why are there an increasing number of mergers with companies in different industries? Give some examples. What industry do you think will be the next for global consolidation?

3. Discuss the problems inherent in developing a cooperative alliance to enhance competitive advantage, but also incurring the risk of developing a new competitor.

4. What are the common sources of incompatibility in cross-border alliances? What can be done to minimize them?

5. Discuss the economic situation in the Russian Federation with your class. What has changed since this writing? What are the implications for foreign companies to start a joint venture there now?

6. What is involved in strategic implementation? What is meant by "creating a *system of fits*" with the strategic plan?

7. Explain how the host government may affect strategic implementation—in an alliance or another form of entry strategy.

8. How might the variable of national culture affect strategic implementation? Use the Wal-Mart example to highlight some of these factors.

Application Exercises

1. At the time of writing, the Daimler-Chrysler alliance had run into considerable trouble. By the time you are using this textbook, the company's situation may have worsened or improved. How is the alliance doing now? Research the events, successes, and problems that DaimlerChrysler AG has experienced so far and report to the class. Were the problems discussed in this chapter avoidable? Are the strategic goals, which led to the alliance, still attainable?

2. Review the featured Management Focus section on Wal-Mart in Japan. Research the company's recent operations in Japan and report to the class. Has Wal-Mart expanded elsewhere in Japan? How are its new stores doing? What, if any, problems has it run into?

Experiential Exercise: Partner Selection in an International Context

—by Professor Anne Smith

Read the following three scenarios and think about the assigned questions before class. Although the names of the specific telecommunications firms have been disguised, each scenario is based on actual events and real companies in the telecommunications service industry.

Scenario 1: TOOLBOX and FROZEN in Mexico

By October 30, 1990, managers from TOOLBOX (A Baby Bell[1] located in the eastern United States) and FROZEN (a Canadian telecommunications service and equipment provider) had been working for months on a final bid for the Telmex privatization. In two weeks, a final bid was due to the Mexican Ministry of Finance for this privatization; TOOLBOX's consortium was competing against four other groups.

Teléfonos de México (Telmex) was a government-run and -owned telecommunications provider, which included local, long-distance, cellular, and paging services in Mexico. Yet, in late 1989, the Mexican government decided to privatize Telmex. Reasons for Telmex's privatization included its need for new technology and installation expertise and the large pent-up demand for phone service in Mexico (where only one in five households had a phone). In early 1990, managers from TOOLBOX's international subsidiary were in contact with many potential partners such as France Telecom, GTE, FROZEN, and Spain's Telefonica. By June 1990, TOOLBOX and FROZEN had chosen each other to partner and bid on the Telmex privatization. During the past six months, discussions had gone smoothly between the international managers at TOOLBOX and FROZEN. With a local Mexican partner (required by the Mexican government), the managers worked out many details related to their Telmex bid, such as who would be in charge of installations and backlog reduction, who would install new cellular equipment, who would upgrade the marketing and customer service function, and who would select and install the central office switches. A TOOLBOX international manager commented, "We got along extremely well with our neighbors to the north. Not surprisingly, given that we speak the same language, have similar business values . . . but, basically we liked their international people, which was essential for our largest international deal ever." A FROZEN international manager stated, "It was ironic that our top executive in charge of business development had been a summer intern at TOOLBOX when he was in college. So, he liked our selection of TOOLBOX for this partnering arrangement, even though he was not familiar with the current TOOLBOX top managers." By September 1990, investment bankers estimated that a winning bid would probably top $1.5 billion. On November 15, 1990, all final bids for the privatization would be due. Having worked out the operational details (contingent on a winning bid), managers from TOOLBOX and FROZEN returned to meet with their top managers one final time to get some consensus on a final bid price for Telmex.

Scenario 2: The Geneva Encounter

At the Telecom 1984 convention in Geneva, Robert and Jim (a GEMS senior vice president and a business development manager, respectively) had just finished hearing the keynote address and were wandering among the numerous exhibits. This convention, hosted every four years in Geneva, included thousands of exhibits of telecommunications services and hardware providers; tens of thousands of people attended. Though GEMS (a Baby Bell in the southwestern United States) did not have a booth at the 1984 convention, Robert and Jim were trying to learn about international telecommunications providers and activities. On the third day of the conference, Robert and Jim were standing at an exhibit of advanced wireless technologies when they struck up a conversation with another bystander who was from Israel.

"You can get lost in this convention," exclaimed Jim. Daniel from Israel agreed, "Yes, this is my first trip to the Telecom convention, and it is overwhelming. . . . Tell me about GEMS. How is life freed from Ma Bell?" Robert, Jim, and Daniel continued their conversation over drinks and dinner. They learned that Daniel was an entrepreneur who was involved in many different ventures. One new venture that Daniel was pursuing was Yellow Pages directories and publishing. Daniel was delighted to meet those high-level executives from GEMS because of the Baby Bells' reputations as high-quality telephone service providers. Several months after the conference, Robert and Jim visited Daniel in Israel to discuss opportunities there. Six months later, GEMS and Daniel's firm were jointly developing software for a computerized directory publishing system in Israel. GEMS had committed people and a very small equity stake ($5 to $10 million) to this venture.

Scenario 3: LAYERS and Jack in UK Cable

In early 1990, LAYERS (another Baby Bell from the western United States) was considering investing in an existing cable television franchise in the United Kingdom. In 1984, pioneer/pilot licenses had been awarded in some cities. Many of these initial licenses were awarded to start-up companies run by entrepreneurs with minimal investment capital. Unfortunately, "the 100 percent capital allowances that were seen as vital to make the financial structuring of the cable build a commercial reality" were abolished, creating a "break in the industry's development [from 1985 to 1989] whilst many companies that were interested in UK cable were forced to reexamine their financial requirements."[2]

Jack had obtained one of these early UK cable licenses in 1984, and his investment capital was quickly consumed from installing cable coupled with slow market penetration. By 1986, his efforts toward this venture had waned. In the 1990 Broadcast Act, the government relaxed its rule for cable operators and allowed non-EC control of UK cable companies. This created incentives for current cable operators to sell an equity stake in their ventures. This allowed U.S. and Canadian telephone companies to bring desperately needed cash as well as marketing and installation expertise to these cable ventures. Aware of the impending changes, Jack was once again focusing on his cable operations. He arranged a meeting with several LAYERS international managers in November 1989, in anticipation of the changes. Turning on his charm and sales abilities, Jack explained to the LAYERS international managers the potential for UK cable television.[3] He also shared with these managers that he was willing to sell a large equity stake in his company to get it growing again. The international managers from LAYERS were impressed by Jack's enthusiasm, but they were even more intrigued by the possibility of learning about the convergence of cable and telephone services from this UK "laboratory." The LAYERS international managers decided that they would discuss this deal with their executive in charge of unregulated activities. By June 1990, LAYERS had an equity stake, estimated to be between $30 and $50 million, in Jack's UK cable venture.

Questions

Think about these questions from the perspective of the Baby Bell in each scenario:

1. In your opinion, which one of these scenarios should lead to a long-term successful international partnering relationship? Based on what criteria?

2. In your opinion, which one of these scenarios has the least chance of leading to a long-term, successful international partnering relationship? Why?

[1] Seven Baby Bells (also know as Regional Bell Operating Companies, or RBOCs for short) were created in 1984, when they were divested from AT&T. The term "Baby Bell" is really a misnomer given their large size, between $7 billion and $10 billion in revenues, at divestiture. In 1984, the Baby Bells were granted discrete territories where they offered local telephone service; these seven firms also were allowed to offer cellular service in their local service territories. From the AT&T divestiture settlement, the Baby Bells were allowed to keep the lucrative yellow pages and directory assistance services. Yet, these seven firms had no international activities or significant international managerial experience at divestiture.
[2] The Cable Companion, The Cable Television Association, pp. 1–12.
[3] In the UK, cable operators were allowed to offer both cable and telephone service.

SOURCE: This exercise was written by Professor Anne Smith, University of New Mexico, based on her research of the firms discussed. Copyright 1998 by Professor Anne Smith. Used with permission.

Internet Resources

Visit the Deresky companion Web site at www.prenhall.com/deresky for this chapter's Internet resources.

NTT DoCoMo, Japan: Global Alliances and Strategy Implementation

NTT DoCoMo was established after a spinoff from NTT in 1991. The company is headquartered in Tokyo. In Japan, NTT DoCoMo was the first company to bring voice to non-voice communications to the market. The company was also the first one to introduce i-mode (Internet-mode) technology and has over 48 million subscribers. The company is composed of 40 consolidated subsidiaries and nine affiliates. In the last eight years, NTT DoCoMo has established itself as the main leader in the wireless industry and its i-mode has been one of the fastest growing products in Japan.[1] NTT DoCoMo's i-mode helps companies to download data and other information. It is interesting to note that the company was ranked first in market value ($175.43 billion) in Japan in 2001.[2] In 2003, NTT DoCoMo's revenues surpassed $40.7 billion and made a profit of $2.1 billion. In Japan, NTT DoCoMo has been one of the leading high-tech companies. Like UK's Vodafone, NTT DoCoMo's early successes benefited from its unique i-mode technology, consumer demand, 1990's Internet revolution, and global alliances.[3] In 2004, NTT DoCoMo's products include Mobile phone services, PHS services, quickcast services, and other miscellaneous services. In mobile phone services, NTT DoCoMo provides cellular services, FOMMA (Freedom of Mobile Multimedia Access), 3G (third generation) mobile phone services, and packet communication services. PHS (personal handy services) encompasses high-performance terminals, PDAs, and notebook PCs. Quickcast provides paging service and other business solutions that require a high scale/volume content. The company's other services include M-Stage,

Infogate, Mzone, Worldcall, Worldwalker, Worldwing, Mobiler's Check, Pre-Call, Satellite Mobile Communications Services, Maritime Telephone Services, and In-Flight Telephone Services.[4]

After establishing itself as the key player in the wireless industry, NTT DoCoMo has sought aggressive global diversification by seeking minority stakes in selected wireless and Internet-type companies in Asia, Europe, and the United States. In 2004, NTT DoCoMo's selected overseas acquisitions and shareholdings include: KPN (The Netherlands), Hutchison Whampoa (Hong Kong), KG Telecom (Taiwan), AT&T Wireless (U.S.), Verio (U.S.A), and SK Telecom (South Korea). In the last three years, the company has created a multitude of alliances and partnerships with companies such as: America Online, Coca-Cola Japan, Denstu, Itochu, Microsoft, SEGA Corp., Sony, Sun Microsystems, 3Com, Walt Disney, and others. Regarding the nature of its long-term shareholdings in foreign markets, NTT DoCoMo has avoided acquiring companies and prefers to take minority ownership in Asia, Europe, and North America. Except for Verio, the company has taken a low-profile approach in its acquisitions but still exercises some control over the management. In the area of alliances and collaborations, the company's strategy is to tie-up with other high-tech and mobile operators that have significant national and global visibility, such as AOL, Coca-Cola, Denstu, Microsoft, and others. This change in NTT DoCoMo's core strategy and overseas expansion signifies its future growth in the wireless and Internet industries. Analysts believe that in the next five years, NTT DoCoMo plans on becoming one of the leading players in the global wireless industry. On the other hand, NTT DoCoMo may face a heightened competition because of the industry's consolidation and alliances that could change the face of this market.[5]

NTT DoCoMo's Alliances and Global Partnership

As mentioned earlier, NTT DoCoMo plans on becoming one of the leading players in the global wireless industry because of its unique product offerings and

---

*The material in this case is intended to be used as a basis for classroom/academic discussion rather than to illustrate either effective or ineffective handling of a managerial situation or business practices.

[1]See www.nttdocomo.com.
[2]*Business Week.* (1999), "Power play: Let the big mobile-phone duel begin," (November 29), pp. 54–55; *The Economist.* (1999), "Mobile warfare," (November 20), pp. 20–22; *The Economist.* (1999b), "A fight to the wire," (November 27), pp. 63–64.
[3]For more information on Vodafone and NTT DoCoMo's global strategies, see: Anwar, Syed T. (2002), "NTT DoCoMo and M-Commerce: A Case Study in Market Expansion and Global Strategy," *Thunderbird International Business Review,* Vol. 44, No. 1, pp. 139–164; Anwar, Syed T. (2003), "Vodafone and the wireless industry: A case in market expansion and global strategy," *Journal of Business and Industrial Marketing,* Vol. 18, No. 3, pp. 270–286; also see: Kodama, Mitsuru. (2003), "Strategic community-based theory of firms: Case Study of NTT DoCoMo," *Journal of High Technology Management Research,* Vol. 14, pp. 307–330.

SOURCE: Written exclusively for this text by Syed Tariq Anwar, Professor, West Texas A&M University. Copyright © Syed Tariq Anwar, 2004.

[4]See www.nttdocomo.com.
[5]Anwar, Syed T. (2002, 2003), op. cit.

FIGURE 1. NTT DoCoMo's Alliances and Partnerships in Global Markets (as of April 2004)

NTT DoCoMo's Alliances & Partnerships

Application: Hewlett-Packard Company, Japan Airlines, Macromedia, Microsoft, Oracle, Samsung, Sony Computer Entertainment, Sun Microsystems, and Visa

Information/Content:
News and Information: CNN, Nihon Keizai Shimbun, Inc., Bloomberg LP, Dow Jones, Bridge Japan, Weathernews, Inc., The Chosun Ilbo, People's Daily, Digital Bridge Communications, The Asahi Shimbun, and Stock Smart
Entertainment: Disney, Hudson, USJ Co. Ltd., Telysys Networks Co., Ltd., and Ima Hima, Inc.
Ringing Tones: Xing Konami and Music Channel Co. Ltd.
Database: NTT Directory Services Co., Nokia Japan, Matsushita Electric Industry Co., Ltd., OG Capital Co., Ltd., and Kimec
Others: Northwest Airlines, Inc., Citibank NA Tokyo, Tokyo-Mitsubishi TD Waterhouse Securities, Ericsson, and Federal Express

Operating Partnerships: KG Telecommunications Co. Ltd. (Taiwan), KPN Mobile (The Netherlands), AT&T Wireless (U.S.), Hutchison 3G Holdings Ltd., (UK), Hutchison Telephone Co. Ltd. (Hong Kong), Bouygues Telecom (France), and Telefonica Moviles Espana (Spain)

Technical Alliances: Hutchison Whampoa Limited (Hong Kong), SingTel Mobile Pte. Ltd. (Singapore), MBNS Multimedia Technologies (Malaysia), PT Telekom (Indonesia), Smart Communications (Philippines), Smart Tone Mobile Communications Limited (Hong Kong), Sonera (Finland), Telecom Italia Mobile (Italy), and TOT (Thailand)

SOURCE: www.nttdocomo.com; *Financial Times; The Wall Street Journal* (various issues).

strong consumer demand in Japan. It is interesting to note that to enter into other markets, NTT DoCoMo has avoided seeking majority ownership in other companies. Unlike Vodafone's aggressive worldwide acquisitions, NTT DoCoMo has pursued a unique international expansion based on taking minority stakes in other telecommunications and high-tech companies. Since 1998, the company has pursued this strategy by seeking alliances and joint ventures with European, Asian, and North American companies. In simple terms, creating alliances and seeking minority stakes are at the heart of NTT DoCoMo's global strategy and its expansion plan that allows the company to reduce risk while respecting the local company's autonomy and the management structure (see Figure 1).

NTT DoCoMo has benefited by sharing its 2G and the 3G mobile technologies while respecting the local partners' needs and day-to-day operations. In 2004, NTT DoCoMo maintained over 48 million customers worldwide and has created alliances and other cooperative agreements in Europe, North America, Asia, and South America (see Figure 1). In its application alliances, NTT DoCoMo's partners are Hewlett-Packard, Japan Airlines, Macromedia, Microsoft, Oracle, Samsung, Sony Computer Entertainment, Sun Microsystems, and Visa. In the area of media and news, the company has alliances with all the major content providers. NTT DoCoMo's operating partnerships include KG Telecommunications (Taiwan), KPN Mobile (The Netherlands), AT&T Wireless (U.S.), Hutchison

3G Holdings (UK), Hutchison Telephone (Hong Kong), Bouygues Telecom (France), and Telefonica Moviles Espana. In addition, NTT DoCoMo's technical alliances are with companies such as Hutchison Whampoa (Hong Kong), SingTel Mobile (Singapore), MBNS Multimedia Technologies (Malaysia), PT Telekom (Indonesia), Smart Communications (Philippines), SmarTone Mobile Communications (Hong Kong), Sonera (Finland), Telecom Italia Mobile (Italy), and TOT (Thailand).[6]

Although, NTT DoCoMo's corporate philosophy puts emphasis on "creating a new communications culture," it falls short of being a market leader and an aggressive wireless operator in global markets. The company's strategic alliances and partnerships are strong but fail to bring a strong visibility in global markets (see Figure 1). NTT DoCoMo's i-mode has been a phenomenal success in Japan but remains weak outside of Japan because of its new 3G W-CDMA (Wideband-Code Division Multiple Access) mobile standard. In 2004, the company's 16 percent stake in AT&T Wireless was affected by Cingular's acquisition of the company. NTT DoCoMo's plans of making W-CDMA the global standard in 3G mobile technology looks slim. It should be noted that global

expansion in the wireless industry is significantly different from the mainstream multinational enterprises (MNEs). Compared to MNEs in the 1980s and 1990s, the wireless industry is an integral part of the Internet world that demands different types of multi-company alliances and partnership and a high level of risk and global initiatives.[7] Unlike Vodafone, NTT DoCoMo seems to be less risk-prone and aggressive in its global acquisitions, alliances, and partnerships.[8] In Internet-related industries, rapid product development and release of new technologies is the norm.[9] Interestingly, there are numerous mobile standards used in Japan, Europe, and North America.[10] In 2003, even China announced the introduction of its own wireless standard.[11] This has caused problems in the introduction of new products and mass marketing. After looking at NTT DoCoMo's global expansion, we can draw the following four conclusions: (a) the company capitalized on its i-mode technology and became a leader in the wireless and Web-based industry; (b) the company's first-mover advantage helped maintain a competitive advantage in the Japanese market; (c) the company targeted those low risk global markets that had a growth potential but limited exposure; and (d) the company fulfilled business and consumer needs but remained to be a weak player in its global launch of W-CDMA mobile standards.

---

[6]For detail, see: www.nttdocomo.com

[7]For detail, see: *Financial Times*. (2003), "DoCoMo to sell out of joint venture with AOL," (December 17), p. 25; *Financial Times*. (2004), "DoCoMo's dilemma: To go or not to go global," (January 23), p. 24; *Financial Times*. (2004), "DoCoMo seeks place in new U.S. mobile network," (February 26), p. 15; *Financial Times*. (2004), "DoCoMo's 3G push remains stuck on hold," (March 3), p. 8; *The Wall Street Journal*. (2004), "DoCoMo unlikely to bid on AT&T Wireless," (February 5), p. B4.

[8]Anwar, Syed T. (2002, 2003), op. cit.

[9]For detail, see: Hanson, Ward. (2000). *Principles of Internet Marketing*, Cincinnati, Ohio: South-Western College Publishing.

[10]*Anwar*, Syed T. (2002, 2003), op. cit.

[11]*The Wall Street Journal*. (2004), "China will keep pursuing digital standards," (April 23), p. B1&B2.

CASE QUESTIONS

1. What are your views of NTT DoCoMo's competitive edge in the global mobile phone industry?
2. Analyze and evaluate NTT DoCoMo's strengths and weaknesses in North America, Asia, and Europe.
3. Analyze and evaluate NTT DoCoMo's alliances and global partnerships. What do you recommend to the company regarding their future plans and strategies?
4. What did you learn from NTT DoCoMo's alliances and global partnerships?

Organization Structure and Control Systems

Outline

Opening Profile: Samsung Electronics Thrives through Its Global Network of R&D Alliances, Streamlined Structure, and Vertical Integration

Korea's Samsung Electronics is emerging as a global enterprise through joint R&D projects with leading overseas companies, along with technology transfer arrangements and joint investments (see Table 8-1). It plans to unseat Sony Corporation as the number one electronics brand and shaper of digital trends. Samsung is the leading producer of digital mobile phones using code division multiple access (CDMA) technology. For 2003, the company had 32 percent global market share in DRAM chips—used in all PCs—while its other market shares included 32 percent in big-screen televisions, 10 percent in cell phones, 18 percent in LCD displays, and 14 percent in flash memory. The company has production, sales, and distribution facilities in Asia, Europe, North America, and South America.

Since CEO and Chairman Yun Jong Yong took over in 1997, he "has been executing Samsung's strategy with ferocious drive over a remarkably broad

Table 8-1   Samsung's Global Alliance Network

Name	Date	Field
Sony (S-LCD)	Mar. 2004	The 7th Generation Semiconductor (1870*2200mm)
IBM	Mar. 2004	Semiconductor 90, 65, 45 Nano Logic Technologies
Maytag	Feb. 2004	Premium Drum Washing Machine
EMC	Feb. 2004	Storage
Sanyo	Feb. 2004	Heat/Cool Inverter Air conditioner
Dell	Jan. 2004	Multi-functional Laser Printer
Sony	Oct. 2003	The Next Generation LCD for TVs
Toshiba	Sept. 2003	Optical Storage
HP	Sept. 2003	Inkjet Printer
Disney	Sept. 2003	Set-top Box
Napster	Sept. 2003	Samsung-Napster Player
NEC	July 2003	High-End Computing System for Businesses
16 partners including MS	July 2003	Home Network
Sanyo	Apr. 2003	Home Air conditioner
Infineon Germany	Feb. 2003	Next-generation Semiconductors for Smart Phone
Kent University	Mar. 2003	CD fundamental technology
Mastushida	Jan. 2003	DVD Recorder
Microsoft	Nov. 2002	Pocket PC
Softbank Japan	Nov. 2002	IP Set Top Box
Bell Canada	Nov. 2002	Next-generation Wireless Technology
HP	Sept. 2002	DDR DRAM
Mitsubishi	Sept. 2002	Core solution chip for camera in mobile devices
Miscrosoft	Aug. 2002	CPU for PDA
Oracle Korea	Aug. 2002	Anycall MITs (Mobile Intelligent Terminals)
T-Mobile	Aug. 2002	Cellular phones
Best Buy	July 2002	Side-by-side refrigerators
ORANGE Group	June 2002	Cellular phones
Mitsubishi	May 2002	Waching Machine
Microsoft	Oct. 2001	Digital Home Technology
Sony	Aug. 2001	flash memory card (memory stick)
AOL–Time Wamer	July 2001	digital products, advertising, marketing
Dell	Mar. 2001	memory chips, display products, ODD
Intel	Feb. 2001	Rambus DRAM
Rockwell	June 1999	automation
Automation	Feb. 2001	
Microsoft	July 2000	Internet TV
SAMSUNG Electro-Mechanics, Internet TV Network:		
Microsoft	June 2000	next-generation mobile communications
Battle Top	June 2000	Internet game
Converge	May 2000	e-commerce
Yahoo!	Mar. 2000	Internet solution
Harris, NDS, 4DL, Sk/Stream	Apr. 2000	interactive digital TV
Warner Bros.	Mar. 2000	DVD player
3com	Feb. 2000	IMT-2000
Comig	Feb. 2000	optics
Thales	Nov. 1999	defense industry
Ame	Sept. 1999	refrigerator
Nortel	June 1999	MT-2000
Adept	Dec. 1998	automation (robot & control system)
Alpha Processor	June 1998	non-memory chps

SOURCE: www.samsung.com, April 27, 2004.

conglomerate."[1] To streamline, Yun reorganized the company by cutting 24,000 workers and selling $2 billion in non-core businesses. The company's managers like the fact that they go through far fewer layers of bureaucracy to get their new products and plans approved; they say that this streamlined organization structure gives them a competitive edge to seize new opportunities.

Samsung remains diversified and vertically integrated; the company's chips and displays go into its own digital products. It has spent $19 billion over five years on new chip facilities. While rivals prefer to buy similar technologies from other companies rather than tying up capital, Yun considers that the company's vertical integration gives it an advantage.

Clearly global competition is fierce in this dynamic, high-technology industry. Time will tell how much of an advantage Samsung has gained through its restructuring and its global networks.

SOURCE: www.samsung.com, Company Profile, April 27, 2004; "The Samsung Way," *Business Week,* June 16, 2003; Kim Sung-hung and Woo In-ho, "Change Everything You've Got, Except for Your Family—Chairman Lee's Iron Will Turns Samsung into New Firm," *The Korea Herald,* May 31, 2003.

S trategic plans are abstract sets of decisions that cannot affect a company's competitive position or bottom line until they are implemented. Having decided on the strategic direction for the company, international managers must then consider two of the key variables for implementing strategy: the organizational structure and the control and coordinating mechanisms. The necessity of adapting organizational structures to facilitate changes in strategy is illustrated in the opening profile detailing some elements of Samsung Electronics' global structure.

ORGANIZATIONAL STRUCTURE

There is no permanent organization chart for the world.... It is of supreme importance to be ready at all times to take advantage of new opportunities.

ROBERT C. GOIZUETA,
(Former) Chairman and Ceo, Coca-Cola Company[2]

Organizational structures must change to accommodate a firm's evolving internationalization in response to worldwide competition. Considerable research has shown that a firm's structure must be conducive to the implementation of its strategy.[3] In other words, the structure must "fit" the strategy, or it will not work. Managers are faced with how best to attain that fit in organizing the company's systems and tasks.

The design of an organization, as with any other management function, should be contingency based, taking into account the variables of that particular system at that specific point in time. Major variables include the firm's strategy, size, and appropriate technology, as well as the environment in those parts of the world in which the firm operates. Given the increased complexity of the variables involved in the international context, it is no easy task to design the most suitable organizational structure and subsystems. In fact, research shows that most international managers find it easier to determine what to do to compete globally (strategy) than to decide how to develop the organizational capability (structure) to do it.[4] Additional variables affecting structural choices—geographic dispersion as well as differences in time, language, cultural attitudes, and business practices—introduce further layers of complication. We will show how organizational structures need to, and typically do, change to accommodate strategies of increasing internationalization.

EVOLUTION AND CHANGE IN MNC ORGANIZATIONAL STRUCTURES

Historically, a firm reorganizes as it internationalizes to accommodate new strategies. The structure typically continues to change over time with growth and with increasing levels of investment or diversity and as a result of the types of entry strategy chosen. Internationalization is the process by which a firm gradually changes in response to international competition, domestic market saturation, and the desire for expansion, new markets, and diversification. As discussed in Chapter 6, a firm's managers weigh alternatives and decide on appropriate entry strategies. Perhaps the firm starts by exporting or by acting as a licensor or licensee, and then, over time, it continues to internationalize by engaging in joint ventures or by establishing service, production, or assembly facilities, or alliances, abroad, moving into a global strategy. At each stage, the firm's managers redesign the organizational structure to optimize the strategy's chances to work, making changes in the firm's tasks and relationships and designating authority, responsibility, lines of communication, geographic dispersal of units, and so forth. This model of **structural evolution** has become known as the **stages model**, resulting from Stopford's research on 187 U.S. multinational corporations (MNCs).[5] Of course, many firms do not follow the stages model because they may start their internationalization at a higher level of involvement—perhaps a full-blown global joint venture without ever having exported, for example.

Even a mature MNC must make structural changes from time to time to facilitate changes in strategy—perhaps a change in strategy from globalization to regionalization (see Chapter 6) or an effort to improve efficiency or effectiveness. The reorganization of Aluminum Company of America (Alcoa), for example, split the company into smaller, more autonomous units, thereby giving more focus to growing businesses, such as automotive products, where the market for aluminum is strong. It also enabled Alcoa to link businesses with similar functions that are geographically divided—that is, to improve previously insufficient communication between Alcoa's aluminum operations in Brazil and its Australian counterparts. Alcoa, as with most MNCs, has found the need to continuously adapt its structure to accommodate global expansion and new ventures. As of 2004, Alcoa had a presence in forty-one countries, and employed 120,000 people worldwide.[6] The typical ways in which firms organize their international activities are shown in the following list. (Larger companies often use several of these structures in different regions or parts of their organization.) After the presentation of some of these structural forms, the focus will turn to transitional organizational arrangements.

- Domestic structure plus export department
- Domestic structure plus foreign subsidiary
- International division
- Global functional structure
- Global product structure

As previously stated, many firms—especially smaller ones—start their international involvement by exporting. They may simply use the services of an export management company for this, or they may reorganize into a simple *domestic structure plus export department*.

To facilitate access to and development of specific foreign markets, the firm can take a further step toward worldwide operations by reorganizing into a *domestic structure plus foreign subsidiary* in one or more countries (see Exhibit 8-1). To be effective, subsidiary managers should have a great deal of autonomy and should be able to adapt and respond quickly to serve local markets. This structure works well for companies with one or a few subsidiaries located relatively close to headquarters.

With further market expansion, the firm may then decide to specialize by creating an *international division,* organized along functional, product, or geographic lines. With this structure, the various foreign subsidiaries are organized under the international division, and subsidiary managers report to its head and are typically given the title Vice President,

EXHIBIT 8-1 Domestic Structure Plus Foreign Subsidary

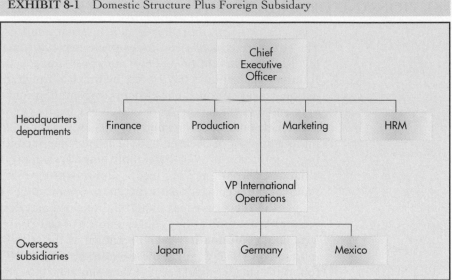

International Division. This vice president, in turn, reports directly to the CEO of the corporation. The creation of an international division facilitates the beginning of a global strategy. It permits managers to allocate and coordinate resources for foreign activities under one roof, and so it enhances the firm's ability to respond, both reactively and proactively, to market opportunities. Some conflicts may arise among the divisions of the firm because more resources and management attention tend to get channeled toward the international division than toward the domestic divisions and because of the different orientations of various division managers.[7] Companies such as IBM, PepsiCo, and Gillette have international divisions, called, respectively, IBM World Trade, PepsiCola International, and Gillette International.

Integrated Global Structures

To respond to increased product diversification and to maximize benefits from both domestic and foreign operations, a firm may choose to replace its international division with an integrated global structure. This structure can be organized along functional, product, geographic, or matrix lines.[8]

The **global functional structure** is designed on the basis of the company's functions—production, marketing, finance, and so forth. Foreign operations are integrated into the activities and responsibilities of each department to gain functional specialization and economies of scale. This form of organization is primarily used by small firms with highly centralized systems. It is particularly appropriate for product lines using similar technology and for businesses with a narrow spectrum of customers. This structure results in plants that are highly integrated across products and that serve single or similar markets.[9]

Much of the advantage resulting from economies of scale and functional specialization may be lost if the managers and the work systems become too narrowly defined to have the necessary flexibility to respond to local environments. An alternative structure can be based on product lines.

For firms with diversified product lines (or services) that have different technological bases and that are aimed at dissimilar or dispersed markets, a **global product (divisional) structure** may be more strategically advantageous than a functional structure. In this structure, a single product (or product line) is represented by a separate division. Each division is headed by its own general manager, and each is responsible for its own production and sales functions. Usually, each division is a **strategic business unit** (SBU)—a self-contained business with its own functional departments and accounting systems. The advantages of this organizational form are market concentration, innovation, and responsiveness to new opportunities in a particular environment. It also facilitates diversification and rapid growth, sometimes at the expense of scale economies and functional

EXHIBIT 8-2   Global Product (Divisional) Structure

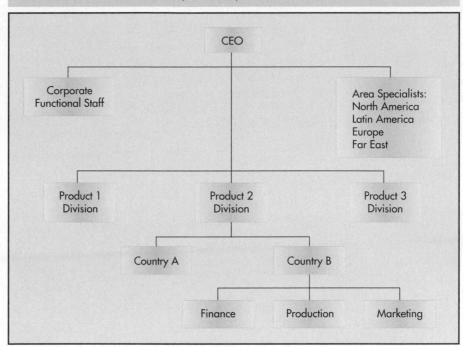

specialization. H. J. Heinz Company CEO William R. Johnson came on board in April 1998 and decided that the company should restructure to implement a global strategy. He changed the focus of the company from a multidomestic international strategy using the global geographic area structure to a global strategy, using the global product divisional structure. His goal was further growth overseas by building international operations; this structure also readily incorporated Heinz's Specialty Pet Food Division for marketing those products around the world.[10] Particularly appropriate in a dynamic and diverse environment, the global product structure is illustrated in Exhibit 8-2.

With the global product (divisional) grouping, however, ongoing difficulties in the coordination of widely dispersed operations may result. One answer to this problem, particularly for large MNCs, is to reorganize into a global geographic structure.

In the **global geographic (area) structure**—the most common form of organizing foreign operations—divisions are created to cover geographic regions (see Exhibit 8-3). Each regional manager is then responsible for the operations and performance of the countries within a given region. In this way, country and regional needs and relative market knowledge take precedence over product expertise. Local managers are familiar with the cultural environment, government regulations, and business transactions. In addition, their language skills and local contacts facilitate daily transactions and responsiveness to the market and the customer. While this is a good structure for consolidating regional expertise, problems of coordination across regions may arise. With the geographic structure, the focus is on marketing, since products can be adapted to local requirements. Therefore, marketing-oriented companies, such as Nestlé and Unilever, which produce a range of products that can be marketed through similar (or common) channels of distribution to similar customers, will usually opt for this structure. Nestlé SA, for example, uses this decentralized structure, which is more typical of European companies, because "it is not Nestlé's policy to generate most of its sales in Switzerland, supplemented by a few satellite subsidiaries abroad. Nestlé strives to be an insider in every country in which it operates, not an outsider."[11]

Grouping a number of countries under a region doesn't always work out, however, as Ford experienced with its European Group. It soon discovered the tensions among the units in Germany, Britain, and France resulting from differences in their national systems and cultures, and in particular management styles. Nevertheless, it has pursued its consolidation into five regionalized global centers for the design, manufacture, and marketing of

EXHIBIT 8-3   Global Geographic Structure

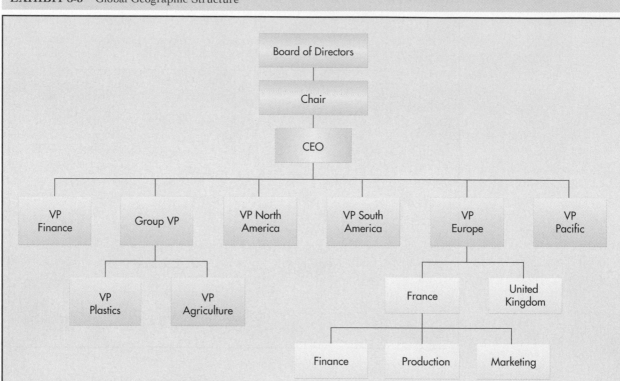

seventy lines of cars around the world.[12] In 2001, under Ford's CEO Jac Nasser—born in Lebanon and raised in Australia—Ford negotiated a presence in more than 200 countries, with 140 manufacturing plants.[13]

A **matrix structure**—a hybrid organization of overlapping responsibilities—is used by some firms but has generally fallen into disfavor recently.

ORGANIZING FOR GLOBALIZATION

> *If you misjudge the market [by globalizing], you are wrong in fifteen countries rather than only in one.*

FORD EUROPEAN EXECUTIVE[14]

No matter what the stage of internationalization, a firm's structural choices always involve two opposing forces: the need for **differentiation** (focusing on and specializing in specific markets) and the need for **integration** (coordinating those same markets). The way the firm is organized along the differentiation–integration continuum determines how well strategies—along a localization–globalization continuum—are implemented. This is why the structural imperatives of various strategies such as globalization must be understood to organize appropriate worldwide systems and connections.

As previously presented, global trends and competitive forces have put increasing pressure on multinational corporations to adopt a strategy of **globalization**, a specific strategy that treats the world as one market by using a standardized approach to products and markets. The following are two examples of companies reorganizing to achieve globalization:

- **IBM.** Big Blue decided to move away from its traditional geographic structure to a global structure based on its fourteen worldwide industry groups, such as banking, retail, and insurance, shifting power from country managers to centralized industry expert teams. IBM hopes the restructuring will help the company take advantage of global markets and break down internal barriers.
- **Bristol-Meyers Squibb.** The international drug company announced the formation of new worldwide units for consumer medicine businesses such as Bufferin, and for its Clairol and hair-care products.[15]

Organizing to facilitate a globalization strategy typically involves rationalization and the development of strategic alliances. To achieve rationalization, managers choose the manufacturing location for each product based on where the best combination of cost, quality, and technology can be attained. It often involves producing different products or component parts in different countries. Typically, it also means that the product design and marketing programs are essentially the same for all end markets around the world—to achieve optimal economies of scale. The downside of this strategy is a lack of differentiation and specialization for local markets.

Organizing for global product standardization necessitates close coordination among the various countries involved. It also requires centralized global product responsibility (one manager at headquarters responsible for a specific product around the world), an especially difficult task for multiproduct companies. Henzler and Rall suggest that structural solutions to this problem can be found if companies rethink the roles of their headquarters and their national subsidiaries. Managers should center the overall control of the business at headquarters, while treating national subsidiaries as partners in managing the business—perhaps as holding companies responsible for the administration and coordination of cross-divisional activities.[16]

A problem many companies face in the future is that their structurally sophisticated global networks, built to secure cost advantages, leave them exposed to the risk of environmental volatility from all corners of the world. Such companies must restructure their global operations to reduce the environmental risk that results from multicountry sourcing and supply networks.[17] In other words, the more links in the chain, the more chances for things to go wrong.

Comparative Management in Focus

The Overseas Chinese Global Network

In increasing strength, overseas Chinese businessmen from Southeast Asia are investing in China, where they possess linguistic and cultural advantages over big Western corporations. Navigating layers of government and the rituals of business etiquette is easier if you speak the language and appreciate the history.
—*The New York Times, December 14, 2003.[18]*

The Chinese who left the mother country had to struggle, and that became a culture of its own. Because we have no social security, the Overseas Chinese habit is to save a lot and make a lot of friends.
—*Lee Shau Kee, 65, Real Estate Developer, Hong Kong (Net Worth $6 Billion)[19]*

Compared to the Japanese *keiretsu,* the emerging Chinese commonwealth is an interconnected, open system—a new market mechanism for conducting global business.[20] It is now becoming apparent to many business leaders, who have finally figured out Japan's *keiretsu,* that they "now need to understand a distinctively Chinese model, where tycoons cut megadeals in a flash and heads of state wheel and deal like CEOs."[21]

The "Chinese commonwealth" is a form of global network that has become the envy of Western multinationals. It is a network of entrepreneurial relationships spread across continents, though primarily in Asia. What is increasingly being referred to as the "big dragon of Greater China" includes mainland China's 1.3 billion citizens and more than 55 million overseas Chinese—most of them from Taiwan, Indonesia, Hong Kong, and Thailand. It is estimated that the Overseas Chinese control $2 trillion in liquid assets and contribute about 80 percent of the capital for the People's Republic of China (PRC). If the Overseas Chinese lived in one country, their GNP would exceed that of mainland China.[22] In addition, this "Bamboo Network," which transcends national boundaries, is estimated to contribute about 70 percent of the private sector in Malaysia, Thailand, Indonesia, and the Philippines."[23] Most observers believe that this China-based informal economy is the world leader in economic growth, industrial expansion, and exports. It comprises mostly mid-sized, family-run firms linked by transnational network channels. These channels for the movement of information, finance, goods, and capital help to explain the relative flexibility and efficiency of the numerous ongoing informal agreements and transactions that bind together the various parts of the Chinese-based trading area.[24] The network alliances bind together and draw from the substantial pool of financial capital and resources available in the region, including those of entrepreneurial services in Hong Kong, technology and manufacturing capability in Taiwan, outstanding communications in Singapore, and vast endowments of land, resources, and labor in mainland China.

The Overseas Chinese, now models for entrepreneurship, financing, and modernization for the world, and in particular for Beijing, are refugees from China's poverty, disorder, and communism. Business became the key to survival for those Chinese emigrants faced with uncertainties, hardships, and lack of acceptance in their new lands. The uncertainties, a survivor mentality, and the cultural basis in the Confucian tradition of patriarchical authority have led to a way of doing business that is largely confined to family and trusted friends. This business mentality and approach to life has led to many self-made billionaires among the Overseas Chinese. Among them is Y. C. Wang, the Taiwanese plastics king, who had to leave school after the sixth grade but taught himself what was necessary to develop a new industry.[25]. More recently, there has been a new wave of investors - overseas Chinese who are attracted by rapid growth in China, compared to slow growth in their home countries, such as Singapore and Indonesia.[26]. The network of alliances of the ethnic Chinese is based on *guanxi*—personal connections—among families, business friends, and political associations, often rooted in the traditional clans. Massive amounts of cross-investment and trade are restricted primarily to families and long-standing connections, including those from the province of the PRC from which the overseas Chinese or their ancestors migrated. As examples, Chinese ties in Hong Kong have provided about 90 percent of the investment in the adjacent province of Guangong; and telephone calls from the special economic zone of Xiamen in the PRC to Taiwan now average 60,000 a month, up from ten a month eight years ago.[27] The web of those connections has created an influential network that is the backbone of the East Asian economy.

The history, culture, and careful, personal approach to business of the Overseas Chinese have led to some underlying values—Kao calls them "life-raft" values—which have shaped a distinctive business culture. These values include thrift and a very high savings level, regardless of need, extremely hard work, trust in family before anyone else, adherence to patriarchal authority, investment strictly based on kinship and affiliations, a preference for investment in tangible goods, and an ever-wary outlook on life.[28] This shared web of culture and contacts has spawned an intensely commercial and entrepreneurial network of capitalists and a dominant power in Asia. Two benefits of such a business culture are speed and patience. Because of their knowledge of and trust in their contacts, the Overseas Chinese can quickly smell profits and make decisions even more quickly; a deal to buy a hotel in Asia can be completed in days, compared to months in the United States.[29]. Patience to invest for the long term is an outcome of closely held ownership and management, often in a single family, so that outside shareholders are not demanding short-term profits. No doubt sharing language and cultural bonds is a vital lubricant for business, especially with people in China, where there are few firm laws on which businesspeople can rely.[30]

Organizing to "Be Global, Act Local"

In their rush to get on the globalization bandwagon, too many firms have sacrificed the ability to respond to local market structures and consumer preferences. Managers are now realizing that—depending on the type of products, markets, and so forth—a compromise must be made along the globalization–regionalization continuum, and they are experimenting with various structural configurations to "be global and act local." Colgate-Palmolive's organizational structure illustrates such a compromise. The primary operating structure is geographic—that is, localized. The presidents of four major regions—North America, Europe, Latin America, and Asia Pacific—report to the COO while other developing regions such as Africa, Eastern Europe, and the Middle East report to the chief of operations of international business development. Then that person reports to the CEO of Colgate-Palmolive, who oversees the centralized coordinating operations (that is, the "globalized" aspects), for technology, finance, marketing, human resources management, and so on.[31]

Levi Strauss is another example of a company attempting to maximize the advantages of different structural configurations. First, the company has ensured its ability to respond to local needs in a different way by allowing its managers to act independently: Levi's success turns on its ability to fashion a global strategy that doesn't snuff out local initiative. It's a delicate balancing act, one that often means giving foreign managers the freedom needed to adjust their tactics to meet the changing tastes of their home markets.[32]

Second, Levi Strauss keeps centralized control of some aspects of its business but decentralizes control to its foreign operations, organized as subsidiaries. These subsidiaries are supplied by a global manufacturing network of Levi plants and contract manufacturers. This approach allows local coordination and the flexibility to respond to ever-changing fashion trends and fads in denim shading.[33]

Another company's plan to go global by acting local does not involve changing the company's basic structure. Fujitsu, a Japanese high-technology conglomerate producing computers, telecommunications equipment, and semiconductors, has found a way to internationalize by proxy. Fujitsu has substantial stakes in two foreign companies—Amdahl, a Silicon Valley maker of IBM-compatible mainframes, and International Computers Ltd. (ICL), Britain's biggest computer company—that accounts for nearly half of Fujitsu's overseas revenues. These firms are run by Westerners, who are given free reign to manage and even compete against each other. The plan is doing so well that Fujitsu is looking for similar deals in Europe. As Fujitsu's president, Takuma Yamamoto, explains, "We are doing business in a borderless economy, but there is a rising tide of nationalism, and you have to find ways to avoid conflict. That is one reason we give our partners autonomy."[34]

Although strategy may be the primary means to a company's competitive advantage, the burden of realizing that advantage rests on the organizational structure and design. Because of the difficulties experienced by companies trying to be "glocal" companies (global and local), researchers are suggesting new, more flexible organizational designs involving interorganizational networks and transnational design.

EMERGENT STRUCTURAL FORMS

Companies are increasingly abandoning rigid structures in an attempt to be more flexible and responsive to the dynamic global environment. Some of the ways they are adapting are by transitioning to formats known as interorganizational networks, global e-corporation network structures, and transnational corporation network structures, as described as follows.

Interorganizational Networks

Whether the ever-expanding transnational linkages of an MNC consist of different companies, subsidiaries, suppliers, or individuals, they result in relational networks. These networks may adopt very different structures of their own because they operate in different local contexts within their own national environments. By regarding the MNC's overall structure as a network of interconnected relations, we can more realistically consider its organizational design imperatives at both global and local levels. Royal Philips Electronics of the Netherlands, one of the world's biggest electronics companies, has operating units in sixty countries, using a network structure. These units range from large subsidiaries, which might be among the largest companies in a country, to very small single-function operations, such as research and development or marketing divisions for one of Philips's businesses. Some have centralized control at Philips's headquarters; others are quite autonomous. For some time, Philips had fallen far behind its Japanese competitors in productivity because of missteps and seemingly endless restructurings. However, when

Philips' Chief executive Gerard J. Kleisterlee—a 30-year Philips veteran—took over in 2001, he again reorganized the company. He divested $850 million in less important or unprofitable businesses and shuttered a dozen factories, outsourced manufacturing for much of the electronics and appliance manufacturing, and chip production.[35] The restructuring seems to be working, with Philips' 2003 sales hitting EUR 29 billion, including a 34 percent increase in sales in China.[36]

The network of exchange relationships, say Ghoshal and Bartlett, is as representative of any MNC as it is of Philips. The network framework makes clear that the company's operating units link vastly different environmental and operational contexts based on varied economic, social, and cultural milieus. This complex linkage highlights the intricate task of a giant MNC to rationalize and coordinate its activities globally to achieve an advantageous cost position while simultaneously tailoring itself to local market conditions (to achieve benefits from differentiation).[37]

The Global E-Corporation Network Structure

The organizational structure for global e-businesses, in particular for physical products, typically involves a network of virtual e-exchanges and "bricks and mortar" services, whether those services are in-house or outsourced. This structure of functions and alliances makes up a combination of electronic and physical stages of the supply chain network, as depicted in Exhibit 8-4.

As such, the network comprises some global and some local functions. Centralized e-exchanges for logistics, supplies, and customers could be housed anywhere; suppliers, manufacturers, and distributors may be in various countries, separately or together, wherever efficiencies of scale and cost may be realized. The final distribution system and the customer interaction must be tailored to the customer-location physical infrastructure and payment infrastructure, as well as local regulations and languages.[38]

The result is a global e-network of suppliers, subcontractors, manufacturers, distributors, buyers and sellers, communicating in real time through cyberspace. This spreads efficiency throughout the chain, providing cost-effectiveness for all parties.[39] Dell Computer is an

EXHIBIT 8-4   The Global E-Corporation Network Structure

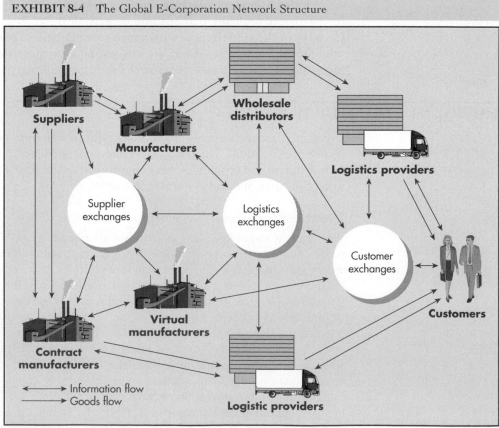

SOURCE: AMR Research.

example of a company that uses the Internet to streamline its global supply systems. It has a number of factories around the world that supply custom-built PCs to customers in that region. Customers' orders are received through call centers or Dell's own Web site. The order for components then goes to its suppliers, which have to be within a fifteen-minute drive of its factory. The component parts are delivered to the factory, and the completed customers' orders are collected within a few hours. Dell maintains Internet connections with its suppliers and connects them with its customer database so that they have direct and real-time information about orders. Customers also can use Dell's Internet system to track their orders as they go through the chain.[40]

The Transnational Corporation (TNC) Network Structure

To address the globalization–localization dilemma, firms that have evolved through the multinational form and the global company are now seeking the advantages of horizontal organization in the pursuit of transnational capability—that is, the ability to manage across national boundaries, retaining local flexibility while achieving global integration.[41] This capability involves linking foreign operations to each other and to headquarters in a flexible way, thereby leveraging local and central capabilities.[42] ABB (Asea Brown Boveri) is an example of such a decentralized horizontal organization. ABB operates in 140 countries with 1,000 companies, with only one management level separating the business units from top management. ABB prides itself on being a truly global company, with eleven board members representing seven nationalities. Thus, this structure is less a matter of boxes on an organizational chart and more a matter of a network of the company's units and their system of horizontal communication. This involves lateral communication across networks of units and alliances rather than in a hierarchy. The system requires the dispersal of responsibility and decision making to local subsidiaries and alliances. The effectiveness of that localized decision making depends a great deal on the ability and willingness to share current and new learning and technology across the network of units.

Whatever the names given to the organizational forms emerging to deal with global competition and logistics, the MNC organizational structure as we know it, with its hierarchical pyramid, subsidiaries, and world headquarters, is gradually evolving into a more fluid form to adapt to strategic and competitive imperatives. Facilitating this change, Kilmann points out, is the information technology explosion fueled by computers, fax machines, teleconferencing, the Internet, and so forth:

> *Competitive companies in the future will be elaborate networks of people and information, each exerting an influence on the other. [These networks will comprise] a small hub of staff connected to each other by their physical proximity, which is electronically connected to global associates who help control assets and negotiate agreements to extend the company's business influence.[43]*

In this new global web, the location of a firm's headquarters is unimportant. It may even be, says Reich, "a suite of rooms in an office park near an international airport—a communications center where many of the web's threads intersect."[44] The web is woven by decisions made by managers around the world, both decisions within the company and those between other companies. Various alliances tie together units and subunits in the web. Corning Glass, for instance, changed from its national pyramidlike organization to a global web, giving it the capability of making optical cable through its European partner, Siemens AG, and medical equipment with Ciba-Geigy.[45]

CHOICE OF ORGANIZATIONAL FORM

Two major variables in choosing the structure and design of an organization are the opportunities and need for (1) globalization and (2) localization. Exhibit 8-5 depicts alternative structural forms appropriate to each of these variables and to the strategic choices regarding the level and type of international involvement desired by the firm. This figure thereby updates the evolutionary stages model to reflect alternative organizational responses to more recent environments and to the anticipated competitive environments ahead. The updated model shows that, as the firm progresses from a domestic

EXHIBIT 8-5   Organizational Alternatives and Development for Global Companies

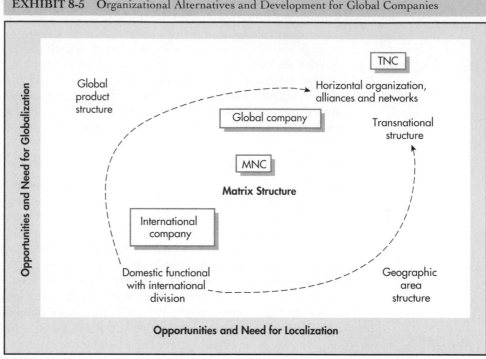

SOURCES: Based on models by R. E. White and T. A. Poynter, "Organizing for Worldwide Advantage," *Business Quarterly* 54 (Summer 1989); John M. Stopford and Louis T. Wells, Jr., *Managing the Multinational Enterprise* (New York: Basic Books, 1972): and C. A. Bartlett, "Organizing and Controlling MNCs, " *Harvard Business School Case Study*, no. 9 (March 1987): 365, 375.

to an international company—and perhaps later to a multinational and then a global company—its managers adapt the organizational structure to accommodate their relative strategic focus on globalization versus localization, choosing a global product structure, a geographic area structure, or perhaps a matrix form. The model proposes that, as the company becomes larger, more complex, and more sophisticated in its approach to world markets (no matter which structural route it has taken), it may evolve into a transnational corporation (TNC). The TNC strategy is to maximize opportunities for both efficiency and local responsiveness by adopting a transnational structure that uses alliances, networks, and horizontal design formats. The relationships between choice of global strategy and the appropriate structural variations necessary to implement each strategic choice are further illustrated in Exhibit 8-6.

EXHIBIT 8-6   Global Strategy–Structure Relationships

	Multidomestic Strategy	**International Strategy**	**Globalization Strategy**	**Transnational Strategy**
	Low ⟷ Need for Coordination ⟷ High			
	Low ⟷ Bureaucratic Costs ⟷ High			
Centralization of authority	Decentralized to national unit	Core competencies centralized; others decentralization to national units	Centralized at optimal global location	Simultaneously Centralized and Decentralized
Horizontal differentiation	Global area structure	International division structure	Global product group structure	Global Matrix Structure "Matrix in the Mind"
Need for complex integrating mechanisms	Low	Medium	High	Very High
Organizational culture	Not important	Quite important	Important	Very important

SOURCE: C. W. L. Hill and E. R. Jones, *Strategic Management*, 3rd ed. (Boston: Houghton Mifflin, 1995), 390.

Organizational Change and Design Variables

When a company makes drastic changes in its goals, strategy, or scope of operations, it will usually also need a change in organizational structure. However, other, less obvious indications of organizational inefficiency also signal a need for structural changes: conflicts among divisions and subsidiaries over territories or customers, conflicts between overseas units and headquarters staff, complaints regarding overseas customer service, and overlapping responsibilities are some of these warning signals. Exhibit 8-7 lists some indications of the need for change in organizational design.

At persistent signs of ineffective work, a company should analyze its organizational design, systems, and work flow for the possible causes of those problems. The nature and extent of any design changes must reflect the magnitude of the problem. In choosing a new organizational design or modifying an existing structure, managers must establish a system of communication and control that will provide for effective decision making. At such times, managers need to localize decision making and integrate widely dispersed and disparate global operations.

Besides determining the behavior of the organization on a macro level (in terms of what the different divisions, subsidiaries, departments, and units are responsible for), the organizational design must determine behavior on a micro level. For example, the organizational design affects the level at which certain types of decisions will be made. Determining how many and what types of decisions can be made and by whom can have drastic consequences; both the locus and the scope of authority must be carefully considered. This centralization–decentralization variable actually represents a continuum. In the real world, companies are neither totally centralized nor totally decentralized: The level of centralization imposed is a matter of degree. Exhibit 8-8 illustrates this centralization–decentralization

---

EXHIBIT 8-7   When Is Change Needed?

- A change in the size of the corporation—due to growth, consolidation, or reduction
- A change in key individuals—which may alter management objectives, interests, and abilities
- A failure to meet goals, capitalize on opportunities, or be innovative
- An inability to get things done on time
- A consistently overworked top management that spends excessive hours on the job
- A belief that costs are extravagant or that budgets are not being met
- Morale problems
- Lengthy hierarchies that inhibit the exercise of strategic control
- Planning that has become increasingly staff-driven and is thus divorced from line management
- Innovation that is stifled by too much administration and monitoring of details
- Uniform solutions that are applied to nonuniform situations. The extreme opposite of this condition—when things that should or could function in a routine manner do not—should also be heeded as a warning. In other words, management by exception has replaced standard operating procedures

The following are a few specific indicators of *international* organizational malaise:

- A shift in the operational scope—perhaps from directing export activities to controlling overseas manufacturing and marketing units, a change in the size of operations on a country, regional, or worldwide basis, or failure of foreign operations to grow in accordance with plans and expectations.
- Clashes among divisions, subsidiaries, or individuals over territories or customers in the field
- Divisive conflicts between overseas units and domestic division staff or corporate staff
- Instances wherein centralization leads to a flood of detailed data that is neither fully understood nor properly used by headquarters
- Duplication of administrative personnel and services
- Underutilization of overseas manufacturing or distribution facilities
- Duplication of sales offices and specialized sales account executives
- Proliferation of relatively small legal entities or operating units within a country or geographic area
- An increase in overseas customer service complaints
- Breakdowns in communications within and among organizations
- Unclear lines of reporting and dotted-line relationships, and ill-defined executive responsibilities

SOURCE: Business International Corporation, *New Directions in Multinational Corporate Organization* (New York: Business International Corporation, 1981).

EXHIBIT 8-8   Locus of Decision Making in an International Organization

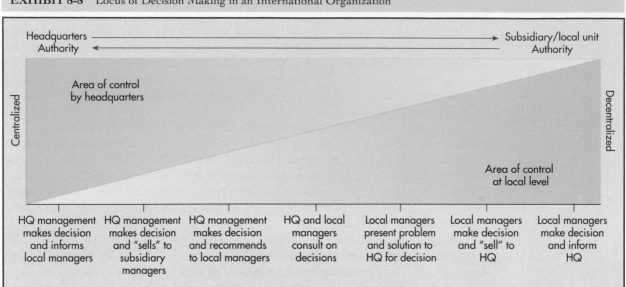

SOURCE: Based on and adapted from R. Tannenbaum and W. Schmidt; and A. G. Kefelas, *Global Business Strategy* (Cincinnati: South-Western, 1990).

continuum and the different ways that decision making can be shared between headquarters and local units or subsidiaries. In general, centralized decision making is common for some functions (finance; research and development) that are organized for the entire corporation, whereas other functions (production; marketing; sales) are more appropriately decentralized. Two key issues are the speed with which the decisions have to be made and whether they primarily affect only a certain subsidiary or other parts of the company as well.

As noted, culture is another factor that complicates decisions on how much to decentralize and how to organize the work flow and the various relationships of authority and responsibility. Part IV more fully presents how cultural variables affect people's attitudes about working relationships and about who should have authority over whom. At this point, it is important merely to note that cultural variables must be taken into account when designing an organization. Delegating a high level of authority to employees in a country where workers usually regard "the boss" as the rightful person to make all the decisions is not likely to work well. Clearly, managers must think through the interactions of organizational, staffing, and cultural issues before making final decisions.

In summary, no one way to organize is best. Contingency theory applies to organizational design as much as to any other aspect of management. The best organizational structure is the one that facilitates the firm's goals and is appropriate to its industry, size, technology, and competitive environment. Structure should be fluid and dynamic—and highly adaptable to the changing needs of the company. The structure should not be allowed to get bogged down in the administrative heritage of the organization (that is, "the way we do things around here" or "what we've always done") to the point that it undermines the very processes that will enable the firm to take advantage of new opportunities.

Most likely, however, the future for MNC structure lies in a global web of networked companies. Ideally, a company tries to organize in a way that will allow it to carry out its strategic goals; the staffing is then done to mesh with those strategic goals and the way the organizational structure has been set up. In reality, however, the existing structural factors often affect strategic decisions, so the end result may be a trade-off of desired strategy with existing constraints. So, too, with staffing: "Ideal" staffing plans have to be adjusted to reflect the realities of assigning managers from various sources and the local regulations or cultural variables that make some organizing and staffing decisions more workable than others.

What may at first seem a linear management process of deciding on strategy, then on structure, and finally on staffing is actually an interdependent set of factors that must be taken into consideration and worked out as a set of decisions. Chapter 9 explores how staffing decisions are—or should be—intricately intertwined with other decisions regarding strategy, structure, and so forth. A unique set of management cadre and skills in a particular location can be a competitive advantage in itself, and so it may be a smart move to build strategic and organizational decisions around that resource rather than risk losing that advantage. The following sections present some other processes that are involved in implementing strategy and are interconnected with coordinating functions through organizational structure.

CONTROL SYSTEMS FOR GLOBAL OPERATIONS

The establishment of a single currency makes it possible, for the first time, to establish shared, centralized accounting and administrative systems.

FRANCESCO CAIO,
CEO, Merloni Elettrodomestici[46]

To complement the organizational structure, the international manager must design efficient coordinating and reporting systems to ensure that actual performance conforms to expected organizational standards and goals. The challenge is to coordinate far-flung operations in vastly different environments with various work processes, rules, and economic, political, legal, and cultural norms. The feedback from the control process and the information systems should signal any necessary change in strategy, structure, or operations in a timely manner. Often, the strategy, the coordinating processes, or both, need to be changed to reflect conditions in other countries.

Monitoring Systems

The design and application of coordinating and reporting systems for foreign subsidiaries and activities can take any form that management wishes. MNCs usually employ a variety of direct and indirect coordinating and control mechanisms suitable for their organization structure. Some of the typical control methods used for the major organizational structures discussed here are shown in Exhibit 8-9. These are self-explanatory. For example, in the transnational network structure, decision-making control is centralized to key network nodes, greatly reducing emphasis on bureaucratic control. Output control in this exhibit refers to the assessment of a subsidiary or unit based only on the results attained. Other specific mechanisms are summarized in the next sections.

EXHIBIT 8-9   Control Mechanisms in Multinational Organizational Structures

Multinational Structures	Output Control	Bureaucratic Control	Decision-Making Control	Organization Control
International division structure	Most likely profit control	Must follow company policies	Some centralization possible	Treated like other divisions
Global geographic structure	Profit center most common	Some policies and procedures necessary	Local units have autonomy	Local subsidiary culture often most important
Global product structure	Unit output for supply; sales volume for sales	Tight process controls for product quality and consistency	Centralized at product division headquarters	Possible for some companies but not always necessary
Transnational network structure	Used for supplier units and some independent profit centers	Less important	Few decisions centralized at headquarters; more decisions centralized in key network nodes	Organizational culture transcends national cultures; supports sharing and learning; the most important control mechanism

SOURCE: Adapted from John B. Cullen, *Multinational Management: A Strategic Approach*, 2nd ed. (Cincinnati: South-Western, 1999), 329.

Direct Coordinating Mechanisms

Direct mechanisms that provide the basis for the overall guidance and management of foreign operations include the design of appropriate structures (discussed previously in this chapter) and the use of effective staffing practices (discussed in Chapter 9). Such decisions proactively set the stage for operations to meet goals, rather than troubleshooting deviations or problems after they have occurred. The accompanying Management Focus: McDonald's in Moscow—A Decade of Control Challenges describes how McDonald's Corporation. successfully set up direct control systems in advance of its entry into Moscow.

Management Focus

McDonald's in Moscow—A Decade of Control Challenges

We have proudly served millions of customers and are looking forward to working with our team of managers and crew to expand our operation to serve many more in communities across Russia.

—Khamzat Khasbulatov, President, McDonald's in Russia[47]

Russians line up to sample McDonald's fare in Moscow; 30,000 were served on opening day.

As of 2001, McDonald's had fifty-eight restaurants in the Moscow region, St. Petersburg, Nizhny Novgorod, Yaroslavl, Samara, and Kazan. The restaurants serve more than 150,000 customers every day, and since opening on January 31, 1990, it has served more than 250 million customers and more than 52 million Big Mac sandwiches.

It all started with a chance meeting between George Cohon, senior chairman, McDonald's Canada, and a Soviet Olympic delegation at the Olympic games in Montreal in 1976. It sparked fourteen years of negotiations and culminated in the opening of the first McDonald's in Russia.

When the restaurant finally opened its doors in Moscow's busy Pushkin Square in January 1990, the largest agreement between the former Soviet Union and a food service company became a reality. The 900-seat restaurant broke several of McDonald's previous records: 30,000 Russians were served on opening day, and 1 million had been served by March. It took twelve years of negotiations by George A. Cohon, president and founder of McDonald's Restaurants of Canada, to open the doors in Pushkin Square. McDonald's has a 49 percent interest in the joint venture with the Moscow City Council Department of Food Service. In all, McDonald's

Canada invested $50 million for construction and personnel training for the processing plant and the restaurant. It agreed to reinvest all its profits in Moscow for a chain of twenty restaurants.

The biggest control problem for McDonald's was that of quality control for its food products. Unlike its Western counterparts, this international joint venture (IJV) has had to adopt a strategy of vertical integration for its sourcing of raw materials. To control the quality, distribution, and reliability of its ingredients, McDonald's built a $40 million, 110,000-square-foot plant in a Moscow suburb to process the required beef, milk, buns, vegetables, sauces, and potatoes. The facility includes laboratories for testing to ensure compliance with quality and consistency standards. Peter Frings, an agronomist with McCain Foods Limited, was brought in to introduce the Russian farmers to the nonnative Russet Burbank potato used to make the famous McDonald's fries. Frings and other experts spent several months working on local farms to advise farmers on such aspects as increasing acreage yields and boosting overall quality.

Operational control was a considerable problem for McDonald's in this historic joint venture, specifically in regard to controlling the quality of food and service. The first challenge was the hiring and training of local employees; Craig Sopkowicz, McDonald's quality-control expert, was in charge of the new employees. "We looked for applicants who lived close to the restaurant, among other things, in order to control the timeliness of employees," explains Sopkowicz.[48] Most of the new hires were between 18 and 27 years old, and this was usually their first job: Teenagers seldom work in Russia because labor laws protect them from conflicts with schoolwork. After selecting the 630-member crew, the all-important training and customer control began. To be flexible when positions changed, the new crew was trained in all aspects of the restaurant's functions; the new staff logged in more than 15,000 training hours to ensure control similar to that in Western operations. In addition, Roy Ellis, the personnel specialist, had some concern about the employees' appearance and decided to construct an on-site laundry room. "It's more practical . . . and it means we can ensure our standards,"

explains Ellis.[49] The four Russian managers (Khamzat Khazbulatov, Vladimir Zhurakovskij, Mikhail Sheleznov, and Georgij Smoleevskij) went through the same rigorous training that any other McDonald's manager would, enabling them to manage any of the 11,000 units worldwide. They went to McDonald's Institute of Hamburgerology in Toronto, Canada, for five months—a 1,000-hour program—and from there they went to Hamburger University in Oakbrook, Illinois, for two weeks training along with 235 managers from around the world. The operating philosophy underlying the training can be summed up as "QSC&V"—quality, service, cleanliness, and value.

Innovative control procedures take place in front of the counter in the Moscow unit as well as behind the cash registers. To control for the timeliness of service, McDonald's tried to reduce the long waiting lines by hiring private security people to keep order and by using public-address systems to tell patrons how to place orders. In addition to verbal instructions, customers are given picture-menus to simplify the ordering process. The Russian menu has also been streamlined to help speed up the service and the decision-making process. McDonald's has combated the growing black market problem by installing a one-door policy; this has eliminated large-scale pilferage, which usually occurs out the back door. A limit of ten Big Macs to each customer helps stop the black market sale to hungry customers anxiously waiting in line.

Top management at McDonald's anticipated difficulties with the setup and daily operations of this IJV and, indeed, had been working toward the opening day for thirteen years. Through careful planning for the control of crucial operational factors, they solved the sourcing, distribution, and employment problems inherent in the former Soviet Union.

More than a decade later, in 2001, McDonald's Russia was still importing chickens from France, cheese, fish, and apple segments from Poland, and potatoes—cut and frozen—from the Netherlands. Now a "chain" in Russia with fifty-eight restaurants, McDonald's says that it sources 75 percent of its supplies within the country but that, for continued quality control, it opened its own "McComplex" farm to supply its outlets.

SOURCE: Updates by the author from www.McDonalds.com, February 20, 2001; A. Jack, "Russians Wake Up to Consumer Capitalism," www.FT.com *(Financial Times),* January 30, 2001; earlier material adapted by the author from a term paper written by Gil George and Karsten Fetten, students at the State University of New York–Plattsburgh (December 1990). Copyright © 2001 by Helen Deresky.

Other direct mechanisms are visits by head-office personnel and regular meetings. Top executives from headquarters may use periodic visits to subsidiaries to check performance, troubleshoot, and help to anticipate future problems. International Telephone and Telegraph Corporation (ITT) holds monthly management meetings at its New York headquarters. Performance data are submitted by each ITT subsidiary general manager from around the world, and problems and solutions are shared.[50] The meetings allow each general manager to keep in touch with her or his associates, with the overall mission and strategy of the organization, and with comparative performance data and new problem-solving techniques. Increasingly, the tools of technology are being applied as direct mechanisms to ensure up front that operations will be carried out as planned, in particular in countries where processes such as efficient infrastructure and goods forwarding cannot be taken for granted. An example of this is the logistics monitoring system set up by Air Express International in Latin America to minimize its many problems there.[51] As another example, Bikeworld.com controls its order fulfillment and customer service as it expands globally by incorporating FedEx e-business technologies to develop a fully automated and scalable fulfillment system (see E-Biz Box).

E-BIZ BOX

Bikeworld Goes Global with E-Commerce Shipping Alliances

Over thirty years ago Bikeworld established itself as the place to go in San Antonio, Texas, for high-quality bicycles and components, expert advice, and personalized service. Then, in 1996, Whit Snell, Bikeworld's founder, realized that he needed to put his company on the Internet in order to keep customers from using out-of-state mail-order houses. For Bikeworld, the Web represented a 24-hour global retail space where small companies had the same reach and potential for success as much larger ones. So, Bikeworld opened its Web site in 1996, and joined the e-commerce opportunities to become a global company.

BIKEWORLD FACES THE CHALLENGES OF GLOBAL SHIPPING AND TRACKING

Bikeworld was soon to encounter one of Internet retailing's highest hurdles: fulfillment and after-sale customer service. Sales of its high-value bike accessories over the Internet were steadily increasing, but the time spent processing orders, manually shipping packages, and responding to customers' order status inquiries threatened to overwhelm the 16-person operation.

In need of help, Bikeworld looked to FedEx and realized FedEx could offer affordable express delivery on every order; exceeding customer expectations while automating the fulfillment process.

"To go from a complete unknown to a reputable worldwide retailer was going to require more than a fair price. We set out to absolutely amaze our customers with unprecedented customer service. FedEx gave us the blinding speed we needed," says Snell.

The FedEx solution was twofold: To better manage the dramatic increase in sales volume, the FedEx PowerShip system was integrated with the Bikeworld.com Web server for a seamless exchange of information—from online selling through fulfillment and reporting. When an order is placed at Bikeworld.com, it is assigned a unique FedEx tracking number. As the order proceeds through the assembly process, a FedEx shipping label is generated automatically.

In search of a solution for its customer inquiry issues, Bikeworld utilized FedExShip Manager API software to develop a custom tracking application. The software code embedded FedEx shipping and package tracking functions into Bikeworld's Web site. It allows customers to follow their orders from the moment they're placed until the FedEx courier arrives. Snell says that it's not unusual for customers to check on their orders several times a day, following their packages through the FedEx delivery network.

- Fully automated and scalable fulfillment system enabled sales value to increase from $1 million to $6 million.
- Access to real-time order status enhances customer service and leads to greater customer retention.
- Bikeworld now has global capacity to service customers.

GROWTH AT THE SPEED OF THE NET

As a traditional shop, Bikeworld's annual sales hovered around $1 million, more than respectable for the category. Four years after venturing online, sales volume has more than quadrupled, and the company is on track to surpass $6 million in 2000. More significantly, Bikeworld.com is consistently profitable, a distinction that places it among the e-commerce elite.

"We had growth but not explosive growth until we went online and chose FedEx as our carrier and offered reliable overnight and two-day service. Just the fact that our product arrives in the FedEx box adds credibility to its value," explains Snell. "The ability to fulfill orders is almost a product by itself. Once you get that done, you can do anything. FedEx helped us get there."

And if you're in San Antonio, you can still visit Bikeworld's Alamo Heights location to buy a bike, find an elusive part, or get a flat fixed.

▷ BIKEWORLD'S ORDER MANAGEMENT PROCESS

❶ Customer places an order on the Internet at www.bikeworld.com.

❷ Bikeworld.com's server, assigns the customer's order a FedEx tracking number, using FedEx PowerShip software. As the order proceeds through assembly, a FedEx shipping label is generated automatically.

❸ Bikeworld.com assembles the customer order and places the shipping air waybill on the package.

❹ By integrating FedEx Ship Manager API into the Bikeworld.com Web site, customers are able to track their orders from the time they are placed until they are delivered.

❺ FedEx picks up the order and delivers overnight or within two to three days, depending on the customer's specifications.

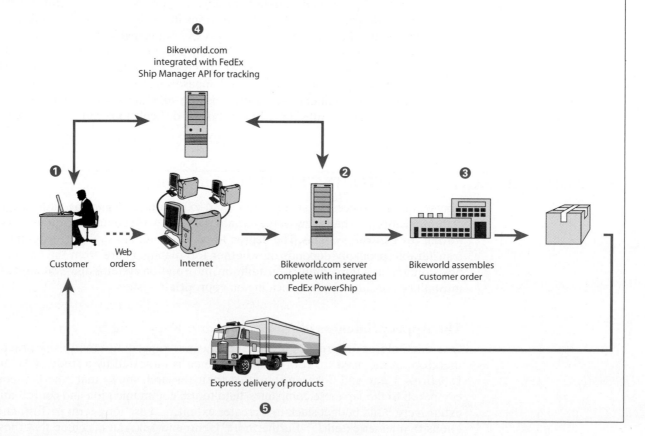

SOURCE: www.bikeworld.com, November 16, 2004, and adapted information from www.Fedex.com, February 22, 2002.

Indirect Coordinating Mechanisms

Indirect coordinating mechanisms typically include sales quotas, budgets, and other financial tools, as well as feedback reports, which give information about the sales and financial performance of the subsidiary for the last quarter or year.

Domestic companies invariably rely on budgets and financial statement analyses, but for foreign subsidiaries, financial statements and performance evaluations are complicated by *financial variables in MNC reports,* such as exchange rates, inflation levels, transfer prices, and accounting standards.

To reconcile accounting statements, MNCs usually require three different sets of financial statements from subsidiaries. One set must meet the national accounting standards and procedures prescribed by law in the host country. This set also aids management in comparing subsidiaries in the same country. A second set must be prepared according to the accounting principles and standards required by the home country. This set allows some comparison with other MNC subsidiaries. The third set of statements translates the second set of statements (with certain adjustments) into the currency of the home country for consolidation purposes, in accordance with FASB Ruling Number 52 of 1982. A foreign subsidiary's financial statements must be consolidated line by line with those of the parent company, according to International Accounting Standard Number 3, adopted in the United States.[52]

Researchers have noted comparative differences between the use of direct versus **indirect controls** among companies headquartered in different countries. One study by Egelhoff examined the practices of fifty U.S., U.K., and European MNCs over their foreign subsidiaries. It compared the use of two mechanisms—the assignment of parent-company managers to foreign subsidiaries and the use of performance reporting systems (that is, comparing behavior mechanisms with output reporting systems).[53] The results of this study show that considerable differences exist in practices across MNC nationalities. For example, says Egelhoff, U.S. MNCs monitor subsidiary outputs and rely more on frequently reported performance data than do European MNCs. The latter tend to assign more parent-company nationals to key positions in foreign subsidiaries and can count on a higher level of behavior control than their U.S. counterparts.[54]

These findings imply that the U.S. system, which measures more quantifiable aspects of a foreign subsidiary, provides the means to compare performance among subsidiaries. The European system, on the other hand, measures more qualitative aspects of a subsidiary and its environment, which vary among subsidiaries—allowing a focus on the unique situation of the subsidiary but making it difficult to compare its performance to other subsidiaries.[55]

MANAGING EFFECTIVE MONITORING SYSTEMS

Management practices, local constraints, and expectations regarding authority, time, and communication are but a few of the variables likely to affect the **appropriateness of monitoring (or control) systems**. The degree to which headquarters' practices and goals are transferable probably depends on whether top managers are from the head office, the host country, or a third country. In addition, information systems and evaluation variables must all be considered when deciding on appropriate systems.

The Appropriateness of Monitoring and Reporting Systems

One example of differences in the expectations regarding monitoring practices, and therefore in the need for coordination systems, is indicated by a study of Japanese and U.S. firms. Ueno and Sekaran state that their research shows that "the U.S. companies, compared to the Japanese companies, tend to use communication and coordination more extensively, build budget slack to a greater extent, and use long-term performance evaluations to a lesser extent."[56] Furthermore, Ueno and Sekaran conclude that those differences in reporting systems are attributable to the cultural variable of individualism in U.S. society, compared to collectivism in Japanese society. For example, U.S. managers are more likely to use formal communication and coordination processes, whereas Japanese managers use informal and implicit processes. In addition, U.S. managers, who are evaluated on individual performance, are more likely to build slack into budget calculations for a safety net than their Japanese counterparts, who are evaluated on group performance. The implications of this study are that managers around the world who understand the cultural bases for differences in control practices will be more flexible in working with those systems in other countries.

The Role of Information Systems

Reporting systems, such as those described in this chapter, require sophisticated information systems to enable them to work properly—not only for competitive purposes but also for purposes of performance evaluation. Top management must receive accurate and timely information regarding sales, production, and financial results to be able to compare actual performance with goals and to take corrective action where necessary. Most international reporting systems require information feedback at one level or another for financial, personnel, production, and marketing variables.

The specific types of functional reports, their frequency, and the amount of detail required from subsidiaries by headquarters will vary. Neghandi and Welge surveyed the types of functional reports submitted by 117 MNCs in Germany, Japan, and the United States.[57] They found that U.S. MNCs typically submit about double the number of reports than do German and Japanese MNCs, with the exception of performance reviews. German MNCs submit a few more reports than do Japanese MNCs. U.S. MNCs thus seem to monitor much more via specific functional reports than do German and Japanese MNCs. The Japanese MNCs put far less emphasis on personnel performance reviews than do the U.S. and German MNCs—a finding consistent with the Japanese culture of group decision making, consensus, and responsibility.

Unfortunately, the accuracy and timeliness of information systems are often less than perfect, especially in less developed countries, where managers typically operate under conditions of extreme uncertainty. Government information, for example, is often filtered or fabricated; other sources of data for decision making are usually limited. Employees are not used to the kinds of sophisticated information generation, analysis, and reporting systems common in developed countries. Their work norms and sense of necessity and urgency may also confound the problem. In addition, the hardware technology and the ability to manipulate and transmit data are usually limited. The **MIS adequacy** in foreign affiliates is a sticky problem for headquarters managers in their attempt to maintain efficient coordination of activities and consolidation of results. Another problem is the **non-comparability of performance data across countries**—the control problem caused by the difficulty of comparing performance data across various countries because of the variables that make that information appear different—which hinders the evaluation process.

The Internet has, of course, made the availability and use of information attainable instantaneously. Many companies are starting to supply Internet MIS systems for supply-chain management. European partners Nestlé S.A. and Danone Group, world leaders in the food industry, set up Europe's first Internet marketplace for e-procurement in the consumer goods sector, called CPGmarket.com:

> *CPGmarket.com will enhance the efficiency of logistics while at the same time reducing procurement costs for businesses producing, distributing and selling consumer goods. CPG (based on mySAP.com e-business platform) allows companies not only to buy and sell, but also to access industry information. . . . Participants will benefit from a more efficient market, reducing costs through higher transaction efficiency and simplified processes.[58]*

Evaluation Variables across Countries

A major problem that arises when evaluating the performance of foreign affiliates is the tendency by headquarters managers to judge subsidiary managers as if all of the evaluation data were comparable across countries. Unfortunately, many variables can make the evaluation information from one country look very different from that of another country, owing to circumstances beyond the control of a subsidiary manager. For example, one country may experience considerable inflation, significant fluctuations in the price of raw materials, political uprisings, or governmental actions. These factors are beyond the manager's control and are likely to have a downward effect on profitability—and yet, that manager may, in fact, have maximized the opportunity for long-term stability and profitability compared with a manager of another subsidiary who was not faced with such adverse conditions. Other variables influencing profitability patterns include transfer pricing, currency devaluation, exchange-rate fluctuations, taxes, and expectations of contributions to local economies.

One way to ensure more meaningful performance measures is to adjust the financial statements to reflect the uncontrollable variables peculiar to each country where a subsidiary is located. This provides a basis for the true evaluation of the comparative return on investment (ROI), which is an overall control measure. Another way to provide meaningful, long-term performance standards is to take into account other nonfinancial measures. These measures include market share, productivity, sales, relations with the host-country government, public image, employee morale, union relations, and community involvement.[59]

CONCLUSION

The structure, control, and coordination *processes* are the same whether they take place in a domestic company, a multinational company with a network of foreign affiliates, or a specific IJV. It is the extent, the focus, and the mechanisms used to organize those activities that differ. More coordination is needed in global companies because of uncertain working environments and information systems and because of the variable loci of decision making. Headquarters managers must design appropriate systems to take into account those variables and to evaluate performance.

Summary of Key Points

1. An organization must be designed to facilitate the implementation of strategic goals. Other variables to consider when designing an organization's structure include environmental conditions, the size of the organization, and the appropriate technology. The geographic dispersion of operations as well as differences in time, language, and culture affect structure in the international context.
2. The design of a firm's structure reflects its international entry strategy and tends to change over time with growth and increasing levels of investment, diversity, or both.
3. Global trends are exerting increasing pressure on MNCs to achieve economies of scale through globalization. This involves rationalization and the coordination of strategic alliances.
4. MNCs can be regarded as interorganizational networks of their own dispersed operations and other strategic alliances. Such relational networks may adopt unique structures for their particular environment, while also requiring centralized coordination.
5. The transnational structure allows a company to "be global and act local" by using networks of decentralized units with horizontal communication. This permits local flexibility while achieving global integration.
6. Indications of the need for structural changes include inefficiency, conflicts among units, poor communication, and overlapping responsibilities.
7. Coordinating and monitoring systems are necessary to regulate organizational activities so that actual performance conforms to expected organizational standards and goals. MNCs use a variety of direct and indirect controls.
8. Financial monitoring and evaluation of foreign affiliates are complicated by variables such as exchange rates, levels of inflation, transfer prices, and accounting standards.
9. The design of appropriate monitoring systems must take into account local constraints, management practices and expectations, uncertain information systems, and variables in the evaluation process.
10. Two major problems in reporting for subsidiaries must be considered: (1) inadequate management information systems and (2) the noncomparability across countries of the performance data needed for evaluation purposes.

Discussion Questions

1. What variables have to be considered in designing the organizational structure for international operations? How do these variables interact, and which do you think are most important?
2. Explain the need for an MNC to "be global and act local." How can a firm design its organization to enable this?
3. What is a transnational organization? Since many large MNCs are moving toward this format, it is likely that you could at some point be working within this structure. How do you feel about that?
4. Discuss the implications of the relative centralization of authority and decision making at headquarters versus local units or subsidiaries. How would you feel about this variable if you were a subsidiary manager?
5. As an international manager, what would make you suggest restructuring your firm? What other means of direct and indirect monitoring systems do you suggest?
6. What is the role of information systems in the reporting process? Discuss the statement "Inadequate MIS systems in some foreign affiliates are a control problem for MNCs."

Application Exercises

1. If you have personal access to a company with international operations, try to conduct some interviews and find out about the personal interactions involved in working with the organization's counterparts abroad. In particular, ask questions about the nature and level of authority and decision making in overseas units compared with headquarters. What kinds of conflicts are experienced? What changes would your interviewees recommend?
2. Do some research on monitoring and reporting issues facing an MNC with subsidiaries in (1) India and (2) the former East Germany. Discuss problem areas and your recommendations to the MNC management as to how to control potential problems.
3. Find out about an IJV in the United States. Get some articles from the library, write to the company for information, and if possible visit the company and ask questions. Present your findings on the company's major control issues to the class—both at the beginning of the venture and now. What is the company doing differently in its control process compared to a typical domestic operation? Are the control procedures having the desired results? What recommendations do you have?

Experiential Exercise

In groups of four, consider a fast-food chain going into Eastern Europe. Decide on your initial level of desired international involvement and your entry strategy. Draw up an appropriate organizational design, taking into account strategic goals, relevant variables in the particular countries in which you will have operations, technology used, size of the firm, and so on. At the next class, present your organization chart and describe the operations and rationale. (You could finalize the chart on an overhead or flip chart before class begins.) What are some of the major control issues to be considered?

Internet Resources

Visit the Deresky companion Web site at prenhall.com/deresky for this chapter's Internet resources.

Asea Brown Boveri (ABB), Sweden, 2004: What Went Wrong?

Since its inception, Asea Brown Boveri (hereafter called ABB) has always attracted the business and academic community because of its unique organizational structure, consistent growth pattern, and extensive worldwide operations.[1] After the merger of Asea and Brown, Boveri and Cie (BBC), ABB had an excellent international expansion. Academics and business practitioners studying multinational corporations (MNCs) and global companies often admired ABB because of its outstanding growth, highly sophisticated management, and peculiar corporate structure.[2] ABB particularly became famous for its unique decentralized horizontal organizational system and global networking, which was based on lateral communication across the company's 1,000 entities around the globe.[3] The phrase "think global, act local" became synonymous with ABB and its former chairman, Percy Barnevik, who aggressively advocated and practiced the concept in the company.[4] In 2004, ABB continues to be global leader in the areas of power and automation technologies although the company's corporate image has been affected because of heavy losses in 2001 and 2002. In 2003, ABB's revenues surpassed $20.4 billion and made a profit of $108 million. During the same period, the company's market value stood at $12.12 billion. On the other hand, in 2000, the Groups' market capitalization exceeded $40 billion. As of 2004, the ABB Group has operations in over 100 countries, employs 116,464 people worldwide, and is listed on the stock exchanges of Zurich, Stockholm, London, Frankfurt, and New York.[5] In the last five years, ABB has not been able to achieve the same growth and expansion because of changing markets and slow demand.

The ABB Group has over 115 years of rich history dating back to the late 1800s. The Group was formed in 1988 when Asea AB of Västerås, Sweden and BBC Brown Boveri Limited of Baden, Switzerland merged their operations and formed ABB (Asea Brown Boveri) Limited. Each company held 50 percent of the new entity and was headquartered in Zurich, Switzerland. The merger was highly rated by the media because of Europe's 1992 economic integration. In 1883, Ludvig Fredholm founded Elektriska Aktiebolaget in Stockholm that in 1890 merged with Wenstroms and Granstroms Elektriska Kraftbolag to form Asea (Allmanna Svenska Elektriska Aktiebolaget). In the next fifty years, Asea grew from an unknown company to an international entity having subsidiaries in Great Britain, Denmark, Finland, and Spain. The company became famous for its transmission lines, generators, transformers, locomotives, and motors.[6]

BBC was founded by Charles E. L. Brown and Walter Boveri in Baden, Switzerland in 1891. By the early 1900, BBC had its operations in Austria, Germany, Italy, and Norway. Like Asea, BBC manufactured power plants, turbines, transformers, hydroelectric power stations, locomotives, and other industrial products. The company invented many new technologies and set the pace for the power generation industry. Before merging with Asea, BBC was operating globally and employed 97,000 workers worldwide.[7] Under the leadership of its former chairman Percy Barnevik, the company launched a massive global expansion program because of growing demand, especially in East Asia and Eastern Europe. Between 1993 and 1998, ABB continued to grow in Europe, Asia, and Latin America by seeking acquisitions, alliances and joint ventures that helped the company to

---

An earlier version of this case was presented at the 2004 Academy of International Business Annual Conference, Stockholm, Sweden, July 10–13, 2004.

The material in this case is intended to be used as a basis for classroom/academic discussion rather than to illustrate either effective or ineffective handling of a managerial situation or business practices.

[1] See company Web site (www.abb.com).

[2] For more information, see: *The Asian Wall Street Journal*. (1995). "U.S. power provider ABB profits from localization," (May 22), p. 4; *The Asian Wall Street Journal*. (1996). Swiss-Swedish ABB is among Europe's leaders in looking to Asia for continued revenue growth, (March 4), p. 19; Belanger, Jacques et al. (editors). (1999). *Being local worldwide: ABB and the challenge of global management*, New York: Cornell University Press; Berggren, Christian. (1996). "Building a truly global organization? ABB and the problems of integrating a multi-domestic enterprise," *Scandinavian Journal of Management*, 12 (2), pp. 123–137.

[3] For detail, see: Deresky, Helen. (2003). *International Management: Managing Across Borders and Cultures*, Upper Saddle River, New Jersey: Prentice Hall, p. 305; Kotabe, Masaaki and Kristiaan, Helsen. (2004). *Global Marketing Management*, New York: John Wiley & Sons, pp. 549–550.

[4] Burham, K. and Heimer, C. (1998). *ABB—the dancing giant*, London, UK: Financial Times/Pitman Publishing.

SOURCE: Written exclusively for this book by Syed Tariq Anwar, May 2004, Copyright © Syed Tariq Anwar.

---

[5] For more information, see company Web site (www.abb.com); *Forbes*. (2004). "The world's 2000 leading companies, (April 12), pp. 144–220; *Value Line*. 2002. Machinery industry, (August 2): 1331; *The Wall Street Journal*. (2003). "The great asbestos swindle," (January 6), A18; *The Wall Street Journal*. (2003). "How 'Europe's GE' and its star CEO tumbled to earth," (January 23), A1&A8.

[6] See company Web site (www.abb.com).

[7] See company Web site (www.abb.com).

consolidate its position in world markets. The year 1998 was particularly important for ABB when it acquired Elsag Bailey Process Automation. The acquisition made ABB a major player in the global automation market.

ABB's current history and corporate profile are incomplete without discussing its two former high-ranking officers, Percy Barnevik (chairman) and Goeran Lindahl (chief executive), who left the company in 2001. Both were criticized by the world media over their generous pension payments received from ABB after departing the company. Barnevik alone received over $87 million in pension benefits. Interestingly, during the same year, ABB lost $691 million. In addition, the company's U.S. subsidiary was sued for asbestos liabilities. Since Barnevik coordinated the merger between Asea and Brown Boveri, he was highly admired by the analysts because of his corporate foresight and making ABB one of the best global companies in the world.[8] In the late nineties, Barnevik was known as another Jack Welch (former CEO of General Electric) because of his leadership, star image, and global vision.[9] Jurgen Dormann, the current CEO who worked for Aventis, took over the company in September 2002 and has brought a multitude of structural changes to avoid bankruptcy. Although ABB lost $691 million in 2001and $161 million in 2002, it earned a net profit of $108 million in 2003.[10]

What Went Wrong with ABB's Organizational Structure?

Global companies formulate their organizational structures on the basis of location, market coverage, competition, and product lines. Like other companies, ABB was severely impacted by the East Asian crisis. The region's currency depreciations and weaker economies had an adverse affect that brought massive reductions in the company's revenues. In addition to the East Asian crisis, ABB's own corporate blunders, complex organizational structure, and reshuffling of the top management added miseries to the company. The net result was a major financial downfall that affected the company's market value, growth, and global operations. ABB's organizational problems and missteps that led to the negative image, lost market share, and corporate retrenchment are as follows:

1. Global diversifications and internationalization issues: In the nineties, ABB expanded operations and sought internationalization at a very fast pace. The

company established hundreds of subsidiaries worldwide that included power/electrical equipment, oil, gas and petrochemicals, automation technologies, and other heavy industries. During the tenure of Barnevik, ABB became highly infatuated with global expansion that eventually brought losses and corporate problems.[11] ABB was famous for its unique matrix structure at the global level. In the seventies and the eighties, many companies capitalized on the matrix structure that was thought to be highly efficient at the multidimensional and global levels.[12] In the initial stages, companies benefited because of the matrix's economies of scale, innovative operations, lateral personal communications, and transfer of resources. The weaknesses of the matrix system were found in the areas of authority and chain of command that led to ambiguity and increased costs.[13] Likewise, ABB encountered problems in its matrix structure and had difficulty materializing its goals at the global level (see Figure 1).

2. Leadership gaps and performance issues: In 2002, ABB started to see the impact of the East Asian crisis and weaker demand from other parts of the world. In addition, ABB's organizational structure and control system made things even worse. This resulted in major restructuring and changes in its top management. From 2000 to 2003, the Group undertook significant corporate changes that led to unloading the company's financial services and oil and gas divisions. As of 2004, ABB has somewhat recovered by restructuring its power and automation technology divisions. Barnevik did an excellent job in the nineties regarding internationalizing ABB. After a period of rapid growth, Barnevik's leadership and management style became ineffective and controversial because of ABB's far-flung operations, complex organizational structure, and widespread international subsidiaries. During Barnevik's long tenure with ABB, the company had no plan of succession. In addition, ABB's top management actively sought decentralization while keeping its global matrix structure in many markets. This impacted the company's performance eventually leading to losses.

3. East-Asian financial crisis: The East Asian financial crisis was triggered by China's devaluation of the yuan and later spread to other parts of East Asia. In the nineties, East Asia's economic health was solid and the region had started a variety of infrastructural projects. ABB was one of the major beneficiaries of the Asian development. After the crisis, large industrial conglomerates

[8]For more discussion, see: Barth, Steve. (1998). "World trade's executive of the decade," *World Trade Magazine,* (December), pp. 1–7, (www.global-insight.com); *Financial Times.* (1998). "All the power but none of the glory", (August 24), p. 7; *Financial Times.* (2001). "Foundations look shady on the house that Percy built," (September 18), p. 24.
[9]*The Economist.* (1988). "Asea-Brown Boveri! Power play," (May 28), pp. 19–22.
[10]*Business Week.* (2002). "Barnevik's fall from grace," (March 25), p. 1; *Business Week.* (2002). "Making a federal case out of overseas abuses," (November 25), p. 78.

[11]For more information, see: *Financial Times.* (1997). "A multinational cadre of managers is the key," (October 8), p. 10; *Financial Times.* (2002). "How a toxic mixture of asbestos liabilities and plummeting demand poisoned an industrial powerhouse," (October 23), p. 13; *The Wall Street Journal.* (2003). "How 'Europe's GE' and its star CEO tumbled to earth," (January 23), pp. A1&A8; *The Wall Street Journal.* (2003). "ABB U.S. unit files for chapter 11, cites asbestos claimants," (February 18), p. A19.
[12]Agthe, Klaus E. (1990). "Managing the mixed marriage," *Business Horizons,* 33 (1), pp. 37–43.
[13]For detail, see: AT Kearney. (2002). *Waging war on complexity: How to master the matrix organizational structure,* Chicago, Illinois: A. T. Kearney, Inc.

like ABB with extensive involvement in the region were unable to deal with the changing markets. Cancellations of projects that led to heavy losses and downsizing were the end result. ABB could not recover from the East Asian crisis and saw its revenues dry up in the region that led to a total loss of over $1 billion in 2001/2002.

4.   Controversy over pension benefits: In the last few years, CEO salaries and their exorbitant pension benefits have been severely criticized by the media. Company executives from Enron, World Com, ImClone, and others have been sent to jails for mishandling the company money and their unethical behavior. In 2002, Barnevik became part of the controversy when it was discovered that he had received from ABB pension benefits worth $87 million. This was major negative publicity for the company when it lost over $500 million during the same period.

5.   Issues of asbestos-related liabilities: Like other companies, ABB was also hit hard by massive asbestos claims because of the U.S. Combustion Engineering Unit that the company had acquired in 1990. In 2003, ABB allocated $1.2 billion to deal with these claims. In 2003, in the U.S. alone, 90,000 new asbestos claims were filed raising the corporate liability to U.S. plaintiffs about $200 billion. According to a survey published by Rand Institute of Civil Justice, in the coming years, there could be another 2.4 million workers affected by the asbestos-related crisis, making new claims of $200 billion.[14] ABB has allocated a significant contingency fund to deal with the current and future asbestos claims. The asbestos issue was a major setback to ABB's global restructuring and recovery.

6.   Changing global competition: Global competition in the power plants and other heavy industry has changed in the last ten years. At the time of the Asea and BBC merger, markets were booming in the Asian region. For a long time, ABB maintained a strong presence in the industry because of its unique organizational structure and worldwide operations. As of 2004, there tends to be more competition in the industry and some of the large market opportunities have disappeared. Like other industries, power plants and infrastructural industries were affected by factors that ABB could not control.

What Lies Ahead?

After 2001, ABB made changes in its top leadership as well as organizational structure. In 2004, ABB announced the appointment of Fred Kindle as its future CEO.[15] The company conducted a thorough evaluation of its global operations and core competencies. In 2004, ABB continues to re-fetch its global growth by being more proactive in its regional growth. For example, the company seems more realistic in its core operations and non-core assets such as oil, gas, and petrochemicals have been unloaded to deal with current financial problems. ABB has cut over 12,000 jobs worldwide to streamline the operations and continues to deal with its asbestos-related liabilities. ABB's poor performance and pension scandals forced the management to concentrate on its regional operations. The company has started to re-design its complex organizational structure and control system based on rationalization, performance, and growth (see Figure 1). On the basis of past events, it is expected that the company will continue to reorganize its global operations. ABB's top management has devised a major restructuring plan that proposes selling its oil, gas, and petrochemical division for $925 million. In 2003, the company proposed a $2.5 billion rights issue, seeking a three-year $1 billion credit facility, and future $750 million bond issue.[16] In the coming years, the company will continue to reformulate its core competencies and more corporate changes are expected. Additional corporate rationalization and organizational streamlining is possible if ABB sees recovery in its global markets.

In conclusion, ABB is an interesting case study in the areas of organizational structure and control systems. Right from its inception (after the merger in 1988), ABB has been the first-mover company and a market leader in the power and oil and gas industry. Led by its former visionary chairman Barnevik, ABB was highly pragmatic and entrepreneurial in its early growth and global expansion. Regarding organizational structure and control systems, the ABB case is relevant from two areas. First, market leaders may not maintain a strong competitive edge forever. Organizational structures and control systems must conform to the markets and competition. Besides this, the design of the global organizational structure must fit the strategy and the environment. Second, very few MNCs exploit new markets by applying the same organizational structures. In the coming years, it will be interesting to see if ABB can maintain worldwide growth by following its newly devised plan or just keep shedding operations and other subsidiaries.

---

[14]*Fortune.* (2002). "The $200 billion miscarriage of justice," (March 4), pp. 154–170.

[15]*Financial Times.* (2004). "ABB surprises with new chief," (March 2), p. 16.

[16]*New York Times.* (2002). "ABB plans to sell part of its financial unit," (April 3), pp. W1&W7.

FIGURE 1. ABB's old versus new corporate strategy and organizational models during the tenures of CEOs Percy Barnevik and Jürgen Dormann (1988–2004)

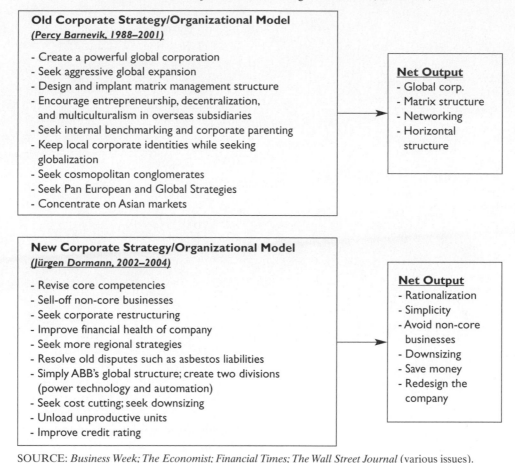

Old Corporate Strategy/Organizational Model
(Percy Barnevik, 1988–2001)

- Create a powerful global corporation
- Seek aggressive global expansion
- Design and implant matrix management structure
- Encourage entrepreneurship, decentralization, and multiculturalism in overseas subsidiaries
- Seek internal benchmarking and corporate parenting
- Keep local corporate identities while seeking globalization
- Seek cosmopolitan conglomerates
- Seek Pan European and Global Strategies
- Concentrate on Asian markets

Net Output
- Global corp.
- Matrix structure
- Networking
- Horizontal structure

New Corporate Strategy/Organizational Model
(Jürgen Dormann, 2002–2004)

- Revise core competencies
- Sell-off non-core businesses
- Seek corporate restructuring
- Improve financial health of company
- Seek more regional strategies
- Resolve old disputes such as asbestos liabilities
- Simply ABB's global structure; create two divisions (power technology and automation)
- Seek cost cutting; seek downsizing
- Unload unproductive units
- Improve credit rating

Net Output
- Rationalization
- Simplicity
- Avoid non-core businesses
- Downsizing
- Save money
- Redesign the company

SOURCE: *Business Week; The Economist; Financial Times; The Wall Street Journal* (various issues).

CASE QUESTIONS

1. What are your views of ABB's position in the global infrastructure industry?

2. Analyze and evaluate ABB's organizational structure and its control systems during the tenures of Percy Barnevik and Jürgen Dormann (see Figure 1). Also, draw a chart to discuss the company's strengths and weaknesses.

3. What specific strategies does ABB need to undertake in the coming years to be a key player in the industry? What structural changes should be made to implement those strategies?

4. What did you learn from ABB's complex organizational structure and its global operations?

Case 9 FedEx vs. UPS — Competing with Contrasting Strategies in China

I don't know that I agree that there's a sort of Chinese way and an American way. I think there is clearly more of an entrepreneurial and establishment way . . . and China at the moment is a country that is very entrepreneurial in nature. We are more consonant with the new China.
—Frederick W. Smith, Chairman and CEO, FedEx Corporation[1]

UPS expects continued strong and robust growth in China. We take a long-term approach to any expansion and believe the opportunity in China is great enough to overcome any business cycle.
—Jim Kelly, Chairman and CEO, UPS[2]

INTRODUCTION

The U.S.-based FedEx Corporation (FedEx),[3] one of the world's largest logistics solutions provider, announced a money-back guarantee scheme in September 2002 for its customers in China. Under the scheme, FedEx offered full refund of customers' money in case of late delivery of shipments. By introducing this scheme, FedEx became the first international logistics company to offer money-back guarantee in China.

Analysts were quick to comment that this measure was taken by FedEx to counterattack the move announced by its global competitor, the U.S.-based United Parcel Service (UPS).[4] UPS had opened two representative offices in the Chinese cities—Shenzhen and Qingdao in early September 2002. UPS had also announced its plans to open four more offices in Xiamen, Dongguan, Hangzhou, and Tianjin by early 2003.

For a long time, FedEx and UPS had been arch-rivals in China competing against each other for more market share in the Chinese logistics market (Refer Exhibit C9-1). According to the analysts, FedEx had adopted an aggressive approach to increase its market share in China. The company invested heavily in procuring air routes and in deploying its own aircrafts within and outside China for shipping goods. FedEx had also developed a vast distribution network with pickup outlets across China. Until 2001, the company used global advertising campaigns to advertise in China.

UPS, on the other hand, followed a more conservative and cautious approach while making inroads into the Chinese market. The company made efforts to position itself as a local company, rather than building an image of a global player. Instead of investing on building its own logistics infrastructure, the company decided to depend on leased facilities. Despite acquiring rights to fly its own plane in 2000, UPS was mostly dependent on its joint venture relationships to ship goods within and outside China. Analysts felt that UPS' advertising was old-fashioned, even compared to the prevalent standards in China.

Until the late 1990s, UPS followed a cautious approach, making limited investments in China compared to that of FedEx. However, with improving business prospects in China following its entry into the World Trade Organization (WTO) in 2001, the company aggressively pursued the Chinese market, helping it to develop its market presence there.

ESTABLISHING PRESENCE IN CHINA

According to the Chinese legal regulations, foreign logistics management companies including FedEx and UPS could do business in China only through a partnership or joint venture with a local company (Refer Exhibit C9-1). Foreign companies were not allowed to independently run businesses in China. Further, they were required to handle only international express cargo business (they were not permitted to do cargo handling business within the Chinese cities).

This case was written by Vivek Gupta, ICFAI Center for Management Research (ICMR). It is intended to be used as a basis for class discussion rather than to illustrate either effective or ineffective handling of a management situation.

The case was compiled from published sources.

[1]As quoted in the article, "Orient Express: Just How Hard Should a U.S. Company Woo Foreign Markets," by Douglas A. Blackmon and Diane Brady in *The Wall Street Journal,* dated April 6, 1998.

[2]As quoted in the article, "UPS Begins Direct Service to China," in www.newswire.ca, dated March 30, 2001.

[3]FedEx is one of the world's largest express transportation companies, providing information and logistics solutions services. For the financial year ending May 2003, the company generated revenues of $22.5 billion and net income of $1.47 billion.

[4]UPS is one of the world's largest express carrier and package delivery company. It is also a leading global provider of specialized transportation and logistics services. For the financial year ending December 2002, UPS generated revenues of $31.3 billion and a net income of $3.18 billion.

EXHIBIT C9-1 A Snapshot of the Logistics Industry in China (2002)

There are about 1,500 licensed international freight-forwarding operators in China. Of these, 450 are Sino-foreign joint ventures, primarily involved in the management of international freight at the international level. Inland transportation is handled by Chinese freight forwarders—mainly single-truck operations subcontracted by international freight forwarders to move goods from warehouses to ports. Foreign logistics companies face a number of hurdles for conducting business in China. An overview of such hurdles and the future scenario is given here.

Entry Barriers
Foreign logistics companies intending to do business in China can enter only through joint ventures with local Chinese companies.

Legal Regulations
Foreign companies cannot:

- Distribute products other than those they manufacture in China
- Own and manage distribution networks, wholesale outlets or warehouses
- Conduct customs brokerage and clearance, ground transportation, warehousing, and related services outside a transport joint venture.
- Hold a majority stake in a joint venture, with limitations on where and how fast joint ventures can expand

Expected Changes over the Next Decade
The Chinese government promised to make significant improvements in the next decade in relation to the regulations, following the commitments made to the WTO. The promised improvements include:

- Foreign companies will be allowed to distribute imported products, besides those made in China.
- China has agreed to phase out all restrictions on distribution services within three years. Restrictions on all services auxiliary to distribution will be phased out in three to four years. These include express delivery services, vehicle rental and leasing, freight forwarding, and storage and warehousing. Foreigners engaged in these businesses will be able to set up their wholly-owned subsidiaries.
- In the most sensitive and protected sectors—chemicals, oil, and petroleum—China will provide distribution rights to foreigners within five years.

Adapted from the article, "FedEx has ideas for China," written by David L Cunningham Jr. in *Nation* (Thailand), dated October 15, 2002.

FEDEX—DEVELOPING THE SERVICES NETWORK

FedEx commenced its operations in April 1973 in Memphis, U.S. In 1984, FedEx entered China after acquiring Gelco Express International, a UK-based courier company which had operations in Europe and Asia Pacific. During the first decade of its operations in China, FedEx focused on establishing the required infrastructure and distribution network to provide reliable express freight and documentation services.

Rather than targeting leading Chinese companies, FedEx focused on those multinational companies which had Chinese operations and were already FedEx's customers in the U.S. or elsewhere. FedEx also targeted those Chinese entrepreneurs who were expanding their business and whom the company believed would readily adopt FedEx's fast and accurate delivery techniques.

To compete effectively with the established local competitors in China, FedEx, in its initial years, invested heavily on building its own distribution network. In 1989, FedEx invested $880 million to acquire Flying Tiger Line Inc (Tiger).[5] The acquisition helped FedEx to get a ready access to Tiger's Asian routes, including a high traffic route between Japan and China.

By 1995, FedEx had started freight operations in China. The company appointed EAS International Transportation Limited (EAS) as a global service participant for China to ship the goods and packages within China. EAS acted as the carrier of the goods and packages of FedEx within China through its network spread across 34 major commercial cities covering nearly 50% of the Chinese population. By mid-1995, FedEx invested another $67.5 million to acquire Evergreen International Airlines,[6] the only cargo carrier with flying rights into China. This allowed FedEx access to an all-cargo route to directly serve the Chinese customers .

---

[5]Founded in 1945 in the U.S. as a coast-coast freight carrier, Tiger was one of the largest air cargo airlines in the country. By the time of its acquisition by FedEx, it became reputed as an all-cargo airline with flying rights to 21 countries.

[6]Headquartered at Oregon, U.S., EIA owned one of the largest all-cargo fleets in the cargo business, with operations across the world.

Following the receipt of the permit from the Civil Aviation Administration of China (CAAC) in January 1996, FedEx earned the distinction of being the only U.S.-based all-cargo carrier with aviation rights to China. Having secured the aviation rights in China and several other Asian countries, FedEx introduced the 'hub and spoke system'[7] in Asia. FedEx had already launched the Asia Pacific hub at Subic Bay, Philippines, in September 1995 in order to expand its operations in other Asian countries. This enabled the company to launch an organized distribution system in Asia, called the FedEx AsiaOne network through which 13 major commercial and financial cities in Asia (spokes) were connected. This network enabled FedEx to provide an overnight delivery of goods shipped within the Asian countries. The Asian shipments could be further routed to the FedEx's global network through the Asia Pacific hub.

In March 1996, FedEx launched its first scheduled air service in China using its own aircraft in and out of China with bi-weekly flights to Beijing and Shanghai. In September 1996, the two cities were integrated into the FedEx AsiaOne network. These enabled the customers in Shanghai and Beijing to ship and receive packages between China and the U.S. and the rest of Asia.

In April 1998, FedEx launched the Express Distribution Centers (EDCs) in Beijing and Hong Kong by entering into an agreement with U-Freight Holdings Limited.[8] The EDCs, which were connected to the AsiaOne network, enabled FedEx to ship the goods to the destination, through the fastest possible route within 24 hours of the receipt of the order. The EDCs were capable of handling huge volumes of inventory and providing distribution services for fast-moving, high turnover goods. The primary target customers for the EDCs were those customers who did not possess warehouses and required express transportation facilities to sell their products.

In 1999, FedEx launched the Chinese version of the "FedEx Internet Ship" software. The software permitted shippers to prepare shipment documentation for consignments to more than 60 countries using from their own offices. It also allowed online tracking of shipment status through FedEx's Web site. In February 1999, the tracking application was enhanced to allow FedEx customers to query and receive package status information for up to 25 shipments simultaneously.

By the late 1990s, FedEx had gained a stronghold in the Chinese market. The company had developed a huge network of purple and orange trucks and express distribution centers. FedEx had built a customer friendly image since the company provided its customers' quicker customs clearance and reliable pick-up and delivery services using its own aircraft linking China to extensive regional and global networks.

DEVELOPING THE SERVICES NETWORK

In 1907, Jim Casey (Jim), a 19-year-old messenger boy, started American Messenger Company (AMC) from a Seattle sidewalk in the U.S. to offer bicycle messenger service with an initial investment of $100. His intention was to offer messenger service of the highest quality at the lowest price to the customers. In 1913, Jim and Evert McCabe, who led rival Motorcycle Delivery Company, agreed to merge with AMC and a new company was formed. It was named as Merchants Parcel Delivery Company (MPDC). In 1919, MPDC was renamed as United Parcel Service (UPS).

UPS commenced its operations in China in 1988 through an agent partnership[9] relationship with China's biggest freight forwarder, *China National Foreign Trade Transportation Group,* popularly known as Sinotrans. In its first move, UPS started offering express delivery of small packages and documents. As per the agreement, UPS delivered the packages/documents to China while Sinotrans was responsible for delivering the packages in China.

Unlike FedEx, rather than using its own aircraft, UPS followed a low investment strategy for almost a decade after its entry into China. During that period, the company entered into alliances with airline companies— Hong Kong Dragon Airlines Limited[10] and China Eastern Airlines Corp[11] that delivered the packages to China.

By 1995, UPS sent its first flight to China from its two hubs located in Hong Kong and Singapore. By the end of 1995, the company had established its presence in 21 cities in China leveraging on its partnership with Sinotrans. In 1996, UPS entered into a 50–50 joint venture with Sinotrans Beijing Airfreight Forwarding Company (Pekair) in China. Through the joint venture, UPS aimed at improving its market share in the growing air freight market in China. The venture had an initial fleet of 12 vehicles, employee strength of 65, and covered 74 Chinese cities. It planned to offer international shipping of documents and parcels and international cargo transport.

During the late 1990s, UPS stepped up its investments in infrastructural facilities and acquisitions in order to expand its presence in China. In June 1998, UPS inaugurated a $2 million air hub facility at the express handling center at the Hong Kong airport. The facility enabled UPS to employ its own people and use its own

[7]According to the system, on a particular day, packages from various cities were sent to a central location called hub where they would be sorted out and then sent across to their ultimate destinations, called spokes through planes by early morning next day.
[8]A global transportation service provider that provides customs clearance, warehousing, domestic distribution, and other value added services.
[9]A relationship between two companies in which the agent company acts on behalf of the principal company, on the basis of mutually agreed terms.
[10]Founded in 1985, Dragon air served 27 passenger destinations across Asia with one of the most advanced aircraft fleets in the region.
[11]China's second largest air carrier, located in Shanghai.

infrastructure for loading and unloading of goods from its cargo carriers. Through this, the customers could be ensured that their baggage was handled carefully, thus further enhancing the reliability of UPS services.

The launch of the hub facility enabled UPS to launch its international shipping processing system in China. The facility was equipped with an electronic data access system, which was interlinked to the Electronic Data Interface (EDI) of the Customs & Excise Department at the airport Express Centre. Through this, UPS could get its packages cleared by the customs authorities even before their arrival into the airport, thereby saving a lot of time required for the customs clearance process.

In order to offer quicker delivery of the packages, UPS opened two spin-off centers in Hong Kong to sort and deliver packages during late 1998. As a result, UPS could increase the productivity of its baggage handling by 100%. Commenting on the launch of the facility, Perry Chao, UPS' Managing Director of Hong Kong operations, said, "Our strategy is to build a flexible, high-tech, reliable, and fully integrated operations network. As a result, our customers will continue to enjoy late cut-off time and speedy delivery even with the airport further away."[12] UPS also launched a new web-based delivery service, UPS document exchange service, which permitted reliable delivery of documents online through the Web site www.exchange.ups.com.

By 1999, UPS had spread its network across 108 cities in China, making it one of the largest networks by an international logistics company in China. In January 1999, UPS announced an agreement with Sinotrans, to expand its operations to 22 more cities in China. Through this agreement, UPS expanded its network to 130 cities in China, competing directly with FedEx, which had operations in 144 cities at that time. UPS and Sinotrans also signed a memorandum of understanding (MOU) stating that UPS would make additional investments to improve its operations, train its own staff by getting the help of Sinotrans. The company also aimed at enhancing its brand identity in China. By signing the MOU, UPS intended to make its uniformed drivers and brown trucks a common site on the streets of major business centers in China.

In April 1999, UPS entered into a strategic alliance with 7-Eleven, a leading convenience store in Hong Kong that operated round-the-clock. Through this agreement, UPS was able to expand its network by 350 locations in Hong Kong. At the stores, express envelopes were accepted, which were charged, depending upon the location to be shipped, irrespective of the weight of the package. In order to encourage the customers to try this service, UPS launched a limited period promotion campaign in which the customers who used the service were given a phone card having three visuals of the Sydney Olympics.

In November 1999, UPS began five-times-weekly scheduled express service to Shenzhen. By opening up an express-handling facility at Shenzhen airport, UPS became the first U.S. carrier to be permitted to handle its own express traffic in Shenzhen. During the period 1996–99, according to reports, UPS had made investments of an estimated $400 million in China.

THE CONTRASTING STRATEGIES

Analysts felt that FedEx and UPS established themselves in China till the late 1990s following different corporate styles. Both the companies followed a significantly different approach, providing different alternatives for companies that are planning to globalize. While FedEx believed in tackling foreign competition head-on, UPS believed in partnering with them. While FedEx followed a high risk approach, putting heavy investments to build its own manufacturing and distribution systems, UPS was happy to enter into lease agreements with companies already having presence in China. While FedEx's main thrust was on capturing the accounts of its multinational customers operating in China, UPS focused on the local customers. To promote its services, FedEx adopted Western-style advertising, while UPS tried to build an image of a local company.

ADVERTISING AND PROMOTION

Till the mid-1990s, the focus on advertising and promotion by both FedEx and UPS was relatively less. However, during the late 1990s, as the competition in the logistics business in China intensified, both FedEx and UPS started emphasizing on promotion to attract the Chinese customers. However, till the late 1990s, there was a marked distinction in the approach of FedEx and UPS towards advertising and promotion of their services in China.

FedEx followed an approach which emphasized heavily publicizing its service offerings in China. It launched intimidating ad campaigns to attract customers. For example, one of its advertisements in 1997 showed the tail of a FedEx plane parked in front of The Forbidden City saying "Call FedEx. It's almost forbidden not to." FedEx stressed promoting its service offerings and enhancing brand awareness among the customers in China. For this purpose, it hired a popular media company, OMD[13] based in Hong Kong.

In contrast to FedEx's approach, UPS used less advertising. It preferred to project itself as a local Chinese company. In a six-week TV campaign in 1997, the company displayed a motorized three wheeler, a larger van, a brown UPS truck, and a Boeing 747 moving together in a line on a runway representing its global image rather

---

[12] As quoted in the press release, "UPS Opens Hub Facility at Airport Express Centre. First Express Carrier Granted Self-Handling Right," posted on www.ups.com, dated June 30, 1998.

[13] Founded in 1996, OMD is the global media partner of three leading advertising agencies in the world—BBDO, DDB, and TBWA. It is a unit of Omnicom Group, the largest marketing and corporate communications company in the world.

than showing it as an American company. To target Chinese customers outside China, UPS-sponsored Chinese New Year celebrations in Toronto and Vancouver, where many Chinese immigrants resided. UPS also sponsored Olympic Games in China in 1996 and 2000.

TARGETING CUSTOMERS

While targeting customers in China, FedEx offered its standardized logistics services. However, FedEx seemed to have annoyed a few companies in China that expected a personalized approach from the company. Li Ping, an executive at Chinatex Cotton Yarns & Fabrics Import & Export Corporation in Beijing commented, "I know they're (FedEx) one of the biggest companies in the U.S., but that doesn't matter here (in China). The personal relationship matters most here. You have to talk to customers and make them feel good. . . . They haven't sent anyone here; so, we don't do business with them."[14]

FedEx targeted those customers who valued a highly controlled distribution system and wanted constant information about the status of shipments. The company focused on providing solutions to all logistics related problems of its customers. For instance, in the mid-1990s, FedEx noticed that Chinese exporters who shipped goods to the U.S. faced problems due to their ignorance of the U.S. customs clearance procedures. This caused unnecessary cost and time overruns since their shipments were held up with the U.S. customs department. FedEx realized that it could cash in on this opportunity to market its pre-clearance service[15] to the Chinese exporters.

During July and August 1996, the company conducted seminars in two major Chinese cities—Shanghai and Hong Kong—explaining to the customers the customs clearance procedure in the U.S. and how FedEx's service could solve their problems. This induced tremendous response and increase in the shipments from China to the U.S.

FedEx's main focus was on providing its customers innovative and value-added services. For instance, in September 2000, FedEx pioneered the launch of two new services for Chinese customers—The Asia One and the North American Next Day Delivery. The new services enabled customers in Beijing, Shanghai, Guangzhou, Shenzhen, and other neighboring cities to deliver their packages to 15 Asian cities (through Asia One) and major U.S. and Canadian cities (through North American Next Day Delivery) on the next working day. As a result, FedEx became the only company in China to offer such services. Commenting on FedEx's focus on

providing best services to the customers, Marco Lee, Managing Director (Regional Sales—China & Mid-Pacific) of FedEx said, "FedEx always wants to add value to our customers' businesses. We are here not only to provide solutions to our customers; we are also committed to help them increase efficiency."[16]

On the contrary, UPS targeted local Chinese customers following a personalized approach. The company attempted to adapt its services according to the customs and traditions of Chinese customers. For instance, the company noticed that Chinese customers attached a lot of importance to interpersonal relationships. Accordingly, UPS sales personnel cordially approached the customers, explained to them about the services and only then struck deals. Even the UPS couriers were recognized for their customer-friendly attitude. This approach enabled the company to develop a very good rapport with the Chinese customers and encouraged those who patronized other companies to shift to UPS. For instance, an advertising executive from a Chinese company shifted his account from a government-owned mail service company to UPS when a UPS executive approached him and explained the utility (both in terms of convenience as well as cost) of using UPS services for their business operations.

THE INVESTMENTS MADE

Since its entry into China, FedEx had invested heavily on building its services network in China with a long-term approach. Wilson Chung, general manager of FedEx China said, "China is one of the most important markets for FedEx. We are dedicated to continually investing in this market."[17] However, the company faced a major setback due to South East Asian currency crisis during 1997–98. Due to the significant currency devaluations in the Southeast Asian countries, FedEx reported its first quarterly loss (quarter ended February 1998) on international operations since 1996. This was largely attributable to the high investments made in its extensive air network in Asia, coupled with declining cargo volume and revenues from troubled Asian countries. Joseph M. Pyne (Vice President—Marketing) of UPS, was quick to comment, "Because of the investment (FedEx) made, they're almost stuck in that market. That's the plan they have to live with. We're looking at the market and moving with it in China."[18]

In contrast to the FedEx approach, UPS decided to make investments according to the market conditions in China. Till 1997, UPS had invested significantly less compared to what FedEx did in China. UPS had stepped

[14]As quoted in the article, "Orient Express: Just How Hard Should a U.S. Company Woo Foreign Markets?" by Douglas A. Blackmon and Diane Brady in *The Wall Street Journal,* dated April 6, 1998.
[15] Through this service, the details regarding goods shipped into a country were intimated in advance to the customs authorities of that country prior to landing of the flight. This enabled faster customs clearance.

[16]As quoted in the press release, "FedEx U.S. Customs Brokerage Specialist Shared with Asian Shippers the Efficient Way of Sending Goods to the U.S.," in www.fedex.com, dated August 6, 1996.
[17]As quoted in the article, "FedEx to Expand Services in China," in *Xinhua,* dated September 22, 2000.
[18]As quoted in the article, "Orient Express: Just How Hard Should a U.S. Company Woo Foreign Markets?" by Douglas A. Blackmon and Diane Brady in *The Wall Street Journal* dated April 6, 1998.

up its operations as the demand increased, sacrificing some market share due to its limited risk strategy. Due to the lack of its own air service, UPS was unable to offer customers in China the range of logistical services that FedEx could. The management of UPS always felt that if the business prospects in China improved later, the company could fly its own aircraft in and out of China. The company's low investment strategy in China saved it from any major losses due to the South East Asian currency crisis. As the freight volumes reduced in China, UPS had to just reduce the space it leased on other companies' planes.

FedEx felt that its high investment strategy had helped in gaining more market share in China. According to Air Cargo Management Group, a Seattle based consultancy, by mid-1998, FedEx had captured 13% of the express market in China, excluding Hong Kong, while UPS had less than 5% share. Alan B. Graf, FedEx's chief financial officer commented, "We knew it was risky when we built so much capacity, but we're staying. And that has just got to have a long-term payoff."[19]

LOGISTICS INDUSTRY IN CHINA— IMPROVING PROSPECTS

China was viewed as the logistics industry's most important emerging market. According to an industry analyst at Merge Global Incorporated,[20] a, U.S.-based research company, China's air-cargo market was the world's fifth-largest, and its emerging express market was valued at $400 million in 1998. According to studies conducted during the late 1990s, China's demand for time-definite express freight was projected to grow by 20% per year till 2002, much faster compared to the global air-freight market.

By 2000, competition in the logistics industry in China had intensified. Both FedEx and UPS were facing competition from MNCs like DHL, and China's state-owned enterprises like China Post. Following the decision of the Chinese government to enter into the World Trade Organization in 2001, the competition in the industry intensified further. With the removal of several rules and regulations which had protected China's government-owned logistics companies, the business prospects for multinational logistics companies improved significantly.

With the improved business prospects, UPS decided to follow a more aggressive approach to expand its market presence in China. The company lobbied intensively in the U.S. to secure a right to operate its own flight directly into China. The company also decided to invest significantly in infrastructural facilities in the new millennium.

In November 2000, the U.S. Department of Transportation (DOT) granted UPS air rights to operate direct flights from the U.S. to China. UPS was allowed six flights between U.S. and China in a week. In December 2000, following DOT's decision to designate UPS as the fourth U.S. air-carrier to service [the] China market, FedEx appealed to U.S. DOT to allow it one more flights per week to China.

RISING COMPETITION

Analysts felt that granting of air rights to UPS would further intensify the competition in China and enable major U.S. freight service carriers to access the Chinese market by offering low cost and better service. Though FedEx had not questioned DOT's decision to permit six flights to UPS, the company objected to the awarding of three flights to United Airlines and Northwest Airlines, its other competitors in China. FedEx called DOT's decision "fundamentally unfair" under the pretext that its contribution to the export growth in the U.S. was significantly high when compared with that of Northwest Airlines or United Airlines.

In March 2001, UPS announced the launch of six weekly flights between China and the U.S. using Boeing 747 aircraft, directly servicing Beijing and Shanghai. Four weekly flights were to start from Ontario International Airport, California and [an]other two at Newark, New Jersey. On April 1, 2001, the first flight landed in China. Commenting on the event, Jim Kelly, Chairman and CEO of UPS said, "This is the first time ever that a U.S. cargo carrier will fly directly from the U.S. to China. We believe this designation is a sign of the growing importance of global trade and UPS['] place in the new global marketplace. With these new flights, UPS will offer the broadest portfolio of services to customers shipping to and from China."[21] The launch of the service turned out to be a successful move by UPS as its business in the U.S.–China region grew by an estimated 40% soon after the launch.

Reacting to the move of UPS, FedEx announced an additional flight to its existing fleet of 11 aircrafts. In April 2001, FedEx also launched the Shanghai Express Freighter service. The newly launched flight service enabled FedEx to improve its services in the express segment between eastern China and the U.S. by reducing the shipment time by three to four hours. FedEx also stated its plans to inaugurate new infrastructure facilities in four Chinese states—Nanjing, Hangzhou, Dongguan, and Ningbo.

UPS further intensified its promotion activities following the launch of its direct flight to China. In May

---

[19] As quoted in the article, "Orient Express: Just How Hard Should a U.S. Company Woo Foreign Markets?" by Douglas A. Blackmon and Diane Brady in *The Wall Street Journal,* dated April 6, 1998.

[20] A specialized strategy consulting firm, which focuses exclusively on developing competitive strategy for firms in the freight transportation and logistics industries. Its clients include many of the world's largest producers of transportation and logistics services.

[21] As quoted in the press release, "FedEx U.S. Customs Brokerage Specialist Shared with Asian Shippers the Efficient Way of Sending Goods to the U.S.," in www.fedex.com, dated August 6, 1996.

2001, UPS launched an advertising campaign developed by reputed advertising agency, McCann-Erickson.[22] In the campaign titled "Brown Survey," a lady was asked to identify, as to what immediately struck her mind when a series of colors were flashed at her. When the color brown flashed, she instantly related it to reliability, and then to UPS. The campaign focused on creating a unique brand identity of UPS, as UPS was traditionally recognized for its fleet of brown trucks, which offered reliable service to the customers, through its customer-friendly employees and courier persons.

In an attempt to sell B2B e-commerce solutions to the cost-conscious Chinese businesses, UPS launched the "Customer Automation Program" in June 2001. Under the program, UPS offered to computerize the business units of its customers by providing the required PCs and software and by linking them to the UPS shipping systems free. The customers could print their own shipping labels. By doing this, UPS enabled its customers to understand the cost benefits of purchasing UPS B2B e-commerce solutions.

To further promote its business and compete effectively with UPS, FedEx implemented few innovative ideas. For instance, in association with OMD, FedEx started sponsoring popular TV shows in China during mid-2001. It first sponsored popular television game show—"Who Wants to Be a Millionaire"[23]—aired on Asia Television (ATV). The purpose of choosing the game show for sponsorship was to associate FedEx with speed and accuracy—the two key ingredients emphasized in the game show. The effort paid off for FedEx, as within three months of sponsoring the show, its top-of-mind recall[24] increased by 42% among the people in China. Encouraged by the success, FedEx sponsored another game show on ATV, "The Vault." The interactive game show was used to display [the] FedEx brand as the backdrop through an attractive FedEx moving TV billboard. This initiative was successful as FedEx's brand awareness increased, and the company was able to position its services for its speed and accuracy.

In October 2001, FedEx introduced a unique service in China. The company inaugurated a massive 6,080 square-meter FedEx–DTW Express Center at Shanghai Pudong International Airport. The integrated warehouse management system[25] at the center comprised a sorting and distribution system which employed state of the art wireless technology to enhance productivity and provide accurate information. The system could handle 6,000 to 12,000 packages per hour. Analysts felt that FedEx launched this system to cope up with the increasing volumes of goods and packages following China's entry into the WTO in 2001.

To counter FedEx's move, UPS launched two new services—UPS Signature Tracking TM and UPS Worldwide Express Plus TM in December 2001. The signature tracking service provided proof of delivery of the package of the recipient (his/her signature) within minutes of its delivery.[26] This service was targeted primarily at business customers who needed to furnish proof of delivery to affect other business transactions. The UPS Worldwide Express plus TM enabled shipping of packages or documents from China to any major U.S. city next day by 8 a.m. or to other non-metropolitan cities in the U.S., 13 European countries and Canada by 8:30 a.m.

THE RIVALRY INTENSIFIES

The rivalry between FedEx and UPS to grab more market share of the Chinese logistics market further intensified in 2002. In April 2002, UPS launched a new intra-Asia hub in the Philippines. The new hub, along with two other UPS located in Singapore, Hong Kong, and Taipei, comprised the worldwide UPS network. This move enabled UPS to significantly enhance its operational capacity in China, apart from enabling it to increase its ability to serve the Chinese customers by offering quicker and more reliable service.

In May 2002, following the launch of an intra-Pacific air hub in the Philippines, which complemented the other hub facilities in Taiwan, Singapore, and Hong Kong, UPS launched an advertising campaign titled "Asia," showcasing UPS as an integrated logistics solutions provider. The campaign, like the previous ad campaign, stressed the reliability of UPS service. It also gave a glimpse of the advanced technology employed at UPS including the WAP-enabled package tracking technology.

In September 2002, FedEx planned to further improve its services in Southern China and the Pearl River Delta region, by upgrading the aircraft serving Shenzhen from a DC-10 to an MD-11. This move also increased the freight capacity by 30 tons.

In order to understand the needs of the Chinese customers in smaller cities better and to offer these customers express delivery service of higher quality, UPS opened two offices in Chinese cities—Shenzhen and Qingdao in September 2002. UPS followed up this move by opening an office at the south Chinese city of Xiamen in October 2002. This was an effort by UPS towards further penetrating into the local Chinese market. Another significant factor of this launch was that all the employees of the office were hired locally.

---

[22]Based in the U.S., it is one of the world's leading integrated brands communications company with operations spread across the world.

[23]The interactive game show comprised a series of rounds in which questions were shot at the participants, who were required to reply with the right answer in quick time.

[24]The immediate company or its brand which flashes to mind upon being confronted with an industry. For example, the brand which might immediately flash when one thinks of a cola drink might be Coke or Pepsi.

[25]The automated system enables unloading and loading of goods, their sorting, and their customs clearance with minimum physical effort.

---

[26]Upon receiving the package, the recipient's signature was taken and converted into the digital format and displayed online. This served as the proof of delivery.

EXHIBIT C9-2 Revenues of Top Five Logistics Companies Operating in China

Company/Revenues	2000 (Rmb-Million)	2001 (Rmb-Million)	Growth (%)
China Couriers Service Company	1562	1600	2.4
DHL–Sinotrans	510	749	46.9
Federal Express Corporation	210	299.9	42.7
UPS	160	249.7	56
TNT Skypak–Sinotrans Ltd	110	149.9	36.3

SOURCE: "Couriers in China," a report published by Euro Monitor in August 2002, executive summary posted on www.euromonitor.com.

STATUS IN 2003

By 2003, the competition between FedEx and UPS was at its peak. Both the companies had been aggressively pursuing the Chinese market by regularly announcing new and better services, agreements, and tie-ups. Both the companies continuously revised their strategies according to the moves announced by their counterpart.

In January 2003, FedEx announced an agreement with Kodak to offer self-delivery services in 28 Kodak Express Shops in Shanghai. FedEx was the first company to offer express shipment delivery services following a retail approach. The Kodak shops that were selected in Shanghai were mainly located in business centers and high-class residential areas, where there was greater demand for these services. FedEx packaging and shipping documents service was available in-store so that consumers could handle the express shipment (below 2.5 kg) on their own with the assistance of [the] Kodak shop's trained staff.

In January 2003, UPS entered into an agreement with Yangtze River Express Airlines Company (Yangtze),[27] a Chinese cargo airline. According to the terms of the agreement, Yangtze would provide regular flights to link UPS hub in Shanghai with four major Chinese cities—Beijing, Qingdao, Xiamen, and Guangzhou. The agreement required six Boeing 737 flights each week on a Shanghai–Xiamen–Guangzhou–Shanghai route. In March 2003, the route was changed to Shanghai–Beijing–Qingdao–Shanghai. This agreement enabled UPS to offer one-day faster service and more reliability for international shipments.

In June 2003, FedEx entered into agreements with two Chinese companies—Trade Port[28] and Sun Logistics[29]—in

an attempt to improve its services. The agreement enabled FedEx to offer quicker delivery of urgent packages by loading and unloading such goods at the 40,000 square feet Trade Port facility located very close to the airport. This proximity to the airport saved costs and time of customers. In the same month, FedEx announced plans to expand its business to 100 more cities in China by the end of 2003. The company expected to register revenue growth rates of 30% in China for the next five years.

In June 2003, UPS signed an agreement with Lucent Technologies, a U.S. company that designed and delivered networks for communication service providers, to undertake management of UPS logistics operations in the Asia-Pacific region. In the same month, UPS also announced plans to enhance its network from 21 to 40 cities in the Asia-Pacific region by the end of 2003. The company also announced plans to open 20 more offices in 2003.

Due to better understanding of local conditions and its aggressive investment strategy during the past couple of years, UPS was able to increase its market share among its existing customers and was able to attract new customers. The efforts made by UPS in China reaped positive results. The company's revenues increased by 56% in 2001 (refer to Exhibit C9-2). For the fourth quarter ending December 2002, UPS registered a significant growth of 60% in revenues with exports in China growing by 40%. According to unconfirmed reports, the market share in 2003 of both FedEx and UPS had increased in China.

---

[27]Yangtze River Express is 85%-controlled by a unit of Hainan Airlines Co. American Aviation fund, controlled by international financier George Soros, is Hainan Airlines' biggest shareholder, with a 14.8% stake.
[28]Trade port Hong Kong is a logistics company, backed by an international conglomerate of prestigious companies including Fraport AG (Frankfurt Airport Services Worldwide), Schiphol Group (Schiphol Amsterdam Airport), China National Aviation Corporation (CNAC),

and Hong kong Land (a listed property developer and part of the Jardine Matheson Group), who possess good track records in specialized fields such as air logistics management, air transportation management, airline management, airport terminal management, and property development and management.
[29]A logistics company, started on August 28, 2000, which offers a one-stop logistics service by consolidating logistics resources and expertise, infrastructure strengths, and web-based technology.

QUESTIONS FOR DISCUSSION

1. FedEx entered into China in 1984 through a joint venture, while UPS entered China in 1988 through an agent partnership relationship. Critically examine the contrasting strategies adopted by both the companies, while entering and expanding their services network in China.
2. FedEx had followed an aggressive, high investment strategy, while UPS followed a conservative, low investment approach. Critically examine the contrasting elements in both the companies' strategies with a focus on advertising and promotion, target customers and the investments made until the late 1990s. What benefits and disadvantages do you perceive in the overall approach of both the companies while expanding in China?
3. In the early years of the new millennium, the rivalry between FedEx and UPS in the Chinese logistics market had intensified further. Examine the moves and countermoves followed by both companies during the period. According to you, what strategies should each company adopt to improve their market share in China?

REFERENCES

"Pass the Parcel," *Economist,* March 18, 1995.

"FedEx Gets Aviation Rights to China," *Asian Business Review,* October 1995.

"FedEx U.S. Customs Brokerage Specialist Shared with Asian Shippers the Efficient Way of Sending Goods to the U.S.," www.fedex.com, August 9, 1996.

White, Michael, "Going UPS in China," *World Trade,* August 1996.

Blackmon, Douglas A., and Brady, Diane, "Orient Express: Just How Hard Should a U.S. Company Woo Foreign Markets?" *The Wall Street Journal,* April 6, 1998.

"UPS in China," pandaexpress.ups.com, August 2, 1999.

"FedEx JV Cements Expansion," *Export Today's Global Business,* January 2000.

"Choose Competition in China Trade," *The Detroit News,* May 1, 2000.

"FedEx's Hub of Supply Chain Activity," www.ebnonline.com, May 10, 2000.

"UPS Appears Set to Win Battle for China Air Routes," *The Wall Street Journal,* September 22, 2000.

"FedEx to Expand Service in China," *XINHUA,* September 22, 2000.

Wallis, Keith, "Cargo 'Capacity Crunch' Seen," *Hong Kong Imail,* December 15, 2000.

Wallis, Keith, "FedEx Mulls Links to Mainland Carriers," *Hong Kong Imail,* February 8, 2001.

"UPS Begins Direct Service to China," www.newswire.ca, March 30, 2001.

Krause, Kristin S., "Battle for China Begins," *Traffic World,* April 2, 2001.

"Foreign Express Companies Make the Cake Bigger," *China Franchise News,* www.chinalaw.cc, April 18, 2001.

Galligan, Jim, "Express Giants UPS, FedEx Depend on Cargo to Set Their Tables for a Chinese Feast," www.ttnews.com, May 16, 2001.

Yan, Wang, "Foreign Businesses Eye China's Express Delivery Market," www.bizshanghai.com, June 1, 2001.

Chen, Anne, "Scaling the Wall," www.eweek.com, June 18, 2001.

Bangsberg, P.T., "FedEx Planning Expansion in China," *JoC Week,* September 4, 2001.

"FedEx Unveils Biggest Express Center in China," *People's Daily,* www.china.org.cn, October 22, 2001.

"FedEx Plans More Flights to Japan," *China Economic Review,* May 2002.

"FedEx to Cover 300 Chinese Cities in 5yrs," www.chinafair.org.cn, October 9, 2002.

Cunningham, David L. Jr., "FedEx Has Ideas for China," *Nation* (Thailand), October 15, 2002.

Wallis, Keith, "Express Cargo Teams Target Curbs," *Hong Kong Imail,* October 30, 2002.

"UPS Opens Representative Office in Xiamen," www.ups.com, October 30, 2002.

Krause, Kristin S., "Hong Kong Competition," *Traffic World,* November 18, 2002.

Sowinski, Lara L., "Good Things Come in Small Packages," www.worldtrademag.com, December 1, 2002.

"OMD's Chan Drives FedEx Branding with Sponsorship," *Media Asia,* December 13, 2002.

"FedEx Offers Money-back Guarantee in China," www.dragonventure.com, 2002.

"FedEx Opens Express Center in Pudong," www.tdctrade.com, 2002.

Armbruster, William, "Questions & Answers with David L. Cunningham Jr.," *Journal of Commerce,* January 20, 2003.

"FedEx Rolls Out New Asia Shipping Service," www.ebnonline.com, April 24, 2003.

"Lucent Signs Five-Year Pact with UPS Supply Chain Solutions," www.logisticsfocus.com, June 9, 2003.

"What Happens When One of the World's Largest Countries Meets the World's Largest Transportation Company?" www.chinaquest.ups.com.

"Press Releases, January 1996 to June 2003," www.fedex.com.

"Press Releases, January 1997 to June 2003," www.ups.com.

Case 10   Pepsi's Entry into India—A Lesson in Globalization

Convincing India that it needs Western junk has not been easy.[1]

—A New Internationalist Magazine Article, commenting on Pepsi's struggle to enter India, in August 1988

A LETTER TO PEPSI

In 1988, the New York office of the President of the multi-billion cola company PepsiCo received a letter from India. The company had been trying for some time to enter the Indian market—without much success. The letter was written by George Fernandes (Fernandes), the General Secretary of one of the country's leading political parties, Janata Dal. He wrote, "I learned that you are coming here. I am the one that threw Coca-Cola out, and we are soon going to come back into the government. If you come into the country, you have to remember that the same fate awaits you as Coca-Cola."[2]

This development did not seem to be a matter that could be ignored. PepsiCo's arch-rival and the world's number one cola company, Coca-Cola, had indeed been forced to close operations and leave India in 1977 after the Janata Dal came to power.[3] Even in the late 1980s, India had a closed economy and government intervention in the corporate sector was quite high. However, multinational companies such as PepsiCo had been eyeing the Indian market for a long time for a host of reasons. As the major market for PepsiCo, the U.S., seemed to be reaching saturation levels, the option to expand on a global scale seemed to have become inevitable for the company.

India was a lucrative destination since its vast population offered a huge, untapped customer base. During the late 1980s, the per capita consumption of soft drinks in India was only three bottles per annum as against 63 and 38 for Egypt and Thailand respectively. Even its neighbor Pakistan boasted of a per capita soft drink consumption of 13 bottles. PepsiCo was also encouraged by the fact that increasing urbanization had already familiarized Indians with leading global brands.

Given these circumstances, PepsiCo officials had been involved in hectic lobbying with the Indian government to obtain permission to begin operations in the country. However, the company could not deny that many political parties and factions were opposed to its entry into the country. It had therefore become imperative for PepsiCo to come up with a package attractive enough for the Indian government.

THE PROMISES THAT HELPED PEPSI ENTER

In May 1985, PepsiCo had joined hands with one of India's leading business houses, the R. P. Goenka (RPG) group, to begin operations in the country. The company, along with the RPG group company Agro Product Export Ltd., planned to import the cola concentrate and sell soft drinks under the Pepsi label. To make its proposal attractive to the Indian government, PepsiCo said that the import of cola concentrate would essentially be in return for exporting juice concentrate from operations to be established in the north Indian state of Punjab.

In its proposal submitted to the Ministry of Industrial Development, company sources said that the objectives of PepsiCo's entry into India revolved around "promoting and developing the export of Indian agro-based products and introducing and developing PepsiCo's products in the country." However, the government rejected this proposal primarily on two grounds: one, the government did not accept the clause regarding the import of the cola concentrate and, two, the use of a foreign brand name (Pepsi) was not allowed as per the regulatory framework. The association with the RPG group too ended at this juncture.

Not willing to sit quietly on the issue, PepsiCo put forward another proposal to the government a few months later. The company knew that the political and social problems[4] that plagued Punjab were an extremely

This case was written by A. Mukund, ICFAI Center for Management Research (ICMR). It is intended to be used as a basis for class discussion rather than to illustrate either effective or ineffective handling of a management situation.

The case was compiled from published sources.

[1]"Pepsi's Push," www.newint.org.

[2]"Coke Returns from India Exile," (Interview with Fernandes), *International Monitor,* July/August 1995.

[3]In the regulatory environment of the late 1970s, foreign enterprises operating in any non-priority sector in India could not own more than a 40% stake in the ventures. Coca-Cola ran its operations through a 100% subsidiary. After the company refused to partner with an Indian company and share its technology, it had to stop its operations and leave the country.

[4]The rise of militant groups demanding the creation of a separate state, Khalistan, led to serious religion-based terrorism in Punjab throughout the 1980s and early 1990s. Hundreds of people were killed in terrorist violence, and security forces and the police had a tough time bringing the situation under control. By the mid-1990s, the terrorist movement had been controlled to a large extent.

sensitive issue for India in the 1980s. PepsiCo's decision to link its entry with the development and welfare of the state was thus a conscious one, aimed at winning the government over. The fact that Punjab boasted a healthy agricultural sector (with good crop yields in the past) also played a role in PepsiCo's decision.

Reportedly, the new proposal gave a lot of emphasis to the effects of PepsiCo's entry on agriculture and employment in Punjab. The company claimed that it would play a central role in bringing about an agricultural revolution in the state and would create many employment opportunities. To make its proposal even more lucrative, PepsiCo claimed that these new employment opportunities would tempt many of the terrorists to return to society. This added a lot of "plus points" to PepsiCo's proposal, since a large number of young people in the state had become terrorists during the 1980s, causing socio-cultural and economic problems of a serious nature for many families in the state.

Reportedly, even as the government contemplated PepsiCo's proposal, many Indian soft drinks companies and social and political groups strongly voiced their opposition to it. Protestors said that the company would siphon out money from the country in the form of profits, promotional fees, and various other means. Protestors argued that the same money could be used for the development of the country.

Some critics even cited the instance of PepsiCo's involvement in Chile's political turmoil to support their opposition to the proposal.[5] Most of the opponents said that allowing a foreign company into a non-priority sector went against the existing government's [of the Congress (I) party, led by the Prime Minister Rajiv Gandhi] foreign trade policies.

Meanwhile, to "sweeten" the proposal, PepsiCo made many commitments to the Indian government—most of them highlighting the company's concern for the development of the areas it planned to operate in. Some of the important commitments were:

- The company would focus on food and agro-processing and only 25% of the investment would be directed towards the soft drinks business.
- The company would not only bring advanced food processing technology to India, but also provide a boost to the image of products made in India in foreign markets.
- Half of the production would be exported and the export–import ratio would be 5:1 for a period of 10 years (80% of the exports to be of food products manufactured by the company and 20% of the

exports to be of food products from a select list manufactured by other companies)
- Creation of jobs for 50,000 people across the nation, of which 25,000 were to be in Punjab.
- Foreign brand names would not be used.
- An agricultural research center would be established.

The government was apparently quite impressed with the terms and conditions PepsiCo had proposed. Thus, despite continuing protests, the Pepsi Foods Ltd. (Pepsi) venture was finally cleared by the government in September 1988. Pepsi was a joint venture between PepsiCo, Punjab Agro Industrial Corporation (PAIC, a body established by the Punjab government) and Voltas India Ltd. (a company owned by the business house of Tatas). While PepsiCo held 36.89% of the venture's stake, PAIC and Voltas held 36.11% and 24% stakes respectively. The company launched the soft drinks business with great fanfare and an elaborate multi-media advertising campaign in 1989.

The success of PepsiCo's efforts to enter India generated a significant amount of attention. While the political groups opposing the company's entry continued to criticize the government's decision, there were many who appreciated the way in which PepsiCo had clinched the deal. Some years later, commenting on how the company effectively used megamarketing[6] to enter the Indian market, renowned marketing expert Philip Kotler said, "Pepsi bundled a set of benefits that won the support of various interest groups in India. Instead of relying on the normal four Ps for entering a market, Pepsi added two additional Ps, namely, Politics and Public Opinion."[7] He added that committing to work towards developing the rural economy and bringing in new food-processing packaging and water-treatment technologies turned a lot of votes in PepsiCo's favor.

PEPSI'S PROMISES—KEEP SOME, BREAK SOME!

Pepsi began by setting up a fruit and vegetable processing plant at Zahura village in Punjab's Hoshiarpur district. The plant would focus on processing tomatoes to make tomato paste. Since the local varieties of tomatoes were found to be of inferior quality, Pepsi imported the required material for tomato cultivation. The company entered into agreements with a few big farmers (well-off farmers with large land holdings) and began growing tomatoes through the contract farming route[8] (though the

[5]In the early 1970s, Chile's pro-socialism President Salvador Allende was killed after a military coup toppled the government. According to reports, the United States (U.S.) had a hidden role to play in this coup as it wanted to curb the growth of socialism in Chile. Reports claim that the then PepsiCo Chairman, Donald Kendall, had personally sought the U.S. government's help for protection of the company's commercial interests in Chile.

[6]Megamarketing refers to the strategic coordination of economic, psychological, political, and public relations skills to gain the cooperation of a number of parties in order to enter or operate in a market.
[7]As mentioned in *Marketing Management* (The Millennium Edition) by Philip Kotler. The four Ps being referred to are "Product," "Place," "Promotion" and "Price."
[8]Contract farming refers to a farming arrangement. Under this arrangement, farmers enter into a contract with a buyer to supply a specific quantity of the produce at a pre-determined price and quality. The buying company provides some inputs and technology to the farmers.

agro-climatic profile of Punjab was not exactly suitable for a crop like tomato, Pepsi had chosen the state because its farmers were progressive, their landholdings were on the larger side, and water availability was sufficient).

Initially, Pepsi had a tough time convincing farmers to work for the company. Its experts from the U.S. had to interact extensively with the farmers to explain how they could benefit from working with the company. Another problem, although a minor one, was regarding financial transactions with the farmers. When the company insisted on payments by cheque, it found out that as many as 80% of the farmers did not even have a bank account!

Soon other problems cropped up. When the crop was harvested at the end of 1990, the Zahura plant had still not been made operational. As a result, the crop could not be utilized as planned and the local farmers had to bear combined losses of Rs 2.5 million.[9] In addition, critics commented that Pepsi paid the farmers only Rs 0.75 per kg of tomatoes, when the market price was Rs 2.00 per kg. Pepsi's detractors also alleged that the company had selected only big farmers, deliberately neglecting the small and medium farmers.

Pepsi received a lot of criticism for failing to create jobs. The company had promised to provide jobs to 50,000 people, but by 1991 it had employed only 783 people as direct employees. By 1992, this figure increased marginally to 909 and by 1996 it rose to 2,400. Pepsi claimed that it had provided employment to around 26,000 people in the country through indirect employment.

Industry observers commented that the company had included even the small vendors who sold its soft drinks as indirect employees. They argued that all these vendors could not be regarded as the employees of Pepsi. Information given by the company revealed that more than 50% of its employees were working for the concentrate and bottling business, and not the food processing activities. This prompted critics to say that Pepsi was not focusing on generating employment in the agriculture sector.

Pepsi had a majority holding in Futura Polymers Ltd. (Futura), a company that was involved in the business of recycling plastic. This company was reported to be working towards replacing many workers with machines. A senior manager at the company, L. R. Subbaraman, said, "Later they will ask for more money, form organizations, maybe unions. We are always trying to be more machine oriented."[10] This attempt at reducing the workforce seemed to go against the company's commitments to create jobs.

Pepsi devised a clever way to handle the commitment it had made that it would not use a foreign brand name in India. Its cola was named "Lehar Pepsi" to differentiate it from Pepsi, as the product was known outside India. In the packaging and promotion, where the product name was visible, the name Pepsi was given a prominent position while the Lehar part of it was relegated to the background. Consumers thus invariably had a stronger, more lasting impression of "Pepsi" than "Lehar Pepsi."

Pepsi also failed to adhere to its commitment to export 50% of its production. Since its agricultural initiatives were not turning out to be as productive as planned, its export of fruit/vegetable-based products was negligible. To make up for this, Pepsi began exporting products such as tea, rice, and shrimp. In addition, it exported glass bottles, leather products, and even champagne. Critics pointed out these products had always been exported from India and that Pepsi was deliberately not meeting its export obligations.

Pepsi's detractors, such as Fernandes, were still focused on proving that allowing the company to operate in India was not a good decision. In fact, the decision to allow the company to enter the country was the subject matter of many heated debates in the Indian parliament. In one such debate in 1991, Fernandes asked the Food Processing Ministry why Pepsi was not being forced to honor its commitments. Another parliament member, S. K. Gangwar, said that the fact that Pepsi was being allowed to function normally even though it had not adhered to many of its commitments was very disturbing. He said, "When the Pepsi company has not fulfilled its commitments, why is it being allowed to continue to function here?"[11]

To deal with this unrest, a team of government officials visited the company's plant in December 1990. The team included a Director (Food, Vegetable Products department) and a Deputy Secretary from the Ministry of Food Processing Industries. The team's findings corroborated most of the charges leveled against Pepsi. It found that Pepsi had not made any efforts to export 40% of the goods it manufactured and that it had not taken any concrete steps to set up an agro-research institute. The team then referred the matter to the Ministry of Commerce, which in turn issued a show-cause notice to the company.

However, even by late 1991, the company had not replied to this notice. Many parliament members demanded closure of the company's operations to punish it for its numerous violations. This was easier said than done, since the closure of a company needed the coordination of the Food Processing Ministry and officers of the Ministries of Commerce, Finance, Industry, and Food Processing. An Inter-Ministerial committee was therefore set up to look into the matter.

All the previously discussed incidents prompted critics to comment that Pepsi never had any serious intentions of developing Punjab's agricultural sector. Many of them felt that Pepsi's proposal to better the

[9]July 2003 exchange rate: Rs 47 = 1 U.S. $.
[10]"Dumping Pepsi's Plastic," www.multinationalmonitor.org, September 1994.
[11]http://alfa.nic.in.

lives of the state's people and develop the rural economy were just ploys to gain entry into the country.

Luckily for Pepsi, it did not have to face criticism on many of the previously discussed grounds for long.

INDIA LIBERALIZES—A BOON FOR PEPSI

In the early 1990s, the Government of India was facing a foreign exchange crisis. The country was finding it extremely difficult to borrow funds from the international markets due to a host of problems on the political, economic, and social fronts. Organizations like the International Monetary Fund agreed to help the Indian government deal with the financial crisis, on condition that it liberalized the Indian economy. As a result, the government decided to liberalize the economy. The removal of the numerous restrictions on foreign trade and the increased role of private equity in Indian markets were the two most prominent features of the government's new economic policy.

Pepsi benefited from the economic changes in many ways. The removal of various restrictions meant that it no longer had to fulfill many of the commitments it had made at the time of its entry. The government removed the restrictions that bound Pepsi's investments in the soft drinks business to 25% of the overall investments and required it to export 50% of its production. The company took full advantage of the new economic policy. In 1994, it bought off its partners in the venture; while Voltas sold off its stake completely, PAIC's stake was reduced to less than 1%.

The company established a wholly-owned subsidiary, PepsiCo Holdings India Pvt. Ltd. (PHI), which was completely devoted to the soft drinks business. Soon, all of Pepsi's investments in the country were being routed through this new company. Under the new economic policy, the use of foreign brand names in India was allowed. Consequently, Pepsi changed its cola's name from Lehar Pepsi to Pepsi.

In 1995, Pepsi's decision to sell off its tomato paste plant to the Indian FMCG major, the Unilever-subsidiary, Hindustan Lever Ltd. (HLL), added to the negative publicity surrounding the company. The only link that Pepsi maintained with its agriculture-related commitments was the contract farming of tomatoes over 3,500 acres of land. HLL used the bulk of the tomato paste produced by the plant for its tomato ketchup and puree offerings. The rest was handed over to Pepsi for export.

Developments over the next few years seemed to support the critics' view that the company's main focus was clearly on the soft drinks business. In 1995, the beverages business grew by as much as 50% and as a result, by 1996, PHI's turnover surpassed Pepsi's turnover by Rs 1.25 billion. By 1996, fruit/vegetable-based products formed a minuscule 1.5% of PHI's exports, whereas

plastic exports (bottles manufactured at Futura) were as high as 67% (it was alleged that the plastic bottles business resulted in the emission of highly toxic material that was polluting the areas around the factory and irreparably damaging the ecosystem). Also, even by 1997, the agro-research center promised by the company was nowhere in sight.

PEPSI GOES FARMING—FINALLY

Though Pepsi attracted a lot of criticism, many people felt there was a positive side to the company's entry into India. According to a www.agroindia.org article, Pepsi's tomato farming project was primarily responsible for increasing India's tomato production. Production increased from 4.24 million tonnes in 1991–92 to 5.44 million tonnes in 1995–96. The company's use of high yielding seeds was regarded as one of the reasons for the increase in productivity in tomato cultivation during the same period.

Commenting on the previously discussed issue, Abhiram Seth [Seth, the company's Executive Director (Exports and External Affairs)] said, "When we set up our tomato paste plant in 1989, Punjab's tomato crop was just 28,000 tonnes, whereas our own requirement alone was 40,000 tonnes. Today, the state produces 250,000 tonnes. Per hectare yields, which used to be 16 tonnes, have crossed 50 tonnes."[12]

Pepsi was, however, not as successful in the chili contract farming venture that was started soon after the tomato venture stabilized. While the area under cultivation was 1,750 acres in 1997, it was reduced to around 300 acres by 2000. According to company sources, the chili venture failed because the main market for Pepsi's processed chili paste was the South-East Asian region. Due to the financial crisis in the region in the late 1990s, the demand for chili paste petered out. As a result, Pepsi decided to cut back on chili farming and focus on more profitable crops.

Pepsi offered its contract farmers advanced equipment such as transplanters (for planting tomato and chili saplings) and seeding machines (for groundnuts) to help them carry out their tasks efficiently and speedily. The equipment, which was offered free of cost to the farmers, had been imported and modified to suit Indian conditions.

Pepsi gradually expanded its contract farming network from Zahura to the districts of Amritsar, Patiala, and Sangrur (in Punjab). Over the next few years, the contract farming initiative (for potatoes) was extended to Uttar Pradesh (in the city of Meerut), Madhya Pradesh (in the city of Indore), Karnataka, and Maharashtra.

In the late 1990s, the company finally met its commitment to set up agro-research centers. Such centers were set up in Jallowal and Channo (in Punjab) and Nelamangala (in Karnataka). These centers carried out

---

[12]"Pepsi into Groundnut Contract Farming," www.hinduonnet.com, March 13, 2000.

field trials for various crops, vegetables and fruits and maintained nurseries for tomato, chili, potato, and basmati rice. Through a "Pepsi Agri Backward Integration Program," Pepsi encouraged Punjab's farmers to cultivate potatoes with low sugar content (potatoes with high sugar content are unsuitable for making chips).

In October 1999, inspired by the promising trial runs of its basmati rice farming efforts, Pepsi decided to give a special thrust on contract farming for this crop. In 2000, the company extended its contract farming initiative to groundnuts. It planned to grow about 34,000 tonnes over the next 3–4 years. Seth said, "The 34,000 tonnes (over two crops) will yield around 20,000 tonnes of shelled nuts, of which we plan to export 12,000 tonnes to European confectioneries, salters and roasters and another 2,000 tonnes to the Far East."[13] Pepsi planned to use a part of the crop to manufacture peanut butter for export.

The company chose Punjab for its groundnut project. It believed that groundnut production in the state had declined over the years only because the state had not paid adequate attention to the crop's cultivation. Pepsi sources also said that as compared to paddy, which required extensive water (a scarce commodity in the monsoon-dependent Indian agriculture sector), growing groundnuts (which requires comparatively less water) in Punjab made more sense.

The fact that the Punjab government was actively looking for means to replace one-third of its paddy cultivation with a less water-intensive crop made Pepsi's new venture very attractive. To encourage farmers to grow groundnuts, the company stated that it would help them in all possible ways to get good yields. Later on, groundnut farming initiatives were introduced in Gujarat also. Pepsi imported superior technology from China and transferred it to groundnut farmers in Punjab and Gujarat. As a result, the yield per hectare improved from 1 tonne to 3.5–4.5 tonnes.

In June 2000, while revealing plans to invest Rs 1.25 billion every year in Karnataka during 2000–02, Pepsi's President P. M. Sinha (Sinha) said that the company planned to further expand its raw material sourcing operations in the state. This was in addition to the Rs 1.4 billion already invested in the state. The company planned to further expand its operations related to the processing of guava, pineapple, sweet lime, and ginger. In this context, it planned to work in association with the Karnataka government and various raw material suppliers.

Sinha said that since its entry into India, Pepsi had invested over Rs 18 billion by 2000 (of this, Rs 1.5 billion had been invested in Punjab, where around 8,000 people were working for the company). He said the company's

agri-program had been successful because of its unique "laboratory-farm-factory approach."

DOING BUSINESS ON ITS OWN TERMS

The company's contract farming initiatives and its focus on improving Punjab's agricultural sector seemed to indicate that Pepsi had been working towards fulfilling its pre-entry commitments. However, the reality was quite different.

In 2000, the company's exports added up to Rs 3 billion. The items exported included not only processed foods, basmati rice, and guar gum,[14] but also soft drink concentrate. Though the company did not make the figures public, in all probability, the portion of soft drink concentrate in its exports was much higher than that of any other product. In fact, the company met the soft drink concentrate requirements of many of its plants worldwide through its Indian operations.

Even by 2000, of its annual requirement of 25,000 tonnes of potatoes per annum, Pepsi got only 3,000 tonnes from its contract farmers. Given these figures, it would be interesting to see how it planned to achieve its objectives of meeting its complete requirement of potatoes through the contract farming route by 2004.

Many analysts said that since the regulatory framework had changed entirely after its entry into India, Pepsi was not at all bound to honor its earlier commitments. They said that given this context, the fact that it had done so much for the country's agriculture sector was something to be appreciated.

Even in 2002, Pepsi entered into various contract farming deals. In August 2002, it joined hands with a Punjab state government body, Punjab Agri Export Corporation (Pagrexco), to process citrus fruits. The company planned to identify, source, and process citrus fruits for its juices venture Tropicana. In the same month, Pepsi began farming two kinds of seaweeds in Tamilnadu that were used to make carrageenan (a product used in many FMCG and food products). This was the first instance of organized, commercial seaweed farming ever in the country.

By 2003, Pepsi's soft drinks, snacks, fruit juices, and mineral water businesses had established themselves firmly in India. While the cola and snack brands had enviable market positions, the mineral water and juices businesses were still experiencing growth pangs.

For millions of Indians, Pepsi had become a part of their lives in many different ways: A far cry indeed from the days when the cola giant was struggling to enter the country and had to use the crutches of agri-business initiatives and export commitments!

---

[13]"Pepsi into Groundnut Contract Farming," www.hinduonnet.com, March 13, 2000.

[14]Guar gum is extracted from the seed of Cyamopsis tetragonoloba, a leguminous plant. It is used as an emulsifier, thickener, and stabilizer in a wide range of foods, cosmetics, and pharmaceuticals.

QUESTIONS FOR DISCUSSION

1. Why do companies like Pepsi need to globalize? What are the various ways in which companies can enter a foreign market? What hurdles and problems did Pepsi face when it tried to enter India during the 1980s?
2. Critically analyze the strategy adopted by Pepsi to sell itself to the Indian government. Do you think the biggest factor responsible for the acceptance of its proposal by the regulatory authorities was its projection of its operations as the solution to many of Punjab's problems? Why/Why not?
3. How did the company react to the changes in the business environment after the liberalization of the

Indian economy in the early 1990s? Critically comment on the allegations that Pepsi deliberately did not adhere to most of its commitments.

4. Examine the contract farming initiatives undertaken by Pepsi in India and explain the rationale for such initiatives from the company's perspective. Why is it important for multinational corporations to work towards the improvement of the economy of the countries in which they operate? What are the various other ways in which this can be done?

ADDITIONAL READINGS & REFERENCES

"Coke Returns from India Exile," *International Monitor*, July 1995.

Chakravarti, V. K., "Pepsi to Experiment with Contract Farming on Basmati, Pulses," *Financial Express*, April 26, 1999.

Singh, Kavaljit, "Broken Commitments: The Case of Pepsi in India," *PIRG Update*, Issue no.1, May 19, 1997.

Srinivas, Nath Nidhi, "Basmati Is the Right Choice for Pepsi," *The Economic Times*, October 26, 1999.

Damodaran, Harish, "Pepsi into Groundnut Contract Farming," www.hinduonnet.com, March 13, 2000.

"Pepsi Foods to Invest Rs 125 Cr. in Karnataka," *Business Line*, June 06, 2000.

"Pepsi to Expand Channo Plant," www.tribuneindia. com, March 29, 2001.

Dutta, Jyothi P. T., "Channo Unit 2nd Phase Launched," *Business Line*, April 01, 2001.

Dutta, Jyothi P. T., "PepsiCo to Invest Rs 200 Cr. in India," April 02, 2001.

"Pepsi Foods Exports to Touch Rs 400 Cr. in 2001," www.expressindia.com, April 03, 2001.

"Contract Farming—PepsiCo Style," www.tribuneindia. com, December 06, 2001.

"Co-operative Models to Help Farmers," www.etagricul-ture.com, January 2002.

"Pepsi, Pagrexco Tie Up for Citrus Cultivation," http://in.biz.yahoo.com, February 13, 2002.

Damodaran, Harish, "Pepsi Forays into Seaweed Farming," *Business Line*, August 01, 2002.

"Pepsi, Punjab Govt. Sign Deal for Citrus Cultivation," *Business Line*, August 20, 2002.

"Pepsi's Push, Indians Open Door," www.newint.org; http://alfa.nic.in.

Case 11   Starbucks' International Operations

Internationally, we are in our infancy.
—*Howard Schultz, Chairman & Chief Global Strategist, Starbucks, in March 2003*

The expansion strategy internationally is not bulletproof as it is in the U.S.
—*Mitchell J. Speiser, Analyst—Lehman Brothers, in June 2003*

ALL'S NOT WELL WITH STARBUCKS

In March 2003, *Fortune* came out with its annual list of "Fortune 500 companies." For Howard Schultz (Schultz),

Chairman of Starbucks Corp. (Starbucks), this list was special as Starbucks [was] featured in the list. It was a dream come true for the Seattle-based entrepreneur.

Though the U.S. economy was reeling under recession and many retail majors were reporting losses and applying for bankruptcy, Starbucks announced a 31%

This case was written by K. Subhadra, under the direction of Sanjib Dutta, ICFAI Center for Management Research (ICMR). It is intended to be used as a basis for class discussion rather than to illustrate either effective or ineffective handling of a management situation.

The case was compiled from published sources.

increase in its net earnings and a 23% increase in sales for the first quarter of 2003. Analysts felt that the success of Starbucks showed that a quality product speaks for itself. The fact that Starbucks spent less than 1% of its sales on advertising and marketing strengthened this view. In addition to being a popular brand among customers, Starbucks was also considered the best place to work due to its employee friendly policies.[1]

However, analysts felt that the success of Starbucks was due to its profitable domestic operations. It was reported that most of Starbuck's international operations were running into losses. In May 2003, Starbuck's Japanese operations reported a loss of $3.9 million (Japan constituted the largest market for the company outside the U.S.), and the company also performed badly in Europe and the Middle East. Analysts pointed out that Starbucks international operations were not as well planned as its U.S. operations. They also observed that the volatile international business environment made it difficult for the company to effectively manage its international operations.

Many analysts felt that it was important for the company to focus on its international operations. With the U.S. market getting saturated, Starbucks would be forced to look outside the U.S. for revenues and growth.

The history of Starbucks dates back to 1971, when Jerry Baldwin, Zev Siegl, and Gordon Bowker launched a coffee bean retailing store named Starbucks to sell specialty whole-bean coffee in Seattle. By 1981, the number of Starbucks stores increased to five and Starbucks also established a small roasting facility in Seattle. Around the same time, Howard Schultz (Schultz) who was working with Hammarplast—a Swedish housewares company which (marketed coffee makers) noticed that Starbucks, a small company from Seattle, was ordering more coffee makers than anyone else. In order to find out more about the company, Schultz visited Seattle. Schultz was so impressed by the company and its founders that he offered to work for the company.

By 1982, Schultz joined Starbucks as marketing manager, with an equity stake in the company. During his first year at Starbucks, he studied the various types of coffee and the intricacies of the coffee business. The turning point came in 1983, when Schultz was sent to Milan (Italy) for an international housewares show. There he observed that every street in the city had an espresso coffee bar, where people met and spent time. Schultz realized that Starbucks could introduce espresso coffee bars in the U.S. Schultz put forward this idea to his partners. But they did not like the idea of selling espresso coffee. However, after a lot of persuasion from Schultz, they agreed to allow him to sell espresso coffee in their retail shop. The business picked up and by the weekend they were making more money by selling the beverage than by selling coffee beans. Still when the

partners refused to venture into the beverage business, Schultz decided to quit the company and start out on his own.

In April 1985, Schultz opened a coffee bar—II Giornale in Seattle—with a seed capital of $150,000 invested by Jerry Baldwin and Gordon Bowker. The rest of the capital was raised through private placement. Soon, the second and third stores were opened in Seattle and Vancouver respectively. During 1987, when Schultz heard that Starbucks' owners were selling off six stores along with a roasting plant and the Starbucks brand name, he raised $3.8 million through private placements and bought Starbucks. As Starbucks was a more established name, Schultz decided to retain it instead of Il Giornale.

Schultz expanded Starbucks to Chicago, Los Angeles, and other major cities. But with increasing overhead expenses, the company reported a loss of $1.2 million in the year 1990. Schultz was, however, confident of his business plan and continued his expansion spree. He even hired employees from companies such as PepsiCo. By 1991, the number of Starbucks stores increased to 116, and it became the first privately owned company to offer employee stock options. In 1992, Starbucks was listed on the stock exchange at a price of $17 per share.

The strategy adopted by Starbucks was to blanket a region with its new stores. By doing so it could reduce the customers' rush in one store and also increase its revenues through new stores. This helped the company to reduce its distribution costs and the waiting period for customers in its stores, thereby increasing the number of customers. It was reported that on an average a customer visited Starbucks stores 18 times a month, a very high number compared to other American retailers. By 1993 there were around 100 Starbucks stores, which increased to 145 in 1994.

Along with serving coffee, Starbucks also sold merchandise. In 1995, it started selling CDs of its famous in-house music program. It also entered into alliances with various players such as Canadian Airlines, United Airlines, Starwood Hotel, and Barnes & Noble Inc., to serve Starbucks coffee.

Analysts attributed the success of Starbucks not only to its aggressive expansion, but also to its product innovation. Starbucks came out with new products to attract customers. For instance in 1995, to cater to the needs of diet conscious youngsters it launched *Frappuccino*—a low fat creamy iced coffee. In 1996, it launched ice cream and ice cream bars through its subsidiary Starbucks and Dreyer's Grand Ice Cream, Inc. In the same year it also entered into an agreement with the cola major PepsiCo to launch bottled Starbucks *Frappuccino*. Due to all these initiatives Starbucks has recorded an average growth of 20% per year since 1991, and its store traffic increased to 6–8% per year.

However, in mid-1990s, with the market reaching saturation, Starbucks could no longer depend on the U.S. market for growth. Analysts felt that to maintain its

[1]Starbucks was the first organization in the U.S. to offer stock options and health care coverage to part-time employees also.

TABLE I   Starbucks International Presence*

Country	Type of Entry	Name of the Partner	Year
Canada	Wholly-owned subsidiary	Starbucks Coffee Canada	1996
Japan	Joint Venture	Sazaby Inc	1996
Malaysia	Licensee	Berajaya Group bhd	1998
New Zealand	Licensee	Restaurant Brands	1998
Taiwan	Joint Venture	President Coffee Corp	1998
Kuwait	Licensee	Alshaya	1999
Philippines	Licensee	Rustan's Coffee Corp	2000
Australia	Joint Venture	Markus Hofer	2000
Israel	Joint Venture	Delek Corporation**	2001
Austria	Licensee	Bon Appetit Group**	2001
Switzerland	Licensee	Bon Appetit Group**	2001
Germany	Joint Venture	Karstadt Qualle AG	2002
Greece	Joint Venture	Marinopoulos Brothers	2002
Mexico	Joint Venture	SC de Mexico	2002
Hawaii	Joint Venture	Café Hawaii Partners	2002
Hong Kong	Joint Venture	Maxim's Caterers Ltd	2000
Indonesia	Joint Venture	PT Mitra A Diperkasa	2002
Puerto Rico	Joint Venture	Puerto Rico Coffee Partners LLC	2002
Lebanon	Licensee	Alshaya	N.A.
Spain	Joint Venture	Grupo Vips	2002

This list is not exhaustive.
** Starbucks closed its operations in Israel and bought out the stakes of its partners in Austria and Switzerland in 2003.*

SOURCE: Compiled from various newspaper articles.

growth rates and to boost revenues, Starbucks should venture abroad. In 1995, Starbucks formed Starbucks Coffee International, its wholly owned subsidiary to monitor the company's international expansion. In 1996, Starbucks entered Japan through a joint venture with the Sazaby's Inc (a leading Japanese teashop and interior-goods retailer) and over the years it expanded into South-East Asia, Europe, and the Middle East. By March 2003, Starbucks had 1,532 stores (23% of its total stores) outside the U.S. (Refer to Table I for Starbucks' international presence).

Starbucks decided to enter the Asia Pacific Rim markets first.[2] Growing consumerism in the Asia Pacific countries and eagerness among the younger generation to imitate Western lifestyles made these countries attractive markets for Starbucks.

Starbucks decided to enter international markets by using a three pronged strategy—joint ventures, licensing and wholly owned subsidiaries, (Refer to Exhibit CII-1 for the modes of entry in international markets.) Prior to entering a foreign market, Starbucks focused on studying the market conditions for its products in the country. It then decided on the local partner for its business. Initially Starbucks test marketed with a few stores that were opened in trendy places, and the company's experienced managers from Seattle handled the operations.

After successful test marketing, local baristas (brew masters) were given training for 13 weeks in Seattle. Starbucks did not compromise on its basic principles. It ensured similar coffee beverage line ups and *No Smoking* rules in all its stores across the globe.

When Starbucks entered into a joint venture with Sazaby Inc. to open Starbucks stores in Japan, analysts felt that Starbucks was unlikely to succeed. They even advised Starbucks to forego its principles such as *No Smoking,* and ensure that the size of the stores would not be more than 500 square feet due to the high rents in Japan. However, Starbucks stuck to its *No Smoking* principle, which attracted young Japanese women to the Starbucks stores, and the size of the stores was 1200–1500 sq ft—similar to the stores in the U.S. Proving analysts wrong, Starbucks became successful and in the first year itself, it opened more than 100 stores.

According to Starbucks' sources, listening to its local partner also helped. Starbucks took advantage of its local partner Sazaby's knowledge about Japanese coffee drinking habits and introduced new products such as Green Tea Frappuccino, which became popular.

Starbucks was successful in attracting a young crowd in all its Asian markets, as young people in these markets were eager to imitate the American culture. It even adapted itself to the local culture to gain market acceptance. For instance Starbucks offered curry puffs and meat buns in Asian markets as Asians generally prefer to eat something while having coffee.

Analysts felt that the strong coffee drinking culture in Europe posed both challenges and opportunities for

[2]Asia Pacific Rim markets consist of Japan, Philippines, Indonesia, Thailand, Taiwan, Malaysia, Singapore, China, South Korea, North Korea, New Zealand, Australia, Vietnam, Cambodia, Papua New Guinea.

There are six primary ways to enter a foreign market. They are: exporting, turnkey projects, licensing, franchising, joint venture with a host country firm, and setting up a wholly-owned subsidiary in the host country. Each mode of entry has its advantages and disadvantages. The method a company chooses depends on a variety of factors including the nature of the particular product or service and the conditions for market penetration in the foreign target market.

Exporting

Most firms begin their global expansion with exports and later switch over to another mode. In the 1990s, the volume of exports in the world economy had increased significantly due to the decline in trade barriers. However, exporting still remains a challenge for smaller firms. Firms planning to export must identify foreign market opportunities, familiarize themselves with the mechanics of exports, and learn to deal with foreign exchange risk.

Turnkey Projects

In a turnkey project, the contractor handles every aspect of the project for a foreign client including the training of operating personnel. After the completion of the contract, the foreign client is handed the "key" to the plant that is ready for operation. Turnkey projects are common in chemical, pharmaceutical, and petroleum refining industry.

Licensing

Licensing is an arrangement whereby a company (licenser) grants the rights to intangible property like patents, inventions, formula, process, designs, copyrights, and trademarks to another company (licensee) for a specified period of time. The licenser receives a loyalty fee from the licensee. For example, in the early 1960s, Xerox licensed its patented xerographic know-how to Fuji–Xerox. It was initially meant for ten years; but the license was extended several times. In return, Fuji–Xerox paid Xerox a royalty fee equal to 5% of the net sales revenue that it earned.

Franchising

Franchising is similar to licensing except that it requires long-term commitments. In franchising, the franchiser not only sells intangible property to the franchisee, but also insists that the franchisee abide by the rules of business. In some cases, the franchiser also assists the franchisee in running the business. The franchiser receives a royalty payment that is usually a percentage of the franchisee's revenues. Service companies usually opt for franchising. For example, McDonald's pursues its expansion abroad through franchising. McDonald's sets down strict rules for the franchisees to operate their restaurants. The rules extend to cooking methods, staffing policy, and design and location of the restaurants. McDonald's also organizes the supply chain and provides management training and financial assistance to the franchisees.

Joint Ventures

In contrast to licensing and franchising arrangements, joint ventures allow companies to own a stake and play a role in the management of the foreign operation. Joint ventures require more direct investment and training, management assistance and technology transfer. Joint ventures can be equity or non-equity partnerships. Equity joint ventures are contractual arrangements with equal partners. Non-equity ventures are the ones where the host country partner has a greater stake. In some countries, a joint venture is the only way for a foreign company to set up operations.

Wholly Owned Subsidiaries

In a wholly owned subsidiary, the firm owns 100% of the stock of the subsidiary. Wholly owned subsidiaries can be established in a foreign country in two ways. A firm can set up new operations in the foreign country or it can acquire a firm and promote its products through that firm.

The following are the advantages and disadvantages of various entry modes.

Entry Mode

Advantage

Disadvantage

EXPORTING

Advantages: Ability to realize location and experience curve economies
Disadvantages: High Transport Costs
Trade Barriers
Problems with local marketing agents

TURNKEY CONTRACTS

Advantages: Ability to earn returns from process technology skills in countries where FDI is restricted
Disadvantages: Creating efficient competitors
Lack of long term market presence

EXHIBIT C11-1   (Cont.)

LICENSING
Advantages: Low development costs and risks
Disadvantages: Lack of control over technology
Inability to realize location and experience curve economies
Inability to engage in global strategic coordination

JOINT VENTURES
Advantages: Access to local partner's knowledge
Sharing development costs and risks
Politically acceptable
Disadvantages: Lack of control over technology
Inability to engage in global strategic coordination
Inability to realize location and experience economies

WHOLLY OWNED SUBSIDIARIES
Advantages: Protection of technology
Ability to engage in global strategic coordination
Ability to realize location and experience economies
Disadvantages: High costs and risks

SOURCE: ICFAI Center for Management Research.

Starbucks. It would face tough competition from the sidewalk cafes of France, coffeehouses of Vienna, and espresso bars of Italy, that had developed a strong coffee drinking culture across the Continent, exposing Europeans to the best coffee in the world. However, Starbucks executives commented that Europe used to make great coffees but by the late 1990s, the taste had gone awry. In 1998, Starbucks opened its first store in England, and soon expanded its presence to Switzerland, Germany, and Greece.

It was generally felt that though old people would stick to the existing coffee houses, the young would be attracted to Starbucks. Said Helmut Spudich, editor, *Der Standard* (a Vienna-based paper), "The coffeehouses in Vienna are nice, but they are old. Starbucks is considered hip."[3] Another important factor that could lead to the success of Starbucks in Europe was its ambience and *No Smoking* environment, unlike traditional European coffee bars. The self-service mode of operation also attracted the young crowd as it was observed that youngsters did not like to wait for the waiter to come and take orders. According to Starbucks sources, it was successful because it was not just selling coffee but an experience, which was unique only to Starbucks stores. Maslen, President–Starbucks International, said, "The coffee is good but it's just the vehicle. The romance of coffee, the occasion, the community, is what Starbucks is selling."[4] In the Middle East, Starbucks went for licensing (except in Israel where it had a joint venture). Respecting the culture in the Middle East, Starbucks stores offered segregated section for ladies.

In September 2002, Starbucks announced that it would increase the number of international stores to 10,000 by 2005. However, analysts pointed out that it would be difficult for Starbucks to make profits in international markets, and they were soon to be proved right.

PROBLEMS IN INTERNATIONAL MARKETS

From the early 2000s, Starbucks faced many problems in its international operations. (Refer to Exhibit CII-2 for risks in international markets.) The volatile political environment in the Middle East created serious problems for Starbucks. In July 2002, Arab students gave a call for a boycott of American goods and services, due to the alleged close relationship between the U.S. and Israel. The boycott targeted U.S. companies including Starbucks, Burger King, Coca Cola, and Estee Lauder. Starbucks topped the list of companies to be boycotted due to Schultz's alleged closeness to the Jewish community.[5]

The problem was aggravated when it was reported that, in one of his lectures to students at the University of Washington, Schultz had said, "one of my missions is to sensitize you; you should not be immune to what is happening in the world. I travel a great deal and one of the things that I see is the rise of anti-Semitism in Europe, especially France and England."[6] His address to Jewish Americans made matters worse. Schultz said, "What is going on in the Middle East is not an isolated part of the world. The rise of anti-Semitism is at an all time high since the 1930s. Palestinians aren't doing their job; they're not stopping terrorism."[7] These comments from Schultz resulted in angry protests from the Arab

---

[3]"Planet Starbucks," *BusinessWeek,* September 9, 2002.
[4]"Starbucks Jolts Europe's Coffee Houses," *Seattle Times,* May 19, 2002.

[5]In 1998, Schultz was honored with the "Israeli 50th Anniversary Tribute Award" by the Jerusalem Fund of Aish Ha-Torah (a group supporting Israel).
[6]"Starbucks: The Cup That Cheers," www.zmag.org, July 11, 2002.
[7]"Starbucks: The Cup That Cheers," www.zmag.org, July 11, 2002.

EXHIBIT C11-2 Types of Risk in International Business

Typically a firm operating internationally is exposed to different types of risk. These can be listed as environmental, financial, organizational, or strategic risks.

Strategic Risk

MNCs typically face a diverse set of risks all of which cannot be assessed quantitatively. Michael Porter defines five forces impacting a firm's competitiveness—threat of substitutes, threat of new entrants in the industry, bargaining power of suppliers, bargaining power of customers, and the intensity of competition within the industry. A firm's strategic decisions to respond to the five forces are a source of risk.

Operational Risk

Operational risk arises out of factors internal to the company such as machinery breakdown, industrial strife, supply and distribution imperfections, excess or shortfall in inventory, and so on. It causes a down-time in the day-to-day operations of the enterprise. Reducing costs by eliminating wastage, reducing variances and lead-time by improving processes are important to bring about global efficiency. The more the number of parts and processes involved in production, the greater the risk of not achieving the desired quality and productivity standards.

Political Risk

Political risk refers to political actions that have a negative impact on the firm's value. The process of establishing a cause-and-effect relationship between political factors and business income is called political risk analysis. Political risk is not confined to developing countries. It exists even in highly industrialized economies. While macro-political risks such as war and anti-globalization efforts affect the value of all firms in the country, micro-political risks like regulation of certain industries affect the value of a firm or firms within that industry, adversely.

Country Risk

Country risk is a wider concept that encompasses economic conditions, government policies, political conditions, and security factors. The challenge of country risk analysis is in the aggregation of risk factors.

Technological Risk

Technological risk means the probability of adverse effects on business due to factors like obsolescence of an existing technology, development costs of new technology, failure of a new technology, and security concerns of electronic transactions.

Environmental Risk

Environmental risk can be of two forms. The company may incur regulators' wrath because it polluted the environment, or there may be a public outcry in the event of an environmental damage caused by the company. Environment risk management might not provide short-term gains like financial risk management does. But in the long run, it can certainly become a source of competitive advantage and also enhance the corporate image.

SOURCE: ICFAI Center for Management Research.

countries and pro-Palestinian groups across the Middle East and Europe. Analysts felt that Schultz's comments strengthened the feeling that he was acting as an Israeli mouthpiece.

Starbucks distanced itself from Schultz's comments, saying that they represented his personal beliefs and not those of the company. Schultz also denied allegations that he was anti-Palestinian and released a personal statement, saying that "my position has always been pro-peace and for the two nations to co-exist peacefully."[8] In addition to the previously mentioned incidents, the U.S. declaration of war on Iraq in early 2003 made matters

worse for the company. Due to increasing security threats, Starbucks closed down its six stores in Israel.

Starbucks also faced criticism from non-governmental organizations (NGOs) who urged the company to acquire certified coffee beans, ensuring that those coffee beans were grown and marketed under certain economic and social conditions. Starbucks also faced problems due to economic recession in countries such as Switzerland, Germany, and Japan in the early 2000s, where it experienced declining sales and revenues.

Starbucks faced stiff competition, high business development costs, and resistance from customers in international markets. Especially in Europe, it was reported that Starbucks faced stiff competition from well-established local players who offered speciality coffee at

---

[8]"Starbucks: The Cup That Cheers," www.zmag.org, July 11, 2002.

EXHIBIT C11-3	Income Statement of Starbucks (All amounts in millions of U.S. Dollars except per share amounts)		
Particulars	**Sep 02**	**Sep 01**	**Sep 00**
Revenue	3,288.90	2,649.00	2,169.20
Cost of Goods Sold	2,582.70	2,068.00	1,684.30
Gross Profit	706.20	581.00	484.90
Gross Profit Margin (%)	21.50	21.90	22.40
SG&A Expense	202.20	151.40	110.20
Depreciation & Amortization	221.10	177.10	142.20
Operating Income	282.90	252.50	232.50
Operating Margin (%)	8.60	9.50	10.70
Total Net Income	215.10	181.20	94.60
Net Profit Margin (%)	6.50	6.80	4.40
Diluted EPS ($)	0.54	0.46	0.25

SOURCE: www.hoovers.com

lower prices when compared to Starbucks. For example in England, while the Starbucks tall latte coffee was sold at $2.93, the same was available for $2.12 at the local coffee shop.

By late 1990s, Starbucks noticed that store traffic in Japan, its largest overseas market, had been reducing. It was observed that over a period of time, customers opted for different stores, as they did not like the taste of Starbucks coffee. Commented a customer, "I never go to Starbucks if I can help it. The coffee tastes artificial."[9] The Starbucks sales in Japan declined by over 17% in 2002. In order to boost its sales, it even introduced food items like rice and salmon wraps, and white peach muffins, yet it failed to gain market acceptance.

It was observed that Starbucks was unable to earn more revenue from its international operations due to its complex joint ventures and licensing agreements. While the company invested huge amounts in imparting training to the employees and promoting its products, it earned only a percentage share in total profits and royalty fees. It was further felt that the company did not have any control over the operational costs.

In addition to its problems in international markets, Starbucks experienced operational problems due to lack of a trained workforce and suitable real estate for its stores. Commenting on the operational hindrances faced by Starbucks, Maslen said, "If we could train the people and find the real estate, the expansion could happen tomorrow, almost. There is demand."[10]

FUTURE PROSPECTS

In order to have better control over operational costs, Starbucks decided to go for new suppliers for items such as mugs. It was reported that the company was thinking of sourcing mugs from low cost Japanese vendors rather than importing them from the U.S. and planning to source its paper goods (such as plates and cups) from Southeast Asia.

Starbucks also announced that it would slow down its pace of expansion by opening around 80 stores in 2003 (compared to the 115 stores opened in 2002). Company sources also revealed that Starbucks would close down its loss making stores. However, analysts pointed out that closing down the loss making stores and adopting cost cutting will increase profitability only in the short run and not drive future growth.

Analysts pointed out that Starbucks should rethink its entry strategy in international markets and focus on pricing. They also felt that the company being relatively debt free, and with around $300 million in free cash flows, it should be able to rebuild its foreign operations.

However, they cautioned Starbucks against the external risks resulting from volatile political and business environments across the world. They felt that with increasing tensions between America and the rest of the world, the business environment, especially in the Middle East and South East Asian regions, was becoming increasingly volatile. Acknowledging the risks involved in the international markets, Schultz said, "We're not taking our success for granted. We also understand that the burden of proof at times is on us given the fact that a lot is being written and there's more sensitivity than ever before about America and American companies. These are the very early days for the growth and development of the company internationally. Clearly, there's a big world out there for Starbucks to expand in."[11]

Only time can tell whether Starbucks will be able to brew its success in the international markets.

---

[9]"For Starbucks, There's No Place Like Home," *BusinessWeek,* June 9, 2003.
[10]"Starbucks Jolts Europe's Coffee Houses," *Seattle Times,* May 19, 2002.

[11]"Starbucks Backlash: The Java Giant's Expansion Brews Dissent Overseas," www.globalexchange.org, April 16, 2003.

QUESTIONS FOR DISCUSSION

1. Analysts feel that MNCs can mitigate some of the risks in international markets by deciding on a suitable mode of entry into these markets. Analyze the entry strategies adopted by Starbucks for its international expansion.
2. Careful analysis and management of risks not only mitigate losses but also provide superior returns. In the light of this statement, do you think Starbucks did not analyze and manage the risks involved in the different markets it entered?
3. A company faces a diverse set of risks in international markets. What were the risks faced by Starbucks in its international operations? Explain how Starbucks can reduce risks in its international business.

ADDITIONAL READINGS & REFERENCES

Reese, Jennifer, "Starbucks," *Fortune*, December 9, 1996.

Ioannau Lori, "King Bean," *Fortune*, May 5, 1998.

"Perky People," *The Economist*, May 28, 1998.

Stone, "Starbucks: The Jolt Is Still There—and Not Just from Java," *BusinessWeek*, April 6, 1999.

Schwartz, Nelson, "Still Perking After All These Years," *Fortune*, May 24, 1999.

Gimein, Mark, "Behind Starbucks' New Venture: Beans, Beatniks, and Booze," *Fortune*, May 15, 2000.

Yang, Jones Dori, "An American (Coffee) in Paris–and Rome," www.ups.edu, February 19, 2001.

Holmes, Stanley, "Starbucks: Keeping the Brew Hot," *BusinessWeek*, August 6, 2001.

"Coffee with Your tea?" *The Economist*, October 4, 2001.

"Starbucks Jolts Europe's Coffee Houses," *Seattle Times*, May 19, 2002.

Erlanger, Steven, "Starbucks Proves a Hit in Vienna, Even with Smoking Banned," www.naplesnews.com, June 1, 2002.

"Israel to Back Out of Starbucks Venture as Arab Boycotts Rage On," www.inminds.co.uk, July 11, 2002.

McDougall, William, "Starbucks: The Cup That Cheers," www.zmag.com, July 11, 2002.

Holmes, Stanley, Bennett Drake, Carlisle Kate, Dawson Chester, "Planet Starbucks," *BusinessWeek*, September 9, 2002.

Dawson, Chester & Holmes Stanley, "Is Japan Losing Its Taste for Latte Already?," *BusinessWeek*, December 9, 2002.

Daniels, Cora, "Mr. Coffee," *Fortune*, March 30, 2003.

Jung, Helen, "Starbucks Backlash: The Java Giant's Expansion Brews Dissent Overseas," www.globalexchange.com, April 16, 2003.

Patsuris, Penelope, "Can Starbucks Get It Wholesale?" *Forbes*, April 25, 2003.

Holmes, Stanley, Kunii M. Irene, Ewing Jack, Capell Kerry, "For Starbucks, There's No Place Like Home," *BusinessWeek*, June 9, 2003.

www.starbucks.com

www.starbucks.co.jp

www.hoovers.com

www.businesswire.com

www.seattletimes.com

Case 12 *DaimlerChrysler AG in 2004: A Global Strategy Gone Sour*

The merger of Daimler-Benz AG[1] and Chrysler Corporation took place in May 1998 with big pomp and circumstance in the world auto industry. Highly publicized in its future outlook and global integration, the merger created a transnational corporation that combined two large auto manufacturers with distinct corporate cultures and governance systems. At the time of the merger, both companies had business operations on every continent of the world. After the merger, in 1999, the new entity's consolidated revenues totaled $154.6 billion with a profit of $5.6 billion and employed 441,502 workers worldwide. During the same year, DaimlerChrysler's market share stood at 7.4% in the global auto industry (see Tables 1 and 2).[2] Interestingly, the merger was considered

SOURCE: written exclusively for this book by Syed Tariq Anwar, Professor of Marketing and International Business, T. Boone Pickens College of Business, West Texas A&M University. Copyright © Syed Tariq Anwar, 2004.

[1]AG: *Aktien–Gesellshaft* (a joint stock company in Germany).

[2] For detail, see: Anwar, Syed T. 2003. "DaimlerChrysler AG: The Making of a New Transnational Corporation," in Deresky, Helen. *International Management: Managing Across Borders and Cultures*, 4th edition, Upper Saddle River, New Jersey: Prentice Hall, pp. 340–356; *The Wall Street Journal*. 1998. Eaton. "DaimlerChrysler Will Be 'Transnational," (August 31): B8. Also see: Marjorie, Sorge and Mark Phelan. 1998. "The Deal of the Century," *Automotive Industries*, (June): 46-69; *The Wall Street Journal*. 1998. "There Are No German or U.S. Companies, Only Successful Ones," (May 7): A1&11; *The New York Times*. 1998c. "Capitalism Victorious (Thanks, Everyone)," (May 10): B1&8; Kogut, Bruce. 1999. "What Makes a Global Company?" *Harvard Business Review*, (January/February): 165–170.

highly unusual since a German company initiated it. Historically, mergers in the European Union (EU) were often discouraged by businesses and regulatory agencies to discourage non-European companies and their foreign direct investment (FDI) from coming into the region.[3] *The Wall Street Journal* noted on the European corporate mergers:

> Many of the biggest deals were negotiated in government offices or between scions of the establishment. Interlocking shareholdings shielded management from the sanctions of the market. Size counted more than profits. Hostile takeovers simply weren't done.[4]

To stockholders, the news of the merger was particularly appealing since DaimlerChrysler was to become the third largest auto manufacturer after General Motors and Ford.[5] Since 1997, both companies had looked for merger partners but encountered difficulties regarding finding the right auto manufacturer. Though perceived as an unlikely marriage, the auto industry welcomed the merger because of its cost savings and global synergies.[6] The Harbour Associates commented:

> *Clearly the story of the year was the fusion of Daimler-Benz and Chrysler Corporation—resulting in the world's fifth-largest producer of vehicles. The announcement sent shock waves through the industry, Aside from the culture shock, there was also the sentimental fallout. Without question, the Big Three entity is gone forever.[7]*

The DaimlerChrysler merger displayed two distinct features regarding its place in the auto industry. First, the Daimler-Benz Mercedes brand ranked as one of most visible luxury brands. Second, in the case of Chrysler, the company's strength lay in its low end/sub-compact cars and trucks and was one of the Big Three auto manufacturers in North America. In 1998, Chrysler's product lines included cars, mini vans, Jeep, and sub-compact

utility vehicles. Chrysler was particularly known for its money-making mini vans, Jeep, and Dodge trucks.

In the early nineties, both companies had encountered problems in their market shares and global operations. In the case of Chrysler, the only alternative for future growth and survival was to merge with another auto company. Since 1995, both companies had investigated the prospects of a merger with Fiat, Honda, BMW, and Renault. Because of logistical issues, national barriers, branding incompatibilities, and corporate cultures, no progress was achieved. Despite the fact that the merger was welcomed by auto analysts and consumers, there were concerns regarding both companies future growth potential, corporate compatibility, and branding issues.[8]

BRIEF HISTORY OF DAIMLER-BENZ AND CHRYSLER CORPORATION

In the late 1800s, Gottlieb Daimler and Karl Benz were the early pioneers in building the motor carriage and two-cylinder V-engine in Germany. Daimler and Benz's early successes helped them establish the auto brand in the growth stage of the industry. In 1924, Benz and Cie and Daimler-Motoren-Gesellschaft merged and formed what today is known as Daimler-Benz. The company was particularly instrumental in establishing a luxury auto brand and commercial vehicles in the German market. Like other new companies, the company was closely linked to the German state.[9] In the coming years, Daimler-Benz expanded beyond Germany and saw its vehicles selling in hundreds of countries. After the eighties, the company became the largest conglomerate in Germany and was highly rated for its luxury cars in the auto industry. In the last fifty years, the Mercedes brand has truly become one of the major luxury brands and captures the attention of consumers worldwide because of its high quality, performance, and rigid safety standards. After the seventies, the company diversified into aerospace, consumer appliances, electronics, locomotives, and IT services.[10] Unlike other German multinational corporations (MNCs), Daimler-Benz mostly remained in Europe because of its rigid corporate culture and regional strategies. Ewing describes this phenomenon that has been unique to German and other European companies in the post-war environment:

> *Devastated spiritually and physically, many of Germany's big companies became defensive and risk-averse. In postwar Germany, they created webs of cross-holdings and reciprocal board memberships. The incestuous system functioned well during the cold*

[3]For more discussion, see: Anwar. 2003, op. cit.; Blasko, Matej, Jeffry M. Netter, and Joseph F. Sinkey. 2000. "Value Creation and Challenges of an International Transaction: The DaimlerChrysler Merger," *International Review of Financial Analysis*, 9(1): 77–102; Karolyi, G. Andrew. 2003. "DaimlerChrysler AG, the First Truly Global Share," *Journal of Corporate Finance*, 9: 409–430; Neubauer, Fred, Ulrich Steger, and Georg Radler. 2000. "The Daimler/Chrysler Merger: The Involvement of the Boards," *Corporate Governance*, 8(4): 376–387.
[4]*The Wall Street Journal*. 1999. "Europe Marks a Year of Serious Flirtation with the Free Markets," (December 30): A1.
[5]See: *The New York Times*. 1998a. "Daimler-Benz Will Acquire Chrysler in $36 Billion Deal That Will Reshape Industry, (May 7), pp. 1&C4; *The Economist*. 1998. A New Kind of Car Company," (May 9): 61–62; *The Wall Street Journal*. 1998b. "Chrysler Might Merge with Daimler-Benz—or Be Taken Over," (May 6): A1&8.
[6]Harbour & Associates, Inc. 1999. *The Harbour Report 1999: North America,* Troy, Michigan: Harbour & Associates, Inc., p. 3; *The Wall Street Journal*. 1998. "Chrysler Approves Deal with Daimler-Benz: Big Question Remain," (May 7): A1&1.
[7]Harbour & Associates, Inc. 1999, op. cit.

[8]Anwar. 2003, op. cit.
[9]*The New York Times*. 1998b. "Rise of [the] Borderless Corporation," (May 8): 1&8.
[10]For detail, see: Turner, Graham. 1986. "Inside Europe's Giant Companies: Daimler-Benz Goes Top of the League," *Long Range Planning*, 19(5): 12–17.

war. But it couldn't cope with the global competition that accelerated after the 1989 fall of the Berlin Wall and, more recently, the introduction of the euro.[11]

It was only in the post cold-war period that Daimler-Benz took interest in other markets and sought FDI in Europe and other parts of the world. Circumstances that led Daimler-Benz to invest overseas included the single European market, the introduction of euro currency, demand in emerging markets, branding issues, and Germany's high manufacturing cost.[12]

In the case of Chrysler, the company was founded by Walter P. Chrysler in 1925 who had worked for Buick Motor Company. Unlike Daimler-Benz, Chrysler manufactured cars for the masses and particularly targeted the mainstream American consumer. Between 1941 and 1960, Chrysler introduced many new auto models and took credit for bringing forth new technologies and innovations in North America. As the third largest auto manufacturer, Chrysler always remained behind GM and Ford and was rated as one of the "late movers" in the industry. Regarding quality and market share, Chrysler often had difficulty positioning itself in the market. The company's products were perceived to be shoddy and sub-standard. During the seventies, Chrysler's problems worsened because of oil crisis, poor quality, and Japanese competition. In the early eighties, the company was on the verge of bankruptcy but was rescued by the U.S. government. After 1980, Chrysler picked Lee Iacocca as its CEO, who rescued the company and made numerous short-term and long-term changes which included alliances with other auto manufacturers, realigning the product lines, and cost cutting. This resulted in new lines of vehicles such as K-cars, mini vans, Jeep Cherokee, and other utility and commercial vehicles. Iacocca's strategies resulted in huge profits for the company and saved the company from bankruptcy.[13]

In the early nineties, Chrysler vehicles started to get good ratings from analysts but continued to remain behind other manufacturers in quality and consumer satisfaction. In the areas of new innovations and technologies, Chrysler's products were no match to American, European, and Japanese cars and had difficulty attracting consumers in North America. During the same time, the auto industry had become global in manufacturing and competition. In the mid-nineties, Chrysler started to face the same problems that engulfed the company in the early eighties. When Daimler-Benz proposed the merger in January 1998, Chrysler's Board saw a major opportunity for survival and access to new

markets. In the next four months, both companies negotiated extensively and closed the deal in May 1998 (see Tables 1 and 2).

After the merger, DaimlerChrysler management sought an organizational structure that was adaptable and ready to combine two different corporate cultures, eventually creating a transnational corporation. The companies were particularly careful not to create a structure that could have jeopardized their global strategy during the transitionary period. In the first twelve months, both companies faced many challenges regarding reorganization, and above all, how best to combine Daimler-Benz's highly hierarchical and rigid management structure with Chrysler's informal corporate practices. Daimler-Chrysler's new organizational structure particularly took into consideration German and American business systems and appointed two co-chairmen, Jürgen Schrempp from Daimler-Benz and Chrysler's Robert E. Eaton.[14]

REASONS FOR THE DAIMLER-BENZ AND CHRYSLER CORPORATION MERGER

As stated earlier, the DaimlerChrysler merger was heavily influenced by the competitive forces of the auto industry. In the nineties, the industry was mired in downsizing, restructuring, low profits, and changing consumer demand. The top eight manufacturers from North America, Japan, and Europe were heavily burdened with debt and high cost issues. Daimler-Benz and Chrysler saw the merger as an opportunity to streamline and reorganize their operations at the global level. Other factors included joint research and development, access to emerging markets, and rationalization.[15] The merger created a company with total revenues of $154 billion and world market share of 7.4%. The major factors that contributed to the merger are as follows:[16]

1. Cost issues: In the nineties, Chrysler was known as a low cost producer and its design and styling departments were known in the industry. Daimler-Benz, on the other hand, was an excellent technology and quality leader in the luxury segments. Daimler-Benz's product development and manufacturing cost remained high and often lagged behind in bringing new products to the market. Hence, both companies saw this opportunity to exchange their know-how by seeking collaboration. In the post merger process, the companies were expected to save $1.2 billion because of collaboration in product development (see Tables 4, 5, and 6).

[11]Ewing, Jack. 2000. "The Show of Muscle Isn't So Scary," *Business Week*, (January 10): p. 24.

[12]In 1999, Germany was the most expensive nation in the world in manufacturing and cost of labor.

[13]Levin, Doron P. 1995. *Behind the Wheel at Chrysler: The Iacocca Legacy*, New York: Harcourt Brace & Co.

[14]Sorge, Marjorie & Mark Phelan. 1998. "The Deal of the Century," *Automotive Industries*, (June): 47.

[15]For detail, see: *The Wall Street Journal*. 1999. "Daimler Faces Big Test in Small-Car Market," (November 29): C14; Cliffe, Sarah. 1999. "Can This Merger Be Saved?" *Harvard Business Review*, 77(1): 29–44; *The Economist*. 1999. "How to Make Mergers Work," (January 9): 15–16.

[16]For detail, see: Anwar. 2003, op. cit.

TABLE 1 Chronology of DaimlerChrysler Merger: Pre- and Post-Merger Period/Developments (1998–2004)

Pre-Merger Period/Developments:	
January 12, 1998:	Jürgen Schrempp (Chairman, Daimler-Benz) proposed to Robert Eaton (Chairman, Chrysler Corp.) for a possible merger while visiting an auto show in Detroit.
February 12–18, 1999:	Both companies' representatives and advisors met to discuss the merger issues and its feasibility.
March 2, 1998:	Both Chairmen (Schrempp and Eaton) met in Lausanne, Switzerland to chalk out future plans.
March–April, 1998:	Working teams from both companies discussed and outlined details of the merger.
April 23–May 6, 1998:	Working teams from both companies finalized the merger agreement and other documentation.
May 6, 1998:	Both companies signed the merger agreement in London, UK.
May 7, 1998:	Merger agreement is announced in the press.
July 23, 1998:	EU's European Commission approved the DaimlerChrysler merger.
July 31, 1998:	U.S.'s Free Trade Commission approved the merger plan.
August 6, 1998:	DaimlerChrysler announced plans to list its share as a global-listed stock instead of ADRs.*
September 18, 1998:	Chrysler shareholders approved the merger with 97.5% agreement of voters.
September 18, 1998:	Daimler-Benz shareholders approved the merger with 99.9% agreement of voters.
November 6, 1998:	To qualify for pooling-of-interests accounting treatment, Chrysler issued 23.5 million shares.
November 9, 1998:	Daimler-Benz receives 98% of stock for its exchange offer.
November 17, 1998:	DaimlerChrysler stock started trading on 21 stock exchanges worldwide under the symbol <u>DCX</u>.
Post-Merger Developments:	
2000:	DaimlerChrysler took a $1.9 billion (37.1%) stake in Mitsubishi Motors Corp. (MMC). Kirk Kerkorian, a Las Vegas casino owner and Chrysler's biggest individual shareholder, filed a $2 billion law suit against DaimlerChrysler citing a $1 billion loss after the merger.
2001:	Chrysler reported losing $1.4 billion euros; U.S. management team is removed by DaimlerChrysler.
2002:	As a head of Chrysler, Dieter Zetsche tries to fix the company but many hurdles remain.
April 2003:	Chrysler Group's turnaround did not work and lost $1 billion because of weak sales, overcapacity, and old factories; MMC also lost money.
August 2003:	DaimlerChrysler agreed to pay $300 million to Kerkorian to settle $2 billion class action lawsuit but continues to fight Tracinda Investment Group's $2 billion suit of post-merger losses and other liabilities.
Dec. 2003/Jan. 2004:	Schrempp appeared in a Delaware court to testify in the lawsuit brought by Tracinda Investment Group against DaimlerChrysler. Schrempp says, "The deal was a merger of equals."
April 2004:	Despite losses in 2004, DaimlerChrysler's supervisory board supports Schrempp; the company refuses to retract from its global strategy; DaimlerChrysler and Hyundai opened talks about their troubled alliance.
May 3, 2004:	DaimlerChrysler and Beijing Automotive Industry Holding Company Ltd. (BAIC) announced the production of Mercedes-Benz C-Class and E-Class cars in Beijing, China. The project's annual capacity will be 25,000 cars per year.
May 5–13, 2004:	Daimler refused to inject capital into the troubled Mitsubishi Motors Corp. DaimlerChrysler announced selling its 10.5% stake in Hyundai Motor Company; also announced realigning its strategic alliance with Hyundai.

Note: * ADR: American Depository Receipts.

SOURCE: DaimlerChrysler, AG. (History/Group Archives & Investor Relations), www.daimlerchrysler.com; Anwar, Syed T. 2003. "DaimlerChrysler AG: The Making of a New Transnational Corporation," in Deresky, Helen. *International Management: Managing Across Borders and Cultures*, 4th edition, Upper Saddle River, New Jersey: Prentice Hall, pp. 340–356; *Business Week*; *The Economist*; *Financial Times*; *The Wall Street Journal* (various issues).

2. Relations with suppliers: In Chrysler's post-restructuring period, the company had created a good supplier network and outsourcing activities.[17] This attracted Daimler-Benz, which had difficulty in these areas. The company also wanted to use Chrysler's suppliers in its small-car and future sub-compact models where the company lacked expertise and manufacturing facilities.

3. Diesel engine technology: At the time of the merger, Daimler-Benz and Chrysler were considered good manufacturers in the diesel technology and were willing to share their know-how in the post-merger period. The diesel engine technology in the sub-compact segments was particularly attractive to Chrysler since it was a low-cost manufacturer in the industry.

4. Dealer network: Historically, Daimler-Benz had a strong dealer network in Europe, Latin America, and North America. On the other hand, Chrysler's dealer network remained inadequate in Europe. The company had limited visibility in the European markets for a long

---

[17]Hartley, Janet, Bertie M. Greer, and Seungwook Park. 2002. "Chrysler Leverages Its Suppliers' Improvement Suggestions," *Interfaces*, 32(4): 20–27.

TABLE 2 DaimlerChrysler: Pre and Post-Merger Financial and Corporate Data (1997 and 2004)

A: Financial Data (1997)	Daimler-Benz	Chrysler
Revenues:	$71.5 billion	$61.1 billion
Profit:	4.6	2.8
Assets:	76.1	60.4
Stockholders' Equity:	19.5	11.3
Market Capitalization:	86.8	35.9
Employees:	300,000	121,000
Unit Sales:	1.1 million	2.9 million
Fortune Global 500 Rank (1998):	17	25

B: Financial Data (2004)	DaimlerChrysler
Revenues:	$157.1 billion
Profit:	5.1
Assets:	195.5
Stockholders' Equity:	19.5
Market Capitalization:	42.5
Fortune Global 500 Rank (2003):	7
Fortune's Most Admired Companies Rank:	10 (score: 4.51 out of 10)
Manufacturing Facilities in 17 countries	
Products sold in 200 countries	

C: Major Brands and Products (2004)

Mercedes-Benz Group:
- Maybach
- Mercedes-Benz Cars (A-Class, C-Class, E-Class, S-Class, SLK Class, SL-Class, CLK Class, CL-Class, SLR, M-Class, and G-Class), MPV, Camper Vans, Trucks, and Buses.

Chrysler Group:
- Dodge Cars (Neon, SRT, Intrepid, Stratus, and Viper), Dodge Trucks, SUVs, and Minivans
- Chrysler (Crossfire, PT Cruiser, Sebring, Chrysler 300, Pacifica, and Town & Country)
- Jeep

Commercial Vehicles Division: Setra Mercedes-Benz, Freightliner, Sterling Trucks, and Western Star Trucks.

DaimlerChrysler Services: DaimlerChrysler Services, and DaimlerChrysler Bank.

Strategic Partners: Mitsubishi Fuso Truck and Bus Corp., Mitsubishi Motors Corp., and Hyundai Motor Company.

SOURCE: Company Web site (www.daimlerchrysler.com); *Business Week*; *The Economist*; *Financial Times*; *Forbes*; *Fortune*; *The Wall Street Journal* (various issues).

time while General Motors and Ford were well established in the same market. This was appealing to Chrysler because of its mini vans, Jeep, and other subcompact brands. Both companies wanted to use each other's dealer network in Europe and Latin America as well.

5. The euro currency and corporate environment: Business environment in the European markets played a major contributing factor behind the merger. Cross-border mergers were on the rise because of Europe's single market, corporate consolidations, and above all, availability of corporate bonds and high-yield debt markets. Companies in Europe and North America wanted to capitalize on these changes to seek expansion.

6. North American Free Trade Agreement-related benefits: In the early nineties, with the passage of the NAFTA Treaty, the U.S. started to attract FDI from Europe because of future corporate expansion and growth

potential. Under NAFTA's rules-of-origin, foreign companies were mandated to invest in auto transplants in North America.[18] To Daimler-Benz, merging with another auto producer was a viable option to comply with NAFTA's rules-of-origin. Earlier, the same rules also prompted the company to start manufacturing its model M-series in Tuscaloosa, Alabama for the North America market. Merging with Chrysler was seen even more promising since it showed additional growth prospects in North America.

7. Daimler-Benz's diversification: As Germany's premier corporation, Daimler-Benz was in a strong position regarding its sales and profits and continued to increase

---

[18]For NAFTA's rules-of-origin, see: Anwar, Syed T. 1996. "The Impact of NAFTA on Canada's Automobile Industry: Issues and Analysis," *World Competition*, 19 (3): 115–136. For M-series and its development, see: Haasen, Adolf. 1999. "M-Class: The Making of a New Daimler-Benz," *Organizational Dynamics*, 27(4): 74–78.

TABLE 3   DaimlerChrysler's Brands and Businesses (as of May 2004)

- ATENA Engineering
- American LaFrance
- Chrysler
- DaimlerChrysler Capital Services
- DaimlerChrysler Commercial Buses North America
- DaimlerChrysler Powersystems Axles
- DaimlerChrysler Research and Technology North America, Inc.
- DaimlerChrysler Services
- DaimlerChrysler Services—Chrysler Financial
- DaimlerChrysler Services Fleet Management
- DaimlerChrysler Vans LLC
- Detroit Diesel Corporation
- Dodge
- Dornier Consulting
- Evobus
- Five Star
- Fleet Operations: The Chrysler Group
- Freightliner Custom Chassis Corporation (FCCC)
- Freightliner LLC
- Freightliner Trucks
- Global Electric Motorcars (GEM)
- Jeep
- LMC Lean Manufacturing Consulting GmbH
- Maybach
- MB-technology GmbH
- Mercedes-Benz
- Mercedes-Benz ATC GmbH
- Mercedes-Benz CharterWay
- Mercedes-Benz Credit Corp.
- Mercedes-Benz FleetBoard
- Mopar Parts
- MTU Friedrichshafen
- Orion Buses
- Protics Technical Information Consulting & Support GmbH
- PUREM Abgassysteme GmbH & Co. KG
- Remarketing Operations: The Chrysler Group
- SelecTrucks
- Setra
- Sterling Trucks
- Smart
- Thomas Built Buses
- Western Star Trucks
- Westfalia Van Conversion

SOURCE: DaimlerChrysler. 2004. Company Web site, May (www.daimlerchrysler.com).

its market share from core businesses (automotive and vehicles) in the eighties. In 1985, the company's profits increased by 52% to $577 million. In the late eighties, the company saw its sales declining and encountered problems in aerospace, computers, and household appliances.[19] In the coming years, the company had to seek major downsizing and laid off thousands of employees. During the same period, the company's profit fell by 30%.[20] In the nineties, Daimler-Benz sought major corporate restructuring and survived by unloading unprofitable non-core operations. This helped the company to streamline operations but future growth did not look promising. Selected options available to the company included a merger or other FDI activities in world markets. Daimler-Benz preferred a merger over FDI activities. Eventually, in 1998, a merger with Chrysler was proposed to capitalize on the North American market. Other contributing factors that encouraged the merger included NAFTA-related market and healthy business conditions in Europe.

---

[19] The companies included Dornier, MTU, and AEG.
[20] *Financial Times*. 1993. "Daimler-Benz Profits to Fall by Up to 30%," (April 17): 1.

8. Issues of globalization: In the Cold War era, markets in the developed countries and emerging markets started to take off because of globalization, FDI, and strong consumer demand. Daimler-Benz realized that it was critical to expand globally not only by exporting products but also getting involved beyond the German market. This encouraged the company to find a merger partner.

9. Brand portfolios and manufacturing strategies: Daimler-Benz and Chrysler's core products were in the automotive sectors. At the time of the merger, Daimler-Benz earned 80% of its revenues from cars and commercial vehicles. Chrysler was even more dependent on its automotive products. The new company's brand portfolio looked so promising that in just a few months, both partners were ready to form a new entity. The major attraction behind the merger was to save money by eliminating corporate duplication and using the same manufacturing platforms worldwide. Except in a few segments, the companies had minimum overlap in their brand portfolios. At the time of the merger, Daimler-Benz led in mostly luxury cars and commercial vehicles while Chrysler concentrated on low-end market.

10. German corporate culture and governance issues: In the post-World War II period, German companies developed a unique corporate structure that was based on hierarchical system, cross-shareholdings, and inward looking/Pan-European strategies. In the post-Cold War period, Europe was engulfed in competition, expansion, and above all, FDI from North America. This forced German companies to seek a different corporate model based on global expansion and openness. Daimler-Benz was influenced by the changes that encouraged the company to expand globally, especially in North America.[21]

WHAT WENT WRONG WITH DAIMLERCHRYSLER'S GLOBAL STRATEGY?

Though in 1999 DaimlerChrysler's merger looked feasible in the auto industry, the company encountered problems and had setbacks that raised questions about its future viability. The company faced the following problems in the post-merger period:

1. Corporate culture and "the merger of equals" issues: In the auto industry, Daimler-Benz was viewed as a conservative and rigid company regarding its corporate bureaucracy, product development, and quality standards. On the other hand, Chrysler's corporate culture was known as informal, outward oriented, and somewhat less rigid in its operations. These characteristic business practices evolved over time from their respective societal cultures. Daimler-Benz lacked exposure to the American way of management and business practices. The mismatch of corporate culture eventually created problems in the areas of future planning, supervisory board, research and development, expatriate management, executive salaries, and labor relations.[22] In the post-World War II era, the German system was developed on the basis of a hierarchical structure that encouraged seniority, consensus building, and above all, the supervisory boards' powers in the day-to-day operations. In the first few years, some of Chrysler's operations in the U.S. took a downturn because of management shakeups, disagreements on joint vision, collective strategies, production, and branding issues. Since DaimlerChrysler was made into a transnational company, dealing with two national cultures with distinct business practices was a daunting task. Neither companies' executives were ready for the changes that were to take place in the transnational structure. Since Chrysler was an independent organization before the merger, American managers disliked Daimler-Benz's control and majority ownership, especially seeing the new entity's headquarters moving to Germany.[23] Some managers resented moving to Stuttgart because of their families not wanting to give up the American way of life. Language problems were cited as another hurdle in the assimilation process; the Germans held meetings using only German, knowing that the Chrysler executives did not understand, reinforcing the notion that this was a takeover, not a merger. After the merger, Daimler-Benz controlled 51% of the company and moved the headquarters to Stuttgart. In addition, DaimlerChrysler's shareholders fretted over the loss of shareholder value that instigated a $9 billion lawsuit and two other class action suits by Chrysler's largest individual investor Kirk Kerkorian. The investor claimed a $1 billion loss because of the company's poor performance in the stock market. In 1999, DaimlerChrysler shares were trading at $108. In 2002, the stock dropped down to $35, losing billions of dollars of shareholder value. According to DaimlerChrysler, Kerkorian "mischaracterized" the merger and refused to

[21]For more discussion, see: Broadbeck, Felix C., Michael Frese, and Mansour Javidan. 2002. "Leadership Made in Germany: Low on Compassion, High on Performance," *Academy of Management Executive*, 16(1): 16–30; *Financial Times*. 2002. "Is Germany's Model Finding Its Level?" (September 5): 7; Kogut, Bruce and Gordon Walker. 2001. "The Small World of Germany and the Durability of National Networks," *American Sociological Review*, 66(3): 317–335; Peck, Simon I. and Winfried Ruigrok. 2000. "Hiding Behind the Flag? Prospects for Change in German Corporate Governance," *European Management Journal*, 18(4): 420–430; Tuschke, Anja and Wm. Gerard Sanders. 2003. "Antecedents and Consequences of Corporate Governance Reform: The Case of Germany," *Strategic Management Journal*, 24: 631–649; *The Wall Street Journal*, 2002. "Behind the Crisis in Germany, a Past That Is Crippling," (December 6): A1&12.

[22]Anwar, 2003. op. cit.; also see: *Financial Times*. 1999. "Two Tribes on the Same Trail," (August 31): 10.

[23]For more discussion on this topic, see: Sorge, Marjorie and Mark Phelan. 1998. "The Deal of the Century," *Automotive Industries*, (June): 47; *Financial Times*. 1998. "Culture Crucial to Synergy Equation," (May 8): 22; *The Wall Street Journal*. 1998. "For Daimler-Benz, a Cultural Road Test," (May 8): B1; *Business Week*. 1998. "A Secret Weapon for German Reform," (October 12): 138; *The Wall Street Journal*. 1999. Daimler Chrysler's Transfer Woes, (August 24): B1; *The Wall Street Journal*. 1999. "Daimler Chrysler Readies Management Recall," (September 15): A25.

TABLE 4   Auto Industry in North America: Selected Manufacturing, Production and Labor Productivity Data (1998)

Company	Annual Capacity	Actual Production	Utilization	Hours Per Vehicle (HPV)*	Workers Per Vehicle (WPV)*
Auto Alliance (Michigan)**	268,464	167,607	62%	25.70	3.07
BMW (South Carolina)	65,800	54,802	83	NA	NA
CAMI (Canada)	26,352	54,819	24	41.60	3.34
DaimlerChrysler (14 plants)	2,906,480	2,906,366	100	33.86	3.27
Ford (22 plants)	4,429,280	4,298,784	97	24.87	3.04
General Motors (29 plants)	6,272,808	4,945,990	79	32.58	3.24
Honda (4 plants)	947,120	881,694	93	21.41	2.49
Mercedes (Alabama)	80,088	68,732	86	NA	NA
Mitsubishi (Illinois)	259,440	157,139	61	NA	NA
Nissan Motors (3 plants)	792,232	498,631	63	19.20***	2.45***
NUMMI (California)****	387,318	361,897	93	21.78	2.69
Subaru–Isuzu (Indiana)	248,160	216,198	87	NA	NA
Toyota Motors (4 plants)	667,400	647,030	97	21.63	2.48
Volkswagen (Mexico)	391,040	338,959	87	NA	NA

Notes: * HPV and WPV data may not include all assembly plants; ** Mazda and Ford; *** Nissan Smyrna plant only; **** NUMMI (New United Motors Manufacturing, Inc.; Joint Venture of GM and Toyota); NA: Not available.

SOURCE: Harbour & Associates. 1998. *The Harbour Report 1999: North America*, Troy, Michigan: Harbour & Associates, Inc.

take responsibility for the investor's losses.[24] While testifying in a federal court in December 2003, Schrempp strongly defended the 1998 $36 billion deal between Daimler-Benz and Chrysler as a "merger of equals."[25] In short, both companies' top managements did not anticipate dealing with so many problems in the areas of cultural assimilation, executive departures, disappearing shareholder value, and weak demand for Chrysler products. Eventually, this resulted in a major distraction for the company. In 2004, DaimlerChrysler continues to struggle with global integration in the areas of manufacturing, low profits, and corporate assimilation.

2. Competition in the global auto industry: Today's auto industry is an integral part of the developed world and is highly competitive and global in its markets and product development. The industry is continuously impacted by cost and labor issues (see Tables 4, 5, 6, and 7).[26] The industry's impact is visible in almost every sector of national economies.[27] In some markets, the competitive environment is further complicated by national subsidies, tariff barriers, and cash rebates.[28] To launch a new auto

model, it takes an investment of $500 million to $1 billion. Sourcing/outsourcing strategies are used by the automakers to control cost and logistical problems. Auto plants are located on the basis of markets and suppliers' networks. The major players in the industry include General Motors, Ford, Toyota, Honda, Nissan, Volkswagen, and others. Toyota is considered the most efficient manufacturer in quality and consumer satisfaction (see Tables 7 and 8).[29] Like other producers, DaimlerChrysler wants to become a major global player but has been unable to materialize its goals. *Financial Times* accurately commented:

> *At DaimlerChrysler, there were fears within the company about the pace at which Mr. Schrempp was driving his concept of 'Welt AG'—a global car maker—at a time when the group's core Mercedes brand needed defending in the face of competitors challenging its traditions of quality and luxury.[30]*

As of 2004, the industry's cut-throat competition and quality issues have become a problem for the company. Ultimately, it is a hindrance in the company's global strategy.

[24]For more information, see: *Financial Times*. 2003. "Corporate Germany Embraces the Global Village," (December 18): 14; *Yahoo! Finance*. 2004. "DaimlerChrysler Says Kerkorian 'Mischaracterized' Merger," (May 14): 1 (http://biz.yahoo.com/); *The Wall Street Journal*, 2000. "The Limits of Schremppism," (December 6): A23; *The Wall Street Journal*. 2003. "Chrysler's Merger Lessons," (December 9): A26.
[25]*Financial Times*. 2003. "Schrempp Says Chrysler Was Merger of Equals," (December 10): 17; *Financial Times*. 2004. "The Battle of DaimlerChrysler," (January 2): 5.
[26]For detail, see: Harbour & Associates. 2003. *The Harbour Report 2003: North America*, Troy, Michigan: Harbour & Associates, Inc.; *Value Line*. 2004. "Auto and Truck Industry," (March 5): 101–109; *Standard & Poor's Industry Surveys*. (2003). "Industry Surveys: Autos and Auto Parts," (December 25): 1–29; *The Wall Street Journal*, 2004. "U.S. Car Makers Lose Market Share," (January 6): A3.
[27]Anwar. 2003, op. cit.

[28]*The Wall Street Journal*, 2004. "Detroit's Challenge: Weaning Buyers from Years of Deals," (January 6): A1&A2.
[29]For more discussion on auto companies, see: Anwar. 2003, op. cit; *Business Week*. 2003. "BMW: Will Panke's High-Speed Approach Hurt the Brand?" (June 9): 57–60; *The Economist*. 2004. "Cadillac Comeback," (January 24): 61–63; *Financial* Times. 2004. "Toyota Leads Japanese Conquest of Europe," (March 2): 7; Harbour & Associates, Inc. 2003, op. cit; *The Wall Street Journal*. "At Ford, High Volume Takes Backseat to Profits," (May 7): A1&A12; *The Wall Street Journal*. "Toyota's Earnings More Than Doubled," (May 12): A3&A6; *The Wall Street Journal*. "As VW Tries to Sell Pricier Cars, Everyman Image Holds It Back," (May 13): A1&A8.
[30]*Financial Times*. 2004. "German Chiefs Watch Their Backs as They Eye the World," (May 14): 14.

TABLE 5 Auto Industry in North America: Selected Manufacturing, Production, and Labor Productivity Data (2002)

Company	Annual Capacity	Actual Production	Utilization	Hours Per Vehicle (HPV)*
Auto Alliance (Michigan)**	256,432	65,925	26%	35.30
BMW (South Carolina)	120,000	123,328	103	NA
CAMI (Canada)	107,160	62,724	59	29.90
DaimlerChrysler (15 plants)	3,001,056	2,664,465	89	28.04
Ford (22 plants)	4,417,098	4,100,326	93	26.14
General Motors (32 plants)	6,207,651	5,507,407	89	24.76
Honda (5 plants)	1,257,795	1,138,821	91	21.41
Mercedes (Alabama)	100,016	88,271	88	NA
Mitsubishi (Illinois)	234,248	204,284	87	NA
Nissan Motors (3 plants)	856,208	758,460	89	19.20***
NUMMI (California)****	361,486	369,853	102	21.78
Subaru–Isuzu (Indiana)	248,160	131,833	53	NA
Toyota Motors (5 plants)	833,554	895,116	107	21.63
Volkswagen (Mexico)	391,040	336,489	86	NA

Notes: * HPV data may not include all assembly plants; ** Mazda and Ford; *** Nissan Smyrna plant only; **** NUMMI (New United Motors Manufacturing, Inc.; Joint Venture of GM and Toyota); NA: Not available.

SOURCE: Harbour & Associates. 2003. *The Harbour Report 2003: North America*, Troy, Michigan: Harbour & Associates, Inc.

3. Depressed demand in the auto industry: The global auto industry is always impacted by weak consumer confidence that is a reflection of countries' economic health. The East Asian crisis impacted DaimlerChrysler's sales. Furthermore, the European and North American markets did not help either because of the economic slowdown and unemployment problems.

4. Production and manufacturing issues: At the time of the merger, Daimler-Benz and Chrysler wanted to streamline their manufacturing by using the same platforms. The idea looked good on paper but companies had a hard time materializing this strategy worldwide because of logistical issues, mismatch of manufacturing and production methods, and cost issues. The cost was hard to be contained and in the North American subcompact market, Chrysler lagged behind in sales and market share (see Table 8).

5. Brand portfolio issues: At the time of merger, Daimler-Benz and Chrysler had a major plan to combine their brands but it never really happened because of the mismatch of brand portfolios. Daimler-Benz targeted the upscale market while Chrysler mostly pursued low end/sub-compact markets in North America. Although both companies cooperated in product development and supplier network, tangible benefits were seen to be limited in the post-merger period (see Table 8).

6. DaimlerChrysler's stalled Asian strategy: To make a strong foothold in Asia, DaimlerChrysler took a 37.1% ($1.9 billion) stake in Mitsubishi Motors Corporation in 2000. At that time, the investment and the alliance looked viable because of Asia's booming sub-compact markets. Though an underdog from Japan, Mitsubishi was not a strong player in North America. In 2004, the company lost over $200 million because of limited

product lines and other marketing issues. DaimlerChrysler refused to inject capital into troubled Mitsubishi. In addition, in May 2004, DaimlerChrysler announced selling its 10.5% stake in Hyundai Motor Company and realigned its strategic alliance with the Korean partner. During the same month, to enter into China, DaimlerChrysler and Beijing Automotive Industry Holding Company Limited announced the production of Mercedes-Benz's C and E-Class cars in China. The project's annual capacity is expected to produce 25,000 cars per year. Though DaimlerChrysler's China venture looks viable in the long term, it will take time to have the project matured.[31]

WHAT LIES AHEAD?

According to DaimlerChrysler, the company's global strategy is based on four competitive areas: global presence, strong brands, broad product range, and technology leadership.[32] The company has been successful in global markets and a force to be reckoned with because of a well diversified brand portfolio (passenger cars and commercial vehicles). The company maintains strong brands and a broad product portfolio but lags in market share and global integration that was envisaged in the merger. In the coming years, the company's management faces an uphill

[31]For more discussion, see: *Business Week*. 2004. "As Shaky Automotive Menage A Trois," (May 10): 40–41; *Financial Times*. 2004. "DaimlerChrysler to Sell Its $1 Billion Hyundai Stake," (May 4): 17; *The Wall Street Journal*. "Mitsubishi Motors to Review Products, Overhaul Its Culture," (May 3): A12; *The Wall Street Journal*. "DaimlerChrysler Agrees to Sell Its 10% Stake in Hyundai Motor," (May 12): A6.
[32]See company Web site (www.daimlerchrysler.com).

TABLE 6   Global Auto Manufacturers: Selected Financial Data (1997–2003)

Company	1997	1998	1999	2000	2001	2002	2003
DaimlerChrysler:							
Revenues ($ mil)	127,131	154,615	151,035	152,446	136,072	156,838	157,125
Net profit ($ mil)	7,279.0	6,448.0	5,173.0	3,338.0	(589.2)	5,114.0	512.3
Pretax profit per vehicle ($)	1,868	1,336	1,470	1,497	170	(1,679)	226
Earnings per share ($)	7.15	6.54	6.25	3.26	(0.59)	5.22	0.55
Net Profit Margin (%)	5.7	4.2	3.4	2.2	NA	3.3	0.3
Ford:							
Revenues ($ mil)	153,627	144,416	162,558	170,064	162,412	163,420	164,196
Net profit ($ mil)	6,920.0	6,570.0	7,237.0	4,823.0	(5,453)	284.0	759.0
Pretax profit per vehicle ($)	NA	NA	NA	709	(1293)	(211)	NA
Earnings per share ($)	5.62	5.28	5.86	3.22	(3.02)	.15	.31
Net Profit Margin (%)	4.5	4.5	4.5	2.8	NA	0.2	0.3
General Motors:							
Revenues ($ mil)	173,168	161,315	176,558	184,632	177,260	186,763	185,524
Net profit ($ mil)	5,972.0	3,662.0	5,576.0	4,452.0	601.0	1,736.0	3,822.0
Pretax profit per vehicle ($)	NA	NA	NA	388	73	267	NA
Earnings per share ($)	7.89	5.24	8.53	6.68	1.77	3.35	4.18
Net Profit Margin (%)	3.4	2.3	3.2	2.4	0.3	0.9	1.5
Honda:							
Revenues ($ mil)	45,111	51,688	57,536	52,170	55,357	66,429	67,439
Net profit ($ mil)	1,959.6	2,430.4	2,475.8	1,874.4	2,727.0	3,555.5	3,610.0
Pretax profit per vehicle ($)	182	1,040	993	1,440	1,294	1,345	1,406
Earnings per ADR ($)*	1.01	1.30	1.27	0.96	1.40	1.83	2.35
Net Profit Margin (%)	4.3	4.9	4.3	3.6	4.9	5.4	5.8
Nissan:							
Revenues ($ mil)	49,358	54,583	56,388	49,110	46,588	56,905	57,770
Net profit ($ mil)	382.0	(229.9)	(6,456)	2,670	2,799.0	4,126.4	4,189.0
Pretax profit per vehicle ($)	301	(66)	(17)	(2,782)	811	1,105	1,975
Earnings per ADR ($)*	0.30	(0.18)	(3.25)	1.26	1.39	1.95	2.25
Net Profit Margin (%)	0.8	NA	NA	5.4	6.0	7.3	6.4
Toyota:							
Revenues ($ mill)	87,807	105,832	119,656	106,030	107,443	128,965	135,819
Net profit ($ mill)	3,416.1	3,747.0	4,540.0	5,447.0	4,177.0	6,247.0	7,992
Pretax profit per vehicle ($)	957	1,239	1,348	1,234	1,464	1,477	1,814
Earnings per ADR ($)*	1.79	1.98	2.02	2.92	2.28	3.52	6.00
Net Profit Margin (%)	3.9	3.35	3.8	5.1	3.9	4.8	6.4

Notes: * Earnings per ADR (American Depository Receipts).

SOURCE: Harbour & Associates. 2003. *The Harbour Report 2003: North America*, Troy, Michigan: Harbour & Associates, Inc.; *Value Line*. 2004. Auto and Truck Industry, March 5: 101–109.

TABLE 7   Top Ten Global Auto Manufacturers Based on Market Capitalization (as of May 2004)

Rank	Company	Market Capitalization
1.	Toyota	$119.6 billion
2.	Nissan	46.9
3.	**DaimlerChrysler**	42.5
4.	Honda	38.4
5.	BMW	25.4
6.	General Motors	24.9
7.	Ford	24.7
8.	Renault	20.0
9.	Volkswagen	13.3
10.	Peugeot	12.6

SOURCE: *Financial Times.* 2004. "Toyota Snaps at GM's Heels as Net Profits Surge," May 12: 17.

TABLE 8 DaimlerChrysler and Other Global Auto Manufacturers: Strengths, Weaknesses, and Current/Future Plans (2004)

DaimlerChrysler	GM	Ford	Volkswagen	Toyota	Honda	Nissan
Sales: $157.12 bill.*	Sales: $185.52 bill.*	Sales: $164.19 bill.*	Sales: $91.33 bill.*	Sales: $135.81 bill.*	Sales: $67.43 bill.*	Sales: $57.77 bill.*
Strengths:	**Strengths:**	**Strengths:**	**Strengths:**	**Strengths:**	**Strengths:**	**Strengths:**
• DaimlerChrysler is the fourth largest automaker in the world; good market coverage in over 100 countries; sells luxury as well as sub-compact vehicles.	• GM is the largest automaker in the world.	• Ford is the third largest automaker in the world.	• Good brand recognition worldwide.	• In sales, Toyota became the second largest auto manufacturer after GM in 2004.	• Strong manufacturer in the sub-compact segments.	• Nissan has made a marvelous recovery under the leadership of Carlos Ghosn.
• Good distribution and sales network; major conglomerate.	• Major player in global markets with many brands; largest exporter of vehicles from the U.S.	• Maintains visible brands and supplier network.	• Strong presence in Europe and Latin American.	• Expanding in many markets worldwide.	• Quality standards are good and are well rated.	• Nissan brand has been reinvigorated by Renault; In 2004, one of the most profitable auto companies in the world.
• Major manufacturer of utility trucks in North America,	• Market share has improved.	• Consumer ratings are better in utility trucks.	• Good distribution network in the European market.	• Maintains outstanding manufacturing plants worldwide; Toyota production system (TPS) continues to be the worldwide benchmark in quality.	• Strong brand in North America and Asia.	• Many new products have been introduced since 2002.
Weaknesses:	• Maintains a good manufacturing and distribution system worldwide.	**Weaknesses:**	**Weaknesses:**	• Toyota products are rated highly in North America and other parts of the world.	• Low cost auto manufacturer; highly focused in product development; maintains good economies of scale.	• Quality has improved; turn-around strategy has received good ratings from the market.
• The merger did not help the company to increase market share and productivity.	**Weaknesses:**	• The "world car" strategy has not materialized.	• Key models in the sub-compact segments are aging.	• Low cost manufacturer in many categories; hybrid cars are doing well in North America.	• Expanding in North America and Asia.	• Renault–Nissan alliance has cut costs and gained market share since 2003.
• Unable to deal with two corporate cultures (American and German) in its global integration.	• GM's global operations have improved since 2001.	• Quality issues are haunting the company.	• Costs are too high.	• Overseas expansion is on track.	**Weaknesses:**	• Overhauled Nissan's corporate culture and business practices.
• Quality and branding issues remain to be resolved; Chrysler brand has not done well in cars.	• Slow to change because of its company size; big organization with a massive bureaucratic structure.	• Distribution system is weak in overseas markets.	• Limited brand visibility in North America, especially in the sub-compact market; dealer network is weak.	**Weaknesses:**	• Honda has a limited presence in some markets of Europe and Latin America.	
	• Product development cost is high.	• Losing market share in North America.	• Limited product offerings and brand portfolio.	• Corporate culture is somewhat rigid.	• Beyond the sub-compact markets, Honda's product portfolio lacks variety in global branding.	
	• Brand Portfolio is diverse.	**Current/Future Plans:**	• Sales and marketing outside of Europe are weak.			
		• Reorganization is being undertaken to address quality issues and market expansion.	• New models have been scarce.			

TABLE 8 (Cont.)

Daimler Chrysler	GM	Ford	Volkswagen	Toyota	Honda	Nissan
• Chrysler cars do not get good ratings in North America. • In 2004, the company's global strategy has stalled; alliances with Mitsubishi and Hyundai are non productive. **Current/Future Plans:** • Reorganization regarding global operations and manufacturing may take place in the coming years. • More cost cutting will take in the coming years.	**Current/Future Plans:** • Asia-Pacific business has improved. • Will target new markets, especially the Chinese market. • Hybrid models will be built in future.	• Profit is preferred over high volume strategy. • Hybrid car is in the pipeline. • Ford is switching to flexible production systems. • Plan on concentrating more on subcompacts.	• Volkswagen does not attract a mass market outside of Europe. **Current/Future Plans:** • Reorganization is in progress; product development issues are being addressed. • Plan on expanding in the Chinese market. • Entry into the high-end market will continue in the coming years.	• Product designs are unappealing and may need an overhaul. • Limited market share in the European luxury segments. **Current/Future Plans:** • Continues to expand worldwide; will be a major player in the coming years. • Overseas manufacturing is a major part of Toyota's global strategy.	• Limited diversification sought by the company from its core business. **Current/Future Plans:** • Future expansion is possible in North America and Europe.	**Weaknesses:** • Still lacks market share in the North America. • Limited product portfolio in global markets. **Current/Future Plans:** • Global reorganization is on track; new models are in the pipeline. • Making big efforts in product development; also will be manufacturing cars in China.

Notes: * 2003 sales.

SOURCE: (1). Anwar, Syed T. 2003. "DaimlerChrysler AG: The Making of a New Transnational Corporation," in Deresky, Helen. *International Management: Managing Across Borders and Cultures*, 4th edition, Upper Saddle River, New Jersey: Prentice Hall, pp. 340–356; Harbour & Associates, Inc. 2003. *The Harbour Report: North America 2003*. Troy, Michigan: Harbour & Associates, Inc.; *Automotive Industries; Business Week; The Economist; Financial Times; Value Line; The Wall Street Journal* (various issues).

task reviving its profits and smooth global integration.[33] If DaimlerChrysler achieves its merger objectives in the areas of cost cutting, global integration, rationalization, and R&D savings, the merger will definitely be rated as a *cause celebre* merger. If all goes well, the company will be credited for making a transatlantic corporation. On the other hand, as of 2004, it remains a question mark regarding the merger's viability and long-term prospects.[34] Hamel correctly comments on mega mergers:

Whatever the rationale for corporate coupling, a spate of academic research has demonstrated that mega-mergers are as likely to destroy shareholder wealth as to create it. In most cases, the costs of integration, both direct and indirect, overwhelm the anticipated economies.[35]

CASE QUESTIONS

1. Analyze and evaluate the Daimler-Benz and Chrysler Corporations' strengths and weaknesses before the merger.
2. What are the differences in the typical German and American cultures and their corporate cultures that contributed to problems with the merger?
3. What did you learn from DaimlerChrysler's post-merger problems and blunders? Evaluate their strategy and how it was implemented.
4. Compare and contrast DaimlerChrysler with other global auto manufacturers (GM, Ford, Toyota, Honda, Volkswagen, Nissan, etc.) regarding their global strategies and competitive issues.

5. Discuss DaimlerChrysler's global branding strategies in the world auto markets. Do you anticipate the company revamping and overhauling its brands in the coming years?
6. Within the time frame of this case (2004), assess what kinds of short-term and long-term global strategies DaimlerChrysler needs to formulate to regain market share in the world automotive industry?
7. Do some research to update this case as of the time of your reading this text. How is DaimlerChrysler's global strategy progressing at this time? What global alliances does the company have?

[33]Harbour & Associates. 2003, op. cit; *The Wall Street Journal.* "Daimler CEO Defends Strategy, Reign," (May 6): A3.

[34]Anwar. 2003, op. cit.
[35]Hamel, Gary. 2004. "When Dinosaurs Mate," *The Wall Street Journal*, (January 22): A12.

Case 13   *Global E-Commerce at United Parcel Service (UPS) 2001*

In November 1999, after being privately held for over ninety years, United Parcel Service (UPS) carried out the largest initial public offering ever by a U.S.-based company at that time. The initial public offering (IPO) raised $5.47 billion, leaving the company cash-rich and able to pursue strategic acquisitions and mergers. After that, the company embarked on aggressive expansion around the world consistent with its new charter to become an enabler of global e-commerce, as well as a leader in parcel delivery service. UPS's broad vision of e-commerce included integrating the flow of information, capital, and

goods around the world. In keeping with that vision, UPS grew its global delivery business, and added powerful units in supply chain management, and global trade financing.

Prior to the IPO, technology and connectivity were already considered strategic company advantages and priorities. Even after an e-commerce marketing unit was formed, company executives still thought about the context of changing business processes. In 1996, UPS formed an e-commerce team to help the company find ways to use the Internet to conduct business. Alan Amling served on that original team.

Alan Amling, director of e-commerce at United Parcel Service, took a break beside the waterfall outside headquarters north of Atlanta. The lush green foliage reminded him of his home in Grant's Pass, Oregon. He thought back to the meeting he'd just left on the redesign of the www.ups.com Web site. He wondered how long it would take the group to reach consensus. He knew that once that happened, they would move quickly ahead to implement the new plan.

Relaxing for a rare moment in the cool spring air, Alan asked himself, "How do you make an elephant dance? How do you get a huge company like UPS to be more nimble?" These questions highlighted the major challenge facing management at UPS. How do you keep a huge company growing in times of rapid change?

UPS earned about $30 billion in revenue in 2000. If the company grows 15% a year, it would have to create the equivalent of a $4.5 billion new company every year. Over the five years from 1996 to 2001, UPS's net income grew at an amazing 22% compound annual rate.

How can UPS keep its competitive edge, achieved by strategic planning, focused long-term vision, hard work, and a $12 billion investment in technology? How do you integrate e-commerce throughout the company's global operations? James Belasco's 1991 business best-seller *Teaching the Elephant to Dance* was all about how to get a large company to welcome change. More recently, *Who Moved My Cheese?* by Spencer Johnson and Kenneth H. Blanchard deals with the same topic. Amling's team needed to find a way to drive these messages through UPS.

HISTORY OF UPS

Four teenagers founded UPS on August 28, 1907, in Seattle, Washington to deliver packages by motorcycle and a Ford for the Bon Marché department stores. From its humble beginnings, UPS has grown into a global giant of the shipping industry. Private and self-effacing UPS was known for its inconspicuous brown delivery trucks and reliability since it began operation. The company didn't even have a marketing department until 1988. The company just made sure their prices were lower than the U.S. Postal Service for years. When Federal Express came on the scene in the 70s and 80s with its flashy marketing campaign, UPS saw the need to communicate more efficiently with the external community, and created a public relations and a marketing department.

By 2001, UPS was one of the world's largest employers with over 359,000 employees (320,500 U.S. and 38,500 international). UPS revenue in 2000 hit $29.8 billion. Worldwide, the company served 7.9 million customers daily. UPS used a fleet of more than 620 aircraft, making it the eleventh largest airline in the world. In 2001, UPS ran a fleet of 152,500 package cars, trucks, and tractor trailers.

Transforming the traditional giant of the shipping industry into a technology-driven global company was not easy. The company invested over $12 billion in technology and infrastructure from 1991 to 2001, more than it spent on its delivery fleet of trucks. The changes transformed the company. Even with that investment in technology and the company's new global orientation, it still took a lot of discussion internally to get the big globe logo and www.ups.com Internet address painted on all UPS trucks. Traditionalists within the company wanted only *ups* in small letters and an 800 phone number painted on the trucks. After much consensus building, the company moved ahead in one direction. Long-time UPSers on the Management Committee subsequently lead the new company charter, providing essential support and direction for UPS's transformation.

In its earliest history, UPS delivered packages to homes and expanded down the West Coast from Seattle. It expanded into air service in 1929, flying up and down the West Coast and as far east as Phoenix. In the Great Depression of the 1930s, the company had to eliminate the air service and go back to ground package delivery. After World War II with the rise of the suburbs, people had their own cars and the country developed a national freeway system. The company went state by state and got approval to go to every address by the 1970s. After the company was able to reach every address in every state, it started looking outside the U.S. at Europe with the same idea of delivery to every address.

In the 1980s, UPS started over with its own air service. In an eighteen-month period, the company created an airline that grew to be the ninth largest airline in the U.S. The company picked Louisville, Kentucky, for its main U.S. hub because of its good weather and location. UPS could deliver overnight from Louisville to a large number of people, since 70% of the U.S. population lived east of the Mississippi. Other U.S. hubs were located in Philadelphia; Dallas; Ontario; California; Rockford, Illinois; Columbia, South Carolina; and Hartford, Connecticut. Miami, Florida, serves as UPS's Latin American and Caribbean hub. In the Asia Pacific region, major hubs were Taipei, Hong Kong, Singapore, and the Philippines. Cologne/Bonn remains the European hub. In Canada, hubs were located in Hamilton, Ontario and Montreal, Quebec.

Each hub was connected to a number of operating centers which served as home base for the familiar brown package trucks, and provided all pickup and delivery service within a specific geographic area. Operating center area boundaries were contiguous to one another so that every address was covered. With this system, next-day ground delivery occurred routinely among all operating center areas that were connected to the same hub. In some cases, next-day ground service was possible to destinations more than 400 miles away.

The UPS Next-Day Air system operated under the same hub-and-spoke principle. Packages picked up by UPS drivers were sorted at the local center and rushed to a nearby airport. UPS aircraft served as "feeder" vehicles, arriving at the air hub with packages and documents heading to hundreds of locations, and departing hours later with a load of packages to be delivered in the airplane's destination service area. The bottom-line benefit of this system to UPS and its customers lay in its being the quickest, most efficient, and most cost-effective way to get packages from point A to point B on a global basis.

UPS's reputation in the shipping business became based on efficiency. With the electronics industry, high tech and computers especially, ground and air delivery within a guaranteed timeframe became critical. Not surprisingly, there was a direct correlation between speed of delivery and price charged for the service. Over time, industrial engineers helped to grow the company. "Planning and execution, especially long-term planning, are what we're known for," says Gary W. Huff, Director of E-commerce international marketing at United Parcel Service.

After Alan Amling joined the start-up UPS e-commerce group in 1996, the company went through major changes. It morphed into a new company that did a lot more than deliver 13.6 million packages and documents daily, 9 million of which come from customers who were connected electronically to UPS. Late in 2000, the Standard and Forrester Research service published a study of the shipping preferences of online buyers. The report states that "given the choice of UPS, U.S. Mail, and FedEx, 62% of online buyers go with UPS most often." The company worked hard to live up to its vision as the connection between the virtual and physical worlds in over 200 countries and territories. The Web site, www.ups.com, dedicated content for 109 countries, in nineteen languages and dialects.

The core business of UPS remained ground and air package operations in the U.S. and internationally. Its non-package operations consisted of the UPS Logistics Groups, the most significant revenue growth driver in the non-package segment. This group operated primarily in Supply Chain Management, Logistics Technologies, Service Parts Logistics, and Transportation Services.

The Supply Chain Management unit offered global distribution services, inventory and order management, transportation network management, and customer service. Major users of this service included Ford, Nike, IBM, Honeywell, and Cisco Systems. The Logistics Technologies unit developed and operated management information systems that provide total visibility of orders and products moving from origin to destination. The Service Parts Logistics unit delivered critical parts in 1-, 2-, 4- and 24-hour windows, using a worldwide network of transportation and central distribution and field stocking facilities. The unit also repaired telecommunications, network, and computer equipment, providing turnaround service for warranties in 24–48 hours. Transportation Services offered re-engineering, design, and management services for transportation networks.

UPS CAPITAL CORPORATION

In the mid-1990s, UPS's management very carefully studied the possibility of starting a finance business. The innovative idea of the world's largest shipping company making loans ran into some resistance at first. Eventually, senior management reached consensus and decided to establish UPS Capital Corporation in May 1998 as a wholly owned subsidiary. UPS Capital (capital.ups.com) offered COD services, asset-based lending, inventory finance, and global trade financing. It helped its customers to expand operations, sell to new accounts, accelerate cash flow, lease new equipment, and expand working capital.

This new idea would definitely keep the elephant dancing, and allow the company to expand its mission to enabling the flow of funds, as well as goods and information. The move into financing gave UPS an opportunity to leverage its access to cash, leverage its brand, and provide financial solutions increasingly tied to the movement of goods and information. UPS's excellent Standard & Poor's rating allows the company to borrow at low rates.

The financial services business is risky. UPS could have made any number of profitable acquisitions tied to its core business, but it wanted to be more deeply involved in commerce. The creation of Capital Corporation was less about abundant cash flow than it was about investing in opportunities to grow the core package business by financially supporting its own customers.

UPS Capital Corporation offered a wide range of financial services. In 2001, the unit had over 170 employees and more than 2,000 customers. The non-shipping business (primarily logistics and UPS Capital) contributed about 5% to UPS's bottom line, and about $300 million to the company's operating profit in 2000. UPS Capital operates in the U.S. and six other countries including the United Kingdom, Hong Kong, and Taiwan. UPS Capital offers its customers asset-based lending, and helps them with cash-flow problems. It paid small and midsize exporters on credit in advance for goods they shipped to their customers abroad.

Assuming these significant new risks for its clients, UPS could help customers to grow, which in turn helped UPS's core shipping business. UPS Capital also does global trade financing against inventory and accounts receivable, provides online bill-paying service, and issues credit cards.

The UPS Strategic Enterprise Fund (SEF) was founded in 1997 as a private equity strategic investment group to invest in start-ups. SEF was a corporate venture capital fund that invested in early-stage, cutting-edge companies strategically aligned with UPS's business model. SEF's mission was to gain insight into the workings of the new economy and to help shape UPS's strategy development.

UPS kept a finger on the pulse of the marketplace through the SEF. More important than the potential financial returns of investing in these start-ups was the prospect of knowledge returns—that is, knowledge capital. The most publicized Strategic Enterprise Fund start-up was UPS E-logistics, which catered to small and mid-sized businesses seeking turnkey warehouse inventory services and shipping management. Another start-up was Air2Web, which deals with wireless technology.

HISTORY OF UPS INTERNATIONAL

Physical reminders of UPS's bold global direction appeared throughout the new corporate headquarters north of Atlanta. Sixty maps were etched into the lobby floor representing all corners of the globe, showing the worldwide reach of the company. Wrapping around the entry wall was a quote from Jim Casey, founder of UPS. "Our horizon is as distant as our mind's eye wishes it to be." It sets the tone for the company's global strategy, a long-term vision of well-planned, focused, and, at times, aggressive expansion.

In 1975, UPS set up its first international operation in Canada. The following year, it started a domestic operation in West Germany. Nine years later, the company began international air service between the U.S. and Belgium, France, Germany, Luxembourg, Netherlands, and the UK. By 1988, the UPS International Express Service network was serving 41 countries, with delivery to virtually every address. The company methodically focused its attention on expansion. After purchasing sixteen European companies, UPS expanded its operations to go to deliver in 700 cities in Europe. By 1987, UPS International Express Service had become available to most of Western Europe, Japan, and Canada.

In April 1989, UPS began expedited document service to 163 countries and territories. Later that same year, UPS started work on an $80 million computer and telecommunications center in Mahwah, New Jersey, to serve as the center of its global computer network. This center was part of a five-year plan and a $1.5 billion investment to develop state-of-the-art technology for UPS's global delivery network.

By 1995, UPS introduced package tracking through the Internet, so customers could have an immediate status report on the whereabouts of their shipments. Two years later, UPS launched UPS OnLine® Tracking Software in five languages. By 1998, UPS customers could track shipments in sixteen local languages and dialects, an industry first. Also in 1998, Ronald G. Wallace, former president of UPS Canada, took over as president of UPS International. Under his leadership, UPS's business continued to grow internationally.

In 2001, UPS acquired six direct flights into Beijing and Shanghai, China, from the U.S. Four flights originated from Ontario, California, while the other two fly out of Newark, New Jersey. With these routes, UPS became the first company in the industry to offer non-stop flights between the United States and China and cut a whole day in delivery time. It also enabled UPS to offer customers more capacity and reliability. Before these flights, UPS could not fly its own planes into China. It had to unload packages in Hong Kong and put them on planes operated by other airlines. For delivery within China, UPS partnered with Sinotrans, one of the largest transportation companies in that country. UPS had branded operations with brown vans and uniformed drivers in 21 major Chinese cities, with plans to expand to 40 cities soon.

By 2001, UPS had a chance to catch up with FedEx, which held an estimated 10% to 15% of the express-delivery market in China, compared to UPS's approximately 5% share. FedEx had direct service to China beginning in 1995, when it bought the only direct all-cargo flight operating authority from Evergreen International Aviation Inc. Both UPS and FedEx lag behind DHL, which held about 30% of the China market. Both companies viewed China as a major future economic opportunity with its 1.2 billion people. If Congress permanently normalized China's trade status, U.S.–China trade would become even more important.

Also in 2001, UPS purchased Fritz, a freight forwarding and customs company. UPS had also been buying smaller freight forwarders in order to break down borders, help with customs, and facilitate shipments. Fritz had 400 facilities in more than 120 countries.

Going international, UPS had a few problems with cultural differences. The color brown had a strong tradition within UPS. Crayola® even named one of its crayons UPS Brown. In 1907, when four teenagers started the company, that brown was the color of first-class Pullman train cars. In some countries, however, the signature shade of brown led to some cultural misunderstandings. For example, in Spain, hearses have the same brown color as the UPS trucks. These problems resolved as people became accustomed to the branding.

Other countries had issues with the color brown as well. For example, the UPS brown uniform looks similar to the one that police wear in Thailand. So when the UPS deliveryman first arrived at some addresses in Bangkok, unsuspecting customers would panic. Again, people eventually got used to the brand. When UPS acquired a company overseas, it used dual logoing for a three-to-five-year period, so customers got used to the brand and the brown color.

Gradually, UPS tried to blend in with the local culture. In the years up to 2001, UPS had approximately 400 expatriates around the world; subsequently, they had thirty. The company preferred to send in UPS executives from the U.S. overseas for short-term overseas assignments, while training local managers to run in-country operations.

The tough part of the international business was translating the virtual to the physical world. In international shipping, there were still many impediments. All goods had to go through the customs process. UPS found that the more information it could streamline, the better. Whenever possible, the company pre-cleared the goods electronically, and gave the customs agents more information than they would normally get. International shipping was at the mercy of the destination country's customs. If customs or government-related issues didn't delay shipments, the technology was in place to get anything anywhere in the world in 24–48 hours. The international dateline was another cause for delay beyond UPS's control.

THE SHIPPING INDUSTRY AND COMPETITORS

In 1998, 1999, and 2000, UPS was ranked as the World's Most Admired Company in the mail, package, and freight industry in a survey by *Fortune Magazine*. The magazine surveyed 12,600 executives, directors, and securities analysts on eight key attributes of reputation including innovation, quality of management, employee talent, and social responsibility. In second place came FedEx, followed by TNT Post Group and Deutsche Post.

In the 1970s, FedEx revolutionized the shipping industry with overnight delivery of packages and the capability to track the progress of packages via computers. Although UPS had experimented with air service for years, it was essentially a trucking company. Only in 1988 did UPS get its own air delivery service up and running. UPS was competing on a par with FedEx in the mid-90s in terms of computer systems, then surpassed their capabilities in many respects beginning in the late 1990s. UPS improved on FedEx's proprietary software by developing their system to work with any corporate computer network.

The Internet hit the industry in the 1990s. UPS's investment in technological infrastructure paid off. By 2001, UPS led the industry by giving customers many choices of guaranteed quick air or inexpensive ground delivery, global trade financing, Web retailing and call centers, and logistic services such as warehousing and supply-chain management.

Both shipping leaders experienced similar growth in 2000. UPS grew 11% to $30 billion in revenues, compared to FedEx's 8.8% increase in revenues up to $18 billion. UPS earned $2.8 billion in profits, which yielded an operating margin of 15.3%. This margin was nearly double that of FedEx, which only earned $688 million in profit.

UPS's growth can be partly attributed to its decision in 1999 to use its huge ground transportation network to assist with overnight deliveries. Its logisticians realized UPS could make mid-range deliveries up to 400 miles by truck rather than plane at great savings to the company. As a result, cost per package was estimated to be $6.65, compared to FedEx's $11.89, according to transportation analysts at Credit Suisse First Boston.[1] The packages carried by UPS tended to be heavier than FedEx's, while more of FedEx's packages traveled by air. So the cost advantage of UPS over rival FedEx was significant. FedEx relied heavily on its air fleet, although from 1997 through 2001, it spent $500 million on a ground network. In 2001, it would spend $150 million more on ground service in an attempt to reach all U.S. homes. FedEx offered night and Saturday deliveries, services that UPS did not provide, although UPS had night and Saturday delivery on its Next Day Air and Second Day Air products.

In foreign markets, only 10% of deliveries were made overnight. In this area, DHL International, owned by Deutsche Post and based in Brussels, was the leader with about 20% to 25% of the European market. FedEx and TNT Post Group tied for second place with 10% to 15% each of the European market. UPS was third in Europe, with 8% to 12% market share.

[1] *BusinessWeek*, May 21, 2001, p. 65

HISTORY OF GLOBAL E-COMMERCE AT UPS

UPS defined e-commerce broadly as using network-compatible technology to conduct business. In 1996, UPS created its e-commerce team to develop ways to use the Internet to conduct business. The company realized that any way companies buy, sell, and do business would affect UPS. The e-commerce team was born out of the Information Technology Strategy Team (ITSC), a cross-functional committee of senior-level managers directing UPS's strategy in the technology area. The ITSC team at the time included current Vice-Chairman, Mike Eskew, current Chief Information Officer, Ken Lacy, and current Senior Vice President of Corporate Development, Joe Pyne.

The global e-commerce team began by looking at where the opportunities were. They saw that the company had a real opportunity to become partners with its customers through e-commerce. The group shared a revolutionary vision. They wanted UPS to be an indispensable branded component of global transportation of hard goods. In this way, UPS would leverage its competency. Once the team agreed on that vision, the rest was simple. Everyone had the same answer: "Build UPS into the business process of our customers." That was the real epiphany the e-commerce group had in its developmental phase.

Handling information became part of their charge. UPS delivered 13.6 million packages every day, and got 250 data elements on each package. UPS was using this data to improve its operations and provide tracking information. Then the e-commerce team asked itself, "How can we provide this information back to our customers to improve their businesses' processes?"

The new e-commerce group had a profound effect on the core business, which UPS saw as customer connectivity. Looking at the core business in a new way, e-commerce team members felt like they were in a start-up company over the next few years. Amling explained, "Every time we were on the Internet, our brand would be there. We could not be separated from our brand. The Internet is not just domestic. It had to be global because the Internet is global. This kept U.S. grounded, to create solutions around our core business. What we know and what we're good at. Our strategy was to integrate and inform."

Working hard through 2001 to smoothly integrate e-commerce with the core operations, Amling said the ultimate goal was for his unit to disappear. When e-commerce became so totally integrated into the entire operations of the company, the separate e-commerce unit would no longer need to exist. "We'll know when we're successful, and when we no longer need an e-commerce unit. That will come when we're woven into every aspect of UPS. We're starting to overlap with traditional marketing and research groups now."

UPS CORPORATE CULTURE

UPS had a strong corporate culture, going back to its roots in Seattle in 1907. The culture had a profound impact on the growth and evolution of the company over the years. UPS had a reputation for methodical, careful planning, and a steady work ethic. This was precisely why Alan Amling was pondering how his team could help make an elephant dance and keep it nimble. The company relied on consensus, seeking buy-in from all constituents before moving ahead. They were not known as flashy marketers like FedEx. Even the company colors reflected their cultures: UPS's conservative brown vs. FedEx's eye-catching orange and purple. The companies' cultures contrasted by the images of UPS's industrial engineers and FedEx's marketing experts.

The UPS culture emphasized consensus and communication. John Flick, director of International Public Relations for UPS, said, "The company speaks with one voice." The corporate culture sent a clear, consistent message through management by consensus. Once agreement was reached, the company could execute. It might take a while to get consensus, but after that, implementation was swift. Then UPS moved forward solidly in agreement, articulating the new direction clearly and consistently. Communicating the major changes in the company posed a major challenge, given the sheer size of the company and number of employees. According to many employees, the company had a great culture and work ethic. Early on, soon after Alan Amling joined UPS, he told his manager, "Well, I'd do this if it were my money." And he replied, "It is your money!" Bonuses were tied to the whole company's performance, rather than the efforts of one unit. UPS employees tended to be very loyal to the company. Turnover at UPS was much lower than for most companies. It wasn't unusual for employees to stay at the company for 25–40 years of service. UPS saw itself as a family organization.

In the lobby at UPS headquarters, visitors saw large words etched on the wall intended to describe the UPS culture: Service, Integrity, Community, Teamwork, Vision, People, Growth. Humility and informality were also important parts of the culture. Many executives like Alan Amling, John Flick, and Gary Huff got their start at the company working part- or full-time in delivery and package sorting. UPS felt that all employees needed to know the bread and butter of the business. Even the newly hired techies were required to spend some time on a package car, learning what it was like to run on a very tight schedule.

In the past, titles didn't have much importance internally. With the company going public, titles began to take on new importance. Although people dressed formally at headquarters, the company had an open door policy. Everyone talked to managers by their first name. At the new UPS Innoplex, the company's e-commerce solutions center, just north of the UPS Atlanta headquarters, employees dressed in business casual, jeans, and t-shirts. At the headquarters, dress was more formal, suit and tie.

But executives at both places all went on first-name basis, even top executives. Employees honored the company's long history and traditions, and remembered past UPS leaders with respect.

Speed and timing were vital to the culture. As an example of this, Chief Executive Officer, Jim Kelly, was known to apologize to employees for wasting their time when he was just five minutes late for a meeting.

Integrity also played an important role in the culture. "Our image is very important to us. INTEGRITY. We'll live and die by this," said Ron Wallace, president of UPS International. "We have very strict rules concerning integrity, appearance of vehicle, service, safety, feeling of UPS family. We promote from within. We insist on what we have works," Wallace added.

Jim Kelly, Chairman and CEO of UPS, spoke about integrity to a Rutgers University Business Forum. He said, "Despite UPS's size and scope, integrity isn't just a line in a statement of company values, hanging on a wall somewhere and gathering dust. Integrity is manifested every day at UPS through three basic working principles: 1) delivering quality; 2) taking care of your people; and 3) taking responsibility for your actions."

UPS also emphasized ethics, doing the right thing at all times. All managers got business ethics training every year. In addition, UPS was the number one corporate contributor to the United Way. The money came from the employees as a payroll deduction. Each work group gave a day of service to the United Way. Some people volunteered a day to work for Goodwill Industries or Habitat for Humanity. The company viewed this volunteering as a great team-building activity as well. Instead of running an obstacle course, the company encouraged employees to do something for the community.

GLOBAL STRATEGY

UPS applied three main global strategies of 1) access, 2) integration, and 3) globalization to grow its business in preparation for long-term development. UPS's global strategy was to be a business partner for companies worldwide, and to make them successful by enabling global commerce to their benefit. The company tried to anticipate business needs ten to twenty years in the future. As president of UPS International, Ron Wallace, said, "A successful strategy must be long-term and focused. At the same time, you must be able to tailor it to each individual marketplace."

In addition to the three main strategies, Wallace identified four key emphases of UPS's global strategy:

1. Logistics
2. Customer relationships and customer service
3. Technology
4. Culture

In the logistics area, supply chain improvements gave UPS a competitive edge over FedEx and DHL. Additionally, UPS executives put customer relationships and customer service at the top of their radar screens. Logistics and customer service were driven by technology. In terms of culture, Wallace saw that UPS needed to have a keen awareness of cultures, and be street smart. He considered all business to be local, and firmly believed that a successful global company needed to show respect for people, cultures, and customers.

The logistics unit, which started up in 1994, was housed in a building south of the Atlanta corporate headquarters. Its growth had been phenomenal. In 2000, the unit grew 58%, with revenues exceeding $1 billion. Analysts and company officials expected the growth to continue. At a huge warehouse in Louisville, Kentucky, UPS Logistics handled distribution for many companies like Nike, Sprint, and Hewlett-Packard in one site. UPS provided a broad menu of services for its clients, including repair, storage, tracking, and shipping. The three main strategies of access, integration, and globalization drove international e-commerce as well as other operations of the company.

Access

UPS was working hard to be within easy reach of every customer worldwide. According to Alan Amling, "We will use digital, wireless and software, whatever vehicle it takes, to connect the physical and virtual worlds. Our goal is to take a page from Coke's plan, to put a Coke within arm's reach of desire. We want to be wherever someone wants to use us."

Many UPS activities and acquisitions aimed to make access to its services as easy as possible for its customers. The company worked to make every point of contact, whether pickup, shipment, package tracking, or delivery, easy and accessible for its clients.

In order to get even closer to its customers, UPS made several major acquisitions. It bought Mail Boxes Etc., a worldwide network of retail shipping stores, in order to have a wider, more visible presence. With the Mail Boxes Etc. stores, it became easier for people to know where to take their packages for UPS shipment.

To extend that access abroad, UPS struck a deal with 500 Texaco stations in the Benelux countries in Europe to act as package pickup stations for UPS customers. The gas stations serve double-duty as satellite pickup stations with e-mail notification to the customers. The program was being expanded to the UK by the end of 2001. In Asia, alliances with convenience stores gave customers greater accessibility to UPS services. UPS customers could send packages from Seven-Eleven in Hong Kong and Singapore, and Family Mart in Taiwan.

UPS provided access globally through different channels and devices, for example wireless technology as well as Web. UPS wanted to be easily accessible by whatever devices the customer used. www.ups.com worked to effect migration from phone to Web, since the Web was a much lower cost channel to serve. It was especially good for small and medium-sized companies. Customer self-service

focused on small and medium businesses. Other ways UPS provided access were through UPS OnLine® Advantage where customers could lease a computer for a dollar a day and UPS OnLine® Worldlink which gave customers free Internet access to www.ups.com.

Since many customers abroad had access to the Internet through their wireless devices, UPS invested heavily in a variety of channels for its wireless online services and tracking systems. Wireless was currently available to UPS customers in Europe, several Asian countries, and the U.S. To provide greater access in the U.S. and abroad, UPS reconfigured its tracking system for wireless access from cell phones and Palm Pilots. For example, there were three times as many wireless Internet users in Europe as in the U.S., so wireless was very important.

Integration

UPS sought to integrate its Web-based business into customer service and inventory control. In this way, the company could get into supply chain management and provide an integrated global network.

Alan Amling stated, "Our strategy is to underlie our clients' business, connect the nodes. UPS works in the background, behind the scenes, the brown truck that is unobtrusive. We're building UPS into the structure of the companies."

UPS wanted customers to look at it like a partner in business, rather than a vendor. UPS recognized that it needed to earn the trust of the clients to encourage clients to turn over a lot of operations usually done internally. Many companies accepted UPS software onto their computers to print labels and track their packages.

UPS wanted to help its online clients with everything that happened after a customer pushed the "buy" button. It wasn't that UPS would develop a company's Web store, since many companies already specialized in that. UPS's philosophy in terms of building Web stores was to do what UPS did best. So the company incorporated UPS into PDG Software and ShopSite applications, and allowed those applications to build the customer's Web store. Both companies became part of the UPS Product Provider Program that could be found at www.ec.ups.com/ecommerce/solutions/ecsolutions.html in 2001.

Broadening its corporate vision beyond pickup and delivery of shipments, UPS saw itself as the glue in the supply chain. It defined the supply chain as everything happening in a shipment from the time the product was ordered, including returns. In terms of supply chain management, if a small company was growing and the garage didn't work anymore for a warehouse, UPS could help.

UPS enabled the flow of information and funds as well, not just goods through UPS Capital Corporation and UPS Logistics units. UPS viewed enabling the information flow as especially critical to their business. Their logistics unit began to show people how they could save a lot of costs if they had better information. Businesses tended to have safety stock, since they didn't want to run out of what they needed. As a result, billions of dollars worth of goods sat in warehouses. If companies had a better understanding of demand and goods, they could save huge sums of money that were used to maintain excess inventories.

Globalization

UPS enabled global commerce in a big way, with its presence in more than 200 countries and territories. The company's $3 billion in cash helped it to purchase dozens of related businesses over the five years from 1996 through 2001.

UPS grew nationally and internationally in three ways: by funding start-ups, buying other companies, and forming alliances with strong partners. Everything the company did related in some way to its core business of transportation of goods, funds, or information. Funding start-ups was difficult due to the expense and time it took to establish a brand presence. So more often, UPS acquired other companies, or formed alliances that advanced its strategies of access, integration, and globalization. As part of its investment strategy, UPS often invested for knowledge capital and to be more nimble, rather than for financial gain. By investing early in a certain area, the company anticipated the needs of the market.

GLOBAL E-COMMERCE INITIATIVES

UPS saw its Web site as a work site where people came to get things done. UPS had Internet shipping in thirty-four origin countries. In 2001, the company received more than four million online tracking requests per day. Customers could track shipments from the Web site where they bought it. UPS saw this as process improvement, driving customers back to the Web site of the company. It also reflected the strategy of integration, being a close partner with the client it served.

The tracking service that UPS provided was significant, since many dot-coms failed for lack of customer service. They only allowed customers to contact them by e-mail, without any means to contact the company by phone. The difference between handling a tracking request via the phone and handling that same request over the Internet was the difference between dollars and dimes. As a result, UPS tried to encourage people to use its Web site by making it responsive to customer needs and easy to use.

www.ec.ups.com.   This Web site offered e-commerce solutions to improve the business process, customer service, and reduce costs. Here, customers could download UPS OnLine® Tools and get help in integrating the tools into their own Web site or business applications. The powerful online tools include tracking, rates and services, time in transit, address validation, and other services. The Brown & Brown OnLine® Store demonstrated the use of UPS's advanced shipping applications to potential e-commerce customers. The online store sold UPS memorabilia such as model package delivery trucks. At www.ec.ups.com, customers could also order UPS OnLine® WorldShip, free software for shipping and tracking.

Returns.   Through its returns service, UPS saved companies much more than they charged for the service. With e-commerce orders, a company usually had double the number of returns that it would have with a bricks-and-mortar operation. Typically, returns over the Web ran 10-12%. To help companies deal with this situation, UPS offered an authorized return service. As part of the service, UPS listed the three closest drop-off places for returns, and even had a map on how to get there.

Tracking.   UPS gave its customers visibility into the supply chain every step of the way. It collected 240 data elements for each package using bar codes. With their DIADs (computer clipboards), UPS drivers electronically scanned the packages. This information was transmitted internally and used for tracking. UPS scanned each package at many stages in the shipment process, so it knew where the package was at all times. Customers could easily get detailed tracking information, as well as the nearest drop-off facility, from the www.ups.com Web site, or wireless devices such as a Palm VII. www.ups.com tracked on a worldwide basis.

In the past, information flowed solely between UPS and its customer. The UPS OnLine® Tools were developed to allow customers to integrate UPS functionality (track a package, get a signature proof of delivery, ship a package, calculate a shipping rate and select a service, calculate time-in-transit, or validate an address) directly into their business processes (integrating tracking into customer service, rating into their order processing system, etc.) They could do this directly on their Web site. For example, UPS gave the ability to clients such as Land's End to track packages on their own Web site, rather than have customers call in for tracking information. The company gave a reference number to its customers for tracking at the time of order.

STRATEGIC ALLIANCES

Additionally, UPS built itself into the commerce platforms that some of its customers used. These were UPS's strategic alliances. Companies like Oracle built UPS transportation into their systems. If a person bought or upgraded to the new Oracle software, UPS was built right in. UPS also struck strategic alliances with companies like eBay where the company put a UPS Service Center right on their site. This was strategic because it helped eBay make it easier for customers to trade on their site, while it also exposed UPS to a whole new customer base.

Information.   Information gives customers access to a great source of power. With information, the consumer starts to drive the supply chain, which causes some displacement of supply chain members. UPS supplied shipping information to companies along their entire supply chains rather than just at the beginning and end. This transparency added a great deal of efficiency to companies. For instance, companies could alter production according to the status of incoming materials.

Security. One of the major concerns of the e-commerce unit at UPS was security. The company had to make sure no one came between UPS and its customer to use the information entrusted to UPS. UPS took its responsibility seriously as custodian of each company's information.

Electronic Signature. The electronic signature that UPS collected when someone signed the electronic clipboard could be very valuable. Many customers had UPS built into their accounts receivable. UPS provided proof of delivery information to the merchant, who in turn could put in a message to overdue accounts.

Nimbleness. An example of nimbleness at UPS was the way the company repurposed its phone centers. UPS always had its own phone center, buildings, technology, facilities, and equipment. Over the years, the company developed competencies in managing phone centers, as it anticipated its package and call volume growing. Then along came the Internet. Instead of getting four million calls a day, UPS handled most requests on the Internet, although it still handled some questions over the phone. Millions of customers each day used UPS's OnLine® Tools to track their own packages. So UPS had to decide, "Do we close down the call center buildings or do we re-purpose?"

UPS decided to sell use of its phone centers to companies like Nike.com. When a customer placed a call to Nike.com, it went to a UPS-managed facility that answered on Nike's behalf, sent goods inbound and outbound, and did most of the final delivery. Companies that used UPS's logistics services were not required to use UPS for shipping. Most did because UPS was the best option, not because it was required.

FOCUS ON USER NEEDS

The Web site, www.ups.com, underwent a complete redesign that was directed by Wharton graduate Rakesh Sapra, the director of Interactive Marketing. The redesign was driven by user needs. Sapra said, "We want unparalleled customer experience onsite." UPS tried to optimize user experience on its global Web sites because they have found this to be an important way to differentiate themselves from competitors. Many of the online services that FedEx and UPS offer were identical, with similar rates. Differentiation boiled down to the experience customers had on the Web and the different channels available to them.

Sapra's team worked to make the site interactive, the branding distinctive, and to give a uniform look and feel to the site around the world. The overall mission of www.ups.com was to enable customers worldwide to do business through the Web site. The company saw the Web as a unique channel to build relationships with customers. Its Web site focused on providing personalized self-service and being relevant to customers' needs.

To update and redesign the site, Sapra's team shadowed customers to see what they did. The group talked to a wide range of people including front-office receptionists, employees in the shipping room, administrative assistants, customer service representatives, and VPs of logistics. The team wanted to discover how www.ups.com could make customers' lives easier. Then they kept redesigning the site until all functions were easy to use. They tested and modified the design until they were satisfied that the Web site met customers' needs.

TAILORING WEB SITES FOR MARKET IN EACH COUNTRY

UPS kept its www.ups.com Web site standard around the globe. In a shipping environment, it made sense to keep the organization of the different country sites very similar. That way, a customer could go to UPS's French or German site, and know where to find which services would be available. The content might vary by country, but the site would have essentially the same look and feel. Some Latin American sites, for example, were offered in the variation of Spanish most relevant to the country. In the latest redesign of www.ups.com, UPS localized country Web sites according to content, language, and cultural sensitivities. These might include sensitivity to color, symbols, or tones that people might find objectionable.

FUTURE CHALLENGES

"We're at the intersection of the physical and virtual world. Internet shoppers can go around the world in 30 seconds or less, but bringing goods back from their virtual world tour is not as easy. That means great opportunity for UPS," said Alan Amling. As UPS continued to build the bridge between the physical and virtual worlds, it faced a number of challenges.

Modernizing customs clearance in many countries would help UPS's business. If customs in a destination country holds a package (called "putting it in jail") for several days, no system can improve efficiency of delivery. Nothing else matters except the customs clearance delays. No process will speed its delivery.

Communication had become an important priority, since in the past people didn't associate UPS with technology. So the new look of the company required a lot of communication externally. UPS established a pressroom Web site to give the media access to press releases, media kits, executive speeches, and other information about the company. Internal communication presented another challenge, with the worldwide reach of UPS and its large number of employees. UPS spent $300 million on training each year to stress the value of innovation, pass on cultural values, and review the policy book. It took time to communicate with over 360,000 employees in 200 countries and territories, and build a good understanding of the company's strategy.

How will UPS continue to embrace change and stay agile? What ways will it find to respond quickly to the changing business environment? How will e-commerce at UPS continue to expand its access, integration, and globalization?

Finally, the way the company addressed the question posed by Alan Amling and his team was critical to its success. "How do you make an elephant dance?" Executives at UPS attribute the company's success to its ability to transform itself over time, the company's strong culture, a united vision, speaking with one voice, and its customer-centered approach. For the time being, UPS is definitely dancing.

ACKNOWLEDGMENTS

This case would not have been possible without the generous support and guidance of Alan Amling, Director of E-Commerce, UPS, and John Flick, Director of International Public Relations, UPS. The author gratefully acknowledges the invaluable assistance of the following UPS employees:

Ron Wallace, President of UPS International

Joe Guerrisi, UPS Capital Corporation

Gary W. Huff, Director E-Commerce, International Marketing, Corporate

Lynette A. McIntyre, Public Relations Director for UPS Logistics Group

Kelly B. Norman, International Marketing Analyst, Corporate

Rakesh Sapra, Director of Interactive Marketing

The author also thanks Robert E. Grosse, Director of Research and Professor of International Management at Thunderbird, The American Graduate School of International Management, for his help with this project.

REFERENCES

Barron, Kelly. "Logistics in Brown. UPS. Company of the Year." *Forbes*. January 10, 2000.

Belasco, James. *Teaching the Elephant to Dance: The Manager's Guide to Empowering Change*, Plume. 1991.

Biederman, David. "The Globetrotting Giant." *Journal of Commerce*. August 21–27, 2000.

Haddad, Charles, & Jack Ewing. "Ground Wars. UPS's Rapid Ascent Leaves FedEx Scrambling," *Business Week*. May 21, 2001, pp. 64–68.

Johnson, Spencer, & Kenneth H. Blanchard. *Who Moved My Cheese?* Putnam Publishing Group. 1998.

Kirby, Julia. "Reinvention with Respect. An Interview with Jim Kelly of UPS." *Harvard Business Review*. November 2001. pp. 116–123.

Levy, Mitchell. Case Study of United Parcel Service, Inc. (UPS). *E-volve-or-Die.com. Thriving in the Internet Age through E-Commerce Management*. Indianapolis, IN: New Riders. 2001, pp. 274–280.

Parker, John G. "UPS's Team Europe." *TrafficWorld*. July 12, 1999.

Somoggi, Luara. "US$1 Billion in Technology." *Dinheiro*. June 21, 2000.

UPS International Update. Winter 2001, pp. 1–4.

Vyas, Rajiv. "UPS Unit Delivering Cash Internationally." *Atlanta Business Chronicle*. 3/17/2000. Vol. 22, issue 42, p. 3A.

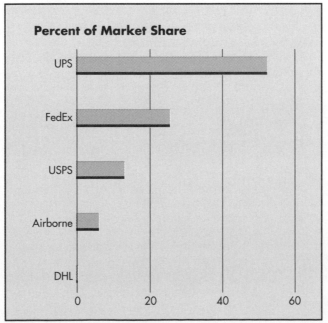

EXHIBIT C13-1   2000 Market Share of Domestic U.S. Parcel and Express Deliveries

SOURCE: SJ Consulting Group.

EXHIBIT C13-2   Transportation Company Fact Sheet 2001

	UPS	FedEx	US Postal Service	Airborne Express	DHL
Founded	Aug. 28, 1907	1971	1775	1946, CA	1969
	Seattle, WA	Little Rock, AR	Philadelphia, PA,		San Francisco, CA
Headquarters	Atlanta, GA	Memphis, TN	Washington, D.C.	Seattle, WA	San Francisco, CA
Chairman and CEO	James P. Kelly	Frederick W. Smith	Postmaster General & CEO John E. Potter	Robert S. Cline	Patrick Lupo
2000 Revenue	$29.8 billion	$18.3 billion	$63 billion	$3.3 billion	$1.5 billion
Daily Delivery Volume	13.6 million packages and documents	5 million packages and documents	668 million pieces of mail	0.9 million packages	Not available
Employees	359,000	215,000	797,795	22,787	68,700
Delivery Fleet (# of vehicles)	152,500	56,000	202,000	15,080	18,576
Jet Aircraft	238	640	Not available	129	254
Chartered	384	—	—	64	—

EXHIBIT C13-3   Transportation Company Fact Sheet 2000

	UPS	FedEx	US Postal Service	Airborne Express	DHL
Non-US Revenue	$ 4.2 billion	$ 4.5 billion	$ 1.7 billion	$0.3 billion	Not available
Daily Overseas Delivery Volume	11 million packages and documents	Not available	3 million pieces of mail	0.01 million packages	Not available
Non-US Employees	38,000	49,000	0	n.a.	
Overseas Delivery Fleet (# of vehicles)	n.a.	n.a.	n.a.	n.a.	
Non-US Jet Aircraft	n.a.		N/A	n.a.	
Non-US Chartered	—	—	—	—	—

CHAPTER 9

Staffing, Training, and Compensation for Global Operations

Outline

Opening Profile: Offshoring IT Jobs—Dell Moves Some Operations Back to the United States

Dell's recent decision to direct some customer service calls to help desks in the United States, rather than to its call center in Bangalore, India, shows how companies with customer support operations overseas are having to tread a fine line with their clients, some of whom are still surprised to talk to technicians on a different continent.

To analysts and consultants, the outsourcing of technology jobs is a trend that will only grow. In Dell's case, some of its most coveted business customers complained to management that Indian technical support workers relied too heavily on scripted answers and were unable to handle more complex computer problems. While most questions phoned in by home computer users tend to be fairly straightforward—like how to update software or install a wireless adaptor—greater expertise is needed to respond to corporate network problems.

A spokesman for Dell, Barry French, said the company was responding to concerns from business customers when it decided last month to route calls from many large business customers to American call centers, though he maintained that it would not be sending fewer calls over all to its operation in India.

"We just flipped a switch," he said, explaining that some consumer calls that had been handled by domestic call centers would now be sent to India.

"What companies are finding is that offshore can be good for generic, commodity services," said Howard Rubin, executive vice president of the Meta Group, a consulting firm. "Corporate customers have problems very local to their applications and very specific to their companies."

Analysts say that along with skill considerations, some companies may be worried about criticism from labor groups and some customers who object to sending jobs overseas. Governments are under particular pressure. This year, half a dozen states are considering that workers hired under state contracts be American citizens or documented workers.

Stephen Lane, research vice president for information technology services at the Aberdeen Group in Boston, said, "There is a backlash and it's building, particularly in sectors like information technology that is still being hard hit by the economy."

Clearly, information technology workers will face more difficulty as technology jobs move to cheaper labor markets abroad. According to a new survey by IDC, a market research company, nearly a quarter of information technology services will be sent offshore by 2007, sharply higher than the 5 percent of technology services being handled offshore this year.

The first wave of offshore outsourcing began with the movement of customer-service call work to offices in India, Malaysia, and Indonesia, but American companies are also beginning to send back-office work, like the processing of forms, abroad as well.

While the outsourcing of technical service jobs is reminiscent of the movement of manufacturing jobs overseas in recent decades, analysts say the difference is that the change in the technology industries is occurring faster. And the jobs that are beginning to leave are considered white-collar jobs that have traditionally been protected from competition with foreign workers.

"Companies are getting more aggressive about it," said Chris Disher, an outsourcing specialist with the consulting firm Booz Allen Hamilton. "The economies are straightforward—you get an $80,000 engineer for $12,000," he said, alluding to wages in India.

The challenge for the United States technology companies, according to industry consultants, is to distinguish between the tasks that can be effectively handled offshore and those that cannot. Some, like Dell, have learned that they need to be sensitive to the reaction of their customers.

"In times like these, your business is attached to customer sentiment," said Atul Vashistha, chief executive of NeoIT, a California company that advises companies on outsourcing to India. "It's primarily a question of market timing."

"There are truly some areas where complexities" make sending work offshore difficult, Mr. Vashistha said. He recounted the experience of one client, a skateboard manufacturer with almost all its customers teenage boys, that found sending its support services overseas disastrous. The cultural nuances, and the constantly changing jargon of skateboarding, made it necessary for support calls to be handled by like-minded young American men. The company, which Mr. Vashistha declined to name, moved its support operations back to the United States last year.

By contrast, Scotiabank, a Canadian company, has kept its customer service operations in Canada, using technology to keep labor costs low. Higher customer satisfaction is worth the slightly higher cost, said John Parkinson, chief technologist for the Americas region at Cap Gemini Ernst & Young, a consulting business that works closely with the bank.

Many offshore call centers are becoming more sensitive to the need to tutor workers in American customs as a crucial part of their training. Some workers in customer service jobs in Bangalore, for example, are being instructed to watch reruns of "Friends" to acquaint themselves with the cultural norms of American consumers, said Mr. Disher, the Booz Allen specialist. Trainees at many firms are also asked to read American newspapers and magazines, and are coached on American consumer habits.

Still, many callers do not seem to care where the help desk is. "Most of the time, they're just happy to be talking to a human," Mr. Parkinson said. "The vast majority of people are indifferent to whether it's an American if they're getting good service."

SOURCE: Copyright 2003 The New York Times Company December 8, 2003 reprinted with permission.

[In the new millennium], the caliber of the people will be the only source of competitive advantage.
—Allan Halcrow, Personnel Journal[1]

Of the top 100 UK firms surveyed by Cendant International Assignment Services, 63 reported failed foreign assignments.
www.FT.com[2]

This chapter's opening profile describes a contemporary problem of where to source employees as service jobs have now joined manufacturing jobs in the category of "boundaryless" human capital. This is a complex issue for human resources (HR) managers as they seek to support strategic mandates (see Chapter 6). This contemporary competitive issue is just one of the many challenges to the human resource management function of any organization, domestic or international. However, given the greater complexity of managing international operations, the need to ensure high-quality management is even more critical than in domestic operations.

A vital component of implementing global strategy is *international human resource management* (IHRM). IHRM is increasingly being recognized as a major determinant of success or failure in international business. In a highly competitive global economy, where the other factors of production—capital, technology, raw materials, and information—are increasingly able to be duplicated, "the caliber of the people in an organization will be the only source of sustainable competitive advantage available to U.S. companies.[3] Corporations operating overseas need to pay careful attention to this most critical resource—one that also provides control over other resources. Most U.S. multinationals underestimate the importance of the human resource planning function in the selection, training, acculturation, and evaluation of managers assigned abroad. Yet the increasing significance of this resource is evidenced by the numbers. More than 37,000 multinational corporations (MNCs) are currently in business worldwide. They have control more than 200,000 foreign affiliates and have more than 73 million employees. In the United States, foreign MNCs employ three million Americans—more than 10 percent of the U.S. manufacturing workforce.[4] In addition, about 80 percent of mid- and large-sized U.S. companies send managers abroad, and most plan to increase that number.[5] The National Foreign Trade Council (NFTC) estimates that 300,000 U.S. expatriates are on assignment at any given time. Of those companies responding to Arthur Andersen's Global Best in Class Study,

Those companies generate 43 percent of their revenues outside their headquarters country; consequently, they need expatriates who can support their expansion through both technical expertise and cultural understanding.[6]

However, recent advances in technology are enabling firms to effectively and efficiently manage the IHRM function and maximize the firm's international management cadre, as illustrated in E-Biz Box: HRMS Goes Global at British Airways.

E-BIZ BOX

HRMS Goes Global at British Airways

Companies operating in several countries need to globalize the human resource management systems (HRMS). Compelling reasons for doing so include the need to get an accurate count of the international workforce, to monitor expatriates, to track and analyze employee benefits, to evaluate compensation models, and to streamline payroll. MNCs also need to access data on knowledge and abilities, make up-to-date information easily accessible to line managers, and study career planning and succession planning models. Creating a global HRMS, however, is not an easy task. The different laws, cultures, business practices, and technological limitations of various countries have to be taken into consideration.

Michael P. Corey, head of HR Systems for British Airways, knows how challenging it is to coordinate HR management systems when your company has a presence in eighty-three countries. Without efficient hardware, software, and HR strategies to back it all up, the corporate data highway can easily resemble a one-lane, unpaved roadway in a developing nation: chaotic, crowded, and swarming with obstacles. But Corey is adamant about implementing a system that provides HR with the tools to truly excel. "In an era of intense competition and pressure, at a time when HR must provide value, it's essential to automate and streamline as much as possible," he explains. With more than 50,000 employees working worldwide, and many of them in a different location every day of the week, it's no simple task.

When HR needs to notify employees of a change in benefits or policy, for example, many of the workers are 40,000 feet above the earth. When it needs to track head count or update employee records, it has to deal with twenty-four time zones and dozens of languages and cultures. In addition, systems and technologies that work in one place can come to a grinding halt elsewhere. Yet British Airways's automated system handles recruiting, benefits, head count, basic recordkeeping, and an array of other functions—cutting across technology platforms and breaking language barriers. Moreover, the system, dubbed ACHORD (Airline Corporate Human and Organisation Resources Database), links to thirty-five other systems that require staff data within British Airways. Plans are now under way to link to forty additional business systems.

When a manager in Kuala Lumpur needs information on terminations or company share schemes, it is accessible within seconds. When an HR specialist in New York requires data on pensions or concessional travel arrangements, it's visible in a flash. With a network of IBM mainframe computers linked to PCs and dumb terminals, data flows seamlessly between offices and across national boundaries. What's more, the worldwide network has almost eliminated duplicate data input, paperwork, disks, and delays in processing work. "It fits into the concept of reengineering and making HR accountable and involved in corporate matters," says Corey. "It provides us with a powerful tool."

SOURCE: Adapted from: S. Greengard, "When HRMS Goes Global: Managing the Data Highway," *Personnel Journal* 7, no. 6 (June 1995): 90–91.

At the first level of planning, decisions are required on the staffing policy suitable for a particular kind of business, its global strategy, and its geographic locations. Key issues involve the difficulty of control in geographically dispersed operations, the need for local decision making independent of the home office, and the suitability of managers from alternate sources.

The interdependence of strategy, structure, and staffing is particularly worth noting. Ideally, the desired strategy of the firm should dictate the organizational structure and staffing modes considered most effective for implementing that strategy. In reality, however, there is usually considerable interdependence among those functions. Existing structural constraints often affect strategic decisions; similarly, staffing constraints or unique sets of competences in management come into play in organizational and sometimes strategic decisions. It is thus important to achieve a system of fits among those variables that facilitates strategic implementation.

STAFFING FOR GLOBAL OPERATIONS

> *We found the most successful formula is to hire people in-country and then bring them to our U.S. headquarters to get acquainted and have them interact with our organization.*
>
> STUART MATHISON,
> *Vice President for Strategic Planning, Sprint International[7]*

Alternate philosophies of managerial staffing abroad are known as the ethnocentric, polycentric, regiocentric, and global approaches. Firms using an **ethnocentric staffing approach** fill key managerial positions with people from headquarters—that is, **parent-country nationals (PCNs)**. Among the advantages of this approach, PCNs are familiar with company goals, products, technology, policies, and procedures—and they know how to get things accomplished through headquarters. This policy is likely to be used where a company notes the inadequacy of local managerial skills and determines a high need to maintain close communication and coordination with headquarters. It is also the preferred choice when the organization has been structured around a centralized approach to globalization and is primarily at the internationalization stage of strategic expansion.

Frequently, companies use PCNs for the top management positions in the foreign subsidiary—in particular, the chief executive officer (CEO) and the chief financial officer (CFO)—to maintain close control. PCNs are usually preferable when a high level of technical capability is required. They are also chosen for new international ventures requiring managerial experience in the parent company and where there is a concern for loyalty to the company rather than to the host country—in cases, for example, where proprietary technology is used extensively.

Disadvantages of the ethnocentric approach include (1) the lack of opportunities or development for local managers, thereby decreasing their morale and their loyalty to the subsidiary and (2) the poor adaptation and lack of effectiveness of expatriates in foreign countries. Procter & Gamble, for example, routinely appointed managers from its headquarters for foreign assignments for many years. After several unfortunate experiences in Japan, the firm realized that such a practice was insensitive to local cultures and also underutilized its pool of high-potential non-American managers.[8] Furthermore, an ethnocentric recruiting approach does not enable the company to take advantage of its worldwide pool of management skill. This approach also serves to perpetuate particular personnel selections and other decision-making processes because the same types of people are making the same types of decisions.

With a **polycentric staffing approach**, local managers—**host-country nationals (HCNs)**—are hired to fill key positions in their own country. This approach is more likely to be effective when implementing a multinational strategy. If a company wants to "act local," staffing with HCNs has obvious advantages. These managers are naturally familiar with the local culture, language, and ways of doing business, and they already have many contacts in place. In addition, HCNs are more likely to be accepted by people both inside and outside the subsidiary, and they provide role models for other upwardly mobile personnel.

With regard to cost, it is usually less expensive for a company to hire a local manager than to transfer one from headquarters, frequently with a family and often at a higher rate of pay. Transferring from headquarters is a particularly expensive policy when it turns out that the manager and her or his family do not adjust and have to be prematurely transferred home. Rather than building their own facilities, some companies acquire foreign firms as a means of obtaining qualified local personnel. Local managers also tend to be instrumental in staving off or more effectively dealing with problems in sensitive political situations. Some countries, in fact, have legal requirements that a specific proportion of the firm's top managers must be citizens of that country.

One disadvantage of a polycentric staffing policy is the difficulty of coordinating activities and goals between the subsidiary and the parent company, including the potentially conflicting loyalties of the local manager. Poor coordination among subsidiaries of a multinational firm could constrain strategic options. An additional drawback of this policy is that the headquarters managers of multinational firms will not gain the overseas experience necessary for any higher positions in the firm that require the understanding and coordination of subsidiary operations.

In the **global staffing approach**, the best managers are recruited from within or outside of the company, regardless of nationality. This practice—recruiting **third country nationals (TCNs)**—has been used for some time by many European multinationals. Recently, as more major U.S. companies adopt a global strategic approach, they are also considering foreign executives for their top positions. General Motors hired J. Ignacio Lopez de Arriortua as vice president for worldwide purchasing, Xerox hired Vittorio Cassoni as executive vice president, and Esprit de Corp hired Fritz Ammann as president.[9] A global staffing approach has several important advantages. First, this policy provides a greater pool of qualified and willing applicants from which to choose, which, in time, results in further development of a global executive cadre. As discussed further in Chapter 10, the skills and experiences that those managers use and transfer throughout the company result in a pool of shared learning that is necessary for the company to compete globally. Second, where third country nationals are used to manage subsidiaries, they usually bring more cultural flexibility and adaptability to a situation, as well as bilingual or multilingual skills, than parent-country nationals, especially if they are from a similar cultural background as the host-country coworkers and are accustomed to moving around. In addition, when TCNs are placed in key positions, they are perceived by employees as acceptable compromises between headquarters and local managers and thus appointing them works to reduce resentment. Third, it can be more cost-effective to transfer and pay managers from some countries than from others because their pay scale and benefits packages are lower. Indeed, those firms with a truly global staffing orientation are phasing out the entire ethnocentric concept of a home or host country. As part of that focus, the term **transpatriate** is increasingly replacing the term *expatriate*.[10] Firms such as Philips, Heinz, Unilever, IBM, and ABB have a global staffing approach, which makes them highly visible and seems to indicate a trend.[11]

Generally, it seems that "the more distant geographically and culturally the subsidiary, the more expatriates are used in key positions, especially in less developed countries."[12] Clearly, this situation arises out of concern about uncertainty and the ability to control implementation of the corporation's goals. However, given the generally accepted consensus that staffing, along with structure and systems must "fit" the desired strategy, firms desiring a truly global posture should adopt a global staffing approach.[13] That is easier said than done. As shown in Exhibit 9-1, such an approach requires the firm to overcome barriers such as the availability and willingness of high-quality managers to transfer frequently around the world, dual career constraints, time and cost constraints, conflicting requirements of host governments, and ineffective human resource management policies.

In a **regiocentric staffing approach**, recruiting is done on a regional basis—say within Latin America for a position in Chile. This staffing approach can produce a specific mix of PCNs, HCNs, and TCNs, according to the needs of the company or the product strategy.[14]

What factors influence the choice of staffing policy? Among them are the strategy and organizational structure of the firm, as well as the factors related to the particular subsidiary (such as the duration of the particular foreign operation, the types of technology used, and the production and marketing techniques necessary). Factors related to the host country also play a part (such as the level of economic and technological development, political stability, regulations regarding ownership and staffing, and the sociocultural setting).[15] As a practical matter, however, the choice often depends on the availability of qualified managers in the host country. Most MNCs use a greater proportion of PCNs (also called **expatriates**) in top management positions, staffing middle and lower management positions with increasing proportions of HCNs ("inpatriates") as one moves down the organizational hierarchy. The choice of staffing policy has a considerable influence on organizational variables in the subsidiary, such as the locus of decision-making

EXHIBIT 9-1   Maintaining a Globalization Momentum

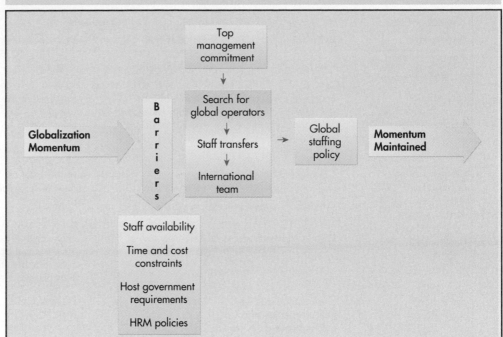

SOURCE: Adapted from D. Welch, "HRM Implications of Globalization," *Journal of General Management* 19, no. 4 (Summer 1994): 52–69.

authority, the methods of communication, and the perpetuation of human resource management practices. These variables are illustrated in Exhibit 9-2. The conclusions drawn by the researchers some time ago are still valid today. The ethnocentric staffing approach, for example, usually results in a higher level of authority and decision making in headquarters compared to the polycentric approach.[16]

A study by Rochelle Kopp found that ethnocentric staffing and policies are associated with a higher incidence of international human resource management problems.[17] In addition, Kopp found that Japanese firms scored considerably lower than European and American firms in their practice of implementing policies such as preparing local nationals for advancement and keeping inventory of their managers around the world for development purposes. As a result of these ethnocentric practices, Japanese firms seem to experience various IHRM problems, such as high turnover of local employees, more than European and American firms.

Without exception, all phases of human resources management should support the desired strategy of the firm.[18] In the staffing phase, having the right people in the right places at the right times is a key ingredient to success in international operations. An effective managerial cadre can be a distinct competitive advantage for a firm. How the "right" selections are made is the focus of the next section.

GLOBAL SELECTION

The initial phase of setting up criteria for global selection, then, is to consider which overall staffing approach or approaches would most likely support the company's strategy, as previously discussed—such as HCNs for localization, the (multilocal) strategic approach, and transpatriates for globalization. These are typically just starting points using idealized criteria, however. In reality, other factors creep into the process, such as host-country regulations, stage of internationalization, and—most often—who is both suitable and available for the position. It is also vital to integrate long-term strategic goals into the selection and development process, especially when rapid global expansion is intended. Insufficient

EXHIBIT 9-2 Relationships among Strategic Mode, Organizational Variables, and Staffing Orientation

Aspects of the Enterprise	Orientation			
	Ethnocentric	**Polycentric**	**Regiocentric**	**Global**
Primary Strategic Orientation/Stage	International	Multidomestic	Regional	Transnational
Perpetuation (recruiting, staffing, development)	People of home country developed for key positions everywhere in the world	People of local nationality developed for key positions in their own country	Regional people developed for key positions anywhere in the region	Best people everywhere in the world developed for key positions everywhere in the world
Complexity of organization	Complex in home country; simple in subsidiaries	Varied and independent	Highly interdependent on a regional basis	"Global Web": complex, independent, worldwide alliances/network
Authority; decision making	High in headquarters	Relatively low in headquarters	High regional headquarters and/or high collaboration among subsidiaries	Collaboration of headquarters and subsidiaries around the world
Evaluation and control	Home standards applied to people and performance	Determined locally	Determined regionally	Globally integrated
Rewards	High in headquarters; low in subsidiaries	Wide variation; can be high or low rewards for subsidiary performance	Rewards for contribution to regional objectives	Rewards to international and local executives for reaching local and worldwide objectives based on global company goals
Communication; information flow	High volume of orders, commands, advice to subsidiaries	Little to and from headquarters; little among subsidiaries	Little to and from corporate headquarters, but may be high to and from regional headquarters and among countries	Horizontal; network relations
Geographic identification	Nationality of owner	Nationality of host country	Regional company	Truly global company, but identifying with national interests ("glocal")

SOURCE: Updated and adapted by H. Deresky in 2002, from original work by D.A. Heenan and H. V. Perlmutter. *Multinational Organization Development* (Reading, MA: Addison-Wesley, 1979), 18–19.

projection of staffing needs for global assignments will likely result in constrained strategic opportunities because of a shortage of experienced managers suitable to place in those positions.

The selection of personnel for overseas assignments is a complex process. The criteria for selection are based on the same success factors as in the domestic setting, but additional criteria must be considered, related to the specific circumstances of each international position. Unfortunately, many personnel directors have a long-standing, ingrained practice of selecting potential expatriates simply on the basis of their domestic track records and their technical expertise.[19] The need to ascertain whether potential expatriates have the necessary cross-cultural awareness and interpersonal skills for the position is too often overlooked. It is also important to assess whether the candidate's personal and family situation is such that everyone is likely to adapt to the local culture. There are five categories of success for expatriate managers: job factors, relational dimensions such as cultural empathy and flexibility, motivational state, family situation, and language skills. The relative importance of each factor is highly situational and difficult to establish.[20]

These *expatriate success factors* are based on studies of American expatriates. One could argue that the requisite skills are the same for managers from any country—and particularly so for third country nationals.

A more flexible approach to maximizing managerial talent, regardless of the source, would certainly consider more closely whether the position could be suitably filled by a host-country national, as put forth by Tung, based on her research.[21] This contingency model of selection and training depends on the variables of the particular assignment, such as length of stay, similarity to the candidate's own culture, and level of interaction with local managers in that job. Tung concludes that the more rigorous the selection and training process, the lower the failure rate.

The selection process is set up as a decision tree in which the progression to the next stage of selection or the type of orientation training depends on the assessment of critical factors regarding the job or the candidate at each decision point. The simplest selection process involves choosing a local national because minimal training is necessary regarding the culture or ways of doing business locally. However, to be successful, local managers often require additional training in the MNC companywide processes, technology, and corporate culture. If the position cannot be filled by a local national, yet the job requires a high level of interaction with the local community, very careful screening of candidates from other countries and a vigorous training program are necessary.

Most MNCs tend to start their operations in a particular region by selecting primarily from their own pool of managers. Over time, and with increasing internationalization, they tend to move to a predominantly polycentric or regiocentric policy because of (1) increasing pressure (explicit or implicit) from local governments to hire locals (or sometimes legal restraints on the use of expatriates) and (2) the greater costs of expatriate staffing, particularly when the company has to pay taxes for the parent-company employee in both countries.[22] In addition, in recent years, MNCs have noted an improvement in the level of managerial and technical competence in many countries, negating the chief reason for using a primarily ethnocentric policy in the past. One researcher's comment represents a growing attitude: "All things being equal, a local national who speaks the language, understands the culture and the political system, and is often a member of the local elite should be more effective than an expatriate alien."[23] However, concerns about the need to maintain strategic control over subsidiaries and to develop managers with a global perspective remain a source of debate about staffing policies among human resource management professionals.[24] A globally oriented company such as ABB (Asea Brown Boveri), for example, has 500 roving transpatriates who are moved every two to three years, thus developing a considerable management cadre with global experience.[25]

For MNCs based in Europe and Asia, human resource policies at all levels of the organization are greatly influenced by the home-country culture and policies. For Japanese subsidiaries in Singapore, Malaysia, and India, for example, promotion from within and expectations of long-term loyalty to and by the firm are culture-based practices transferable to subsidiaries. At Matsushita, however, selection criteria for staffing seem to be similar to those of Western companies. Its candidates are selected on the basis of a set of characteristics the firm calls SMILE: specialty (required skill, knowledge); management ability (particularly motivational ability); international flexibility (adaptability); language facility; and endeavor (perseverance in the face of difficulty).[26]

Problems with Expatriation

> *While 89 percent of companies formally assess a candidate's job skills prior to a foreign posting, less than half go through the same process for cultural suitability. Even fewer gauge whether the family will cope.*
>
> www.FT.com[27]

Deciding on a staffing policy and selecting suitable managers are logical first steps but do not alone ensure success. When staffing overseas assignments with expatriates, for example, many other reasons, besides poor selection, contribute to *expatriate failure* among U.S. multinationals. A large percentage of these failures can be attributed to poor preparation and planning for the entry and reentry transitions of the manager and his or her family. One important variable, for example, often given insufficient attention in the selection, preparation, and support phases, is the suitability and adjustment of the spouse. The inability of the spouse to adjust to the new environment has been found to be a major—in fact, the most frequently cited—reason for expatriate failure in United States and European companies.[28] Yet only about half of those companies studied had included the spouse in the interviewing process. In addition, although research shows that human relational skills are critical for overseas work (a fact acknowledged by the companies in a study by Tung), most of the U.S. firms surveyed failed to include this factor in their assessment of candidates.[29] The following is a synthesis of the factors frequently mentioned by researchers and firms as the major causes of expatriate failure:

- Selection based on headquarters criteria rather than assignment needs
- Inadequate preparation, training, and orientation prior to assignment
- Alienation or lack of support from headquarters
- Inability to adapt to local culture and working environment
- Problems with spouse and children—poor adaptation, family unhappiness
- Insufficient compensation and financial support
- Poor programs for career support and repatriation

After careful selection based on the specific assignment and the long-term plans of both the organization and the candidates, plans must be made for the preparation, training, and development of expatriate managers.

TRAINING AND DEVELOPMENT

It is clear that preparation and training for cross-cultural interactions are critical. In earlier discussions of the need for cultural sensitivity by expatriate managers, reports indicate that up to 40 percent of expatriate managers end their foreign assignments early because of poor performance or an inability to adjust to the local environment.[30] Moreover, about half of those who do remain function at a low level of effectiveness. The direct cost alone of a failed expatriate assignment is estimated to be from $50,000 to $150,000. The indirect costs may be far greater, depending on the expatriate's position. Relations with the host-country government and customers may be damaged, resulting in a loss of market share and a poor reception for future PCNs.

Both cross-cultural adjustment problems and practical differences in everyday living present challenges for expatriates and their families. Examples are evident from a survey of expatriates when they ranked the countries that presented the most challenging assignments to them, along with some pet peeves from their experiences:

China: a continuing problem for expatriates; one complained that at his welcome banquet he was served duck tongue and pigeon head.

Brazil: Expatriates stress that cell phones are essential because home phones don't work.

India: Returning executives complain that the pervasiveness of poverty and street children is overwhelming.

Indonesia: Here you need to plan ahead financially because landlords typically demand rent two to three years in advance.

Japan: Expatriates and their families remain concerned that, although there is excellent medical care, the Japanese doctors reveal little to their patients.

After these five countries, expatriates also rank Russia, Mexico, Saudi Arabia, South Korea, and France as challenging.[31]

Even though cross-cultural training has proved to be effective, less than a third of expatriates are given such training. In a study by Harvey of 332 U.S. expatriates (dual-career couples), the respondents stated that their MNCs had not provided them with sufficient training or social support during the international assignment.[32] Much of the rationale for this lack of training is an assumption that managerial skills and processes are universal. In a simplistic way, a manager's domestic track record is used as the major selection criterion for an overseas assignment.

In most countries, however, the success of the expatriate is not left so much to chance. Foreign companies provide considerably more training and preparation for expatriates than U.S. companies. Therefore, it is not hard to understand why Japanese expatriates experience significantly fewer incidences of failure than their U.S. counterparts, although this may be partially because fewer families accompany Japanese assignees. Japanese multinationals typically have recall rates of below 5 percent, signifying that they send abroad managers who are far better prepared and more adept at working and flourishing in a foreign environment.[33] While this success is largely attributable to training programs, it is also a result of intelligent planning by the human resource management staff in most Japanese organizations, as reported by Tung.[34] This planning begins with a careful selection process for overseas assignments, based on the long-term knowledge of executives and their families. An effective selection process, of course, will eliminate many potential "failures" from the start. Another factor is the longer duration of overseas assignments, averaging almost five years, which allows the Japanese expatriate more time to adjust initially and then to function at full capacity. In addition, Japanese expatriates receive considerable support from headquarters and sometimes even from local divisions set up for that purpose. At NEC Corporation, for example, part of the Japanese giant's globalization strategy is its permanent boot camp, with its elaborate training exercises to prepare NEC managers and their families for overseas battle.[35]

The demands on expatriate managers have always been as much a result of the multiple relationships that they have to maintain as they are of the differences in the host-country environment. Those relations include family relations, internal relations with people in the corporation, both locally and globally, especially with headquarters, external relations (suppliers, distributors, allies, customers, local community, etc.), and relations with the host government. It is important to pinpoint any potential problems that an expatriate may experience with those relationships so that these problems may be addressed during predeparture training. Problem recognition is the first stage in a comprehensive plan for developing expatriates (see Exhibit 9-3). The three areas critical to preparation are cultural training, language instruction, and familiarity with everyday matters.[36] In the model shown in Exhibit 9-3, various development methods are used to address these areas during predeparture training, postarrival training, and reentry training. These methods continue to be valid and used by many organizations. Two-way feedback between the executive and the trainers at each stage helps to tailor the level and kinds of training to the individual manager. The desired goal is the increased effectiveness of the expatriate as a result of familiarity with local conditions, cultural awareness, and an appreciation of his or her family's needs in the host country.

Cross-cultural Training

Training in language and practical affairs is quite straightforward, but cross-cultural training is not; it is complex and deals with deep-rooted behaviors. The actual process of cross-cultural training should result in the expatriate learning both content and skills that will improve interactions with host-country individuals by reducing misunderstandings and inappropriate behaviors. Black and Mendenhall suggest that trainers should apply social learning theory to this process by using the behavioral science techniques of incentives and rehearsal until the trainee internalizes the desired behaviors and reproduces them.[37] The result is a state of adjustment, representing the ability to effectively interact with host nationals.

Culture Shock

The goal of this training is to ease the adjustment to the new environment by reducing **culture shock**—a state of disorientation and anxiety about not knowing how to behave in an unfamiliar culture. The cause of culture shock is the trauma people experience in new and different cultures, where they lose the familiar signs and cues that they had used to interact in daily life and where they must learn to cope with a vast array of new cultural cues and expectations.[38] The symptoms of culture shock range from mild irritation to deep-seated psychological panic or crisis. The inability to work effectively, stress within the family, and hostility toward host nationals are the common dysfunctional results of culture shock—often leading to the manager giving up and going home.

It is helpful to recognize the stages of culture shock to understand what is happening. Culture shock usually progresses through four stages, as described by Oberg: (1) *honeymoon,* when positive attitudes and expectations, excitement, and a tourist feeling prevail (which may last up to several weeks); (2) *irritation and hostility,* the crisis stage when cultural

EXHIBIT 9-3 IHRM Process to Maximize Effectiveness of Expatriate Assignments

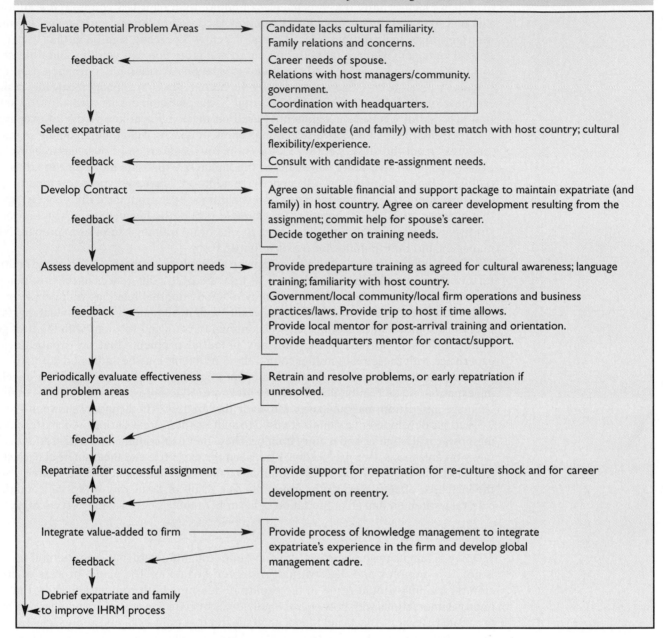

differences result in problems at work, at home, and in daily living—expatriates and family members feel homesick and disoriented, lashing out at everyone (many never get past this stage); (3) *gradual adjustment,* a period of recovery in which the "patient" gradually becomes able to understand and predict patterns of behavior, use the language, and deal with daily activities, and the family starts to accept their new life; and (4) *biculturalism,* the stage in which the manager and family members grow to accept and appreciate local people and practices and are able to function effectively in two cultures.[39] Many never get to the fourth stage—operating acceptably at the third stage—but those who do report that their assignment is positive and growth oriented.

Subculture Shock

Similar to culture shock, though usually less extreme, is the experience of **subculture shock**. This occurs when a manager is transferred to another part of the country where there are cultural differences—essentially from what she or he perceives to be a "majority" culture to a "minority" one. The shock comes from feeling like an "immigrant" in one's own country and being unprepared for such differences. For instance, someone going from New York to Texas will experience considerable differences in attitudes and lifestyle between those two states. These differences exist even within Texas, with cultures that range from roaming ranches and high technology to Bible-belt attitudes and laws and to areas with a mostly Mexican heritage.[40]

Training Techniques

Many training techniques are available to assist overseas assignees in the adjustment process. These techniques are classified by Tung as (1) *area studies,* that is, documentary programs about the country's geography, economics, sociopolitical history, and so forth; (2) *culture assimilators,* which expose trainees to the kinds of situations they are likely to encounter that are critical to successful interactions; (3) *language training;* (4) *sensitivity training;* and (5) *field experiences*—exposure to people from other cultures within the trainee's own country.[41] Tung recommends using these training methods in a complementary fashion, giving the trainee increasing levels of personal involvement as she or he progresses through each method. Documentary and interpersonal approaches have been found to be comparable, with the most effective intercultural training occurring when trainees become aware of the differences between their own cultures and the ones they are planning to enter.[42]

Similarly categorizing training methods, Ronen suggests specific techniques, such as workshops and sensitivity training, including a field experience called the *host-family surrogate,* where the MNC pays for and places an expatriate family with a host family as part of an immersion and familiarization program.[43]

Most training programs take place in the expatriate's own country prior to leaving. Although this is certainly a convenience, the impact of host-country (or in-country) programs can be far greater than those conducted at home because crucial skills, such as overcoming cultural differences in intercultural relationships, can actually be experienced during in-country training rather than simply discussed.[44] Some MNCs are beginning to recognize that there is no substitute for on-the-job training (OJT) in the early stages of the careers of those managers they hope to develop into senior-level global managers. Colgate-Palmolive—whose overseas sales represent two-thirds of its $6 billion in yearly revenue—is one company whose management development programs adhere to this philosophy. After training at headquarters, Colgate employees become associate product managers in the United States or abroad—and, according to John R. Garrison, manager of recruitment and development at Colgate, they must earn their stripes by being prepared to country-hop every few years. In fact, says Garrison, "That's the definition of a global manager: one who has seen several environments firsthand."[45] Exhibit 9-4 shows some other global management development programs for junior employees.

EXHIBIT 9-4   Corporate Programs to Develop Global Managers

- ABB (Asea Brown Boveri) rotates about 500 managers around the world to different countries every two to three years in order to develop a management cadre of transpatriates to support their global strategy.
- PepsiCo has an orientation program for its foreign managers, which brings them to the United States for one-year assignments in bottling division plants.
- British Telecom uses informal mentoring techniques to induct employees into the ways of their assigned country; existing expatriate workers talk to prospective assignees about the cultural factors to expect (www.FT.com).
- Honda of America Manufacturing gives its U.S. supervisors and managers extensive preparation in Japanese language, culture, and lifestyle and then sends them to Tokyo for up to three years to the parent company.*
- General Electric likes its engineers and managers to have a global perspective whether or not they are slated to go abroad. The company gives regular language and cross-cultural training for them so that they are equipped to conduct business with people around the world (www.GE.com).

The importance of developing a global orientation in one's career development is illustrated by the advice offered to potential applicants to Citibank given on their Web site, as described in Management Focus: Citibank Gives Advice on Career Planning. Citibank is now part of Citigroup—a global financial and insurance institution—since the merger of Citicorp and Travelers Insurance in 1998.

Management Focus

Citibank Gives Advice on Career Planning

BE MOBILE: TO GET SOMEWHERE, YOU HAVE TO GO PLACES!

As Citibank continues to expand globally, there is a growing need for a cadre of professionals with the global perspective to lead the organization. Two-thirds of Citibank's current management team have already had international experience. While living and working in other countries are probably the most direct ways to gain a global perspective, there are alternate routes to accomplish this objective. These are well worth exploring if your road to career growth lies over Citibank's global horizons.

A GLOBAL MOVE IS A GOOD CAREER MOVE

Expatriate assignments offer an extraordinary opportunity for experience, learning, and personal and career enrichment. Our goal is to have each expatriate assignment fulfill a business need and to provide each person who accepts an expatriate assignment with professional as well as personal growth opportunities.

SOME CAREER ADVANTAGES OFFERED BY AN EXPATRIATE ASSIGNMENT

- Develop a global business outlook and an understanding of how to leverage the bank's global position.

- Gain the broader perspective through working in different cultures, geographies, businesses, and functions.
- Interact with a wide range of customers and work with globally focused managers and colleagues, so you can stretch beyond your current environment and add breadth and depth to your work experience.
- Apply your solutions to truly unique problems within different cultures and environments.
- Take on new challenges that stretch and develop your skills by requiring you to take educated risks.

OTHER WAYS TO GAIN A GLOBAL PERSPECTIVE

While advantageous for some, international assignments aren't right for everyone. Only you and those close to you can decide if you want to live and work in a different country, and if so, at which point in time. If success on your career path requires international experience and you are unable to take on an international assignment at this time for any reason, there are other ways to gain global exposure. These might include short-term assignments in other locations, jobs that involve cross-border interaction, or a task force made up of a global team.

SOURCE: www.Citibank.com.

Integrating Training with Global Orientation

In continuing our discussion of "strategic fit," it is important to remember that training programs, like staffing approaches, be designed with the company's strategy in mind. Although it is probably impractical to breakdown those programs into a lot of variations, it is feasible to at least consider the relative level or stage of globalization that the firm has reached because obvious major differences would be appropriate, for example, from the initial export stage to the full global stage. Exhibit 9-5 suggests levels of rigor and types of training content appropriate for the firm's managers, as well as those for host-country nationals, for four globalization stages—export, multidomestic, multinational, and global. It is noteworthy, for example, that the training of host-country nationals for a global firm has a considerably higher level of scope and rigor than that for the other stages and borders on the standards for the firm's expatriates.

As a further area for managerial preparation for global orientation–in addition to training plans for expatriates and for HCNs separately–there is a particular need to anticipate potential problems with the interaction of expatriates and local staff. In a 2003 study

EXHIBIT 9-5   Stage of Globalization and Training Design Issues

Export Stage	MNC Stage
Degree of Rigor: Low to moderate	*Degree of Rigor:* High moderate to high
Content: Emphasis should be on interpersonal skills, local culture, customer values, and business behavior.	*Content:* Emphasis should be on interpersonal skills, two-way technology, transfer, corporate value transfer, international strategy, stress management, local culture, and business practices.
Host-Country Nationals: Low to moderate training of host nationals to understand parent country products and policies.	*Host-Country Nationals:* Moderate to high training of host nationals in technical areas, product and service systems, and corporate culture.
MDC Stage	**Global Stage**
Degree of Rigor: Moderate to high	*Degree of Rigor:* High
Content: Emphasis should be on interpersonal skills, local culture, technology transfer, stress management, and business practices and laws.	*Content:* Emphasis should be on global corporate operations and systems, corporate culture transfer, customers, global competitors, and international strategy.
Host-Country Nationals: Low to moderate training of host nationals; primarily focusing on production and service procedures.	*Host-Country Nationals:* High training of host nationals in global organization production and efficiency systems, corporate culture, business systems, and global conduct policies.

SOURCE: J. S. Black, Mark. E. Mendenhall, Hal B. Gregersen, and Linda K. Stroh, *Globalizing People Through International Assignments* (Reading, MA: Addison Wesley Longman, 1999).

of expatriates and local staff (inpatriates) in Central and Eastern European joint ventures and subsidiaries, Peterson found that managers reported a number of behaviors by expatriates that helped them to integrate with local staff, but also some which were hindrances (see Exhibit 9-6). Clearly, this kind of feedback from MNC managers in the field can provide the basis for expatriate training and also help HCNs to anticipate and work with the expatriates in order to meet joint strategic objectives.

Training Host-Country Nationals

We found that the key human resource role of the MNC [in Central and Eastern Europe] was to expose the local staff to a market economy; to instill world standards of performance; and provide training and functional expertise.

RICHARD PETERSON,
"The Use of Expatriates and Inpatriates in Central and Eastern Europe Since the Wall Came Down," Journal of World Business, 2003[46]

The continuous training and development of HCNs and TCNs for management positions is also important to the long-term success of multinational corporations. As part of a long-term staffing policy for a subsidiary, the ongoing development of HCNs will facilitate the transition to an indigenization policy. Furthermore, multinational companies like to have well-trained managers with broad international experience available to take charge in many intercultural settings, whether at home or abroad. Such managerial skills are increasingly needed in U.S.–Japanese joint ventures—a good example being G.M.–Toyota in Fremont, California. There, managers as well as employees from both the United States and Japan learn to work side by side and adjust to a unique blend of country and corporate culture. For the Americans in this organization, helping to acculturate the Japanese employees not only demonstrates friendly goodwill but also is a necessary part of securing their own future in the company.

Many multinationals, in particular "chains," wish to train their local managers and workers to bridge the divide between the firm's successful corporate culture and practices, on the one hand, with the local culture and work practices on the other. One example of how to do this in China is the Starbucks firm, featured in Management Focus: Success! Starbucks' Java Style Helps to Recruit, Train, and Retain Local Managers in Beijing.

EXHIBIT 9-6 Factors That Help or Hinder the Integration of Expatriate Staff with Local Staff

Factors helping	Factors hindering
Forming close working relationships	Not using team concept
Learning local language	Not learning local language
Transferring technical/business knowledge	Arrogance
Ability to integrate into local life	Spouse and family problems in adjusting
Professionalism in behavior	Being autocratic
Cultural sensitivity	Low level of delegating by expatriate
Willingness to learn	Expatriate not being talented
Providing model of competitiveness	Lack of cultural sensitivity
Adaptability	Reluctance to change and adapt
Team building skills	We–they mentality
Introducing effective management control system	Too short expatriate assignment to nation
Focus on service dimension	"Home country" mentality
Teaching locals about market economy	Poor cross-cultural mentality
Marketing know-how	Lack of curiosity
Friendliness/openness	Acting like back home
Deep financial knowledge	Different way of thinking than local staff
Self-confidence	
Strong work ethic	
Previous assignments in the region	
Treating local staff with respect	
Listening skills	
Acceptance of local culture	

SOURCE: Reprinted from *Journal of World Business*, 38, R. B. Peterson, "The Use of Expatriates and Inpatriates in Central and Eastern Europe Since the Wall Came Down," 55–69, 2003, with permission from Elsevier.

Management Focus

Success! Starbucks' Java Style Helps to Recruit, Train, and Retain Local Managers in Beijing

When we first started, people didn't know who we were and it was rough finding sites. Now landlords are coming to us.
David Sun, President of Beijing Mei Da Coffee Company (Franchisee for Northern China) (The Economist, October 6, 2001)
Starbucks Coffee International opened its 34th retailer in Beijing on July 16, 2003, in the Zhongguancun area known as "China's Silicon Valley," making it the 70th café in China's mainland.
—Info-Prod (Middle East) Ltd., July, 2003

As we see from the above quote, Starbucks has achieved a remarkable penetration rate in China, given that it is a country of devoted tea drinkers who do not take readily to the taste of coffee.

Starbucks is no stranger to training leaders from around the world into the Starbucks style (the company has over 6,500 coffee shops in Europe, Latin America, North America, the Middle East, and the Pacific Rim). Company managers nevertheless have had quite a challenge in recruiting, motivating, and retaining managers for its Beijing outlets. Starbucks' primary challenge has been to recruit good managers in a country where the demand for local managers by foreign companies expanding there is far greater than the supply of managers with any experience in capitalist-style companies.

Chinese recruits have stressed that they are looking for opportunity to get training and to advance in global companies rather than for money. They know that managers with experience in Western organizations can always get a job. The brand's pop-culture reputation is also an attraction to young Beijingers.

In order to expose the recruits to java-style culture as well as to train them for management, Starbucks brings them to Tacoma, Washington, for three months to give them a taste of the West Coast lifestyle and the company's informal culture, such as Western-style backyard barbecues. Then they are exposed to the art of cappuccino-making at a real store before dawn and concocting dozens of fancy coffees. They get the same intensive training as anyone else anywhere in the world. One recruit, Mr. Wang, who worked in a large Beijing hotel before finding out how to make a triple grand latte, said that he enjoys the casual atmosphere and respect. The training and culture are very different from what one would expect at a traditional state-owned company in China, where the work is strictly defined and has no challenge for employees.

Starbucks has found that motivating their managers in Beijing is multifaceted. They know that people won't switch jobs for money alone. They want to work for a company that gives them an opportunity to learn. They also want to have a good working environment and a company with a strong reputation. The recruits have expressed their need for trust and participation in an environment where local nationals are traditionally not expected to exercise initiative or authority. In all, what seems to motivate them more than anything else is dignity.

SOURCES: www.Starbucks.com; "China: Starbucks Opens New Outlet in Beijing," *Info-Prod (Middle East) Ltd.,* July 20, 2003; "Coffee with Your Tea? Starbucks in China," *The Economist,* October 6, 2001; "Starbucks' Expansion in China Is Slated," *Wall Street Journal,* October 5, 1998.

Many HCNs are, of course, receiving excellent training in global business and Internet technology within their home corporations. Kim In Kyung, twenty-four, for example, has a job involving world travel and high technology with Samsung Electronics Company of Seoul, South Korea. Part of Samsung's strategy is to promote its new Internet focus, and this strategy has landed the farmer's daughter a $100,000 job. Her situation reflects Seoul's sizzling tech boom, where IT comprises 11 percent of its $400 billion economy and is expected to reach 20 percent by 2010.[47]

Whether in home corporations or in MNC subsidiaries or joint ventures in any country, managerial training to facilitate e-business adoption is competitively taking on increasing importance in order to take advantage of new strategic opportunities. While large companies are well ahead on the curve for information and communication technologies (ICT), there is considerable need for small and medium-sized enterprises (SMEs) to adopt such knowledge-creating capabilities. Managerial training in ICT is particularly critical for firms in new economy and emerging markets, and, in the aggregate, can provide leverage for rapid economic growth in regions such as Eastern Europe. Research in 2003 by Damaskopoulos and Evgeniou addressed these needs by surveying more than 900 SME managers in Slovenia, Poland, Romania, Bulgaria, and Cyprus. While most managers recognized the opportunities in implementing e-business strategies, they also noted the urgent need of training in order to take advantage of those opportunities. Exhibit 9-7 shows, in order of priority, the training needs and issues as perceived by those SME managers. Some

EXHIBIT 9-7   SME Managers in Eastern Europe: Training Priorities for E-Business Development

Addressing security and privacy concerns
Developing a business plan
Developing an e-business strategy
Understanding of electronic payment methods
Financing e-business initiatives
Personalisation and customer relationship management on the Internet
Sourcing e-business solutions and expertise
Developing the right partnerships for e-business
Training in technology management
Implementation of e-business strategy
Learning how to collect marketing intelligence online
Crafting the right business model for the Internet
Developing marketing strategies for the Internet
Collecting marketing intelligence online
Opportunities and pitfalls of online advertising
Understanding mobile commerce
Devising a sustainable revenue model
Understanding business-to-business marketplaces and virtual value chains

SOURCE: Reprinted from Panagiotis Damaskopoulos and Theodoros Evgeniou, "Adoption of New Economy Practices by SMEs in Eastern Europe," *European Management Journal,* 21, 2, 133–145, 2003. With permission from Elsevier.

of these factors are at the firm level, while other issues relate to the market and regulatory levels, such as the need to increase security for commercial activity on the Internet.[48] Such findings highlight the need to recognize the strategy-staffing-training link, and the importance to the overall growth of emerging economies.

In another common scenario also requiring management of a mixture of executives and employees, American and European MNCs presently employ Asians as well as Arab locals in their plants and offices in Saudi Arabia, bringing together three cultures: well-educated Asian managers living in a Middle Eastern, highly traditional society who are employed by a firm reflecting Western technology and culture. This kind of situation requires training to help all parties effectively integrate multiple sets of culturally based values, expectations, and work habits.

COMPENSATING EXPATRIATES

The significance of an appropriate compensation and benefits package to attract, retain, and motivate international employees cannot be overemphasized. Compensation is a crucial link between strategy and its successful implementation: There must be a fit between compensation and the goals for which the firm wants managers to aim.[49] So that they will not feel exploited, MNC employees need to perceive equity and goodwill in their compensation and benefits, whether they are PCNs, HCNs, or TCNs. The premature return of expatriates or the unwillingness of managers to take overseas assignments can often be traced to their knowledge that the assignment is detrimental to them financially and usually to their career progression.

From the firm's perspective, the high cost of maintaining appropriate compensation packages for expatriates has led many companies—Colgate-Palmolive, Chase Manhattan Bank, Digital Equipment, General Motors, and General Electric among them—to cut back on PCN assignments as much as possible. "Transfer a $100,000-a-year American executive to London—and suddenly he [or she] costs the employer $300,000," explains the *Wall Street Journal*. "Move him to Stockholm or Tokyo, and he [or she] easily becomes a million-dollar [manager]."[50]

Designing and maintaining an appropriate compensation package is more complex than it would seem because of the need to consider and reconcile parent and host-country financial, legal, and customary practices. The problem is that although little variation in typical executive salaries at the level of base compensation exists around the world, a wide variation in net spendable income is often present. U.S. executives may receive more in cash and stock, but they have to spend more for what foreign companies provide, such as cars, vacations, and entertainment allowances. In addition, the manager's purchasing power with that net income is affected by the relative cost of living. The cost of living is considerably higher in most of Europe than in the United States. In designing compensation and benefit packages for PCNs, then, the challenge to IHRM professionals is to maintain a standard of living for expatriates equivalent to their colleagues at home, plus compensating them for any additional costs incurred. This policy is referred to as "keeping the expatriate whole."[51]

To ensure that expatriates do not lose out through their overseas assignment, the **balance sheet approach** is often used to equalize the standard of living between the host country and the home country and to add some compensation for inconvenience or qualitative loss. This approach is illustrated in Exhibit 9-8. However, recently some companies have begun to base their compensation package on a goal of achieving a standard of living comparable to that of host-country managers, which does help resolve some of the problems of pay differentials.

In fairness, the MNC is obliged to make up additional costs that the expatriate would incur for taxes, housing, and goods and services. The tax differential is complex and expensive for the company, and MNCs generally use a policy of tax equalization: The company pays any taxes due on any type of additional compensation that the expatriate receives for the assignment; the expatriate pays in taxes only what she or he would pay at home. The burden of foreign taxes can be lessened, however, by efficient tax planning—a fact often overlooked by small firms. The timing and methods of paying people determine what foreign taxes are incurred. For example, a company can save on taxes by renting an

EXHIBIT 9-8   The Balance Sheet Approach

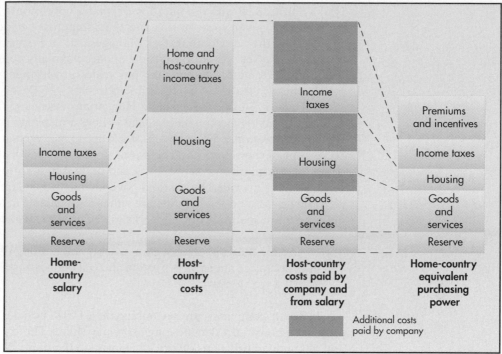

SOURCE: C. Reynolds, "Compensation of Overseas personnel, " in J. Famularo, *Handbook of Human Resource Administration*, 2ed. © 1989 McGraw-Hill, reproduced by permission of McGraw-Hill.

apartment for the employee instead of providing a cash housing allowance. All in all, MNCs have to weigh the many aspects of a complete compensation package, especially at high management levels, to effect a tax equalization policy. The total cost to the company can vary greatly by location; for example:

> *Expatriates in Germany may incur twice the income tax they would in the U.S., and they are taxed on their housing and cost-of-living allowances as well. This financial snowball effect is a great incentive to make sure we really need to fill the position with an expatriate.*

> JOHN DE LEON,
> *Vice President IHRM, CH2MHill, 2003[52]*

Managing PCN compensation is a complex challenge for companies with overseas operations. All components of the compensation package must be considered in light of both home- and host-country legalities and practices. Those components include:

Salary: Local salary buying power and currency translation, as compared with home salary; bonuses or incentives for dislocation

Taxes: Equalize any differential effects of taxes as a result of expatriate's assignment

Allowances: Relocation expenses; cost-of-living adjustments; housing allowance for assignment and allowance to maintain house at home; trips home for expatriate and family; private education for children

Benefits: Health insurance; stock options

Most important, to be strategically competitive, the compensation package must be comparatively attractive to the kinds of managers the company wishes to hire or relocate. Some of those managers will, of course, be local managers in the host country. This, too, is a complex situation requiring competitive compensation policies that can attract, motivate, and retain the best local managerial talent. In many countries, however, it is a considerable challenge to develop compensation packages appropriate to the local situation and culture, while also recognizing the differences between local salaries and those expected by expatriates or transpatriates (that difference itself often being a source of competitive advantage).

COMPENSATING HOST-COUNTRY NATIONALS

How do firms deal with the question of what is appropriate compensation for host country nationals, given local norms and the competitive needs of the firm? This issue is explored further in Comparative Management in Focus: Compensating Russians. Of course, no one set of solutions can be applicable in any country. Many variables apply—including local market factors and pay scales, government involvement in benefits, the role of unions, the cost of living, and so on.

In Eastern Europe, for example, Hungarians, Poles, and Czechs spend 35 to 40 percent of their disposable income on food and utilities, which may run as high as 75 percent in the Russian Federation.[53] Therefore, East European managers must have cash for about 65 to 80 percent of their base pay, compared to about 40 percent for U.S. managers (the rest being long-term incentives, benefits, and perks). In addition, they still expect the many social benefits provided by the "old government." To be competitive, MNCs can focus on providing goods and services that are either not available at all or are extremely expensive in Eastern Europe. Such upscale perks can be used to atttract high-skilled workers.

> Nestlé Bulgaria offers a company car and a cellular phone to new recruits. . . .
> Fuel prices are about $2 per gallon and cell phones cost $1,200 a year—equivalent
> to half a year's salary.[54]

In Japan, companies are revamping their HRM policies to compete in a global economy, in response to a decade-long economic slump. The traditional lifetime employment and guaranteed tidy pension are giving way to the more Western practices of competing for jobs, of basing pay on performance rather than seniority, and of making people responsible for their own retirement fund decisions.[55]

In China, too, change is underway. University graduates may now seek their own jobs rather than be assigned to state-owned companies, though nepotism is still common. In a study of HRM practices in China, Bjorkman and Lu found that a key concern of Western managers in China was the compensation of the HCNs. In Beijing and Shanghai, top Chinese managers have seen their salaries increase by 30 to 50 percent in the last few years. They have also received considerable fringe benefits, such as housing, company cars, pensions, and overseas training. The difficulty, too, was that in Western–Chinese joint ventures, the Chinese partner opposed pay increases.[56] Yet when trying to introduce performance-based pay, the Western companies ran into considerable opposition and usually gave up, using salary increases instead. Setting up some kind of housing scheme, such as investing in apartments, seemed to be one way that foreign-owned firms were able to compete for good managers. Those managers were, understandably, maximizing their job opportunities now that they did not have to get permission to leave the Chinese state-owned companies.[57]

According to Citigroup, it is also imperative to make clear what benefits, as well as salary, come with a position because of the way compensation is perceived and regulated around the world.[58] In Latin America, for example, an employee's pay and title are associated with what type of car they can receive.

Comparative Management in Focus

Compensating Russians

Korean companies are cashing in by signing up low-cost Russian engineers.
—*www.Businessweek.com, March 8, 2004*[59]

Russia is our No.1. destination for technology outsourcing.
—*Cha Dae Sung, Samsung, March 8, 2004*[60]

Samsung, LG Electronics, Daewoo Electronics, and many other Korean companies take advantage of the enormous pool of scientific and engineering talent in Russia. Samsung employs eighty engineers and scientists, many in suboffices in Moscow.

They pay electrical engineers in Russia the equivalent of $3,000 to $5,000 a month, which is five times the pay from a local Russian company, still a substantial saving over Korean employees at that level.

Generally, however, MNCs operating in Russia, with local employees at various levels, continue to face many complicating factors involved in compensating Russian nationals: the ongoing transition to a market economy; the Russians' past practices and resultant expectations from their background of employment and compensation in state-owned enterprises; and the cultural norms and work behaviors resulting from their social system. Puffer and Shekshnia recommend tailoring compensation packages to the Russian culture and the prevailing economic and market situation. They examined compensation surveys conducted by Otis Elevator Company and the U.S. Embassy and found that trends of Western firms compensating Russian nationals typically included three components: a base salary, incentive pay, and a variety of nonmonetary fringe benefits. Puffer and Shekshnia felt that these three components satisfied the prevailing Russian situation and the Russian culture—which they conclude, using Hofstede's categories, to be that of high power distance, high uncertainty avoidance, high collectivism, high femininity, and high short-term orientation. For example, some hard-currency and some nonmonetary fringe benefits allow Russian employees to have things that are otherwise simply not available to them because of inflation or nonavailability—in other words, to combat the uncertainty avoidance of the value of basic compensation.[61] However, based on their research and experiences in Russia, Puffer and Shekshnia recommend that Western firms need to design compensation packages that will meet their business objectives as well as reward Russians equitably and appropriately. To achieve this end, they give the following recommendations, designed to "reinforce those aspects of Russian culture that help achieve corporate objectives, while reducing the influence of other cultural dimensions that could undermine objectives:"[62]

1. Select Russian employees who are achievement-oriented and willing to take risks (that is, those who do not fit the cultural profile of the majority of Russian workers).
2. Tie individual bonuses to initiative and personal accountability (to encourage individual goal setting).
3. Organize social events and other group activities.
4. Provide small-group incentives (to encourage team achievement with Western managers).
5. Provide a mix of short- and long-term incentives (to transition to a focus on long-term corporate objectives).
6. Tailor the compensation package to individual preferences (to enjoy choices they have not had before).

CONCLUSION

The effectiveness of managers at foreign locations is crucial to the success of the firm's operations, particularly because of the lack of proximity to, and control by, headquarters executives. The ability of expatriates to initiate and maintain cooperative relationships with local people and agencies will determine the long-term success, even viability, of the operation. In a real sense, a company's global cadre represents its most valuable resource. Proactive management of that resource by headquarters will result in having the right people in the right place at the right time, appropriately trained, prepared, and supported. MNCs using these IHRM practices can anticipate the effective management of the foreign operation, the fostering of expatriates' careers, and ultimately, the enhanced success of the corporation.

Summary of Key Points

1. Global human resource management is a vital component of implementing global strategy and is increasingly being recognized as a major determinant of success or failure in international business.
2. The main staffing alternatives for global operations are the ethnocentric, polycentric, regiocentric, and global approaches. Each approach has its appropriate uses, according to its advantages and disadvantages.

3. The causes of expatriate failure include the following: poor selection based on inappropriate criteria, inadequate preparation before assignment, alienation from headquarters, inability of manager or family to adapt to local environment, inadequate compensation package, and poor programs for career support and repatriation.
4. The three major areas critical to expatriate preparation are cultural training, language instruction, and familiarity with everyday matters.
5. Common training techniques for potential expatriates include area studies, culture assimilators, language training, sensitivity training, and field experiences.
6. Appropriate and attractive compensation packages must be designed by IHRM staffs to sustain a competitive global management cadre. Compensation packages for host-country managers must be designed to fit the local culture and situation, as well as the firm's objectives.

Discussion Questions

1. What are the major alternative staffing approaches for international operations? Explain the relative advantages of each and the conditions under which you would choose one approach over another.
2. Why is the HRM role so much more complex, and important, in the international context?
3. Explain the common causes of expatriate failure. What are the major success factors for expatriates? Explain the role and importance of each.
4. What are the common training techniques for managers going overseas. How should these vary as appropriate to the level of globalization of the firm?
5. Explain the balance sheet approach to international compensation packages. Why is this approach so important? Discuss the pros and cons of aligning the expatriate compensation package with the host-country colleagues compared to the home-country colleagues.

Application Exercises

1. Make a list of the reasons you would want to accept a foreign assignment and a list of reasons you would want to reject it. Do they depend on the location? Compare your list with a classmate and discuss your reasons.
2. Research a company with operations in several countries and ascertain the staffing policy used for those countries. Find out what kinds of training and preparation are provided for expatriates and what kinds of results the company is experiencing with expatriate training.

Experiential Exercise

This can be done in groups or individually. After the exercise, discuss your proposals with the rest of the class.

You are the expatriate general manager of a British company's subsidiary in Brazil, an automobile component parts manufacturer. You and your family have been in Brazil for seven years, and now you are being reassigned and replaced with another expatriate—Ian Fleming. Ian is bringing his family—Helen, an instructor in computer science, who hopes to find a position; a son, age twelve; and a daughter, age fourteen. None of them has lived abroad before. Ian has asked you what he and his family should expect in the new assignment. Remembering all the problems you and your family experienced in the first couple of years of your assignment in Brazil, you want to facilitate their adjustment and have decided to do two things:

1. Write a letter to Ian, telling him what to expect—both on the job and in the community. Tell him about some of the cross-cultural conflicts he may run into with his coworkers and employees, and how he should handle them.
2. Set up some arrangements and support systems for the family and design a support package for them, with a letter to each family member telling them what to expect.

Internet Resources

Visit the Deresky companion Web site at prenhall.com/deresky for this chapter's Internet resources.

Fred Bailey in Japan: An Innocent Abroad

Fred Bailey gazed out the window of his twenty-fourth-floor office at the tranquil beauty of the Imperial Palace amid the hustle and bustle of downtown Tokyo. It had been only six months since Fred had arrived with his wife and two children for this three-year assignment as the director of Kline & Associates' Tokyo office. Kline & Associates was a large multinational consulting firm with offices in nineteen countries worldwide. Fred was now trying to decide whether he should simply pack up and tell headquarters that he was coming home or whether he should try to convince his wife, and himself, that they should stay and finish the assignment. Given how excited they all were about the assignment to begin with, it was a mystery to Fred how things had gotten to this point. As Fred watched the swans glide across the water in the moat that surrounds the Imperial Palace, he reflected on the past seven months.

Seven months ago, Dave Steiner, the managing partner of the main office in Boston, asked Fred to lunch to discuss business. To Fred's surprise, the business they discussed was not about the major project that he and his team had just finished; instead, it was about a very big promotion and career move. Fred was offered the position of managing director of the firm's relatively new Tokyo office, which had a staff of forty, including seven Americans. Most of the Americans in the Tokyo office were either associate consultants or research analysts. Fred would be in charge of the whole office and would report to a senior partner. Steiner implied to Fred that if this assignment went as well as his past projects, it would be the last step before becoming a partner in the firm.

When Fred told his wife about the unbelievable opportunity, he was shocked at her less than enthusiastic response. His wife, Jennifer (or Jenny as Fred called her), thought that it would be rather difficult to have the children live and go to school in a foreign country for three years, especially when Christine, the oldest, would be starting middle school next year. Besides, now that the kids were in school, Jenny was thinking about going back to work, at least part time. Jenny had a degree in fashion merchandising from a well-known private university and had worked as an assistant buyer for a large women's clothing store before having the two girls.

Fred explained that the career opportunity was just too good to pass up and that the company's overseas package would make living overseas terrific. The company would pay all the expenses to move whatever the Baileys wanted to take with them. The company had a very nice house in an expensive district of Tokyo that would be provided rent free, and the company would rent their house in Boston during their absence. Moreover, the

firm would provide a car and driver, education expenses for the children to attend private schools, and a cost-of-living adjustment and overseas compensation that would nearly triple Fred's gross annual salary. After two days of consideration and discussion, Fred told Steiner he would accept the assignment.

The current Tokyo office managing director was a partner in the firm but had been in the new Tokyo office for less than a year when he was transferred to head a long-established office in England. Because the transfer to England was taking place right away, Fred and his family had about three weeks to prepare for the move. Between transferring responsibilities at the office to Bob Newcome, who was being promoted to Fred's position, and getting furniture and the like ready to be moved, neither Fred nor his family had much time to really find out much about Japan, other than what was in the encyclopedia.

When the Baileys arrived in Japan, they were greeted at the airport by one of the young Japanese associate consultants and the senior American expatriate. Fred and his family were quite tired from the long trip, and the two-hour ride to Tokyo was a rather quiet one. After a few days of just settling in, Fred spent his first full day at the office.

Fred's first order of business was to have a general meeting with all the employees of associate consultant rank and higher. Although Fred didn't notice it at the time, all the Japanese staff sat together and all the Americans sat together. After Fred introduced himself and his general idea about the potential and future directions of the Tokyo office, he called on a few individuals to get their ideas about how the things for which they were responsible would likely fit into his overall plan. From the Americans, Fred got a mixture of opinions with specific reasons about why certain things might or might not fit well. From the Japanese, he got very vague answers. When Fred pushed to get more specific information, he was surprised to find that a couple of the Japanese simply made a sucking sound as they breathed and said that it was "difficult to say." Fred sensed the meeting was not achieving his objectives, so he thanked everyone for coming and said he looked forward to their all working together to make the Tokyo office the fastest-growing office in the company.

After they had been in Japan about a month, Fred's wife complained to him about the difficulty she had getting certain everyday products like maple syrup, peanut butter, and good-quality beef. She said that when she could get it at one of the specialty stores it cost three and four times what it would cost in the States. She also complained that since the washer and dryer were much too small, she had to spend extra money by sending things out to be dry-cleaned. On top of all that, unless she went to the American Club in downtown Tokyo, she never had anyone to talk to. After all, Fred was gone ten to sixteen hours a day. Unfortunately, while Jenny talked, Fred was preoccupied, thinking about a big upcoming meeting between his firm and a significant prospective client, a top-100 Japanese multinational company.

The next day, Fred, along with the lead U.S. consultant for the potential contract, Ralph Webster, and one of the Japanese associate consultants, Kenichi Kurokawa, who spoke perfect English, met with a team from the Japanese firm. The Japanese team consisted of four members: the vice president of administration, the director of international personnel, and two staff specialists. After shaking hands and a few awkward bows, Fred said that he knew the Japanese gentlemen were busy and he didn't want to waste their time, so he would get right to the point. Fred then had the other American lay out their firm's proposal for the project and what the project would cost. After the presentation, Fred asked the Japanese what their reaction to the proposal was. The Japanese did not respond immediately, so Fred launched into his summary version of the proposal, thinking that the translation might have been insufficient. Again, the Japanese had only the vaguest of responses to his direct questions.

The recollection of the frustration of that meeting was enough to shake Fred back to reality. The reality was that in the five months since that first meeting little progress had been made and the contract between the firms was yet to be signed. "I can never seem to get a direct response from Japanese," he thought to himself. This feeling of frustration led him to remember a related incident that happened about a month after this first meeting with this client.

Fred had decided that the reason not much progress was being made with the client was that he and his group just didn't know enough about the client to package the proposal in a way that was appealing to the client. Consequently, he called in Ralph Webster, the senior American associated with the proposal, and asked him to develop a report on the client so that the proposal could be reevaluated and changed where necessary. Jointly, they decided that one of the more promising Japanese research associates, Tashiro Watanabe, would be the best person to take the lead on this report. To impress upon Tashiro the importance of this task and the great potential they saw in him, they decided to have the young Japanese associate meet with both Fred and Ralph. In the meeting, Fred and Ralph laid out the nature and importance of the task, at which point Fred leaned forward in his chair and said to Tashiro, "You can see that this is an important assignment and that we are placing a lot of confidence in you by giving it to you. We need the report by this time next week so that we can

revise and represent our proposal. Can you do it?" After a somewhat pregnant pause, Tashiro responded hesitantly, "I'm not sure what to say." At that point, Fred smiled, got up from his chair, walked over to the young Japanese associate, extended his hand, and said, "Hey, there's nothing to say. We're just giving you the opportunity you deserve."

The day before the report was due, Fred asked Ralph how the report was coming. Ralph said that, since he had heard nothing from Tashiro, he assumed everything was under control but that he would double-check. Ralph later ran into one of the U.S. research associates, John Maynard. Ralph knew that John was hired for Japan because of his Japanese language ability and that, unlike any of the other Americans, John often went out after work with some of the Japanese research associates, including Tashiro. So Ralph asked John if he knew how Tashiro was coming on the report. John then recounted that at the office the previous night Tashiro had asked if Americans sometimes fired employees for being late with reports. John had sensed that this was more than a hypothetical question and asked Tashiro why he wanted to know. Tashiro did not respond immediately, and since it was 8:30 in the evening, John suggested they go out for a drink. At first Tashiro resisted, but then John assured him that they would grab a drink at a nearby bar and come right back. At the bar, John got Tashiro to open up.

Tashiro explained the nature of the report that he had been requested to produce. He continued to explain that, even though he had worked long into the night every night to complete the report, it was just impossible and that he had doubted from the beginning whether he could complete the report in a week.

At this point, Ralph asked John, "Why didn't he say something in the first place?" Ralph didn't wait to hear whether or not John had an answer to this question. He headed straight to Tashiro's desk.

Ralph chewed out Tashiro and then went to Fred, explaining that the report would not be ready and that Tashiro, from the start, didn't think it could be. "Then why didn't he say something?" Fred asked. No one had any answers, and the whole episode left everyone more suspect and uncomfortable with each other.

Other incidents, big and small, had made the last two months especially frustrating, but Fred was too tired to remember them all. To Fred it seemed that working with Japanese both inside and outside the firm was like working with people from another planet. Fred felt he couldn't communicate with them, and he never could figure out what they were thinking. It drove him crazy.

On top of all this, Jennifer laid a bombshell on him. She wanted to go home, and yesterday was not soon enough. Even though the kids seemed to be doing all right, Jennifer was tired of Japan—tired of begin stared at, of not understanding anybody or being understood, of not being able to find what she wanted at the store, of not being able to drive and read the road signs, of not having anything to watch on television, of not being involved in anything. She wanted to go home and could not think of any reason why they shouldn't. After all, she reasoned, they owed nothing to the company because the company had led them to believe this was just another assignment, like the two years they spent in San Francisco, and it was anything but that!

Fred looked out the window once more, wishing that somehow everything could be fixed, or turned back, or something. The traffic below was backed up. Though the traffic lights changed, the cars and trucks didn't seem to be moving. Fortunately, beneath the ground, one of the world's most advanced, efficient, and clean subway systems moved hundreds of thousands of people about the city and to their homes.

CASE QUESTIONS

1. You are Fred. What should you do now?
2. Turn back the clock to when Fred was offered the position in Tokyo. What, if anything, should have been done differently, and by whom?

Source: J. Stewart Black, in *International human Resource Management*, eds. M. Mendenhall and Gary Oddou (Boston: PWS-Kent, 1991).

CHAPTER
10
Developing a Global Management Cadre

Outline

Opening Profile: Foreign from the Start

By Philip Shearer, Group President, Clinique, Estée Lauder, NY: (Written with Abby Ellin)

MY mother was French, my father British, and I was born in Morocco. Life there was a dream: we lived on the sea; we went to the beach. It was a great combination of the easy life and hard work. It was also extraordinarily romantic, and when I say I met my wife in high school in Casablanca, everyone thinks of Humphrey Bogart.

At the same time, you learned what it was like to live in a developing country. You learned about humility and the notion that nothing is easy for everyone.

When you're born and raised in a country like this, you also know you won't stay forever; you're a foreigner. In the 1960's and early 70's the energy was in North America, so after graduating from college in France I came to the United States for business school at Cornell.

From there, I worked at a pharmaceutical company in Minneapolis. Then I worked in France, Mexico, Britain, Japan, and again in the United States for companies like L'Oréal and the Elizabeth Arden division of Eli Lilly.

You learn common themes when you live all over the world. Most important: You have to remain yourself. People will trust you and relate to you whatever your culture is, provided you are trustworthy and credible.

Still, you have to get used to other cultures. In Mexico, when you drive around the country, you ask for directions and you say, "Is such and such a place far away?" Depending on whom you ask the answer could be, "Yes, very far." On a bus, it is, "Not so far." If the person is in a car, the reply is, "Next door."

In Japan, where I lived when I was working for Elizabeth Arden, when you have a meeting the most important person will sit the farthest from the door. So, we had this lunch where I was with my boss, who then became the most important person in the room. But he said, "I don't believe in all this; I'm going to sit in the middle of the table." That created total chaos.

Americans show off a little more than people in other parts of the world; it's the cowboy culture. But in the end, you have to deliver. And that's the same all over the world.

Growing up in Morocco certainly helped my career. For example, I learned to drive at 10. My father taught me on the side of the road. After that, I caught the driving bug. I wanted to go to racing school but my father said he would pay only for college, so that's where I went.

I later went to racing school in Britain. My claim to fame is that I was the North American Ferrari Challenge champion in 2001.

Car racing is a little macho, but I am also obsessed with beauty products. A few nights ago my wife and I had dinner with a friend of mine who also races. He told me how he had just found this magical shaving cream that he absolutely loves. It turns out it is one of my products. I told him if you want your shave to be more sensual and smooth, you need to use the "post-shave healer," too. We were eating sushi, and our wives looked at us in surprise.

Not too long ago, I became an American citizen. I went from the beach of Casablanca to the corporate world of New York City. Who would have thought?

SOURCE: www.nytimes.com, September 21, 2003. Reprinted by permission of *The New York Times* Copyright 2003. The New York Times Company.

A crucial factor in global competitiveness is the ability of the firm to maximize its global human resources in the long term. To do this, attention must be paid to several important areas:

1. To maximize long-term retention and use of international cadre through career management so that the company can develop a top management team with global experience.
2. To develop effective global management teams.
3. To understand, value, and promote the role of women and minorities in international management in order to maximize those underutilized resources.
4. To work with the host-country labor relations system to effect strategic implementation and employee productivity.

PREPARATION, ADAPTATION, AND REPATRIATION

We began to realize that the entire effectiveness of the assignment could be compromised by ignoring the spouse.

STEVE FORD,
Corporation Relocations, Hewlett-Packard[1]

Effective human resource management of a company's global cadre does not end with the overseas assignment. It ends with the successful repatriation of the executive into company headquarters. Long-term, proactive management of critical resources should begin with the end of the current assignment in mind—that is, it should begin with plans for the repatriation of the executive as part of his or her career path. The management of the reentry phase of the career cycle is as vital as the management of the cross-cultural entry and training. Otherwise, the long-term benefits of that executive's international experience may be negated.[2] Shortsightedly, many companies do little to minimize the potential effects of **reverse culture shock** (return shock). In fact, a survey of companies belonging to the American Society of Personnel Administration International (ASPAI) revealed that only 31 percent had formal repatriation programs for executives and only 35 percent of those included spouses. In addition, only 22 percent of those had conducted the programs prior to the executive's departure for the assignment.[3] Those U.S. companies without programs had various explanations: a lack of expertise in repatriation training, the cost of the programs, or a lack of a perceived need for such training.

The long-term implications of ineffective repatriation practices are clear—few good managers will be willing to take international assignments because they will see what happened to their colleagues. If a certain manager lost out on promotion opportunities while overseas and is now, in fact, worse off than before he or she left, the only people willing to take on foreign assignments in the future will be those who have not been able to succeed on the home front or those who think that a stint abroad will be like a vacation. Research has shown that employees commonly see overseas assignments as negative career moves in many U.S. multinational companies.[4] In contrast, such moves are seen as positive in most European, Japanese, and Australian companies because they consider international experience necessary for advancement to top management.

In a recent study of dual-career couples, "the perceived impact of the international assignment upon returning to the U.S." was one of the most important issues stated by managers regarding their willingness to relocate overseas.[5]

Reverse culture shock occurs primarily because of the difficulty of reintegrating into the organization but also because, generally speaking, the longer a person is away, the more difficult it is to get back into the swing of things. Not only might the manager have been overlooked and lost in the shuffle of a reorganization, but her or his whole family might have lost social contacts or jobs and feel out of step with their contemporaries. These feelings of alienation from what has always been perceived as "home"—because of the loss of contact with family, friends, and daily life—delay the resocialization process. Such a reaction is particularly serious if the family's overall financial situation has been hurt by the assignment and if the spouse's career has also been kept "on hold" while he or she was abroad.

For companies to maximize the long-term use of their global cadre, they need to make sure that the foreign assignment and the reintegration process are positive experiences. This means careful career planning, support while overseas, and use of the increased experience and skills of returned managers to benefit the home office. Research into the practices of successful U.S., European, Japanese, and Australian multinational corporations (MNCs) indicates the use of one or more of the following support systems, as recommended by Tung, for a successful repatriation program:

- A mentor program to monitor the expatriate's career path while abroad and upon repatriation.
- As an alternative to the mentor program, the establishment of a special organizational unit for the purposes of career planning and continuing guidance for the expatriate.
- A system of supplying information and maintaining contacts with the expatriate so that he or she may continue to feel a part of the home organization.[6]

The Role of the Expatriate Spouse

Many companies are beginning to recognize the importance of providing support for spouses and children—in particular because both spouses are often corporate fast trackers and demand that both sets of needs be included on the bargaining table. Firms often use informal means, such as intercompany networking, to help find the trailing spouse a position in the same location. They know that, with the increasing number of dual-career couples (65 percent in the United States), if the spouse does not find a position the manager will very likely turn down the assignment. They decline because they cannot afford to lose the income or because the spouse's career may be delayed entirely if he or she is out of the workforce for a few years. As women continue to move up the corporate ladder, the accompanying ("trailing") spouse is often male—estimated at 25 percent in the year 2000.[7] Companies such as Hewlett-Packard, Shell, Medtronic, and Monsanto offer a variety of options to address the dual-career dilemma.

At Procter & Gamble, employees and spouses destined for China are sent to Beijing for two months of language training and cultural familiarization. Nissho Iwai, a Japanese trading company, gets together managers and spouses who are leaving Japan with foreign managers and spouses who are on their way there. In addition, the firm provides a year of language training and information and services for Japanese children to attend schools abroad. Recent research on 321 American expatriate spouses around the world shows that effective cross-cultural adjustment by spouses is more likely (1) when firms seek the spouse's opinion about the international assignment and the expected standard of living and (2) when the spouse initiates his or her own predeparture training (thereby supplementing the minimal training given by most firms).[8]

Expatriate Career Management

Support services provide timely help for the manager and, therefore, are part of the effective management of an overseas assignment. The overall transition process experienced by the company's international management cadre over time is shown in Exhibit 10-1. It comprises three phases of transition and adjustment that must be managed for successful socialization to a new culture and resocialization back to the old culture. These phases are (1) the exit transition from the home country, the success of which will be determined largely by the quality of preparation the expatriate has received; (2) the entry transition to the host country, in which successful acculturation (or early exit) will depend largely on monitoring and support; and (3) the entry transition back to the home country or to a new host country, in which the level of reverse culture shock and the ease of re-acculturation will depend on previous stages of preparation and support.[9]

A company may derive many potential benefits from carefully managing the careers of its expatriates. By helping managers make the right moves for their careers, the company will be able to retain people with increasing global experience and skills. But from the

EXHIBIT 10-1   The Expatriate Transition Process

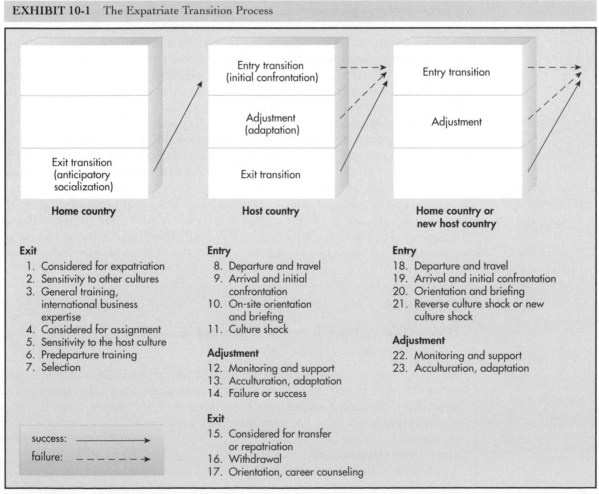

SOURCE: P. Asheghian and B. Ebrahimi, International Business (New York: Harper Collins, 1990), 470.

individual manager's perspective, most people understand that no one can better look out for one's interests than oneself. With that in mind, managers must ask themselves, and their superiors, what role each overseas stint will play in career advancement and what proactive role each will play in one's own career.

The Role of Repatriation in Developing a Global Management Cadre

Managers returning from expatriate assignments are two to three times more likely to leave the company within a year because attention has not been paid to their careers and the way they fit back into the corporate structure back home.

www.FT.com,
March 5, 2001[10]

In the international assignment, both the manager and the company benefit from the enhanced skills and experience gained by the expatriate. Many returning executives report an improvement in their managerial skills and self-confidence. Some of these acquired skills, as reported by Adler, include the following:

- **Managerial Skills, Not Technical Skills:** learning how to deal with a wide range of people, to adapt to their cultures through compromise, and not to be a dictator.
- **Tolerance for Ambiguity:** making decisions with less information and more uncertainty about the process and the outcome.
- **Multiple Perspectives:** learning to understand situations from the perspective of local employees and businesspeople.
- **Ability to Work with and Manage Others:** learning patience and tolerance—realizing that managers abroad are in the minority among local people; learning to communicate more with others and empathize with them.[11]

In addition to the managerial and cross-cultural skills acquired by expatriates, the company benefits from the knowledge and experience those managers gain about how to do business overseas, and about new technology, local marketing, and competitive information. The company should position itself to benefit from that enhanced management knowledge if it wants to develop a globally oriented and experienced management cadre—an essential ingredient for global competitiveness—in particular where there is a high degree of shared learning among the organization's global managers. If the company cannot retain good returning managers, then their potential shared knowledge is not only lost but also conveyed to another organization that hires that person. This can be very detrimental to the company's competitive stance. Some companies are becoming quite savvy about how to use technology to utilize shared knowledge to develop their global management cadre, to better service their customers, and—as a side benefit—to store the knowledge and expertise of their managers around the world in case they leave the company. That knowledge, it can be argued, is an asset in which the company has invested large amounts of resources. One such savvy company is Booz-Allen & Hamilton, which instituted a Knowledge On-Line intranet, as featured in the following E-Biz Box:

E-BIZ BOX

Booz-Allen & Hamilton Uses Intranet Technology to Share Technology around the Globe

Since 1914, senior executives of world-class organizations in both the public and private sectors have selected Booz-Allen & Hamilton to carry out their management and technology consulting assignments. Booz-Allen recently solved a problem for itself that it is often called upon to solve for its clients: how to bridge islands of information that are isolated due to geographical constraints, computing platforms, and different applications.

After eliminating groupware, document management, and homegrown systems as possible solutions, Booz-Allen decided on intranet technology. For its Knowledge

On-Line (KOL) intranet, the firm chose Netscape Enterprise Server and Netscape News Server to support a variety of intranet applications, including:

- A database-driven expert skills directory
- A firmwide knowledge repository able to retrieve information in multiple data types
- Employee directories
- Newsgroups that facilitate global project collaboration

Using a series of benchmarks to evaluate intranet solutions vendors, Booz-Allen determined Netscape software to be the best solution. Netscape met the firm's requirements for:

- Industry-leading Web-based server software
- Outstanding performance, reliability, security, and pricing
- Interoperability, application portability, scalability, and systems network management

Booz-Allen has achieved a tremendous return on investment from its intranet, according to an International Data Corporation study.

Booz-Allen & Hamilton relies on its Knowledge On-Line intranet to enhance knowledge sharing among its employees worldwide and to improve client service. By using its intranet to link islands of information separated by geography and platform-specific applications, the renowned consulting firm has enabled its 2,000 private sector consultants to collect and share firmwide their best thinking and expertise.

COLLECTING AND SHARING KNOWLEDGE IN MULTIPLE DATA TYPES

One of the most valued applications supported by KOL is a knowledge repository whereby Booz-Allen can capture, classify, and quantify the firm's knowledge and expertise. The idea behind the knowledge repository is to package knowledge within context. Consultants can do a quick search for best practices, frameworks, business intelligence, competitive data, comparative analysis, business tools, and techniques to help them solve client problems as well as locate the leading experts on a topic.

CYBERSPACE COLLABORATION

Booz-Allen uses the secure Netscape News Server to let global teams of consultants discuss a variety of company- and noncompany-related topics via message threading and real-time discussion groups.

Consultants all over the world take great advantage of the communicative and collaborative capabilities inherent to KOL. Using the news readers built into Netscape Navigator, consultants can engage in either private or public discourse within Booz-Allen. For more general communication across the entire firm, KOL provides public discussion folders accessible to all users.

SOURCE: Excerpted from Netscape.com case studies.

Black and Gregersen's research of 750 U.S., European, and Japanese companies concluded that those companies that reported a high degree of job satisfaction and strong performance, and that experienced limited turnover, used the following practices when making international assignments:

- They focus on knowledge creation and global leadership development.
- They assign overseas posts to people whose technical skills are matched or exceeded by their cross-cultural abilities.
- They end expatriate assignments with a deliberate repatriation process.[12]

A successful repatriation program, then, starts before the assignment. The company's top management must set up a culture that conveys the message that the organization regards international assignments as an integral part of continuing career development and advancement, and that it values the skills of the returnees. The company's objectives should be reflected in its long-range plans, commitment, and compensation on behalf of the expatriate. GE sets a model for effective expatriate career management. With its 500 expatriates worldwide, it takes care to select only the best managers for overseas jobs and then commits to placing them in specific positions upon reentry.[13] A study of the international human resource management (IHRM) policies of British multinationals indicates that careful planning for foreign assignments pays off. Farsighted policies, along with selection criteria based more on the adaptability of the manager and her or his family to the culture than on technical skills, apparently account for the low expatriate failure rate—estimated at less than 5 percent.[14]

GLOBAL MANAGEMENT TEAMS

MNCs, today, realize it is essential to maximize their human assets in the form of global management teams so they can share resources and manage the transnational transfer of knowledge. The term, **global management teams,** describes collections of managers in or from several countries who must rely on group collaboration if each member is to experience optimum success and goal achievement.[15] Whirlpool International, for example, is a U.S.–Dutch joint venture, with administrative headquarters in Comerio, Italy, where it is managed by a Swede and a six-person management team from Sweden, Italy, Holland, the United States, Belgium, and Germany. To achieve the individual and collective goals of the team members, international teams must "provide the means to communicate corporate culture, develop a global perspective, coordinate and integrate the global enterprise, and be responsive to local market needs."[16] The role and importance of international teams increase as the firm progresses in its scope of international activity. Similarly, the manner in which multicultural interaction affects the firm's operations depends on its level of international involvement, its environment, and its strategy. In domestic firms, the effects of cross-cultural teams are limited to internal operations and some external contacts. In international firms that export products and produce some goods overseas, multicultural teams and cultural diversity play important roles in the relationships between buyers, sellers, and other intermediaries at the boundary of the organization. For multinational firms, the role of multicultural teams again becomes internal to the company; the teams consist of culturally diverse managers and technical people who are located around the world and are also working together within subsidiaries. The team's ability to work effectively together is crucial to the company's success. In addition, technology facilitates effective and efficient teamwork around the world. This was found by the Timberland U.K. sales conference planning team. In the past, the company's large sales conferences were cumbersome to organize because their offices were in France, Germany, Spain, Italy, and the United Kingdom. Then the team started using the British Telecom Conference Call system for the arrangements, which saved them much travel and expense. The company subsequently adopted the BT Conference Calls for the executive team's country meetings.

Global management teams play a vital role in global organizations.

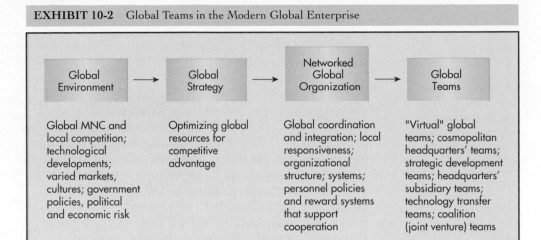

EXHIBIT 10-2   Global Teams in the Modern Global Enterprise

SOURCE: Adapted from T. Gross, E. Turner, and L. Cederholm, "Building Teams for Global Operations," *Management Review* (June 1987): 34.

There really was no point in traveling for two-hour meetings. So we would lock diaries for a couple of hours over BT Conference Call.

www.BritishTelecom.com/cases,
February 19, 2001[17]

For global organizations and alliances, the same cross-cultural interactions hold as in MNCs, and, in addition, considerably more interaction takes place with the external environment at all levels of the organization. Therefore, global teamwork is vital, as are the pockets of cross-cultural teamwork and interactions that occur at many boundaries.[18] For the global company, worldwide competition and markets necessitate global teams for strategy development, both for the organization as a whole and for the local units to respond to their markets.

As shown in Exhibit 10-2, when a firm responds to its global environment with a global strategy and then organizes with a networked "glocal" structure (see Chapter 8), various types of cross-border teams are necessary for global integration and local differentiation. These include teams between and among headquarters and subsidiaries, transnational project teams, often operating on a "virtual" basis, and teams coordinating alliances outside the organization. In joint ventures, in particular, multicultural teams work at all levels of strategic planning and implementation, as well as on the production and assembly floor.

"Virtual" Transnational Teams

Virtual groups, whose members interact through computer-mediated communication systems (such as desktop video conferencing systems, e-mail, group support systems, internets, and intranets), are linked together across time, space, and organizational boundaries.[19]

Increasingly, advances in communication now facilitate **virtual global teams**, a horizontal networked structure, with people around the world conducting meetings and exchanging information via the Internet, enabling the organization to capitalize on twenty-four-hour productivity. In this way, too, knowledge is shared across business units and across cultures.[20] The advantages and cost savings of virtual global teams are frequently offset by their challenges—including cultural misunderstandings and the logistics of differences in time and space, as shown in Exhibit 10-3. Group members must build their teams while bearing in mind the group diversity and the need for careful communication.[21]

Managing Transnational Teams

The ability to develop and lead effective transnational teams (whether they interact "virtually", or physically, or, as is most often the case, a mixture of both) is essential in light of the increasing proliferation of foreign subsidiaries, joint ventures, and other transnational alliances. As noted by David Dotlich of Honeywell Bull. (HBI), an international computer firm, effective international teamwork is essential because cross-cultural "double-talk, double agendas, double priorities, and double interests can present crippling business

EXHIBIT 10-3   Operational Challenges for Global Virtual Teams

Geographic Dispersal:	The complexity of scheduling communications such as teleconferences and videoconferences across multiple time zones, holidays, and so on.
	Lack of face-to-face meetings to establish trust or for cross-interaction processes such as brainstorming.
Cultural Differences:	Variations in attitudes and expectations toward time, planning, scheduling, risk taking, money, relationship building, and so on.
	Differences in goal sets and work styles arising out of such variables as individualism/collectivism, the relative value of work compared with other life factors; variable sets of assumptions, norms, patterns of behavior.
Language and Communications:	Translation difficulties, or at least variations in accents, semantics, terminology, or local jargon.
	Lack of personal and physical contact, which greatly inhibits trust and relationship building in many countries; the social dynamics change.
	Lack of visibility of nonverbal cues makes interpretation difficult and creates two-way noise in the communication process.
Technology:	Variations in availability, speed, acceptability, cost of equipment necessary for meetings and communications through computer-aided systems.
	Variable skill levels and willingness to interact through virtual media.

risks when your storefront stretches for 6000 miles."[22] HBI represents a joint venture of NEC (Japan), Campagnie de Machines Bull (France), and Honeywell (United States). To coordinate this joint venture, HBI considered it important to have transnational teams for front-end involvement in strategic planning, engineering, design, production, and marketing. Dotlich notes that HBI's primary corporate question is how to integrate a diverse pool of cultural values, traditions, and norms in order to be competitive.[23]

Teams comprising people located in far-flung operations are faced with often-conflicting goals of achieving greater efficiency across those operations, responding to local differences, and facilitating organizational learning across boundaries; conflicts arise based on cultural differences, local work norms and environments, and varied time zones. A recent study by Joshi et al. of a thirty-member team of human resources (HR) managers in six countries in the Asia–Pacific region showed that network analysis of the various interactions among team members can reveal when and where negative cross-cultural conflicts occur and so provide MNC top management with information for conflict resolution so that a higher level of synergy may be attained among the group members. The advantages of synergy include a greater opportunity for global competition (by being able to share experiences, technology, and a pool of international managers) and a greater opportunity for cross-cultural understanding and exposure to different viewpoints. The disadvantages include problems resulting from differences in language, communication, and varying managerial styles; complex decision-making processes; fewer promotional opportunities; personality conflicts, often resulting from stereotyping and prejudice; and greater complexity in the workplace.[24] In the Joshi study, the greatest conflict, and therefore lack of synergy, was not, as one would expect, resulting from the headquarters–subsidiary power divide. Rather, the critical conflicts radiated from the Country A subsidiary and Country B subsidiary, given the required communication and workflow patterns between them. (Country names were kept confidential so that individuals in the study would not be identified).

What are other ways that management can ascertain how well its international teams are performing and what areas need to be improved? The following criteria for evaluating the success of such teams have been proposed by Indrei Ratiu of the Intercultural Management Association in Paris:

- Do members work together with a common purpose? Is this purpose spelled out, and do all feel it is worth fighting for?
- Has the team developed a common language or procedure? Does it have a common way of doing things, a process for holding meetings?

- Does the team build on what works, learning to identify the positive actions before being overwhelmed by the negatives?
- Does the team attempt to spell out matters within the limits of the cultural differences involved, delimiting the mystery level by directness and openness regardless of the cultural origins of participants?
- Do the members recognize the impact of their own cultural programming on individual and group behavior? Do they deal with, not avoid, their differences in order to create synergy?
- Does the team have fun? (Within successful multicultural groups, the cultural differences become a source of continuing surprise, discovery, and amusement rather than irritation or frustration.)[25]

The actual level of success of global teams seems disappointing as reported by MNC managers of seventy global teams in a recent study by Govindarajan and Gupta. Of those managers, 82 percent said their teams fell short of their intended goals, and one-third of the teams rated their performance as largely unsuccessful. In recognizing the areas needing better team management, fifty-eight of those executives in the study ranked five key tasks based on their level of importance and also on how difficult it is to accomplish that task. The results are shown in Exhibit 10-4. The researchers concluded from their study that the ability to cultivate trust among team members is critical to the success of global business teams if they want to minimize conflict and encourage cooperation.[26]

Following are some general recommendations the researchers make for improving global teamwork:

- Cultivating a culture of trust: One way to do this is by scheduling face-to-face meetings early on, even if later meetings will be "virtual".
- Rotating meeting locations: This develops global exposure for all team members and also legitimizes each person's position.
- Rotating and diffusing team leadership
- Linking rewards to team performance
- Building social networks among managers from different countries[27]

What other techniques do managers actually use to deal with the challenge of achieving cross-cultural collaboration in multinational horizontal projects? A comparative study of European project groups in several countries by Sylvie Chevrier, published in 2003, revealed three main strategies:[28]

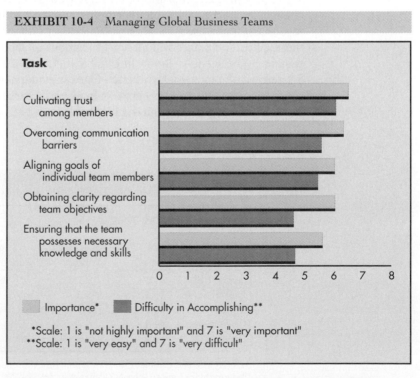

EXHIBIT 10-4 Managing Global Business Teams

SOURCE: Adapted from V. Govindarajan and A. K. Gupta, "Building an Effective Global Business Team," *MIT Sloan Management Review,* Summer 2001, v42, i4, 63.

- **Drawing upon individual tolerance and self-control:** In this R&D consortium, the Swiss manager treated all team members the same, ignoring cultural differences, and the team members coexisted with patience and compromise. Many of the members said they were used to multinational projects and just tried to focus on technical issues.
- **Trial and error processes coupled with personal relationships:** This is a specific strategy in which the project manager sets up social events to facilitate the team members getting acquainted with one another. Then, they discover, through trial and error, what procedures will be acceptable to the group.
- **Setting up transnational cultures:** Here the managers used the common professional, or occupational, culture, such as the engineering profession, to bring the disparate members together within a common understanding and process.

The managers in the study admitted their solutions were not perfect, but met their needs as best they could in the situation. Chevrie suggests that, where possible, a "cultural mediator" should be used who helps team members interpret and understand one another and come to an agreement about processes to achieve organizational goals.[29]

THE ROLE OF WOMEN IN INTERNATIONAL MANAGEMENT

Around the world, women are remaking companies, society, and themselves. But in each country, women have achieved different things, fought different battles—and made different sacrifices.[30]

Opportunities for indigenous female employees to move up the managerial ladder in a given culture depend on the values and expectations regarding the role of women in that society. In Japan, for example, the workplace has traditionally been a male domain as far as managerial careers are concerned (although rapid changes are now taking place). To the older generation, a working married woman represented a loss of face to the husband because it implied that he was not able to support her. Women were usually only allowed clerical positions, under the assumption that they would leave to raise a family and perhaps later return to part-time work. Employers, thus, made little effort to train them for upper level positions.[31] As a result, very few women workers have been in supervisory or managerial posts—thus, limiting the short-term upward mobility of women through the managerial ranks.[32]

The younger generation and increased global competitiveness have brought some changes to traditional values regarding women's roles in Japan. More than 60 percent of Japanese women are now employed, including half of Japanese mothers. But how and when these cultural changes will affect the number of Japanese women in managerial positions remains to be seen. As shown in Exhibit 10-5, as of 2003, Japanese women represented only 8.9 percent of managerial workers.[33] One can understand the problems Japanese women face when trying to enter and progress in managerial careers when we review the experiences of Yuko Suzuki (see Management in Focus: Japan's Neglected Resource—Female Workers).

EXHIBIT 10-5 How Women Fare: A Comparison of Professional Women in Japan to Those in Other Industrialized Countries.

Women as a percentage of . . .	All workers	Managerial workers	Civil service workers General	Managerial	National Parliament/ Congress
Japan	41.0%	8.9%	20.2%	1.4%	7.3%
United States	46.6	46.0	49.3	23.1	14.3
Sweden	48.0	30.5	43.0	51.0	45.3
Germany	44.0	26.9	39.0	9.5	32.2
Britain	44.9	30.0	49.1	17.2	17.9

SOURCES: The Cabinet Office of Japan: International Labor Organization; Inter-Parliamentary Union. www.NYTimes.com, July 24, 2003. Reprinted with permission Copyright 2003 The New York Times Company The New York Times.

Management Focus

Japan's Neglected Resource: Female Workers

Tokyo, July 24—When Yuko Suzuki went into business for herself after the advertising company she worked for went bankrupt, no amount of talk she had heard about the hardships facing professional women here prepared her for the humiliations ahead.

As an independent saleswoman, she found that customers merely pretended to listen to her. Time and again when she finished a presentation, men would ask who her boss was. Eventually she hired a man to go along with her, because merely having a man by her side—even a virtual dummy—increased her sales significantly, if not her morale.

"If I brought a man along, the customers would only establish eye contact with him, even though I was the representative of the company, and doing the talking," she said. "It was very uncomfortable."

Japan has tried all sorts of remedies to pull itself out of a 13-year economic slump, from huge public works projects to bailouts of failing companies. Many experts have concluded that the expanding role of women in professional life could provide a far bigger stimulus than any scheme tried so far.

But it often seems that the Japanese would rather let their economy stagnate than send their women up the corporate ladder. Resistance to expanding women's professional roles remains high in a country where the economic status of women trails far behind that of women in other advanced economies.

"Japan is still a developing country in terms of gender equality," Mariko Bando, an aide to Prime Minister Junichiro Koizumi, recently told reporters. This year the World Economic Forum ranked Japan 69th of 75 member nations in empowering its women.

While 40 percent of Japanese women work, a figure that reflects their rapid, recent entry into the job market, they hold only about 9 percent of managerial positions, compared with about 45 percent in the United States, according to the government and the International Labor Organization. Women's wages, meanwhile, are about 65 percent of those of their male counterparts, one of the largest gaps in the industrial world.

Japanese labor economists and others say it is no wonder, then, that Japan, which looked like a world beater 20 years ago, is struggling to compete economically today. With women sidelined from the career track, Japan is effectively fighting with one hand tied behind its back.

"Japan has gone as far as it can go with a social model that consists of men filling all of the economic, management and political roles," said Eiko Shinotsuka, assistant dean of Ochanomizu University and the first woman to serve on the board of the Bank of Japan.

"People have spoken of the dawn of a women's age here before," she said, "but that was always in relatively good times economically, and the country was able to avoid social change. We've never had such a long economic crisis as this one, though, and people are beginning to recognize that the place of women in our society is an important factor."

By tradition Japanese companies hire men almost exclusively to fill career positions, reserving shorter-term work, mostly clerical tasks and tea serving, for women, who are widely known in such jobs here as office ladies, or simply O.L.'s.

Ms. Suzuki, who went into business for herself, is the exception. These days Ms. Suzuki, an impeccably groomed 32-year-old who dresses in crisp suits and speaks at a rapid, confident clip, is the proud owner of her own company, a short-term office suite rental business in one of Tokyo's smartest quarters. "I am the only professional out of all of my girlhood friends," she said. "The rest are housewives or regular office ladies, and they all say that what has happened to me is unbelievable."

Whatever a woman's qualifications, breaking into the career track requires overcoming entrenched biases, not least the feeling among managers that childbearing is an insupportable disruption.

That is so even though the country faces a steep population decline and keeping women sidelined has had economic costs. Women's relative lack of economic participation may be shaving 0.6 percent off annual growth, a study presented to the Labor Ministry estimated last year.

Meanwhile, at companies where women make up 40 to 50 percent of the staff, average profits are double those where women account for 10 percent or less, the Economy Ministry reported last month.

A recent issue of Weekly Women magazine nonetheless recounted the stories of women who said they had been illegally dismissed because of pregnancy or had sought abortions for fear of being dismissed.

"I reported to my boss that I was pregnant and would like to take off for a medical check," Masumi Honda, a 33-year-old mother was quoted as saying. "When I came home from the hospital, I was shocked that he had just left a message saying that I needn't bother coming to work any more."

Other women say the intense competitive pressure in the workplace can lead to resentment, even in progressive companies, against mothers who avail themselves of child care leave or flexible work hours.

One woman, who abandoned a career in marketing after similar experiences in two companies, recounted taking leave for three days to look after a sick child.

"After that I was not included in new projects," said the woman, who spoke on condition that she not be identified, "and after that I felt they saw me as an unreliable person. I finally decided that if I work in a company,

I must understand the company's spirit, which means I couldn't feel comfortable taking maternal benefits."

The growing sense of urgency in official circles about these issues is driven largely by the projections of a population decline that could cause huge labor shortages over the next half-century and possibly even economic collapse. So far, though, government efforts to expand women's place in the economy have been modest and halting.

An advisory panel appointed by Prime Minister Koizumi recommended recently that the public and private sectors aim to have at least 30 percent of managerial positions filled by women by 2020. These days there is growing talk of affirmative action in Japan.

But changing mind-sets will be difficult. Earlier this year, former Prime Minister Yoshiro Mori, a member of a government commission charged with finding solutions to the population crisis, was widely quoted as saying the main reason for Japan's falling birthrate was the overeducation of its women.

Mr. Koizumi's top aide, Yasuo Fukuda, was recently quoted as saying that often women who are raped deserve it, while a legislator from the governing party said, approvingly, that the men who carried out such acts were virile and "good specimens." The latter comment came last month at a seminar about the falling birthrate.

While senior politicians bemoan overeducation as the cause of Japan's population problems, women unsurprisingly cite other reasons that make it difficult for them to have children and also play a bigger role in the country's economic life.

Foremost is the lack of day care, which for many forces stark choices between motherhood and career. There are also the working hours of many offices, which extend deep into the evening and sometimes all but require social drinking afterward.

Haruko Takachi, 37, a postal manager, is luckier than most. Her child was accepted into a 20-student nursery school opened last year by the Ministry of Education.

It is the only public nursery school available for the 38,000 government employees who work in Kasumigaseki, central Tokyo's administrative district. Unlike most private nurseries, which close earlier, the school remains open until 10 p.m.

"I work until 8 in the evening, but there are plenty of times when I work much later," she said. "That's just the social reality in Japan. There are some other women in my milieu, but most of them have just one child and don't plan for more."

Ms. Suzuki, who founded her own business, has been married for several years and has no children. She regards day care as just a small piece of what is needed in Japan. Men and women, she says, must rethink gender roles—an idea that she hesitantly concludes makes her a feminist.

"Men are really intimidated by professional women in Japan," she said. "But this is still a society where even when it looks like a woman has some authority, the men usually manage to stay on top."

Where one finds limitations on managerial opportunities for women in their own country, obviously even more limitations on their opportunities apply to them as expatriates. Overall, more managerial opportunities are available for American women than for women in most other countries. However, even for American women, who now fill more than 46 percent of the managerial positions at home, commensurate opportunities are not available to them abroad: About 6 percent of North American expatriate managers are women.[34] While in the 1990s, less than 3 percent of German expatriates were women, this figure has steadily increased to 10 percent in 2002.[35] However, opportunities for women at the top ranks in Germany remain very limited. In a Deutsche Bank lecture in May 2004, statistics were discussed that showed that, although women accounted for 47 percent of the total labor force, only 3.7 percent of senior managers in Germany are women.

> *More than any other European economy, Germany has stunted the development of its female business community. None of the Dax index of Germany's top companies has a woman on the board.*
>
> THE FINANCIAL TIMES,
> *June 15, 2004*[36]

The reasons for the different opportunities for women among various countries can often be traced to the cultural expectations of the host countries—the same cultural values that keep women in these countries from the managerial ranks. In Germany, for example, the disparity in opportunities for women can be traced in part to the lifestyles and laws. For example, children attend school only in the mornings, which restricts the ability for both parents to work. Cultural expectations may also contribute to different opportunities for women at the top levels between northern and southern Europe.

The North-South Divide in Europe, Inc. ... Women are far more likely to serve on the boards of Scandanavia's biggest companies than Italy's or Spain's, and attitudes to their promotion remain deeply split.

THE FINANCIAL TIMES,
June 14, 2004[37]

While top boardrooms in Spain and Italy remain almost exclusively male, women occupy 22 percent of board seats in the largest companies in Norway and 20 percent in Sweden. While this phenomenon can be attributed to complex social and cultural issues, firms ought to be aware of the effects on their bottom line. Research by Catalyst, published in 2004, showed that—of the 353 Fortune 500 companies they surveyed—the quartile with the largest proportion of women in top management had a return on equity of 35.1 percent higher than the quartile with the lowest female representation.[38]

The lack of expatriates who are female or represent other minority groups does not reflect their lack of desire to take overseas assignments. Indeed, studies indicate women's strong willingness to work abroad and their considerable success on their assignments. For example, Adler's major study of North American women working as expatriate managers in countries around the world showed that they are, for the most part, successful.[39]

The most difficult job seems to be getting the assignment in the first place. North American executives are reluctant to send women and minorities abroad because they assume they will be subject to the same culturally based biases as at home, or they assume a lack of understanding and acceptance, particularly in certain countries. Research on fifty-two female expatriate managers, for example, shows this assumption to be highly questionable. Adler showed, first and foremost, that foreigners are seen as foreigners; furthermore, a woman who is a foreigner (a *gaijin* in Japan) is not expected to act like a local woman. According to Adler and Izraeli, "Asians see female expatriates as foreigners who happen to be women, not as women who happen to be foreigners." The other women in the study echoed this view. One woman based in Hong Kong noted, "'It doesn't make any difference if you are blue, green, purple, or a frog. If you have the best product at the best price, they'll buy."[40]

Women and minorities represent a significant resource for overseas assignments— whether as expatriates or as host-country nationals—which is underutilized by U.S. companies. Adler studied this phenomenon regarding women and recommends that businesses (1) avoid assuming that a female executive will fail because of the way she will be received or because of problems experienced by female spouses; (2) avoid assuming that a woman will not want to go overseas; and (3) give female managers every chance to succeed by giving them the titles, status, and recognition appropriate to the position—as well as sufficient time to be effective.[41]

WORKING WITHIN LOCAL LABOR RELATIONS SYSTEMS

A New Deal in Europe? With labor's power flagging, serious reforms may be around the corner.

www.businessweek.com,
July14, 2003[42]

The unions are taking it on the chin everywhere.

JOHN C. KORNBLUM,
Chairman, German Unit, Lazard, Freres & Co., July 2003[43]

If you have to close a plant in Italy, in France, in Spain or in Germany, you have to discuss the possibility with the state, the local communities, the trade unions; everybody feels entitled to intervene ... even the Church.

JACOB BITTORELLI,
Former Deputy Chairman of Pirelli[44]

An important variable in implementing strategy and maximizing host-country human resources for productivity is that of the labor relations environment and system within which the managers of a multinational enterprise (MNE) will operate in a foreign country. Differences in economic, political, and legal systems result in considerable variation in labor relations systems across countries. Pan-European firms, for example, are still dealing with disparate national labor and social systems as the European Commission (EC) directors wrestle with the goal of the harmonization of labor laws.[45] In addition, European businesses continue to be undermined by their poor labor relations and by inflexible regulations. As a result, businesses are having to move jobs overseas to cut labor costs, resulting from a refusal of unions to grant any reduction in employment protection or benefits in order to keep the jobs at home. In addition, non-European firms wishing to operate in Europe have to carefully weigh the labor relations systems and their potential effect on strategic and operational decisions. However, some change may be on the horizon to provide relief to businesses in Europe. Recently, unions in Germany, France, and Italy have been losing their battle to derail labor-market reforms by the governments in those countries who are increasingly concerned that excess regulation and benefits to workers are smothering growth opportunities.[46]

The term **labor relations** refers to the process through which managers and workers determine their workplace relationships. This process may be through verbal agreement and job descriptions, or through a union's written labor contract, which has been reached through negotiation in **collective bargaining** between workers and managers. The labor contract determines rights regarding workers' pay, benefits, job duties, firing procedures, retirement, layoffs, and so on.

The prevailing labor relations system in a country is important to the international manager because it can constrain the strategic choices and operational activities of a firm operating there. The three main dimensions of the labor–management relationship that the manager will consider are (1) the participation of labor in the affairs of the firm, especially as this affects performance and well-being; (2) the role and impact of unions in the relationship; and (3) specific human resource policies in terms of recruitment, training, and compensation.[47] Constraints take the form of (1) wage levels that are set by union contracts and leave the foreign firm little flexibility to be globally competitive; (2) limits on the ability of the foreign firm to vary employment levels when necessary; and (3) limitations on the global integration of operations of the foreign firm because of incompatibility and the potential for industrial conflict.[48]

Organized Labor around the World

The percentage of the workforce in trade unions in industrialized countries has declined in the last decade, most notably in Europe (see Exhibit 10-6). This trend is attributable to various factors, including an increase in the proportion of white-collar and service workers as proportionate to manufacturing workers, a rising proportion of temporary and part-time workers, and a reduced belief in unions in the younger generations. However, the numbers do not show the nature of the system in each country. In most countries, a single dominant industrial relations system applies to almost all workers. Both Canada and the United States have two systems—one for the organized and one for the unorganized. Each, according to Adams, has "different rights and duties of

EXHIBIT 10-6	Union Membership as a Percentage of the Workforce	
	1990	**2000**
France	9.2	9.1
Germany	38.5	29.7
Italy	39.2	35.4
Spain	16.8	15
U.K.	38.1	29

"Marching in Place, Europe's Businesses Say They Need a More Flexible Labor Force," *Time International*, May 6, 2002, v159, 17, 58.

the parties, terms and conditions of employment, and structures and processes of decision making." Basically, in North America, an agent represents unionized employees, whereas unorganized employees can only bargain individually, usually with little capability to affect major strategic decisions or policies or conditions of employment.[49]

The traditional trade union structures in Western industrialized societies have been in *industrial unions,* representing all grades of employees in a specific industry, and *craft unions,* based on certain occupational skills. More recently, the structure has been conglomerate unions, representing members in several industries—for example, the metal workers unions in Europe, which cut across industries, and general unions, which are open to most employees within a country.[50] The system of union representation varies among countries. In the United States, most unions are national and represent specific groups of workers—for example, truck drivers or airline pilots—so a company may have to deal with several different national unions. A single U.S. firm—rather than an association of firms representing a worker classification—engages in its own negotiations. In Japan, on the other hand, it is common for a union to represent all workers in a company. In recent years, company unions in Japan have increasingly coordinated their activities, leading to some lengthy strikes.

Industrial labor relations systems across countries can only be understood in the context of the variables in their environment and the sources of origins of unions. These include government regulation of unions, economic and unemployment factors, technological issues, and the influence of religious organizations. Any of the basic processes or concepts of labor unions, therefore, may vary across countries, depending on where and how the parties have their power and achieve their objectives, such as through parliamentary action in Sweden. For example, collective bargaining in the United States and Canada refers to negotiations between a labor union local and management. However, in Europe collective bargaining takes place between the employer's organization and a trade union at the industry level.[51] This difference means that North America's decentralized, plant-level, collective agreements are more detailed than Europe's industry-wide agreements because of the complexity of negotiating myriad details in multi-employer bargaining. In Germany and Austria, for example, such details are delegated to works councils by legal mandate.[52]

The resulting agreements from bargaining also vary around the world. A written, legally binding agreement for a specific period, common in Northern Europe and North America, is less prevalent in Southern Europe and Britain. In Britain, France, and Italy, bargaining is frequently informal and results in a verbal agreement valid only until one party wishes to renegotiate.[53]

Other variables of the collective bargaining process are the objectives of the bargaining and the enforceability of collective agreements. Because of these differences, managers in MNEs overseas realize that they must adapt their labor relations policies to local conditions and regulations. They also need to bear in mind that, while U.S. union membership has declined by about 50 percent in the last twenty years, in Europe, overall, membership is still quite high—though it, too, has been falling but from much higher levels.

Most Europeans are covered by collective agreements, whereas most Americans are not. Unions in Europe are part of a national cooperative culture between government, unions, and management, and they hold more power than in the United States. In June 1998, for example, thousands of employees at the state-owned Air France Airline staged protests in Paris airports against proposed job and pay cuts, thereby causing the government to back down.[54]

Increasing privatization will make governments less vulnerable to this kind of pressure. It is also interesting to note that some labor courts in Europe deal separately with employment matters from unions and works councils. In Japan, labor militancy has long been dead, since labor and management agreed forty years ago on a deal for industrial peace in exchange for job security. Unions in Japan have little official clout, especially in the midst of the Japanese recession.

In addition, not much can be negotiated, since wage rates, working hours, job security, health benefits, overtime work, insurance, and the like are legislated. Local working conditions and employment issues are all that are left to negotiate. In addition, the managers and labor union representatives are usually the same people, a fact that serves to limit confrontation, as well as does the cultural norm of maintaining harmonious relationships. In the industrialized world, tumbling trade barriers are also reducing the power of trade unions because competitive multinational companies have more freedom to choose alternative productive and sourcing locations. Most new union workers—about 75 percent—will be in emerging nations, like China and Mexico, where wages are low and unions are scarce.

In China, although all Chinese and foreign firms with more than 100 employees are required by law to open a branch of the national union, that law is usually ignored, or instituted in name only, putting managers in charge and seldom including workers in any meetings. In Shenzhen, Guangdong, for example, which has become the world's largest and most dynamic manufacturing center—making everything from shoes to Sony PlayStations—workers often work seven days a week, twelve hours a day, at pay often below legal minimums.[55] The order was in response to a sharp rise in labor tension and protests about poor working conditions and industrial accidents. The All-China Federation of Trade Unions claimed that foreign employers often force workers to work overtime, pay no heed to labor-safety regulations, and deliberately find fault with the workers as an excuse to cut their wages or fine them.

> *Liao Yuanxin, local chief of the government's All-China Federation of Trade Unions, listed candidates to represent workers of Neil Pryde, a foreign-run sportswear factory. For union committee member: two workers and two company managers. For vice chairman: the human resources director. For chairman: Huang Hongguang, a top factory boss.*
>
> THE NEW YORK TIMES,
> *December 29, 2003*[56]

Although China wishes to take advantage of capitalism, the police crush efforts to set up independent unions as threats to the Communist Party. Workers feel that local authorities ignore workers rights in order to keep the investors happy.[57]

Convergence versus Divergence in Labor Systems

> *In South Africa, the elimination of apartheid has given rise to a rapidly growing labor movement. The African National Congress is pro-union, and local unions receive assistance from the AFL-CIO branch in Johannesburg.*[58]

Although no clear direction is evident at this point, political changes, external competitive forces, increased open trade, and frequent moves of MNCs around the world are forces working toward convergence in labor systems. **Convergence** occurs as the migration of management and workplace practices around the world reduce workplace disparities from one country to another. This occurs primarily as MNCs seek consistency and coordination among their foreign subsidiaries and as they act as catalysts for change by "exporting" new forms of work organization and industrial relations practices.[59] It also occurs as harmonization is sought, such as for the EC countries, and as competitive pressures in free-trade zones, such as the NAFTA countries, eventually bring about demands for some equalization of benefits for workers.[60] This trend is highlighted in the Management Focus: Unions without Borders? The Case of the Duro Bag Factory in Rio Bravo. It would appear that economic globalization is leading to labor transnationalism and will bring about changes in labor rights and democracy around the world.[61] In East European societies in transition to market economies, for example, newly structured industrial relations systems are being created.[62] Trends in industrial relations, such as the flattening of organizations and the decline in the role of trade unions are viewed by many as global developments pointing to convergence in labor systems.[63]

Management Focus

Unions without Borders? The Case of the Duro Bag Factory in Rio Bravo

In the dusty border town of Rio Bravo, just across the Rio Grande from Pharr, Texas, the Duro Bag Factory churns out the chichi paper bags sold for a dollar at suburban shopping malls throughout the United States.

Eluid Almaguer, an intense, stocky labor activist in his 30s, got a job at the plant in 1998. There he says he saw people lose fingers in machines cutting the cardboard used to stiffen the bottoms of the bags. Safety guards, he explains, were removed from the rollers that imprint designs on the paper lining—the extra time required to clean them was treated as needless lost production. Almaguer recalls that solvent containers didn't carry proper danger warnings, and while workers got dust masks, they were useless for filtering out toxic chemical fumes. "In terms of safety, well, there just wasn't any," he remembers bitterly.

No help was forthcoming from the union at Duro, a *sección,* or local, of the Paper, Cardboard, and Wood Industry Union. The *sección*—part of the Confederation of Mexican Workers (CTM), a pillar of support for the country's ruling bureaucracy since the 1930s—has a contract with the company, a protection agreement in which government-affiliated union leaders are paid to guarantee labor peace. But Duro workers did find assistance abroad, in a nascent cross-border solidarity movement that is emerging as labor's answer to the globalization of capital.

The battle to change conditions in this plant is one of many labor conflicts that have erupted in the past decade from one end of the border to the other. Duro is just one of 3,611 foreign-owned factories employing more than 1.3 million people in Mexico, according to the National Association of Maquiladoras. In cities like Rio Bravo, Ciudad Juarez, and Tijuana, hundreds of thousands of workers stream through plant gates at each shift change—a human wave pouring into communities of cardboard houses and dirt streets.

As *maquiladora*-style production has transformed the Mexican economy, it has also provided a proving ground for a new model of international relationships between workers and unions. This cross-border solidarity movement has created new leverage against employers and has energized the rank-and-file union base in Mexico, Canada, and the United States, while providing immediate material support for embattled workers like those at Duro. Five years ago the AFL-CIO administration of John Sweeney broke from the old cold war policy of former AFL-CIO presidents George Meany and Lane Kirkland, which defended free trade, corporate interests, and U.S. foreign policy. Yet, the newest vision of what an international labor movement could become—based on solidarity from below—is being born not in an office in Washington but in shantytowns along the border.

For Duro workers, this support network is based partly in the Coalition for Justice in the Maquiladoras (CJM), which brings together unions, churches, and community organizations in Mexico, Canada, and the United States. For more than a decade, the coalition has functioned as a resource for Mexican workers trying to fight an economic policy that uses their low wages to encourage further *maquiladora* investment. At Duro, with CJM support, workers began the effort to change conditions by trying to enforce provisions of the union-protection agreement (and Mexican law) that, at least on paper, guarantee overtime pay, profit-sharing, and other rights. As an initial step, they expelled the *seccion*'s general secretary, Jose Ángel García Garces, whom they viewed as too close to company managers. In his place the members elected Almaguer.

Duro's vice president of plastics, Bill Forstrom, says wages start at 60 pesos a day (about $6). A gallon of milk in the supermarket costs 20 pesos—a third of a day's work. According to Consuelo Moreno, a Duro worker, "My daughter had to drop out of school this year because we didn't have the money for her to continue."

Nevertheless, says Almaguer, "people were willing to work at bad-paying jobs. But not under those conditions." The new leaders brought repeated grievances before the plant's human relations manager, Alejandro de la Rosa. "We'd take (our complaints) to his office, and he'd throw us out," Almaguer says. "The company was in violation of at least 50 percent of the contract." In October 1999, the company fired Almaguer. The union's leaders in Mexico City cooperated, excluding him from union membership. Police and guards were called into the plant. But after three days of turmoil, workers forced Almaguer's reinstatement as general secretary. Then, on April 14, 2000, 400 workers refused to go to work as a protest against abusive treatment, and they were later joined by 800 more.

In spring 2000, the contract at Duro expired, and workers drew up a list of demands for a new agreement. They asked for two pairs of safety shoes each year, work clothes, contributions to a savings plan, and a doctor at the plant to take care of injuries. "The company said it owned the factory—they would decide what would be done here," Almaguer recalls.

When workers wouldn't budge, their union's national officials signed a new agreement with the company on June 11, ignoring their demands. By then, workers had decided that enforcing the protection agreement was no longer possible. They struck again. And in front of the factory gates, they began organizing a new, independent, and democratic union.

With the cooperation of the CJM, there was a public protest in August 2000 of hundreds of advocates of independent unionism from Mexico and the United States. In the face of such pressure, the Tamaulipas labor board finally granted the Duro union legal status. Almaguer's house, made of shipping pallets and cardboard, was later burned down in an arson attack, a crime local police refuse to investigate.

SOURCE: Adapted and excerpted from D. Bacon, "Unions without Borders: A New Kind of Internationalism Is Challenging Neoliberal Globalism," *The Nation,* 272, no. 3 (January 22, 2001): 20.

Other pressures toward convergence of labor relations practices around the world come from the activities and monitoring of labor conditions worldwide by various organizations. One of these organizations is the International Labor Organization (ILO)—comprising union, employer, and government representation—whose mission is to ensure that humane conditions of labor are maintained. Other associations of unions in different countries include various international trade secretariats representing workers in specific industries. These include the International Confederation of Free Trade Unions (ICFTU) and the World Confederation of Labor (WCL). The activities and communication channels of these associations provide unions and firms with information about differences in labor conditions around the world.[64] One result of their efforts to provide awareness and changes in labor conditions was the pressure they brought to bear on MNCs operating in South Africa in the late 1980s. The result was the exodus of foreign companies and the eventual repeal of apartheid laws. Now there is a rapidly growing labor union movement there, thanks to the pro-union African National Congress. The AFL-CIO opened an office in Johannesburg and assists the South African unions.[65]

Political and cultural shifts are also behind the new labor law in South Korea, as the country moves from a system founded on paternalism and authoritarianism to one based on more liberal values.[66]

Although forces for convergence are found in labor relations systems around the world, as discussed previously, for the most part, MNCs still adapt their practices largely to the traditions of national industrial relations systems, with considerable pressure to do so. Those companies, in fact, act more like local employers, subject to local and country regulations and practices. Although the reasons for continued divergence in systems seem fewer, they are very strong: Not the least of these reasons are political ideology and the overall social structure and history of industrial practices. It is highly unlikely that China, for example, would accept Western practices that threaten their political ideology. In the European Union (EU), where states are required to maintain parity in wage rates and benefits under the Social Charter of the Maastricht Treaty, a powerful defense of cultural identity and social systems still exists, with considerable resistance by unions to comply with those requirements. Managers in those MNCs also recognize that a considerable gap often exists between the labor laws and the enforcement of those laws—in particular in less developed countries. Exhibit 10-7 shows the major forces for and against convergence in labor relations systems.

The NAFTA and Labor Relations in Mexico

About 40 percent of the total workforce in Mexico is unionized, with about 80 percent of workers in industrial organizations that employ more than twenty-five workers, unionized. However, government control over union activities is very strong, and although some strikes occur, union control over members remains rather weak.[67] MNCs are required by government regulation to hire Mexican nationals for at least 90 percent of their workforce; preference must be given to Mexicans and to union personnel. In reality, however, the government permits hiring exceptions.

EXHIBIT 10-7   Trends in Global Labor Relations Systems

Forces for Global Convergence ← Current System →	Forces to Maintain or Establish Divergent Systems
Global competitiveness	National labor relations systems and traditions
MNC presence or consolidation initiatives	Social systems
Political change	Local regulations and practices
New market economies	Political ideology
Free-trade zones: harmonization	Cultural norms
(EU), competitive forces (NAFTA)	
Technological standardization, IT	
Declining role of unions	
Agencies monitoring world labor practices	

Currently, the only labor issues that are subject to a formal traditional review under the NAFTA labor side pact are minimum wages, child labor, and safety issues. Foreign firms, such as Honeywell, operating in Mexico are faced with pressures from various stakeholders in their dealings with unions. In fact, in early 1998, AFL-CIO president John Sweeney flew to Mexico to try to develop coordinated cross-border organizing and bargaining strategies. Although no deals were made at that time, the seeds were sown in the direction of more open union activity and benefits for employees.

Many foreign firms set up production in Mexico at least in part for the lower wages and overall cost of operating there—utilizing the advantages of the NAFTA—and the Mexican government wants to continue to attract that investment, as it has for many years before NAFTA. Mexican workers claim that some of the large U.S. companies in Mexico violate basic labor rights and cooperate with pro-government labor leaders in Mexico to break up independent unions. Workers there believe that MNCs routinely use blacklists, physical intimidation, and economic pressure against union organization and independent labor groups that oppose Mexican government policies or the pro-government Confederation of Mexican Workers (CTM). GE, for example, has been accused of firing eleven employees in its Juarez plant who were involved in organizing a campaign for the Authentic Labor Front, Mexico's only independent labor group. The company was also accused of blacklisting union activists and circulating the list to some employers. In February 1994, formal complaints were filed with the Department of Labor, National Administration Office (NAO), by two U.S. unions—the Teamsters and the United Electrical, Radio, and Machine Workers Union. (U.S. unions have an interest in increasing wages and benefits in Mexico to offset some of the reasons that American companies take productive facilities there, along with U.S. jobs.) The NAO—set up by the NAFTA to monitor labor policies in the United States, Mexico, and Canada—reviewed complaints that GE may have violated Mexican labor law. That office later ruled that those claims against GE were unsubstantiated; they also ruled that neither the NAO nor its Mexican counterpart could punish other nations for failing to address union-organization rights, although they could issue formal complaints.[68]

This incident illustrates the complexities of labor relations when a firm operates in other countries—particularly with linkages and interdependence among those countries, such as through the NAFTA or the EC. Of interest are the differences among NAFTA nations in labor law in the private sector. For example, while the minimum wage in Mexico is far less than that in Canada or the United States, a number of costly benefits for Mexican workers are required, such as fifteen days of pay for a Christmas bonus and 90 days of severance pay. For comparison, the following section examines labor relations in Germany.

Comparative Management in Focus

Labor Relations in Germany

Companies adopting the voluntary EU company statute, to take effect in October, could be obliged to introduce co-determination if the new company includes significant German interests.

FINANCIAL TIMES,
January 16, 2004[69]

IG Metall has established Germany as a high-wage, high-quality production center. . . . (but) the fact that companies are transferring jobs to other countries is an omen.

M. FICHTER,
Center for Labor Relations, Free University of Berlin[70]

DaimlerChrysler employees at Mercedes factories in Germany have agreed to smaller raises and increased hours after the carmaker threatened to shed 6,000 jobs, adding to pressure for a longer workweek nationwide.

www.nytimes.com,
July 24, 2004[71]

Germany's **codetermination** law *(mitbestimmung)*—which refers to the participation of labor in the management of a firm—mandates representation for unions and salaried employees on the supervisory boards of all companies with more than 2,000 employees and "works councils" of employees at every work site. Unions are well integrated into managerial decision making and can make a positive contribution to corporate competitiveness and restructuring; this seems different from the traditional adversarial relationship of unions and management in the United States. However, the fact is that firms, in the form of affiliated organizations of companies, have to contend with negotiating with powerful industrywide unions. Employment conditions that would be negotiated privately in the United States, for example, are subject to federal mandates in Germany—a model unique in Europe. Under the pressures of global competition, though, German Chancellor Gerhard Schroder proposed reforms in the summer of 2003 that would put downward pressure on the unions' power by making it easier for firms to hire and fire, while simultaneously trimming jobless, health, and pension benefits.[72] The average metalworker, for example, earns around $2,500 a month, works a thirty-five-hour week, and has six weeks of annual vacation. In 2003, Germans on average worked fewer hours than those in any other country than the Netherlands.[73]

Union membership in Germany is voluntary, usually with one union for each major industry, and union power traditionally has been quite strong. Negotiated contracts with firms by the employers' federation stand to be accepted by firms that are members of the federation, or used as a guide for other firms. These contracts, therefore, result in setting the pay scale for about 90 percent of the country's workers.[74]

The union works councils play an active role in hiring, firing, training, and reassignment during times of reorganization and change.[75] Because of the depth of works council penetration into personnel and work organization matters, as required by law, their role has been described by some as "co-manager of the internal labor market."[76] This situation has considerable implications for how managers of MNCs plan to operate in Germany. IG Metall, for example, which is Germany's largest metalworking union, with 2.6 million workers, negotiates guidelines regarding pay, hours, and working conditions on a regional basis. Then, works councils use those guidelines to make local agreements. IG Metall's proactive role on change illustrates the evolving role of unions by leading management thinking instead of reacting to it. In addition, management and workers tend to work together because of the unions' structure. Indeed, such institutional accord is a powerful factor in changing deeply ingrained cultural traits.

Codetermination has clearly helped to modify German managerial style from authoritarian to something more akin to humanitarian, without, it should be noted, altering its capacity for efficiency and effectiveness.[77] This system compares to the lack of integration and active roles for unions in the U.S. auto industry—for example, conditions that limit opportunities for change.

DaimlerChrysler, the German-American company headquartered in Germany, includes a works council in its decision making, as mandated by German law. This means that the company's labor representatives pay close attention to U.S. attitudes, which may lead to changes in the tone of the collective bargaining processes. The two-tiered system of a supervisory and a management board will remain. DaimlerChrysler was one of several companies to exert pressure in 2004 to bring down the high labor costs and taxes in Germany, under the threat of moving its plants elsewhere to remain globally competitive. With the DaimlerChrysler company accounting for about 13 percent of the DAX index of thirty German blue-chip stocks, U.S. shareholders and managers in the company hold some power to bring about change and reduce operating costs in the company—and perhaps eventually in the country. Pay for German production workers has been among the highest in the world, about 150 percent of that in the United States and about ten times that in Mexico. German workers also have the highest number of paid vacation days in the world and prefer short workdays. However, in July 2004, Jürgen Peters, chairman of Germany's powerful IG Metall engineering trade union, announced the agreement with DaimlerChrysler to accept smaller raises and increased working hours, after the company threatened to move 6,000 jobs elsewhere.[78] The agreement followed one by 4,000 Siemens employees in June 2004 to extend their workweek. The DaimlerChrysler agreement prompted the German chancellor, Gerhard Schröder to announce:

> *The agreement between the management board, the works council and IG Metall is a victory for reason.*
>
> GERHARD SCHRÖDER,
> *July 23, 2004*[79]

Foreign companies operating in Germany also have to be aware that termination costs are very high—including severance pay, retraining costs, time to find another job, and so on—and that is assuming the company is successful in terminating the employee in the first place, which is very difficult to do in Europe. This was brought home to Colgate-Palmolive when it tried to close its factory in Hamburg in 1996. The company offered the 500 employees an average of $40,000 each, but the union would not accept, and eventually Colgate had to pay a much higher (undisclosed) amount.

The German model, according to Rudiger Soltwedel of the Institute for the World Economy at Kiel, holds that competition should be based on factors other than cost.[80] Thus, the higher wage level in Germany should be offset by higher-value goods like luxury cars and machine tools, which have been the hallmark of Germany's products. To the extent that the West German unions have established the high-wage, high-skill, and high-value-added production pattern, they have also become dependent on the continued presence of that pattern.[81] In recognition of that dependency, German auto firms are in the process of remaking themselves after the Japanese model—reducing supplies and cutting costs so they can compete on a global scale. However, this social contract, which has underpinned Germany's manufacturing success, is fraying at the edges as Germany's economy weakens under the $100 billion cost of absorbing East Germany and under competitive EU pressures.[82]

Conflicting opinions over the value of co-determination were evident in 2004, as business practices became increasingly subject to EU policies. A major concern was that firms from other countries which were considering cross-border mergers would be discouraged by the EU statute which would oblige them to incorporate co-determination if the new company includes significant German interests.

CONCLUSION

The role of the IHRM department has expanded to meet the strategic needs of the company to develop a competitive global management cadre. Maximizing human resources around the world requires attention to the many categories and combinations of those people, including expatriates, host-country managers, third-country nationals, female and minority resources, global teams, and local employees. Competitive global companies need top managers with global experience and understanding. To that end, attention must be paid to the needs of expatriates before, during, and after their assignments in order to maximize their long-term contributions to the company.

Summary of Key Points

1. Support programs for expatriates should include information from and contact with the home organization, as well as career guidance and support after the overseas assignment.
2. The expatriate's spouse plays a crucial role in the potential retention and effectiveness of the manager in host locations. Companies should ensure the spouse's interest in the assignment, include him or her in the predeparture training, and provide career and family support during the assignment and upon return.
3. Global management teams offer greater opportunities for competition—by sharing experiences, technology, and international managers—and greater opportunities for cross-cultural understanding and exposure to different viewpoints. Disadvantages can result from communication and cross-cultural conflicts and greater complexity in the workplace.

4. Women and minorities represent an underutilized resource in international management. A major reason for this situation is the assumption that culturally based biases may limit the opportunities and success of females and minorities.
5. Labor relations refers to the process through which managers and workers determine their workplace relationships. The labor relations environment, system, and processes vary around the world and affect how the international manager must plan strategy and maximize the productivity of local human resources.

Discussion Questions

1. What steps can the company's IHRM department take to maximize the effectiveness of the expatriate's assignment and the long-term benefit to the company?
2. Discuss the role of reverse culture shock in the repatriation process. What can companies do to avoid this problem? What kinds of skills do managers learn from a foreign assignment, and how can the company benefit from them? What is the role of repatriation in the company's global competitive situation?
3. What are the reasons for the small numbers of American female expatriates? What more can companies do to use women and minorities as a resource for international management?
4. Discuss the role of international management teams relative to the level of a company's global involvement. Give some examples of the kinds of teams that might be necessary and what issues they would face.

Application Exercise

Interview one or more managers who have held positions overseas. Try to find a man and a woman. Ask them about their experiences both in the working environment and in the foreign country generally. How did they and their families adapt? How did they find the stage of reentry to headquarters, and what were the effects of the assignment on their career progression? What differences do you notice, if any, between the experiences of the male and the female expatriates?

Experiential Exercise

Form groups of six students, divided into two teams, one representing union members from a German company and the other representing union members from a Mexican company. These companies have recently merged in a joint venture, with the subsidiary to be located in Mexico. These union workers, all line supervisors, will be working together in Mexico. You are to negotiate six major points of agreement regarding union representation, bargaining rights, and worker participation in management, as discussed in this chapter. Present your findings to the other groups in the class and discuss.

Internet Resources

Visit the Deresky companion Website at http://prenhall. com/deresky for this chapter's Internet resources.

Avon in Global Markets: Managing and Developing a Global Workforce

Avon is ready to speak your language, in over 100 countries across the globe. We are knocking on more doors than ever, looking for you—to buy or to sell Avon products—in your own special corner of the world.—Avon is a leader in beauty and a powerhouse in direct selling. For our customer, we are a trusted name—ever constant, ever changing. We're getting bigger and bolder every day, and this is our mission.

www.avon.com,
May 2004

Avon Products, Inc. (hereafter called Avon) is the largest direct seller of personal care products and is the brand to be reckoned with. The company targets young as well as middle-aged customers in over 100 countries. In 2004, Avon has 45,900 associates and over 4 million independent representatives worldwide. The company is one of the well-established brands in the $90 billion toiletries/cosmetics and household nondurables industry.[1] In 1999, Andrea Jung was named the first female CEO of the company. Since taking charge, Jung has reinvigorated the company and implemented many timely changes in the U.S. and global markets. It is no longer the same company that faced sluggish sales and debt problems in the eighties.[2] In 2003, Avon's revenues surpassed $6.87 billion and profit was $664.8 million. Over 60 percent of the company's revenues come from selling its products in international markets. According to *Fortune* magazine's 2004 annual business rankings, the company is one of the most admired companies in the area of household nondurables and personal products and consistently receives good ratings from the industry (see Table 1 and Figure 1). Regarding brand identity, corporate reputation, and sales network, Avon is truly a global brand for the masses. In addition, in the area of minority recruitment, Avon always receives good ratings by the analysts.[3]

Right from its inception, direct selling has been Avon's major strength in the U.S. and global markets. Other companies (Mary Kay and Amway) that capitalized on the direct selling model equally excel in their target markets and have made phenomenal expansion overseas.[4] In global markets, Avon's major competitors include Proctor & Gamble, Johnson & Johnson, Pfizer, Sara Lee, Gillette, Wyeth, Estée Lauder, L'Oreal, and Unilever.[5] Avon also sells through catalogs, mall kiosks, and a Web-based store. Beyond its personal care products and cosmetics, the company has expanded in other areas that include fragrances, toiletries, jewelry, apparel, and home furnishings. Avon's products/brand names include Avon Color, Avon Skincare, Avon Bath & Body, Avon Hair Care, Avon Wellness, Avon Fragrance, beComing, and Mark.[6]

Managing and Developing a Global Workforce

In global business, a company's workforce and sales people are the main representatives, taking orders and dealing with customers on a daily basis in consumer and industrial markets. Becoming aware of intercultural differences and getting the appropriate training play an important role in the development of a productive sales force. Areas that are important in the development of a good workforce include cultural sensitivity, motivation, ethical

SOURCE: Written exclusively for this book by Syed Tariq Anwar. Copyright © Syed Tariq Anwar, May 2004. *The material in this case is intended to be used as a basis for classroom/academic discussion rather than to illustrate either effective or ineffective handling of a managerial situation or business practices.*
[1]See: Company Web site (www.avon.com); *Standard & Poor's Industry Surveys.* (2003). "Industry surveys: Household nondurables," (December 18), pp. 1–25; *Value Line.* (2004). "Avon Products", (April 2), p. 821; *The Wall Street Journal.* (2003). "An unlikely rival challenge L'Oreal in beauty market," (January 9), pp. A1 & A6.
[2]*Business Week.* (1991). "Despite the face-lift, Avon is sagging," (December 2), pp. 101–102; *The Economist.* (1996). "Scents and sensibility," (July 13), pp. 57–58.
[3]For detail, see: *Business Week.* (2000). "Avon: The new calling," (September 18), pp. 136–148; *Fortune.* (2004). *Fortune* Global 500, (April 5), pp. F1–F72; *Fortune.* (2004). "America's most admired companies," (March 8), p. 112; *Business Week.* (2003). "The 100 top brands," (August 4), pp. 72–78; Hoover's.com (www.hoover.com).

[4]In 2003, Mary Kay's worldwide revenues surpassed $1.2 billion and maintained operations in thirty countries. Amway, on the other hand, had operations in eighty countries and its sales totaled $4.5 billion. For more information, see: www.marykay.com; www.amway.com; Cort, Kathryn T. and William L. Shanklin. (1999)." The Wall: How Mary Kay Cosmetics knocks it down," *Marketing Management,* (Fall/Winter), 42–46; Underwood, Jim. (2004). *More Than a Pink Cadillac: Mary Kay Inc.'s 9 Leadership Keys to Success,* New York: American Media International; Cross, Wilbur. (1999). *Amway: The True Story of the Company that Transformed the Lives of Millions,* New York: Berkeley Publishing Group.
[5]For detail, see: Hoover's.com (www.hoover.com); *Standard & Poor's Industry Surveys.* (2003). "Industry surveys: Household nondurables," (December 18), pp. 1–25; *The Wall Street Journal.* (2003). "An unlikely rival challenge L'Oreal in beauty market, (January 9), pp. A1 & A6.
[6]For detail, see: Company Web site (www.avon.com).

Table 1   Avon Products, Inc.: Selected Company Data

A. Company data (2003):

Senior Management:

Chairman and CEO:	Andrea Jung
President and COO:	Susan J. Kropf
Senior VP, Corporate Strategy/Bus. Development:	Gina Boswell
Executive VP & CFO:	Robert J. Corti

Financial Data (2003):

Sales:	$6.87 bil. (change: 1.4%)
Net income:	$664.8 mil. (change: 24.4%)
Market value:	$16.83 bil. (March 2004)
Assets:	$3.36 bil.
Company type:	Public (listed on NYSE)

Other Data and Rankings:

Total employees:	45,900 (change: 2%)
Independent sales representatives:	4.4 mil.
Ranking in *Fortune* 500 (2004):	275 (based on sales)
Ranking in *Fortune's* "most admired companies" (household/personal products; 2004):	3 (score: 6.59 out of 10)
Ranking in *Business Week's* 100 most valuable global brands (2003):	57 (brand value: $4.63 bil.)
Percentage of global sales (2003):	
North America:	38%
Europe:	20%
Latin America:	28%
Asia/Pacific:	13%

B. Major competitors of Avon:

Total global cosmetics/beauty Industry (2003): $90 billion

Major competitors: Proctor & Gamble, Johnson & Johnson, Pfizer, Sara Lee, Gillette Company, Wyeth, Estée Lauder, Tommy Hilfiger, L'Oreal, and Unilever.

SOURCE: Company Web site, May 2004, (www.avon.com); Hoover's.com (www.hoovers.com); *Business Week.* (2003). "The 100 top brands," (August 4), pp. 72–78; *Forbes.* (2004). "The world's 2000 leading companies, (April 12), pp. 144–22; *Fortune.* (2004). "America most admired companies," (March 8), p. 112; *Fortune.* (2004). *Fortune* Global 500, (April 5), pp. F1–F72; *Standard & Poor's Industry Surveys.* (2003). "Industry surveys: Household nondurables," (December 18), pp. 1–25; *Value Line.* (2004). "Avon Products," (April 2), p. 821.

standards, relationship building, and organizational skills.[7] Standard international human resource training encompasses areas that deal with hiring and firing, absenteeism, team building, and creating good leadership skills. In addition, valuing workplace diversity and providing equal opportunity is important as well.[8] No matter what HR programs pursued by companies, commitment on the part of top management is critical in developing the workforce. The jobs of sales people and company representatives become even more critical with door-to-door selling and diverse markets. Organizing the workforce in the new markets and dealing with a variety of industrial labor relations around the world can be a daunting task.

Equally important areas are hiring, training, and, above all, retaining the best employees (see Table 2). In the case of Avon, effective management of its global workforce is crucial to the company's strategy since it maintains over 4 million independent representatives and 45,900 associates in hundred countries (see Figure 1). In international business, consumer companies cannot operate efficiently without having the best and [most] well-trained workforce. Like other companies, Avon runs leadership programs and on-the job training seminars on a regular basis. The company particularly maintains high standards in four areas that affect the sales force productivity and future retention (i.e., compensation, fringe benefits, professional development, and workforce environment). Avon's five values and principles include: trust, respect, belief, humility, and integrity. Interestingly, Avon has also been one of the first-movers in workforce diversity and minority recruitment in the United States and over 86 percent of management positions in the

---

[7]Kotabe, Masaaki and Kristiaan Helsen. (2004). *Global Marketing Management,* 3rd edition, New York: John Wiley & Sons, pp. 452–476.
[8]Deresky, Helen. (2003). *International Management: Managing across Borders and Cultures,* 4th edition, Upper Saddle River, New Jersey: Prentice Hall, pp. 415–441.

FIGURE 1. Avon's Global Operations in 2004

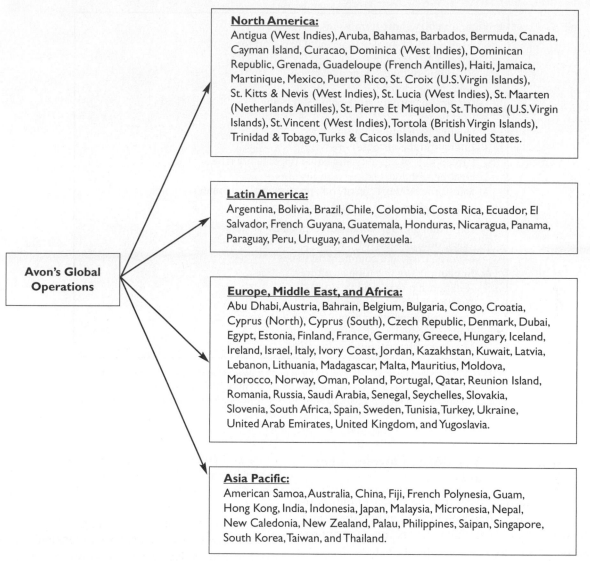

North America:
Antigua (West Indies), Aruba, Bahamas, Barbados, Bermuda, Canada, Cayman Island, Curacao, Dominica (West Indies), Dominican Republic, Grenada, Guadeloupe (French Antilles), Haiti, Jamaica, Martinique, Mexico, Puerto Rico, St. Croix (U.S. Virgin Islands), St. Kitts & Nevis (West Indies), St. Lucia (West Indies), St. Maarten (Netherlands Antilles), St. Pierre Et Miquelon, St. Thomas (U.S. Virgin Islands), St. Vincent (West Indies), Tortola (British Virgin Islands), Trinidad & Tobago, Turks & Caicos Islands, and United States.

Latin America:
Argentina, Bolivia, Brazil, Chile, Colombia, Costa Rica, Ecuador, El Salvador, French Guyana, Guatemala, Honduras, Nicaragua, Panama, Paraguay, Peru, Uruguay, and Venezuela.

Avon's Global Operations

Europe, Middle East, and Africa:
Abu Dhabi, Austria, Bahrain, Belgium, Bulgaria, Congo, Croatia, Cyprus (North), Cyprus (South), Czech Republic, Denmark, Dubai, Egypt, Estonia, Finland, France, Germany, Greece, Hungary, Iceland, Ireland, Israel, Italy, Ivory Coast, Jordan, Kazakhstan, Kuwait, Latvia, Lebanon, Lithuania, Madagascar, Malta, Mauritius, Moldova, Morocco, Norway, Oman, Poland, Portugal, Qatar, Reunion Island, Romania, Russia, Saudi Arabia, Senegal, Seychelles, Slovakia, Slovenia, South Africa, Spain, Sweden, Tunisia, Turkey, Ukraine, United Arab Emirates, United Kingdom, and Yugoslavia.

Asia Pacific:
American Samoa, Australia, China, Fiji, French Polynesia, Guam, Hong Kong, India, Indonesia, Japan, Malaysia, Micronesia, Nepal, New Caledonia, New Zealand, Palau, Philippines, Saipan, Singapore, South Korea, Taiwan, and Thailand.

SOURCE: Company Web site (www.avon.com).

company are held by women. The company conspicuously follows what it preaches in its corporate philosophy. Avon's vision states:

> To be the company that best understands and satisfies the product, service and self-fulfillment needs of women—globally.[9]

In addition, 50 percent of the company's Board of Directors is female.[10] The same is true in international markets where the majority of the company staff and independent representatives are females, making the company a good employer and a role model in women's well-being and employment opportunities. Of course, the nature of the company's product lines and operations deal with areas that attract women from all walks of life.[11] Furthermore, through the Avon Foundation, the company generously provides funding for cancer research, education, and other charitable programs. The company has been one of the major supporters of women's issues in North America and overseas. This creates commitment, harmony, and a supportive work environment that has been beneficial to the company. In 2004, Avon foundation's projects include breast cancer programs in the areas of education, outreach and support services, screening, diagnostic and treatment services, and medical research and clinical care. Besides this, the company supports various programs in women's empowerment, and arts and humanities.[12]

[9]See: Company Web site (www.avon.com).
[10]See: Company Web site (www.avon.com).

[11]For a good discussion on this topic, see: Martin, Joanne, Kathleen Knopoff, and Christine Beckman. (2001). "An alternative to bureaucratic impersonality and emotional labor: Bounded emotionality at the Body Shop," *Administrative Science Quarterly,* Vol. 43, pp. 429–469.
[12]For detail see: Company Web site (www.avon.com).

Table 2   Human Resource Issues of Market Entry and Workforce Management

Pre-market entry/short-term issues:
  - Availability of local management and workforce
  - Expatriate recruiting
  - Recruitment methods and selection
  - Sales force training
  - Cultural sensitivity/cross-cultural training
  - Cost issues
  - Dealing with labor relations/laws
  - Intercultural considerations
  - Perceptions of equality and equal opportunity issues
  - Dealing with local labor relations/laws
  - Salesforce strategy (territorial, product, and customer)

Post-market entry/long-term issues:
  - Job training/professional development
  - Sales force productivity issues
  - Control, trust, and commitment issues
  - Implanting organizational culture
  - Relationship marketing
  - Acculturation/adaptation issues
  - Supervision/mentoring (motivation and ethical perceptions)
  - Building global/local management teams
  - Managing diversity/multiculturalism

SOURCE: Deresky, Helen. (2003). *International Management: Managing across Borders and Cultures,* 4th edition, Upper Saddle River, New Jersey: Prentice Hall, pp. 415–441; Kotabe, Masaaki and Kristiaan Helsen. (2004). *Global Marketing Management,* 3rd edition, New York: John Wiley & Sons, pp. 452–476.

Future Growth and Workforce Development in Multicultural Markets

In 2004, the toiletries/cosmetics and household non-durables industry has done well in the United States and global markets. In international markets, methods of production, manufacturing, and competition have become truly global, fetching companies additional opportunities and growth.[13] This is also attributed to the globalization phenomenon, strong consumer demand, changing demographics, better household income, and supply chain efficiencies.[14] Like other manufacturers, Avon has done well, and the company's sales and profits have gone up. Avon's market share is growing in China, Russia, Eastern Europe, emerging markets, and selected developing countries. In the coming years, from population and growth perspectives, countries such as China, India, Indonesia, Brazil, Pakistan, Bangladesh, and Russia carry huge opportunities for Avon and other players in the toiletries/cosmetics and household nondurables industry. These countries either have a large population or maintain a well-educated middle class which is a prerequisite for the toiletries/cosmetics industry (see Table 3). Like

other companies, Avon may have to adapt its business model because of local considerations and supply chain issues. Consequently, these forces will help expand Avon's workforce as well as its market share.

In global markets, Avon is in a better position to attract productive workforce because of its well-established sales network and a strong brand identity.[15] Avon is particularly interested in expanding operations in China, although in 1998 the Chinese government banned door-to-door selling and made changes in the industry. Since China became a member of the World Trade Organization (WTO) in 2001, more structural changes are expected in the Chinese market.[16] For Avon, the Chinese market is a win-win situation and is expected to generate 10 percent of the company's Asian revenues. Currently, Avon maintains 5,500 beauty boutiques in China and over 700,000 loyal members. In 2004, the company announced plans to open 500 additional boutiques and will acquire its

---

[13]Mytelka, Lynn K. (2000). "Local systems of innovation in a globalized world economy," *Industry and Innovation,* Vol. 7, No. 1, pp. 15–32.
[14]Ghemawat, Pankaj. (2003). "Globalization: The strategy of differences," *HBS Working Knowledge,* (November 10), pp. 1–4 (www.hbswk.hbs.edu).

[15]*Business Week.* (2003). "The 100 top brands," (August 4), pp. 72–78; *Global Cosmetics Industry.* (2003). "Top Global Brands," (February), pp. 28–33.
[16]For more discussion, see: Yeung, Godfrey and Vincent Mok. (2003). "WTO accession and the managerial challenge for manufacturing sectors in China," *Asia Pacific Business Review,* Vol. 9, No. 2, pp. 1360–1380; Zhang, Xin. (2001). "Distribution rights in China: Regulatory barriers and reform in the WTO context," *Journal of World Trade,* Vol. 35, No. 6, pp. 1247–1291.

Table 3   Most Populous Countries and Per Capita GDP

Rank/Country	Population (2003)	Population (2025)	Per Capita GDP (2003)
1. China	1,288.7 mil.	1,454.7 mil.	$1,090 (exchange rate based)
2. India	1,068.6	1,363.0	480
3. United States	291.5	351.1	32,000
4. Indonesia	220.5	281.9	796
5. Brazil	176.5	211.2	2,820
6. Pakistan	149.1	249.7	2,100 (PPP)
7. Bangladesh	146.7	208.3	389
8. Russia	145.5	136.9	2,320

Purchasing power parity.
Standard & Poor's Industry Surveys. (2003). Industry surveys: Household nondurables, (December 18), pp. 1-25;
Bureau of Public Affair. (2004). "Background Notes," *U.S. Department of State,*
(http://www.state.gov/r/pa/ei/bgn/).

Chinese partner Masson for $50 million.[17] Because of shorter life cycles and [a] rising middle class, new products and markets are the key to success in the emerging markets. Since the company continues to grow in international markets, it will keep hiring and training the new workforce in its door-to-door selling model. The company's distribution strategies may have to be adapted to the local needs because of working women or other cultural and logistical considerations and include mail, phone, fax, retail outlets, and Web sites.[18] Market

entry issues and workforce management will have a big impact on Avon's future expansion in international markets. In conclusion, Avon definitely carries a significant advantage over its rivals because of a well-organized and trained sales force, and above all, 4.4 million independent representatives in global markets. *Financial Times* correctly comments on Jung's future strategies:

The younger generation is just one area where Ms. Jung sees growth potential. Another is China and the emerging markets, a region she calls 'Avon heaven.' Ms. Jung believes China, which is among Avon's top markets, offers its biggest growth opportunity.[19]

[17]For more information, see: *Chinadaily.* (2004). "Avon moves to enhance presence in China," (March 22), pp. 1–2 (www.chinadaily.com); *Far Eastern Economic Review.* (1998). "Cosmetic surgery," (October 22), pp. 64–65; *The Wall Street Journal.* (2003). "Avon, seeing China's potential, sets aggressive plan for growth," (October 23), p. B2.
[18]*Standard & Poor's Industry Surveys.* (2003). "Industry surveys: Household nondurables," (December 18), pp. 1–25.

[19]*Financial Times.* (2003). "Mistress of the turnaround answers Avon's calling," (November 3), p. 8.

CASE QUESTIONS

1. Evaluate Avon's operations in global markets regarding the use of international cadre development and building company associates and independent representatives.
2. Since 60 percent of Avon's revenues are generated outside the United States, what recommendations do you provide to the company regarding dealing with culturally diverse workforce and multicultural marketplace in the coming years?
3. In the coming years, Avon's future global expansion is contingent on hiring and retaining the best workforce and sales people in global markets. What training and cross-cultural strategies do you recommend to the company to deal with this area?
4. China is expected to be a major market for Avon. If you were to advise Avon, how would you develop a competitive IHR plan for the company?

CHAPTER

11

Motivating and Leading

Outline

Opening Profile: Fujitsu Uses Pay Cuts as a Motivational Tool

TOKYO, Jan. 26, 2004 Taking a page from Japan's human resource handbook, Fujitsu will cut the salaries of around 14,000 managers to motivate them—and their subordinates—to work harder.

Fujitsu, one of the world's largest makers of computer and telecommunications equipment, hopes to return to a profit soon for the first time in three years. The company is betting that the pay cuts will push managers to rally rank-and-file workers in the remaining months of the fiscal year, which ends March 31.

The pay cuts, will be "several percent" from each paycheck and will start at the section chief level and go up, a spokeswoman for Fujitsu, Yuri Momomoto, said. The cuts will take effect from now to March. If Fujitsu meets its goal of 30 billion yen ($281.6 million) in profit for the year, the managers might have their full salaries restored, Ms. Momomoto said.

The pay cuts are not meant to meet any particular financial goal, she said, but rather to build a sense of urgency and team spirit. While the step might seem counterintuitive to American sensibilities, in Japan it makes sense. Workers here often feel a strong kinship to their employers, especially in times of crisis. Under this logic, employees will work harder if they see their managers making sacrifices for the sake of the group.

> Top executives in Japan often volunteer to take temporary pay cuts when a company performs poorly or is embroiled in scandal, even if the executives are not directly responsible.
>
> In Fujitsu's case, by forcing all managers, regardless of rank or division, to take pay cuts, the company can distribute the pain evenly and avoid blaming any one group for the company's shortcomings.
>
> By cutting salaries, Fujitsu can also avoid eliminating jobs, a process that is complicated by Japan's labor laws.
>
> ---
>
> SOURCE: www.nytimes.com, January 27, 2004, Copyright © 2004. *The New York Times Company,* used with permission.

Motivating

The Westerners can't understand that we need the fork on our neck, not all these nice words and baby techniques. The Technique is the fork.

Russian Middle Manager, 2002[1]

After managers set up a firm's operations by planning strategy, organizing the work and responsibilities, and staffing those operations, they turn their attention to everyday activities. This ongoing behavior of individual people carrying out various daily tasks enables the firm to accomplish its objectives. Getting those people to perform their jobs efficiently and effectively is at the heart of the manager's challenge.

Motivation—and therefore appropriate leadership style—is affected by many powerful variables (societal, cultural, and political). When considering the Japanese culture, for example, discussed throughout this book, it is not surprising to find that Fujitsu uses some motivational techniques very different from those in the West, as illustrated in the opening profile. Clearly Fujitsu's decision to cut pay is based on the Japanese tradition of "sink or swim" with co-workers and employer.

Our objective in this chapter is to consider motivation and leadership in the context of diverse cultural milieus. We need to know what, if any, differences exist in the societal factors that elicit and maintain behaviors leading to high employee productivity and job satisfaction. Are effective motivational and leadership techniques universal or culture based?

CROSS-CULTURAL RESEARCH ON MOTIVATION

Motivation is very much a function of the context of a person's work and personal life. That context is greatly influenced by cultural variables, which affect the attitudes and behaviors of individuals (and groups) on the job. The framework of this context was described in Chapter 3 and illustrated in Exhibit 3-1. In applying Hofstede's research on the cultural dimensions of individualism—uncertainty avoidance, masculinity, and power distance, for example—we can make some generalized assumptions about motivation, such as the following:

- High uncertainty avoidance suggests the need for job security, whereas people with low uncertainty avoidance would probably be motivated by more risky opportunities for variety and fast-track advancement.
- High power distance suggests motivators in the relationship between subordinates and a boss, whereas low power distance implies that people would be more motivated by teamwork and relations with peers.

- High individualism suggests people would be motivated by opportunities for individual advancement and autonomy; collectivism (low individualism) suggests that motivation will more likely work through appeals to group goals and support.
- High masculinity suggests that most people would be more comfortable with the traditional division of work and roles; in a more feminine culture, the boundaries could be looser, motivating people through more flexible roles and work networks.

Misjudging the importance of these cultural variables in the workplace may result not only in a failure to motivate but also in demotivation. Rieger and Wong-Rieger present the following example:

> In Thailand, the introduction of an individual merit bonus plan, which runs counter to the societal norm of group cooperation, may result in a decline rather than an increase in productivity from employees who refuse to openly compete with each other.2

In considering what motivates people, we have to understand their needs, goals, value systems, and expectations. No matter what their nationality or cultural background, people are driven to fulfill needs and to achieve goals. But what are those needs, what goals do they want to achieve, and what can motivate that drive to satisfy their goals?

The Meaning of Work

Because the focus in this text is on the needs that affect the working environment, it is important to understand first what work means to people from different backgrounds. For most people, the basic meaning of work is tied to economic necessity (money for food, housing, and so forth) for the individual and for society. However, the additional connotations of work are more subjective, especially about what work provides other than money—achievement, honor, social contacts, and so on.

Another way to view work, however, is through its relationship to the rest of a person's life. The Thais call work *ngan,* which is the same as the Thai word for "play," and they tend to introduce periods of play in their workdays. On the other hand, most people in China, Germany, and the United States have a more serious attitude toward work. Especially in work-oriented China, seven-day work weeks with long hours and few days off are common. A study of average work hours in various countries conducted by Steers found that Koreans worked longer hours and took fewer vacation days than workers in Thailand, Hong Kong, Taiwan, Singapore, India, Japan, and Indonesia.[3] The study concluded that the Koreans' hard work was attributable to loyalty to the company, group-oriented achievement, and emphasis on group harmony and business relationships.

Studies on the meaning of work in eight countries were carried out by George England and a group of researchers who are called the Meaning of Work (MOW) International Research Team.[4] Their research sought to determine a person's idea of the relative importance of work compared to that of leisure, community, religion, and family. They called this concept of work **work centrality,** defined as "the degree of general importance that working has in the life of an individual at any given point in time." The mean score on the work centrality index for the eight countries studied is shown in Exhibit 11-1. Clearly the Japanese hold work to be very important in their lives.

The obvious general implication from these findings is that the higher the mean work centrality score, the more motivated and committed the workers will be. Of even more importance to managers (as an aid to understanding culture-based differences in motivation) are the specific reasons for valuing work. What kinds of needs does the working environment satisfy, and how does that psychological contract differ among populations?

The MOW research team provided some excellent insights into this question when it asked people in the eight countries to what extent they regarded work as satisfying six different functions: Work (1) provides a needed income, (2) is interesting and satisfying, (3) provides contacts with others, (4) facilitates a way to serve society, (5) keeps one occupied, and (6) gives status and prestige. The results are shown in Exhibit 11-2. Note the similarities of some of these functions with Maslow's need categories and Herzberg's categories of motivators and maintenance factors. Clearly, these studies can help international managers

EXHIBIT 11-1   The Relative Meaning of Work in Eight Countries

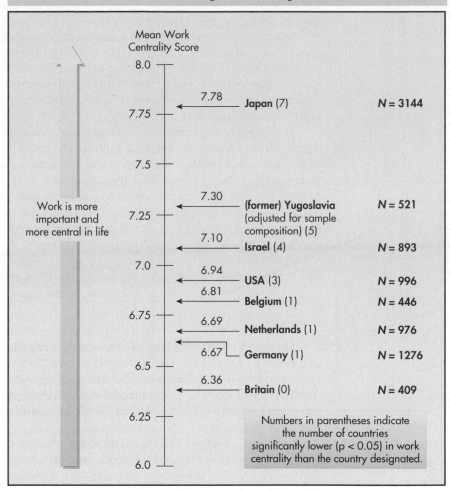

SOURCE: MOW International Research Team, *The Meaning of Working: An International Perspective* (London: Academic Press, 1985).

EXHIBIT 11-2   The Perceived Utility of the Functions of Work (Mean Number of Points)

Country	N	Working provides you with an income that is needed	Working is basically interesting and satisfying to you	Working permits you to have interesting contacts with other people	Working is a useful way for you to serve society	Working keeps you occupied	Working gives you status and prestige
Japan	3180	45.4	13.4	14.7	9.3	11.5*	5.6‡
Germany	1264	40.5	16.7	13.1	7.4	11.8	10.1
Belgium	447	35.5	21.3	17.3	10.2	8.7	6.9
Britain	471	34.4	17.9	15.3	10.5	11.0	10.9
Yugoslavia	522	34.1	19.8	9.8	15.1	11.7	9.3
United States	989	33.1	16.8	15.3	11.5	11.3	11.9
Israel	940	31.1	26.2	11.1	13.6	9.4	8.5
Netherlands	979	26.2	23.5	17.9	16.7	10.6	4.9
All countries combined	8792	35.0†	19.5	14.3	11.8	10.8	8.5

*Working keeps you occupied *was translated in Japan in such a manner that there is real question about how similar its meaning was to that intended.*

†*The combined totals weight each country equally regardless of sample size.*

‡*The mean points assigned by a country to the six functions add to approximately 100 points.*

SOURCE: Meaning of Work International Research Team, *The Meaning of Working: An International Perspective* (London: Academic Press, 1985).

to anticipate what attitudes people have toward their work, what aspects of work in their life context are meaningful to them, and therefore what approach the manager should take in setting up motivation and incentive plans.

In addition to the differences among countries within each category—such as the higher level of interest and satisfaction derived from work by the Israelis as compared with the Germans—it is interesting to note the within-country differences. Although income was the most important factor for all countries, it apparently has a far greater importance than any other factor in Japan. In other countries, such as the Netherlands, the relative importance of different factors was more evenly distributed.

The broader implications of such comparisons about what work means to people are derived from considering the total cultural context. The low rating given by the Japanese to the status and prestige found in work, for instance, suggests that those needs are more fully satisfied elsewhere in their lives, such as within the family and community. In the Middle East, religion plays a major role in all aspects of life, including work. The Islamic work ethic is a commitment toward fulfillment, and so business motives are held in the highest regard.[5] The origin of the Islamic work ethic is in the Muslim holy book, the Qur'an, and the words of the Prophet Mohammed:

> On the day of judgment, the honest Muslim merchant will stand side by side with the martyrs.

> MOHAMMED

Muslims feel that work is a virtue and an obligation to establish equilibrium in one's individual and social life. The Arab worker is defined by his or her level of commitment to family, and work is perceived as the determining factor in the ability to enjoy social and family life.[6] A study of 117 managers in Saudi Arabia by Ali found that Arab managers are highly committed to the Islamic work ethic and that there is a moderate tendency toward individualism.[7]

Exhibit 11-3 shows the results of the study and gives more insight into the Islamic work ethic. Another study by Kuroda and Suzuki found that Arabs are serious about their work and that favoritism, give-and-take, and paternalism have no place in the Arab

EXHIBIT 11-3 The Islamic Work Ethic: Responses by Saudi Arabian Managers

Item	Mean*
Islamic Work Ethic	
1. Laziness is a vice.	4.66
2. Dedication to work is a virtue.	4.62
3. Good work benefits both one's self and others.	4.57
4. Justice and generosity in the workplace are necessary conditions for society's welfare.	4.59
5. Producing more than enough to meet one's personal needs contributes to the prosperity of society as a whole.	3.71
6. One should carry work out to the best of one's ability.	4.70
7. Work is not an end in itself but a means to foster personal growth and social relations.	3.97
8. Life has no meaning without work.	4.47
9. More leisure time is good for society.	3.08
10. Human relations in organizations should be emphasized and encouraged.	3.89
11. Work enables man to control nature.	4.06
12. Creative work is a source of happiness and accomplishment.	4.60
13. Any man who works is more likely to get ahead in life.	3.92
14. Work gives one the chance to be independent.	4.35
15. A successful man is the one who meets deadlines at work.	4.17
16. One should constantly work hard to meet responsibilities.	4.25
17. The value of work is derived from the accompanying intention rather than its results.	3.16

*On scale of 1–5 (5 highest)

SOURCE: Adapted from Abbas J. Ali, "The Islamic Work Ethic in Arabia," *Journal of Psychology* 126 (5) (1992): 507–519 (513).

workplace. They contrasted this attitude to that of the Japanese and Americans, who consider friendship to be an integral part of the workplace.[8]

Other variables affect the perceived meaning of work and how it satisfies various needs, such as the relative wealth of a country.[9] When people have a high standard of living, work can take on a meaning different from simply providing the basic economic necessities of life. Economic differences among countries were found to explain variations in attitudes toward work in a study by Furnham et al. of over 12,000 young people from forty-one countries on all five continents. Specifically, the researchers found that young people in Far East and Middle Eastern countries reported the highest competitiveness and acquisitiveness for money, while those from North America and South America scored highest on work ethics and "mastery" (that is, continuing to struggle to master something).[10] Such studies show the complexity of the underlying reasons for differences in attitudes toward work—cultural, economic, and so on—which must be taken into account when considering what needs and motivations people bring to the workplace. All in all, research shows a considerable cultural variability affecting how work meets employees' needs.

The Needs Hierarchy in the International Context

How can a manager know what motivates people in a specific country? Certainly, by drawing on the experiences of others who have worked there and also by inferring the likely type of motivational structure present by studying what is known about the culture in that region. In addition, some research and comparative studies about needs in specific countries are available and can provide another piece of the puzzle.

Some researchers have used Maslow's hierarchy of needs to study motivation in other countries. A classic study by Haire, Ghiselli, and Porter surveyed 3,641 managers in fourteen countries. They concluded that Maslow's needs, in particular the upper-level ones, are important at the managerial level, although the managers reported that the degree to which their needs were fulfilled did not live up to their expectations.[11]

In a similar study, Ronen investigated whether work-related values and needs are similar across nationalities and whether the motivation categories of Maslow and Herzberg apply universally. Studying trained, nonmanagerial male employees (in Germany, Canada, France, Japan, and the United Kingdom), he found that such similarities do exist and that there are common clusters of needs and goals across nationalities. These clusters include (1) job goals, such as working area, work time, physical working conditions, fringe benefits, and job security; (2) relationships with co-workers and supervisors; and (3) work challenges and opportunities for using skills.[12] Ronen concludes that need clusters are constant across nationalities and that Maslow's need hierarchy is confirmed by those clusters. In addition, he claims that Herzberg's categories are confirmed by the cross-national need clusters in his study.

People's opinions of how best to satisfy their needs vary across cultures also. As shown in Exhibit 11-4, priorities vary regarding sources of job-related satisfaction. For example, China, Israel, and Korea gave the highest score to "achievement" as satisfying self-actualization needs, whereas the first choice was an "interesting job" for Germany, Holland, and the United States.

One clear conclusion is that managers around the world have similar needs but show differing levels of satisfaction of those needs derived from their jobs. Variables other than culture may be at play, however. One of these variables may be the country's stage of economic development. With regard to the transitioning economy in Russia, for example, a study by Elenkov found that Russian managers stress security and belongingness needs as opposed to higher-order needs.[13] Whatever the reason, many companies that have started operations in other countries have experienced differences in the apparent needs of the local employees and how they expect work to be recognized. Mazda, of Japan, experienced this problem in its Michigan plant. Japanese firms tend to confer recognition in the form of plaques, attention, and applause, and Japanese workers are likely to be insulted by material incentives because such rewards imply that they would work harder to achieve them than they otherwise would. Instead, Japanese firms focus on groupwide or companywide goals, compared with the American emphasis on individual goals, achievement, and reward.

EXHIBIT 11-4 Comparative Job Motivational Components

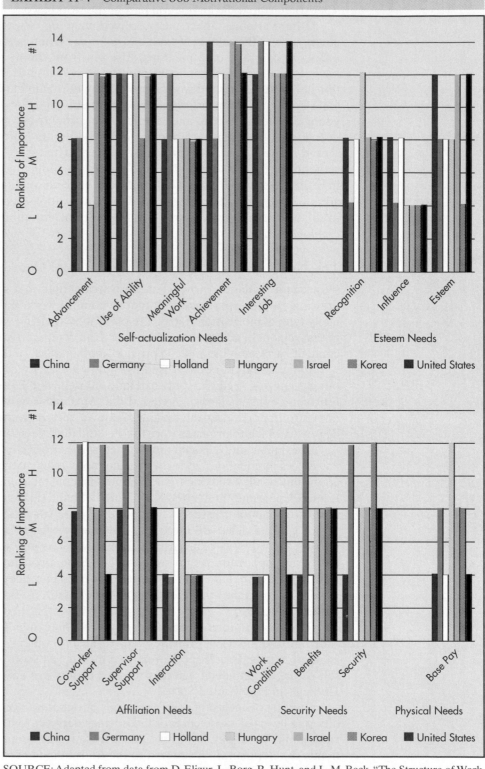

SOURCE: Adapted from data from D. Elizur, L. Borg, R. Hunt, and L. M. Beck, "The Structure of Work Values: A Cross-Cultural Comparison," *Journal of Organizational Behavior* 12 (1991): 21–28.

When considering the cross-cultural applicability of Maslow's theory, then, it is not the needs that are in question as much as the ordering of those needs in the hierarchy. The hierarchy reflects the Western culture where Maslow conducted his study, and different hierarchies might better reflect other cultures. For example, Eastern cultures focus on the needs of society rather than on the needs of individuals. Nevis proposes that a hierarchy more accurately reflecting the needs of the Chinese would comprise four levels: (1) belonging, (2) physiological needs, (3) safety, and (4) self-actualization in the service of society.[14] It is difficult to observe or measure the individual needs of a Chinese person because, from childhood, these are intermeshed with the needs of society. Clearly, however, along with culture, the political beliefs at work in China dominate many facets of motivation. As the backbone of the industrial system, cadres (managers and technicians) and workers are given exact and detailed prescriptions of what is expected of them as members of a factory, workshop, or work unit. This results in conformity at the expense of creativity. Workers are accountable to their group, which is a powerful motivator. Because being "unemployed" is not an option in China, it is important for employees to maintain themselves as cooperating members of the work group.[15] Money is also a motivator, stemming from the historical political insecurity and economic disasters that have perpetuated the need for a high level of savings.[16] A Gallup opinion poll cited in the 1998 *World Competitiveness Yearbook* found that a priority among Chinese is to "work hard and get rich," compared to Europeans and Americans, who value self-achievement over wealth.[17]

The Intrinsic–Extrinsic Dichotomy in the International Context

The intrinsic–extrinsic dichotomy is another useful model (researched by a number of authors) for considering motivation in the workplace. Herzberg's research, for example, found two sets of needs: (1) motivational factors (intrinsic) and (2) maintenance factors (extrinsic).

Results from others' research using Herzberg's model provide some insight into motivation in different countries and help us to determine whether the intrinsic–extrinsic dichotomy is generalizable across cultures. Research on managers in Greece and on workers in general in an Israeli kibbutz indicate that all these people are motivated more by the nature of the work itself; dissatisfactions resulted from the conditions surrounding the work.[18] Another study in Zambia generally found the same dichotomy. Work motivation was found to result from the intrinsic factors of the opportunity for growth and the nature of the work and, to some extent, physical provisions. Factors that produced dissatisfaction and were not motivators were extrinsic—relations with others, fairness in organizational practices, and personal problems.[19]

In addition to research on single countries, Herzberg's theory has been used to compare different countries on the basis of job factors and job satisfaction. A study of MBA candidates from the United States, Australia, Canada, and Singapore, for example, indicated that Herzberg's motivational factors were more important to these prospective managers than hygiene factors.[20] In a broader study of managers from Canada, the United Kingdom, France, and Japan to determine the relative importance of job factors to them and how satisfied they were with those factors, Kanungo and Wright drew a number of interesting conclusions. Interpreting their results, we can draw some overall conclusions: The managers indicated that internally mediated factors (intrinsic, job content factors) were more important than organizationally controlled factors (extrinsic, job context factors). However, they found differences across countries, in particular between the United Kingdom and France, in how much importance the managers placed on job outcomes and also in their relative levels of satisfaction with those outcomes.[21] As a practical application of their research results, Kanungo and Wright suggest the following implications for motivation in the workplace:

> *Efforts to improve managerial performance in the UK should focus on job content rather than on job context. . . . Job enrichment programs are more likely to improve performance in an intrinsically oriented society such as Britain, where satisfaction tends to be derived from the job itself, than in France, where job context factors, such as security and fringe benefits, are more highly valued.*[22]

To answer common questions about whether Japanese-style management practices—work groups, quality circles, and long-term employment—make a difference to commitment and job satisfaction, Lincoln studied 8,302 workers in 106 factories in the United States and Japan (though not specifically using Herzberg's factors). He concluded that those practices had similar positive or negative effects on work attitudes in both countries. However, while the level of commitment to the company was essentially the same in both samples, the Japanese indicated a lower level of job satisfaction.[23]

The lower level of satisfaction is contrary to popular expectations because of the well-known Japanese environment of teamwork, productivity, long-term employment, and dedication to the company. However, previous research has also found a lower level of job satisfaction in Japan.[24] Lower work satisfaction indicates a higher level of motivation to fulfill personal and company goals (that is, to do better), compared to a lower level of motivation indicated by complacency. As Lincoln points out, however, these research findings could be the result of another cultural variable introducing a measurement bias: the Japanese tendency to "color their evaluations of nearly everything with a large dose of pessimism, humility and understatement" in their persistent quest to do better.[25] This underscores the need to consider carefully all the cultural variables involved in observing or managing motivation.

Although, more cross-cultural research on motivation is needed, one can draw the tentative conclusion that managers around the world are motivated more by intrinsic than by extrinsic factors. Considerable doubt remains, however, about the universality of Herzberg's or Maslow's theories because it is not possible to take into account all of the relevant cultural variables when researching motivation. Different factors have different meanings within the entire cultural context and must be considered on a situation-by-situation basis. The need to consider the entire national and cultural context is shown in Comparative Management in Focus: Motivation in Mexico, which highlights motivational issues for Mexican workers and indicates the importance to them of what Herzberg calls maintenance factors. As you read, consider whether this situation supports or refutes Herzberg's theory.

Comparative Management in Focus

Motivation in Mexico

In Mexico, everything is a personal matter; but a lot of managers don't get it.
To get anything done here, the manager has to be more of an instructor, teacher,
or father figure than a boss.
—*Robert Hoskins, Manager, Leviton Manufacturing, Juarez*

It is particularly important for an aspiring international manager to become
familiar with Mexican factory workers because of the increasing volume of
manufacturing that is being outsourced there.[26]

To understand the cultural milieu in Mexico, we can draw on research that concludes that Latin American societies, including Mexico, rank high on power distance (the acknowledgment of hierarchical authority) and on uncertainty avoidance (a preference for security and formality over risk). In addition, they rank low on individualism, preferring collectivism, which values the good of the group, family, or country over individual achievement.[27] In Mexico, the family is of central importance; loyalty and commitment to family and friends frequently determine employment, promotion, or special treatment for contracts. Unfortunately, it is this admirable cultural norm that often results in motivation and productivity problems on the job by contributing to very high absenteeism and turnover, especially in the *maquiladoras*. This high turnover and absenteeism are costly to employers, thereby offsetting the advantage of relatively low labor cost per hour. "Family reasons" (taking care of sick relatives or elderly parents) are the most common reasons given for absenteeism and for failing to return to work.[28] Workers often simply do not come back to work after vacations or holidays. For many Mexican males, the value of work lies primarily in its ability to fulfill their culturally imposed responsibilities as head of household and breadwinner rather than to seek individual achievement.[29] Machismo (sharp role differentiation based on gender) and prestige are important characteristics of the Mexican culture.

As a people, speaking very generally, Mexicans are very proud and patriotic; *respeto* (respect) is important to them, and a slight against personal dignity is regarded as a grave provocation.[30] Mexican workers expect to be treated in the same respectful manner that they use toward one another. As noted by one U.S. expatriate, foreign managers must adapt to Mexico's "softer culture"; Mexican workers "need more communication, more relationship-building, and more reassurance than employees in the U.S."[31] The Mexican people are very warm and have a leisurely attitude toward time; face-to-face interaction is best for any kind of business, with time allowed for socializing and appreciating the Mexicans' cultural artifacts, buildings, and so forth. Taking time to celebrate a worker's birthday, for instance, will show that you are a *simpático* boss and will increase workers' loyalty and effort. The workers' expectations of small considerations that seem inconsequential to U.S. managers should not be discounted. In one maquiladora, when the company stopped providing the annual Halloween candy, the employees filed a grievance to the state Arbitration Board—Junta de Conciliación y Arbitraje.

Most managers in Mexico find that the management style that works best there is authoritative and paternal. Paternalism is expected; the manager is regarded as *el patrón* (pronounced pah-trone), or the father figure, whose role it is to take care of the workers as an extended family.[32] Employees expect managers to be the authority; they are the "elite"—power rests with the owner or manager and other prominent community leaders. For the most part, if not told to do something, the workers will not do it, nor will they question the boss or make any decisions for the boss.[33] Nevertheless, employees perceive the manager as a person, not as a concept or a function, and success often depends on the ability of a foreign manager to adopt a personalized management style, such as by greeting all workers as they arrive for their shifts.

Generally speaking, many Mexican factory workers doubt their ability to personally influence the outcome of their lives. They are apt to attribute events to the will of God, or to luck, timing, or relationships with higher authority figures. For many, decisions are made on the basis of ideals, emotions, and intuition rather than objective information. However, individualism and materialism are increasingly evident, particularly among the upwardly mobile high-tech and professional Mexican employees.

Corrective discipline and motivation must occur through training examples, cooperation, and, if necessary, subtle shaming. As a disciplinary measure, it is a mistake to directly insult a Mexican; an outright insult implies an insult to the whole family. As a motivation, one must appeal to the pride of the Mexican employees and avoid causing them to feel humiliated. Given that, "getting ahead" is often associated more with outside forces than with one's own actions; the motivation and reward system becomes difficult to structure in the usual ways. Past experiences have indicated that, for the most part, motivation through participative decision making is not as effective as motivation through the more traditional and expected autocratic methods. With careful implementation, however, the mutual respect and caring that the Mexican people have for one another can lead to positive team spirit needed for the team structure to be used successfully by companies, such as GM in its highest-quality plant in the world in Ramos Arizpe, near Saltillo, Mexico.[34] Although a study by Nicholls, Lane, and Brechu concluded cultural constraints are considerable when it comes to using self-managing teams in Mexico, the Mexican executives surveyed suggested that the relative success depends on the implementation. The conflicts are between the norms of behavior in self-managed teams typical of U.S. and Canadian culture (such as initiative and self-leadership, bottom-up decision making), and typical values in Mexican business culture (such as resistance to change, adherence to status roles, and top-down hierarchical structure). These differences in work-role norms seem to create a behavioral impasse, at least initially, when it comes to the potential for setting up self-managed teams.[35]

Although self-managed teams require individual leaders to take risks by spearheading team initiatives, those behaviors, according to the survey of Mexican executives, "are in sharp contrast to the behavioral norms of the paternalistic and hierarchical tradition of managers and workers in the Mexican work place." The workers expect the managers to give instructions and make decisions.[36] The business culture in Mexico is also attributable to prevailing economic conditions in Mexico of low levels of education, training, and technical skills. The Mexican executives surveyed gave some suggestions for implementing work teams and cautioned that the process of implementation will take a long time. They suggested the following:

- Foster a culture of individual responsibility among team members.
- Anticipate the impact of changes in power distribution.
- Provide leadership from the top throughout the implementation process.
- Provide adequate training to prepare workers for teamwork.
- Develop motivation and harmony through clear expectations.
- Encourage an environment of shared responsibility.[37]

For the most part, Mexican workers expect that authority will not be abused but rather that it will follow the family model in which everyone works together in a dignified manner according to their designated roles.[38] Any event that may break this harmony, or seems to confront authority, will likely be covered up. This may result in a supervisor hiding defective work, for example, or, as in the case of a steel conveyor plant in Puebla, a total worker walkout rather than using the grievance process.[39] Contributing to these kinds of problems is the need to save face for oneself and to respect others' place and honor. Public criticism is regarded as humiliating. Employees like an atmosphere of formality and respect. They typically use flattery and call people by their titles rather than their names to maintain an atmosphere of regard for status and respect.

A context of continuing economic problems and a relatively low standard of living for most workers help explain why Maslow's higher-order needs (self-actualization, achievement, status) are generally not very high on most Mexican workers' lists of needs. In discussing compensation, Mariah de Forest, who consults for American firms in Mexico, suggests the following:

> Rather than an impersonal wage scale, Mexican workers tend to think in terms of payment now for services rendered now. A daily incentive system with automatic payouts for production exceeding quotas, as well as daily/monthly attendance bonuses, works well.[40]

As a result of economic reforms and the peso devaluation, money is now a pressing motivational factor for most employees. Since workers highly value the enjoyment of life, many companies in Mexico provide recreation facilities—a picnic area, a soccer field, and so forth. Bonuses are expected regardless of productivity. In fact, it is the law to give Christmas bonuses of fifteen days of pay to each worker. Fringe benefits are also important to Mexicans; because most Mexican workers are poor, the company provides the only source of such benefits for them. In particular, benefits that help to manage family-related issues are positive motivators for employees at least to turn up for work. To this end, companies often provide on-site health care facilities for workers and their families, nurseries, free meals, and even small loans in crisis situations.[41] In addition, those companies that understand the local infrastructure problems often provide a company bus to minimize the pervasive problems of absenteeism and tardiness.

The foregoing statements are broad generalizations about Mexican factory workers. Increasing numbers of American managers are in Mexico because the NAFTA has encouraged more U.S. businesses to move operations there. For firms on U.S. soil, managers may employ many Mexican-Americans in an intercultural setting. As the second-largest and fastest-growing ethnic group in the United States, Mexican-Americans represent an important subculture requiring management attention as they take an increasing proportion of the jobs there. Yet, they remain the least assimilated ethnic group in the majority mainstream, partially from economic or occupational causes and partially from choice.[42]

Research shows that little conclusive information is available to answer a manager's direct question of exactly how to motivate in any particular culture. The reason is that we cannot assume the universal applicability of the motivational theories, or even concepts, that have been used to research differences among cultures. Furthermore, the entire motivational context must be taken into account. For example, Western firms entering markets in Eastern Europe invariably run into difficulties in motivating their local staffs. Those workers have been accustomed to working under entirely different circumstances and usually do not trust foreign managers. Typically, then, the work systems and responsibilities must be highly structured because workers in Eastern Europe are not likely to use their own judgment in making decisions and because managerial skills are not developed.[43]

A principal rule in the [Russian] workplace is "Superiors know better."

SNEJINA MICHAILOVA,
2002[44]

A study by Michailova in 2002 found that most Russian employees are still used to the management style that prevailed in a centrally planned economic system. This context resulted in vertically managed hierarchies, one-man authority, and anti-individualism. The employees in the study experienced conflict when faced with different managerial styles from their Russian and Western managers in joint venture situations. Those employees were in traditional industries, were on average forty-five years old, and were more motivated by the authoritarianism of their Russian managers than the attempts at empowerment by their Western managers. More importantly, the conflicting motivational techniques left them in a "double bind", as shown in Exhibit 11-5.

In sum, motivation is situational, and savvy managers use all they know about the relevant culture or subculture—consulting frequently with local people—to infer the best means of motivating in that context. Furthermore, tactful managers consciously avoid an ethnocentric attitude in which they make assumptions about a person's goals, motivation, or work habits based on their own frames of reference, and they do not make negative value judgments about a person's level of motivation because it differs from their own.

Many cultural variables affect people's sense of what is attainable, and thus affect motivation. How much control people believe they have over their environment and their destiny—whether they believe that they can control certain events, and not just be at the mercy of external forces—is one example. Although Americans typically feel a strong internal locus of control, others attribute results to, for example, the will of God (in the case of Muslims) or to the good fortune of being born in the right social class or family (in the case of many Latin Americans). For example, whereas Americans feel that hard work will get the job done, many Hong Kong Chinese believe that outcomes are determined by *joss*, or luck. Clearly, then, managers must use persuasive strategies to motivate employees when they do not readily connect their personal work behaviors with outcomes or productivity.

The role of culture in the motivational process is shown in Exhibit 11-6. An employee's needs are determined largely by the cultural context of values and attitudes—along with the national variables—in which he or she lives and works. Those needs then determine the meaning of work for that employee. The manager's understanding of what work means in that employee's life can then lead to the design of a culturally appropriate

---

EXHIBIT 11-5   Conflicting Motivational Techniques in Western–Russian Joint Ventures

Western managers to Russian employees	Russian managers to Russian employees
Take initiative and come with suggestions	Do what you are supposed to do and obey the established rules
Learn from the mistakes and don't repeat them	Mistakes are not allowed and should be punished
Be longer term and future oriented	Concentrate on here and now (and don't forget how it was before)
Think of the company as an integrated entity	Act according to your own job description and don't interfere in other people's job

SOURCE: Reprinted from S. Michailova, "When Common Sense Becomes Uncommon: Participation and Empowerment in Russian Companies with Western Participation," *Journal of World Business* 37 (2002) 180–187, with permission from Elsevier.

EXHIBIT 11-6 The Role of Culture in Job Motivation

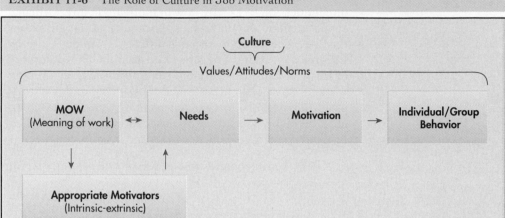

job context and reward system to guide individual and group employee job behavior to meet mutual goals.

Reward Systems

Incentives and rewards are an integral part of motivation in a corporation. Recognizing and understanding different motivational patterns across cultures leads to the design of appropriate reward systems. In the United States, there are common patterns of rewards, varying among levels of the company and types of occupations and based on experience and research with Americans. Rewards usually fall into five categories: financial, social status, job content, career, and professional.[45] The relative emphasis on one or more of these five categories varies from country to country. In Japan, for example, reward systems are based primarily on seniority, and much emphasis is put on the bonus system. In addition, distinction is made there between the regular workforce and the temporary workforce, which usually comprises women expected to leave when they start a family. As is usually the case, the regular workforce receives considerably more rewards than the temporary workforce in pay and benefits and the allocation of interesting jobs.[46] For the regular workforce, the emphasis is on the employee's long-term effectiveness in terms of behavior, personality, and group output. Rewarding the individual is frowned on in Japan because it encourages competition rather than the desired group cooperation. Therefore, specific cash incentives are usually limited. In Taiwan, recognition and affection are important; company departments compete for praise from top management at their annual celebration.

In contrast, the entire reward system in China is very different from that of most countries. The low wage rates are compensated for by free housing, schools, and medical care. While egalitarianism still seems to prevail, the recent free-enterprise reform movements have encouraged *duo lao, duo de* ("more work, more pay"). One important incentive is training, which gives workers more power. One approach used in the past—and one that seems quite negative to Americans—is best illustrated by the example of a plaque award labeled "Ms. Wong—Employee of the Month." While Westerners would assume that Ms. Wong had excelled as an employee, actually this award given in a Chinese retail store was for the worst employee; the plaque was designed to shame and embarrass her.[47] Younger Chinese in areas changing to a more market-based economy have seen a shift toward equity-based rewards, no doubt resulting from a gradual shift in work values.[48]

No doubt culture plays a significant role in determining the appropriate incentive and reward systems around the world. Employees in collectivist cultures such as Japan, Korea, and Taiwan would not respond well to the typical American merit-based reward system to motivate employees because that would go against the traditional value system and would disrupt the harmony and corporate culture.

Leading

The manager's quintessential responsibility is to help his people realize their own highest potential.

JACQUES MAISONROUGE,
IBM World Trade Corporations[49]

This section on leadership prompts consideration of the following questions: To what extent, and how, do leadership styles and practices around the world vary? What are the forces perpetuating that divergence? Where, and why, will that divergence continue to be the strongest? Is there any evidence for convergence of leadership styles and practices around the world? What are the forces leading to that convergence, and how and where will this convergence occur in the future? What implications do these questions have for cross-cultural leaders?

The task of helping employees realize their highest potential in the workplace is the essence of leadership. The goal of every leader is to achieve the organization's objectives while achieving those of each employee. Today's global managers realize that increased competition requires them to be open to change and to rethink their old culturally conditioned modes of leadership.

THE GLOBAL LEADER'S ROLE AND ENVIRONMENT

The greatest competitive advantage global companies in the twenty-first century can have is effective global leaders. Yet this competitive challenge is not easy to meet. People tend to rise to leadership positions by proving themselves able to lead in their home-country corporate culture and meeting the generally accepted behaviors of that national culture. However, global leaders must broaden their horizons—both strategically and cross-culturally—and develop a more flexible model of leadership that can be applied anywhere—one that is adaptable to locational situations around the world.[50] From their recent research involving 125 global leaders in fifty companies, Morrison, Gregersen, and Black concluded that effective leaders must have global business and organizational savvy. They explain global business savvy as the ability to recognize global market opportunities for a company and having a vision of doing business worldwide. Global organizational savvy requires an intimate knowledge of a company's resources and capabilities in order to capture global markets, as well as an understanding of each subsidiary's product lines and how the people and business operate on the local level. Morrison, Gregersen, and Black outline four personal development strategies through which companies and managers can meet these requirements of effective global leadership: travel, teamwork, training, and transfers (the four "T's").[51]

Travel, of course, exposes managers to various cultures, economies, political systems, and markets. Working on global teams teaches managers to operate on an interpersonal level while dealing with business decision-making processes that are embraced by differences in cultural norms and business models. Although formal training seminars also play an important role, most of the global leaders interviewed said that the most influential developmental experience in their lives was the international assignment. Increasingly, global companies are requiring that their managers who will progress to top management positions must have overseas assignment experience.[52] The benefits accruing to the organization depend on how effectively the assignment and repatriation are handled, as discussed in Chapter 10.

Effective global leadership involves the ability to inspire and influence the thinking, attitudes, and behavior of people anywhere in the world.[53] The importance of the leadership role cannot be overemphasized because the leader's interactions strongly influence the motivation and behavior of employees, and ultimately, the entire climate of the organization. The cumulative effects of one or more weak managers can have a significant negative impact on the ability of the organization to meet its objectives.

Managers on international assignments try to maximize leadership effectiveness by juggling several important, and sometimes conflicting, roles as (1) a representative of the

EXHIBIT 11-7 Factors Affecting Leadership Abroad

Content	
Attributes of the Person	**Characteristics of Decisions Situation**
Job position knowledge, experience, expectations	Degree of complexity, uncertainty, and risk
Longevity in company, country, functional area	In-country information needs and availability
Intelligence and cultural learning or change ability	Articulation of assumptions and expectations
Personality as demonstrated in values,	Scope and potential impact on performance
beliefs, attitudes toward foreign situations	Nature of business partners
Multiple memberships in work and professional groups	Authority and autonomy required
Decision and personal work style	Required level of participation and acceptance by employees, partners, and government
	Linkage to other decisions
	Past management legacy
	Openness to public scrutiny and responsibility
Context	
Attributes of the Job or Position	**Characteristics of the Firm and Business Environment**
Longevity and past success of former role occupants in the position	Firm structure: size, location, technology, tasks, reporting, and communication patterns
Technical requirements of the job	Firm process: decision making, staffing control system, reward system, information system, means of coordination, integration, and conflict resolution
Relative authority or power	
Physical location (e.g., home office, field office)	
Need for coordination, cooperation, and integration with other units	Firm outputs: products, services, public image, corporate culture, local history, and community relations
Resource availability	Business environment: social-cultural, political-economic, and technological aspects of a country or market
Foreign peer group relations	

SOURCE: R. H. Mason and R. S. Spich, *Management: An International Perspective* (Homewood, IL: Irwin, 1987), 186.

parent firm, (2) the manager of the local firm, (3) a resident of the local community, (4) a citizen of either the host country or of another country, (5) a member of a profession, and (6) a member of a family.[54]

The leader's role comprises the interaction of two sets of variables—the content and the context of leadership. The content of leadership comprises the attributes of the leader and the decisions to be made; the context of leadership comprises all those variables related to the particular situation.[55] The increased number of variables (political, economic, and cultural) in the context of the managerial job abroad requires astute leadership. Some of the variables in the content and context of the leader's role in foreign settings are shown in Exhibit 11-7. The multicultural leader's role thus blends leadership, communication, motivational, and other managerial skills within unique and ever-changing environments. We will examine the contingent nature of such leadership throughout this section.

The E-Business Effect on Leadership

An additional factor—technology—is becoming increasingly pervasive in its ability to influence the global leader's role and environment and will, perhaps, contribute to a lessening of the differences in motivation and leadership around the world. More and more often, companies like Italtel Spa, featured in E-Biz Box: Italtel Spa's Leadership Style Empowers Global Employees with Technology, are using technology in global leadership techniques to set up systems for their geographically dispersed employees to enable them to expand and coordinate their global operations. In the case of Italtel, this required wide delegation and empowerment of their employees so that they could decentralize.

Individual managers are realizing that the Internet is changing their leadership styles and interactions with employees, as well as their strategic leadership of their organizations. They are having to adapt to the hyperspeed environment of e-business, as well as to the need for visionary leadership in a whole new set of competitive industry dynamics. Some of these new-age leadership issues are discussed in Management Focus: Leadership in a Digital World.

E-BIZ BOX

Italtel Spa's Leadership Style Empowers Global Employees with Technology

EXECUTIVE SUMMARY

Company: Italtel Spa
Industry: Telecommunications
Business Challenge: To "flatten" the organization and expand globally.
Solution: An Intranet based on Netscape products that enables Italtel to share knowledge and product information throughout the company.
Plant operations, antenna functioning, and network traffic are monitored online.
Solution Features: Employees can access Italtel's technical product documentation online.
Employees can book training courses via the Intranet.
Reduced costs for information, documentation, and software distribution.
Business Benefits: Network and service monitoring online contributes to improved customer service. Centralized employee database and single network login for every user dramatically reduce system administration time and costs.

Italtel spa is an international supplier of telecommunications networks that specializes in the design, development, and installation of integrated telecommunications systems. The company employs 16,000 people, 21 percent of whom are involved in research and development. Italtel invests 12 percent of its annual revenues in R&D, addressing a wide range of applications.

BUSINESS CHALLENGE

With the globalization of the telecommunications market, Italtel had to expand internationally in order to compete successfully. To do so, Italtel management felt that it should "flatten" the organization, moving from a hierarchical structure to one in which employees are empowered with all the tools and information they need to do their jobs better, thereby improving customer service and time to market.

In addition to the business challenges associated with international expansion, the company faces several technical challenges. Sweeping changes spurred by the convergence of communication and information technologies force Italtel to innovate faster than ever before. As a result, Italtel needs to share knowledge and information and improve communication throughout the company—all within a distributed, extremely heterogeneous computing environment. This environment includes a wide range of client systems, such as Unix workstations and PCs running Windows software, and servers that include Digital, Hewlett-Packard, IBM, Sun, and Windows NT-based systems. The company needed a new information technology solution that would provide global information access, flexibility, and ease of use. Among the goals for the new system were to create a centralized, easily accessible source for all company information resources, to monitor the company's telecommunications services and network online for better performance, to organize training courses, and to set up working groups in different departments.

SOLVING THE CHALLENGE

Italtel selected key components of the Netscape SuitSpot server software family to deploy an enterprisewide Intranet and messaging solution. Netscape Enterprise Server distributes Wed-based Intranet and Internet services.

SOURCE: www.Netscape.com case studies.

Management Focus

Leadership in a Digital World

What does leadership mean in a digital world in which organizations are flexible and fluid and the pace of change is extremely rapid? What's it like to lead in an e-business organization? Jomei Chang of Vitria Technology describes it as follows: "There's no place to hide. [The Internet] forces you to be on your toes every minute, every second." Is leadership in e-businesses really all that different from traditional organizations? Managers who've worked in both think it is. How? Three differences seem to be most evident: the speed at which decisions must be made, the importance of being flexible, and the need to create a vision of the future.

Making Decisions Fast.   Managers in all organizations never have all the data they want when making decisions, but the problem is multiplied in e-business. The situation is changing rapidly and the competition is intense. For example, Meg Whitman, president and CEO of eBay, says, "We're growing at 40 percent to 50 percent per quarter. That pace absolutely changes the leadership challenge. Every three months we become a different company. In one year, we went from 30 employees to 140, and from 100,000 registered users to 2.2 million. At Hasbro [where she was previously an executive], we would set a yearlong strategy, and then we would simply execute against it. At eBay, we constantly revisit the strategy—and revise the tactics."

Leaders in e-businesses see themselves as sprinters and their contemporaries in traditional businesses as long-distance runners. They frequently use the term "Internet time," which is a reference to a rapidly speeded-up working environment. "Every [e-business] leader today has to unlearn one lesson that was drilled into each one of them: You gather data so that you can make considered decisions. You can't do that on Internet time."

Maintaining Flexibility.   In addition to speed, leaders in e-businesses need to be highly flexible. They have to be able to roll with the ups and downs. They need to be able to redirect their group or organization when they find that something doesn't work. They have to encourage experimentation. This is what Mark Cuban, president and co-founder of Broadcast.com, had to say about the importance of being flexible. "When we started, we thought advertising would be the core of our business. We were wrong. We thought that the way to define our network was to distribute servers all over the country. We were wrong. We've had to recalibrate again and again—and we'll have to keep doing it in the future."

Focusing on the Vision.   Although visionary leadership is important in every organization, in a hyperspeed environment, people require more from their leaders. The rules, policies, and regulations that characterize more traditional organizations provide direction and reduce uncertainty for employees. Such formalized guidelines typically don't exist in e-businesses, and it becomes the responsibility of the leaders to provide direction through their vision. For instance, David Pottruck, co-CEO of Charles Schwab, gathered nearly 100 of the company's senior managers at the southern end of the Golden Gate Bridge. He handed each a jacket inscribed with the phrase "Crossing the Chasm" and led them across the bridge in a symbolic march to kick off his plan to turn Schwab into a full-fledged Internet brokerage. Getting people to buy into the vision may require even more radical actions. For instance, when Isao Okawa, chairman of Sega Enterprises, decided to remake his company into an e-business, his management team resisted—that is, until he defied Japan's consensus-charged, lifetime-employment culture by announcing that those who resisted the change would be fired, risking shame. Not so amazingly, resistance to the change vanished overnight.

SOURCE: S. P. Robbins and M. Coulter, *Management,* 7th ed. (Upper Saddle River, NJ: Prentice Hall), 2001.

CROSS-CULTURAL RESEARCH ON LEADERSHIP

Numerous leadership theories focus in various ways on individual traits, leader behavior, interaction patterns, role relationships, follower perceptions, influence over followers, influence on task goals, and influence on organizational culture.[56] Here it is important to understand how the variable of societal culture fits into these theories and what implications can be drawn for international managers as they seek to provide leadership around the world. Although the functions of leadership are similar across cultures, anthropological studies, such as those by Margaret Mead, indicate that while leadership is a universal phenomenon, what makes effective leadership varies across cultures.[57]

In addition to research studies that indicate variations in leadership profiles, the generally accepted image that people in different countries have about what they expect and admire in their leaders tends to become a norm over time, forming an idealized role for these leaders. Industry leaders in France and Italy, for example, are highly regarded for their social prominence and political power. In Latin American countries, leaders are respected as total persons and leaders in society, with appreciation for the arts being important. In Germany, polish, decisiveness, and a wide general knowledge are respected, with their leaders granted a lot of formality by everyone. Foreigners are often surprised at the informal off-the-job lifestyles of executives in the United States and would be surprised to see them pushing a lawn mower for example.[58]

Most research on U.S. leadership styles describes managerial behaviors on, essentially, the same dimension, variously termed *autocratic* versus *democratic, participative* versus *directive, relations-oriented* versus *task-oriented,* or *initiating structure* versus *consideration continuum.*[59] These studies were developed in the West, and conclusions regarding employee responses largely reflect the opinions of U.S. workers. The democratic, or participative, leadership style has been recommended as the one more likely to have positive results with most U.S. employees.

CONTINGENCY LEADERSHIP: THE CULTURE VARIABLE

Modern leadership theory recognizes that no single leadership style works well in all situations.[60] A considerable amount of research, directly or indirectly, supports the notion of cultural contingency in leadership. This means that, as a result of culture-based norms and beliefs about how people in various roles should behave, what is expected of leaders, what influence they have, and what kind of status they are given vary from nation to nation. Clearly, this has implications for what kind of leadership style a manager should expect to adopt when going abroad.

The GLOBE Project

Recent research by the Global Leadership and Organizational Behavior Effectiveness (GLOBE) research program comprised a network of 170 social scientists and management scholars from sixty-two countries for the purpose of understanding the impact of cultural variables on leadership and organizational processes. Using both quantitative and qualitative methodologies to collect data from 18,000 managers in those countries, representing the majority of the world's population, the researchers wanted to find out which leadership behaviors are universally accepted and which are culturally contingent. Not unexpectedly, they found that the positive leadership behaviors generally accepted anywhere are behaviors such as being trustworthy, encouraging, an effective bargainer, a skilled administrator and communicator, and a team builder; the negatively regarded traits included being uncooperative, egocentric, ruthless, and dictatorial.[61] Those leadership styles and behaviors found to be culturally contingent are charismatic, team-oriented, self-protective, participative, humane, and autonomous.

The results for some of those countries researched are shown in Exhibit 11-8. The first column *(N)* is the sample size within that country. The scores for each country on those leadership dimensions are based on a scale from 1 (the opinion that those leadership behaviors would not be regarded favorably) to 7 (that those behaviors would substantially facilitate effective leadership). Note that reading from top to bottom on a single

EXHIBIT 11-8 Culturally-Contingent Beliefs Regarding Effective Leadership Styles

Country	N	Charisma	Team	Self-Protective	Participative	Humane	Autonomous
Argentina	154	5.98	5.99	3.46	5.89	4.70	4.55
Australia	345	6.09	5.81	3.05	5.71	5.09	3.95
Austria	169	6.03	5.74	3.07	6.00	4.93	4.47
Brazil	264	6.01	6.17	3.50	6.06	4.84	2.27
Canada (English-speaking)	257	6.16	5.84	2.96	6.09	5.20	3.65
China	160	5.57	5.57	3.80	5.05	5.18	4.07
Denmark	327	6.01	5.70	2.82	5.80	4.23	3.79
Egypt	201	5.57	5.55	4.21	4.69	5.14	4.49
England	168	6.01	5.71	3.04	5.57	4.90	3.92
Germany [Former FRG (WEST)]	414	5.84	5.49	2.97	5.88	4.44	4.30
Germany [Former GDR (EAST)]	44	5.87	5.51	3.33	5.70	4.60	4.35
Greece	234	6.02	6.12	3.49	5.81	5.16	3.98
Hong Kong	171	5.67	5.58	3.68	4.87	4.89	4.38
Hungary	186	5.91	5.91	3.24	5.23	4.73	3.23
India	231	5.85	5.72	3.78	4.99	5.26	3.85
Indonesia	365	6.15	5.92	4.13	4.61	5.43	4.19
Ireland	157	6.08	5.82	3.01	5.64	5.06	3.95
Israel	543	6.23	5.91	3.64	4.96	4.68	4.26
Italy	269	5.99	5.87	3.26	5.47	4.37	3.62
Japan	197	5.49	5.56	3.61	5.08	4.68	3.67
Malaysia	125	5.89	5.80	3.50	5.12	5.24	4.03
Mexico	327	5.66	5.75	3.86	4.64	4.71	3.86
Netherlands	289	5.98	5.75	2.87	5.75	4.81	3.53
Nigeria	419	5.77	5.65	3.90	5.19	5.48	3.62
Philippines	287	6.33	6.06	3.33	5.40	5.53	3.75
Poland	283	5.67	5.98	3.53	5.05	4.56	4.34
Portugal	80	5.75	5.92	3.11	5.48	4.62	3.19
Russia	301	5.66	5.63	3.69	4.67	4.08	4.63
Singapore	224	5.95	5.77	3.32	5.30	5.24	3.87
South Africa (Black sample)	241	5.16	5.23	3.63	5.05	4.79	3.94
South Africa (White sample)	183	5.99	5.80	3.20	5.62	5.33	3.74
South Korea	233	5.53	5.53	3.68	4.93	4.87	4.21
Spain	370	5.90	5.93	3.39	5.11	4.66	3.54
Sweden	1,790	5.84	5.75	2.82	5.54	4.73	3.97
Switzerland (German)	321	5.93	5.61	2.93	5.94	4.76	4.13
Taiwan	237	5.58	5.69	4.28	4.73	5.35	4.01
Thailand	449	5.78	5.76	3.91	5.30	5.09	4.28
Turkey	301	5.96	6.01	3.58	5.09	4.90	3.83
USA	399	6.12	5.80	3.16	5.93	5.21	3.75
Venezuela	142	5.72	5.62	3.82	4.89	4.85	3.39

Scale 1 to 7 in order of how important those behaviors are considered for effective leadership (7 = highest).

SOURCE: Selected data from Den Hartog, R. House, et al. (GLOBE Project) *Leadership Quarterly*, 10, no. 2 (1999).

dimension allows comparison among those countries on that dimension. For example, being a participative leader is regarded as more important in Canada, Brazil, and Austria than it is in Egypt, Hong Kong, Indonesia, and Mexico. In addition, reading from left to right for a particular country on all dimensions allows development of an effective leadership style profile for that country. In Brazil, for example, one can conclude that an effective leader is expected to be very charismatic, team-oriented and participative, and relatively humane but not autonomous.

The charismatic leader shown in this research is someone who is, for example, a visionary, an inspiration to subordinates, and performance-oriented. A team-oriented leader is someone who exhibits diplomatic, integrative, and collaborative behaviors toward the team. The self-protective dimension describes a leader who is self-centered, conflictual, and status conscious. The participative leader is one who delegates decision making and encourages subordinates to take responsibility. Humane leaders are those who are compassionate to their employees. An autonomous leader is, as expected, an individualist, so countries that ranked participation as important tended to rank autonomy in leadership as relatively unimportant. In Egypt, participation and autonomy were ranked about equally.[62]

This broad, path-breaking research by the GLOBE researchers can be very helpful to managers going abroad, enabling them to exercise culturally appropriate leadership styles. In another stage of this ongoing research project, interviews with managers from various countries led the researchers, headed by Robert House, to conclude that the status and influence of leaders vary a great deal across countries or regions according to the prevailing cultural forces. Whereas Americans, Arabs, Asians, the English, Eastern Europeans, the French, Germans, Latin Americans, and Russians tend to glorify leaders in both the political and organizational arenas; those in the Netherlands, Scandinavia, and Germanic Switzerland have very different views of leadership.[63] Following are some sample comments made by managers from various countries:

- Americans appreciate two kinds of leaders. They seek empowerment from leaders who grant autonomy and delegate authority to subordinates. They also respect the bold, forceful, confident, and risk-taking leader, as personified by John Wayne.
- The Dutch place emphasis on egalitarianism and are skeptical about the value of leadership. Terms like *leader* and *manager* carry a stigma. If a father is employed as a manager, Dutch children will not admit it to their schoolmates.
- Arabs worship their leaders—as long as they are in power!
- Iranians seek power and strength in their leaders.
- Malaysians expect their leaders to behave in a manner that is humble, modest, and dignified.
- The French expect leaders to be "cultivated"—highly educated in the arts and in mathematics.[64]

Other research also provides insight on the relative level of preference for autocratic versus participative leadership styles. For example, Hofstede's four cultural dimensions (discussed in Chapter 3) provide a good starting point to study leader–subordinate expectations and relationships. We can assume, for example, that employees in countries that rank high on power distance (India, Mexico, the Philippines) are more likely to prefer an autocratic leadership style and some paternalism because they are more comfortable with a clear distinction between managers and subordinates rather than with a blurring of decision-making responsibility.

Employees in countries that rank low on power distance (Sweden and Israel) are more likely to prefer a consultative, participative leadership style, and they expect superiors to adhere to that style. Hofstede, in fact, concludes that participative management approaches recommended by many American researchers can be counterproductive in certain cultures.[65] The crucial fact to grasp about leadership in any culture, he points out, is that it is a complement to subordinateship (employee attitudes toward leaders). In other words, perhaps we concentrate too much on leaders and their unlikely ability to change styles at will. Much depends on subordinates and their cultural conditioning, and it is that subordinateship to which the leader must respond.[66] Hofstede points out that his research reflects the values of subordinates, not the values of superiors. His descriptions of the types of subordinateship a leader can expect in societies with three different levels of power distance are shown in Exhibit 11-9.

In another part of his research, Hofstede ranked the relative presence of autocratic norms in the following countries, from lowest to highest: Germany, France, Belgium, Japan, Italy, the United States, the Netherlands, Britain, and India. India ranked much higher than the others on autocracy.[67]

Expectations about managerial authority versus participation were also among the managerial behaviors and philosophies studied by Laurent, a French researcher. In a

EXHIBIT 11-9   Subordinateship for Three Levels of Power Distance

Small Power Distance	Medium Power Distance (United States)	Large Power Distance
Subordinates have weak dependence needs.	Subordinates have medium dependence needs.	Subordinates have strong dependence needs.
Superiors have weak dependence needs toward their superiors.	Superiors have medium dependence needs toward their superiors.	Superiors have strong dependence needs toward their superiors.
Subordinates expect superiors to consult them and may rebel or strike if superiors are not seen as staying within their legitimate role.	Subordinates expect superiors to consult them but will accept autocratic behavior as well.	Subordinates expect superiors to act autocratically.
Ideal superior to most is a loyal democrat.	Ideal superior to most is a resourceful democrat.	Ideal superior to most is a benevolent autocrat or paternalist.
Laws and rules apply to all, and privileges for superiors are not considered acceptable.	Laws and rules apply to all, but a certain level of privilege for superiors is considered normal.	Everybody expects superiors to enjoy privileges; laws and rules differ for superiors and subordinates.
Status symbols are frowned upon and will easily come under attack from subordinates.	Status symbols for superiors contribute moderately to their authority and will be accepted by subordinates.	State symbols are very important and contribute strongly to the superior's authority with the subordinates.

SOURCE: Reprinted from Geert Hofstede, "Motivation, Leadership, and Organization: Do American Theories Apply Abroad?" *Organizational Dynamics* (Summer 1980): 42–63. Copyright © Geert Hofstede, with permission from Elsevier.

study conducted in nine Western European countries, the United States, Indonesia, and Japan, he concluded that national origin significantly affects the perception of what is effective management.[68] For example, Americans and Germans subscribe more to participation than do Italians and Japanese; Indonesians are more comfortable with a strict autocratic structure. Managers in Sweden, the Netherlands, the United States, Denmark, and Great Britain believe that employees should participate in problem solving rather than simply be "fed" all the answers by managers, compared with managers in those countries on the higher end of this scale, such as Italy, Indonesia, and Japan. Laurent's findings about Japan, however, seem to contradict common knowledge about Japan's very participative decision-making culture. In fact, research by Hampden-Turner and Trompenaars places Japan as second highest, after Sweden, in the extent to which leaders delegate authority.[69] Findings regarding the other countries are similar—shown in Exhibit 11-10. However, participative leadership should not mean a lack of initiative or responsibility.

Other classic studies indicate cross-cultural differences in the expectations of leadership behavior. Haire, Ghiselli, and Porter surveyed more than 3,000 managers in fourteen countries. They found that, although managers around the world consistently favored delegation and participation, those managers also had a low appreciation of the capacity and willingness of subordinates to take an active role in the management process.[70]

In addition, several studies of individual countries or areas conclude that a participative leadership style is frequently inappropriate. Managers in Malaysia, Indonesia, Thailand, and the Philippines were found to prefer autocratic leadership, whereas those in Singapore and Hong Kong are less autocratic.[71] Similarly, the Turks have been found to prefer authoritarian leadership, as do the Thais.[72]

In the Middle East, in particular, little delegation occurs. A successful company there must have strong managers who make all the decisions and who go unquestioned. Much emphasis is placed on the use of power through social contacts and family influence, and the chain of command must be rigidly followed.[73] A comparison of these and other management dimensions between Middle Eastern and Western managers is shown in Exhibit 11-11.

The effects of participative leadership can vary even in one location when the employees are from different cultural backgrounds—from which we can conclude that a subordinate's culture is usually a more powerful variable than other factors in the environment.

EXHIBIT 11-10   Comparative Leadership Dimensions: Participation and Initiative

Managerial Initiative, Managers' Sense of Drive and Responsibility		Extent to Which Leaders Delegate Authority	
0 = low; 100 = high		0 = low; 100 = high	
USA	73.67	Sweden	75.51
Sweden	72.29	Japan	69.27
Japan	72.20	Norway	68.50
Finland	69.58	USA	66.23
Korea	67.86	Singapore	65.37
Netherlands	67.11	Denmark	64.65
Singapore	66.34	Canada	64.38
Switzerland	65.71	Finland	62.92
Belgium/Lux	65.47	Switzerland	62.20
Ireland	64.76	Netherlands	61.33
France	64.64	Australia	61.22
Austria	62.56	Germany	60.85
Denmark	62.79	New Zealand	60.54
Italy	62.40	Ireland	59.53
Australia	62.04	UK	58.95
Canada	61.56	Belgium/Lux	54.55
Spain	61.55	Austria	54.29
New Zealand	59.46	France	53.62
Greece	58.50	Italy	46.80
UK	58.25	Spain	44.31
Norway	54.50	Portugal	42.56
Portugal	49.74	Greece	37.95

SOURCE: C. Hampden-Turner and A. Trompenaars, *The Seven Cultures of Capitalism* (New York: Doubleday, 1993).

Research that supports this conclusion includes a study conducted in Saudi Arabia that found participative leadership to be more effective with U.S. workers than with Asian and African employees, and a study in a U.S. plant that found that participative leadership resulted in greater satisfaction and communication among U.S. employees than among Mexican employees.[74]

Exhibit 11-12 depicts an integrative model of the leadership process that pulls together the variables described in this book and in the research on culture, leadership, and motivation—and shows the powerful contingency of culture as it affects the leadership role. Reading from left to right, Exhibit 11-12 presents culture from the broad environmental factors to the outcomes affected by the entire leadership situation. As shown, the broad context in which the manager operates necessitates adjustments in leadership style to all those variables relating to the work and task environment and the people involved. Cultural variables (values, work norms, the locus of control, and so forth), as they affect everyone involved—leader, subordinates, and work groups—then shape the content of the immediate leadership situation.

The leader–follower interaction is then further shaped by the leader's choice of behaviors (autocratic, participative, and so on) and by the employees' attitudes toward the leader and the incentives. Motivation effects—various levels of effort, performance, and satisfaction—result from these interactions, on an individual and a group level. These effects determine the outcomes for the company (productivity, quality) and for the employees (satisfaction, positive climate). The results and rewards from those outcomes then act as feedback (positive or negative) into the cycle of the motivation and leadership process.

Clearly, then, international managers should take seriously the culture contingency in their application of the contingency theory of leadership: They must adjust their leadership behaviors according to the context, norms, attitudes, and other variables in that society. One example of the complexity of the leadership situation involving obvious

Managerial Function	Middle Eastern Stereotype	Western Stereotype
Organizational design	Highly bureaucratic, overcentralized with power and authority at the top. Vague relationships. Ambiguous and unpredictable organization environments.	Less bureaucratic, more delegation of authority. Relatively decentralized structure.
Patterns of decision making	Ad hoc planning, decisions made at the highest level of management. Unwillingness to take high risk inherent in decision making.	Sophisticated planning techniques, modern tools of decision making, elaborate management information systems.
Performance evaluation and control	Informal control mechanisms, routine checks on performance. Lack of vigorous performance evaluation systems.	Fairly advanced control systems focusing on cost reduction and organizational effectiveness.
Manpower policies	Heavy reliance on personal contacts and getting individuals from the "right social origin" to fill major positions.	Sound personnel management policies. Candidates' qualifications are usually the basis for selection decisions.
Leadership	Highly authoritarian tone, rigid instructions. Too many management directives.	Less emphasis on leader's personality, considerable weight on leader's style and performance.
Communication	The tone depends on the communicants. Social position, power, and family influence are ever-present factors. Chain of command must be followed rigidly. People relate to each other tightly and specifically. Friendships are intense and binding.	Stress usually on equality and a minimization of differences. People relate to each other loosely and generally. Friendships not intense and binding.
Management methods	Generally old and outdated.	Generally modern and more scientific.

SOURCE: Copyright © 1980 by The Regents of the University of California. Reprinted from the *California Management Review* 22, no. 3. By permission of The Regents.

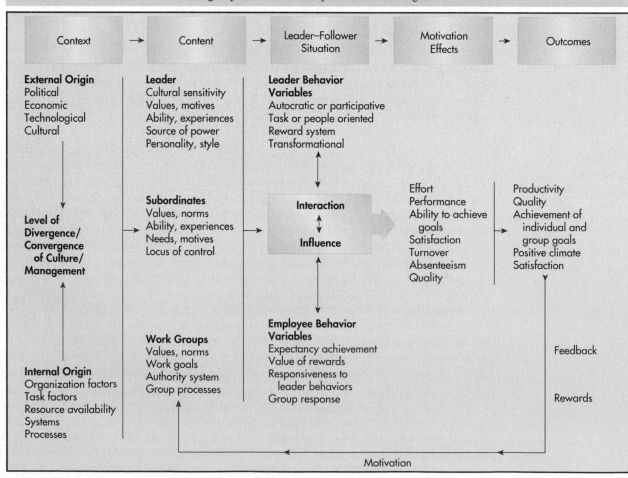

contextual as well as cultural factors can be seen in the results of a study of how Russian employees responded to the participative management practices of North American managers. It was found that the performance of the Russian workers decreased, which the researchers attributed to a history of employee ideas being ignored by Russian managers, as well as cultural value differences.[75] To gain more insight into comparative leadership situations, Comparative Management in Focus: Leadership in India highlights the leadership context in India, along with the implications for appropriate leadership by expatriates.

Comparative Management in Focus

Leadership in India

The most effective leadership style in India would thus combine integrity, being organized, an action orientation, being a self starter, charisma, and a collective orientation; with being a problem solver, a visionary, entrepreneurial, and inspirational, in that order.
—*Jagdeep S. Chhoker, 2001*[76]

Results from the recent GLOBE research program confirm the continued diversity and complexity of Indian society and culture, demanding unique skills and behaviors from leaders in India. Although Indian culture is ancient, the society also appears to be transitioning toward power equalization. Although humane orientation and collectivism are still the most important aspects of Indian culture, at the same time there is an increasing preference for individualism.[77]

Many subtle effects of the caste system remain and still affect life in organizations in the form of a strict adherence to hierarchy. Indians are disposed to hierarchically structure all relationships.[78] Management in India is often autocratic, based on formal authority and charisma. Family norms emphasizing loyalty to the family authority figure underlie the limited decision-making experience and lack of familiarity with responsibility exhibited by some employees. Consequently, decision making is centralized, with much emphasis on rules and a low propensity for risk.[79] In addition, intricate family ties and strong authority figures perpetuate a managerial style of paternalism.

Under the pervasive influences of religion, caste, and family on the life of Hindus (about 75 percent of the population), the Indian culture stresses moral orientation and loyalty, as in the pursuit of dharma (one's obligation to society, rather than personal goals). Work tends to be viewed primarily in the context of family or intercaste relationships, rather than being valued for itself.[80]

Since the original source of power is family and friends, nepotism is common at both the lowest and highest levels. Not surprisingly, power based on expertise frequently takes a backseat to power based on position.[81] In India, it is difficult for nonfamily members to advance into upper management. Such strong cultural influences in managers' origins affect managerial style.

Because of the respect for authority and obedience within the Indian family system, attempts by managers—whether Indian or otherwise—to delegate authority often result in confusion and a lack of respect for the manager; Indian employees expect the managers to make the decisions. The norm is to "check with the boss." Any introduction of participative management requires careful training because it is so unlike the cultural norms. Generally, U.S. or other "foreign" managers in India need to make connections with the right families, make contact at the highest levels, and provide incentives for middle managers and assistants to help nudge proposals upward.[82]

Relationship orientation seems to be a more important characteristic of effective leaders in India than performance or task orientation.
—*Jagdeep S. Chhoker, 2001*[83]

On the micro level of leadership—manager to employees—managers from other cultures are wise to tread slowly while trying to understand the culture and find what works, and to realize that they will encounter a wide range of organizational practices. Research by the GLOBE project researchers found that other important characteristics for effective leadership in India are an action orientation and charisma. They found that management tends to be formal in what has become known as a "vertical collectivist" culture and that autocratic and bureaucratic leadership styles usually work best.[84]

Various other proposals have been put forward to help managers move toward more effective leadership. Tripathi suggests that "indigenous values, such as familism, need to be synthesized with the values of industrial democracy."[85] Similarly, Sinha proposes that, while a leader in India has to be a "nurturant," taking a personal interest in the well-being of each subordinate, he or she can use that nurturance to encourage increasing levels of participation. The manager may accomplish this by guiding and directing subordinates to work hard and maintain a high level of productivity, reinforcing each stage with increased nurturance.[86] According to Sinha and Sinha, a prerequisite to effective cross-cultural leadership in India is to establish work as the "master value." Once this is done, "other social values will reorganize themselves to help realize the master value."[87]

Multiple problems abound on the macro level of leadership of a global enterprise in India, as discovered by companies such as Gillette, Texas Instruments, and Hewlett-Packard. Investment opportunities are very attractive, with a potential for great sales and a pool of cheap, highly educated, and skilled labor. Even after getting through the entrenched bureaucracy to set up business, though, managers may face many operating problems because of the undeveloped infrastructure and difficult climate. Gaining control and integrating leadership styles with local managers are additional hurdles. Western managers, used to being boss in their own companies, may have difficulty taking orders from Indian partners and prefer to operate at a faster pace.[88] Gill, of Gillette, suggests, "You've got to find the right partner and convince him to give you complete management control."[89] Failure to include an Indian partner or to build local support was behind the cancellation of Enron's $2.8 billion power project in Dhabol, as part of a resurgence of economic nationalism in India pending national elections in 1995. The project was reinstated in 1999; but as of 2001, problems between Enron and the Indian government continued and Enron decided not to build more plants in India.[90] In other areas, such as telecommunications, liberalization is progressing well, to the benefit of companies such as AT&T, Motorola, and Texas Instruments (TI). It is noteworthy that these companies have Indian joint-venture partners and Indian CEOs. TI India's managing director, Srini Rajam, noted that the Bangalore plant was responsible for one-third of TI's design automation for semiconductor products worldwide.[91]

India is expected to be an economic giant someday. Meanwhile, U.S. managers must realize that setting up and running a successful business in India requires astute leadership skills, including integrating and collaborating at all levels of the community for the long term.

As noted, leadership refers not just to the manager–subordinate relationship, but to the important task of running the whole company, division, or unit for which a manager is responsible. When that is a global responsibility, it is vital to be able to adapt one's leadership style to the local context on many levels. Nancy McKinstry, an American leader in Europe, is very sensitive to that imperative. Since she moved to Europe a year ago, charged with the task of turning around the troubled Wolters Kluwer, the Dutch publishing group, she "has had plenty of experience of the way national and cultural differences can both bedevil and enliven business."[92] One immediate difference she noticed is that she is one of few women in senior management in Holland. That fact, added to the focus of the Dutch media on the executive as a person and the views of the employees, rather than the focus on the company as in the United States, was surprising to her. As she continues her restructuring plan, Ms. McKinstry (whose physician husband commutes every two weeks between his hospital job in New York and his family in Amsterdam) has found that there is a misconception that she is going to apply an American, bottom-line- leadership style. However, she says:

> *There isn't that one-size-fits-all approach, not even within Europe. . . . If you*
> *have a product or a customer problem in France, there might be an approach*
> *that works extremely well. But if you took that same approach and tried to*
> *solve the exact same problem in Holland, you might fail.* [93]

NANCY MCKINSTRY,
Chairman and CEO, Wolters Kluwer Publishing Group, Holland, July 15, 2004[94]

Ms McKinstry explains that in southern Europe, there's far more nuance to what people are saying compared to northern Europe, and in particular compared to the U.S. direct, optimistic style. She finds that they often don't want to say 'No' to her, even though they may not be able to achieve what she is asking them. Her leadership approach is to listen hard and say "How are you going to go about meeting this goal?"[95].

CONCLUSION

Because leadership and motivation entail constant interactions with others (employees, peers, superiors, outside contacts), cultural influences on these critical management functions are very strong. Certainly, other powerful variables are intricately involved in the international management context, particularly those of economics and politics. Effective leaders carefully examine the entire context and develop sensitivity to others' values and expectations regarding personal and group interactions, performance, and outcomes— and then act accordingly.

Summary of Key Points

1. Motivation and leadership are factors in the successful implementation of desired strategy. However, while many of the basic principles are universal, much of the actual content and process are culture-contingent—a function of an individual's needs, value systems, and environmental context.

2. One problem in using content theories for cross-cultural research, such as those created by Maslow and Herzberg, is the assumption of their universal application. Because they were developed in the United States, even the concepts, such as achievement or esteem, may have different meanings in other societies, resulting in a noncomparable basis of research.

3. Implicit in motivating an employee is an understanding of which of the employee's needs are satisfied by work. Studies on the "meaning of work" indicate considerable cross-cultural differences.

4. Other studies on cross-cultural motivation support Herzberg's two-factor theory. They also indicate, as do studies using Maslow's theory, support for the greater importance of intrinsic factors to motivation, at least on the managerial level. One problem with Herzberg's theory is that it does not account for all relevant cultural variables.

5. A reexamination of motivation relative to Hofstede's dimensions of power distance, uncertainty avoidance, individualism, and masculinity provides another perspective on the cultural contexts that can influence motivational structures.

6. Incentives and reward systems must be designed to reflect the motivational structure and relative cultural emphasis on five categories of rewards: financial, social status, job content, career, and professional.

7. Effective leadership is crucial to the ability of a company to achieve its goals. The challenge is to decide what is effective leadership in different international or mixed-culture situations.

8. The perception of what makes a good leader—both traits and behaviors—varies a great deal from one society to another. The recent GLOBE leadership study across sixty-two countries provides considerable insight into culturally appropriate leadership behaviors.

9. Contingency theory is applicable to cross-cultural leadership situations because of the vast number of cultural and national variables that can affect the dynamics of the leadership context. These include leader–subordinate and group relations, which are affected by cultural expectations, values, needs, attitudes, perceptions of risk, and loci of control.

10. Joint ventures with other countries present a common but complex situation in which leaders must work together to anticipate and address cross-cultural problems.

Discussion Questions

1. Discuss the concept of work centrality and its implications for motivation. Use specific country examples and discuss the relative meaning of work in those countries.
2. What are the implications for motivation of Hofstede's research findings on the dimensions of power distance, uncertainty avoidance, individualism, and masculinity?
3. Explain what is meant by the need to design culturally appropriate reward systems. Give some examples.
4. Develop a cultural profile for workers in Mexico and discuss how you would motivate them.
5. Describe the variables of content and context in the leadership situation. What additional variables are involved in cross-cultural leadership?
6. Explain the theory of contingency leadership and discuss the role of culture in that theory.
7. How can we use Hofstede's four dimensions—power distance, uncertainty avoidance, individualism, and masculinity—to gain insight into leader–subordinate relationships around the world? Give some specific examples.
8. Describe the autocratic versus democratic leadership dimension. Discuss the cultural contingency in this dimension and give some examples of research findings indicating differences among countries.
9. Discuss how you would develop a profile of an effective leader from the research results from the GLOBE project. Give an example.

Application Exercises

1. Using the material on motivation in this chapter, design a suitable organizational reward system for the workers in your company's plant in Mexico.
2. Choose a country and do some research (and conduct interviews, if possible) to create a cultural profile. Focus on factors affecting behavior in the workplace. Integrate any findings regarding motivation or work attitudes and behaviors. Decide on the type of approach to motivation you would take and the kinds of incentive and reward systems you would set up as manager of a subsidiary in that country. Use the theories on motivation discussed in this chapter to infer motivational structures relative to that society. Then decide what type of leadership style and process you would use. What major contingencies did you take into account?
3. Try to interview several people from a specific ethnic subculture in a company or in your college regarding values, needs, expectations in the workplace, and so on. Sketch a motivational profile of this subculture and present it to your class for discussion.

Experiential Exercises

1. Bill Higgins had served as the manager of a large U.S. timber company located in a rather remote rain forest in a South American country. Since it began its logging operations in the 1950s, a major problem facing the company has been the recruitment of labor. The only nearby source of labor is the sparsely populated local Indian group in the area. Bill's company has been in direct competition for laborers with a German company operating in the same region. In an attempt to attract the required number of laborers, Bill's company invested heavily in new housing and offered considerably higher wages than the German company, as well as a guaranteed forty-hour work week. Yet the majority of the available workers continued to work for the German company, despite its substandard housing and minimum hourly wage. Bill finally brought in several U.S. anthropologists who had worked among the local Indians. The answer to Bill's labor recruitment problem was quite simple, but it required looking at the values of the Indian labor force rather than simply building facilities that would appeal to the typical U.S. laborer.

   What did the anthropologists tell Bill?

   SOURCE: Gary P. Ferraro, *The Cultural Dimensions of International Business*, 2ed (Upper Saddle River, NJ: Prentice Hall, 1994).

2. Meet with another student, preferably one whom you know well. Talk with that person and draw up a list of leadership skills you perceive him or her to possess. Then consider your research and readings regarding cross-cultural leadership. Name two countries where you think the student would be an effective leader and two where you think there would be conflict. Discuss those areas of conflict. Then reverse the procedure to find out more about yourself. Share with the class, if you wish.

Internet Resources

Visit the Deresky companion Web site at prenhall. com/ deresky for this chapter's Internet resources.

Sir Richard Branson's Planes, Trains, Resorts, and Colas in 2004: A Case in Global Leadership

Sir Richard Branson, long considered king of the über-stretch, has successfully wrapped his core Virgin brand (which began as a student magazine and small mail order record company in the 1970s) around everything from wine to bridal to travel and financial services. No matter what type of business it is, the autographed Virgin identity and/or signature red and white colors are prominently incorporated within the business unit's visual identity.

—de Mesa, Alycia. www.brandchannel.com[1]

In today's competitive world, running a global company requires strong leadership skills based on creative thinking, sound judgment, and visionary attitude. Motivating company employees who may be located in far-flung corners of the world can be a daunting task. Companies may have powerful brands, but weaker leadership can impinge smooth operations. In any company, corporate leadership requires two important areas, content leadership (leader's attributes and decision making skills) and context leadership (variables dealing with a particular situation).[2] Corporate leadership in global business becomes even more complex when companies enter into other markets. Global managers understand that the magic formula for success is how to adapt their organizational skills to local cultures. This may include changing corporate and functional strategies on a regular basis. The challenge of working and dealing with people in the international environment can be a complex task. Virgin Group's Chairman, President and CEO, Sir Richard Branson is a good example, who in many categories fits well with the qualities needed to be a role model in global leadership. As a founder of the group, he continues to inspire and lead Virgin and has made the company one of the top global brands. Under the leadership of Sir Branson, Virgin Group has over 200 companies, selling books, music, colas, mobile phone, and aggressively competing in large industries such as airlines, trains, and resorts. In 2004, Virgin is a $7 billion successful empire and employs 36,000 workers all over the world

(see Table 1).[3] Virgin's success can be attributed to Sir Branson's charismatic personality and down-to-earth leadership style, often using common sense strategies and openness. Often called flamboyant and charismatic, Sir Branson is a highly effective leader and tough negotiator. His outward-oriented approach was a big plus in the establishment of the company. Media often called him a "walking billboard" and a "one man brand." As a tireless worker, Sir Branson has converted Virgin into a top tier brand in Europe and other parts of the world.[4] One analyst commented:

Yet Branson himself is the opposite of elitist, his company is one of the least hierarchical one could come across. To the annoyance of his senior managers, Branson seems to pay as much attention to a chat with a clerk in the airline's mailroom as to a memorandum from his marketing director. Letters from his staff are always read first. . . . He manages and motivates his staff by example. Branson is highly energetic.[5]

Another analyst observed:

In the modern world of business, Richard Branson is an anomaly. In an era dominated by strategists, he is an opportunist. Through his company, the Virgin Group, he has created a unique business phenomenon. Never before has a single brand been so successfully deployed across such a diverse range of goods and services."[6]

From the corporate perspective, Sir Branson is famous for his team building skills and consultative approach in day-to-day business. On many occasions, he quietly but firmly initiated new ventures from scratch and built them into large and profitable entities (see Table 1). Virgin Atlantic Airways, the flagship of the group, fits in this category, having started as a small entity

---

[1]de Mesa, Alycia, "How Far Can a Brand Stretch?" BrandChannel.com, February 23, 2004, p. 1.

[2]Deresky, Helen. (2003). *International Management: Managing Across Borders and Cultures,* Upper Saddle River, New Jersey: Prentice Hall, p. 305.

[3]For detail, see: *Hoover's Online* (2004). "Virgin Group, Ltd.," (April), p. 1, (www.hoover.com).

[4]For detail, see: Brandchannel.com, "Brand of the Year 2003," (www.brandchannel.com); *Financial Times.* (2002). "Mature, Experienced Virgin Seeks Out Bright City Lights," (May 7), p. 24.

[5]Jackson, Tim. (1996). *Richard Branson—Virgin King: Inside Richard Branson's Business Empire,* Rocklin, California: Prima Publishing, pp. 6–7.

[6]Dearlove, Des. (1999). *Business the Richard Branson Way: 10 Secrets of the World's Greatest Brand-Builder,* New York: American Management Association., p. 1.

Table 1   Virgin Group: Company Data and Selected Brands

A. Company data (2003)	
Chairman, President, and CEO:	Sir Richard Branson
Company type:	Private
Sales:	$7.00 billion (estimated)
Sales growth:	7.7%
Total employees:	36,000 (estimated)
B: Selected companies and brands in 2004	
Virgin Atlantic	Virgin Mobile Australia
Virgin Blue	Virgin Mobile
Virgin Trains	Virgin Drinks
Virgin Balloon Flights	Train.com
Virgin Mobile	Limited Edition by Virgin
Virgin Active	Virgin Credit Card
Virgin V2 Music	Virgin Cola
V.Shop	Virgin Publishing
Virgin Bride	Virgin Net
Virgin Wines	Virgin Energy
Virgin Cosmetics	Virgin Cars
Virgin One	Virgin Direct
London Broncos	VirginMoney.com
The Roof Gardens	Virgin Rapido
Virgin Express	Strom Model Agency
Virgin Holidays	Virgin Student.com
Virgin Pulse	Virgin Galactic.com
Virgin Megastores	

SOURCE: Company Web site (www.virgin.com); Adbrand.net (www.mind-advertising.com); Hoover's.com (www.hoover.com).

and later becoming a huge success. As a company's main spokesperson, Sir Branson is always "visible" and does not miss any opportunity to promote the Virgin brand, often seeking "daring personal exploits."[7] For example, on many occasions, Sir Branson attempted daredevil stunts and balloon rides across the globe to get free publicity for the company. At the micro level, Sir Branson is highly involved with the management for corporate growth and expansion. At the macro level, Sir Branson personally gets involved in the risky yet profitable ventures that the company starts. Virgin Group avoids large acquisitions and aggressively develops smaller companies for future growth in new industries. For this reason, Virgin's corporate culture keeps Sir Branson busy and well informed about the company's global operations.

Customer service is Sir Branson's utmost priority. It is one of the reasons that in customer service, Virgin Atlantic Airways is among the top brands in the airline industry. To be a successful corporate leader, one has to deal with the day-to-day activities of their companies. Sir Branson is good at leading his $7 billion empire in a variety of industries and markets where environments are dynamic and changing (see Table 1).[8] In 2004, Sir Branson's Virgin is one of the highly rated companies in the areas of airlines, resorts, auto rentals, mobile phones, and other products. Although a latecomer in the U.S., Virgin Group plans on starting a low cost airline, Virgin USA in 2004.[9] Virgin Mobile's operations are booming in the UK and have entered into the U.S. by making a joint venture with Sprint. In Australia, Virgin Blue, a low

---

[7]De Vries, Manfred and F. R. Kets. (1998). "Charisma in Action: The Transformational Abilities of Virgin's Richard Branson and ABB's Percy Barnevik," *Organizational Dynamics*, (Winter), p. 9. For a good discussion on global leadership, see: Dalton, Maxine, et al. (2002). *Success for the New Global Manager: How to Work Across Distances, Countries, and Cultures,* San Francisco, California: Jossey-Bass; McCall, Morgan and George P. Hollenbeck. (2002). *Developing Global Executives,* Boston, Massachusetts: Harvard Business School Press.

[8]*The Wall Street Journal.* (2004). "Virgin Atlantic plans to boost fleet, routes and work force," (March 24), p. D8.
[9]For more information, see: *Financial Times.* (2004). "U.S. efforts to woo Virgin verge on the ridiculous," (February 24), p. 16; *Financial Times.* (2004). "Virgin set to reveal plans for expansion," (March 24), p. 18.

cost airline, is doing well. In conclusion, Sir Branson has created an umbrella of companies where cooperation rather than intra-company competition is encouraged. Although Virgin Group does face problems in some of its new ventures and markets, the company as a whole is a classic case in the areas of global leadership-infact one could say "outerworld leadership", with his latest venture into space travel, Virgin Galactic LLC. Sir Branson's common sense leadership skills and strategies are a great asset to Virgin. The company's Web site accurately affirms this corporate philosophy that states:

Our companies are part of a family rather than a hierarchy. They are empowered to run their own affairs, yet other companies help one another, and solutions to problems come from all kinds of sources. In a sense, we are community, with shared ideas, values, interests, and goals. The proof of our success is real and tangible."[10]

[10]See: Company Web site (www.virgin.com).

CASE QUESTIONS

1. What are your views of Sir Richard Branson's leadership style and his motivational skills?
2. Analyze and discuss the transformation and future prospects of the company in global markets under the leadership of Sir Richard Branson.
3. What did you learn from the leadership style of Sir Richard Branson?

SOURCE: Written especially for this book by Syed Tariq Anwar, May 2004. Copyright © Syed Tariq Anwar.

**The material in this case is intended to be used as a basis for classroom/academic discussion rather than to illustrate either effective or ineffective handling of a managerial situation or business practices.

Case 14 Management of Human Assets at Infosys

"Our assets walk out of the door each evening. We have to make sure that they come back the next morning."(Narayana Murthy, CEO Infosys).

At a time when organizations are debating the strategic importance of their human resources, Infosys, a consulting and software services organization, includes its human resources on its Balance Sheet to affirm their asset value.[1] Mr. Mohandas Pai, Chief Financial Officer of Infosys, provides a rationale for this practice:

"Investors examine financial and non-financial parameters that determine long-term success of a company. These new non-financial parameters challenge the usefulness of evaluating companies solely on traditional measures as they appear in a typical financial report. Human resources represent the collective expertise, innovation, leadership, entrepreneurial and managerial skills endowed in the employees of an organization. Our representation is based on the belief that intangible assets provide a tool to our investors for evaluating market-worthiness of Infosys."

As a knowledge-intensive company, Infosys recognizes the value of its human assets in maintaining and increasing its competitive position. At the same time, Infosys realizes that these assets can easily "walk away," as competitors in India and abroad covet its IT talent. Consequently, the challenge facing Infosys is: "How can it attract, retain and develop its human assets in a highly competitive and dynamic environment?" The answer to this question may lie in the management of the 9,000 plus Infocians (as the employees are referred to), and that of many more to be hired in the future.

OVERVIEW

Infosys, one of India's leading information technology ("IT") services companies, uses an extensive non-U.S. based ("offshore") infrastructure to provide managed software solutions to clients worldwide.[2] Headquartered in Bangalore, India, Infosys has seventeen state-of-the-art software development facilities throughout India and one development center in Canada. These enable it to provide quality, cost-effective services to clients in a resource-constrained environment.

Through its worldwide sales headquarters in Fremont, California (and nineteen other sales offices located in the United States, Canada, the United Kingdom, Belgium, Sweden, Germany, Australia, Japan, and India), Infosys markets its services to large IT-intensive businesses. During fiscal 2000, Infosys derived 78.0% of its revenues from North America, 14.8% from Europe and 1.4% from India. Although most Infosys revenues are from the United States, Infosys maintains a diversified client base, with its largest client representing 7.2% of fiscal 2000 revenues. As of March 31, 2000, Infosys had approximately 194 clients. This client base [is] comprised of mainly Fortune 500 companies, growing Internet companies, and other multinational companies. As a result of its commitment to quality and client service, Infosys has a high level of repeat business. For fiscal 2000 and 1999, existing clients from the previous fiscal year generated 87.0% and 90.0%, respectively, of Infosys's revenues.[3]

HISTORY

Seven software professionals founded Infosys in 1981 with the goals of leveraging sweat equity and creating wealth legally and ethically in India. This was a daunting task in a country where the government was allegedly more concerned with redistributing wealth than creating it. Most of India's commerce was owned and controlled by an oligarchy of families to which Infosys had no ties.

Infosys's competitive advantage has historically been derived from low wage costs in India relative to service providers in the United States and Europe. Their initial foray into the U.S. market was through a company called Data Basics Corp. as a "body-shop" or on-site developer of software for U.S. customers. Later, in 1987, Infosys formed a joint venture with Kurt Salmon Associates to handle marketing in the U.S. These initial entries into the U.S. market were a stepping stone for Infosys's growth in later years.[4]

The years between 1981 and 1991 were not easy for Infosys, which aimed to create large-scale software

---

*Sumita Raghuram (Assistant Professor of Management, Fordham University, New York) wrote this case to facilitate classroom discussion rather than to illustrate either effective or ineffective handling of a business situation. The case has benefited from the input of many key employees at Infosys.

[1]For details about the accounting model used to calculate human asset value, please see Appendix A.

[2]For details about their products, please see Appendix B.

---

[3]Annual Report 2000.

[4]"Infosys: Can They Make It?" *Business World* 7–21, November 1998, p. 19–22.

factories in India using contemporary technology, methodology, and software tools. However there were many obstacles. First, data and satellite communications were not readily available in India. Second, importation of equipment from abroad was difficult and expensive because of high tariffs. Third, the premium at which one could value shares in an IPO was decided by a government officer, not by the market, and it was generally low; hence, equity was not a viable option for financing. Debt equity was the only remaining option.[5]

In 1991, partly from International Monetary Fund pressure and shrinking currency reserves, the Indian government began liberalizing the economy. The office through which an IPO was valued was abolished and the market was allowed to decide what the stock premium would be. The government also abolished duty on all imports brought in for export purposes and foreign investment was allowed. This governmental change brought both new opportunities and new threats to Infosys, opportunities to raise capital and threats from increased competition.

In 1993, Infosys went public on the Indian stock exchange with a market capitalization of $10 million. Infosys's initial public offering ("IPO") raised approximately $4.4 million in gross aggregate proceeds. In 1999 Infosys was listed on NASDAQ with a market capitalization of $10 billion.[6] A NASDAQ listing was significant for Infosys in many ways. As Nandan Nilekani, co-founder and COO of Infosys explains, "We wanted to be recognized as a global company, and it was imperative that we were listed on the largest and deepest capital markets in the world." Infosys expects NASDAQ trading will attract global investors and thus raise the capital it can use for future growth. A NASDAQ listing also helps Infosys in other ways. For example, it helps it build brand equity that enhances the company's visibility beyond India. It also enables Infosys to offer employees stock options overseas. This will enable Infosys to attract top-notch talent globally.

The liberalization of the Indian economy also brought unprecedented competition to India. Such multinational corporations as IBM, Sun Microsystems, and Motorola could leverage their vast financial resources to compete for India's most valuable resources, its people. MNCs could provide the Indian people with never before available salaries and compensation competitive on a global scale.[7] Competition for IT talent was further aggravated in 2000 by the increase in the quota of H-1 visas that allow organizations to hire professionals overseas.

LEADERSHIP AND CULTURE

Most of the current human resource practices at Infosys result from the vision of the leaders and the culture that

they have created. Narayana Murthy, known for his leadership and vision, is the public image of Infosys. His leadership style is humble and straight-forward, quite uncommon in the world of Indian business. Narayana Murthy believes in sharing wealth with his employees and in leading by example. In a knowledge-based business like Infosys, he sees the importance of consistency in rhetoric and action in empowering employees. Narayana Murthy is credited with creating a culture of closeness and empowerment at Infosys. His management style, rare among Indian business leaders, is based on [W]estern management.[8]

The other founding members of Infosys contribute their own specialties. Though less known, they each play a critical part in shaping the culture and running the operations at Infosys. These unique personalities, with their particular strengths, create the basis for an uncommon culture at Infosys. Infosys was voted India's most admired company by a January 2000 survey in *The Economic Times.*[9] According to Narayana Murthy, what Infosys has on its side is "youth, speed, and imagination, and [they] are constantly innovating in every area of [their] operation."[10] The founders' efforts have been paying off. According to a California-based management consultant working in India, "Infosys has been critical in changing the mind-set of India."[11] Transparency is one of the important values held by Infosys. A practice illustrative of this value is its very early decision to adopt the U.S. GAAP standards, the most stringent standards, for reporting its financial results.

Hema Ravichandar, the Senior VP of Human Resources, sums up the characteristics of the culture that distinguish Infosys from its competitors

> *"Our emphasis on transparency and communication sets us apart from the prevalent family owned businesses operating in India. Our emphasis on getting the employees' emotional buy-in into the company distinguishes us from the MNCs that have recently entered the Indian business scene."*

The attempt to ensure emotional buy-in is evident in their effort to provide a self-sufficient work environment for their employees. Infosys inaugurated its facilities in Bangalore under the name of "Infosys City" in November 2000. Spread over 44.225 acres, it is claimed to be the largest software services campus in the world. It has the largest "video wall" in Asia which allows for video conferencing simultaneously from multiple centers. The existing buildings also form part of the Infosys City. The City contains food courts that serve Chinese, North Indian, South Indian, and Western cuisine. A state-of-the-art gym, golf course, pool tables, table tennis

[5]"Ten Minutes with NR Narayana Murthy," *NASDAQ/AMEX International Magazine,* Issue 24, September 1999.

[6]"Infosys, The First Indian Company to Trade on NASDAQ," *Forbes* 23 August 1999, p. 22.

[7]"The Lightening Spark," *Silicon Technology and Business Magazine,* August 1998, p. 50–51.

[8]Joshi, Rahul. "Infosys Has Completed the Infancy Stage." *The Economic Times* 3 January 2000.

[9]"Infosys Voted India's Most Admired Company, Followed by HLL, Wipro." *The Economic Times* 3 January 2000.

[10]"Ten Minutes with N.R. Narayana Murthy" *NASDAQ/AMEX International Magazine* 24 September 1999, p. 13.

[11]"Start Up: From India to America." *Forbes* 23 August 1999, p. 22–23.

tables, and dance floor are already in place. The sauna, grocery store, an Infosys Store, 50,000 square feet [of] swimming pool, and a lake with paddling boats will soon be part of the City. The eco-friendly campus now has 3,500 trees, with another 2,500 more when the City is complete. The landscape includes stone paths, rose beds, bamboo clusters with benches beneath them, fountains, and water recycling plants. Besides the enticing work environment, Infosys provides state of the art technology to its employees. For example, PCs used by Infocians are upgraded every two years.

MANAGEMENT OF THE HUMAN RESOURCE ASSETS

As of March 31, 2000, Infosys had approximately 5,400 employees. The current employee strength represents a growth rate between 40–50% since 1996. Of these about 86% are engaged in software development (including trainees) and the other 14% are in support services. fifty seven percent of the employees are aged between 20–25 years, 31 percent are aged between 26–30 years, and the other 12% are over 31 years of age. Approximately 85% of the employees are males, and 15% are females.

Infosys invests heavily in its programs to recruit, train, and retain qualified employees. Further, management believes that Infosys has established a reputation as one of the most preferred employers for software engineers in India. Elsewhere in the software industry, employee attrition rate is around 30%; Infosys boasts an employee attrition rate of only 9.8%.

SELECTION

The first step in the strategic management of a company's human resources is selection of assets with skills and potential consistent with its business requirements. Infosys's business requirements are flexibility and innovation. Accordingly, it has developed clear selection criteria consistent with this business need. Selection is based on [an] individual's ability to learn, academic achievement, [and] conceptual knowledge, as well as temperament for (and fit with) Infosys's culture. Further, because of Infosys's reputation as a premier employer, it can select from a large pool of qualified applicants within India. Competition among applicants is intense.

One selection criteria in particular stands out: the learnability. At Infosys, *learnability* is defined as the ability of an individual to derive general conclusions from specific situations and then apply them to a new unstructured situation.

P.S. Srivathsa, the Senior Manager of Human Resource Development, adds:

"Learnability is considered an important criterion because the project life cycle is short and technology is changing rapidly—so the ability of the person to take the concept learnt in one setting and to apply it to another is very important. At Infosys learnability is assessed through written tests that include mathematical and analytical questions geared towards assessing the aptitude of a person to derive generic patterns from a situation."

For its entry-level positions, Infosys focuses its recruiting efforts on students with excellent academic background from engineering departments of Indian schools. The first step in the hiring process is manpower planning, where the numbers are determined. This planning usually takes place 20 months ahead of the hiring process. Recruitment includes campus interviews, as well as inviting applications over the Internet, newspaper ads, through job fairs, and HR consultants. The initial screening is based on such criteria as academics and experience. In 1999, 185,000 resumes were processed and, after the initial screening, were reduced to 40,000 resumes. The shortlisted applicants undergo a selection test.

The test comprises two main components: arithmetic reasoning and logical reasoning. Because of time pressures involved in testing the large volume of candidates across the country, the reading comprehension section has been eliminated, cutting down the testing time to one hour. Tutorials or coaching classes offered by third parties are popular among individuals who wish to prepare for these competitive tests. Infosys has a question bank system from which questions are picked randomly for each test center. Those who score above the cut-off in the selection test are called for an interview.

Interviews are conducted jointly by the human resource managers and the technical manager. At the interview stage, screening criteria used are aspirations, expectations, flexibility, presentation skills, and communication skills. In 1999, 10,000 candidates were interviewed, and offers were extended to approximately 3,330. Of these, approximately 2,050 accepted.

Rejected candidates may reapply after nine months. People do come back and, if they have picked up the necessary skills, they are hired.

TRAINING AND DEVELOPMENT

At Infosys, training and development [constitute] the next step in building its human assets where the objective is to match the available skills and abilities to its business requirements. In the headquarters at Bangalore, the education and research center is housed in a building that can train 1,000 software engineers simultaneously. It comprises fully equipped classrooms, labs with video-conferencing units, individual faculty rooms, and a 30,000 square foot library with a capacity for 10,000 books. In addition, under construction are a management development training center and a Wireless Center for Excellence to be built by Nortel Networks. The Wireless Center is expected to be the e-commerce research center with a capacity for 650 people working on research in wireless Internet capabilities.

The education and research department of Infosys offered 241 courses in 1998–1999, including courses in business, database management, e-commerce, quality systems, programming language (e.g., Java, C++), networking concepts, software development, languages (e.g., French, Japanese), interpersonal skills (e.g., communication), and managerial skills (leadership, team management, negotiation). Full-time faculty teaches 75% of these courses; professionals teach 10% of the courses and outside vendors offer rest of the courses. The full time faculty comprises 40 individuals from academics and industry. The human resources department supplies 5 additional facilitators, who provide the soft-skills training; the quality control department delivers the training for quality.

All fresh technology entrants receive 14.5 weeks of training: 3 days of orientation (e.g. corporate culture, customers), 5 weeks of foundation courses (e.g., programming, systems development, interpersonal skills), 7 weeks of technology courses (e.g. C++, UNIX, HTML), and 2 weeks of group project. In 1998–1999, 1,750 new entrants received the basic training. In addition, training is provided as a part of the continuing education. In 1998–1999, 2,000 employees received training as continuing education: about 8 days/person in technical and software engineering, 1.5 days/person in managerial skills, and 3 days/person in project management.

Beyond entry-level training, people may nominate themselves for the scheduled courses. Close to 100 courses are offered each quarter, with duration from 1 day to 6 days. Most courses are presented in classrooms, some in labs. In addition, course may be offered on request.

Training needs are assessed through various mechanisms; the objective is to fine-tune them to business needs. First the corporate management determines segment-wise technology requirements. These expectations are communicated to the education and research department. So, for instance, the education and research department may be informed of the requirement for 500 people with knowledge in Internet technology in the near future. Specific skill needs such as interfacing with Microsoft or Java may be determined through a deeper analysis. Typically, about 3–6 months advance notice is provided.

Training needs may also be assessed through the regular planning meetings. In these meetings, the expected projects for the coming year are forecasted. These projections determine skill requirements (e.g., 300–400 project managers for 500 projects). Based on current skill availability and skill demand, training needs are determined. The education and research department also tracks specific technologies; the number of requests for the technology from clients may also determine course offerings.

Infosys also offers training and development support to academic institutions by providing exposure to industry, in the form of sabbaticals at Infosys, training programs, and sharing courseware.

CAREERS

Charged with the responsibility of developing human assets in a fast paced environment, career management at Infosys faces two challenges: a shift from a focus on technical expertise in the career to a focus on management expertise, and the speed with which this refocusing must be accomplished.

Nandita Gurjar, the Corporate Development Manager describes the first challenge as follows:

"Management skills have become increasingly relevant for Infosys because of its ever-increasing volume of business as well as its shift towards consulting business. As the number of projects to be handled has increased, the demand for project management skills in goal setting, communication, coaching, delegation and team management has also increased. Invariably the technical personnel are chosen to move to a management track. This choice is ironic in some ways because the better an individual is in technical skills (such as writing code) the more likely he/she is to be moved away from using the technical expertise into a management track requiring management expertise. Technical expertise provides an individual legitimacy and respect from co-workers making them a natural choice as a team leader. Within a short time span the team leaders are required to manage projects, clients and the people working on these projects. It, therefore, becomes necessary for the individual to abandon their technical expertise—something that has been very salient to their identity in the course of education and early career, when they aspire to be smart "techies," and start collecting a repertoire of managerial capabilities.

While developing management skills by attending management development programs 2–3 years ago was one of the "nice things to do," it has now become a business necessity. The nature of management skills required is further complicated by the fact that at Infosys, managers are also required to manage from remote. Team members are spread geographically and may not meet each other or the team leader for a year or perhaps never. As hiring overseas gathers momentum, the demands may be further exacerbated by the fact that team members may belong to different backgrounds and may not completely understand the organization and the country culture."

The second challenge facing career management is the "compression" in career, an effect of the speed at which employees must move from one stage in their career to another. The new hires are very young (22 years old) and they are put under managers who are 24 years old. At 30 these employees are managers of managers. At 35 an individual can potentially become a vice-president. Management skills become necessary at a very early stage in the life and career of an individual at Infosys. Rapid change is a constant challenge. Nandita summarizes this challenge as follows:

"It is a challenge to teach a 24-year-old to become a manager. The young individual believes, "I have not yet grown," but you are saying, "you have to do it".

Just when you become used to something you are pulled out of it and it is time to move on to something else. Those who can cope with this change emerge as leaders (perhaps at the age of 32); others fall back and become comfortable where they are. The whole career development progress in Infosys is therefore comparatively shorter than in other companies."

To address the pressing need for management development, Infosys has put in place some training programs. These include:

- **First time manager program:** This is a 5-day program for new managers, designed to change a manager's mind-set from an individual to a more managerial one, where the focus has to shift from managing individual performance to managing team performance.
- **The manager of managers program:** The program is geared towards teaching managerial skills (such as delegation, team management) to more senior managers.
- **Infosys leadership program:** The program emphasizes the dynamic environment outside of Infosys and the adaptation to its environment. Once again, the objective is to create a "mind-shift" for the senior managers, from looking inward at the internal operations to becoming aware of external change factors.

Compressed careers bring with them other challenges: stress and burnout. With technology-assisted communication devices (e.g., Palm Pilots, cell phones and home computers) employees are multi-tasking, even in meetings. The potential for stress is enormous, intensified by the time zone differences that make the employees accessible around the clock. Thus, working around the clock, coupled with extensive travel and minimal time to manage work and nonwork needs may cause many employees in the future to burnout.

PERFORMANCE APPRAISAL

Perfomance appraisal is a rigorous comprehensive process at Infosys, tied to the future development of the individual's skills and capabilities. First, an evaluation of personal skills is carried out for the tasks assigned to an individual during the appraisal period. The criteria used to evaluate performance on tasks are derived from the business goals and include: timeliness, quality of work, customer satisfaction, developing others, knowledge dissemination, peer satisfaction in the team, increased business potential, and developing optimal task solutions. The evaluation of personal skills and abilities is carried out for the following: learning and analytical ability, decision making, team leadership, change management, communication skills, teamwork, planning, and organizing skills. Each criterion is described and measured on a 5-point

scale. Further, each of the scale points are anchored to descriptions of expected behavior.[12]

Performance appraisal is carried out semi-annually, in July and January. [A] 360-degree appraisal is carried out for all employees. Appraisals are sought from peers, direct supervisors, subordinates, and customers. A minimum of 6 to 7 appraisal reports are collected for each employee. All appraisal forms are completed online and the data is maintained in a central database. The appraisal information is used to identify training courses and other developmental interventions. Future objectives for both task accomplishment and individual skills development are based on the results of the semi-annual evaluation.

COMPENSATION

"We compensate our human assets in three ways. We add learning value through training and development and appraisal practices. We add emotional value through initiatives directed towards supporting employees with their work and personal needs, and we add financial value through monetary compensation." (Hema Ravichandar, Senior Vice President Human Resource Development)

Although Infosys faces strong domestic and international competition for its human assets, through enticing offers from competitors, the compensation level at Infosys equals the average industry level for each country. It is neither above market nor below the market level. The belief is that financial value, when combined with learning and emotional values, yields a total compensation greater than that offered elsewhere in the industry.

Infosys is one of the first Indian companies to offer stock option plans to their employees.[13] Currently Infosys offers three option plans that cover all Infosys employees:

1994 Employees Stock Offer Plan: Established in September 1994, the plan provides for the issuance of 6,000,000 warrants to eligible employees.

1998 Stock Option Plan: Infosys's 1998 Stock Option Plan provides for the grant of non-statutory stock options and incentive stock options to employees. A total of 1,600,000 equity shares are currently reserved for issuance pursuant to the 1998 Plan. Unless terminated sooner, the 1998 Plan will terminate automatically in January 2008. All options under the 1998 Plan will be exercisable for ADSs represented by ADRs.

1999 Stock Option Plan: The 1999 Plan provides for the issue of 6,600,000 equity shares to employees. A compensation committee comprising a maximum of seven members administers the 1999 Plan. Options will be issued to employees at an exercise price not less than the Fair Market Value. Fair Market Value

---

[12]Please see Appendix C for description of one such scale.

[13]"The Lightening Spark," *Silicon Technology and Business Magazine,* August 1998, pp. 50–51.

means the closing price of Infosys's shares on the stock exchange where there is the highest trading volume on a given date, and if the shares are not traded on that day, the closing price on the next trading day. Under the 1999 Plan, options may also be issued to employees at exercise prices that are less than Fair Market Value, only if specifically approved by the members of Infosys in a general meeting.[14]

In addition [to] such statutory benefits as pension, medical and leave, Infosys also offers a loan program that employees find very attractive. Loans may be taken for pursuing a degree program such as an MBA, or to meet such personal needs as purchasing a car or a house. The interest rate varies (4% for a car purchase and 0–4% for [a] house purchase). To date, almost all loans have been repaid.

INFOSYS OVERSEAS HRM

Overseas, the main thrust of human resource management at Infosys has come from its Global Delivery Model. The objective of this model is to support customers using virtual teams that span geographic locations. Recently, however, the focus has shifted from producing at lowest cost and selling at maximum price to producing at locations that provide other benefits. For example, production demands arising from customer needs in Canada, London, or the USA may require that production be carried out in that specific country. Or, in another instance, the "dot com" customers require [the] latest technical expertise that may not be available in India, so that developers must be hired from Silicon Valley in California.

Currently, the greatest need at Infosys is to hire people at all overseas locations, with about 1,000 hires in the next year in the U.S. and 100 in Canada. Before the NASDAQ listing, Infosys could not pay overseas hires, because Indian stock options are not fungible. However, since 1999, Infosys has been recruiting actively in North America (including Canada). A drawback that Infosys faces in attracting candidates is that it has very low brand equity in the U.S. The NASDAQ listing helped build the brand equity for Infosys in its own immediate market, but to most people it is still relatively unknown.

The recruitment strategies being used at the campuses in the U.S. are similar to those used by all other companies. These include lobbying with campus career centers, giving talks to student groups, sending email campaigns, participating in career fairs, and so on. However, certain aspects of the recruitment unique to Infosys offer it a recruiting advantage.

Prasad Tadimeti, the HR manager of Infosys, USA describes these recruiting practices:

"We offer to provide extensive training, that few other companies will offer. The training includes

classroom training and mock projects. After a year our employees are as good as the best Bachelor of Science computer scientist in the world. Subsequently, employees have the opportunity to sign up for any course as a part of their continuous learning process. With an increasing hiring rate, Infosys plans to set up training facilities in [the] U.S. itself. The other aspect of recruitment that provides an advantage to Infosys is our willingness to hire anyone with any reasonable math or science background (for example, economics, math, statistics, physics or chemistry. This is a departure from the hiring practices of other firms that focus on the traditional computer science, computer engineering, and electrical engineering backgrounds. This approach to hiring is attracting a lot of attention. Given our proven track record of training non-computer background people in India, we can do it again here, as long as there is some degree of analytical background in the curriculum and the person has a good GPA."

Although *learnability* is an important criterion for hiring even in North America, the written test used in India to screen out applicants cannot be used in the USA. Instead, the screening criterion is a GPA of 3.0. This compares to a 70% cutoff used by Infosys for students from Indian universities. The other characteristics considered important are interpersonal skills and communication ability, ability to work under pressure, and to travel extensively. While hiring in North America, Infosys particularly emphasizes communication and interpersonal skills, because of their experience that candidates in North America possess these more than candidates in India. In contrast employees hired in India are stronger in technical skills. A team comprising both skills is therefore very advantageous, and can potentially create learning from each other's skills.

Subject knowledge is a distant third or fourth level criterion, based on an assumption that, if the person has applied his/her mind to understand a concept in his/her own discipline, then it is very probably not difficult to teach the person software programming.

Overseas, Infosys maintains the same compensation strategy as in India, namely, that they are not industry leaders in pay. To attract candidates they emphasize the entire employment package. Features of the package include career advancement opportunities, long term careers, job challenge, training opportunities, autonomy, and more early career responsibility compared to competitors.

Culture has so far not been a major barrier in Infosys'[s] ability to do business in India. Prasad provides insight into one significant difference in the managerial approach.

"The employment relationship in Indian businesses is implicit in that there is a mutual understanding that the manager will act in the best interest of the employee. Several employment related issues are left implicit— short-term needs may not be fulfilled with the

[14]Infosys, Annual Report 2000, p.155.

expectation that benefits may be forthcoming in the long run. The employment is expected to last a long time period. Even if performance is sub-par, efforts are made to help the person by either transferring to another line of business or by providing remedial training. In the Western context, on the other hand, employment contracts are more explicit. Employees may want to know the performance criteria and the performance goals against which they will be evaluated. They are less tolerant of ambiguity in the relationships and expectations have to be met instantly for trust to be generated. This difference in expectations from the employment relationship is a challenge that Infosys is facing and expects to continue facing as it diversifies into a global company with heavier influx of different cultures."

FUTURE PLANS

Infosys plans to maintain its growth rate in India and to expand overseas. It has already set up a software development center in Toronto and plans to set up more centers soon. It plans to hire [a] substantial number of employees over the next few years in its overseas offices (e.g., 100 employees in Toronto by mid 2001).

As a part of its growth strategy, Infosys is exploring possible candidates for acquisitions in [the] United States. Infosys believes that pursuing selective acquisitions of IT services and software applications firms could expand its technical expertise, facilitate expansion into new vertical markets, and increase its client base.

As part of its business strategy Infosys is gearing to move up the "value chain" and provide end-to-end solutions to clients.[15]

Infosys will have to achieve these objectives in the face of many challenges.[16] These include increased global competition and labor cost, rapid growth, and increased employee diversity. As Infosys expands overseas, it will experience increased competition from firms with potentially lower labor costs and with a greater ability to respond to changing client IT preferences. Historically Infosys'[s] labor costs have been lower than those of service providers in the United States and Europe. However, because wages in India are currently increasing at a faster rate than in the United States, Infosys will experience shrinking profit margins in future. The rapid growth of Inofsys challenges its ability to transmit its corporate culture worldwide[,] as well as its ability to attract and retain skilled personnel. Overseas hires and acquisitions will result in Infosys experiencing increased employee diversity of cultures. Increased diversity will also come from a different set of skills required for expansion into consulting business.

Infosys'[s] human resource management practices will have to be assessed in light of these challenges. What adjustment will Infosys have to make to harness its human assets as [it moves into] the future?

APPENDIX A: HUMAN CAPITAL ACCOUNTING MODEL

Infosys places an asset value on its human capital based on an accounting model put forth by Lev and Schwartz in 1971.[17] The model is based on human capital theory, which recognizes human capital as one of several forms of holding wealth for a business enterprise, such as money, securities, and physical capital. Accordingly, human capital is treated like other forms of earning assets and thus is an important factor explaining and predicting the future economic growth of the company.

Their accounting model is based on the measurement of human capital using the formula, $V_r = \Sigma\ T_{t=r}\ I(t)/(1 + r)^{t-r}$, where Vr = the human capital value of a person "r" years old; $I(t)$ = the person's annual earnings up to retirement; r = a discount rate specific to the person; T = retirement age. The formula uses an earnings profile, which is a graphic mathematical representation of the income stream generated by a person. Typically, earnings increase with age. As the person reaches retirement age, productivity declines as a result of technological obsolescence and health deterioration.

The model postulated in 1971 remains largely unused because accountants argue that human capital cannot be purchased or owned by the firm and therefore would not be recognized as an asset. Additionally, critics of human capital theory state that labor force does not have a "service potential," meaning employees are paid for rendering current services, and no asset is formed by these payments. Regardless, this model is one of few that exist to value human capital, a source of knowledge for companies. While very basic, the Lev and Schwartz model provides a means by which to disclose human capital values to stakeholders.

The Lev and Schwartz model has been used by Infosys to compute the value of the human resources as of March 31, 1999. The evaluation is based on the present value of the future earnings of the employees and on the following assumptions:

1. Employee compensation includes all direct and indirect benefits earned both in India and abroad.
2. The incremental earnings are based on group/age have been considered.
3. The future earnings have been discounted at 25.32% (previous year—26.95%), this rate being the cost of capital for Infosys. Beta has been assumed at 1.48 based on average beta for software stocks in the U.S.

APPENDIX B: PRODUCTS

Infosys's services include software development, maintenance and re-engineering services, e-commerce and I[I]nternet/intranet consulting[,] as well as dedicated

---

15For details about Infosys's strategy, please see Appendix D.
16For details of competition and risk factors, please see Appendixes E & F.

17L. Baruch and A. Schwartz. "On the Use of the Economic Concept of Human Capital in Financial Statements." *The Accounting Review* 44(1971): 103–110.

As of March 31	2000		1999	
	No. of Employees	Value of human resources (Rs. in lakhs)	No. of Employees	Value of human resources (Rs. in lakhs – 1 lakh = 1,000,00)
Production	4,292	196,513.84	2,854	76,984.25
Support–Technical*	450	8,165.20	389	7,168.97
Support–Others	647	19,062.73	523	10,416.52
	5,389	223,741.77	3,766	94,569.74

* *Note:* Support–Technical includes trainees, employees in R&D activities, and support personnel allocated to production.

	2000	1999
Number of employees	5,389	3,766
Value of human resources	223,741.77	94,569.74
Total revenue	92,146.48	51,273.84
Software revenue	88,232.37	50,889.12
Employee cost	33,455.91	16,605.64
Value-added	72,330.70	37,411.49
Net profits excluding extraordinary income	28,594.86	13,291.54
Total revenue/Human resources value (ratio)	0.41	0.54
Total software revenue/Human resources value (ratio)	0.39	0.54
Value-added/Human resources value (ratio)	0.32	0.40
Value of human resources per employee	41.52	25.11
Employee cost/Human resources value (%)	14.95%	17.56%
Return on human resources value (%)	12.78%	14.05%

Value-added statement

Year ending March 31	2000	1999
Total revenue	92,146.48	51,273.84
Less:		
Software and development expenses (other than employee costs and provision for post-sales client support)	12,916.31	9,326.92
Administration expenses (other than provisions)	6,854.47	4,535.43
Subtotal	19,815.78	13,862.35
Total value-added	72,330.70	37,411.49
Applied to meet:		
Employee costs	33,455.91	16,605.64
Provision for post-sales client support	209.63	219.19
Provision for bad and doubtful debts and doubtful loans and advances	94.03	39.87
Provision for contingencies	333.00	666.00
Provision for e-investing the company	350.00	–
Provision for investment in subsidiary	–	705.96
Income tax	3,970.00	2,294.00
Dividends (including Dividend tax)	3,303.65	1,331.83
Retained in business	30,614.48	15,549.00
	72,330.70	37,411.49

The figures above are based on Indian GAAP financial statements.

SOURCE: 1999–2000 Annual Report

OSDCs for certain clients. In each of its service offerings Infosys assumes full project management responsibility for each project it undertakes.

Dedicated Offshore Software Development Centers

Infosys has pioneered the concept of dedicated Offshore Software Development Centers (OSDCs) in which a software development team that is dedicated to a single client uses technology, tools, processes, and methodologies unique to that client. Each dedicated OSDC is located at a company facility in India and is staffed and managed by Infosys. Once the project priorities are established by the client, Infosys, in conjunction with the client's IT department, manages the execution of the project. By focusing on a single client over an extended time frame, the dedicated OSDC team gains a deeper understanding of the client's business and technology and can being to function as a virtual extension of the client's software team.

The Indian offshore development model became popular in the mid-1990's as a method of dividing software project activities between a service provider's offshore software development facility and a client's on-site location. This model contains many features that are attractive to IT consumers who are primarily located in the United States, Europe, and Japan. These features include: (i) access to a large pool of highly skilled, English-speaking IT professionals, (ii) relatively low labor costs of IT professionals offshore, (iii) the ability to provide high-quality IT services at internationally recognized standards, (iv) the capability to work on specific projects on a 24-hour basis by exploiting time zone differences between India and client sites, and (v) the ability to accelerate the delivery time of larger projects by parallel processing different phases of a project's development. While some U.S. and European companies have commenced their own operations in India, most large corporations have opted to form strategic alliances with local Indian IT companies to reduce the risks and start-up costs of operations in India.

Infosys has a long history of executing projects between its clients' sites in North America, Europe, and Asia and the company's offshore software development facilities in India. In a typical software development or re-engineering assignment, Infosys assigns a small team of two to five IT professionals to visit a client's site and determine the scope and requirements of the project. Once the initial specifications of the engagement have been established, the project managers return to India to supervise a much larger team of 10 to 50 IT professionals dedicated to the development of the required software or system. A small team remains at the client's site to track changes in scope and address new requirements as the project progresses. The client's systems are then linked via satellite to Infosys's facilities[,] enabling simultaneous processing in as many as four offshore software development facilities. Once the development stage of the assignment is completed and tested in India,

a team returns to the client's site to install the newly developed software or system and ensure its functionality. At this phase of the engagement, Infosys will often enter into an ongoing agreement to provide the client with comprehensive maintenance services from one of its offshore software development facilities. In contrast to development projects, a typical maintenance assignment requires a larger team of 10 to 20 IT professionals to travel to the client's site to gain a thorough understanding of all aspects of the client's system. The majority of the maintenance team subsequently returns to the offshore software development facility, where it assumes full responsibility for day-to-day maintenance of the client's system, while coordinating with a few maintenance professionals who remain stationed at the client's site.

By pursuing this model, Infosys completes approximately 68% of its project work at its offshore software development facilities in India. Its project management techniques, risk management processes and quality control measures enable it to complete projects seamlessly across multiple locations with a high level of client satisfaction. Certified under ISO 9001, TickIT, and at Level 5 of the Capability Maturity Model, Infosys rigorously adheres to highly evolved processes. These processes govern all aspects of the software product life cycle, from requirements to testing and maintenance.

Infosys has invested in redundant infrastructure with "warm" backup sites and redundant telecommunication capabilities with alternate routings to provide its clients with high service levels. Additionally, Infosys utilizes two telecommunications carriers in India and has installed in its principal facilities multiple international satellite links connecting with network hubs in Fremont, California and in Quincy, Massachusetts. A different ocean cable connecting Europe and the United States serves each of these hubs. Moreover, Infosys has installed wireless links among its facilities in Bangalore and intends to install wireless links among its other Indian facilities by the end of 2000.

Software Development

Infosys provides turnkey software development with projects varying in size. These include development of new applications or development of new functions for existing applications. Each development project typically involves all aspects of the software development process, including definition, prototyping, design, pilots, programming, testing, installation, and maintenance. In the early stage of a development project, Infosys personnel often work at a client's site to help determine project definition and to estimate the scope and cost of the project. Infosys then performs design review, software programming, program testing, module testing, integration, and volume testing primarily at its own facilities in India.

Software Maintenance

Infosys also provides maintenance services for large legacy software systems. Maintenance services include minor and major modifications and enhancements (including Year 2000 and Eurocurrency conversion) and production support. Such systems are either mainframe-based or client/server and are typically essential to a client's business. Infosys's IT professionals take an engineering approach to software maintenance, focusing on the long-term functionality and stability of the client's overall system. Infosys performs most of the maintenance work at its own facilities using satellite-based links to the client's system. In addition, Infosys maintains a small team at the client's facility to coordinate support functions.

Software Re-Engineering

Infosys's re-engineering services assist clients in migrating to new technologies while extending the life cycle of existing systems that are rich in functionality. Projects include re-engineering software to migrate applications from mainframe to client/server architectures, to extend existing applications to the Internet, to migrate from existing operating systems to UNIX or Windows NT, or to update from a non-relational to a relational database technology. For companies with extensive proprietary software applications, implementing such technologies may require rewriting and testing millions of lines of software code. Infosys has developed proven methodologies that govern the planning, execution, and testing of the software re-engineering process.

New Services

Infosys is also focused in certain new service areas such as (i) Internet consulting, which includes developing applications for Internet/intranet solutions and e-commerce solutions; (ii) Euro conversion, which assists clients in making their systems Euro compliant; and (iii) engineering services, which include software product design. For example, Infosys recently developed an integrated e-commerce online shopping site for one of its U.S. clients, which [includes] four different systems and gave the company complete cycle responsibility for the project.

SOURCE: Infosys 2000 Annual Report.

APPENDIX C: PERFORMANCE APPRAISAL—EXAMPLE OF ONE BEHAVIORALLY ANCHORED RATING SCALE

Timeliness (includes the ability to plan, schedule, and track the assigned, in such a manner that the work flows as envisaged and the work is completed on time).

| A | Way above expectations | Displays abilities to plan, schedule, and track work independently. Accomplishes work well in advance resulting in being able to contribute towards other activities of the project. |

B+	Exceeded expectations	Displays ability to plan, schedule, and track work. Accomplishes work within allocated time.
B	Met expectations	Displays ability to plan, schedule, and track work. Able to meet project deadlines.
B-	Met expectations with assistance	Needs assistance in planning tracking work. Unable to meet project deadlines independently.
C	Below expectations	Not able to plan, schedule, and track work for most of the assigned responsibilities. Severe impact on the project deadlines.

APPENDIX D: INFOSYS STRATEGY

Business Strategy

Pursue World-Class Operating Model. The management believes that one of the most critical contributing factors to Infosys's success has been its commitment to pursue high-quality standards in all aspects of its business including deliverables to the customers, human resource management, investor relations, planning, finance, physical and technological infrastructure, and sales and marketing.

Invest Heavily in Human Resources. Infosys believes that its continued success will depend upon its ability to recruit, train, deploy, and retain highly talented IT professionals. Even as the field of software engineering has been attracting the best and brightest Indian students, management believes Infosys has become, for Indian engineering graduates, one of the most sought after employers.

Focus on Managed Software Solutions. Since its inception, Infosys has dedicated itself to providing managed software solutions, many of which are offered on a fixed-price, fixed-time frame basis. By taking full project management responsibility in every project, Infosys provides its clients high-quality, cost-effective solutions with low risk.

Capitalize on a Well-Established Offshore Development Model. As one of the pioneers of the offshore software development model, Infosys has made significant investments in its infrastructure and has developed the advanced processes and expertise necessary to manage and successfully execute projects in multiple locations with seamless integration.

Maintain Disciplined Focus on Business and Client Mix. Infosys provides a wide range of software services and maintains a disciplined focus on its business mix in an effort to avoid service or client concentration. Beginning in fiscal 1996, Infosys aggressively sought to minimize its client concentration and to accept as clients only those that met strict guidelines for overall revenue potential and profitability.

Growth Strategy

From fiscal 1994 to fiscal 2000, Infosys experienced compounded annual revenue and net income growth rates of 62% and 73%, respectively, and grew from approximately 480 IT professionals to approximately 4,625. The following are the key elements of Infosys's growth strategy:

Broaden Service Offerings. To meet all of its clients' IT needs, Infosys strives to offer a comprehensive range of services by continuously evaluating new and emerging technologies.

Increase Business with Existing Clients. In fiscal 2000, Infosys provided software services for more than 190 clients in the United States, Europe, Australia, Asia, and Japan.

Develop New Clients. Infosys pursues several new client development strategies.

Increase Revenue Per IT Professional. To increase its revenue per IT professional, Infosys continually focuses on building expertise in vertical markets, refining its software development tools and methodologies, and storing and disseminating experiential knowledge in order to improve efficiency and productivity.

Expand and Diversify Base of IT Professionals. Management believes that a critical element of Infosys's growth strategy is its ability to increase its base of IT professionals.

Pursue Selective Strategic Acquisitions. Infosys believes that pursuing selective acquisitions of IT services and software applications firms could potentially expand Infosys's technical expertise, facilitate expansion into new vertical markets, and increase its client base.

APPENDIX E: COMPETITION

The market for IT services is highly competitive. Competitors include IT services companies, large international accounting firms and their consulting affiliates, systems consulting and integration firms, temporary employment agencies, other technology companies, and client in-house MIS departments.

Infosys expects that future competition will increasingly include firms with operations in other countries, potentially including countries with lower personnel costs than those prevailing in India. Part of Infosys's competitive advantage has historically been a cost advantage relative to service providers in the United States and Europe. Since wage costs in India are presently increasing at a faster rate than those in the United States, Infosys's ability to compete effectively will become increasingly dependent on its reputation, the quality of its services and its expertise in specific markets.

Infosys believes that its ability to compete also depends in part on a number of factors outside its control, including the ability of its competitors to attract, train, motivate and retain highly skilled IT professionals, the price at which its competitors offer comparable services, and the extent of its competitors' responsiveness to client needs.[18]

APPENDIX F: RISK FACTORS

Management Of Growth. Infosys has experienced significant growth in recent periods. The company's revenues in fiscal 2000 grew 68.2% over fiscal 1999. As of March 31, 2000, Infosys employed approximately 4,625 software professionals worldwide with 17 software development facilities in India, and one global development center in Canada, operationalized in fiscal 2000. In comparison[,] Infosys employed 3,160 employees in 11 facilities as of March 31, 1999 and 2,190 in 9 facilities as of March 31, 1998. In fiscal 1999, Infosys approved major expansions to its existing facilities and the building of new facilities. Infosys's inability to manage its growth effectively could have a material adverse effect on the quality of the company's services and projects, its ability to attract clients as well as skilled personnel, its business prospects, and its results of operations and financial condition.

Political and Economic Environment. During the past decade, and particularly since 1991, the Government of India has pursued policies of economic liberalization, including significant relaxation of restrictions on the private sector. The current Government of India, formed in October 1999, has announced policies and taken initiatives that support the continuation of the economic liberalization policies pursued by previous governments and has, in addition, set up a special IT task force to promote the IT industry. However, the speed of economic liberalization could change, and specific laws and policies affecting IT companies, foreign investment, currency exchange rates, and other matters affecting investment in Infosys's securities could change as well.

Government of India Incentives and Regulation. Infosys benefits from a variety of incentives given to software firms in India, such as relief from import duties on hardware, a tax exemption for income derived from software exports, and tax holidays and infrastructure support for companies, such as Infosys, operating in specially designated "Software Technology Parks". There can be no assurance that these incentives will continue in [the] future.

Restrictions on U.S. Immigration. Infosys's professionals who work on-site at client facilities in the United States on temporary and extended assignments are typically required to obtain visas. As of March 31, 2000, substantially all of Infosys's personnel in the United States were working pursuant to H-1B visas (745 persons) or L-1 visas (218 persons). Although there is no limit to new L-1 petitions, there is a limit to the number of new H-1B petitions that the United States Immigration and Naturalization Service may approve in any government fiscal year. In years in which this limit is reached, Infosys may be unable to obtain

[18]Infosys, Annual Report 2000, p.143.

the H-1B visas necessary to bring its critical Indian IT professionals to the United States on an extended basis. The U.S. Government reached this limit in March 2000 for its fiscal year ended September 30, 2000 and in May 1999 for the fiscal year ended September 30, 1999. While Infosys anticipated that such limit would be reached prior to the end of the U.S. government's fiscal year and made efforts to plan accordingly, there can be no assurance that Infosys will continue to be able to obtain a sufficient number of H-1B visas. Changes in existing U.S. immigration laws that make it more difficult for Infosys to obtain H-1B and L-1 visas could impair its ability to compete for and provide services to clients and could have a material adverse effect on the results of its operations and financial condition.

Dependence on Skilled Personnel: Risks of Wage Inflation. Infosys's ability to execute project engagements and to obtain new clients depends, in large part, on its ability to attract, train, motivate, and retain highly skilled IT professionals, particularly project managers, software engineers, and other senior technical personnel. An inability to hire and retain additional qualified personnel will impair Infosys's ability to bid for or obtain new projects and to continue to expand its business. Infosys believes that there is significant competition for IT professionals with the skills necessary to perform the services offered by the company. There can be no assurance that Infosys will be able to assimilate and manage new IT professionals effectively. Any increase in the attrition rates experienced by Infosys, particularly that of experienced software engineers and project managers, would adversely affect Infosys's operational and financial results. There can be no assurance that Infosys will be successful in recruiting and retaining a sufficient number of replacement IT professionals with the requisite skills to replace those IT professionals who leave. Further, there can be no assurance that Infosys will be able to re-deploy and retrain its IT professionals to keep pace with continuing changes in IT, evolving standards, and changing client preferences. Historically, Infosys's wage costs in India have been significantly lower than wage costs in the United States for comparably skilled IT professionals. However, at present wage costs in India are increasing at a rate faster than in the United States. In the long-term, wage increases may have an adverse effect on Infosys's profit margins unless it is able to continue increasing the efficiency and productivity of its professionals.

Infrastructure and Potential Disruption in Telecommunications. A significant element of Infosys's business strategy is to continue to leverage its eight software development centers in India and to expand the number of such centers in India as well as outside India. Infosys believes that the use of [a] strategically located network of software development centers will help in many ways. It will provide it with cost advantages, the ability to attract highly skilled personnel in various regions, the ability to service clients on a regional and global basis, and the ability to provide 24-hour service to its clients. Pursuant to its service delivery model, Infosys must maintain active voice and data communication between its main offices in Bangalore, the offices of its clients, and its other software development facilities. Although Infosys maintains redundant software development facilities and satellite communications links, any significant loss of the company's ability to transmit voice and data through satellite and telephone communications would have a material adverse effect on its results of operations and financial condition.

Risks Associated with Possible Acquisitions. Infosys intends to evaluate potential acquisitions on an ongoing basis. As of [this] date, however, Infosys has no understanding, commitment, or agreement with respect to any material future acquisition. Since Infosys has not made any acquisitions in the past, there can be no assurance that the company will be able to identify suitable acquisition candidates available for sale at reasonable prices, consummate any acquisition, or successfully integrate any acquired business into its operations. Further, acquisitions may involve a number of special risks. These include diversion of management's attention, failure to retain key acquired personnel and clients, unanticipated events or circumstances, legal liabilities, and amortization of acquired intangible assets, some or all of which could have a material adverse effect on the company's results of operations and financial condition. Under Indian law, except in certain limited circumstances, Infosys may not make any acquisition of, or investment in, a non-Indian company without RBI and, in most cases, Government of India approval. Even if Infosys does encounter an attractive acquisition candidate, there can be no assurance that RBI and, if required, Government of India approval can be obtained.

QUESTIONS

1. What do you think of the way that human assets are valued at Infosys?
2. Will the company be successful in attracting a similar profile of employees (talented and committed) overseas?
3. How might the company culture/philosophy be a hindrance/facilitator for overseas operations?
4. How does approach taken by Infosys towards its employees compare with that taken by other companies? How does it compare with the HRM approach 15 years ago?

Case 15   West Indies Yacht Club Resort: When Cultures Collide

In early December 1994, Patrick Dowd, a thirty-year-old management consultant, stared out his office window at the snowy Ithaca, New York landscape. Dowd reflected on his recent phone conversation with Jim Johnson, General Manager of the 95-room West Indies Yacht Club Resort (WIYCR) located in the British Virgin Islands. Johnson sounded desperate on the phone to pull the resort out of its apparent tailspin and noted three primary areas of concern. First, expatriate manager turnover was beginning to become problematic. In the past two years the resort had hired and then failed to retain three expatriate Waterfront Directors and three expatriate Food and Beverage Directors. Second, although the resort had not initiated a formal guest feedback program, Johnson estimated that guest complaints had increased from ten per week to more than thirty per week over the past two years. The complaints were usually given by guests to staff at the front desk, written down, passed on to Johnson, and usually centered on the deteriorating level of service provided by local British Virgin Islands employees. Many repeat guests claimed, "The staff just doesn't seem as motivated as it used to be." And third, there appeared to be an increasing level of tension between expatriate and local staff members. In the past, expatriates and locals seemingly found it natural to work side by side[;] now there was a noticeable gap between these groups that appeared to be growing.

Johnson had come to know Dowd and his reputation for being one of the few expatriate management consultants in the region who seemed to have a real grasp on what it took to manage effectively in the Caribbean. The two had become better acquainted in 1993 when the world-renowned sailing school that Dowd was working for, Tradewind Ventures, was contracted to develop new family-focused programs to be offered by the resort. Through this experience, Dowd gained in-depth knowledge of the resort. Dowd's reputation and knowledge of the resort prompted Johnson's call to see if Dowd would be interested in working as a participant observer at the resort to determine the underlying reasons behind his three major concerns. Johnson requested that Dowd work at the resort during three Christmas holiday weeks to observe resort staff during the peak season. Dowd would then present an analysis of his observations and make recommendations regarding what actions could be taken to improve the situation.

SOURCE: Dr. Jeffrey P. Shay, University of Montana. Reprinted by permission of the *Case Research Journal*, Copyright by Jeffrey Shay and the North American Case Research Association. All rights reserved.

Although Dowd had never provided consulting in this specific area (i.e., an analysis of the cultural influences on the behavior of workers in the Caribbean), he gladly accepted the challenge as it coincided with his personal experience in the region and recent courses on cross-cultural management that he had taken at Cornell University. Dowd moved over to his bookcase and pulled books, brochures, and other information off the shelf and began reading. He was departing for the British Virgin Islands in one week and wanted to get a head start on his background research.

BRITISH VIRGIN ISLANDS TOURISM MARKET

Thirty-six islands, 16 of which are inhabited, comprise the 59 square mile chain of British Virgin Islands (BVIs) (see Exhibit C15-1). Unlike neighboring islands, St. Thomas and St. Croix, that underwent extensive tourism development during the 1970s and 1980s, the BVI government carefully planned and restricted growth. The result was a carefully carved niche in the Caribbean market—positioning the island chain in the exclusive/ecotourism market segment.

From 1950–1970, the BVIs hosted the traveling elite. During the early 1970s, the introduction and rapid growth of bareboat chartering (boats ranging from 28 to 50 feet, chartered (rented) to tourists qualified to take the boats out without the assistance of a licensed captain) made the small island chain affordable for tourists with moderate budgets as well. Bareboat charters offered a unique vacation opportunity—one that connected tourists with the islands' rich natural beauty and intriguing history by allowing tourists to visit quiet harbors and villages that were void of larger cruise ships and large hotels. The BVI's calm waters and steady trade winds were soon filled with charter boats as the chain of islands quickly became known as the premier chartering location in the world. By the early 1990s, there were more than 500 charter boats available in the Virgin Islands, with the largest company, The Moorings, managing more than 190 charter boats in the BVIs alone. Although charter industry growth in the BVIs drew the attention of major developers, the combination of strict government regulations constraining the size of new hotels and resorts, along with limited access provided by the small Beef Island Airport, kept these developers and mass tourism out. As a result, smaller mid-scale to upscale hotels and resorts were developed in the BVIs.

EXHIBIT C15-1   Map of the British Virgin Islands and location of luxury hotels and resorts

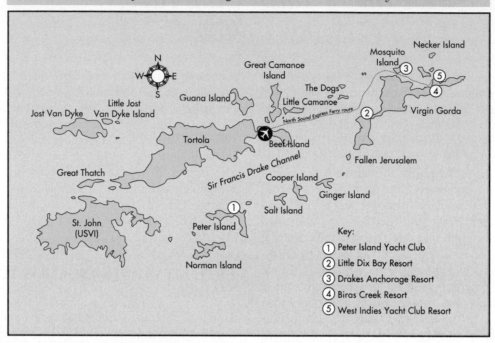

UPSCALE HOTELS IN THE BRITISH VIRGIN ISLANDS

Although several mid-scale hotels were developed and operating in the BVIs by the mid-1980s, there were only four truly upscale hotels in the island chain in addition to WIYCR (discussed in detail later) (see Exhibit C15-1 for hotel locations). Each of these hotels provided three meals per day (not including alcoholic drinks) and access to activities (e.g., water sports equipment) as part of the price for the room. Biras Creek was an independent resort located adjacent to WIYCR's property and overlooked North Sound of Virgin Gorda (see Exhibit C15-2). This resort featured 34 rooms, one restaurant, three tennis courts, a private beach with a bar, a small marina, and several miles of nature trails. Peak season double occupancy rates in 1994 for Biras Creek ranged from $395–695 per night and, similar to WIYCR, this resort was only accessible by sea. After facing high turnover of expatriate resort managers and expatriate assistant managers for the past five years, Biras Creek implemented a policy of hiring individuals for these positions for three-year contracts. After the contract was completed, managers were required to seek employment elsewhere. The owners felt that most managers became less effective after three years because they suffered from burnout.

EXHIBIT C15-2   Virgin Gorda and its luxury hotels

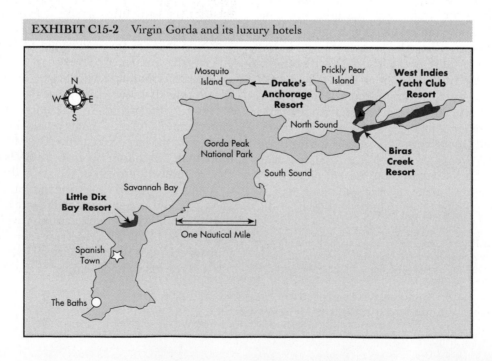

Drakes Anchorage was an independent resort located on the 125-acre Mosquito Island, an island situated at the northern entrance to North Sound (see Exhibit C15-2). This small resort offered 12 rooms, a beachfront restaurant, a protected anchorage for charter boats, a picturesque hiking trail, and four secluded sandy beaches. Peak season double occupancy rates in 1994 ranged between $400–600 per night. Expatriate managers oversaw operations at this resort as well. Guests staying at this resort were primarily interested in a relaxing, secluded vacation with limited activities.

Little Dix Bay Resort opened in 1964 as part of the Rockefeller Resort chain. In 1993, after a multimillion-dollar renovation project, Rosewood Hotels and Resorts, a Dallas-based company, acquired the management contract for the resort. This resort offered 98 rooms ranging in price from $480–1000 per night in 1994 during peak season for a double occupancy room. This resort was located on the northwestern shore of Virgin Gorda and overlooked the Sir Francis Drake Channel, a channel cutting through the heart of the BVI chain (see Exhibit C15-2). In addition to a fine dining restaurant, the resort offered small boats (i.e., sunfish, lasers, whalers, etc.), water-skiing, and day excursions to snorkeling and diving sites for guests. These amenities made Little Dix the WIYCR's strongest local competitor. Under the management of Rosewood Hotels and Resorts, expatriate managers often rotated every two to three years from one Rosewood property to another. Its prices and impeccable service attracted some of the most affluent tourists visiting the region.

Located on Peter Island, the Peter Island Yacht Club was operated by JVA Enterprises, a Michigan-based firm that acquired the resort in the early 1970s (see Exhibit C15-1). The resort had 50 rooms, a fine dining restaurant, a marina, and a beautiful secluded beach. Peak season double occupancy rates ranged from $395–525 per night in 1994. This resort was also managed by expatriates and had been recently remodeled after being struck by two hurricanes in the early 1990s. Similar to Drake's Anchorage, this resort primarily attracted guests looking for a secluded island vacation with limited activity.

BVI LABOR MARKET LAWS AND REGULATIONS

All hotels operating in the BVIs faced a number of challenges beyond the strict regulations on development. Perhaps the most significant challenge was dealing with local labor market laws and regulations. Despite the restricted growth in tourism, the supply of qualified service employees severely lagged demand. Four general government restrictions and policies exacerbated the challenge of hiring and managing staff. First, organizations were granted only a limited number of work permits to attract more experienced service employees from foreign countries. Expatriate work permits were granted based on the total number of employees working at a resort

(i.e., the more employees a resort had, the greater the number of expatriates it could get permits for) and the availability of locals who possessed the skills requisite for the position. The latter meant that resorts had to post positions in local newspapers for at least one month before requesting a permit for an expatriate.

Second, organizations were not permitted to lay off staff during slow seasons. This created significant challenges for resorts like WIYCR that ran at nearly 100% occupancy during the peak season (December through May) and as low as 40% during the off season (June through November). Especially hurt by this were luxury resorts that required high staffing levels to provide the services that guests expected during the peak months but were then left overstaffed during the off season periods.

Third, policies restricting the conditions under which an employee could be fired severely limited an organization's ability to retain only the best workers. For example, one hotel manager claimed, "It is hard to fire a local employee even if he steals from us. We are often required to file documents with the government and then attend a formal hearing on why we dismissed an employee. Since it is so difficult to fire someone who steals, imagine how difficult it is to fire someone who doesn't work hard, is always late, or forgets to come to work! Our hands are really tied by these regulations."

Finally, organizations were under extreme pressure to promote BVI locals into management positions whenever possible. As previously noted, before hiring an expatriate manager a resort had to advertise the position for at least a month. In addition, if a local approached the resort with minimal requisite skills for the job but was enthusiastic and willing to learn, the resort found it difficult in the current environment to overlook the local and hire the expatriate. As a result of these restrictions and policies, managers often found themselves overstaffed with underqualified workers.

Managers overcame these dilemmas in a number of ways. To combat regulations on foreign employees, organizations often paid foreign staff through their offshore corporate headquarters and limited the amount of time they actually spent at the resort, hotel, or other service site. In response to restrictions on laying off staff, organizations offered attractive vacation components to their employment contracts. This allowed the organization to pay lower wages and to decrease excess labor during off-seasons. Managers, forced to retain staff regardless of their productivity levels, rationalized that excess labor costs were offset by lower wages in the region, avoidance of costs associated with training a new employee, and the need for extra staff during peak season.

Hotels and resorts also realized that although many entry-level employees could continue to be trained on-the-job, locals seeking managerial positions would require more formalized training. Unfortunately, neither the BVI nor the United States Virgin Islands had developed hospitality management training programs because there wasn't the critical mass of local managers required to start such programs. Instead hotels and resorts sent promising young staff to service training programs in the Bahamas and Bermuda in an effort to prepare them for management positions.

THE WEST INDIES YACHT CLUB RESORT

In 1964 the Kimball family sailed into the North Sound of Virgin Gorda (see Exhibits C15-2 and C15-3). The Sound's natural beauty captivated the family and they knew it was a place to which the family would soon return. Nestled on the mountainside of the innermost point, the Kimballs found a shorefront pub and five cottages known as The West Indies Resort. The cottages were rustic with only cold water running in the bathrooms. It was at the resort's pub that Joe Kimball met Armin Dubois, the property's eccentric owner. Dubois had been a pioneer Virgin Islands yachtsman who had found paradise on these shores and never left.

Under Dubois's management, an old diesel generator supplied lighting, and water was collected on the roofs and stored in cisterns that doubled as cottage foundations. The pub and restaurant served mariners when Dubois felt like it. Dubois established his own protocol. Mariners blew foghorns just off the main dock and Dubois responded as to whether or not he was open for business. Even after being invited ashore, guests were unsure as to how long the hospitality would last. Dubois was notorious for turning off the generator to let guests know they had outstayed their welcome.

By early 1973, after several visits to North Sound, Kimball asked Dubois if he would sell or lease property so that he could build a family cottage. Dubois replied several months later that he wasn't interested in selling or leasing a small piece of property but would entertain an offer to buy out the whole property. In late 1973, Kimball did just that.

Kimball's painstaking attention to detail fostered development of the property's unique character. His vision was to provide a truly eco-conscious and comfortable place for travelers to enjoy an environment perfect for sailing, fishing, snorkeling, diving, and combing beaches. To accomplish this, Kimball maintained many of Dubois's earlier practices. For example, the resort continued to generate its own electricity, and collect and distill its own water. In addition, the resort used gray water (partially treated water) to irrigate the hillsides and used solar power wherever possible. In sharp contrast to the multi-story designs used by other Caribbean developers, Kimball constructed 55 individual bungalows that were scattered along the hillside and preserved the natural beauty for which the resort was known. Kimball differentiated the resort from others in the region by acquiring the world's largest resort fleet of sailboats (e.g., J24's, JY15's, Cal 27's, Freedom 30's, Lasers, Sunfish, Rhodes l9's, Mistral sailboards) and powerboats (e.g., Boston Whalers and sport fishing boats). These carefully selected boats were easy for even inexperienced guests to handle. These acquisitions in conjunction with the resort's sailing instruction program established the resort's reputation as one of the premier water sports resorts in the world. Subsequently, Kimball changed the resort's name to The West Indies Yacht Club Resort to leverage the distinct aquatic recreational activities that the resort offered.

In 1987, with the resort's reputation growing and business booming, Kimball acquired a fifteen-year renewable

---

EXHIBIT C15-3   Recent Marketing Initiatives

Fast Tacks Weeks: Initial efforts to fill slow season periods centered on leveraging the resort's competitive advantage. Fitch developed The Fast Tack Program which targeted specific sailing groups and utilized the resort's vast sailing resources. These groups ranged from racing to cruising, from families to couples, from senior citizens to young adults. During certain weeks in the historically slow fall season, sailing celebrities were invited and gave specialized seminars to guests. Perhaps the most widely noted week is the ProAm week in which guests are assigned to teams with some of the top match racing skippers in the world. In addition to becoming a major source of income to the resort, the weeks have become a key free advertising vehicle. Articles in sailing magazines have served not only to promote the week's themselves, but have increased reader awareness of the sailing experience that the resort can offer.

Family Weeks: To change the resort's image Fitch marketed special programs during traditional school break periods to families. These weeks provided special services, in including instructional and recreational programs, for children and young adults. By providing a fun yet safe environment for children, parents were free to spend time alone enjoying activities designed for their tastes (e.g., harbor sunset cruises). In additional, there were several family excursions planned throughout the week which offered an opportunity to enjoy exploring reefs and other islands together.

Capturing the Market Earlier: In addition to the family weeks and Fast Tacks weeks, marketers realized that there was another market that they had been ignoring which could significantly reduce some of its occupancy cycle troubles. Instead of waiting until a couple had established themselves or started a family, why not get them when they were tying the knot? After all, the resort provided one of the most romantic atmospheres in the Caribbean. Moreover, the majority of weddings in North America, the primary market for the resort occur during the slow periods of summer and fall. In response to this revelation the resort began to actively marketing wedding and honeymoon packages. The resort hoped that these guests would return for future second, third, and fourth honeymoons[,] as well as bring their children when they started their families.

management contract for The Sandy Point Resort, located adjacent to his property. The additional facilities, including 40 more rooms, a second restaurant, a swimming pool, a fuel dock, and beach, gave the property the critical mass necessary to compete with local and international competitors. The resort also outsourced the provision of Scuba services from the Virgin Islands Dive Company. By 1990, the property had become a fully operational, water sports oriented, ecology-conscious resort that encompassed more than 75 acres and a mile of beachfront.

The resort faced two major challenges: an occupancy cycle with high peaks and low valleys and changing market demographics. Resort managers estimated that occupancy rates from 1985–1990 had ranged from between 80–100% during the peak season from mid-December until the end of May and between 40–60% from June until early December. These fluctuations were thought to occur because key customer markets sought Caribbean vacations during the colder winter months but found it hard to justify a trip to the tropics during spring, summer, and fall when the weather at home was more acceptable. It wasn't until the resort was forced to carry Sandy Point's additional overhead that management realized the need to address occupancy rate fluctuations. One of the most difficult costs to manage was labor. To provide the high-end service that the resort was known for, the number of staff employed by the resort had increased substantially. According to Jim Johnson, the resort was barely able to meet its guests' needs during peak season, while during slow season the resort was overstaffed.

Changing market demographics also posed a challenge. In the past, the resort predominantly attracted couples of all ages. However, changing market demographics severely hampered its ability to attract both new and repeat guests. Former guests who had begun to raise families of their own recalled the intimate moonlit dinners and walks on the beach but couldn't recall ever seeing any children and therefore did not identify the resort as "family friendly". The resort had never turned away families but had focused marketing efforts primarily on affluent couples without children. Changing demographics forced the resort to reexamine the message conveyed by its advertising.

As a result, the resort launched a new marketing campaign in 1990. Advertising targeted families and the staff prepared to cater to family-specific needs. The resort created sailing instruction programs for children and a host of activities designed to keep children busy while their parents enjoyed quiet time together. Family excursions onboard some of the resort's larger yachts provided the opportunity for families to sail together and explore some of the less inhabited islands. In addition, the resort added special Christmas, Easter, and Thanksgiving family programs that offered an entertaining atmosphere for the whole family. The resort changed

and the market was responding favorably as occupancy rates began to climb, even during the difficult slow season. Tom Fitch, the Director of Marketing and Special Promotions, also implemented several additional marketing initiatives in an attempt to increase occupancy during slower periods (see Exhibit C15-3 for examples).

By 1994, the resort began to see initial indications that the marketing initiatives were working. Although the resort still had some difficulty in attracting guests during the period between June and August, the resort increased its occupancy rates during the period between September and December to between 70–80%. The resort was rated as one of the best tropical resorts in the world by *Condé Nast Traveler* and maintained a strong position in the upscale segment of the BVIs. Peak season rates for double occupancy rooms ranged from $390–595 per day with meals and access to all water sports equipment included.

Despite the resort's prime location for water sports activities and strong reputation as the premier water sports resort in the Caribbean, management remained concerned about being able to match the service levels provided by their competitors. Increased availability of water sports at competing resorts threatened the resort's differentiated market position. WIYCR managers knew that some of their former guests were vacationing at nearby Little Dix Bay because that resort now offered similar water sports activities, had rates that overlapped those offered at WIYCR, and guests had been dissatisfied with the declining level of service they experienced during their last visit to WIYCR. WIYCR managers feared that this trend might continue if changes were not implemented soon.

THE WIYCR ORGANIZATION

Company Headquarters. Kimball insisted on managing strategic planning, finance, and reservations activities from an office in Chicago, Illinois (see organization chart in Exhibit C15-4). He wanted to live in the United States and attend to other investments (none of which were in hospitality) and argued that these activities were easily separated from the day-to-day operations management activities that took place at the resort. As the resort expanded and Kimball grew older (he was now in his seventies), he visited WIYCR less frequently and never during peak weeks. Moreover, Kimball, who once prided himself for knowing the names of each employee at the resort, knew fewer and fewer of his employees by name. As a result, when he did visit the resort the local employees thought that Kimball seemed increasingly removed and distant.

Marketing and Special Promotions. Kimball firmly believed that marketing activities should take place close to the consumer. As a result, Tom Fitch, the thirty-two-year-old Marketing and Special Promotions Director, managed from a small office in the southwestern corner of Connecticut. Fitch grew up as an active sailing competitor on the

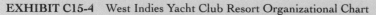

EXHIBIT C15-4   West Indies Yacht Club Resort Organizational Chart

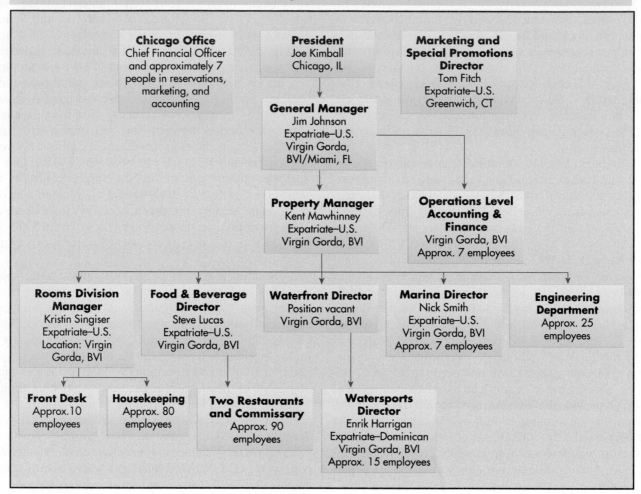

Long Island Sound (an area that stretches from New York City to the southeastern tip of Connecticut) sailing circuit and was well connected within the sailing industry. Fitch's strong sailing background coupled with being centrally located within the U.S.'s largest sailing community afforded great opportunities for promoting the resort with its most major target market area. Unlike Kimball, Fitch was always on-property during the high season and special promotions weeks. Fitch believed that it was important during these weeks for him to tend to the special needs of guests he had attracted to the resort. Local employees often underestimated the work required to plan and market these programs. Seeing him socialize with guests while on property, local employees questioned whether or not his job was really full time once he left the resort and returned to the States. After all, they only saw him periodically when he came in for a few weeks, threw large parties, and frantically tried to ensure that the guests' needs were met.

Jim Johnson, General Manager.   In the WIYCR organization, the General Manager traditionally oversaw all functional areas of the hotel and also played an important role in strategic planning. Jim Johnson, the forty-eight-year-old expatriate General Manager originally from the United States, was hired in 1990 based on his extensive

hospitality experience and academic training. His experience included several years as Assistant Manager of Little Dix Bay Resort and a master's degree in hospitality management from Cornell University. Johnson worked from his home in Miami, Florida most of the time in order to spend more time with his family, provide his children with stronger educational opportunities than those offered in the BVIs, and to reduce the number of expatriate permits that the resort required. Johnson averaged approximately 2 weeks at the resort per month, staying for longer periods of time during the high season and shorter periods of time during the low season. Johnson spent most of the time while at the resort in his office and in meetings with the heads of the various departments. Local employees often referred to him as a "behind the scenes" type manager; he provided detailed goals, objectives, and actions for his staff but was not present for the execution of plans. Johnson generally felt confident in his management team, especially his Property Manager whom he personally recruited and hired.

Kent Mawhinney, Property Manager.   The Property Manager was generally the second in command at the WIYCR and was responsible for implementing the General Manager's plans and monitoring the results. Kent

Mawhinney, the forty-year-old Property Manager from the United States, was hired by Johnson in 1992 and had an impressive background that included working on the management staff for six years at Caneel Bay, a Rockefeller Resort located on nearby St. John (in the United States' Virgin Islands). Mawhinney was a "hands on" manager who believed that "management by walking around" was needed in the Caribbean. Resort employees knew Mawhinney as a manager who was willing to get his hands dirty, and greatly appreciated this attitude.

Kristin Singiser, Rooms Division Manager. The Rooms Division Manager was responsible for two departments at the WIYCR: Housekeeping and the Front Desk. To many guests it seemed like Singiser had been at the resort forever. In fact, Singiser had been hired in 1985 as part of the front desk staff and was now thirty-five years old. She was born and raised in the Midwestern United States. She came to the resort with little hotel industry experience, had only been to the Caribbean as a tourist prior to taking the job, and proceeded to work her way up in the WIYCR organization to her current position. She was well respected by the guests and local staff because of her never-ending energy and constant smile. However, after 11 years at the property Singiser was beginning to get more frustrated with problems she faced over and over again. Her staff knew how Singiser felt but also knew that the issues were mainly between her and the Chicago office.

Steve Lucas, Food and Beverage Director. The Food and Beverage Director was responsible for two restaurants, a commissary, an employee dining facility, and three bars that were located on the WIYCR property. The resort had experienced high turnover in this position with three Food and Beverage Directors resigning to return to the United States within the past two years alone. Steve Lucas, a twenty-eight-year-old with recent experience working as the Food and Beverage Director for an exclusive California resort, was currently filling this position. Lucas was from the United States and had an impressive restaurant industry track record. He was hired by the resort in the middle of November 1994 and arrived at the property during the first week of December. Lucas had no previous experience working outside of the United States.

Nick Smith, Marina Director. The Marina Director was responsible for the resorts growing marina operations, run largely out of the Davey Jones marina. This marina included dock space for up to 35 boats, a fuel and water dock, and yacht maintenance services. The marina attracted yachting enthusiasts who were seeking a short stay in a resort environment. Nick Smith was promoted eight years ago to his current position as Marina Director. Smith, now forty-five years old, was originally from the United States and had been working at the resort for nearly fifteen years. He lived on the property along with his wife and their six-year-old daughter.

Waterfront Director. The Waterfront Director's position was created to assign responsibility to oversee the growing waterfront activities at the resort. The Director's responsibilities included overseeing the Watersports Department and its Director, as well as the resort's fleet of day excursion boats, planning and promoting day excursions, and developing and maintaining relationships with the sites that day excursions visited. The resort hired several expatriates for the Waterfront Director position. For a variety of reasons these expatriates didn't work out. Two had become alcoholics, and one had mysteriously packed his belongings and departed in the middle of the night. This position was currently vacant, with most responsibilities assumed by Nick Smith and Enrik Harrigan (the Watersports Director—see as follows).

Enrik Harrigan, Watersports Director. The Watersports Director was primarily responsible for the resort's fleet of small- to medium-sized boats and its windsurfing program. From 1986 until 1992, the Watersports Department had been under the leadership of Bill Jones, a Canadian who fell in love with the resort while staying there as a guest. His easygoing management style was well respected by a staff that would seemingly do anything for him. Unfortunately for the resort, Bill returned to Canada in 1992. The next most senior member of the water sports staff was twenty-seven-year-old Enrik Harrigan, a windsurfing guru from Dominica (part of the Windward Island chain located in the Southern Caribbean Sea) who had been working at the resort for about five years. Harrigan assumed the responsibilities as Watersports Director and was well respected by the staff as well but found he had difficulty assigning tasks and managing the operation.

DOWD ARRIVES IN THE BRITISH VIRGIN ISLANDS

On December 15, 1994, Dowd arrived at WIYCR. He found it hard to imagine the imminent transformation of the serene British Virgin Islands into an environment overwhelmed by a frenzy of holiday tourist activity. Within a few days thousands of tourists would invade the BVIs, stretching its natural, human, and capital resources to their limits. The natural beauty that the islands offered was a familiar sight for Dowd who had spent ten years working as a management consultant for small- to medium-sized hotels in the Caribbean. Tradewind Ventures, a world renowned sailing school, introduced him to the British Virgin Islands through summer employment as a Skipper and Operations Director in 1986. For the next six years, Dowd worked year-round for Tradewind Ventures as a management consultant during the winter months and Operations Director during the summer. During his tenure with Tradewind Ventures, Dowd added the Cabarete Beach Hotel (Cabarete, Dominican Republic) and the West Indies

Yacht Club Resort (Virgin Gorda, British Virgin Islands) to his client base. In addition, Dowd had completed his Bachelor of Science and Master's in Business Administration at Babson College. The primary point of differentiation between Dowd's consulting services and those offered by the larger consulting companies rested in his understanding of the Caribbean market and, most importantly, its people. His understanding had evolved through interactions both professionally and socially with local nationals from the region. Mike McClane, manager of a nearby charter boat company, respected Dowd's ability to understand the local nationals, saying "You really must understand my employees. Heck, Small Craft (employee's nickname) considers you a friend and I'm the only other outsider I know of to accomplish that. It took me five years[—]you've done it in two summers!"

Dowd had entered the doctoral program in Hotel Administration at Cornell University in September 1994; driven largely by his desire to study the challenges associated with expatriate management assignments. Dowd hoped that his understanding of the local culture was enhanced by what he had learned over the past semester in the classroom at Cornell. His first semester introduced him to new theoretical explanations for differences in behaviors across cultures. He wondered whether these tools would be helpful for interpreting behaviors and then communicating what they mean to Johnson and his managers.

DOWD'S OBSERVATIONS OF OPERATIONS

Checking in. Night had fallen on the Caribbean and as the North Sound Express ferry (a ferry that takes passengers from the Beef Island Airport on Tortola to various resort locations on Virgin Gorda (see Exhibit C15-1) approached the main dock at WIYCR, Dowd noticed the familiar stride of a former colleague from Tradewind Ventures. Dave Pickering, a twenty-two-year-old Cleveland native, had been working in the water sports department for nearly a month and was looking forward to Dowd's arrival. Pickering had worked with Dowd for the past three summers as a Skipper and Program Director at Tradewind Ventures. Although Pickering worked in the Caribbean for these three summers, his interactions had been primarily with the expatriate staff that Tradewind Ventures brought down each summer. Working side-by-side with the locals was a much different experience. Pickering had been hired by WIYCR in early December of 1994 as part of the water sports staff. He was primarily responsible for teaching sailing lessons, taking guests out on the larger boats, and signing out water sports equipment to guests.

Pickering extended an enthusiastic and firm handshake as Dowd got off the ferry. "Welcome to The Rock," he said. "The Rock" was the phrase coined by expatriates to describe living at the secluded resort. The two walked up the dock and Pickering paused for a minute. "Looks like someone forgot to come out and greet the guests again. It will take me a few minutes to give the briefing so go along to the front desk if you want. I'm sure you're familiar with the routine. We're going out to Saba Rock (a small island about 300 feet off the resort's North beach) in about a half-hour, so why don't you drop your stuff in your room and meet me at the dinghy dock[?]" Dowd nodded and headed for the front desk.

Kristin Singiser met Dowd at the front desk, exchanged greetings, and then Singiser suddenly looked confused. "Who met you down on the docks?" she asked.

"Dave was down there and is giving the guest briefing", he replied.

"That's odd. Dave is supposed to be off tonight. I wonder who was supposed to meet you down there?" Singiser said with a disturbed look on her face. She assigned Dowd to his room, picked up the radio microphone, and called one of the golf cart chauffeurs to come pick him up. As Dowd walked out of the lobby he thought, "What would have happened if nobody showed up to greet us? Sure I'm working here, but those people who were on the boat with me are paying thousands of dollars to be [here. What] would they think?"

A Night at Saba Rock. Although Dowd knew that he had an 8:00 a.m. meeting with Johnson, he couldn't help but enjoy the company of his island friends. Saba Rock was the only real hideout for expatriates and local national employees from WIYCR. A few tourists managed to find a dinghy ride out to the small pub on the one-half acre island, but they were usually the more adventurous types and were always welcome.

Pickering always had such a positive disposition; however, tonight a hint of irritability seemed to come across in his voice. "You know why I am here . . . right?" Dowd asked.

"Yes, I think so. Kent Mawhinney told me something about you coming down here to observe operations and make some suggestions for improvements. Boy, do I have some suggestions. How about firing everyone and bringing down our old staff from Tradewind Ventures?" he candidly replied. Dowd couldn't help but inquire further. Pickering said that when he arrived a few weeks prior the employees really welcomed him aboard. This seemed normal; Pickering had always been considered one of the more affable members of the Tradewind Ventures staff. Pickering said that each day co-workers in the water sports department distanced themselves more and more. Pickering said, "The harder I work, the greater the distance between us becomes."

"I don't understand," Pickering continued, "I've even tried to do some of their work to get back in good favor with them. But nothing seems to work. It's gotten to the point where I think some of these guys don't like me at all."

As Pickering continued, he questioned whether the resort's compensation system could ever work. Employees were paid an hourly rate based on their tenure at the resort. As Pickering understood the resort's compensation system, each year resort employees were given a raise without any performance review. Dowd asked Pickering for some concrete examples why the system wasn't working. Pickering explained, "Even some of the most senior guys in the water sports department hide from work. These senior employees know that they will get raises even if they don't do a good job ... excuse me, these guys get raises even if they don't do their job at all."

Pickering was very confused why the locals weren't taking advantage of the opportunity to get tips. Pickering was making $US50–100 extra per day on tips alone and when he told his fellow employees this they laughed and said it wasn't worth that much to them to have to work so hard. Dowd asked if Pickering had discussed his concerns with any of the managers. Pickering replied that he had a few conversations with Mawhinney about it but hadn't been able to find an opportunity to speak with Johnson. The discussion continued until Dowd's eyes began to grow heavy and he climbed in a resort dinghy and headed back to the resort.

Meeting with Johnson.   Johnson arrived in the Clubhouse Restaurant just a few minutes past eight. Dowd had already found his way to the breakfast buffet and sat with a plate full of local fruits and pastries. Johnson seemed rushed and told Dowd that he would have to keep the meeting short. Johnson told Dowd that he didn't want to influence Dowd's observations by explaining what he thought were the problem areas at the resort. Instead, Johnson would rather point out departments generating complaints and let Dowd observe without any biases. Dowd realized that this would be difficult because he knew so many of the employees but it was a role in which Dowd had been successful in the past. Dowd found that getting to the bottom of problems in organizations in the Caribbean often required gaining acceptance by the group, a status that was only achieved through gaining local employees' trust and establishing friendships. It was only then that employees would open up. Johnson wanted Dowd to focus on front desk, food and beverage, and water sports services and indicated that the resort's staff was at Dowd's service in terms of discussing operations. Johnson finished his coffee, wished Dowd luck, and left. As he watched Johnson walk out the door, Dowd thought, "Its always so easy to pick out the expatriate down here ... we always seem in such a hurry."

Property Tour with Kent Mawhinney.   Dowd finished up his breakfast and made his way down the shoreline to meet with Mawhinney, the property manager. He was greeted by Mawhinney at the top of the spiral staircase leading to the administrative offices. Mawhinney informed Dowd that he was leaving on his daily rounds and asked Dowd to join him. Mawhinney had extensive experience working in the Caribbean, and Dowd knew he would be a rich resource. As they walked off to their first stop[,] Dowd bluntly asked Mawhinney what he thought the main problems were at the resort. Mawhinney replied that the most basic problem was getting plans implemented. When Mawhinney managed in the United States, his employees were concerned with the opportunity for advancement and really worked hard to prove themselves. In the Caribbean, things were different. Local employment laws almost guaranteed jobs, and employees knew this. As a result, employees were more concerned with fitting in with their co-workers than making any type of an impression. The resort had provided opportunities for some of the locals to be promoted but few seemed interested. In his opinion, locals didn't want the added responsibility even if it meant more money. In some cases, the resort thought that rewarding the best employees with a title and some authority would help management gain more control over their employees. The result was an employee with a title who was unwilling to take on any of the job's responsibilities. "If the employees only realized what they could have if they worked a little harder, took these positions seriously, and moved up in the organization," Mawhinney commented.

The property tour took about an hour. Mawhinney visited with each department head, a mix of local nationals, and expatriates (see Exhibit C15-4). His conversations instilled a sense of urgency to get the resort in shape for the coming week. In each case, he offered assistance in any way necessary to ensure reaching the resort's desired goals and objectives. Dowd was particularly impressed by the amount of detail that Mawhinney recalled regarding each manager's immediate challenges. Mawhinney pointed out to Dowd that one of the main differences between managing in the United States and managing in the Caribbean is how managers have to communicate with employees. Because there is a 70% functional illiteracy rate on the property, he could not rely on memos as he had in the States. Instead he managed by physically demonstrating to his staff what had to be done. For example, Mawhinney's maintenance staff had been told several times that garbage was to be placed in a specific storage area. The staff continued storing the trash in the wrong place until Mawhinney physically showed them where and how it was to be stored.

Steve Lucas.   By 10:30 a.m., Mawhinney and Dowd had completed the tour of the resort with the exception of the restaurants. As the two approached the Clubhouse dining area, Dowd noticed a man in his early thirties arguing with a local cook who looked to be in his fifties (later Dowd would find out that this was the Head Chef who had worked at the resort for more than 20 years).

"Why didn't you tell me that you couldn't get the ingredients for cheesecake? The menus have already been printed and now we're going to look like fools! What is wrong with you people?" the man asked the cook.

Mawhinney interrupted, "Steve, what seems to be the problem?"

"Well, once again they failed to tell me that something was wrong," Lucas replied.

Mawhinney looked at the cook and asked if he could have a moment alone with Lucas. The cook welcomed the opportunity to leave the tense situation. Mawhinney calmed Lucas down and said that it was just part of the challenge of working in paradise. Mawhinney guided Lucas back over to Dowd, introduced the two, and informed Dowd that he had to get back to his office for a conference call with the resort's head office in Chicago.

Lucas and Dowd exchanged stories of their background. Lucas had been hired two weeks ago because the former Food and Beverage Director quit. When Dowd asked him whether he liked his new job, Lucas replied:

> "It's a bit early to tell. One thing is for sure. . . it's a lot more challenging than I ever imagined! I know the staff has been here for a while but I don't know how they ever managed. They seem to work as a "seat of your pants" type operation. No planning, no commitment, no enthusiasm. It's surprising because I have heard that this resort is one of the best places for people down here to work. I guess the biggest challenge is the fact that I know the people in Chicago expect big things from me and I plan to deliver . . . no matter what it takes. I just wish I had more time to train these people properly before we are hit with the big rush next week. Did you know that The Clubhouse and The Carvery are expected to serve 1,000 dinners on New Year's Eve? After dinner we expect that another 500–800 charterboat tourists will be coming ashore for the entertainment at the bar. Meanwhile, my staff is accustomed to our average nightly seating of about 100 for the rest of the year. This will be a big test for them . . . and, I guess for me as well."

Dowd asked Lucas how he was adjusting to the local culture. "I am having a great time so far. It's so much fun hanging out with a different group of guests every week. I am not looking forward to the slow season around here though. Then, who will I have to hang around with? I haven't made very many local friends and that's mostly because I want to keep business and pleasure separate anyway."

Their conversation went on for another 20 minutes. Finally, Lucas looked anxious to get back to overseeing the preparations for tonight's meal, so Dowd closed the conversation and moved on. As Dowd walked away, he stopped to take a glance back at Lucas. Lucas was hovering over one of his staff, checking to make sure that each ingredient was properly measured before being added to the pot. "What a way to have to manage?" Dowd thought.

Meeting with Kristin Singiser. Singiser entered the restaurant with an apologetic look on her face. "Sorry I am so late. Glad you found yourself a Pina Colada to keep you occupied," she said.

"So, what took you so long?" Dowd asked jokingly.

Singiser explained that it had been a long day. The Chicago office had overbooked the resort by 20% for the coming week without telling the guests that there might be some inconveniences. Therefore, it was her job to greet guests on the dock and inform some of them that they would have to stay onboard one of the resort's larger charter boats for a few nights until rooms became available. Meanwhile, other families were informed that the children and parents would be staying at opposite ends of the resort. As if dealing with understandably irate guests wasn't enough, her staff made several disturbing remarks.

> "They asked me, 'Why is everyone always coming down on us about providing good service when Chicago pulls a stunt like this?' I just don't know how to reply. My staff faces angry guests all day as a result of this fiasco. How can I expect them to be courteous when the guests are so mad and the staff had no influence on the situation? The worst part is that Chicago has done this to us for the past three years and each time I tell my staff to just manage this time and I'll try to make sure it doesn't happen again. I go to bat for them but seem to strike out every time," Singiser said.

Over a lobster dinner, the two discussed many other challenges that Singiser had faced over the years. Much of the locals' behavior she had become accustomed to, but some things were still frustrating. "Sometimes you feel like the only way you can manage these people is to bash them over the head with it," she commented. Apparently her style was to demonstrate exactly what she expected of her front desk staff a few times, knowing that some of them would get it right and others would continue to do it their own way. When they continued to do it their own way, it was time for "bashing them over the head with it." Despite all of her frustrations, Singiser was probably the most respected expatriate on the WIYCR staff. Over her long tenure she had adapted to the local culture, made close friends with the locals, and recognized what it took to get things done. However, she still felt challenged when trying to motivate her staff. "Money, opportunity for advancement, all of the normal incentives, they all don't seem to make any impact," she said.

In previous conversations with Singiser's staff, Dowd had solicited their opinions. Most staff said that Singiser was "different." She had a sincere interest in them and was involved with the local culture. She frequently took trips with her staff to the neighboring islands and had them over to her bungalow for dinner on occasion. Sure, she was tough, but her staff felt that managers had to be that way sometimes.

A Day at Water Sports: As they finished their meals and enjoyed an after dinner drink, Singiser suggested that Dowd spend at least one day working alongside the staff at water sports. That would give him an inside look at a department critical to the resort's success. After all, water sports were the main reason why guests chose the resort for their vacation.

Walking down the path to the water sports shack, Dowd knew that he had an interesting day ahead of him. He had extensive water sports experience but had only observed WIYCR's operations from a guest's perspective. Throughout the day, Dowd took mental notes on how the department operated and how the locals worked (or didn't work). Harrigan was behind the desk at the shack most of the day, while his assistant Mitchell (a twenty-five-year-old local Virgin Gordan) raced about the harbor on a 15-foot whaler (a small power boat) taking guests out to boats. It was surprising that Harrigan allowed some of his senior staff to noticeably avoid work. Fergus and Muhammad (both in their late twenties and from Virgin Gorda), for example, conveniently wondered off during the peak morning rush. Guests were left standing in line for 15 minutes because the desk was short-staffed. With Fergus and Mohammad's help at the desk, Dowd thought that the wait could be reduced to 5 minutes. The daylight sun was waning and guests wanted to get out on the water. When some of the senior staff did interact with guests, they were reserved and not overly courteous. Guests asked questions and the staff mumbled incoherent responses. However, one group of guests did have an advantage— guests who had bought several rounds of drinks for the staff the night before. When one of these guests arrived at the desk, the senior staff would jump to their feet and greet them like these guests were part of the local family. Dowd jokingly referred to this as "pre-service tipping".

Working at the Water Sports Department, Dowd found himself hustling the whole day, thinking that maybe some of it would rub off on his fellow workers. He had a slight advantage over Pickering's socialization into the group because Dowd had worked alongside the local staff during the three previous Thanksgiving vacations as part of a joint project between WIYCR and Tradewind Ventures. The group accepted him long ago. He thought, "Maybe if they see me working hard they will think its OK." By the end of his first day, Dowd had earned $100 in tips. He told the local staff and they didn't believe him until he laid the money out on the counter. He explained how they could easily do the same thing and make a killing this week. They reluctantly replied, "Yeah, right, like we could do that."

At the end of the day, Dowd, Fergus, and Muhammad stopped for a beer at the Commissary (a small snack bar). Dowd asked them how they thought things were going in the Water Sports Department. Fergus replied, "Things went more smoothly when Bill (Jones) was around. He gave us clear directions regarding what we had to do for the day and we did it. Things are different with Enrik (Harrigan). He's really laid back and we often don't know what we're supposed to be doing." Dowd also inquired about how they felt about the expatriates that worked at the resort, and Muhammad's comments summarized the discussion: "We have so many managers from the States and they don't stay here very long. Many of them think they can just come in here and we'll instantly be their friends. I'm tired of making friends just to have them leave a year later. The worst part is that they think we want to become managers like them. Managing people takes too much effort. I'm just not interested in leaving my friends behind just to make a little more money."

Talking with Guests. When Dowd was not speaking with the resort's management or its employees, he spent his time with the guests. The following quotes summarized the comments made by guests regarding guest interactions with the resort's staff:

> "There was nothing for us to do at night from December 23rd until the 26th. I know that the staff has to celebrate Christmas, but it would have been nice for us to have something to do."

> "I was waiting in line for almost 10 minutes at the bar. They only had two bartenders on and they moved so slowly. Plus, since all the guests are getting their own drinks why do they have five waitresses. They just stood there. Can't they work behind the bar too?"

> "We were out on the Almond Walk (a terrace area attached to the resort's main restaurant) and thought that a waiter would come by. When we asked one of the waitresses she said that she was assigned to the dining room. The dining room had served its last guest an hour before and was located about twenty-five feet from the Almond Walk. Someone should tell them that its OK to go out onto the Walk and serve other guests."

> "I asked the restaurant manager to call a waiter over for me but I'll never do that again. He went over to his wait staff and told them that they were incompetent. I felt so bad. I think that the staff purposely avoided our table for the rest of the night because they were afraid of getting into trouble again."

> "I was looking forward to being greeted at the docks by someone who would help me with my bags. After all, I'd just finished a 10-hour trip and am paying a lot of money to be here. When I asked the front desk staff they apologized and said that someone must have forgotten. It's surprising that I am paying

this much money for people to forget. What's that about first impressions being the most important?"

"Reading the brochure, I really thought that the programs for the kids sounded great. However, the first few days my kids said that the staff weren't very interested in making them have a good time. They seemed like they were more interested in when they got off work than with making my kids have a good time. Then they had Dave. What a difference! The kids came back excited about everything they did that day. He was so energetic and interested in my kids."

"I told the front desk that they should really spray for bugs out on the terrace or get one of those bug lamps. There are so many mosquitoes out there in the evening. The staff doesn't seem to be too interested in responding though."

"We called maintenance the other day to tell them that our rooms are not fully operational in terms of things like showers, screens and faucets working. It's kind of surprising to be at a resort like this without at least the basics. They said they would send someone by today, but that was three days ago. I think I will go to one of the other managers next."

"Today I went to the beach at around 10 a.m. and they were already out of towels again. The beach attendant said that he would bring some back as soon as he found them. I guess he didn't find any because it's been three hours, although I did see him standing around at the other end of the resort talking with some friends. Do you think he ever even looked for them?"

Listening to these comments, Dowd wondered which problems related to poor management relations with local staff, which related to simply poor work by the local staff, and which related to poor managing by the expatriates. One thing was sure—issues in all of these areas were beginning to affect the guests.

MAKING SENSE OF IT ALL

Dowd had been at the resort for just one week and the information from interviews with managers, local employees, and resort guests along with personal observations filled his head as he sat down to begin preparing for his meeting with Johnson the following morning. It was clear that there needed to be some changes at the resort if Johnson was going to resolve the issues concerning expatriate turnover, increasing guest complaints, and the level of tension between some of the expatriate managers and the local employees. The first wave of peak season guests, those coming for the Christmas holiday, would arrive tomorrow and stretch the resort's resources to their limits. Dowd wondered how he could best utilize the information gathered to analyze the current situation and provide some course of action for Johnson to take that would address his concerns. Dowd sat at his table and began to organize his thoughts.

Case 16   A First-Time Expatriate's Experience in a Joint Venture in China

THE LONG TRIP HOME

James Randolf was traveling back to his home state of Illinois from his assignment in China for the last time. He and his wife were about three hours into the long flight when she fell asleep, her head propped up by the airline pillow against the cabin wall. James was exhausted,

This case was prepared by Dr. John Stanbury, Assistant Professor of International Business at Indiana University, Kokomo, with enormous assistance from Rina Dangarwala and John King, MBA students. It is not intended to illustrate either effective or ineffective handling of a managerial situation. The views represented here are those of the case author and do not necessarily reflect those of the Society for Case Research. The author's view is based on his own professional judgments. The names of the organization, and the industry in which it operates, and individuals' names and the events described in this case have been disguised to preserve anonymity.
Presented to and accepted by the Society for Case Research. All rights reserved to the author and SCR. Copyright © 1997.

but for the first time in many days he had the luxury of reflecting on what had just happened in their lives.

He was neither angry nor bitter, but the disruption of the last few weeks was certainly unanticipated and in many ways unfortunate. He had fully expected to complete his three-year assignment as the highest ranking U.S. manager of his company's joint venture (JV) near Shanghai. Now, after only 13 months, the assignment was over, and a manager from the regional office in Singapore held the post. Sure, the JV will survive, he thought, but how far had the relationship that he had been nurturing between the two partnered companies been set back? His Chinese partners were perplexed by his company's actions and visibly affected by the departure of their friend and colleague.

Was this an error in judgment resulting from Controls' relative inexperience as a multinational company and a partner in international joint ventures, James wondered?

Or, had something else caused the shift in policy which resulted in the earlier-than-planned recall of several of the corporation's expatriates from their assignments? There had always been plans to reduce the number of expatriates at any particular location over time, but recently the carefully planned timetables seem to have been abandoned. Next week, James had to turn in his report covering the entire work assignment. How frank should he be? What detail should he include in his report? To whom should he send copies? There had been rumors that many senior managers were being asked to take early retirement. James did not really want to retire but could hardly contain his dissatisfaction as to how things had turned out. Maybe it would be better to take the offer, if it was forthcoming, and try to find some consulting that would make the best use of his wide spectrum of technical and managerial experience which now included an expatriate assignment in what was considered to be one of the most difficult locations in the world.

James reflected with satisfaction on his accomplishment of the initial primary objectives[,] which were to establish a manufacturing and marketing presence. In fact, he was quite pleased with his success at putting many things in place [that] would allow the operation to prosper. The various departments within the joint venture were now cooperating and coordinating, and the relationships he had established were truly the evidence of this achievement. He would like to have seen the operations become more efficient, however.

The worklife that awaited him upon his return was a matter of considerable concern. Reports from the expatriates who preceded him in the last few months indicated that there were no established plans to utilize their talents, and often early retirement was strongly encouraged by management. Beyond the obligatory physical examinations and debriefings, he had been told there was little for them to do. Many of the recalled expatriates found themselves occupying desks in Personnel waiting for responses about potential job opportunities.

He gazed at his wife, Lily, now settled into comfortable slumber. At least she had had a pretty good experience. She was born in Shanghai but left China in 1949. The country was then in the middle of a revolution, but, aside from her memory of her parents appearing extremely anxious to leave, she remembered little else about the issues surrounding their emigration to the United States. Most of her perceptions about "what it was like" in China came from U.S. television coverage, some fact, some fiction.

As the plane droned on into the night, James thought back to how this experience began.

THE COMPANY

Controls' world headquarters were in Chicago, Illinois. It had operations in several countries in Europe, Asia, and South America, but, with the exception of several *maquiladoras,* all of its expansion had occurred very recently. Its first involvement in joint ventures began only three years ago. As an in-house supplier to "Filtration, Inc.," a huge Chicago-based international manufacturing conglomerate, specializing in the design and production of temperature control and filtration systems, it had been shielded from significant competition, and most of its product lines of various electronic control mechanisms had been produced in North America. Ten years ago, however, Controls became a subsidiary of Filtration, Inc. and was given a charter to pursue business beyond that transacted with its parent. At the same time, the rules for acquiring in-house business changed as well. Controls now bid for Filtration, Inc.'s business against many of the world's best producers of this equipment. The need to utilize cheaper labor and to be located closer to key prospective customers drove the company to expand internationally at a rate that only a few years earlier would have been completely outside its corporate comfort zone.

A JV in China would provide Controls with an opportunity to gain a foothold in this untapped market for temperature control systems. This could pave the way for a greater thrust into the expanding Chinese economy. If the JV was successful, it could also lead to the establishment of plants to manufacture various products for the entire Asia/Pacific market.

The corporation's involvement in the joint venture seemed less planned than its other expansion efforts. The Freezer and Cooler Controls Business Unit (one of Controls' key business units), headquartered in Lakeland, Minnesota sent a team of four, consisting of two engineers and two representatives from the Finance and Business Planning Departments, to investigate the possibility of partnering with a yet-to-be-identified Chinese electronics assembly operation. The team was not given an adequate budget and was limited to a visit of one month. Not being experienced international negotiators, they were only able to identify one potential partner, a Chinese state-owned firm. They quickly realized that they did not have time to conclude negotiations, and returned to HQ without having met their objective. After debriefing them upon their return to the United States, the corporation's planners decided that the Chinese JV presented a good opportunity and sent another team to continue these negotiations. Eventually, an agreement was reached with the Chinese state-owned firm. Exhibit C16-1 shows the organizational relationships between Filtration, Inc. and its subsidiaries.

HOW IT ALL BEGAN

James had always been intrigued by the idea of securing an international assignment. His interest heightened on the day that Controls, Inc. announced its intentions to expand the business through establishing a more international presence, worldwide. By age 51, James had worked

EXHIBIT C16-1   Filtration Inc. Organization Chart

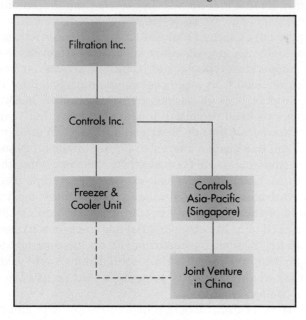

in managerial positions in Engineering, Quality Control, Customer Support, and Program Management for the last 15 of his 23 years with the company, but always in positions geographically based in Pauley, Illinois. He frequently mentioned the idea of working on an international assignment to his superiors during performance reviews and in a variety of other settings. He did not mentally target any specific country, but preferred an assignment in the Pacific Rim, due to his lifelong desire to gain an even deeper understanding of his wife's cultural heritage.

Finally, two years ago, he was able to discuss his interests with the corporation's International Human Resources manager. During this interview he was told of the hardships of functioning as an expatriate. There could a language problem as well as difficulties caused by the remoteness from home office. He remained interested.

A year later, James was first considered for a position that required venture development in Tokyo. At one point he was even told he had been chosen for that position. With little explanation, the company instead announced the selection of a younger, more "politically" connected "fast-tracker."

When, a few months later, a discussion about the position in China was first broached by Personnel, it was almost in the context of it being a consolation prize. The position, however, appeared to be one for which James was even better suited and one which would be challenging enough to "test the mettle" of any manager in the company. The assignment was to "manage a joint venture manufacturing facility" located on Chongming Dao Island, about 25 miles north of Shanghai. The strategic objective of the JV was market entry into China.

Soon thereafter, in mid-August of 1992, James was asked to go immediately to Lakeland to meet one-on-one with Joe Whistler, the director of the Freezer and Cooler Controls Business Unit to discuss the JV. The negotiating team was still in China in the process of "finalizing" the JV agreement with the Chongming Electro-Assembly Company, a state-owned electronic device assembly operation. The corporation felt that there was a dire need to put someone on site. Joe asked if he could leave next week! James indicated that he was interested in accepting the position and that he was willing to do whatever the corporation required of him to make it happen as soon as possible. It was understood that a formal offer for the position would be processed through Personnel and communicated through James's management. When this trip didn't materialize, James wondered if this was going to be a repeat of the Tokyo assignment. Finally, in late September, James's supervisor approached him and said, "if you still want it, you've got the prize."

ORIENTATION

Filtration, Inc. has a defined set of procedures to deal with expatriate work assignment orientation. When it was determined that James was a strong candidate to go overseas, it was arranged for James and his wife to go to Chicago for orientation training. The training began with a day-long session conducted by Filtration, Inc.'s International personnel function. James thought the training was exceptionally well done. Filtration, Inc. brought in experts to discuss pay, benefits, moving arrangements, and a multitude of other issues dealing with working for the corporation in an international assignment. Part of the orientation process was a "look-see trip," the normal length of which was seven days. The trip was quickly arranged to begin two weeks later. The Randolfs were extremely excited. This would be Lily's first trip back to China. They even extended the duration of the trip to ten days to do some investigation on their own time.

There was a considerable mix-up in the planning of the "look-see" trip. Although the Personnel Department in Pauley wanted to arrange the entire trip, Controls' Asia-Pacific regional office in Singapore insisted it was better for them to handle it locally. The Randolfs were supposed to have a rental car available upon arrival but discovered that no arrangements had been made, and so they were forced to secure their own car. Their itinerary indicated that they had reservations at the Shanghai Inn, but they soon discovered that no reservations had been made there either.

In Shanghai they went sightseeing on their own for three days. Afterward, they were scheduled for seven days of official activities. They spent the following two days with an on-site consultant, who was on retainer from the JV, and who showed the potential expatriates around the city. Her tour consisted of what she perceived a typical American might most like to see.

The wife of an expatriate herself, the consultant didn't speak Shanghainese or any other Chinese dialects. Travel with her was somewhat of a nightmare. As opposed to discussing the planned locations with the Chinese driver at the beginning of a day, she directed the trip one step at a time. She would show the driver a card on which was written the address of the next location and say "[G]o here now." This approach caused considerable delays due to the inefficiencies of [traversing] the city numerous times and touring in a disorderly sequence. They were shown American-style shopping, American-style restaurants, and potential living accommodations. The Randolfs were told that leasing a good apartment commonly required a "kickback."

After visiting the JV's factory near Shanghai they traveled to the regional headquarters, Controls Asia-Pacific, in Singapore to participate in an extensive orientation workshop. Again, the topics included compensation policies and other matters of interest to potential expatriates, this time from the perspective of Controls, Inc. James and Lily both noted a significant contrast in dealings with the regional Controls, Inc. personnel staff as opposed to the "first rate" Filtration, Inc. International Human Resources people. The former was by far a less polished and informed operation. Even as they departed Singapore for the United States, they were still unsure that the move was right for them. They spent the next several days reflecting on the trip and discussing their decision. They were discouraged by the lack of maintenance apparent in the factory, which was clearly inferior to U.S. standards. Things were dirty, and little effort was expended on environmental controls. The days seemed awfully gray. However, they had quickly become enamored with the Shanghai people and this became a key factor in their ultimate decision to accept the position. As the result of their interactions with the Chinese partners and Shanghai area residents, James and Lily truly felt the promise of exciting, new, deep, long-lasting relationships.

Once they were firmly committed to the assignment, they attended a two-day orientation on living and working in China. This was provided by Prudential Relocation Services Inc. in Boulder, Colorado, and was tailored to the needs and desires of the participants. Optional curriculum tracks included: the history, culture, political climate, business climate, and the people of the region. James focused his training on a business-related curriculum which was taught by professors from a local university. Additionally, whenever an expatriate returned from China to the home office on home leave, James was given an opportunity to interface with him. Exhibit C16-2 summarizes the key characteristics of Chinese culture and management.

Between November (1992) and January (1993), James worked an exhausting schedule, alternating two-week periods in Pauley and at the JV in China, where lodging and meals were provided in a hotel. During this time, his wife, Lily, remained in Lakewood preparing for their permanent relocation to China. Also, Filtration, Inc. held scheduled, intensive Mandarin language courses in Chicago, which James planned to attend, but due to his work schedule he was unable to take advantage of the opportunity. Finally, in January, James attended the language school for a week. Fortunately, he and Lily already spoke some Cantonese, another Chinese dialect. After James was finally on-site full-time in February, he hired a language tutor to supplement this training. The orientation procedure concluded with a checklist of things that James and Controls were to accomplish after the commencement of his on-site assignment. While all of these checklist items were eventually accomplished, priorities on the job didn't allow them to be completed in a very timely manner.

WORKPLACE ORIENTATIONS

Mandarin, China's official language, was spoken at the factory. In regions where Mandarin is not the primary language of the people, it is the language most commonly used in industry and trade, and in dealing with the government. Most residents were not proficient in Mandarin, although the oldest members of the population had learned it only after they had completed their formal education, if at all. Mandarin became China's official language when the alphabet was standardized in 1955. Away

EXHIBIT C16-2   Survey of Key Characteristics of Chinese Culture and Management

Culture

One of the strong cultural beliefs among the Chinese is that their culture is the oldest and the best. It is the center of the universe, the *Zhong guo*—center country. They believe themselves to be totally self-sufficient. In Chinese, the character of the word China means "middle kingdom," thus implying that everyone other than themselves is beneath them.

Concept of Face and Time

The concept of face is of paramount importance in China. It is a person's most precious possession. Without it, one cannot function in China. It is earned by fulfilling one's duties and other obligations. Face often requires little effort, but merely an attention to

courtesy in relationships with others. Face involves a high degree of self-control, social consciousness, and concern for others. In Chinese society, display of temper, sulking, loss of self-control, or frustration create further loss of face rather than drawing respect.

Despite having invented the clock, the Chinese never define or segment time in the way that it is approached in the West. Even today, for Chinese, time simply flows from one day to another. If a job is not completed today, they will carry it forward to the next day or the day after next. This is a manifestation of the concept of Polychronic (non-linear) time. In Western cultures, people see time as Monochronic (linear).

An important cultural difference between the West and China is the Chinese custom of giving precedence to form and process in completing a task, over the task itself, an approach which is typically more time-consuming.

Behavior

Chinese behavior is influenced by their brutal history. This has created a careful people. They give consideration to the repercussions of every move or decision that they make.

An important aspect of behavior involves the way the Chinese think. They think about thinking and relationships, whereas the Westerner would think in linear patterns of cause and effect.

Another aspect, which confuses the Westerner, is the willingness to discuss endless possibilities even when things look hopeless.

A Chinese philosophy that relates to interacting with Westerners, can be stated: Whereas a Westerner will try to tell you everything he knows in a conversation, a Chinese will listen to learn everything the Westerner knows, so that, at the end of the day, he would know both what he knew and what the Westerner knew.

Gift Giving

Chinese are conditioned to express appreciation in tangible ways, such as by giving gifts and other favors. They regard the Westerner's frequent use of "thank you" as a glib and insincere way of passing off obligations to return favors. When they do someone a favor, they expect appreciation to be expressed in some very concrete way. If all you choose to do is say "thanks," it should be very specific and sincere, and then stop. The Chinese do not like gushy thanks. Gift giving in China is a highly developed art. Although it has greatly diminished today (there is a law forbidding government officials from accepting gifts of any kind or value), the practice remains a vital aspect of creating and nurturing relationships with people.

Living as a Foreign Guest in the People's Republic of China

Foreigners, who have gone to the People's Republic of China in the last decade to help the Chinese, have been given preferential treatment. Their quarters are often far more modern than those of a typical Chinese. The expatriate is given perquisites in excess of those available to all but the top officials, fed with highest quality food, and paid salaries many times higher than paid to their Chinese counterpart of the same status. They are sheltered from the harsh realities of Chinese life and are recipients of enormous courtesy and care.

There are three main reasons for this preferential treatment. First, as a poverty-stricken nation, the Chinese need to attract and retain foreigners to help them achieve a higher standard of living, by increasing their economic and technical level. Second, the Chinese believe that people from the developed nations are so used to modern comforts that they would not be able to function competently without them. Finally, there is simple pride. They want their country to be thought of favorably.

Social

Generally, the sociocultural behavior of the Chinese differs greatly from that of Western societies. Family is very important to them, and obligation to them takes precedence when it conflicts with work responsibilities. Those outside the family are treated with indifference and sometimes with contempt. Decision making evolves from the opinion and support of the family. The

highest respect is given to elders and ancestors. The reverence for authority and order explains why the Chinese are so careful about getting consensus from everyone. An important ideal that is fostered by the family is harmony.

The Chinese do not believe in the concept of privacy. This absence of individuality and freedom is a way of life in China.

Laws Made to Be Broken

Due to their history of being encumbered by rules and taboos, the Chinese have developed a perverse and seemingly contradictory attitude toward laws and regulations. They tend to ignore them and break them to suit their purpose, as long as they think they can get away with it. A significant proportion of public Chinese behavior is based on political expediency, and not on their true feelings. Since their public, official behavior is more of a survival technique than anything else, they do not feel guilty about ignoring or subverting the system. It is something they do naturally as a way of getting by.

Importance of Human Resources Management in Organizations in China

The labor environment in China is influenced by six major factors. They are National Economic Plans, the Four Modernization Programs, Political Leadership, Chinese Cultural Values, Labor Unions, and the Special Economic Zones—that is, SEZs. The SEZs were created specially for the conduct of the joint ventures with overseas countries. The main characteristics of the SEZs that are found in a joint venture are their dominating influence on matters pertaining to the employment wage system, organizational structure, management roles, and decision making.

One of the most interesting aspects of Chinese HRM is the unmistakable influence of some of the traditional cultural values such as *guanxi* (relationship), *renqing* (favor), *mianzi* (face), and *bao* (reciprocation) in recruitment and selection, training and development, and placement and promotion.

There is a definite political element involved in the behavior of Chinese Personnel managers; those who are more party-oriented base their decisions on party policies rather than for the good of the company.

Maintaining Personnel Files and Their Implications

Chinese-style personnel management generally does not forgive or forget any real or imagined past transgressions by employees under their jurisdiction. Any past mistakes or offenses committed by the employee are duly recorded in the employee's file and are often used against that person.

To hire someone from another company, the other company must release the prospective employee's file. This contains the employee's work record and entitles him or her to benefits accorded to workers in the state sector. If the employer is not willing to release the file and the employee leaves, he or she loses the benefits, a risk few Chinese are willing to take. Many foreign companies have been able to complete transfers only after compensating the other company. The average payoff has been about 1,000 yuan (in 1992), a very modest amount in $US but one-half of one month's salary for a translator.

The Chinese can be said to be ethnocentric, that is, the belief that one's own national or regional management practices are superior. This can carry over into the review and acceptance of

EXHIBIT C16-2 (Cont.)

an employee's file from other provinces. The employee's previous place of employment can impact his future job prospects. In this case, the Shanghainese would look with disfavor on an employee file (and therefore the individual) from the poorer, less sophisticated Chongming Dao area.

A related culture difference is that a foreign manager would examine an employee's file from the perspective of performance, whereas a Chinese manager would review the file to learn of an individual's seniority and to see if there is a history of causing dissention.

Rank
There are no official class distinctions in China, but rank among businesspeople and government bureaucrats is very important. It is very important that you know the rank of the individual you are likely to deal with and your response should be consistent with the rank. Connections and rank gain one access to the *tequari* or special privileges. If the top official is accompanied by the second in rank, all the discussion should be directed toward the top official and the second in rank might as well not be present.

Manufacturing and Quality Control in China
In general, the Chinese have only a rudimentary understanding of quality concepts. They almost always carry out 100% inspections to "control" quality. Because the Chinese have become accustomed to inferior quality goods, producing goods of high quality is often not perceived by workers to be important. Those items that do not pass quality control are offered to the employees free of charge.

There is great variety in the quality of technology used in China. For the most part the technological level resembles that

of the United States in the 1950s. There is scant computerization. Materials handling is done manually. Machinery is bulky and frequently needs repair.

Scheduling of work is almost nonexistent, though work itself is assigned to groups. A typical manufacturing operation is very labor-intensive, and in most cases there is an excessively large workforce. Production planning is usually based on the number of hours to be worked rather than on the number of units to be manufactured.

Infrastructure
China's economy suffers from weak infrastructure. Electricity is unavailable at times (especially if the firm has exceeded its quota). Roads need repairs, train shipments are more often than not late, factory allocations of raw materials are (occasionally) routed to other units, and the communication systems can be considered a nightmare.

Additional Note
Neither Geert Hofstede's original study (Hofstede, 1980) nor his later work (Hofstede and Bond, 1988) included China as a country of analysis. However, Hong Kong and Taiwan were included in both instances. The results were similar for Power Distance (Large), Individualism (Low), Uncertainty Avoidance (Low), and Confucianism (High), differing only in Masculinity (Hong Kong, high, and Taiwan, low). We would therefore expect top-down decision making, centralized authority, little participative management, tolerance of uncertainty, and authority vested only in the most senior employees. This confirms the events described in the case.

---

from the work-place, people preferred to speak Shanghainese or Chongming Dao's own similar dialect.

Chongming Dao, the actual site of the factory, was situated in the Chuang Yangtze River. At approximately 50 miles long and 18 miles wide, it is China's third largest island. Its population is approximately one million people. The residents were perceived by the Shanghainese to be poor, backward farmers.

James found that he was able to maintain residencies in Shanghai and in Chongming Dao, although all the Chinese workers, including managers, lived close to their place of work. The trip from downtown Shanghai to the plant took more than two hours. First there was a half-hour trip to the site of the ferry departure, then came a 20-minute ferry ride, followed by another 20 minutes of travel by car. Work days at the factory were scheduled from Tuesdays through Saturdays. As is common in China, the schedules were centrally planned to alternate with those of other factories in a manner which conserved power consumption.

The Chinese partner had warehouses and a business center on the island, which, in addition to the factory, became part of the JV. The people worked under conditions that would be totally unacceptable to most American workers. There were no temperature or humidity controls.

In the winter the plant was so cold that workers wore up to six layers of clothing. In contrast, summers were very hot and humid. None of the machinery had safety guards. Tools were generally either nonexistent or inadequate. Lighting was also very poor.

The Chinese factory's workforce was primarily young women. This was in contrast to the Chinese partner's factories that James had visited, where most of the workers were men who appeared to be over the age of 40. The plant's organization and operation fostered considerable inefficiencies. There were not process controls to prevent errors and scrap. The only visible methods of quality control were extensive amounts of 100% testing and inspection performed after the product was completely assembled. The layout of the plant was awkward. There were numerous little rooms and no large expansive production areas. Operations were not laid out sequentially or even in a line. The typical mode of operations was to have numerous workers working elbow to elbow around the perimeter of a large table.

Material movement was most commonly performed by dragging large tubs of materials across the floor. Storage was disorderly and bins were generally not stacked, due to a lack of shelving. Consequently, containers of parts, partially assembled products, scrap materials, and finished assemblies could be found anywhere and everywhere. Instead of scheduling plant output, the system scheduled only the number of man-hours to be expended. This lack of direction caused a considerable amount of confusion and inefficiency. It was really more of a way of accounting for the use of the excessive labor force that existed in the factory and in the area. James often commented that he could produce as much or more output with only the number of Quality Control (QC) operators that were in the plant. By his estimates, the JV employed three times as many people as were needed. James did not think that he could change this immediately but felt that he could convince the Chinese management that this practice needs to be change eventually.

ADAPTING TO LIFE IN CHINA

Beyond some terrific people in the Personnel Department in Pauley, who could help with specific employment-related issues, James quickly came to realize that there would be little operational support from the home office. His links back to his corporation came more from Filtration, Inc. than from Controls. Filtration, Inc. at least sent a monthly package of news clippings, executive briefs, and memos that had been specifically prepared for expatriates. The package allowed James to keep up somewhat on what was happening in the larger corporate setting.

Filtration, Inc. had a couple of dozen employees in Shanghai. It was their role to establish and implement a joint venture that the parent had negotiated with a different Chinese manufacturer than the one with which Controls had partnered. As part of this team, there were also a few representatives from Controls, Inc. They were all co-located in a small office building in downtown Shanghai. It was in this corporate office environment that James found a great deal of support, a lot of helpful advice, and his unofficial mentor, a Filtration, Inc. manager who had spent four years in China. At the time, James wondered why he hadn't visited this office during his orientation trip.

The help that James received from Controls, Inc.'s subsidiary, Controls Asia-Pacific, was often ineffective and inconsistent. Nagging policies and obligatory paperwork were typical characteristics of their assistance. There were ongoing problems finding and retaining a qualified translator for James. In the agreement, the JV was responsible for providing each expatriate with a translator. Controls Asia-Pacific was responsible for the wage structure at the JV. The Personnel Department in Singapore established a maximum wage rate for the translator position at 2,000 yuan. This rate was fair for the area, but there were few high quality translators available. When an area translator was identified, he would often be lost to another multinational company in the area who offered a salary of 3,000 yuan. To attract translators from Shanghai would require a wage comparable to the

wages one would receive in Shanghai, and 2,000 yuan was significantly lower than that paid in the city.

Another aspect of employment in China which merited consideration was the movement of one's "personnel file" from a former employer to the present one. This is the rough equivalent of changing one's residency to another state in the United States. The reputation and perception of Chongming Dao was that of a rural community. This would have a negative impact on transferring a translator's file back to Shanghai in the future. Singapore didn't understand the economics and implications of this situation and refused to increase the wage rate to a level that would entice qualified translators to accept the position. James, as a result, was without a qualified translator for significant periods during his time in China. The impact on his ability to function in that setting was therefore also significant, resulting in less being accomplished than if Singapore had been more flexible.

The residence in Shanghai was available because the JV had committed to a two-year lease of an executive apartment on the 22nd floor of the Shanghai Inn. These accommodations were quite nice and offered most of the comforts of home. The hotel complex included a supermarket, exercise facilities, a theater, and several restaurants, including Shanghai's Hard Rock Cafe. The three-bedroom apartment, which James measured to be around 1,500 square feet, was converted into a two-bedroom apartment to his specifications. Amenities included cable TV with five English language channels. Accommodations on the island were significantly rougher. The original plan was for James to temporarily stay at the government's guest house on the factory grounds, until a 12-unit housing compound was constructed in the immediate vicinity. The small rooms, intense heat, and fierce mosquitoes at the guest house proved to be unbearable and, by June, James decided to make other arrangements. These entailed staying in a hotel 17 miles away with the two other expatriates from Controls, Inc. to manage the JV. Although the building was new, the quality of the construction was quite poor, which seemed to be common in China. The costs associated with constructing their compound were, by this time, estimated to be much larger than expected. Eventually, a solution was reached to fix up certain aspects of the guest house and retain it as the long-term island living arrangements for them. After this, Lily always traveled with him to and from the factory.

ADAPTING TO THE WORK

In addition to James, there were three other Controls, Inc. expatriates assigned to the JV. The director of Engineering and the director of Manufacturing were on assignment from the United States. The director of Finance was from Singapore. Each of these individuals had dual roles, that of heading up their respective departments, and the assignment to bring to the JV new technology associated with their departments. The Finance

EXHIBIT C16-3 Controls' Joint Venture in China: Organization Chart

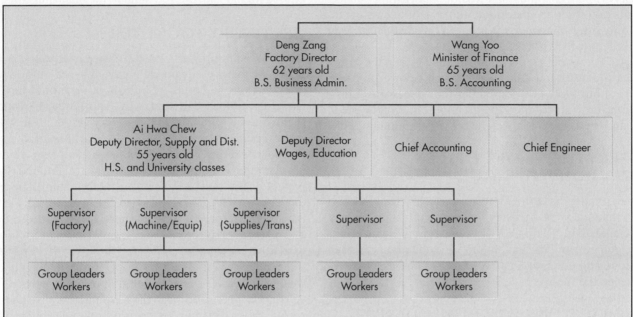

director had the particularly challenging assignment of introducing a new accounting system to the JV, one that was compatible with the Controls, Inc. system. The existing system, installed by the Chinese partner, was not designed to report profits and losses, irrelevant concepts in the formerly state-owned company.

The other expatriates occasionally complained of not getting good cooperation from the Chinese workers. James never encountered this problem, as he always communicated his requests directly to the workers.

One of the first problematic situations that evolved related to differences between expatriate conditions of employment for Filtration, Inc. and Controls, Inc. employees. Most Filtration employees enjoyed a per diem of US$95[,] but Controls employees were limited to US$50 per day. Additionally, the Filtration, Inc.'s visitation policies were more liberal in terms of allowing college-age children to visit their expatriate parents.

ONGOING NEGOTIATIONS

In China, a JV contract is [a] "nice framework" from which to begin the real negotiation process. The Controls JV negotiating team viewed the contract as a conclusion to negotiations and returned to the United States in late December of 1992. James soon discovered that the process of negotiations would be ongoing. On almost a daily basis, some element of the agreement was adjusted or augmented with new understanding.

A misconception held by the Controls negotiating team related to the ease of obtaining appropriate governmental approvals. There were various annexes and subcontracts which were yet to be finalized and approved when they departed. Some of these approvals

were required from government officials with whom they had had very little interface. The impact of this miscalculation was that production in the JV didn't commence on January 1, 1993, as anticipated. Instead it took until August 1, 1993 to get the operation going.

One of the most serious issues affecting the operation of the JV which directly impacted James'[s] effectiveness was the JV's organization structure which was negotiated by the Controls team. The organization chart for the JV is shown in Exhibit C16-3. Controls perceived the position of Chairman (COB) of the Board of Directors to be of greater importance in operating the company than that of managing director, thinking that they could "run the company" from that position. Consequently, when the organization chart was drawn up, Controls conceded the position of managing director to the Chinese partner in exchange for the right to appoint the COB for the first three of the five years. James noted that in Chinese JVs negotiated by Filtration, Inc., the U.S. partner always secured the position of managing director.

OBSERVATIONS OF CHINESE MANAGEMENT METHODS

James observed that when Chinese managers were dealing with subordinates, decision making was very top-down. This resulted in virtually all decisions of any consequence being made by the managing director. James was extremely fortunate that the managing director appointed by the Chinese partner was willing to share his power. He and the managing director developed an excellent relationship, which James consciously worked on in the firm belief that this was the key to business success in China. Toward the end of his time at the

JV, James was frequently left in charge of running the factory while the managing director was visiting outside friends of influence, customers, and potential customers. The only other manager who shared this distinction was the director of Personnel.

The Personnel Department, in this JV, as in the state-owned Chinese companies, was unusually powerful when compared to most U.S. companies that James was familiar with. They maintained the all-important employment files and were very connected to the Communist Party.

OBSERVATIONS OF CHINESE MANAGEMENT TEAM

Chinese managers at the JV were considerably more educated than the workers. They had matriculated at various universities and graduated with degrees in Engineering, Management, and the like. In one case, the manager's experience and education came from his time as a career-soldier in the Army.

INTERACTIONS WITH THE CHINESE GOVERNMENT

Prior to the formation of the JV, the secretary for the Communist Party and the managing director were co-equals when it came to "running the Chongming Electro-Assembly Company." About 325 of the 1,819 employees at the JV were communists. After James's arrival, there was always a question as to what would happen to the party office, which was located adjacent to the managing director's office. In many ways the party served a function similar to that of labor unions in the United States. It represented the workers and entered into discussions related to labor relations issues. The Communist Party could be viewed as a different channel to deal with issues, and James quickly recognized it as an ally.

James's only personal experience with a government bureau was while getting his residency papers established. The rules he encountered were extremely inflexible, everything had to be just right, and no copies were allowed as the Bureau required originals. The Bureau office, which was the size of a walk-in closet in the United States, was extremely crowded and the process required forcing one's way up through the lines to get to the table where female police officers would process the paperwork. After it was all over, he noticed that they had spelled his name wrong. He did not return to correct the mistake.

INTERACTION WITH THE UNION

The JV also had a labor union, but by comparison to the United States, the organization was extremely weak and superficial. James's only dealing with the union related to a request for donations for a retirees' party the union wanted

to hold. Since the JV had no retirees, and this was new ground for him, he referred them to the managing director.

GETTING IT TOGETHER

James loved to walk the floor and see what was happening in the factory. His position gave him the authority to direct actions to be taken, but often he did not have to use this authority in that way. The Chinese workers seemed to be influenced by his every action. If he would make a point to pick up trash in the parking lot, the next day he would observe that the trash had all been cleaned up. Another example was when he straightened some papers in the pigeon holes of a filing system. The next day every stack of papers was perfectly arranged. He felt that there was never a time where he walked the floor and it didn't pay off in some way. He found Chinese workers to be very attentive to detail.

He was often tested by the Chinese managers and workers alike, as is not uncommon in other parts of the world. He perceived that they would test his commitment, leadership, and his decision-making ability. They would determine how far this manager could be pushed. These tests provided him with the opportunity to do the right thing. A case in point was when a drunken sales-person accosted a woman in a nightclub. James took him to a private place and severely chastised him.

During his assignment, he remained cognizant of the fact that one of his jobs was to make the [managing director] look good. This required him to fire a translator on the spot when the translator remarked that anyone who wanted to stay in China was stupid.

He had great admiration for the Chinese workers at the JV. They proved to be very cooperative people. They had a great deal of pride and were very loyal to their company and the industry in which they worked. James often commented that, with informed leadership, Chinese workers would be as good as workers anywhere in the world.

What James liked best[,] however, was his interactions with the Chinese people. Every day brought him a new experience.

OBSERVATIONS ABOUT THE CHINESE PEOPLE

Most of the Chinese people were not communists. They would rather ignore the political situation going on around them and get on with their lives. They were eager to learn anything they could about what Western-ers could teach them. Almost without exception, they looked up to Americans and would begin to imitate them after a while. James found it very gratifying. He was also delighted with their treatment of his wife, Lily, which bordered on reverence. James wondered as to the reasons for this. Perhaps it had something to do with the fact that she, through her parents, had previously escaped communist oppression and found a better life, which symbolized to the Chinese that there was hope for all. James never saw a Chinese man leering at a woman, as is common in the United States. In China, sexuality was a private matter. They tended to live a simpler life than do most [W]esterners. Their children were treated with reverence, even doted on. Their chaotic traffic jams seemed always to be dealt with very calmly. James never observed swearing or anger, as is common in the United States. James also found that the Chinese have an attitude that they know more than [W]esterners do, but that this never manifested itself in a boastful way. The attitude was more that at some point in time, [W]esterners would come around to their way of thinking. It was almost as though they played the role of a wiser urban patriarch guiding his young country cousin during the latter's first visit to the city. See Exhibit C16-2 for more information on Chinese culture and management.

ACTIVITIES AWAY FROM THE JOB

James and Lily had a different social life than that enjoyed in the United States. They spent hours walking and talking. Occasionally, when they were in Shanghai they had the opportunities to see shows. They saw the acrobats, went to symphony concerts and ballet, even joining crowds when Foster Beer brought Australian bands to perform in a Shanghai park.

The concerns Lily had expressed prior to expatriating disappeared as she made friends and became integrated into the social fabric of the area. Because her appearance was indistinguishable from the indigenous Shanghai-area people, she was more readily accepted and learned more about local happenings that most Westerners. At one point, two months after their arrival, Lily was hospitalized with a lung infection. Even this was resolved satisfactorily. She particularly noted that the skill level of the medical practitioners seemed to be very good, from the diagnosis to the way they painlessly took blood samples. Overall she found it easy to occupy her time. She was a traditional wife, who had not worked full time since her children were born and never had difficulty occupying the time in her life as she was a woman who was compelled to learn about everything and everybody. She spent much of her time traveling with James to and from the site, and when he was working she sought out the people and assisted at a mission nearby as she had some experience in nursing, having earned her [nursing degree] before marrying James.

The Randolfs preferred to eat food with fresh ingredients and were happy away from the "supermarket" society, so Lily also spent a lot of time shopping. They felt that they were able to eat quite well in China.

James and Lily learned as much of the local Shanghai dialect as they could. In spite of never becoming fully proficient, the fact that they attempted to speak it greatly pleased the local residents. They spent much of their spare time interacting with the people of the area.

Sometimes Filtration, Inc. would put on a social affair for the expatriates in Shanghai. James and Lily were always invited. While on the island, however, they always ate at the restaurant in the factory. Contrary to what they were told at their orientation training, they found the Chinese to be gregarious and fun-loving during meals. Meals were used as an opportunity to build relationships and share experiences.

JAMES'S RECALL AND DEPARTURE

Then one day, early in February 1994, James received the call from Singapore, which proved to be the most disappointing news he had heard during his entire China experience. Controls had chosen to recall him back to home office. He was directed to train his replacement and return home within the month.

Things had been going very well for several months now, and he was accomplishing a great many things. There was still so much he planned to do, including to convince the Chinese JV partner that they needed to reduce the number of workers significantly.

While he and Lily handled the news and the return arrangements with a great deal of dignity, there was a great sense of disbelief and sadness associated with the recall. Jimmy Chao, his replacement, arrived two weeks later. Jimmy was a Singaporean engineer whose experience was limited to supervising production at one of Controls' factories in that country. James spent as much time getting him up to speed as was possible. Jimmy was 18 years younger than James, quite cocky, and very opinionated and aggressive. While James provided all the coaching that he could, Jimmy was bound to do things his way.

The scene at the ferry when they departed the island for the last time was incredible. Many of the workers and all of the managers supplied by the Chinese partner were there to see them off. Many tokens of appreciation and affection were exchanged.

The plane droned inexorably on. James had, by this point in the trip, "rerun the tapes" of his whole experience over and over in his mind, and again thought about how blessed he felt to have had the experience at all: ["]What recommendations should I make in my report and during my debriefings? If I really think they are heading for the "ditch," it is my responsibility to steer them away from it. Oh well, these questions will have to wait until another day. It is time to get some sleep. I wonder what the temperature is in Pauley?["]

CASE QUESTIONS

1. Critique the apparent expatriate selection process used by Controls, Inc.

2. Comment on the orientation programs that James undertook.

3. What other concerns do you have about Controls' HRM strategy? What changes would you recommend to Controls' management? Or its parent?

4. Was James Randolf a good choice for this position? Justify your arguments.

5. Which of the following is the most appropriate course of action for Controls, Inc. (the subsidiary)?

   a. To continue with their present, haphazard, unplanned approach, and learn through experience and inevitable mistakes?

   b. To hire, at considerable expense, a seasoned international HRM specialist, such as a VP from another firm in the "auto" industry?

   c. To move more slowly and ensure that all involved in the formulation and implementation of International Human Resources Strategy are well trained in the field before undertaking these responsibilities?

6. What are the consequences of poorly managed expatriate management programs, especially in large organizations trying to significantly increase the percentage of total revenue earned from international and foreign activities, and their international market share?

7. What were some of the aspects of the Chinese business environment (including culture) that James had to deal with? Comment on his effectiveness as a manager in a JV in China.

8. What reasons can you give to legitimately explain his removal and replacement? How would you assess his replacement? Do you think that he will be successful? Why or why not?

9. What should James include in his report? How frank should he be? What recommendations should he make? To whom should he send copies?

NOTES

Hendryx, Steven R. "The China Trade: Making the Deal Work." *Harvard Business Review* (July–August 1986): 75–84.

Hofstede, Geert. *Cultures' Consequences: International Differences in Work Related Values,* Beverly Hills, CA: Sage Publications, 1980.

———, and Bond, Michael H. "The Confucius Connection: From Cultural Roots to Economic Growth." *Organizational Dynamics* (Spring 1988): 5–21.

Hu, Wenzhong, and Grove, Cornelius. *Encountering the Chinese: A Guide for the Americans.* Yarmouth, ME: Intercultural Press, Inc., 1993.

Kumar, Saha Sudhir. "Managing Human Resources in China." *Canadian Journal of Administrative Science* 10, no. 2 (Summer 1991): 167–177.

Macleod, Roderick. *How to Do Business with the Chinese.* New York: Bantam Books, 1988.

Wall, Jr., James J. "Managers in the People's Republic of China." *Academy of Management Executives* 4, no. 2 (1990): 19–32.

Yeung, Irene Y. M., and Tung, Rosalie L. "Achieving Business Success in Confucian Societies: The Importance of Guanxi." *Organizational Dynamics* (Autumn 1996): 54–65.

Integrative Term Project

This project requires research, imagination, and logic in applying the content of this course and book.

In groups of three to five students, create an imaginary company that you have been operating in the domestic arena for some time. Your group represents top management, and you have decided it is time to go international.

- Describe your company and its operations, relative size, and so forth. Give reasons for your decision to go international.
- Decide on an appropriate country in which to operate, and give your rationale for this choice.
- State your planned entry strategy, and give your reasons for this strategy.
- Describe the environment in which you will operate and the critical operational factors that you must consider and how they will affect your company.
- Give a cultural profile of the local area in which you will be operating. What are the workers going to be like? What kind of reception do you anticipate from local governments, suppliers, distributors, and so on?

- Draw up an organization chart showing the company and its overseas operations, and describe why you have chosen this structure.
- Decide on the staffing policy you will use for top-level managers, and give your rationale for this policy.
- Describe the kinds of leadership and motivational systems you think would be most effective in this environment. Give your rationale.
- Discuss the kinds of communication problems your managers might face in the host-country working environment. How should they prepare for and deal with them?
- Explain any special control issues that concern you for this overseas operation. How do you plan to deal with them?

Identify the concerns of the host country and the local community regarding your operations there. What plans do you have to deal with their concerns and to ensure a long-term cooperative relationship?

Wal-Mart's German Misadventure

"I don't think that Wal-Mart did their homework as well as they should have. Germany is Europe's most price-sensitive market. Wal-Mart underestimated the competition, the culture, the legislative environment."

—Steve Gotham, Retail Analyst—Verdict Retail Consulting, in October 2002[1]

"We screwed up in Germany. Our biggest mistake was putting our name up before we had the service and low prices. People were disappointed."

—John Menzer, Head—Wal-Mart International, in December 2001[2]

GERMAN BLUES

For the world's largest retailing company—Wal-Mart Inc. (Wal-Mart), the German market was proving difficult to crack. By 2003, even after 5 years of entering Germany, Wal-Mart was making losses. Though Wal-Mart did not reveal these figures, analysts estimated losses of around $200–300 million per annum in Germany, over the five-year period.

According to analysts, the main reason for Wal-Mart's losses was its failure to understand German culture and the shopping habits of Germans. Though Wal-Mart was famous the world over for its Every Day Low Pricing (EDLP),[3] which turned it into the world's number 1 retailer, it could not make an impact in Europe's most price-sensitive market—Germany. Wal-Mart also ran into [a] series of problems with German regulatory authorities for its pricing strategies and faced considerable opposition from German suppliers to its centralized distribution system. It had problems with its German workers too.

To order copies, call 0091-40-2343-0462/63/64 or write to ICFAI Center for Management Research, Plot # 49, Nagarjuna Hills, Hyderabad 500 082, India or email icmr@icfai.org. Web site: www.icmrindia.org.
This case was written by K. Subhadra, under the direction of Sanjib Dutta, ICFAI Center for Management Research (ICMR). It is intended to be used as a basis for class discussion rather than to illustrate either effective or ineffective handling of a management situation. The case was compiled from published sources.

[1]Pommereau, Isabelle de, "Wal-Mart lesson: Smiling Service Won't Win Germans," www.csmonitor.com, October 17, 2002.
[2]Rubin, Daniel, "Grumpy German Shoppers Distrust the Wal-Mart style," www.gaccwa.org, December 30, 2001.
[3]EDLP was a pricing strategy adopted by Wal-Mart to ensure lowest [prices] among all retail chains on its products.

However, Wal-Mart was not the only retailer to do badly in Germany in the 1990s. German retailers too faced losses in the period because of the flat economy and rising unemployment.

Though Wal-Mart was confident that there would be a turnaround in its fortunes in the German market by late 2003, this opinion was not shared by most independent analysts.

BACKGROUND NOTE

In 1962, Sam Walton (Walton) and his brother opened the first Wal-Mart store in Rogers (Arkansas), USA. In the first year of its operations, the store registered sales of over $1 million. Initially, the Waltons concentrated on opening stores in small towns and introduced innovative concepts such as self-service. By 1967, Wal-Mart had 24 stores with sales of $12.6 million.

Encouraged by the early success of Wal-Mart, Sam Walton expanded Wal-Mart's operations to Oklahoma and Missouri in 1968. In the following year, Wal-Mart was incorporated as a company under the name Wal-Mart Stores Inc. In 1970, Wal-Mart established its first distribution center in Bentonville, Arkansas. It floated its first public issue the same year. Wal-Mart continued to grow in the 1970s, benefiting from its highly automated distribution system, which reduced shipping costs and time, and its computerized inventory system, which speeded up the checkout and reordering of stocks. In 1977, Wal-Mart acquired 16 Mohr-Value stores based in Michigan and Illinois. In 1978, it purchased the Hutcheson Shoe Company, and later set up pharmacy, auto service center, and jewelry divisions.

By 1980, Wal-Mart had 276 stores with annual sales of $1.4 billion. The number of stores increased to 640 with annual sales of $4.5 billion and profits of over $200 million by 1984. In the 1980s, strong customer demand in small towns drove the rapid growth of Wal-Mart. Walton said, "When we arrived in these small towns offering low prices every day, customer satisfaction guaranteed, and hours that were realistic for the way people wanted to shop, we passed right by that old variety of store competition, with its 45 percent mark ups, limited selection and limited hours."

In 1988, Walton appointed David Glass (Glass) as CEO of Wal-Mart. Soon after taking over, Glass started Hypermart USA. It was originally a joint venture with Cullum Companies (a Dallas-based supermarket chain). In the following year Wal-Mart bought out Cullum's stake in the venture. The Hypermart was a discount store/supermarket chain, which sprawled over 200,000 square feet. It featured branch banks, fast food outlets, photo developers, and playrooms for shoppers' children. This concept was later retooled as Wal-Mart's Supercenters.

In 1990, Wal-Mart acquired McLane Company (a grocer and retail distributor) and launched a new retail format—Bud's Discount City. Sam Walton died in 1992 after a prolonged illness. Under Glass, Wal-Mart continued its impressive growth. In the 1990s, Wal-Mart entered the international markets. In 1999, Wal-Mart was the largest private employer in [the] U.S. with 1,140,000 Associates.[4] In the same year Cone/Roper Report[5] named Wal-Mart as #1 Corporate Citizen of America. In 2000, Wal-Mart was ranked 5th in *Fortune* magazine's Global Most Admired All-Stars List. Lee Scott (Scott) became the CEO of the company in 2000. In 2002, Wal-Mart was ranked #1 [on the] *Fortune* 500 list. It recorded [its] largest single day [of] sales in the company's history, in 2002, when on the day after Thanksgiving it reported sales of $1.43 billion. In 2003, Wal-Mart was the world's largest retailer with a total of 4,688 stores (3,400 stores in the U.S. and 1,288 stores in other countries). It reported sales of $244.5 billion for the year 2003[,] with a net income of $8.03 billion.

BUSINESS SEGMENTS

Wal-Mart had two types of divisions—Retail divisions and Specialty divisions. Retail divisions were further classified into Wal-Mart Stores, Sam's Clubs, Neighborhood Market, International, and walmart.com (Refer [to] Table I). The specialty division was divided into Tire & Lube Express, Wal-Mart Optical, Wal-Mart Pharmacy, Wal-Mart Vacations, and Wal-Mart's Used Fixture Auctions (Refer [to] Table II).

WAL-MART'S INTERNATIONAL OPERATIONS

In [the] early 1990s, Wal-Mart announced that it would go global. It wanted to look for international markets for the following reasons:

- Wal-Mart was facing stiff competition from Kmart[7] and Target,[8] which adopted aggressive expansion strategies and started eating into Wal-Mart's market share.
- Wal-Mart also realized that the U.S. population represented only 4 percent of the world's population and confining itself to the U.S. market would mean missing the opportunity to tap potentially vast market elsewhere.
- In the early 1990s, globalization and liberalization opened up new markets and created opportunities for discount stores such as Wal-Mart across the world.

During the first five years of its globalization initiative (1991–1995), Wal-Mart concentrated on Mexico,

TABLE I Wal-Mart Retail Divisions

Store Name	Description
Wal-Mart stores	Wal-Mart stores were considered to be the flagship stores of the company offering merchandise in some 36 departments such as apparel, health and beauty aids, household needs, toys, fabrics, jewelry, shoes, and so on. These stores operated on the EDLP philosophy.
Sam's Clubs	Sam's Clubs were members-only warehouse clubs, started in 1983. The Clubs acted as purchasing agents for their members and offered branded merchandise at "members only" prices, both for business and personal use. The Clubs operated by selling high volumes of goods at very low profit margins.
Neighborhood Markets	Neighborhood Markets were located in markets together with Wal-Mart Supercenters.[6] Neighborhood Markets featured a wide variety of products, including fresh produce, deli foods, fresh meat and dairy items, health and beauty aids, one-hour photo and traditional photo developing services, drive-through pharmacies, stationery and paper goods, pet supplies, and household chemicals.
Wal-Mart International	There were international stores of Wal-Mart in 9 countries. The Wal-Mart International division oversaw day-to-day management of its international stores.
Wal-Mart.com	e-business venture of Wal-Mart.

SOURCE: www.walmartstores.com

[4]Wal-Mart's employees are called Associates.
[5]An annual national survey on philanthropy and corporate citizenship.
[6]Wal-Mart Supercenters were opened in 1988. They combined full grocery lines and general merchandise under one roof, giving customers the opportunity to purchase food and non-food products from a single retail outlet in a one-stop family shopping experience.
[7]Kmart is a leading U.S. retailer.
[8]Target is one of the leading discount retail chains in [the] U.S.

TABLE II Wal-Mart Specialty Divisions

Division Name	Description
Tire & Lube Express	This division provided tire and lube service to its customers. Started in early 1990s, by 2003 this division had over 1,300 stores in 40 states in the U.S.
Wal-Mart Optical	This division provided optical services to its customers.
Wal-Mart Pharmacy	This division operated pharmacy stores in Wal-Mart stores and also in medical clinics across the U.S. It employed around 6,500 pharmacists.
Wal-Mart Vacations	Wal-Mart Vacations provided customers travel packages on cruises, holiday packages, car rental and hotel discounts, select theme park tickets, and resorts.
Wal-Mart's Used Fixture[s] Auctions	Through this division, Wal-Mart helped customers to resale fixtures for reuse. Auctions were open to the public and were held at Wal-Mart locations.

SOURCE: www.walmartstores.com

TABLE III Wal-Mart's International Presence in 2003

Country	Mode of Entry	Year of Entry	JV Partner/Company Acquired	No. of Stores
Mexico	Joint Venture	1991	Cifra	597
Canada	Acquisition	1994	Woolco Stores	213
Argentina	Greenfield operations	1995	–	11
Brazil	Joint Venture	1995	Lojas Americanas'	22
China	Greenfield operations	1996	–	26
South Korea	Acquisition	1998	Makro Stores	15
Germany	Acquisition	1997	Wertkauf and Interspar	94
United Kingdom	Acquisition	2000	Alda	258
Puerto Rico	Wholly owned subsidiary	1993	Wal-Mart Puerto Rico, Inc	52

SOURCE: Compiled from various newspapers and Wal-Mart annual reports

Canada, Argentina, and Brazil, which were close to its home market. It started with Canada and Mexico due to the similarities in people's habits, culture, and the business environments in these countries, and also because the North American Free Trade Agreement (NAFTA)[9] made it easier for U.S. companies to enter these markets. Wal-Mart's decision to enter Argentina and Brazil was based on the high growth rates of the Latin American markets.

Wal-Mart expanded its international operations through acquisitions, joint ventures, greenfield operations, and wholly owned subsidiaries. In 1991, Wal-Mart entered Mexico through a joint venture with Mexican

company Cifra, and opened Sam's Clubs in Mexico. Wal-Mart's globalization plans got a boost in 1993, when the Wal-Mart International division was created. In the same year it acquired 122 former Woolco stores from Woolworth in Canada. By 2003 Wal-Mart had a presence in 9 countries with 1,288 stores, which included 942 discount stores, 238 supercenters, 71 Sam's Clubs, and 37 Neighborhood stores (Refer [to] Table III for Wal-Mart's International Presence).

By 2003, Wal-Mart was the largest retailer in Mexico, Argentina, Canada, and Puerto Rico, and one of the top three retailers in the UK. In 2003, Wal-Mart's operating income from international operations was $2.033 billion, 15 percent higher than in the previous year (Refer [to] Table IV). However, Wal-Mart was not successful in all the markets it entered. It failed to make an impact in Europe's most price-sensitive market—Germany.

[9]NAFTA, signed in 1993, removed most of the trade and investment barriers between the United States, Canada, and Mexico.

TABLE IV Operating Income from International Operations	
Fiscal Year	**Operating Income (in $ billions)**
2003	2.033
2002	1.305
2001	0.949

SOURCE: Wal-Mart 2003 Annual Report

WAL-MART IN GERMANY

Most American companies entering Europe started with the UK due to the similarities between the U.S. and the UK in culture, language, and legal environment. Wal-Mart, however, decided to enter Germany first. Analysts were critical of this decision as the German retailing industry was experiencing slow growth rates and retailers were indulging in price wars which eroded margins badly. Additionally, Germany had high labour costs, high real estate prices, and a very inflexible business environment (Refer [to] Exhibit I).

But Wal-Mart felt it was right to venture into the German market. Ron Tiarks, President, Wal-Mart's German [O]perations said, "Germany, being the third-largest economy in the world, is very important to us and one obviously that we can't ignore." *Fortune* wrote in 1999, "Germany offers Wal-Mart a central base from which it can expand to almost anywhere on the Continent. Wal-Mart clearly wants to be a pan-European player, a goal made more feasible by the Euro's promise to ease business across national boundaries."[10] As Germany was considered a price-sensitive market, analysts felt that Wal-Mart's EDLP philosophy would be successful in the country. German stores usually offered seasonal discounts sales

[10]Khan, Jeremy, "Wal-Mart Goes Shopping in Europe," *Fortune*, June 7, 1999.

EXHIBIT I   A Note on the Retailing Industry in Germany

As the world's third largest economy, Germany has attracted the attention of the retailers from around the world such as Marks & Spencers, Toys R Us, for several decades. With a GNP of 2 trillion and population of around 80 million, Germany was rated as one of the biggest retail markets in Europe. In 2002, Germany accounted for 15 percent of Europe's 2 trillion retail market. The West German retail industry saw tremendous growth rates till the early 1990s. However after the unification of Germany in 1990, the Germany economy went through a tough phase of restructuring, which had an impact on the retailing industry too. The difference between the levels of economic prosperity in West and East Germany pulled down the average growth rates in the German retail industry. By the late 1990s, the German retail industry was growing slowly.

The German retail market was oligopolistic with a few players dominating the industry. In early 2000s, the top ten players accounted for 84 percent of sales and the top 5 players in the market garnered around 63 percent of market share. German consumers reportedly attached more importance to value and price, than customer service. According to analysts, German market was one of the most price-sensitive markets in Europe.

Till the late 1990s, discount stores concentrated only on food and other grocery items; but in the late 1990s, the trend changed and the discount stores moved to non-food items also. For instance, the discount store Aldi emerged as the largest seller of personal computers under its own brand name.

In the early 2000s, with the slowdown in the economy, the German retail industry experienced the lowest profit levels of all the developed countries. The profit margin in grocery retailing was just 1.1 percent in 2002, and in the food segment, it was only 0.5 percent. Another important feature of the German retailing industry was the domination of family-owned enterprises. Most of the retailing enterprises were not listed on stock exchanges.

German retailing industry is highly regulated. Analysts believed that the regulatory environment in Germany hindered the development of retailing in the county. There were many legislations relating to the competition and corporate strategies of retailers. The German government also pursues protectionist policies to support small and medium scale German retailers. Some of the legislations which affect the retail industry in Germany significantly are summarized as follows:

- A retailer can operate for a maximum of 80 hours/week. The store working hours are the shortest in Europe. Retailers are not allowed to work on Sundays and holidays. Because of this regulation, Wal-Mart was not able to operate its 24/7 convenience stores in Germany.

- Retailers are not allowed to sell below cost for an extended period of time. However, a merchant can discount his goods for a limited period of time.

As regards German consumers, for cultural reasons, they were less friendly and less outgoing compared with American and British consumers. In line with this, in Germany, the number of employees per store was low compared to the U.S. and other developed markets.

In order to increase consumer spending, the German government undertook major tax reforms in 2001. This was expected to boost retail sales in the country. However, though government tax reforms boosted consumer spending, it did not benefit retail industry as expenditure took place in the housing, tourism, and communications sectors.

During 2003 too, the German retailing industry was expected to have slow growth because of the macroeconomic conditions. The increasing unemployment affected the food retailing sector in the country.

SOURCE: Adapted from various newspaper articles and Web sites

and special sales to increase their sales. With its customer-focused service, it was felt that Wal-Mart would be able gain market share in Germany. However, Wal-Mart faced a number of serious problems in Germany.

ENTRY STRATEGY GONE WRONG?

Wal-Mart expanded its presence into Germany through acquisitions. It acquired the 21 hypermarket stores of Wertkauf in 1997. The Wertkauf stores offered both food and general merchandise to the customers. Wal-Mart sources said that Wertkauf stores would provide the necessary footage in the German market. However, as Wertkauf covered only southwestern Germany, it failed to provide the required market penetration to Wal-Mart in Germany. In 1998, Wal-Mart acquired Interspar's 74 hypermarket stores to raise the total number of Wal-Mart stores in Germany to 95.

With the acquisition of Interspar's stores, Wal-Mart became the fourth largest hypermarket retailer in Germany. However, both the Wertkauf and the Interspar stores were not popular with German consumers. A major challenge for Wal-Mart was to change customer perceptions of the stores. Wal-Mart was criticized for acquiring Interspar's stores as they had made heavy losses and had a poor brand image in the public mind.

Wal-Mart also faced a major problem in trying to integrate the operations of the two companies (Wertkauf and Interspar). John Menzer (Menzer), Head of Wal-Mart International said, "The challenge of putting the two chains together was more than we thought. We knew Interspar was losing money and we had to turn it around. We had to reconstruct it and lose more money before it could turn around."[11]

Wal-Mart found out that the store layout and design of Interspar stores did not conform to Wal-Mart's store layout and design worldwide. Interspar stores were of varied sizes and formats and most of the stores were situated in interior areas, where customers opted for general grocery chains. After acquiring Interspar chain stores, Wal-Mart embarked on a renovation program to bring them to Wal-Mart standards. Wal-Mart reportedly spent around $150 million to renovate the Interspar stores.

Though acquisitions may not have been the ideal route for Wal-Mart to take in Germany, the company, in fact, had little choice. The German government was refusing new licenses for food and grocery retailing, so if it wanted to enter the German market, Wal-Mart had to go in for acquisitions.

PROBLEMS IN OPERATING ENVIRONMENT

Soon after acquiring the stores, Wal-Mart hurried through with their renovation and put its brandname on them to make sure its EDLP message went across. But it was unable to cash in on its EDLP selling point, chiefly because of the strong competition from German retailers (Refer to Exhibit II).

EXHIBIT II   Profiles of German Retailers

ALDI: The history of Aldi dates back to the 1940s. In 1946, Theo Abrecht and Karl Abrecht inherited convenience stores from their parents. In 1960, Albrecht Discount Stores began to be called "Aldi," and there were 300 such stores. In 1961, a hard discount format was formulated by Theo Abrecht and Karl Abrecht. This combined ultra-low prices and high product quality with a very limited product assortment of around 600–700 products with a no-frills shopping experience. In 1962, the company was split into two independent operations—Aldi Nord (Aldi North) and Aldi Sud (Aldi South). Aldi's northern operations were headed by Theo Abrecht, and its southern operations were headed by Karl Abrecht, who operated independently, coordinating major decisions such as suppliers and pricing. The company continued to be known as the Aldi group. By 2002, the Aldi group had around 3,741 stores in Germany and had around 2,643 stores internationally. It had a presence in Australia, United Kingdom, United States, France, Denmark, Belgium, Luxembourg, Netherlands, Ireland, Spain, and Austria.

METRO AG: Metro AG was formed in 1996 after the merger of Metro Cash & Carry (established in 1964), Kaufhof Holding AG (established in 1879), and Asko Deutsche Kaufhaus AG (established in 1880). With the merger, the Metro AG group became [the] world's third biggest supermarket group, with around 2,300 sales outlets, and a distribution network in around 26 countries in the world covering not only European countries but also countries such as China, Turkey, Eastern Europe, and Morocco. The Metro group divided its business into five segments: Cash & Carry, under brand name Metro, Makro and Spar (since March 2002); Real (800 hypermarkets) and Extra (supermarkets) in the food sector; Mediamarkt and Saturn selling electronic goods; Praktiker selling home improvement products; and Galeria and Kaufhof, general stores offering consumer goods. More than 40 percent of Metro AG's

---

[11]"Operations Evolve to Offset Doldrums in Deutschland," *DSN Retailing Today,* June 5, 2001.

EXHIBIT II   (Cont.)

turnover was generated from its international stores. For the year 2002, Metro AG reported sales of 51.5 billion when compared to 2001 sales of 49.5 billion.

EDEKA GROUP: The history of the Edeka group dates back to late 1890s. Edeka group was the brainchild of Friedrich William Raiffeisen and Hermann Schulze Delizsch. Their idea was to set up a purchase association where goods were made available to buyers at low prices. In October 1907, the Edeka Foundation was formed with 23 purchase associations. In the same year, central procurement office called Edeka Center AG was established. Over the years, the group was able to maintain low prices because of its strong relations with its suppliers. Edeka procured goods from regional wholesalers. The Edeka group was made up of a number of independent retailers and co-operative societies. Edeka's product range included organic fruits, vegetables, dairy products, and cereals. The food products were marketed under the brand name Bio Wertkost. The group's brands also included Rio Grande and Mibell. The group also had presence in pharmacy retailing, food processing and wine operations, publishing, and banking services.

SOURCE: Compiled from various newspapers and company Web sites

Whenever Wal-Mart lowered its prices on commodities, German retailers such as Aldi, Lidl, Rewe, and Edeka also lowered their prices to keep their customers, so Wal-Mart found it difficult to get a foothold. German retailer Edeka put it plainly, saying, "The prices Wal-Mart offers are not lower than ours." In response to Wal-Mart's slashing of prices in 2000 German competitor Real—the hypermarket chain—also decreased prices on around 3,000 items. One of the German retailers Rewe even copied Wal-Mart's slogan—"*Jeden Tag Tiefpriese.*" In 2000, Wal-Mart also introduced its private label—"*Smartprice*"—to Germany. However, the German discount retailers had a strong relationship with consumers, and Wal-Mart's private labels were not considered low-priced by the German public.

The lack of strong vendor relations also affected Wal-Mart's operations in Germany. Wal-Mart's success in its home market was mainly due to its efficient supply chain and vendor relations. Unlike in the U.S., where the company and its suppliers were accustomed to the centralized distribution, in Germany suppliers were not comfortable with the centralized distribution system that Wal-Mart adopted. As in the U.S., Wal-Mart in Germany too wanted to rely on inputs from suppliers to decide on product assortments. However, in Germany, Wal-Mart's relationship with its suppliers was not mature enough to make this possible. Thus, Wal-Mart ended up trying to sell goods which its customers did not want but which suppliers wanted to push.

Wal-Mart also had a number of inventory problems. Initially Wal-Mart had only one stockroom which stocked all merchandise. The company found it difficult to hire employees for its stockroom due to the low wages it was offering. The shortage of workers delayed the movement of goods leading to excessive stockpiling.

Another operational problem Wal-Mart faced was employee unrest. It was accused of paying low wages and not providing good working conditions. Wal-Mart did not understand the German work culture. As in its U.S. operations, it discouraged employees from forming unions. After acquiring Interspar and Wertkauf, Wal-Mart prohibited members of the work councils of the erstwhile separate companies from meeting each other. The company also rarely consulted the elected representatives of its employees.

Wal-Mart ran into trouble with German unions when it announced employee lay-offs and store closures in 2002 in order to reduce its personnel costs.[12] In addition it also refused to accept the centralized wage-bargaining process[13] in the German retail industry. Because of this, the trade unions organized a walk-out from Wal-Mart stores which led to bad publicity for the company. Wal-Mart employees also went on a two-day strike in July 2002 demanding negotiation of wage contract by the company.

PROBLEMS IN EXTERNAL ENVIRONMENT

Wal-Mart faced several problems on the legal front as well. It was accused of breaching various German laws. The company was accused of having violated Section (IV) (2) of "Act Against Restraints of Competition"—(Gesetz gegen Wettbewerbsbeschrankungen or GWB) and Section 335a of the "Commercial Act" (Handelsgesetzbuch or HGB). Section (IV) (2) of GWB forbids companies "with superior market power in relation to small- and medium-sized competitors" from lowering their prices and engaging in price wars with small companies. Such large companies were allowed to lower

---

[12] It was reported that Wal-Mart had the highest employee costs among German retailers. The high costs were attributed to heavy recruiting by Wal-Mart anticipating huge business and its misreading of the German retailing environment. For instance, Wal-Mart had to lay off employees who were taken on as greeters as the German public did not take to the idea, and it also had to cut down the number of employees in many stores due to low sales.

[13] In a centralized wage bargaining process, the wages across all companies in a particular industry are decided according to the average productivity in the industry.

prices only after providing justification for the lower prices.

Wal-Mart had lowered the prices of some commodities[,] namely sugar, milk, and margarine, in May 2000. The new prices were reportedly lower than the cost price at which Wal-Mart had bought them. In making this move, Wal-Mart was alleged to have violated Section (IV) (2). In response to Wal-Mart's move, the German retailers Aldi and Lidl also lowered their prices. As the price war continued, the German Federal Cartel Office (FCO) launched an investigation in September 2000. It ordered the retailers to stop selling the commodities below cost price as it would hurt small and medium[-sized] retailers and lead to unfair competition.

In response to the FCO order, Wal-Mart took the case to the Appeals court in Dusseldorf. The Appeals court ruled in favor of Wal-Mart stating that Section (IV) (2) prohibited big players from selling at lower prices, and Wal-Mart could not be considered as a big player in Germany as it did not have a considerable market share nor market capitalization. However, the FCO took the case further up to the Supreme Court against the verdict of the Appeals court. In November 2002, the German Supreme Court gave its verdict, declaring that Wal-Mart's selling goods at prices below cost price would result in unfair competition against small and medium[-sized] retailers, and that Wal-Mart should abandon its pricing strategies.[14]

Wal-Mart was also hauled up for violating the Commercial Act's Section 335a by not publishing financial data such as balance sheet and profit and loss account statements on its operations in Germany. The trade unions alleged that they were not given access to accounts of the company. In order to gain access to financial information, the trade unions filed a suit against Wal-Mart in the state court. In its verdict the court ruled that Wal-Mart should publish the required financial information; it also fined Wal-Mart senior executives for not providing the required financial information. Wal-Mart sources said that since the company was a limited partnership, it was not mandatory for it to publish financial information under German laws. However, according to the trade unions, under the altered German commercial code, even limited partnership firms were required to publish their financial accounts. In November 2002, Wal-Mart filed a suit in the German Supreme Court against the verdict of the state court asking it to stay state court's decision till the European Court of Justice came out with its decision on disclosure provisions by foreign companies.[15]

CULTURAL MISMATCH

Apart from the operational and regulatory problems, Wal-Mart also faced cultural problems in Germany. It found it difficult to integrate the two companies (Wertkauf and Interspar) which it had acquired. The companies had completely different work cultures; while Interspar had decentralized operations with independent regional units, Wertkauf was highly centralized with the head office making all decisions. Addtionally, Wal-Mart found it difficult to integrate the two companies' cultures with its own.

Employee morale in Wal-Mart Germany was also reported to have been badly affected by the changes in the internal rules and regulations affected by Wal-Mart. The earlier managements of both Interspar and Wertkauf had given their executives liberal expense accounts. But after Wal-Mart's acquisition of the firms, the executives' expense accounts were reduced. For instance, during business trips, they were required to share rooms—which came as a culture shock to the Germans.

Wal-Mart also faced a language problem in Germany. When Wal-Mart entered Germany, the top management who came from the U.S., did not show any inclination to learn German. Within a few weeks, English became the official language of the company in Germany. This resulted in serious communication problems for the German employees. Making English the official language affected employee morale with employees starting to feel like outsiders, and getting increasingly frustrated. The German public also found it difficult to pronounce Wal-Mart's name correctly. They pronounced it as Vawl-Mart.

In Germany, Wal-Mart's world-famous customer service methods fell flat. For example, Wal-Mart's famous Ten-Foot Rule[16] was not implemented in Germany, as German customers did not like strangers interfering with their shopping. Commenting on this, Tiarks said, "You can't beat those things into your people. They have to be genuine, or the customer sees right through them." For the same reason, Wal-Mart also did away with the idea of greeters at German stores. In the U.S., Wal-Mart used to employ greeters at all its stores to welcome customers as they entered. However, in Germany, the company found that customers did not appreciate this idea at all. Apart from this, the German consumers realized that they were the ones who would be paying more because of "the guy standing at the door"—which is why they did not appreciate it. Wal-Mart in Germany could not offer loyalty cards[17] as they were banned in Germany.

---

[14]The German Supreme Court felt that Wal-Mart pricing margarine below cost was legal as it was done for only a brief period. However the court was against Wal-Mart's pricing of sugar and milk below cost prices.
[15]Many European firms had filed [a] case against Germany's alterations to its commercial code which required the firms to publish financial information. The European Court of Justice's decision was still awaited.

---

[16]As per [the] Ten-Foot Rule of the company, whenever an employee comes within 10 feet of a customer, the employee should look up to the customer, greet him and ask him if he needs any help.
[17]Loyalty Cards were offered by supermarkets and big retail chains to select loyal customers. The businesses offered special prices for the customers possessing loyalty cards. However, in 2002, many customer groups accused companies of using loyalty cards to track down the purchasing patterns of the customers and started opposing loyalty card schemes.

FUTURE PROSPECTS

Even after five years of entering the German market, Wal-Mart had not made a significant impact in the German retail industry. Wal-Mart reported losses over all the four years up to 2002 in its German operations (Refer to Table V). It was reported that between 1999–2002 Wal-Mart's sales declined by 5 percent on average. Increasing costs also pushed up losses for the company. Wal-Mart sources indicated that personnel costs accounted for around 17 percent of sales; these high costs prompted Wal-Mart to freeze new recruitment. Commenting on the operations in the Germany, Wal-Mart CEO, Scott said, "We just walked in and said, 'We're going to lower prices, we're going to add people to the stores, we're going to remodel the stores because inherently that's correct,' and it wasn't. We didn't have the infrastructure to support the kind of things we were doing."[18]

Though Wal-Mart claimed that sales were picking up, analysts felt otherwise, and said that Wal-Mart in Germany had failed on its customer service promise. Independent studies conducted by some newspapers indicated

TABLE VI   Customer Satisfaction Ratings of German Retailers

Retailer Name	Rank
Aldi Group	1
Globus	2
Kaufland	3
Lidl	4
Norma	5
Marktkauf	6
Wal-Mart	7
Metro	8
Penny	9
Real	10

SOURCE: www.hicbusiness.org

that Wal-Mart was rated seventh out of the ten major retailers in Germany in terms of overall customer satisfaction (Refer to Table VI).

Wal-Mart announced that it would not be looking for further acquisitions in Germany and would concentrate on stabilizing its business in the country. Commenting on the company's plans, Dave Ferguson—Head, European Operations, said, "What we first have to achieve is that the existing stores are operating optimally."

To revive its fortunes in Germany, Wal-Mart announced that it would be focusing on bringing down its capital costs. It announced that instead of opening Wal-Mart supercenters, the company would focus on opening smaller stores in Germany. Only time will tell whether Wal-Mart will become a significant player in the German retail market.

TABLE V   Sales and Operating Profit in Germany

Year	Sales	Operating Profit/(Loss) (in $ millions)
1999	2,815	(192)
2000	2,468	(181)
2001	2,506	(164)
2002	2,420	(108)

SOURCE: Adapted from www.mventures.com

QUESTIONS FOR DISCUSSION

1. Wal-Mart started its global operations in the early 1990s when it opened its first international store in Mexico. Analyze the reasons for Wal-Mart's decision to go global.
2. When Wal-Mart announced that it would be entering the German markets, analysts were surprised. Usually, the cultural affinity between the U.S. and the UK led American companies to target the UK first, before launching onto the European continent. Do you think Wal-Mart's decision to enter the German market was correct? Justify your stand.
3. Even after fives years of doing business in Germany, Wal-Mart had failed to make an impact on the German market and had been incurring losses year after year. Analyze the reasons for Wal-Mart's problems in the German market. Do you think the company would be able to improve its performance in Germany?

ADDITIONAL READINGS & REFERENCES

1. Zellener, Wendy, "Wal-Mart's Newest Accent Is German," *BusinessWeek*, December 18, 1997.
2. Troy, Mike, "Wal-Mart Germany's New President Faces Culture, Customer Challenges," *Discount Store News*, February 9, 1998.
3. Schmid, John, "In Europe, Wal-Mart Pursues a Big Dream," *International Herald Tribune*, October 2, 1998.
4. "Wal-Mart Acquires Interspar Hypermarkets," www.prnewswire.com, December 9, 1998.
5. Troy, Mike, "Wal-Mart Germany Beefs Up," *Discount Store News*, January 4, 1999.

---

[18]Zellner, Wendy, "How Well Does Wal-Mart Travel?" *BusinessWeek*, September 3, 2001.

6. Kahn, Jeremy, "Wal-Mart Goes Shopping in Europe," *Fortune*, June 7, 1999.

7. Dawley, Heidi, "Watch Out Europe: Here Comes Wal-Mart," *BusinessWeek*, June 28, 1999.

8. "Wal-Mart in Germany Is Not Doing Well," www.union-network.org, March 7, 2000.

9. "Wal-Mart Makes Bigger than Expected Losses in Germany," www.union-network.org, March 10, 2000.

10. "The Wal-Mart Effect," *Business Europe*, May 17, 2000.

11. "Wal-Mart's Low Prices too Low for Germany's Retail Regulators," www.enquirer.com, September 9, 2000.

12. "Germany: Stop Bullying Wal-Mart," *BusinessWeek*, September 25, 2000.

13. Marino David, "Wal-Mart Steps Up German Invasion," www.fool.com, March 26, 2001.

14. "Wal-Mart Continues to Lose Money in Germany—Responds through Escalating Price War," www.union-network.org, March 29, 2001.

15. "Operations Evolve to Offset Doldrums in Deutschland," *DSN Retailing Today*, June 5, 2001.

16. Zellner, Wendy; Schmidt Katharine A; Ihlwan, Moon; Dawley Heidi, "How Well Does Wal-Mart Travel?" *BusinessWeek*, September 3, 2001.

17. Rubin, Daniel, "Grumpy German Shoppers Distrust the Wal-Mart Style," www.gaccwa.org, September 30, 2001.

18. "The First 'Real' Wal-Mart Is a Flop?" www.union-network.org, February 12, 2002.

19. Pommereau, Isabelle de, "Wal-Mart Lesson: Smiling Service Won't Win Germans," www.csmonitor.com, October 17, 2002.

20. www.walmartstores.com

21. www.planetretail.net

22. www.forbes.com

23. www.hicbusiness.org

24. www.mventures.com

25. www.wilmercutler.com

Glossary

affective appeals Negotiation appeals based on emotions and subjective feelings.

appropriability of technology The ability of an innovating firm to protect its technology from competitors and to obtain economic benefits from that technology.

attribution The process in which a person looks for an explanation of another person's behavior.

axiomatic appeals Negotiation appeals based on the ideals generally accepted in a society.

B2B Business-to-business electronic transactions.

B2C Business-to-consumer electronic transactions.

balance sheet approach An approach to the compensation of expatriates that equalizes the standard of living between the host and home countries, plus compensation for inconvenience.

chaebol South Korea's large industrial conglomerates of financially linked, and often family-linked, companies that do business among themselves whenever possible—for example, Daewoo.

codetermination *(mitbestimmung)* The participation of labor in the management of a firm.

collective bargaining In the United States, for example, negotiations between a labor union local and management; in Sweden and Germany, for example, negotiations between the employer's organization and a trade union at the industry level.

collectivism The tendency of a society toward tight social frameworks, emotional dependence on belonging to an organization, and a strong belief in group decisions.

communication The process of sharing meaning by transmitting messages through media such as words, behavior, or material artifacts.

comparative advantage A mutual benefit in the exchange of goods between countries, where each country exports those products in which it is relatively more efficient in production than other countries.

competitive advantage of nations The existence of conditions that give a country an advantage in a specific industry or in producing a particular good or service.

context in cultures (low to high) Low-context cultures, such as Germany, tend to use explicit means of communication in words and readily available information; high-context cultures, such as those in the Middle East, use more implicit means of communication, in which information is embedded in the nonverbal context and understanding of the people.

contract An agreement by the parties concerned to establish a set of rules to govern a business transaction.

control system appropriateness The use of control systems that are individually tailored to the practices and expectations of the host-country personnel.

convergence (of management styles, techniques, and so forth) The phenomenon of increasing similarity of leadership styles resulting from a blending of cultures and business practices through international institutions, as opposed to the **divergence** of leadership styles necessary for different cultures and practices.

core competencies Important corporate resources or skills that bring competitive advantages.

creeping expropriation A government's gradual and subtle action against foreign firms.

creeping incrementalism A process of increasing commitment of resources to one or more geographic regions.

cultural noise Cultural variables that undermine the communications of intended meaning.

cultural savvy A working knowledge of the cultural variables affecting management decisions.

cultural sensitivity (cultural empathy) A sense of awareness and caring about the culture of other people.

culture The shared values, understandings, assumptions, and goals that over time are passed on and imposed by members of a group or society.

culture shock A state of disorientation and anxiety that results from not knowing how to behave in an unfamiliar culture.

culture-specific reward systems Motivational and compensation approaches that reflect different motivational patterns across cultures.

degree of enforcement The relative degree of enforcement, in a particular country, of the law regarding business behavior, which therefore determines the lower limit of permissible behavior.

differentiation Focusing on and specializing in specific markets.

direct control The control of foreign subsidiaries and operations through the use of appropriate international staffing and structure policies and meetings with home-country executives (as compared with **indirect control**).

distinctive competencies Strengths that allow companies to outperform rivals.

divergence *See* **convergence**.

domestic multiculturalism The diverse makeup of the workforce comprising people from several different cultures in the home (domestic) company.

E-business The integration of systems, processes, organizations, value chains, and entire markets using Internet-based and related technologies and concepts.

E-commerce The selling of goods or services over the Internet.

e-commerce enablers Fulfillment specialists who provide other companies with services such as Web site translation.

economic risk The level of uncertainty about the ability of a country to meet its financial obligations.

environmental assessment The continuous process of gathering and evaluating information about variables and events around the world that may pose threats or opportunities to the firm.

environmental scanning The process of gathering information and forecasting relevant trends, competitive actions, and circumstances that will affect operations in geographic areas of potential interest.

ethical relativism An approach to social responsibility in which a country adopts the moral code of its host country.

ethnocentric approach An approach in which a company applies the morality used in its home country—regardless of the host country's system of ethics.

ethnocentric staffing approach An approach that fills key managerial positions abroad with persons from headquarters—that is, with parent-country nationals (PCNs).

ethnocentrism The belief that the management techniques used in one's own country are best no matter where or with whom they are applied.

expatriate One who works and lives in a foreign country but remains a citizen of the country where the employing organization is headquartered.

expressive-oriented conflict Conflict that is handled indirectly and implicitly, without clear delineation of the situation by the person handling it.

expropriation The seizure, with inadequate or no compensation, by a local government of the foreign-owned assets of an MNC.

Foreign Corrupt Practices Act A 1977 law that prohibits most questionable payments by U.S. companies to officials of foreign governments to gain business advantages.

foreign direct investment (FDI) Multinational firm's ownership, in part or in whole, of an operation in another country.

franchising An international entry strategy by which a firm (the franchiser) licenses its trademark, products, or services and operating principles to the franchisee in a host country for an initial fee and ongoing royalties.

fully owned subsidiary An overseas operation started or bought by a firm that has total ownership and control; starting or buying such an operation is often used as an entry strategy.

generalizabilty of leadership styles The ability (or lack of ability) to generalize leadership theory, research results, and effective leadership practices from one country to another.

geocentric staffing approach A staffing approach in which the best managers are recruited throughout the company or outside the company, regardless of nationality—often, third-country nationals (TCNs) are recruited.

global corporate culture An integration of the business environments in which firms currently operate, resulting from a dissolution of traditional boundaries and from increasing links among MNCs.

global functional structure Operations are integrated into the activities and responsibilities of each department to gain functional specialization and economies of scale.

globalism Global competition characterized by networks of international linkages that bind countries, institutions, and people in an interdependent global economy and a one-world market.

global geographic (area) structure Divisions are created to cover geographic regions; each regional manager is responsible for operations and performance of the countries within a given region.

globalization The global strategy of the integration of worldwide operations and the development of standardized products and marketing approaches.

global management The process of developing strategies, designing and operating systems, and working with people around the world to ensure sustained competitive advantage.

global management team Collection of managers in or from several countries who must rely on group collaboration if each member is to experience optimum success and goal achievement.

global product (divisional) structure A single product (or product line) is represented by a separate division; each division is headed by its own general manager; each is responsible for its own production and sales functions.

global staffing approach Staff recruited from within or outside of the company, regardless of nationality.

global strategic alliances Working partnerships that are formed around MNCs across national boundaries and often across industries.

governmentalism The tendency of a government to use its policy-setting role to favor national interests rather than relying on market forces.

guanxi The intricate, pervasive network of personal relations that every Chinese person carefully cultivates.

guanxihu A bond between specially connected firms, which generates preferential treatment to members of the network.

haptic Characterized by a predilection for the sense of touch.

high-contact culture One in which people prefer to stand close, touch a great deal, and experience a "close" sensory involvement.

high-context communication One in which people convey messages indirectly and implicitly.

horizontal organization (dynamic network) A structural approach that enables the flexibility to be global and act local through horizontal coordination, shared power, and decision making across international units and teams.

host-country national (HCN) A worker who is indigenous to the local country where the plant is located.

human capital those direct or subcontracted employees whose labor becomes part of the value-added of the firm's product or service. MNCs are increasingly offshoring (outsourcing) that asset around the world in order to lower the cost of human capital

IJV control How a parent company ensures that the way a joint venture is managed conforms to its own interest.

indirect control The control of foreign operations through the use of reports, budgets, financial controls, and so forth. *See* also **direct control**.

individualism The tendency of people to look after themselves and their immediate families only and to value democracy, individual initiative, and personal achievement.

information privacy The right to control information about oneself.

information technology (IT) Electronic systems to convey information.

instrumental-oriented conflict An approach to conflict in which parties tend to negotiate on the basis of factual information and logical analysis.

integration Coordination of markets.

intercultural communication Type of communication that occurs when a member of one culture sends a message to a receiver who is a member of another culture.

internal analysis Determines which areas of a firm's operations represent strengths or weaknesses (currently or potentially) compared to competitors.

internal versus external locus of control Beliefs regarding whether a person controls his own fate and events or they are controlled by external forces.

international business The profit-related activities conducted across national boundaries.

international business ethics The business conduct or morals of MNCs in their relationships to all individuals and entities with whom they come in contact when conducting business overseas.

international codes of conduct The codes of conduct of four major international institutions that provide some consistent guidelines for multinational enterprises relative to their moral approach to business behavior around the world.

international competitor analysis The process of assessing the competitive positions, goals, strategies, strengths, and weaknesses of competitors relative to one's own firm.

internationalization The process by which a firm gradually changes in response to the imperatives of international competition, domestic market saturation, desire for expansion, new markets, and diversification.

international joint venture (IJV) An overseas business owned and controlled by two or more partners; starting such a venture is often used as an entry strategy.

international management The process of planning, organizing, leading, and controlling in a multicultural or cross-cultural environment.

international management teams Collections of managers from several countries who must rely on group collaboration if each member is to achieve success.

international social responsibility The expectation that MNCs should be concerned about the social and economic effects of their decisions regarding activities in other countries.

keiretsu Large Japanese conglomerates of financially linked, and often family-linked, groups of companies, such as Mitsubishi, that do business among themselves whenever possible.

kibun Feelings and attitudes (Korean word).

kinesics Communication through body movements.

kinesic behavior Communication through posture, gestures, facial expressions, and eye contact.

knowledge management the process by which the firm integrates and benefits from the experiences and skills learned by its employees, for example when repatriating managers from the host country.

labor relations The process through which managers and workers determine their workplace relationships.

licensing An international entry strategy by which a firm grants the rights to a firm in the host country to produce or sell a product.

locus of decision making The relative level of decentralization in an organization—that is, the level at which decisions of varying importance can be made—ranging from all decisions made at headquarters to all made at the local subsidiary.

love–hate relationship An expression describing a common attitude of host governments toward MNC investment in their country—they love the economic growth that the MNC brings but hate the incursions on their independence and sovereignty.

low-contact culture Cultures that prefer much less sensory involvement, standing farther apart and touching far less; a "distant" style of body language.

low-context communication One in which people convey messages directly and explicitly.

macropolitical risk event An event that affects all foreign firms doing business in a country or region.

managing environmental interdependence The process by which international managers accept and enact their role in the preservation of ecological balance on the earth.

managing interdependence The effective management of a long-term MNC subsidiary–host-country relationship through cooperation and consideration for host concerns.

maquiladoras U.S. manufacturing or assembly facilities operating just south of the U.S.–Mexico border under special tax considerations.

masculinity The degree to which traditionally "masculine" values—assertiveness, materialism, and the like—prevail in a society.

material culture *See* **object language**.

matrix structure A hybrid organization of overlapping responsibilities.

micropolitical risk event An event that affects one industry or company or only a few companies.

MIS adequacy The ability to gather timely and accurate information necessary for international management, especially in less developed countries.

monochronic cultures Those cultures in which time is experienced and used in a linear way; there is a past, present, and future, and time is treated as something to be spent, saved, wasted, and so on. *See also* **polychronic cultures**.

moral idealism The relative emphasis on long-term, ethical, and moral criteria for decisions versus short-term, cost-benefit criteria. *See also* **utilitarianism**.

moral universalism A moral standard toward social responsibility accepted by all cultures.

multicultural leader A person who is effective in inspiring and influencing the thinking, attitudes, and behavior of people from various cultural backgrounds.

multidomestic strategy Emphasizing local markets, allowing more local responsiveness and specialization.

multinational corporation (MNC) A corporation that engages in production or service activities through its own affiliates in several countries, maintains control over the policies of those affiliates, and manages from a global perspective.

nationalism The practice by a country of rallying public opinion in favor of national goals and against foreign influences.

nationalization The forced sale of an MNC's assets to local buyers with some compensation to the firm, perhaps leaving a minority ownership with the MNC; often involves the takeover of an entire industry, such as the oil industry.

negotiation The process by which two or more parties meet to try to reach agreement regarding conflicting interests.

noise Anything that serves to undermine the communication of the intended meaning.

noncomparability of performance data across countries The control problem caused by the difficulty of comparing performance data across various countries because of the variables that make that information appear different.

nontask sounding (*nemawashi*) General, polite conversation and informal communication before meetings.

nonverbal communication (body language) The transfer of meaning through the use of body language, time, and space.

object language (material culture) How we communicate through material artifacts, whether architecture, office design and furniture, clothing, cars, or cosmetics.

objective–subjective decision-making approach The relative level of rationality and objectivity used in making decisions versus the level of subjective factors, such as emotions and ideals.

open systems model The view that all factors inside and outside a firm—environment, organization, and management—work together as a dynamic, interdependent system.

openness Traits such as open-mindedness, tolerance for ambiguity, and extrovertedness.

outsourcing or offshoreing The use of professional, skilled, or low-skilled workers located in countries other than that in which the firm is domiciled.

paralanguage How something is said rather than the content—the rate of speech, the tone and inflection of voice, other noises, laughing, or yawning.

parent-country national (PCN) An employee from the firm's home country sent to work in the firm's operations in another country (*see also* **expatriate**)

parochialism The expectation that "foreigners" should automatically fall into host-country patterns of behavior.

political risk The potential for governmental actions or politically motivated events to occur in a country that will adversely affect the long-run profitability or value of a firm.

polycentric staffing approach An MNC policy of using local host-country nationals (HCNs) to fill key positions in the host country.

polychronic cultures Those cultures that welcome the simultaneous occurrence of many things and emphasize involvement with people over specific time commitments or compartmentalized activities. *See also* **monochronic cultures**.

posturing General discussion that sets the tone for negotiation meetings.

power distance The extent to which subordinates accept unequal power and a hierarchical system in a company.

privatization The sale of government-owned operations to private investors.

projective cognitive similarity The assumption that others perceive, judge, think, and reason in the same way.

proxemics The distance between people (personal space) with which a person feels comfortable.

protectionism A country's use of tariff and nontariff barriers to partially or completely close its borders to various imported products that would compete with domestic products.

questionable payments Business payments that raise significant ethical issues about appropriate moral behavior in either a host nation or other nations.

regiocentric staffing approach An approach in which recruiting for international managers is done on a regional basis and may comprise a specific mix of PCNs, HCNs, and TCNs.

regionalization strategy The global corporate strategy that links markets within regions and allows managers in each region to formulate their own regional strategy and cooperate as quasi-independent subsidiaries.

regulatory environment The many laws and courts of the nation in which an international manager works.

relationship building The process of getting to know one's contacts in a host country and building mutual trust before embarking on business discussions and transactions.

repatriation The process of the reintegration of expatriates into the headquarters organization and career ladder as well as into the social environment.

resilience Traits such as having an internal locus of control, persistence, a tolerance of ambiguity, and resourcefulness.

reverse culture shock A state of disorientation and anxiety that results from returning to one's own culture.

ringi system "Bottom-up" decision-making process used in Japanese organizations.

self-reference criterion An unconscious reference to one's own cultural values; understanding and relating to others only from one's own cultural frame of reference.

separation The retention of distinct identities by minority groups unwilling or unable to adapt to the dominant culture.

stages model *See* **structural evolution**.

stereotyping The assumption that every member of a society or subculture has the same characteristics or traits, without regard to individual differences.

strategic alliances (global) Working partnerships between MNCs across national boundaries and often across industries.

strategic business unit (SBU) A self-contained business within a company with its own functional departments and accounting systems.

strategic freedom of an IJV The relative amount of control that an international joint venture will have, compared with the parents, in choosing suppliers, product lines, customers, and so on.

strategic implementation The process by which strategic plans are realized through the establishment of a *system of fits* throughout an organization with the desired strategy—for example, in organizational structure, staffing, and operations.

strategic planning The process by which a firm's managers consider the future prospects for their company and evaluate and decide on strategy to achieve long-term objectives.

strategy The basic means by which a company competes: the choice of business or businesses in which it operates and how it differentiates itself from its competitors in those businesses.

structural evolution (stages model) The stages of change in an organizational structure that follow the evolution of the internationalization process.

subculture shock A state of disorientation and anxiety that results from the unfamiliar circumstances and behaviors encountered when exposed to a different cultural group in a country than one the person is familiar with.

SWOT analysis An assessment of a firm's capabilities (**s**trengths and **w**eaknesses) relative to those of its competitors as pertinent to the **o**pportunities and **t**hreats in the environment for those firms.

subsidiary A business incorporated in a foreign country in which the parent corporation holds an ownership position.

synergy The greater level of effectiveness that can result from combined group effort than from the total of each individual's efforts alone.

technoglobalism A phenomenon in which the rapid developments in information and communication technologies (ICTs) are propelling globalization and vice versa.

terrorism The use of, or threat to use, violence for ideological or political purposes.

transnational corporations (TNCs) Multinational corporations that are truly globalizing by viewing the world as one market and crossing boundaries for whatever functions or resources are most efficiently available; structural coordination reflects the ability to integrate globally while retaining local flexibility; typically owned and managed by nationals from different countries.

transpatriate A term similar to expatriates but referring to managers who may be from any country other than that in which the firm is domiciled, and who tends to work in several countries over time – that is who has no true corporate "home."

turnkey operation When a company designs and constructs a facility abroad, trains local personnel, and turns the key over to local management, for a fee

uncertainty avoidance The extent to which people feel threatened by ambiguous situations; in a company, this results in formal rules and processes to provide more security.

utilitarianism The relative emphasis on short-term cost-benefit (utilitarian) criteria for decisions versus those of long-term, ethical, and moral concerns. *See also* **moral idealism**.

values A person or group's ideas and convictions about what is important, good or bad, right or wrong.

virtual global teams Employees in various locations around the world who coordinate their work and decisions through teleconferencing, e-mail, and so on.

work centrality The degree of general importance that working has in the life of an individual at any given time.

workforce diversity The phenomenon of increasing ethnic diversity in the workforce in the United States and many other countries because of diverse populations and joint ventures; this results in intercultural working environments in domestic companies.

works council In Germany, employee group that shares plant-level responsibility with managers.

World Trade Organization (WTO) A formal structure for continued negotiations to reduce trade barriers and settling trade disputes.

Endnotes

Chapter 1

1. W. Arnold, "Business Goes on in Jakarta Despite Threat of Terrorism," www.nytimes.com October 22, 2003.
2. D. Pearl and A. Freedman, "Behind Cipla's Offer of Cheap AIDS Drugs," *Wall Street Journal*, March 12, 2001, p. 5.
3. K. Ohmae, "Putting Global Logic First," *Harvard Business Review* (January–February 1995): 119–125.
4. *Business Week*, August 31, 1998, p. 31–33
5. "For Avon, China Is a Beauty," www.businessweek.com, January 12, 2004.
6. J. L. Levere, "A Small Company, a Global Approach," www.nytimes.com, January 1, 2004.
7. *Business Week*, November 10, 1998, p. 18–20
8. Peter Drucker, Interview, in *Fortune*, January 12, 2004.
9. Ohmae
10. Stefan Wagstyl, "The next investment wave: companies in east and west prepare for the risks and opportunities of an enlarged EU," *Financial Times*, April 27, 2004.
11. George Parker and Quentin Peel, "A fractured Europe," *Financial Times*, September 17, 2003, p. 15.
12. L. Miller, "Go East, Young Company," www.businessweek.com, January 12, 2004.
13. *Financial Times*, September 17, 2003, p. 15.
14. J. Edwards, "East Asia is an economic dynamo," *Financial Times*, January 6, 2004, p. 13.
15. Ibid.
16. FT Summer School, "China: rough but ready for outsiders," *Financial Times*, August 26, 2003, p. 7
17. …. "Worrying about China," www.businessweek.com, January 19, 2004.
18. Naomi Koppel, Associated Press, "Agreement reached allows China entry into WTO," *The Press Republican*, September 16, 2001, p. 1.
19. H. Kumar, "South Asia looks to sign Free Trade Pact," www.nytimes.com, December 31, 2003.
20. …. "Mexico: was NAFTA worth it?" www.businessweek.com, December 22, 2003.
21. The Carnegie Endowment Report, November, 2003.
22. The World Bank report, November, 2003.
23. Mexican Central Bank, quoted in www.businessweek.com, December 22, 2003.
24. www.businessweek.com, December 22, 2003.
25. E. Becker, "A pact on Central America Trade Zone, minus one," www.nytimes.com, December 18, 2003.
26. W. E. Halal and A. I. Nikitin, "One World: The coming synthesis of New Capitalism and a New Socialism," *Futurist* (November/December 1990): 8–14.
27. Andrew Jack, Special report: Russia, "A new dawn brightens Moscow's skyline," *Financial Times*, October 9, 2003, p. 1–3.
28. *American Banker-Bond Buyer*, January 2, 2004, p. 1.
29. E. Arvelund, "Russian growth accelerates, stoked by oil," www.nytimes.com, January 1, 2004.
30. *Financial Times*, October 9, 2003.
31. *Ibid.*
32. N. Itano, "South African companies fill a void," www.nytimes.com, November 4, 2003.
33. UPI Newswire, November 7, 1995.
34. K. Ohmae, 1990 p. 119–125
35. Hewitt Associates Study press release, quoted on CNBC, March 5, 2004.
36. B. Delong, "Globalisation means we share jobs as well as goods," *Financial Times*, August 27, 2003, p. 13.
37. Ibid.
38. *Forrester research report*, November, 2002.
39. J. Fox, "Where your job is going," *Fortune*, November 24, 2003, p. 84–87.
40. … "Outsourcing: Make way for China," www.businessweek.com, July 29, 2003.
41. B. Weiner, "What Executives Should Know About Political Risks," *Management Review* (January 1991): 19–22.
42. Ibid.
43. … "Argentina Strips French Company of License," www.FT.com, *January 27, 2004.*
44. S. H. Robock and K. Simmonds, *International Business and Multinational Enterprises*, 4th ed. (Homewood, IL: Irwin, 1989), 378.
45. Ibid.
46. D. F. Simon, "After Tiananmen: What Is the Future for Foreign Business in China?" *California Management Review* (Winter 1990): 106–108.
47. E. F. Micklous, "Tracking the Growth and Prevalence of International Terrorism," in *Managing Terrorism: Strategies for the Corporate Executive*, eds. P. J. Montana and G. S. Roukis (Westport, CT: Quorum Books, 1983), 3.
48. Robock and Simmonds, p. 378
49. G. M. Taoka and D. R. Beeman, *International Business* (New York: HarperCollins, 1991), p. 112
50. D. R. Beeman, "An Empirical Analysis of the Beliefs Held by the International Executives of United States Firms Regarding Political Risks and Risk Reduction Methods in Developing Nations" (unpublished doctoral dissertation, Indiana University Graduate School of Business, 1978), reprinted in G. M. Taoka and D. R. Beeman, *International Business* (New York: HarperCollins, 1991), 36–41.
51. T. W. Shreeve, "Be Prepared for Political Changes Abroad," *Harvard Business Review* (July–August 1984): 111–118.
52. M. C. Schnitzer, M. L. Liebrenz, and K. W. Kubin, *International Business* (Cincinnati, OH: South-Western, 1985) pp. 45–47
53. C. Erol, "An Exploratory Model of Political Risk Assessment and the Decision Process of Foreign Direct Investment," *International Studies of Management and Organization* (Summer 1985): 75–90.
54. Ibid.
55. T. Morrison, W. Conaway, and J. Bouress, *Dun & Bradstreet's Guide to Doing Business Around the World* (Upper Saddle River, NJ: Prentice Hall, 1997).

56. Schnitzer, Liebrenz, and Kubin, pp. 45-47

57. P. Smith Ring, S. A. Lenway, and M. Govekar, "Management of the Political Imperative in International Business," *Strategic Management Journal* 11 (1990): 141–151.

58. Taoka and Beeman, p. 112

59. Ibid.

60. Overseas Private Investment Corporation, *Investment Insurance Handbook*, 4, 2000

61. Schnitzer, Liebrenz, and Kubin, pp. 45-47.

62. B. O'Reilly, "Business Copes with Terrorism," *Fortune*, January 6, 2004, 48.

63. *Wall Street Journal*, December 29, 2000 p. 3.

64. J. Dahl, "Firms Warn Workers Traveling Abroad," *Wall Street Journal*, April 10, 1989, B1.

65. *Wall Street Journal*, February 20, 2002, p. 5

66. F. John Mathis, "International Risk Analysis," in *Global Business Management in the 1990s*, ed. R. T. Moran (Washington, DC: Beacham, 1990): 33–44.

67. Mathis, 40.

68. … "Why Sweet Deals Are Going Sour in China," *Business Week*, December 19, 1994, 50–51.

69. M. Loeb, "China: A Time for Caution," *Fortune*, February 20, 1995, p. 32-34.

70. P. Hui-Ho Cheng, "A Business Risk in China: Jail," *Asian Wall Street Journal*, April 22, 1994, p. 12

71. M. Litka, *International Dimensions of the Legal Environment of Business* (Boston: PWS-Kent, 1988), 5.

72. Ibid.

73. Rahul Jacob, "Asian Infrastructure: The biggest bet on earth," *Fortune*, October 31, 1994, p. 139-146.

74. Litka, p. 5.

75. Jacob, p. 139-146.

76. Ibid.

77. R. J. Radway, "Foreign Contract Agreements," in *Global Business Management in the 1990s*, ed. R. T. Moran (Washington, DC: Beacham, 1990), 93–103.

78. S. P. Robbins and R. Stuart-Kotze, *Management* (Scarborough, Ontario: Prentice Hall Canada, 1990), 4–11.

79. Ibid.

80. … "Lacking Roads, Village Building Information Highway," *Wall Street Journal*, December 29, 2001, p. 7.

81. B. Delong, "Globalisation means we share jobs as well as goods," *Financial Times*, August 27, 2003, p. 13.

82. Sylvia Ostry, "Technological Productivity and the Multinational Enterprise," *Journal of International Business Studies* 29, 1 (1st quarter, 1998): 85–99.

83. Ibid.

84. … "Where Technology Is the Appropriate Word," *The Economist*, April 18, 1987, 83.

85. … "How to Sell Soap in India," *The Economist*, September 1988, 82.

86. A. Kyte, Gartner, Inc., England, in www.businessweek.com, May 17, 2003.

87. Richard Waters and Chris Nuttall, "Going global: from shopping to search, America's online giants have their sights set on international expansion," *Financial Times*, June 10, 2004.

88. Hans Dieter Zimmerman, "E-Business," www.businessmedia.org, June 13, 2000.

89. "What Is E-Business?" PriceWaterhouseCoopers, www.pwcglobal.com, July 21, 2000.

90. J. Rajesh, "Five E-Business Trends," Net.Columns, www.indialine.com, February 18, 1999.

91. … "E-Management," *The Economist*, November 11, 2000, p. 32-34

92. … "E-Commerce Report, *New York Times*, March 26, 2001, pp. 7-8

93. "Europe's borderless market: the Net," www.businessweek.com, May 17, 2003.

94. S. Mohanbir, M. Sumant, "Go Global," *Business 2.0*, May, 2000, pp. 178-213.

95. A. Chen and M. Hicks, "Going Global? Avoid culture clashes," *PC Week*, April 3, 2000, pp. 9-10.

96. PriceWaterhouseCoopers. This section draws from a term paper by Ms. Laura Harrison, student at the State University of New York, December 2000.

97. PriceWaterhouseCoopers, "What Is E-Business," www.pwcglobal.com, July 21, 2000.

Chapter 2

1. J. Birchall, "UN Ethics Guidelines May Alarm Multinationals," www.FT.com (*Financial Times*), August 11, 2003.

2. A. Maitland, "No Hiding Place for the Irresponsible Business," *Financial Times Special Report*, September 29, 2003, 4.

3. Ibid.

4. J. C. Laya, "Economic Development Issues," in *Multinational Managers and Host Government Interactions*, ed. Lee A. Tavis (South Bend, IN: University of Notre Dame Press, 1988).

5. John A. Quelch and James E. Austin, "Should Multinationals Invest in Africa?" *Sloan Management Review* (Spring 1993): 107–119.

6. Milton Friedman, *Capitalism and Freedom* (Chicago: University of Chicago Press, 1962).

7. S. Prakash Sethi, "A Conceptual Framework for Environmental Analysis of Social Issues and Evaluation of Business Response Patterns," *Academy of Management Review* (January 1979): 63–74.

8. John Dobson, "The Role of Ethics in Global Corporate Culture," *Journal of Business Ethics* 9 (1990): 481–488.

9. Ibid.

10. N. Bowie, "The Moral Obligations of Multinational Corporations," in *Problems of International Justice*, ed. LuperFay (New York: Westview Press: 1987), 97–113.

11. A. C. Wicks, "Norman Bowie and Richard Rorty on Multinationals: Does Business Ethics Need 'Metaphysical Comfort'?" *Journal of Business Ethics* 9 (1990): 191–200.

12. Birchall, *Financial Times*.

13. Joanna Ramey, "Clinton Urges Industry to Enlist in the War Against Sweatshops," www.labordepartment.com, April 15, 1997.

14. Shu Shin Luh, "Report Claims Abuses by Nike Contractors," *Wall Street Journal*, February 22, 2001, 7.

15. *Asian Wall Street Journal*, April 8.

16. "Staunching the Flow of China's Gulag Exports," *Business Week*, April 13, 1992.

17. J. Carlton, "Ties with China Will Be Severed by Levi Strauss," *Wall Street Journal*, May 5, 1993, A3.

18. G. P. Zachary, "Levi Tries to Make Sure Contract Plants in Asia Treat Workers Well," *Wall Street Journal*, July 28, 1994.

19. "Sweatshop Police," *Business Week*, October 20, 1997, 30–32.

20. Kathleen A. Getz, "International Codes of Conduct: An Analysis of Ethical Reasoning," *Journal of Business Ethics* 9 (1990): 567–577.

21. Adrian Michaels and Joshua Chaffin, "Banks 'were aware of Enron fraud'," *Financial Times,* July 29, 2003, 2.
22. James Glassman, quoting Stephen Cutler (Securities Enforcement Director), "A ringing endorsement of fraud," *Financial Times,* July 29, 2003, 5.
23. Peter Gumbel, "Enron, Italian Style," *Time,* January 12, 2003, 53.
24. Swee Hoon Ang, "The Power of Money: A Cross-Cultural Analysis of Business-Related Beliefs," *Journal of World Business* 35, no. 1 (Spring 2000): 43.
25. C. J. Robertson and W. F. Crittenden, "Mapping Moral Philosophies: Strategic Implications for Multinational Firms," *Strategic Management Journal* 24 (2003): 385–392.
26. A. Singer, "Ethics—Are Standards Lower Overseas?" *Across the Board,* September 1991, 31–34.
27. Ibid.
28. Peter Eigen, www.TransparencyInternational.org, October 7, 2003.
29. G. R. Laczniak and J. Naor, "Global Ethics: Wrestling with the Corporate Conscience," *Business,* July–August–September, 1985, 152.
30. Singer.
31. G. A. Steiner and J. F. Steiner, *Business, Government and Society,* 6th ed. (New York: McGraw-Hill, 1991).
32. J. T. Noonan, Jr., *Bribes* (New York: Macmillan, 1984), ii.
33. T. L. Carson, "Bribery and Implicit Agreements: A Reply to Philips," *Journal of Business Ethics* 6 (1987): 123–125.
34. M. Philips, "Bribery," *Ethics* 94 (July 1984) 50.
35. Laczniak and Naor, 1985.
36. L. H. Newton and M. M. Ford, *Taking Sides* (Guilford, CT: Dushkin, 1990).
37. Ibid.; K. Gillespie, "Middle East Response to the U.S. Foreign Corrupt Practices Act," *California Management Review* (Summer 1987): 9.
38. K. M. Bartol and D. C. Martin, *Management* (New York: McGraw-Hill, 1991).
39. D. Vogel, "Is U.S. Business Obsessed with Ethics?" *Across the Board,* November/December, 1993: 31–33.
40. A. Cadbury, *Harvard Business Review* (September–October 1987): 63–73.
41. M. E. Shannon, "Coping with Extortion and Bribery," in *Multinational Managers and Host Government Interactions,* ed. Lee A Tavis (South Bend, IN: University of Notre Dame Press, 1988).
42. Laczniak and Naor.
43. "A World of Greased Palms," *Business Week,* November 6, 1995.
44. D. E. Sanger, "Nippon Telegraph Executive Demoted for Role in Scandal," *New York Times,* December 10, 1988.
45. Susan Chira, "Another Top Official in Japan Loses Post in Wake of Scandal," *New York Times,* January 25, 1989, 1, 5; and "Remember the Recruit Scandal? Well...," *Business Week,* January 8, 1990, 52.
46. A. Michaels and J. Chaffin, "Banks 'Were Aware of Enron Fraud'," *Financial Times,* July 29, 2003: 3.
47. Sadahei Kusumoto, "We're Not in Honshu Anymore," *Across the Board* (June 1989): 49–50.
48. Ibid.
49. P. W. Beamish et al., *International Management* (Homewood, IL: Irwin, 1991).
50. Adapted from Asheghian and Ebrahimi.

51. R. Grosse and D. Kujawa, *International Business* (Homewood, IL: Irwin, 1988), 705.
52. R. H. Mason and R. S. Spich, *Management: An International Perspective* (Homewood, IL: Irwin, 1987).
53. Yves L. Doz and C. K. Prahalad, "How MNCs Cope with Host Government Intervention," *Harvard Business Review* (March–April 1980).
54. Mason and Spich.
55. Simcha Ronen, *Comparative and Multinational Management* (New York: John Wiley and Sons, 1986), 502–503.
56. R. T. De George, *Competing with Integrity in International Business* (New York: Oxford University Press, 1993), 3–4.
57. B. Ward and R. Dubois, *Only One Earth* (New York: Ballantine Books, 1972).
58. Ronen.
59. S. Tifft. "Who Gets the Garbage," *Time,* July 4, 1988, 42–43.
60. Jang B. Singh and V. C. Lakhan, "Business Ethics and the International Trade in Hazardous Wastes," *Journal of Business Ethics* 8 (1989): 889–899.
61. R. A. Peterson and M. H. Sauber, "International Marketing Ethics: Is There a Need for a Code?" Paper presented at the International Studies Association Southwest, Houston, TX, March 16–19, 1984.
62. M. Reza Vaghefi, S. K. Paulson, and W. H. Tomlinson, *International Business Theory and Practice* (New York: Taylor and Francis, 1991), 249–250.
63. T. E. Graedel and B. R. Allenby, *Industrial Ecology* (Upper Saddle River, NJ: Prentice Hall, 1995).
64. M. Sharfman, Book Review of Graedel and Allenby, *Academy of Management Review* 20, no. 4 (1995): 1,090–1,107.
65. Ronen, 1986.
66. P. Asheghian and B. Ebrahimi, *International Business* (NY: Harper and Row, 1990), 640–641.
67. Becker and Fritzsche.

Chapter 3

1. David A. Ricks, *Big Business Blunders: Mistakes in Multinational Marketing* (Homewood, IL: Dow Jones–Irwin, 1983).
2. Carla Joinson, "Why HR Managers Need to Think Globally," *HR Magazine,* April 1998, 2–7.
3. Ibid.
4. J. Stewart Black and Mark Mendenhall, "Cross-Cultural Training Effectiveness: A Review and a Theoretical Framework for Future Research," *Academy of Management Review* 15, no. 1 (1990): 113–136.
5. Adapted from Bernard Wysocki, Jr., "Global Reach: Cross-Border Alliances Become Favorite Way to Crack New Markets," *Wall Street Journal,* March 26, 1990, A1, A4.
6. Geert Hofstede, *Culture's Consequences: International Differences in Work-Related Values* (Beverly Hills, CA: Sage Publications, 1980), 25; E. T. Hall, *The Silent Language* (Greenwich, CT: Fawcett, 1959). For a more detailed definition of the culture of a society, see A. L. Kroeber and C. Kluckholhn, "A Critical Review of Concepts and Definitions," in *Peabody Museum Papers* 47, no. 1 (Cambridge, MA: Harvard University Press, 1952), 181.
7. David Dressler and Donald Carns, *Sociology, The Study of Human Interaction* (New York: Knopf, 1969), 56–57.

8. K. David, "Organizational Processes for Intercultural Management," paper presented at the Strategic Management Association, San Francisco, CA, 1989.

9. *Wall Street Journal*, February 20, 2001; and *Wall Street Journal*, February 2, 1990, A15.

10. Lane Kelley, Arthur Whatley, and Reginald Worthley, "Assessing the Effects of Culture on Managerial Attitudes: A Three-Culture Test," *Journal of International Business Studies* (Summer 1987): 17–31.

11. J. D. Child, "Culture, Contingency and Capitalism in the Cross-National Study of Organizations," in *Research in Organizational Behavior,* ed. L. L. Cummings and B. M. Shaw (Greenwich, CT: JAI Publishers, 1981), 303–356.

12. Jangho Lee, T. W. Roehl, and Soonkyoo Choe, "What Makes Management Style Similar and Distinct Across Borders? Growth Experience and Culture in Korean and Japanese Firms," *Journal of International Business Studies* 31, no. 4 (4th Quarter 2000): 631–652.

13. James A. Lee, "Cultural Analysis in Overseas Operations," *Harvard Business Review* (March–April 1966).

14. E. T. Hall, "The Silent Language in Overseas Business," *Harvard Business Review* (May–June 1960).

15. "American Culture Is Often a Puzzle for Foreign Managers in the U.S.," *Wall Street Journal*, February 12, 1986, 34.

16. "One Big Market," *Wall Street Journal*, February 6, 1989, 16.

17. D. A. Ralston, Yu Kai-Ceng, Xun Wang, R. H. Terpstra, and He Wel, "An Analysis of Managerial Work Values Across the Six Regions of China," paper presented at the Academy of International Business, Boston, November 1994.

18. Philip R. Harris and Robert T. Moran, *Managing Cultural Differences* (Houston, TX: Gulf Publishing, 1987).

19. K. David, "Field Research," in *The Cultural Environment of International Business*, 3rd ed., ed. V. Terpstra and K. David (Cincinnati, OH: South-Western, 1991), 176.

20. "Sharia Loosens Its Grip," *Euromoney* (May 1987): 137–138.

21. Mansour Javidan and Robert J. House, "Cultural Acumen for the Global Manager: Lessons from Project GLOBE," Organizational Dynamics (Spring 2001): 289–305.

22. V. Gupta, P. J. Hanges, and P. Dorfman, "Cultural Clusters: Methodology and Findings," *Journal of World Business,* 37 (2002) 11–15.

23. Ibid.

24. Geert Hofstede, *Cultures and Organizations: Software of the Mind* (New York: McGraw-Hill, 1997) 79–108.

25. Elizabeth Weldon and Elisa L. Mustari, "Felt Dispensability in Groups of Coactors: The Effects of Shared Responsibility on Cognitive Effort" (unpublished manuscript, Kellogg Graduate School of Management, Northwestern University).

26. P. Christopher Earley, "Social Loafing and Collectivism: A Comparison of the United States and the People's Republic of China," *Administrative Science Quarterly* 34 (1989): 565–581.

27. H. K. Steensma, L. Marino, and K. M. Weaver, "Attitudes towards Cooperative Strategies: A Cross-Cultural Analysis of Entrepreneurs," *Journal of International Business Studies* 31, no. 4 (4th Quarter 2000): 591–609.

28. F. Trompenaars, *Riding the Waves of Culture* (London: Nicholas Brealey, 1993).

29. L. Hoeklin, *Managing Cultural Differences: Strategies for Competitive Advantage* (New York: The Economist Intelligence Unit/Addison-Wesley, 1995).

30. Ross A. Webber, *Culture and Management, Text and Reading in Comparative Management* (Homewood, IL: Irwin, 1969), 186.

31. Hwang Kyu-june at Hanaro Company, Broadband Service Provider, quoted in Andrew Ward, "Love Affair Starts to Grip South Korea's Internet generation," *Financial Times*, October 14, 2003, p. 6.

32. A. Ward, p. 6

33. Ibid.

34. H. Jeff Smith, "Information Privacy and Marketing: What the U.S. Should (and Shouldn't) Learn from Europe," *California Management Review* 43, no. 2 (Winter 2001) 30–34.

35. Ibid.

36. Ibid.

37. "Data Privacy Deal," *Journal of Commerce*, March 28, 2000, 4.

38. R. Howells, "Update on Safe Harbor for International Data Transfer," *Direct Marketing* 63, no. 4 (August 2000): 40.

39. Smith, 2001, p. 30–34.

40. D. Darlin and J. B. White, "GM Venture in Korea Nears End, Betraying Firm's Fond Hopes," *Wall Street Journal*, January 16, 1992, 1.

41. Geert Hofstede, *Culture's Consequences: International Differences in Work-Related Values* (Beverly Hills, CA: Sage Publications, 1980).

42. George W. England, "Managers and Their Value Systems: A Five-Country Comparative Study," *Columbia Journal of World Business* (Summer 1978): 35–44.

43. Lennie Copeland and Lewis Griggs, *Going International* (New York: Random House, 1985); Boye De Mente, *Japanese Etiquette and Ethics in Business* (Lincolnwood, IL: NTC Business Books, 1989); George W. England and R. Lee, "Organizational Goals and Expected Behavior among American, Japanese and Korean Managers: A Comparative Study," *Academy of Management Journal* 14, no. 4 (1971): 425–438; R. L. Tung, *Business Negotiations with the Japanese* (Lexington, MA: Lexington Books, 1984); W. G. Ouchi and A. M. Jaeger, "Theory Z Organization: Stability in the Midst of Mobility," *Academy of Management Review* 3, no. 2 (1978): 305–314; T. Seth, "Management and Its Environment in India," in *Management in an International Context*, ed. Joseph L. Massie and J. Luytjes (New York: Harper and Row, 1972), 201–225; Nam-Won Suh, "Management and Its Environment in Korea," in *Management in an International Context*, ed. Joseph L. Massie and Jan Luytjes (New York: Harper and Row, 1972), 226–244; Philip R. Harris and Robert T. Moran, *Managing Cultural Differences* (Houston, TX: Gulf Publishing, 1991); Fernando Quezada and James E. Boyce, "Latin America," in *Comparative Management*, ed. Raghu Nath (Cambridge, MA: Ballinger Publishing, 1988), 245–270; Simcha Ronen, *Comparative and Multinational Management* (New York: John Wiley and Sons, 1986); and V. Terpstra and K. David, *The Cultural Environment of International Business*, 3rd ed. (Cincinnati, OH: South-Western, 1991).

44. Akio Kuzuoka, Forty-year Employee at a Japanese Company, quoted in *Wall Street Journal,* December 29, 2000.

45. R. G. Linowes, "The Japanese Manager's Traumatic Entry in the United States: Understanding the American–Japanese

Cultural Divide," *Academy of Management Review* (1993): 21–38.

46. Ibid.

47. Yumiko Ono and William Spindle, "Japan's Long Decline Makes One Thing Rise—Individualism," *Wall Street Journal*, December 29, 2000 p. 5.

48. Ibid, p. 5.

49. E. T. Hall and M. R. Hall, *Understanding Cultural Differences* (Yarmouth, ME: Intercultural Press, 1990), 4.

50. P. R. Haris and R. T. Moran, *Managing Cultural Differences*, 4th ed. (Houston, TX: Gulf Publishing Co., 1996).

51. Robert Moore, "Saudi Arabia," Chapter 11, in Harris and Moran.

52. John A. Pearce II and Richard B. Robinson, Jr., "Cultivating *Guanxi* as a Foreign Investor Strategy," *Business Horizons* 43, 1 (January 2000): 31.

53. M. Chen, *Asian Management Systems: Chinese, Japanese and Korean Styles of Business* (New York: Routledge, 1995).

54. Anne Marie Francesco and Barry Allen Gold, *International Organizational Behavior* (Upper Saddle River, NJ: Prentice Hall, 1997).

55. J. Lee, "Culture and Management—A Study of Small Chinese Family Business in Singapore," *Journal of Small Business Management*, July 1996: 17–24.

56. R. Sheng, "Outsiders' Perception of the Chinese," *Columbia Journal of World Business* 14 (2) (Summer 2000), 16–22.

57. Lee, p. 17–24

58. Ralston et al.

Chapter 4

1. E. T. Hall and M. R. Hall, *Understanding Cultural Differences* (Yarmouth, ME: Intercultural Press, 1990), 4.

2. E. Wilmott, "New Media Vision," *New Media Age*, September 9, 1999, 8.

3. Hall and Hall; K. Wolfson and W. B. Pearce, "A Cross-cultural Comparison of the Implications of Self-discovery on Conversation Logics," *Communication Quarterly* 31 (1983): 249–256.

4. H. Mintzberg, *The Nature of Managerial Work* (New York: Harper and Row, 1973).

5. L. A. Samovar, R. E. Porter, and N. C. Jain, *Understanding Intercultural Communication* (Belmont, CA: Wadsworth Publishing Co., 1981).

6. P. R. Harris and R. T. Moran, *Managing Cultural Differences,* 3rd ed. (Houston, TX: Gulf Publishing, 1991).

7. H. C. Triandis, quoted in *The Blackwell Handbook of Cross-cultural Management,* eds. M. Gannon and K. Newman (Oxford, England: Blackwell Publishers, 2002).

8. Samovar, Porter, and Jain.

9. Hall and Hall, 15.

10. James R. Houghton, Former Chairman of Corning, Inc., quoted in *Organizational Dynamics*, Spring 2001.

11. J. Child, "Trust: The Fundamental Bond in Global Collaboration," *Organizaional Dynamics* 29, no. 4 (Spring 2001): 274–288.

12. Ibid.

13. World Values Study Group (1994), *World Values Survey, ICPSR Version* (Ann Arbor, MI: Institute for Social Research); R. Inglehart, M. Basanez, and A. Moreno, *Human Values and Beliefs: A Cross-cultural Sourcebook* (Ann Arbor: University of Michigan Press, 1998).

14. Mansour Javidan and Robert J. House, "Cultural Acumen for the Global Manager," *Organizational Dynamics* 29, no. 4 (Spring 2001), 289–305.

15. Samovar and Porter; Harris and Moran.

16. M. L. Hecht, P. A. Andersen, and S. A. Ribeau, "The Cultural Dimensions of Nonverbal Communication, in *Handbook of International and Intercultural Communication*, ed. M. K. Asante and W. B. Gudykunst (Newbury Park, CA: Sage Publications, 1989), 163–185.

17. H. C. Triandis, *Interpersonal Behavior* (Monterey, CA: Brooks/Cole, 1977).

18. Harris and Moran.

19. Adapted from N. Adler, *International Dimensions of Organizational Behavior,* 2nd ed. (Boston: PWS-Kent, 1991).

20. D. A. Ricks, *Big Business Blunders: Mistakes in Multinational Marketing* (Homewood, IL: Dow Jones–Irwin, 1983).

21. Vern Terpstra and K. David, *The Cultural Environment of International Business*, 3rd ed. (Cincinnati, OH: South-Western, 1991).

22. L. Copeland and L. Griggs, *Going International* (New York: Random House, 1985).

23. J. R. Schermerhorn, "Language Effects in Cross-cultural Management Research: An Empirical Study and a Word of Caution," *National Academy of Management Proceedings* (1987): 103.

24. Jiatao Li, Katherine R. Xin, Anne Tsui, and Donald C. Hambrick, "Building Effective International Joint Venture Leadership Teams in China," *Journal of World Business* 34, no. 1 (1999): 52–68.

25. R. L. Daft, *Organizational Theory and Design*, 3rd ed. (St. Paul, MN: West Publishing, 1989).

26. Li et al., 1999.

27. O. Klineberg, "Emotional Expression in Chinese Literature," *Journal of Abnormal and Social Psychology* 33 (1983): 517–530.

28. P. Ekman and W. V. Friesen, "Constants Across Cultures in the Face and Emotion," *Journal of Personality and Social Psychology* 17 (1971): 124–129.

29. J. Pfeiffer, "How Not to Lose the Trade Wars by Cultural Gaffes," *Smithsonian* 18, no. 10 (January 1988).

30. E. T. Hall, *The Silent Language* (New York: Doubleday, 1959).

31. Hall and Hall.

32. Ibid.

33. N. M. Sussman and H. M. Rosenfeld, "Influence of Culture, Language, and Sex on Conversational Distance," *Journal of Personality and Social Psychology* 42 (1982): 66–74.

34. Copeland and Griggs.

35. Hecht, Andersen, and Ribeau.

36. Li et al., 1999.

37. Pfeiffer.

38. Hall and Hall.

39. Ibid.

40. Hecht, Andersen, and Ribeau.

41. P. A. Andersen, "Explaining Differences in Nonverbal Communication," in *Intercultural Communication: A Reader*, ed. L. A. Samovar and R. E. Porter (Belmont, CA: Wadsworth, 1988); S. Scott Elliot, A. D. Jensen, and M. McDonough, "Perceptions of Reticence: A Cross-cultural Investigation," in *Communication Yearbook* 5, ed. M. Burgoon (New Brunswick, NJ: Transaction, 1982).

42. Hall and Hall.

43. R. Axtell, ed., *Do's and Taboos Around the World*, 2nd ed.

(New York: John Wiley and Sons, 1985).

44. Copeland and Griggs.

45. M. K. Nydell, *Understanding Arabs* (Yarmouth, ME: Intercultural Press, 1987).

46. Harris and Moran.

47. E. T. Hall, *The Hidden Dimension* (New York: Doubleday, 1966), 15.

48. A. Almaney and A. Alwan, *Communicating with the Arabs* (Prospect Heights, IL: Waveland, 1982).

49. E. T. Hall, "The Silent Language in Overseas Business," *Harvard Business Review* (May–June 1960).

50. Ibid.

51. Based largely on the work of Nydell; and R. T. Moran and P. R. Harris, *Managing Cultural Synergy* (Houston, TX: Gulf Publishing, 1982), 81–82.

52. Ibid.

53. Copeland and Griggs.

54. Hall and Hall.

55. D. C. Barnlund, "Public and Private Self in Communicating with Japan," *Business Horizons* (March–April 1989): 32–40.

56. Hall and Hall.

57. A. Goldman, "The Centrality of 'Ningensei' to Japanese Negotiating and Interpersonal Relationships: Implications for U.S.–Japanese Communication," *International Journal of Intercultural Relations* 18, no. 1 (Winter 1994).

58. Jean-Louis Barsoux and Peter Lawrence, "The Making of a French Manager," *Harvard Business Review* (July–August 1991): 58–67.

59. D. Shand, "All Information Is Local: IT Systems Can Connect Every Corner of the Globe, But IT Managers Are Learning They Have to Pay Attention to Regional Differences," *Computerworld*, April 10, 2000, 88 (1).

60. T. Wilson, "B2B Links, European Style: Integrator Helps applications Cross Language, Currency and Cultural Barriers," *InternetWeek*, October 9, 2000, 27.

61. Shand.

62. Wilmott.

63. *Business Week*, February, 1998, 14–15.

64. Wilson.

65. D. Ricks, *Big Business Blunders* (Homewood, IL: Dow Jones–Irwin, 1983).

66. Adler.

67. P. G. W. Keen, "Sorry, Wrong Number," *Business Month* (January 1990): 62–67.

68. R. B. Ruben, "Human Communication and Cross-cultural Effectiveness," in *Intercultural Communication: A Reader*, ed. L. Samovar and R. Porter (Belmont, CA: Wadsworth, 1985), 339.

69. D. Ruben and B. D. Ruben, "Cross-cultural Personnel Selection Criteria, Issues and Methods," in *Handbook of Intercultural Training*, Vol. 1, *Issues in Theory and Design*, ed. D. Landis and R. W. Brislin (New York: Pergamon, 1983), 155–175.

70. Young Yun Kim, *Communication and Cross-cultural Adaptation: An Integrative Theory* (Clevedon, England; Multilingual Matters, 1988).

71. Ibid.

72. R. W. Brislin, *Cross-cultural Encounters: Face-to-Face Interaction* (New York: Pergamon, 1981).

Chapter 5

1. CNN and other newscasts during April, 2001.

2. John Pfeiffer, "How Not to Lose the Trade Wars by Cultural Gaffes," *Smithsonian* 18, no. 10 (January 1988): 145–156.

3. Nancy J. Adler, *International Dimensions of Organizational Behavior*, 4th ed., 2002, (Boston: PWS-Kent), 208–232.

4. Philip R. Harris and Robert T. Moran, *Managing Cultural Differences*, 3rd ed., 1991, (Houston, TX: Gulf Publishing).

5. John L. Graham and Roy A. Herberger, Jr., "Negotiators Abroad—Don't Shoot from the Hip," *Harvard Business Review* (July–August 1983): 160–168; Adler; John L. Graham, "A Hidden Cause of America's Trade Deficit with Japan," *Columbia Journal of World Business* (Fall 1981): 5–15.

6. Phillip D. Grub, "Cultural Keys to Successful Negotiating," in *Global Business Management in the 1990s*, ed. F. Ghader et al. (Washington, DC: Beacham, 1990): 24–32.

7. R. Fisher and W. Ury, *Getting to Yes* (Boston: Houghton Mifflin, 1981).

8. "Soviet Breakup Stymies Foreign Firms," *Wall Street Journal*, January 23, 1992.

9. S. Weiss, "Negotiating with 'Romans,'" *Sloan Management Review* (Winter 1994): 51–61.

10. John A. Reeder, "When West Meets East: Cultural Aspects of Doing Business in Asia," *Business Horizons* (January–February 1987): 72.

11. Adler, 197.

12. Fisher and Ury.

13. Lennie Copeland and Lewis Griggs, *Going International* (New York: Random House, 1985), 85.

14. Ibid.

15. Adler, 197–198.

16. Fisher and Ury.

17. R. Tung, "Handshakes across the Sea," *Organizational Dynamics*, Winter 1991, 30–40.

18. John L. Graham, "The Influence of Culture on Business Negotiations," *Journal of International Business Studies* 16, no. 1 (Spring 1985): 81–96.

19. G. Fisher, *International Negotiation: A Cross-cultural Perspective* (Chicago: Intercultural Press, 1980).

20. Pfeiffer.

21. *Wall Street Journal*, February 2, 1994.

22. John L. Graham, "Brazilian, Japanese, and American Business Negotiations," *Journal of International Business Studies* (Spring–Summer 1983): 47–61.

23. T. Flannigan, "Successful Negotiating with the Japanese," *Small Business Reports* 15, no. 6 (June 1990): 47–52.

24. Graham, 1983; Boye De Mente, *Japanese Etiquette and Ethics in Business* (Lincolnwood, IL: NTC Business Books, 1989).

25. Robert H. Doktor, "Asian and American CEOs: A Comparative Study," *Organizational Dynamics* (Winter 1990): 49.

26. Harris and Moran, 461.

27. Adler, 181.

28. These profiles are adapted from Pierre Casse, *Managing Intercultural Negotiations: Guidelines for Trainers and Negotiators* (Washington, DC: Society for Intercultural Education, Training and Research, 1985).

29. D. K. Tse, J. Francis, and J. Walls, "Cultural Differences in Conducting Intra- and Inter-Cultural Negotiations:

A Sino-Canadian Comparison," *Journal of International Business Studies* (3rd Quarter 1994): 537–555.

30. B. W. Husted, "Bargaining with the Gringos: An Exploratory Study of Negotiations between Mexican and U.S. Firms," *International Executive* 36, no. 5 (September–October 1994): 625–644.

31. Pierre Casse, *Training for the Cross-cultural Mind*, 2nd ed. (Washington, DC: Society for Intercultural Education, Training, and Research, 1981).

32. Nigel Campbell, John L. Graham, Alain Jolibert, and Hans Meissner, "Marketing Negotiations in France, Germany, the United Kingdom, and the United States," *Journal of Marketing* 52 (April 1988): 49–63.

33. Neil Rackham, "The Behavior of Successful Negotiators" (Reston, VA: Huthwaite Research Group, 1982).

34. J. Teich, H. Wallenius, and J. Wallenius, "World-Wide-Web Technology in Support of Negotiation and Communication," *International Journal of Technology Management* 17, nos. 1/2 (1999): 223–239.

35. Ibid.

36. Ibid.

37. *Newsweek,* May 2001.

38. J. A. Pearce II and R. B. Robinson, Jr., "Cultivating *Guanxi* as a Foreign Investor Strategy," *Business Horizons* 43, no. 1 (January 2000): 31.

39. Ibid.; R. L. Tung, *U.S.-China Trade Negotiations* (New York: Pergamon Press, 1982).

40. Joan H. Coll, "Sino–American Cultural Differences: The Key to Closing a Business Venture with the Chinese," *Mid-Atlantic Journal of Business* 25, no. 2, 3 (December 1988/January 1989); 15–19.

41. M. Loeb, "China: A Time for Caution," *Fortune*, February 20, 1995, 129–130.

42. O. Shenkar and S. Ronen, "The Cultural Context of Negotiations: The Implications of Chinese Interpersonal Norms," *Journal of Applied Behavioral Science* 23, no. 2 (1987): 263–275.

43. Tse et al.

44. J. Brunner, teaching notes, the University of Toledo.

45. Ibid.

46. Joanna M. Banthin and Leigh Stelzer, "Ethical Dilemmas in Negotiating Across Cultures: Problems in Commercial Negotiations between American Businessmen and the PRC," paper presented at 1st International Conference on East–West Joint Ventures, October 19–20, 1989, State University of New York–Plattsburgh; and J. M. Banthin and L. Stelzer, "'Opening' China: Negotiation Strategies When East Meets West," *The Mid-Atlantic Journal of Business* 25, no. 2, 3 (December 1988/January 1989).

47. Brunner.

48. Pearce and Robinson.

49. Ibid.

50. Ibid.

51. C. Blackman, "An Inside Guide to Negotiating," *China Business Review*, 27, no. 3 (May 2000): 44–45.

52. Brunner.

53. Boye De Mente, *Chinese Etiquette and Ethics in Business* (Lincolnwood, IL: NTC Business Books, 1989), 115–123.

54. S. Stewart and C. F. Keown, "Talking with the Dragon: Negotiating in the People's Republic of China," *Columbia Journal of World Business* 24, no. 3 (Fall 1989): 68–72.

55. Banthin and Stelzer, "'Opening' China."

56. Blackman.

57. Ibid.

58. Lucian Pye, *Chinese Commercial Negotiating Style* (Cambridge, MA: Oelgeschlager, Gunn and Hain, 1982).

59. W. B. Gudykunst and S. Ting Tomey, *Culture and Interpersonal Communication* (Newbury Park, CA: Sage Publications, 1988).

60. L. Copcland and L. Griggs, *Going International* (New York: Random House, 1985), 80.

61. M. A. Hitt, B. B. Tyler, and Daewoo Park, "A Cross-cultural Examination of Strategic Decision Models: Comparison of Korean and U.S. Executives," in *Best Papers Proceedings of the 50th Annual Meeting of the Academy of Management* (San Francisco, CA, August 12–15, 1990), 111–115; G. Fisher, *International Negotiation: A Cross-cultural Perspective* (Chicago: Intercultural Press, 1980); G. W. England, "Managers and Their Value Systems: A Five-Country Comparative Study," *Columbia Journal of World Business* 13, no. 2 (Summer 1978); W. Whitely and G. W. England, "Variability in Common Dimensions of Managerial Values Due to Value Orientation and Country Differences," *Personnel Psychology* 33 (1980): 77–89.

62. Hitt, Tyler, and Park, 114.

63. B. M. Bass and P. C. Burger, *Assessment of Managers: An International Comparison* (New York: Free Press, 1979), 91.

64. D. K. Tse, R. W. Belk, and Nan Zhan, "Learning to Consume: A Longitudinal and Cross-cultural Content Analysis of Print Advertisements from Hong Kong, People's Republic of China and Taiwan," *Journal of Consumer Research* (forthcoming).

65. Copeland and Griggs; M. K. Badawy, "Styles of Mideastern Managers," *California Management Review* 22 (1980): 51–58.

66. N. Namiki and S. P. Sethi, "Japan," in *Comparative Management—A Regional View,* ed. R. Nath (Cambridge, MA: Ballinger Publishing, 1988), 74–76.

67. De Mente, *Japanese Etiquette,* 80.

68. S. Naoto, *Management and Industrial Structure in Japan* (New York: Pergamon Press, 1981); Namiki and Sethi.

69. Harris and Moran, 397.

70. S. P. Sethi and N. Namiki, "Japanese-Style Consensus Decision-Making in Matrix Management: Problems and Prospects of Adaptation," in *Matrix Management Systems Handbook*, ed. D. I. Cleland (New York: Van Nostrand, 1984), 431–456.

Chapter 6

1. Bernard Wysocki, Jr., "U.S. Firms Increase Overseas Investments," *Wall Street Journal*, April 9, 1990.

2. D. Kirkpatrick, "A Growing AOL Europe Now Sets Example for U.S.," www.nytimes.com, September 8, 2003.

3. "The Stateless Corporation," *Business Week*, May 14, 1990, 100–101.

4. A. E. Serwer, "McDonald's Conquers the World," *Fortune*, October 17, 1994.

5. "The Avon Lady of the Amazon," *Business Week*, October 24, 1994.

6. Susan Kropf, President of Avon, interviewed in "For Avon, China Is a Beauty," www.businessweek.com, January 12, 2004.

7. "The Avon Lady of the Amazon," *Business Week,* October 24, 1994.
8. A. K. Gupta and V. Govindarajan, "Managing Global Expansion: A Conceptual Framework," *Business Horizons* (March/April 2000).
9. G. Melloan, "Global Manufacturing Is an Intricate Game," *Wall Street Journal*, November 29, 1988.
10. "The Avon Lady of the Amazon."
11. "The Stateless Corporation."
12. "Trinidad and Tobago," *Wall Street Journal*, May 23, 1990, special advertising section.
13. Robert Weigand, "International Investments: Weighing the Incentives," *Harvard Business Review* (July–August 1983): C1.
14. M. McCarthy, M. Pointer, D. Ricks, and R. Rolfe, "Managers' Views on Potential Investment Opportunities," *Business Horizons* (July–August 1993): 54–58.
15. Anant R. Negandhi, *International Management* (Boston: Allyn and Bacon, 1987), 230.
16. Henry Mintzberg, "Strategy Making in Three Modes," *California Management Review* (Winter 1973): 44–53.
17. Arvind V. Phatak, *International Dimensions of Management*, 2nd ed. (Boston: PWS-Kent, 1989).
18. Joseph V. Micallef, "Political Risk Assessment," *Columbia Journal of World Business* 16 (Summer 1981): 47–52; Mark Fitzpatrick, "The Definition and Assessment of Political Risk in International Business: A Review of the Literature," *Academy of Management Review* 8 (1983): 249.
19. M. Porter, *Competitive Strategy* (New York: Free Press, 1980).
20. D. J. Garsombke, "International Competitor Analysis," *Planning Review* 17, no. 3 (May–June 1989): 42–47.
21. A. Swasy, "Procter & Gamble Fixes Aim on Tough Market: The Latin Americans," *Wall Street Journal*, June 15, 1990.
22. W. H. Davidson, "The Role of Global Scanning in Business Planning," *Organizational Dynamics* 19 (Winter 1991).
23. Garsombke.
24. Joann S. Lublin, "Japanese Auto Makers Speed into Europe," *Wall Street Journal*, June 6, 1990.
25. K. R. Andrews, *The Concept of Corporate Strategy* (Homewood, IL: Dow Jones–Irwin, 1979).
26. A. Shama, "After the Meltdown: A Survey of International Firms in Russia," *Business Horizons* 43, no. 4 (2001): 73.
27. C. K. Prahalad and Gary Hamel, "The Core Competence of the Corporation," *Harvard Business Review* (May–June 1990): 79–91.
28. Ibid.
29. M. E. Porter, "Changing Patterns of International Competition," in *The Competitive Challenge*, ed. D. J. Teece (Boston: Ballinger, 1987), 29–30.
30. P. W. Beamish et al., *International Management* (Homewood, IL: Irwin, 1991).
31. A. Palazzo, "B2B Markets—Industry Basics," www.FT.com, January 28, 2001.
32. N. S. Levinson and M. Asahi, "Cross-National Alliances and Interorganizational Learning," *Organizational Dynamics* (Autumn 1995): 50–62.
33. A. J. Morrison, D. A. Ricks, and K. Roth, "Globalization versus Regionalization: Which Way for the Multinational?" *Organizational Dynamics* 19 (Winter 1991).
34. Ibid.
35. G. M. Taoka and D. R. Beeman, *International Business* (New York: HarperCollins, 1991).
36. Beamish et al.
37. B. Schlender, "Matsushita Shows How to Go Global," *Fortune,* July 11, 1996.
38. Yoram Wind and Susan Douglas, "International Portfolio Analysis and Strategy: The Challenge of the 1980s," *Journal of International Business Studies* (Fall 1991): 69–82.
39. R. Gross and D. Kujawa, *International Business* (Homewood, IL: Irwin, 1989), 372.
40. www.ibm.com, April 10, 2001.
41. P. Greenberg, "It's Not a Small eCommerce World, After All," www.ecommercetimes.com, February 23, 2001.
42. Ibid.
43. M. Porter, *The Competitive Advantage of Nations* (New York: Free Press, 1990).
44. S. Butler, "Survivor: B2B Style," www.emarketer.com/analysis/ecommerce, April 13, 2001.
45. "eBusiness Trends," www.idc.com/ebusinesstrends, April 12, 2001.
46. "Fuji–Xerox Teams Up for New E-Marketplace." www.fujixerox.com, April 14, 2001.
47. "Online Auctions Free Procurement Savings," BHP Corporate Services, www.bhp.com, April 20, 2001.
48. M. Sawhney and S. Mandal, "Go Global," *Business 2.0,* May 2000.
49. Ibid.
50. "Small Businesses Take Part in Export Boom," *Investor's Daily*, July 10, 1991.
51. John Garland, Richard N. Farmer, and Marilyn Taylor, *International Dimensions of Business Policy and Strategy*, 2nd ed. (Boston: PWS-Kent, 1990), 106.
52. Phatak, 58.
53. R. J. Radway, "International Franchising," in *Global Business Management in the 1990s*, ed. R. T. Moran (Washington, DC: Beacham, 1990), 137.
54. P. Engardio, A. Bernstein, and M. Kripalani, "Is Your Job Next?" *Business Week,* February 3, 2003: 50–60.
55. Ibid.
56. Hewitt Associates Research Press Release, CNBC TV, March 5, 2004.
57. F. R. Root, *Entry Strategies for International Markets* (Lexington, MA: Lexington Books, 1987).
58. S. Zahra and G. Elhagrasey, "Strategic Management of IJVs," *European Management Journal* 12, no. 1 (1994): 83–93.
59. Yigang Pan and Xiaolia Li, "Joint Venture Formation of Very Large Multinational Firms," *Journal of International Business Studies* 31, no. 1 (First Quarter 2000): 179–181.
60. Dorothy B. Christelow, "International Joint Ventures: How Important Are They?" *Columbia Journal of World Business* (Summer 1987): 7–13.
61. Kenichi Ohmae, "The Global Logic of Strategic Alliances," *Harvard Business Review* (March–April 1989): 143–154.
62. Zahra and Elhagrasey.
63. "The Partners," *Business Week*, February 10, 1992.
64. Stefan Wagstyl, "The Next Investment Wave: Companies in East and West Prepare for the Risks and Opportunities of an Enlarged EU," *Financial Times,* April 27, 2004: 13.
65. L. Miller, "Go East, Young Company . . ." www.businessweek.com, October 22, 2003.
66. N. G. Carr, "Managing in the Euro Zone," *Harvard Business Review* (January/February 1999): 47–57.

67. L. Miller.
68. N. G. Carr.
69. N. G. Carr.
70. Dana Milbank, "Can Europe Deliver?" *Wall Street Journal,* September 30, 1994: 6.
71. "Creating Global Airlines," www.nytimes.com, October 7, 2003.
72. A. Cowell, "Zeneca Buying Astra as Europe Consolidates," *New York Times,* December 10, 1998.
73. D. Sanger, "Backing Down on Steel Tariffs, U.S. Strengthens Trade Group," www.nytimes.com, December 5, 2003.
74. Daniel Dombey, "Microsoft's Day of Reckoning in Europe," *Financial Times,* March 24, 2004: 3.
75. L. E. Brouthers, S. Werner, and E. Matulich, The Influence of TRIAD Nations' Environments on Price-quality Product Strategies and MNC Performance," *Journal of International Business Studies* 31, 1 (First quarter, 2000): 39–62.
76. Ibid.
77. Yigang Pan and David K. Tse, "The Hierarchical Model of Market Entry Modes," *Journal of International Business Studies* 31, no. 4 (Fourth Quarter 2000): 535–554.
78. Gupta and Govindarajan.
79. Ibid.
80. A. E. Serwer, "McDonald's Conquers the World," *Fortune,* October 17, 1994.
81. K. R. Harrigan, "Joint Ventures and Global Strategies," *Columbia Journal of World Business* 19, no. 2 (Summer 1984): 7–13.
82. G. Hofstede, *Cultures and Organizations: Software of the Mind* (London: McGraw-Hill, 1991).
83. Pan and Tse.
84. Hofstede.
85. Pan and Tse.
86. Hofstede.
87. Pan and Tse.

Chapter 7

1. B. R. Schlender, "How Toshiba Makes Alliances Work," *Fortune,* October 4, 1993, 116–120.
2. D. Lei and J. W. Slocum, Jr., "Global Strategic Alliances: Payoffs and Pitfalls," *Organizational Dynamics* (Winter 1991).
3. M. A. Hitt, R. D. Ireland, and R. E. Hoskisson, *Strategic Management* (Cincinnati, OH: South-Western, 1999).
4. .... www.FT.com, February 2, 2004.
5. J. Tagliabue, "Thomson and TCL to Join TV Units," www.nytimes.com, November 4, 2003.
6. Arvind Parkhe, "Global Business Alliances," *Business Horizons* 43, no. 5 (September 2000): 2.
7. "U.S. Eclipsed by Europe in the M&A Stakes," *Financial Times,* November 17, 2003.
8. "EU Agrees to Rules on Mergers," *Financial Times,* November 28, 2003.
9. Daniel Dombey, "European Takeover Proposals Anger U.S.," *Financial Times,* November 2, 2003, 1.
10. "The Return of the Deal," www.businessweek, November 24, 2003.
11. www.e4engineering.com, January 4, 2001.
12. Tim Burt, "Disney's Asian Adventure," *Financial Times,* October 30, 2003, 8.
13. Ibid.
14. Ibid.
15. Ibid.
16. Ibid.
17. D. Lei, "Offensive and Defensive Uses of Alliances," in Heidi Vernon-Wortzel and L. H. Wortzel, *Strategic Management in a Global Economy,* 3rd ed. (New York: John Wiley & Sons, 1997).
18. Danny Hakim, "DaimlerChrysler Heads to Court over 1998 Merger," www.nytimes.com, November 28, 2003.
19. ... www. FT.com, April 27, 2004.
20. *New York Times,* November 28, 2003
21. R. N. Osborn and C. C. Baughn, "Forms of Interorganizational Governance for Multinational Alliances," *Academy of Management Journal* 33, no. 3 (1990): 503–519.
22. Lei, 1997.
23. Steve Lohr, "China Poses Trade Worry as It Gains in Technology," www.nytimes.com, January 13, 2004.
24. Ibid.
25. Lei, 1997.
26. T. L. Wheelen and J. D. Hunger, *Strategic Management and Business Policy,* 6th ed. (Reading, MA: Addison-Wesley, 1998).
27. Lei, 1997.
28. Wheelen and Hunger.
29. *International Petroleum Finance,* November, 2003.
30. Andrew Jack, "A New Dawn Brightens Moscow's Skyline," *Financial Times,* October 9, 2003, 1–3.
31. Ibid.
32. "In Post-USSR Russia, Any Job Is a Good Job," www.nytimes.com, January 11, 2004.
33. Arkady Ostrovsky, "Threat to Sell Yukos Arm Fuels Concerns," *Financial Times,* July 21, 2004, 1, 17.
34. *Financial Times,* October 9, 2003.
35. A. Jack, "Russians Wake Up to Consumer Capitalism," www.FT.com, January 30, 2001.
36. *Agence France Presse*, August 26, 2003.
37. *International Petroleum Finance*, November 2003.
38. "GM Stepping on the Gas in Russia," www.businessweek.com, December 29, 2003.
39. A. Shama, "After the Meltdown: A Survey of International Firms in Russia," *Business Horizons* 43, no. 4 (July 2000): 73.
40. Ibid.
41. Jack, 2001.
42. S. B. Novikov, "Soviet–American Joint Ventures: The Problems of Establishment and Activities," paper presented to the 1st International Conference on East–West Joint Ventures, State University of New York–Plattsburgh, October 19–20, 1989.
43. K. R. Harrigan, "Joint Ventures and Global Strategies," *Columbia Journal of World Business* 19, no. 2 (Summer 1984): 7–13.
44. M. Brzezinski, "Foreigners Learn to Play by Russia's Rules," *Wall Street Journal*, May 14, 1998.
45. P. Lawrence and C. Vlachontsicos, "Joint Ventures in Russia: Put the Locals in Charge," *Harvard Business Review*, January–February 1993, 44–54.
46. A. E. Serwer, "McDonald's Conquers the World," *Fortune,* October 17, 1994.
47. Jack Welch (then CEO of G.E.) interviewed in *Fortune,* March 8, 1999.
48. Theodore Herbert and Helen Deresky, "Should General Managers Match Their Strategies?" *Organizational*

Dynamics 15, no. 3 (Winter, 1987): 12; R. H. Mason and R. S. Spich, *Management: An International Perspective* (Homewood, IL: Irwin, 1987), 177.

49. E. Anderson and H. Gatignon, "Modes of Foreign Entry: A Transaction Cost Analysis and Propositions," *Journal of International Business Studies* (Fall 1986): 1–26.

50. J. L. Schaan, "Parent Control and Joint Venture Success: The Case of Mexico," unpublished doctoral dissertation, University of Western Ontario, 1983.

51. H. W. Lane and P. W. Beamish, "Cross-Cultural Cooperative Behavior in Joint Ventures in Less Developed Countries," *Management International Review* 30 (Special Issue 1990): 87–102.

52. J. M. Geringer, "Strategic Determinants of Partner Selection Criteria in International Joint Ventures," *Journal of International Business Studies* (First Quarter 1991): 41–62.

53. J. M. Geringer and L. Hebert, "Control and Performance of International Joint Ventures," *Journal of International Business Studies* 20, no. 2 (Summer 1989).

54. Geringer, 1991.

55. P. W. Beamish et al., *International Management* (Homewood, IL: Irwin, 1991).

56. J. P. Killing, *Strategies for Joint Venture Success* (New York: Praeger, 1983).

57. J. L. Schaan and P. W. Beamish, "Joint Venture General Managers in Less Developed Countries," in *Cooperative Strategies in International Business*, ed. F. Contractor and P. Lorange (Toronto: Lexington Books, 1988), 279–299.

58. Oded Shenkar and Yoram Zeira, "International Joint Ventures: A Tough Test for HR," *Personnel* (January 1990): 26–31.

59. Ibid.

60. J. M. Geringer and L. Hebert, "Control and Performance of International Joint Ventures," *Journal of International Business Studies* 20, no. 2 (Summer 1989): 235–254.

61. M. Geringer, "Criteria for Selecting Partners for Joint Ventures in Industrialized Market Economies," doctoral dissertation, University of Washington, Seattle, 1986; Schaan and Beamish.

62. R. Mead, *International Management* (Cambridge, MA: Blackwell Publishers, 1994).

63. I. Berdrow and H. W. Lane, "International Joint Ventures: Creating Value through Successful Knowledge Management," *Journal of World Business,* vol. 38, 1, February, 2003, 15–30.

64. Ibid.

65. Ibid.

66. Lisa Shuchman, "Reality Check," *Wall Street Journal,* April 30, 1998.

67. J. Pura, "Backlash Builds Against Suharto-Lined Firms," *Wall Street Journal,* May 27, 1998.

68. W. M. Danis, "Differences in Values, Practices, and Systems among Hungarian Managers and Western Expatriates: An Organizing Framework and Typology," *Journal of World Business,* August 2003, 224–244.

69. P. Rosenzweig, "Why Is Managing in the United States so Difficult for European Firms?" *European Management Journal* 12, no. 1 (1994): 31–38.

70. "In Alabama, the Soul of a New Mercedes?" *Business Week,* March 31, 1997.

71. Ibid.

72. J. A. Pearce II and R. B. Robinson, Jr., "Cultivating *Guanxi* as a Foreign Investor Strategy," *Business Horizons* 43, no 1 (January 2000): 31.

73. Ibid.

74. www.NextLinx.com, September 10, 2001.

Chapter 8

1. "The Samsung Way," *Business Week,* June 16, 2003.

2. Roberto C. Goizueta, (Former) Chairman and CEO, Coca-Cola Company.

3. A. D. Chandler, *Strategy and Structure: Chapters in the History of the American Industrial Enterprise* (Cambridge, MA: MIT Press, 1962); R. E. Miles et al., "Organizational Strategy, Structure, and Process," *Academy of Management Review* 3, no. 3 (July 1978): 546–562; and J. Woodward, *Industrial Organization: Theory and Practice* (Oxford University Press, 1965).

4. C. A. Bartlett and S. Ghoshal, *Managing Across Borders* (Boston: Harvard Business School Press, 1989).

5. J. M. Stopford and L. T. Wells, Jr., *Managing the Multinational Enterprise* (New York: Basic Books, 1972).

6. Alcoa Corporate Information, www.alcoa.com, accessed July 25, 2004.

7. P. Asheghian and B. Ebrahimi, *International Business* (New York: Harper and Row, 1990).

8. Ibid.

9. R. H. Mason and R. S. Spich, *Management: An International Perspective* (Homewood, IL: Irwin, 1987).

10. "Heinz's Johnson to Divest Operations, Scrap Management of Firm by Regions," *Wall Street Journal,* December 8, 1997, B22.

11. www.Nestle.com, December 7, 2000.

12. A. Taylor III, "Ford's Really Big Leap at the Future," *Fortune,* September 18, 1995, 134–144.

13. L. Greenhalgh, "Ford Motor Company's CFO Jac Nasser on Transformational Change, E-Business, and Environmental Responsibility (Interview)," *Academy of Management Executive* 14, no. 13 (August 2000): 46.

14. "Borderless Management," *Business Week,* May 23, 1994.

15. Ibid.; "Power at Multinationals Shifts to Home Office," *Wall Street Journal,* September 9, 1994; "Big Blue Wants the World to Know Who's Boss," *Business Week,* September 26, 1994.

16. H. Henzler and W. Rall, "Facing Up to the Globalization Challenge," *McKinsey Quarterly* (Fall 1986): 52–68.

17. T. Levitt, "The Globalization of Markets," *Harvard Business Review* (May–June 1983): 92–102; and S. P. Douglas and Yoram Wind, "The Myth of Globalization," *Columbia Journal of World Business* (Winter 1987): 19–29.

18. Jane Perlez, "Chinese Born Overseas Invest in a Distant Homeland," www.nytimes.com, December 14, 2003.

19. L. Kraar, "The Overseas Chinese," *Fortune,* October 31, 1994.

20. J. Kao, "The Worldwide Web of Chinese Business," *Harvard Business Review* (March–April 1993): 24–35.

21. "Asia's Wealth," *Business Week,* November 29, 1993.

22. Kao.

23. "The New Power in Asia," *Fortune,* October 31, 1994.

24. M. Weidenbaum, "The Rise of Great China: A New Economic Superpower," in *Annual Editions, 1995/96* (Guilford, CT: Dushkin Publishing Group), 180–185.

25. Perlez, 2003.
26. Weidenbaum.
27. Kraar.
28. Weidenbaum.
29. Kao.
30. Kraar.
31. P. M. Rosenzweig, "Colgate-Palmolive: Managing International Careers," Harvard Business School Case, 1995.
32. "For Levi's, a Flattering Fit Overseas," *Business Week,* November 5, 1990, 76–77.
33. Ibid.
34. B. R. Schlender, "How Fujitsu Will Tackle the Giants," *Fortune,* July 1, 1991.
35. Andy Reinhardt, "Philips: Back on the Beam," www.businessweek.com, May 3, 2004.
36. Press release, www.Philips.com, accessed July 25, 2004.
37. S. Ghoshal and C. A. Bartlett, "The Mulinational Corporation as an Interorganizational Network," *Academy of Management Review* 15, no. 4 (1990): 603–625.
38. Mohanbir Sawhney and Sumant Mandal, "Go Global," *Business 2.0* (May 5, 2001): 178–213.
39. J. D. Daniels, L. H. Radebaugh, and D. P. Sullivan, *Globalization and Business* (Upper Saddle River, NJ: Prentice Hall, 2002).
40. "Energizing the Supply Chain," *The Review,* Deloitte & Touche, January 17, 2000, p. 1.
41. C. A. Bartlett and S. Ghoshal, "Organizing for Worldwide Effectiveness: The Transnational Solution," *California Management Review* (Fall 1988): 54–74.
42. Ibid., 66.
43. R. H. Kilmann, "A Networked Company that Embraces the World," *Information Strategy* 6 (Spring 1990): 23–26.
44. R. B. Reich, "Who Is Them?" *Harvard Business Review* (March–April 1991): 77–88.
45. Ibid.
46. Francesco Caio, CEO, Merloni Elettrodomestici, interview in *Harvard Business Review*, January/February 1999.
47. www.McDonalds.com, February 20, 2001.
48. Andrew Jack, "Russians Wake up to Consumer Capitalism," www.FT.com January 30, 2001.
49. Ibid.
50. A. V. Phatak, *International Dimensions of Management*, 2nd ed. (Boston: PWS-Kent, 1989).
51. G. Rohrmann, CEO, AEI Corp., press release.
52. Phatak.
53. W. G. Egelhoff, "Patterns of Control in U.S., U.K., and European Multinational Corporations," *Journal of International Business Studies* (Fall 1984): 73–83.
54. Ibid.
55. Ibid.
56. S. Ueno and U. Sekaran, "The Influence of Culture on Budget Control Practices in the U.S.A. and Japan: An Empirical Study," *Journal of International Business Studies* 23 (Winter 1992): 659–674.
57. A. R. Neghandi and M. Welge, *Beyong Theory Z* (Greenwich, CT: J.A.I. Publishers, 1984), 18.
58. www.Nestle.com, press release, March 21, 2000.
59. Phatak.

Chapter 9

1. Allan Halcrow, Editor, *Personnel Journal*, February 1996.
2. www.FT.com, March 5, 2001.
3. J. L. Laabs, "HR Pioneers Explore the Road Less Traveled," *Personnel Journal* (February 1996): 70–72, 74, 77–78.
4. Ibid.
5. J. Stewart Black and Hal B. Gregersen, "The Right Way to Manage Expats," *Harvard Business Review* (March/April 1999): 52–62.
6. C. Joinson, "Why HR Managers Need to Think Globally," *HR Magazine*, April 1998, 2–7.
7. Stuart Mathison, Vice President for Strategic Planning, Sprint International.
8. C. A. Bartlett and S. Ghoshal, "Matrix Management: Not a Structure, a Frame of Mind," *Harvard Business Review* (July–August 1990).
9. J. S. Lublin, "Foreign Accents Proliferate in Top Ranks as U.S. Companies Find Talent Abroad," *Wall Street Journal*, May 21, 1992.
10. S. J. Kobrin, "Is There a Relationship Between a Geocentric Mind-Set and Multinational Strategy?" *Journal of International Business Studies* (Third Quarter 1994); N. J. Adler and S. Bartholomew, "Managing Globally Competent People," *Academy of Management Executive*, August 6, 1992, 52–65; P. Dowling and R. S. Schuler, *International Dimensions of Human Resource Management* (Boston: PWS-Kent, 1990).
11. G. Hedlund, "Who Manages the Global Corporation?" unpublished working paper, Stockholm School of Economics, 1990.
12. D. Welch, "HRM Implications of Globalization," *Journal of General Management* 19, no. 4 (Summer 1994): 52–69.
13. T. T. Herbert and H. Deresky, "Should General Managers Match Their Business Strategies?" *Organizational Dynamics* 15, no. 3 (Winter 1987); and "Senior Management Implications of Strategic Human Resource Management Programs," *Proceedings of the Association of Human Resource Management and Organizational Behavior Conference* (New Orleans, November 1986).
14. D. A. Heenan and H. V. Perlmutter, *Multinational Organization Development* (reading, MA: Addison-Wesley, 1979), 18–19.
15. S. B. Prasad and Y. K. Krishna Shetty, *An Introduction to Multinational Management* (Upper Saddle River, NJ: Prentice Hall, 1979).
16. Rochelle Kopp, "International Human Resource Policies and Practices in Japanese, European, and United States Multinationals," *Human Resource Management* 33, no. 4 (Winter 1994): 581–599.
17. Ibid.
18. Herbert and Deresky.
19. M. Mendenhall and G. Oddou, "The Dimensions of Expatriate Acculturation: A Review," *Academy of Management Review* 10, no. 1 (1985): 39–47.
20. S. Ronen, *Comparative and Multinational Management* (New York: John Wiley and Sons, 1986) and R. L. Tung, "Selection and Training of Personnel for Overseas Assignments," *Columbia Journal of World Business* (Spring 1981): 68–78.
21. Tung, "Selection and Training of Personnel for Overseas Assignments."
22. Dowling and Schuler.
23. S. J. Kobrin, "Expatriate Reduction and Strategic Control in American Multinational Corporations," *Human Resource Management* 27, no. 1 (1988): 63–75.
24. P. J. Dowling, "Hot Issues Overseas," *Personnel Administrator* 34, no. 1 (1989): 66–72.

25. Company information, www.ABB.com, accessed July 26, 2004.

26. Hem C. Jain, "Human Resource Management in Selected Japanese Firms, the Foreign Subsidiaries and Locally Owned Counterparts," *International Labour Review* 129, no. 1 (1990): 73–84; Bartlett and Ghoshal.

27. www.FT.com, March 5, 2001.

28. Rosalie Tung, "American Expatriates Abroad: From Neophytes to Cosmopolitans," *Journal of World Business*, 33 (1998),125–144.

29. R. D. Hays, "Expatriate Selection: Insuring Success and Avoiding Failure," *Journal of International Business Studies* 5, no. 1 (1974): 25–37; Tung, 1998.

30. J. S. Black, "Work Role Transitions: A Study of American Expatriate Managers in Japan," *Journal of International Business Studies* 19 (1988): 277–294.

31. "They're Sending You Where?" www.businessweek.com, January 3, 2000.

32. M. Harvey, "Dual-Career Expatriates: Expectations, Adjustment and Satisfaction with International Relocation," *Journal of International Business Studies* 28, no. 3 (1997).

33. Tung, "U.S., European, and Japanese Multinationals."

34. Ibid.

35. B. Wysocki, Jr., "Prior Adjustment: Japanese Executives Going Overseas Take Anti-Shock Courses," *Wall Street Journal*, December 4, 1987.

36. Mendenhall and Oddou.

37. J. S. Black and M. Mendenhall, "Cross-cultural Training Effectiveness: A Review and a Theoretical Framework for Future Research," *Academy of Management Review* 15, no. 1 (1990): 113–136.

38. K. Oberg, "Culture Shock: Adjustments to New Cultural Environments," *Practical Anthropology* (July–August 1960): 177–182.

39. Ibid.

40. Ibid.

41. P. R. Harris and R. T. Moran, *Managing Cultural Differences,* 4th ed. (Houston, TX: Gulf Publishing, 1996), 139.

42. Tung, "Selection and Training of Personnel for Overseas Assignments."

43. P. C. Earley, "Intercultural Training for Managers: A Comparison of Documentary and Interpersonal Methods," *Academy of Management Journal* 30, no. 4 (December 1987): 685–698.

44. Ronen.

45. Kealey, 81.

46. R. Peterson, "The Use of Expatriates and Inpatriates in Central and Eastern Europe Since the Wall Came Down," *Journal of World Business,* 38 (2003) 55–69.

47. "Seoul Is Supporting a Sizzling Tech Boom," www.businessweek.com, September 25, 2000.

48. P. Damaskopoulos and T. Evgeniou, "Adoption of New Economy Practices by SMEs in Eastern Europe," *European Management Journal,* 21, 2, 133–145, 2003.

49. Herbert and Deresky.

50. "Living Expenses," www.economist.com, July 22, 2000; "Runzheimer International Compensation Worksheet," www.runzheimer.com, 2000.

51. B. W. Teague, *Compensating Key Personnel Overseas* (New York: Conference Board, 1972).

52. S. F. Gale, "Taxing Situations for Expatriates," *Workforce,* June 2003, vol. 82, 6, 100(3).

53. D. Kiriazov, S. E. Sullivan, and H. S. Tu, "Business Success in Eastern Europe: Understanding and Customizing HRM," *Business Horizons* (January/February 2000): 39–43.

54. Ibid.

55. Y. Ono and W. Spindle, "Japan's Long Decline Makes One Thing Rise: Individualism," *Wall Street Journal,* January 3, 2001.

56. Ingmar Bjorkman and Yuan Lu, "The Management of Human Resources in Chinese-Western Joint Ventures," *Journal of World Business* 34, no. 3 (Fall 1999): 306.

57. Ibid.

58. "Personnel Demands Attention Overseas," *Mutual Fund Market News,* March 19, 2001, 1.

59. Moon Ihlwan, "Want Innovation? Hire a Russian," www.businessweek.com, March 8, 1994.

60. Cha Dae Sung, Samsung, Inc., quoted in Moon Ihlwan, "Want Innovation? Hire a Russian," www.businessweek.com, March 8, 2004.

61. Sheila M. Puffer and Stanislav V. Shekshnia, "Compensating Nationals in Post-Communist Russia: The Fit Between Culture and Compensation Systems," paper presented at the Annual Academy of International Business Conference, Boston, November 1994).

62. Ibid.

Chapter 10

1. Charlene M. Solomon, "One Assignment, Two Lives," *Personnel Journal* (May 1996): 36–47.

2. N. J. Adler, *International Dimensions of Organizational Behavior,* 2nd ed. (Boston: PWS-Kent, 1991); M. Mendenhall, E. Dunbar, and G. Oddou, "Expatriate Selection, Training, and Career-Pathing: A Review and Critique," *Human Resource Management* 26 (1987): 331–345.

3. M. G. Harvey, "Repatriation of Corporate Executives: An Empirical Study," *Journal of International Business Studies* 20 (Spring 1989): 131–144.

4. Rosalie Tung, "Career Issues in International Assignments," *Academy of Management Executive* 2, no. 3 (1988): 241–244.

5. M. Harvey, "Dual-Career Expatriates: Expectations, Adjustments and Satisfaction with International Relocation," *Journal of International Business Studies* 28, no. 3 (1997): 627.

6. Tung.

7. Solomon.

8. R. Pascoe, *Surviving Overseas: The Wife's Guide to Successful Living Abroad* (Singapore: Times Publishing, 1992); and R. Pascoe, "Employers Ignore Expatriate Wives at Their Own Peril," *Wall Street Journal,* March 29, 1992.

9. P. Asheghian and B. Ebrahimi, *International Business* (NY: HarperCollins,1990), 470.

10. www.FT.com

11. N. J. Adler, *International Dimensions of Organizational Behavior,* 4th ed (Boston: PWS-Kent, 2002).

12. J. S. Black and H. B. Gregersen, " The Other Half of the Picture: Antecedents of Spouse Cross-cultural Adjustment," *Journal of International Business Studies* (Third Quarter 1992): 461–477.

13. Based on D. C. Feldman, "The Multinational Socialization of Organization Members," *Academy of Management Review* 6, no. 2 (April 1981): 309–318.

14. J. Hamill, "Expatriate Policies in British Multinationals, *Journal of General Management* 14, no. 4 (Summer 1989): 18–33.

15. Based on W. Dyer, *Team Building* (Reading, MA: Addison-Wesley, 1987).

16. T. Gross, E. Turner, and L. Cederholm, "Building Teams for Global Operations," *Management Review* (June 1987): 32–36.

17. www.BritishTelecom.com/cases, February 19, 2001.

18. Based largely on Adler, 2002.

19. T. R. Kayworth and D. E. Leidner, "Leadership Effectiveness in Global Virtual Teams," *Journal of Management Information Systems,* Winter 2001–2002, Vol.18, 3,7–40.

20. C. Solomon, "Building Teams Across Borders," *Global Workforce* (November 1998): 12–17.

21. Ibid.

22. T. Brown, "Building a Transnational Team," Industry Week, May 16, 1988, 13.

23. Ibid.

24. A. Joshi, G. Labianca, P. M. Caligiuri, "Getting Along Long Distance: Understanding Conflict in a Multinational Team through Network Analysis," *Journal of World Business* 37 (2002) 277–284.

25. I. Ratiu, "International Consulting News," in *Managing Cultural Differences,* 3rd ed., P. R. Harris and R. T. Moran (Houston, TX: Gulf Publishing 1991).

26. V. Govindarajan and A. K. Gupta, "Bulding an Effective Global Business Team," *MIT Sloan Management Review,* Summer 2001, vol. 42, issue 4, 63.

27. Ibid.

28. S. Chevrier, "Cross-cultural Management in Multinational Project Groups," *Journal of World Business,* 38 (2), May 2003, 141–149.

29. Ibid.

30. *Wall Street Journal,* July 26, 1995.

31. M. Kaminski and J. Paiz, "Japanese Women in Management: Where Are They?" *Human Resource Management* 23, no. 2 (Fall 1984): 277–292.

32. P. Lansing and K. Ready, "Hiring Women Managers in Japan: An Alternative for Foreign Employers," *California Management Review* 26, no. 4 (1988): 112–127.

33. Howard W. French, "Japan's Neglected Resource: Female Workers,"www.nytimes.com, July 24, 2003.

34. "Women in Business: A Global Report Card," *Wall Street Journal,* July 26, 1995.

35. G. K. Stahl, E. L. Miller, and R. L. Tung, "Toward the Boundaryless Career: A Closer Look at the Expatriate Career Concept and the Perceived Implications of an International Assignment," *Journal of World Business,* 37 (2002) 216–227.

36. Patrick Jenkins and Bettina Wassener, "How Germany Keeps Women off the Board," *FinancialTtimes,* June 15, 2004.

37. Alison Maitland, "The North-South Divide in Europe, Inc.," *Financial Times,* June 14, 2004.

38. Ibid.

39. M. Jelinek N. Adler. "Women: World Class Managers for Global Competition," *Academy of Management Executive* 11, no. 1 (February 1988): 11–19.

40. N. J. Adler and D. N. Izraeli, *Women in Management Worldwide* (Armonk, NY: M. E. Sharpe, 1988), 245.

41. Ibid.

42. www.businessweek.com, July 4, 2003.

43. John C. Kornblum, Chairman German Unit, Lazard Freres and Co., July 2003.

44. Jacob Vittorelli, Former Deputy Chairman of Pirelli.

45. P. J. Dowling, R. S. Schuler, and D. E. Welch, *International Dimensions of Human Resource Management,* 2nd ed. (Belmont, CA: Wadsworth, 1994).

46. "A New Deal in Europe?" www.businessweek.com, July 14, 2003.

47. M. R. Czinkota, I. A. Ronkainen, and M. H. Moffett, *International Business,* 3rd ed. (New York: Dryden Press, 1994).

48. C. K. Prahalad and Y. L. Doz, *The Multinational Mission: Balancing Local Demands and Global Vision* (New York: Free Press, 1987).

49. R. J. Adams, *Industrial Relations under Liberal Democracy* (University of South Carolina Press, 1995).

50. J. S. Daniels and L. H. Radebaugh, *International Business,* 10th ed. (Reading, MA: Addison-Wesley, 2004).

51. Dowling, Schuler, and Welch.

52. Adams.

53. Ibid.

54. "Unions Feel the Beat," *U.S. News and World Report,* January 24, 1994.

55. Ibid.

56. *The New York Times,* December 20, 2003.

57. "World Wire: China to Unionize Foreign Firms," *Wall Street Journal,* May 1, 1996.

58. J. T. Barrett, "Trade Unions in South Africa: Dramatic Change after Apartheid Ends," *Monthly Labor Review* 199, no. 5 (May 1996): 37.

59. M. M. Lucio and S. Weston, "New Management Practices in a Multinational Corporation: The Restructuring of Worker Representation and Rights?" *Industrial Relations Journal* 25, no. 2, 110–121.

60. Ibid.

61. D. B. Cornfield, "Labor Transnationalism?" *Work and Occupations* 24, no. 3 (August 1997): 278(10).

62. R. Martin, A. Vidinova, and S. Hill, "Industrial Relations in Transition Economies: Emergent Industrial Relations Institutions in Bulgaria," *British Journal of Industrial Relations* 34, no. 1 (March 1996): 3.

63. "Labour Relations: Themes for the 21st Century," *British Journal of Industrial Relations* 33, no. 4 (December 1995): 515.

64. Daniels and Radebaugh.

65. Barrett.

66. "Culture Clash: South Korea," *The Economist* 342 (7999), January 11, 1997.

67. A. M. Rugman and R. M. Hodgetts, *International Business* (New York: McGraw-Hill, 1995).

68. Daniels and Radebaugh, 2004.

69. ... *Financial Times,* January 16, 2004.

70. "Marching in Place, Europe's Businesses Say They Need a More Flexible Labor Force," *Time International,* May 6, 2002.

71. Bloomberg News, "Concessions by Employees at Daimler," www.nytimes.com, July 24, 2004.

72. Hugh Williamson, "German Union Chief Warns Cost-cutting Deals Threaten Stability in Labour Force," *Financial Times,* July 22, 2004.

73. "A New Deal in Europe?" www.businessweek.com; *BW Online,* July 14, 2003.

74. J. Hoerr, "What Should Unions Do?" *Harvard Business Review* (May–June 1991): 30–45.

75. H. C. Katz, "The Decentralization of Collective Bargaining: A Literature Review and Comparative Analysis," *Industrial and Labor Relations Review* 47, no. 1 (October 1993).

76. Adams.

77. Williamson, *Financial Times,* July 22, 2004.

78. www.nytimes.com, July 24, 2004.

79. Adams.

80. "The Perils of Cosy Corporatism," *The Economist,* May 21, 1994.

81. Wofgang Streeck, "More Uncertainties: German Unions Facing 1992," *Industrial Relations* (Fall 1991): 30–33.

82. "Germany's Economic Future Is on the Bargaining Table," *Business Week*, March 30, 1992.

Chapter 11

1. S. Michailova, "When Common Sense Becomes Uncommon: Participation and Empowerment in Russian Companies with Western Participation," *Journal of World Business*, 37 (2002) 180–187.

2. F. Rieger and D. Wong-Rieger, "A Configuration Model of National Influence Applied to Southeast Asian Organizations," *Proceedings of the Research Conference on Business in Southeast Asia*, Mary 12–13, 1990, University of Michigan.

3. R. M. Steers, *Made in Korea: Chung Ju Yung and the Rise of Hyundai* (New York: Routledge, 1999).

4. Meaning of Work International Research Team, *The Meaning of Working: An International Perspective* (New York: Academic Press, 1985).

5. D. Siddiqui and A. Alkhafaji, *The Gulf War: Implications for Global Businesses and Media* (Apollo, PA: Closson Press, 1992), 133–135.

6. Ibid.

7. A. Ali, "The Islamic Work Ethic in Arabia," *Journal of Psychology* 126 (1992): 507–519.

8. Yasamusa Kuroda and Tatsuzo Suzuki, "A Comparative Analysis of the Arab Culture: Arabic, English and Japanese Language and Values," paper presented at the 5th Congress of the International Association of Middle Eastern Studies, Tunis (September 20–24, 1991), quoted in Siddiqui and Alkhafaji.

9. J. R. Hinrichs, "Cross-National Analysis of Work Attitudes," paper presented at the American Psychological Association Meeting, Chicago, 1975.

10. A. Furnham, B. D. Kirkcaldy, and R. Lynn, "National Attitudes to Competitiveness, Money, and Work among Young People: First, Second, and Third World Differences," *Human Relations* 47, no. 1 (1994): 119–132.

11. M. Haire, E. E. Ghiselli, and L. W. Porter, "Cultural Patterns in the Role of the Manager," *Industrial Relations* 12, no. 2 (February 1963): 95–117.

12. S. Ronen, *Comparative and Multinational Management* (New York: John Wiley and Sons, 1986).

13. D. S. Elenkov, "Can American Management Concepts Work in Russia? A Cross-cultural Comparative Study," *California Management Review* 40, no. 4 (Summer 1998): 133–157.

14. E. C. Nevis, "Cultural Assumptions and Productivity: The United States and China," *Sloan Management Review* 24, no. 3 (Spring 1983): 17–29.

15. R. L. Tung, "Patterns of Motivation in Chinese Industrial Enterprises," *Academy of Management Review* 6, no. 3 (1981): 481–489.

16. Swee Hoon Ang, "The Power of Money: A Cross-cultural Analysis of Business-Related Beliefs," *Journal of World Business* 35, no. 1 (Spring 2000): 43.

17. *World Competitiveness Yearbook (1998)* (Lausanne, Switzerland: Institute for Management Development).

18. D. D. White and J. Leon, "The Two-Factor Theory: New Questions, New Answers," *National Academy of Management Proceedings* (1976): 358; D. Macarov, "Work Patterns and Satisfactions in an Israeli Kibbutz: A Test of the Herzberg Hypothesis," *Personnel Psychology* (Autumn 1973): 483–493.

19. P. D. Machungwa and N. Schmitt, "Work Motivation in a Developing Country," *Journal of Applied Psychology* (February 1983): 31–42.

20. G. E. Popp, H. J. Davis, and T. T. Herbert, "An International Study of Intrinsic Motivation Composition," *Management International Review* 26, no. 3 (1986): 28–35.

21. R. N. Kanungo and R. W. Wright, "A Cross-cultural Study of Managerial Job Attitudes," *Journal of International Business Studies* (Fall 1983): 115–129.

22. Ibid., 127–128.

23. J. R. Lincoln, "Employee Work Attitudes and Management Practice in the U.S. and Japan: Evidence from a Large Comparative Survey," *California Management Review* 32, no. 1 (Fall 1989): 89–106.

24. J. R. Lincoln and K. McBride, "Japanese Industrial Organization in Comparative Perspective," *Annual Review of Sociology* 13 (1987): 289–312.

25. Lincoln.

26. "Detroit South," *Business Week,* March 16, 1992.

27. Geert Hofstede, "National Cultures in Four Dimensions," *International Studies of Management and Organization* (Spring–Summer 1983).

28. M. B. Teagarden, M. C. Butler, and M. Von Glinow, "Mexico's Maquiladora Industry: Where Strategic Human Resource Management Makes a Difference," *Organizational Dynamics* (Winter 1992): 34–47.

29. T. T. Herbert, H. Deresky, and G. E. Popp, "On the Potential for Assimilation and Integration of Sub-Culture Members into the U.S. Business System: The Micro-Cultural Effects of the Mexican-American National Origin, Culture, and Personality," *Proceedings of the International Business Association Conference* (London, November 1986).

30. John Condon, *Good Neighbors: Communication with the Mexicans* (Yarmouth, ME: Intercultural Press, 1985).

31. G. K. Stephens and C. R. Greer, "Doing Business in Mexico: Understanding Cultural Differences," *Organizational Dynamics* (Summer 1995): 39–55.

32. Teagarden, Butler, and Von Glinow.

33. Stephens and Greer.

34. Ibid.

35. C. E. Nicholls, H. W. Lane, and M. B. Brechu, "Taking Self-Managed Teams to Mexico," *Academy of Management Executive* 13, 3 (1999): 15–25.

36. Ibid.

37. Ibid.

38. Mariah E. de Forest, "Thinking of a Plant in Mexico?" *Academy of Management Executive* 8, no. 1 (1994): 33–40.

39. Ibid.

40. Ibid.

41. Teagarden, Butler, and Von Glinow.

42. Herbert, Deresky, and Popp; R. S. Bhagat and S. J. McQuaid, "Role of Subjective Culture in Organizations: A Review and Direction for Future Research," *Journal of Applied Psychology Monograph* 67, no. 5 (1982): 669.

43. Malgorzata Tarczynska, "Eastern Europe: How Valid Is Western Reward/Performance Management?" *Benefits and Compensation International* 29, no. 8 (April 2000): 9–16.

44. Snejina Michailova, "When Common Sense Becomes Uncommon: Participation and Empowerment in Russian Companies with Western Participation," *Journal of World Business* 37 (2002), 180–187.

45. M. A. Von Glinow and M. B. Teagarden, "The Transfer of Human Resource Management Technology in Sino–U.S. Cooperative Ventures: Problems and Solutions," *Human Resource Management* 27, no. 2 (1988): 201–229.

46. M. A. Von Glinow and Byung Jae Chung, "Comparative HRM Practices in the U.S., Japan, Korea and the PRC," in *Research in Personnel and HRM—A Research Annual: International HRM,* ed. A. Nedd, G. R. Ferris, and K. M. Rowland (London: JAI Press, 1989).

47. A. Ignatius, "Now if Ms. Wong Insults a Customer, She Gets an Award," *Wall Street Journal,* January 24, 1989, 1, 15.

48. T. Saywell, "Motive Power: China's State Firms Bank on Incentives to Keep Bosses Operating at Their Peak," *Far Eastern Economic Review* (July 8, 2000): 67–68.

49. Jacques Maisonrouge, IBM World Trade Corporation, 1998.

50. A. Morrison, H. Gregersen, and S. Black, "What Makes Savvy Global Leaders?" *Ivey Business Journal* 64, no. 2 (1999): 44–51; and *Monash Mt. Eliza Business Review* 1, no. 2 (1998).

51. Ibid.

52. Ibid.

53. Morrison et al.; J. W. Gardner, *John W. Gardner on Leadership* (New York: Free Press, 1989); W. Bennis and B. Nanus, *Leaders* (New York: Harper and Row, 1985); and R. D. Robinson, *Internatinalization of Business* (Hinsdale, IL: Drysden Press, 1984), 117.

54. R. H. Mason and R. S. Spich, *Management: An International Perspective* (Homewood: IL: Irwin, 1987).

55. Ibid., 184.

56. B. M. Bass, *Bass & Stogdill's Handbook of Leadership* (New York: Free Press, 1990).

57. See, for example, M. Mead, *Sex and Temperament in Three Primitive Societies* (New York: Morrow, 1935); and M. Mead et al., *Cooperation and Competition among Primitive Peoples* (New York: McGraw-Hill, 1937).

58. L. Copeland and L. Griggs, *Going International* (New York: Random House, 1985), 131.

59. D. McGregor, *The Human Side of Enterprise* (New York: McGraw-Hill, 1960). See, for example, R. M. Stogdill, *Manual for the Leader Behavior Description Questionnaire—Form XII* (Columbus: Ohio State University, Bureau of Business Research, 1963); R. R. Blake and J. S. Mouton, *The New Managerial Grid* (Houston, TX: Gulf Publishing, 1978).

60. F. E. Fiedler, "Engineering the Job to Fit the Manager," *Harvard Business Review* 43, no. 5 (1965): 115–122.

61. Den Hartog, N. Deanne, R. J. House, Paul J. Hanges, P. W. Dorfman, S. Antonio Ruiz-Quintanna, et al., "Culture Specific and Cross-culturally Generalizable Implicit Leadership Theories: Are Attributes of Charismatic/Transformational Leadership Universally Endorsed?" *Leadership Quarterly* 10, no. 2, (1999): 219–256.

62. Ibid.

63. R. House et al., "Cultural Influences on Leadership and Organizations: Project GLOBE," *Advances in Global Leadership*, Vol. 1, (JAI Press, 1999).

64. Ibid.

65. Geert Hofstede, "Motivation, Leadership and Organization: Do American Theories Apply Abroad?" *Organizational Dynamics* (Summer 1980): 42–63.

66. Ibid.

67. Geert Hofstede, "Value Systems in Forty Countries," Proceedings of the 4th International Congress of the International Association for Cross-Cultural Psychology (1978).

68. Andre Laurent, "The Cultural Diversity of Western Conceptions of Management," *International Studies of Management and Organization* 13, no. 1–2 (Spring–Summer 1983): 75–96.

69. C. Hampden-Turner and A. Trompenaars, *The Seven Cultures of Capitalism* (New York: Doubleday, 1993).

70. M. Harie, E. E. Ghiselli, and L. W. Porter, *Managerial Thinking: An International Study* (New York: John Wiley and Sons, 1966).

71. S. G. Redding and T. W. Case, "Managerial Beliefs among Asian Managers," *Proceedings of the Academy of Management* (1975).

72. I. Kenis, "A Cross-cultural Study of Personality and Leadership," *Group and Organization Studies* 2 (1977): 49–60; F. C. Deyo, "The Cultural Patterning of Organizational Development: A Comparative Case Study of Thailand and Chinese Industrial Enterprises," *Human Organization* 37 (1978): 68–72.

73. M. K. Badawy, "Styles of Mid-Eastern Managers," *California Management Review* (Spring 1980): 57; various newscasts, 2001.

74. A. A. Algattan, *Test of the Path-Goal Theory of Leadership in the Multinational Domain,* paper presented at the Academy of Management Conference, 1985, San Diego, CA; J. P. Howell and P. W. Dorfman, "A Comparative Study of Leadership and Its Substitutes in a Mixed Cultural Work Setting," unpublished manuscript, 1988)

75. D. H. Welsh, F. Luthans, and S. M. Sommer, "Managing Russian Factory Workers: The Impact of U.S.-Based Behavioral and Participative Techniques," *Academy of Management Journal* 36 (1993): 58–79.

76. Jagdeep S. Chhoker, "Leadership and Culture in India: The GLOBE Research Project," www.mgmt3.ucalgary.ca/web/globe.nsf/index, November 10, 2001.

77. Ibid.

78. Jai B. P. Sinha and D. Sinha, "Role of Social Values in Indian Organizations," *International Journal of Psychology* 25 (1990): 705–715.

79. Hofstede, "Motivation, Leadership and Organization."

80. Jai B. P. Sinha, "A Model of Effective Leadership Styles in India," *International Studies of Management and Organization* (Summer–Fall 1984): 86–98.

81. Ibid.

82. B. M. Bass and P. C. Burger, *Assessment of Managers: An International Comparison* (New York: Free Press, 1979).

83. Chhoker.

84. Ibid.

85. R. C. Tripathi, "Interplay of Values in the Functioning of Indian Organizations," *International Journal of Psychology* 25 (1990): 715–734.

86. Sinha.

87. Sinha and Sinha.

88. A. Spaeth, "India Beckons—and Frustrates: The Country Needs Foreign Investment, But Investors May Find that Hard to Believe," *Wall Street Journal,* September 22, 1989, R23–R25.

89. Ibid.

90. "Enron Switches Signals in India," *Business Week,* January 8, 2001. "Enron Calls on Guarantees by India to Collect Debts," *Wall Street Journal*, February 9, 2001.

91. S. S. Rao, "Yankee, Be Good," *Financial World*, November 7, 1995, 54–68.

92. Alison Maitland, "An American Leader in Europe," leadership interview with Nancy McKinstry, Wolters Kluwer, *Financial Times*, July 15, 2004, 10.

93. Ibid.

94. Ibid.

95. Ibid.

Name and Subject Index